Context and Learning

Context and Learning

edited by

Peter D Balsam
Barnard College of Columbia University

Arthur Tomie
Rutgers University

LEA   LAWRENCE ERLBAUM ASSOCIATES, PUBLISHERS
1985   Hillsdale, New Jersey   London

Lawrence Erlbaum Associates, Inc., Publishers
365 Broadway
Hillsdale, New Jersey 07642

Library of Congress Cataloging in Publication Data
Main entry under title:

Context and learning.

  Bibliography: p.
  Includes index.
  1. Conditioned response.   2. Learning, Psychology of.
3. Performance.   I. Balsam, Peter D.   II. Tomie, Arthur.
BF319.C578   **1985**   156'.315   84-13479
ISBN 0-89859-442-1

Printed in the United States of America
10 9 8 7 6 5 4 3 2 1

Contents

Contributors   vii

Preface   xi

1. The Functions of Context in Learning and Performance
   Peter D Balsam   1

2. Contextual Learning in Pavlovian Conditioning
   Robert A. Rescorla, Paula J. Durlach, and James W. Grau   23

3. Effects of Test Context on the Acquisition of Autoshaping to a Formerly Random Keylight or a Formerly Contextual Keylight
   Arthur Tomie   57

4. Some Effects of Contextual Conditioning and US Predictability on Pavlovian Conditioning
   A. G. Baker, Maharaj Singh, and Dalbir Bindra   73

5. Contextual Stimuli Mediate the Effects of Pre- and Postexposure to the Unconditioned Stimulus on Conditioned Suppression
   Alan Randich and Robert T. Ross   105

6. Contexts, Event-Memories, and Extinction

   Mark E. Bouton and Robert C. Bolles   133

7. The Several Roles of Context at the Time of Retrieval

   Ralph R. Miller and Todd R. Schachtman   167

8. Contextual Control and Excitatory Versus Inhibitory Learning:
   Studies of Extinction, Reinstatement,
   and Interference

   Peter S. Kaplan and Eliot Hearst   195

9. Contextual Control of Taste-Aversion Conditioning and
   Extinction

   Trevor Archer, Per-Olow Sjödén, and Lars-Göran Nilsson   225

10. Pitch Context and Pitch Discrimination by Birds

    Stewart H. Hulse, Jeffrey Cynx, and John Humpal   273

11. Contextual Stimulus Control of Operant Responding in Pigeons

    David R. Thomas   295

12. Cue-Context Interactions in Discrimination,
    Categorization, and Memory

    Douglas L. Medin and Thomas J. Reynolds   323

13. Contextual Stimulus Effects of Drugs and Internal States

    Donald A. Overton   357

14. Cognitive Maps and Environmental Context

    Lynn Nadel, Jeffrey Willner, and Elizabeth M. Kurz   385

Author Index   407

Subject Index   417

Contributors

TREVOR ARCHER
  Astra Läkemedel AB
  S-15185 Södertälje, Sweden

ANDREW G. BAKER
  Department of Psychology, McGill University
  Montreal, Quebec, Canada H3A 1B1

PETER D BALSAM
  Department of Psychology, Barnard College of Columbia University
  New York, New York 10027

ROBERT C. BOLLES
  Department of Psychology, University of Washington
  Seattle, Washington 98195

MARK E. BOUTON
  Department of Psychology, University of Vermont
  Burlington, Vermont 05405

JEFFREY CYNX
  Department of Psychology, The Johns Hopkins University
  Baltimore, Maryland 21218

PAULA J. DURLACH
  Department of Experimental Psychology, University of Cambridge
  Cambridge, England CB2 3EB

JAMES W. GRAU
  Department of Psychology, University of Pennsylvania
  Philadelphia, Pennsylvania 19104

ELIOT HEARST
  Department of Psychology, Indiana University
  Bloomington, Indiana 47405

STEWART H. HULSE
  Department of Psychology, The Johns Hopkins University
  Baltimore, Maryland 21218

JOHN HUMPAL
  Department of Psychology, The Johns Hopkins University
  Baltimore, Maryland 21218

PETER S. KAPLAN
  Department of Psychology, University of Colorado
  Boulder, Colorado 80309

ELIZABETH M. KURZ
  School of Social Sciences, University of California at Irvine
  Irvine, California 92717

DOUGLAS L. MEDIN
  Department of Psychology, University of Illinois
  Champaign, Illinois 61820

RALPH R. MILLER
  Department of Psychology, State University of New York
  Binghamton, New York 13901

LYNN NADEL
  School of Social Sciences, University of California at Irvine
  Irvine, California 92717

LARS-GÖRAN NILSSON
  Department of Psychology, University of Umeå
  Umeå, Sweden

DONALD A. OVERTON
    Department of Psychology, Temple University
    Philadelphia, Pennsylvania 19122

ALAN RANDICH
    Department of Psychology, University of Iowa
    Iowa City, Iowa 52242

ROBERT A. RESCORLA
    Department of Psychology, University of Pennsylvania
    Philadelphia, Pennsylvania 19104

THOMAS J. REYNOLDS
    Ayerst Laboratories, Princeton Division
    64 Maple St., Rouses Point, New York 12979

ROBERT T. ROSS
    Department of Psychology, University of Iowa
    Iowa City, Iowa 52242

TODD R. SCHACHTMAN
    Department of Psychology, State University of New York
    Binghamton, New York 13901

PER-OLOW SJÖDÉN
    Department of Applied Psychology, University of Uppsala
    Uppsala, Sweden

DAVID R. THOMAS
    Department of Psychology, University of Colorado
    Boulder, Colorado 80309

ARTHUR TOMIE
    Department of Psychology, Rutgers University
    New Brunswick, New Jersey 08903

JEFFREY WILLNER
    Department of Psychology, University of Virginia
    Charlottesville, Virginia 22903

Preface

The effects of contextual stimuli on the performance of conditioned behaviors have recently become the object of intense theoretical and empirical scrutiny. This book presents the work of researchers who have attempted to characterize the role of context in learning through direct experimental manipulation of these stimuli. Their work reveals that context has important and systematic effects upon the learning and performance of conditioned responses.

The roles played by context are diverse and the problems confronted in attempting to evaluate and differentiate contextual functions are formidable. These considerations are discussed in Balsam's introductory chapter. The remaining chapters present an analysis of the role of context in Pavlovian, operant, and discrimination learning paradigms.

Researchers who are interested in these problems will find that this work poses strong challenges to traditional views of learning. It is our hope, in bringing this work together in one place, that the empirical findings and theoretical tensions developed in this volume will lead to further debate, research, and insight into the fundamental nature of learning.

P. Balsam
A. Tomie

1 The Functions of Context in Learning and Performance

Peter D Balsam
Barnard College of Columbia University

CONTEXT

At a logical and procedural level, all learning occurs in context. Learning occurs in a cognitive or associative context of what has been learned before and in an environmental context that is defined by the location, time, and specific features of the task at hand. The chapters of this book focus primarily on the latter meaning of context, although discussions throughout the book make reference to the influence of past learning on present learning and performance. The common assumption of the chapters presented in this volume is the belief that by analyzing the functional control of behavior by physically defined contextual cues we will arrive at a deeper understanding of the laws of learning and performance. The motivation for this collective undertaking arises, in large part, from the failures of traditional association theories.

General problems with traditional association theory have provided the impetus for exploring alternative systems of analysis. As Estes (1976) has pointed out, the structure of these traditional theories (Guthrie, 1935; Hull, 1943; Pavlov, 1927; Skinner, 1938; Thorndike, 1931) consists of an association between two elements. In some cases, both elements are stimuli, and in others the elements are stimuli and responses. As a consequence, the utility of these theories rests solely on the power of binary associations to account for the data. Two general problems provide a challenge to this approach. First, challenges to the notion that only two elements are involved in the associative learning process, and, second, the great difficulty in specifying objectively what the elements or units of association are, in even the simplest sort of learning experiment, has created a need for major revisions in theories of learning.

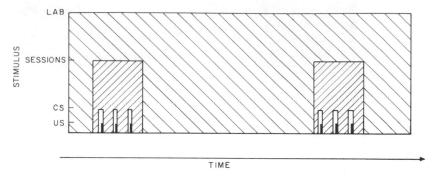

FIG. 1.1.   Schematic representation of the hierarchical structure of contexts in a Pavlovian-conditioning experiment. (After Balsam, 1984; copyright Ballinger Publishing Company. Adapted with permission.)

Consider the simple conditioning experiment depicted in Fig. 1.1. Across days subjects are placed into experimental chambers. In the presence of the experimental apparatus conditioned stimuli (CSs) are presented. In the context of a CS unconditioned stimuli (USs) are presented. After a number of such experiences, the CS will evoke a conditioned response (CR). That CR, however, is not solely a reflection of the CS–US association. If that CS is tested in a different context, CR strength will be affected. The effectiveness of that CS is modulated by context-US associations (Durlach, 1982; Gabriel, 1972; McAllister & McAllister, 1965; Randich & Ross, Chapter 5; Rescorla, Durlach, & Grau, Chapter 2; Tomie, Chapter 3), context-CS associations (Rescorla, 1984; Rescorla, Durlach & Grau, Chapter 2), and by the potentiation of CS–US associations by the context (Bouton & Bolles, Chapter 6; Holland, 1983; Miller & Schactman, Chapter 7). A simple associative learning experiment is, therefore, quite complex. There are many first-order associations that influence performance, but even more difficult for simple association theories is the demonstration that a given stimulus may control an excitatory CR, no CR, or even a different CR, depending on the context in which the stimulus appears (Archer, Sjödén, & Nilsson, Chapter 9; Bouton & Bolles, Chapter 6; Hulse, Cynx, & Humpal, Chapter 10; Kaplan & Hearst, Chapter 8; Medin & Reynolds, Chapter 12; Rescorla, Durlach, & Grau, Chapter 2; Thomas, Chapter 11; Tomie, Chapter 3). One function of context, then, is to modulate the strength and type of control that is exerted by stimuli. Such an effect is not easily accommodated by traditional association theories, and several models that are based on hierarchical associative networks have been developed to account for this sort of control (Estes, 1972, 1976; Medin & Reynolds, Chapter 12).

Loosely speaking, context has been invoked in circumstances where it "disambiguates" (Bouton & Bolles, Chapter 6; Thomas, Chapter 11) or gives an ambiguous stimulus meaning. The importance of context is nowhere clearer than in the analysis of relational stimuli. Hulse, Cynx, & Humpal (Chapter 10), for example, have been studying melody perception in starlings. What is the stimulus that the birds learn about? There is no absolute physical feature of the stimuli that is relevant. It is the relation between stimuli that defines the relevant cue. Again, it is only in the context of other stimuli that any stimulus has meaning.

This discussion of how simple association theory fails and how the idea of context has been crucial to the development of learning theory comes quite close to a discussion presented by Kohler (1929). Kohler argued that the formation of perceptual organizations was primarily what associative learning was about. When elements were integrated into an organizational unit, they belonged together (i.e., they were associated). Kohler, furthermore, suggested that the context in which things are presented will be an important determinant of whether or not they are perceived as belonging together.

None of the chapters of this book abandon the language of association for the study of perceptual organization. There is clearly a concerted attempt to build upon the historical foundations of association theory. This book represents work that takes associationistic psychology into new domains. Each of the chapters challenges existing theory and provides new insights and questions about the nature of learning.

The purpose of this chapter is to provide a guide to the remainder of the book. The following sections provide an introduction to the methods of studying context and to the conceptual issues that arise throughout the book.

THE FUNCTIONS OF CONTEXT

Context has been defined both structurally and functionally by the various contributors to this volume. When it is defined structurally, context generally refers to all the aspects of an experimental environment that are presented concurrently with a conditioned stimulus, including those cues that remain constant throughout a session. When it is defined functionally, it is used to mean any stimulus that modulates the control exerted by other stimuli (Medin & Reynolds, Chapter 12; Thomas, Chapter 11). A number of descriptions have been offered as to how the context influences behavior. Some functions of context imply that it is just like any other cue, whereas other functions are uniquely ascribed to contexts. The various ways in which contexts might function to modulate learning and performance are described in the following.

Competition. Some accounts of the role of contextual cues in learning claim that the context competes with cues for associative strength (Rescorla & Wagner, 1972) or attention (Mackintosh, 1975). In these theories, cues and contexts are functionally equivalent. The competition between them implies that to the extent that one is learned about or attended to the other will suffer. There are other forms of competition, however, that occur between context and cue. Cues and contexts may also compete with one another at a peripheral level. Behavior controlled by the context may interfere with behavior controlled by a cue (Balsam, 1984; Tomie, Chapter 3).

Comparison.   Features of cues and contexts may be compared to one another to determine learning and/or performance. In a comprehensive analysis of the major animal learning paradigms, John Gibbon and his colleagues (Gibbon, 1977, 1979; Gibbon & Balsam, 1981; Gibbon & Church, 1984) have proposed that a ratio comparison of an overall delay to reinforcement in a context with a local delay of reinforcement underlies the performance of learned behavior. In nondiscriminated procedures (e.g., reinforcement schedules and Sidman avoidance procedures), subjects compare an estimate of the delay remaining to reinforcement to an estimate of the overall reinforcement delay, whereas, in discriminated procedures (e.g., discrete trial and classical conditioning procedures), subjects compare an average delay of reinforcement in the signal to the overall delay in the context. When this expectancy ratio exceeds a threshold, subjects respond. In this view, subjects learn about both cues and contexts, and performance is a function of the ratio of their expectancy or associative values. Performance is clearly thought to be a function of this ratio at the time of learning, and by implication the same rule may apply if cue and/or context values are altered after initial training. A similar role for context has been proposed for cases of inhibitory learning (Balsam, in press; Kaplan & Hearst, Chapter 8; Miller & Schachtman, Chapter 7).

Summation.   In contrast to the comparison function, Konorski (1967) suggested that drive conditioned to contextual cues might summate with the associative value of a CS and thus augment the strength of the CR. This sort of summation of context and CS value has been invoked to explain the facilitated responding that is found when a CS is tested in a context associated with the same US that was used to condition the CS (Bouton & Bolles, Chapter 6; Miller & Schachtman, Chapter 7; Rescorla, Durlach, & Grau, Chapter 2).

Retrieval.   A fourth function of context can be to act as a retrieval cue. Such a cue can be part of an association between other stimuli and responses. The probability of recall is, therefore, influenced by whether or not the test context is similar to the training context (Medin & Reynolds, Chapter 12). Context can also serve as a retrieval cue for other associations. For example, Miller and Schachtman (Chapter 7) suggest that context acts as a retrieval cue for a CS–US association. Similarily, a context may act as a retrieval cue for an instrumental CR–US association (Spear, Smith, Bryan, Gordon, Timmons, & Chiszar,

1980). This latter function is quite similar to the one described in the next section, in which context acts like a gate for other associations.

Occasion Setting.   This function of context is based on Holland's (1983) analysis of positive and negative feature discriminations. In these arrangements, a cue is repeatedly presented and occasionally reinforced. In a positive feature procedure, this cue is accompanied by a distinct cue on reinforced occasions. In a negative feature procedure, the cue is accompanied by a distinct stimulus when it is not reinforced. These features, therefore, set the occasions on which the common cues will be differently reinforced. In this paradigm, particularly when the distinctive feature precedes the common cue, the feature serves to enable or gate a particular CS–US relationship. Rescorla, Durlach, and Grau (Chapter 2) report a similar result in which a positive feature acts to enable a particular CS–US relationship, independently of the occasion setter's association with the US.

Similarly, the occasion-setting function of a stimulus can gate an instrumental CR–US relationship. This is an alternate description of the discriminative function of stimuli. A discriminative stimulus performs a contextual function in the sense that it signals when a particular response-reinforcer relationship is in effect (Medin & Reynolds, Chapter 12; Overton, Chapter 13; Thomas, Chapter 11).

Response Selection.   The context in which a cue is reinforced may also determine the specific form of a conditioned response. Unconditioned or conditioned properties of the context may modulate either the learning or performance of a particular CS–CR connection. For example, Joan Graf, Rae Silver, and I have been studying the development of pecking in young Ring Doves. We have found that after associations between seed and food have been formed, the specific form of the CR depends on the context in which squab are tested. The squab will peck at seed but if they are tested in the presence of their parents they will also beg at the *seed,* the food-getting behavior that is usually directed at the parents. The form of the CR directed at the CS (seed) is, therefore, modulated by either the conditioned or unconditioned properties of the context.

Tomie (Chapter 3) shows that the form of the CR in autoshaping may be modulated by the strength of the context-US association at the time of learning. A similar effect on response topography is documented later in this chapter.

Stimulus Generalization.   The physical context in which a stimulus occurs affects the sensory input and/or perception of that stimulus. It is always the relation between cue and context that defines a physical stimulus. This is true even in situations in which there is a single stimulus presented, as well as situations in which the relationship between cue and context is treated explicitly (Hulse et al., Chapter 10). Alterations in context may therefore affect behavior through stimulus generalization processes.

Seven functions of context have been described here and are documented throughout the book. These functions need not be mutually exclusive.

MEASURING CONTEXTUAL CONTROL

There are two general strategies that have been used to assay the strength of associations with the context. One strategy is to examine the effect of contextual manipulations on the control exerted by a nominal CS or discriminative stimulus. The second strategy is to study contextual control by examining the acquisition or maintenance of behavior that is controlled directly by contextual cues.

Context-Shift Test. One technique for studying the influence of context on performance is to first train a subject in one context and then compare performance in the original training context to performance in contexts that differ in various ways from the training context. In general, performance in a context other than the training context will be decremented (Archer et al., Chapter 9; Medin & Reynolds, Chapter 12; Miller et al., Chapter 7; Nadel, Willner, & Kurz, Chapter 14; Overton, Chapter 13). The decrement in performance may be reflected in the level of excitatory control exerted by a stimulus and/or the degree of dimensional stimulus control (Thomas, Chapter 11). Performance is also modulated by the strength of between association between the test context and the US. Strong context-US associations sometimes enhance performance (Bouton & Bolles, Chapter 6; Rescorla et al., Chapter 2; Miller & Schachtman, Chapter 7), whereas under some circumstances strong context-US associations reduce the excitatory control exerted by a stimulus (Balsam, 1982; Kaplan & Hearst, Chapter 8; Miller & Schachtman, Chapter 7; Randich & Ross, Chapter 5). These discrepancies are discussed later.

Retardation Test. Another technique for demonstrating an effect of context conditioning on learning is to examine CS conditioning following pretraining of contextual cues. For example, acquisition speed in a pretrained context has been used extensively as an index of prior context conditioning (Baker, Singh, & Bindra, Chapter 4; Balsam, 1984; Balsam & Schwartz, 1981; Randich & Ross, Chapter 5; Tomie, 1976, 1981, Chapter 3). The rationale for this technique assumes that prior context conditioning will interfere with subsequent acquisition at the learning (Rescorla & Wagner, 1972) and/or performance (Gibbon & Balsam, 1981) level.

The preceding two techniques use responsiveness to a stimulus both as the assay of learning about the stimulus and as the assay of learning about the context. It is often necessary to assay these values independently. Inasmuch as performance to a given stimulus is always modulated by the context in which it is tested, it is impossible to have a "context-free" measure of stimulus learning. It is possible, however, to measure what is known about a context in the absence of the stimulus. Several techniques have been developed for assaying context conditioning by measuring a response that is directly controlled by contextual cues.

Preference Test.   Another procedure that has been used to study learning about the context is a test of preference for different contexts that have undergone different training histories. Subjects are given a choice between staying in a pretrained and nonpretrained context (Bouton & Bolles, Chapter 6; Odling–Smee, 1975; Randich & Ross, Chapter 5), or between two contexts that have been pretrained in different ways (Fanselow, 1980). This technique has been used exclusively in studies of aversive conditioning. The results of the preference test presumably reflect differences in learning about the contexts. The interpretation of what learning they reflect, however, is not so straightforward.

For example, subjects prefer contexts in which shocks are reliably predicted by signals to ones in which shocks are not preceded by reliable signals (Bouton & Bolles, Chapter 6; Fanselow, 1980; Odling–Smee, 1975). These preferences have been interpreted as reflecting the strength of the context-US association. If we allow, however, that (1) context-CS associations and (2) the hierarchical association of the context with the CS–US association itself might influence choices, the preference score tells us which context is preferred but not why that is so. In light of experiments that show that subjects sometimes prefer signaled appetitive stimuli (Fantino, 1977) as well as signaled aversive stimuli to unsignaled USs, only cautious interpretation of preference tests of context value seems appropriate. The analysis of the bases of these preferences, however, will provide an important insight into the nature of learning and into the bases of preferences in general.

Summation Test.   A fourth technique for evaluating context conditioning is to examine the effects of presenting contextual cues on ongoing operant behavior. In conditioned emotional response (CER) procedures, Baker (Baker et al., Chapter 4; Baker, Mercier, Gabel, & Baker, 1981) has argued that, when aversive classical conditioning occurs in the same apparatus as was used for appetitive operant training, ongoing response rates can serve as an assay of contextual conditioning. Presumably, the context affects response rates in the same way as a nominal CS in the standard CER paradigm. Patterson and Overmier (1981) have, in fact, shown this to be the case. When subjects are given off-baseline conditioning sessions, context conditioning can be inferred from the effects of nonreinforced presentation of contextual cues on ongoing operant behavior.

Resistance of Context to Reinforcement.   Tomie (Chapter 3) has developed a fifth technique for studying context conditioning. In these procedures, subjects are first exposed to a pretraining procedure. In a subsequent phase of the experiment, a feature of the pretrained context is presented as a discrete CS paired with a US. In this procedure, context conditioning is inferred from the effectiveness of the former contextual cue to act as a CS (Tomie, Chapter 3). As Tomie points out, the effects of this procedure are modulated by the associative status of the remaining contextual cues present during testing. When training and test contexts are the same, acquisition is retarded, whereas a change of context between training and testing results in facilitated acquisition to the target feature. Tomie's results highlight the difficulties of inferring a level of contextual conditioning solely from behavior controlled by the CS. Strong contextual conditioning may be reflected in either high- or low-CR strength. It is therefore imperative that measures other than a single test based on reponsiveness to a CS be employed in measuring context conditioning (Balsam, 1984; Bouton & Bolles, Chapter 6; Randich & Ross, Chapter 5; Rescorla, Durlach, & Grau, Chapter 2; Tomie, Chapter 3).

Context CRs.   The most direct way to infer the presence of associations to any stimulus is to measure the behavior that is differentially controlled by that stimulus after it has been paired with a US. CRs conditioned to contextual cues can therefore serve as an assay of learning about contexts.

In appetitive conditioning, general activity appears to meet these requirements (Balsam, 1984; Balsam, in preparation; Durlach, 1984; Rescorla, Durlach, & Grau, Chapter 2). These properties are illustrated in an experiment conducted in our laboratory in which two groups of Ring Doves were exposed to 25 sessions of unsignaled food presentation. Following this phase of training, all the subjects

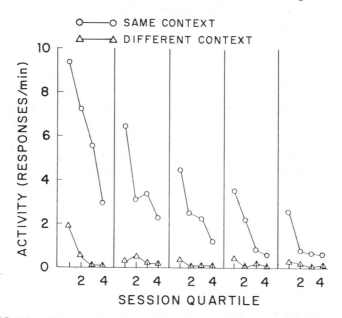

FIG. 1.2.   Mean level of general activity during quartiles of extinction sessions is shown for groups of pigeons that were tested in a context that was either the same as or different from the original training context in which grain had been presented.

were given five sessions of nonreinforced exposure to contextual cues. Figure 1.2 shows, in blocks of quarter sessions, activity levels during these extinction sessions. For half the subjects the extinction context was identical to the training context (circles), and the remainder of the subjects (triangles) were tested in a context that differed from the training context in visual, auditory, and tactile cues. Only those subjects tested in the training context show substantial activity during the test. Activity levels decline within sessions and across days. Spontaneous recovery occurs from the end of one session to the beginning of the next. General activity exhibits the basic properties of a CR and, therefore, can serve as an assay of contextual conditioning. Both context-US (Balsam, 1984; Durlach, 1984) and context-CS (Rescorla, 1984; Rescorla et al., Chapter 2) associations are reflected in conditioned activity controlled by the context.

In summary, a variety of means for studying context conditioning has been developed. Some procedures examine the effects of context on responding to a stimulus embedded in that context, whereas other procedures examine behavior controlled by the context itself. Under the assumption that cues and contexts are independent elements of associations, no one measure provides a clear-cut answer to the question of what is the nature of the associations formed during learning. We must therefore require convergent operations in which more than one measure is used to analyze the role of context in learning.

THE DOMAIN AND CONDITIONS OF CONTEXTUAL CONTROL

Contextual modulation of learning has been documented in birds, rodents, and primates. It has, furthermore, been observed in both appetitive and aversive learning paradigms with phasic and static cues, and with both intereoceptive (see Overton, Chapter 13) and extereoceptive stimuli. All basic learning phenomena that have been studied (excitation, inhibition, extinction, discrimination learning), have been shown to be modulated by contextual manipulations. There is, therefore, great species and procedural generality to these phenomena. But what are their limits? Is there learning that is not contextually bound? If so, what are the conditions that modulate these processes?

When posed in this form, these questions are not easily answered. If we find that learning does not transfer across contexts, we are safe in concluding that such learning is contextually bound. On the other hand, if we find that learning transfers across contexts, can we then conclude that the learning is context free? The transfer finding can be equally well explained by a failure to define the relevant context. This is a familiar problem in the stimulus control literature (Mackintosh, 1977; Terrace, 1966). Failures of stimulus control may mean that there is complete generalization or that the subject is under the control of dimensions other than the manipulated one. It is difficult to conceive of behavior that is not under stimulus control, and, at least in the abstract, it is difficult to conceive of learned behavior that would not be modulated by the context in which it is learned and tested. Nadel, Willner, & Kurz (Chapter 14) argue that contexts are the fundamental organizers of all learning. It is clear, though, that there can be no definitive answer to the question of whether or not learning can be context free.

There can, however, be an answer to the question of what are the necessary conditions for an arbitrarily defined context to exert an influence on learning and performance. A sufficient condition for establishing contextual control is that there be differential reinforcement of a cue signaled by changes in contextual cues. Conditional discriminations arrange these conditions for two cues and contexts (Medin & Reynolds, Chapter 12). This is also illustrated in positive-feature and negative-feature procedures, in which a common cue is rewarded or extinguished only in the presence of a distinctive feature. Under these circumstances, the context in which the common cue is presented will determine whether or not a CR occurs (Archer et al., Chapter 9; Bouton & Bolles, Chapter 6; Medin & Reynolds, Chapter 12; Rescorla et al., Chapter 2).

Differential reinforcement of a cue in more than one context, however, appears not to be a necessary condition for contextual control to develop. Thomas (Chapter 11) and Medin & Reynolds, (Chapter 12) present evidence for contextual control even when cue and context are only experienced together during experimental sessions. Subjects do, however, experience contexts other than the ones that define experimental sessions, and, in fact, experimental chambers are often differentially reinforced with respect to other contexts (Balsam 1984; Mackintosh, 1977; Thomas, Chapter 11). It may be that differential reinforcement of contexts or that simple exposure to changes in context is necessary for achieving control by contextual cues.

CONTEXT EFFECTS ON LEARNING AND PERFORMANCE

Given the potentially ubiquitous nature of contextual influences in learning, it is worth surveying the empirical domain in which contextual functions have been analyzed.

Context learning rate

The domain of contextual functions will be determined in part by the rate at which each of the functions develops. More specifically, the various functions of context might take more or less time and experience to develop. The time course with which each of the contextual functions develops has not been studied in all cases. Those that have provide an interesting pattern of results.

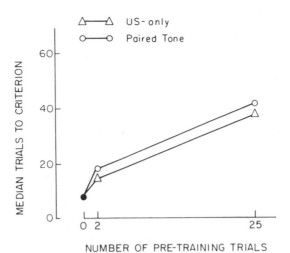

FIG. 1.3.   Median keypeck acquisition speed (number of trials to satisfy a criterion of pecks on three out of four consecutive trials) is shown as a function of the number of pretraining trials. For half the pretrained subjects all grain presentations were preceded by a tone (circles) whereas pretraining consisted of unsignaled US presentation for the remaining subjects (triangles).

Context-US associations develop rapidly. In aversive conditioning procedures, context learning has been demonstrated after just a few US presentations (Archer et al., Chapter 9; Bouton & Bolles, Chapter 6; Odling–Smee, 1975; Randich & Ross, Chapter 5) as well as after a small number of CS–US pairings (McAllister, McAllister, & Benton, 1983). In appetitive preparations, we (Balsam, 1984; Balsam & Gibbon, in preparation; Balsam & Schwartz, 1981) have shown that context-US associations are formed quite rapidly using both retardation and activity measures of learning. Furthermore, context learning is rapid even when US presentations are preceded by signals. Figure 1.3 shows the results of a retardation test (Balsam, 1984; Balsam & Gibbon, in preparation), in which pigeons were exposed to differing numbers of US presentations prior to autoshaping in which the illumination of a keylight was followed by grain presentation. For half the subjects, the pretraining USs were unsignaled, whereas for the remainder of the subjects USs were preceded by a tone. As Fig. 1.3 shows, subsequent keypeck acquisition is a function of the number of pretraining trials but not a function of whether or not those USs are signaled. Associations with the context are, therefore, formed quite rapidly in both appetitive and aversive conditioning.

Over time, the effects of these associations appear to be maintained, as evidenced by their continued influence on asymptotic performance levels (Balsam, 1984; Balsam & Gibbon, in preparation; Balsam & Schwartz, 1981; Durlach, 1984; Randich & LoLordo, 1979; Randich & Ross, Chapter 5; Rescorla,

Durlach, & Grau, Chapter 2; Tomie, 1981, Chapter 3), and by the demonstrable effects of contextual manipulations after substantial training (Bouton & Bolles, Chapter 6; Overton, Chapter 13; Rescorla et al., Chapter 2; Thomas, Chapter 11).

Context-US interference with the CR

Evidence for the competitive (Rescorla & Wagner, 1972) and comparison (Gibbon & Balsam, 1981) functions of contextual cues come from studies that document an inverse relation between the associative value of the context and the strength of the conditioned response. There is strong empirical support for the proposition that context-US associations can interfere with either the learning or expression of CS–US associations (Baker et al., Chapter 4; Balsam, 1984); Balsam & Gibbon, in preparation; Balsam & Schwartz, 1981; Durlach, 1984; Rescorla, Durlach, & Grau, Chapter 2; Tomie, 1981, Chapter 3). The majority of this evidence comes from studies showing that acquisition is decremented by prior context conditioning, that massed trials produce poorer acquisition than spaced trials, and that US presentations during the ITI period also interfere with CR acquisition. The experimental analysis of these effects indicates that contextual interference with the CR is the result of both learning and performance mechanisms.

Performance.   In all these paradigms, at least some of the contextual interference with CR production appears to be due to performance factors. Tomie (Chapter 3), for example, has shown that, under some circumstances, the retarded acquisition following US-only pretraining is due to an effect on CR topogaphy rather than a failure of a CS–US association. Similarly, Jenkins and his colleagues (Jenkins & Lambos, 1983; Lindblom & Jenkins, 1981) have shown that autoshaped responding, eliminated by presenting reinforcers during the ITI (noncontingent condition), recovers completely in extinction. Thus the decrement in responding produced by the noncontingent procedure is due to performance factors rather than a loss of the CS–US association. In our laboratory (Balsam, 1984) we have investigated how temporal variables may contribute to performance deficits. Subjects were exposed to a massed-trial autoshaping procedure that did not result in keypecking. After five subsequent sessions of nonreinforced exposure to the context, the CS was again presented and all subjects pecked the key more often in this phase of the experiment than they had in the conditioning phase. Thus, the failure of subjects to peck the key during the autoshaping phase was due at least in part to a performance block rather than a failure of the CS–US association. Similarly, Randich & Ross (Chapter 5) report that post-conditioning exposure to a US-only procedure results in small decrements in CR strength.

There are several mechanisms that might mediate a performance block. The context might control responses that are incompatible with those controlled by the cue. The topography of the CR controlled by the cue might be altered by context manipulations (see Tomie, Chapter 3). Finally, the context-US or context-CR association might inhibit the response production mechanism controlled by the CS.

There is, unfortunately, little evidence to assess how much each of these mechanisms contributes to contextual interference with the CR. In autoshaping, extinction of the context sometimes reestablishes keypecking to the CS, suggesting that some interference is due to response competition or inhibition by the context. Furthermore, when pigeons are physically restrained in front of the keylight and feeder, acquisition is rapid and the trial spacing effects are severely attenuated (Locurto, Travers, Terrace, & Gibbon, 1980). Thus by preventing subjects from engaging in the behaviors usually conditioned to contextual cues, the effect of varying temporal parameters is attenuated. These data suggest that the inverse relation between background value and keypecking may be due, in part, to the contextual control of behaviors incompatible with keypecking. Data from other preparations also show that CR form and strength are influenced by the ongoing behavioral context in which the CS is presented (Anokhin, 1958; Henton, 1981; Konorski, 1972; Kupalov, 1969).

Learning.   Although some contextual interference with the CR is likely to be mediated by performance factors, the contextual associations that are present at the time a CS is initially learned about exert a long-lasting and powerful effect on CR strength. Even when contextual associations are altered prior to testing the CS, CR strength is still largely a reflection of the performance generated by the original training conditions. For example, in autoshaping initial exposure to a random control procedure does not educe any keypecking (Durlach, 1984; Lindblom & Jenkins, 1981). Subsequent exposure either to CS and context extinction (Lindblom & Jenkins, 1981) or to a test of the CS in a nonreinforced context (Durlach, 1984) also does not result in keypecking. The absence of pecking during random control procedures, therefore, involves more than a performance deficit. Furthermore, asymptotic response strength is inversely related to the degree of prior context conditioning (Balsam & Schwartz, 1981). Hence, there is a strong influence of initial associations on CR performance across a variety of changes in the associative value of the test context. These data argue for a learning component in the interference generated by the context-US association.

The nature of the learning that underlies the context interference effect might be of two sorts. On one hand, it might be that the context-US association blocks the formation of the CS–US association. Alternatively, the context-US association might change the CS–CR association. This latter notion deserves some amplification because it has not been previously suggested.

The basic idea is that the specific CR topography controlled by the CS might be modulated by the context-US association. For example, imagine that very infrequently projectiles are thrown at you and that before each projectile I yell a warning. The topography that is controlled by the warning is very likely to be quite different from the behavior that might be controlled by the warning when the projectiles occur very frequently. In the former case you are likely to dodge the projectile, whereas in the latter case you would most likely protect yourself with your hands. Although there is great danger in generalizing from an example such as this to a general rule of conditioning, it does provide some face validity for the notion that "associative" manipulations, such as trial spacing, might affect the CR form.

According to this logic there is no way for us to distinguish between a failure of CS–US association and the failure of CS's to control the same topographies under different conditions. There seem to be two ways out of this dilemma. One strategy is to try to measure all the CRs that a stimulus might come to control as a result of a CS–US association. A second strategy is to try to employ topography-free tests of associative value. An example of the former strategy is presented in the following.

At this time we do not have a description of precisely how topographies change with changes in the context-US association, but we do have some evidence that in autoshaping CS–US associations may be reflected in topographies other than keypecking. The way in which we have ascertained this is through the measurement of general activity controlled by both the CS and the context. General activity has often proved to be a useful measure of conditioned behavior in situations where the particular CR topographies may be unknown or variable from one trial to the next (Balsam, 1984; Durlach, 1984; Killeen, 1975; Rescorla, Durlach, & Grau, Chapter 2). In the experiments described here, the floor of the experimental chamber was divided into six panels that were hinged on the front and rear walls. Any horizontal movement across these panels was mechanically transduced into a signal and recorded. This has turned out to be a useful technique for measuring the behavior that is conditioned to both the cue and the context in autoshaping experiments with pigeons and ring doves.

One experiment serves to illustrate how general activity can be used to measure both the CS–US and context-US associations. What we wished to investigate was whether or not a response is conditioned to the CS under regimens that do not give rise to keypecking. In an experiment described earlier, we exposed subjects to a 1 to 1 ratio of ITI to trial times, a condition in which subjects typically do not keypeck. For 7 days subjects were exposed to pairings of a 36-sec keylight with grain. Twenty of these pairings occurred each day with an ITI of 36 sec. This procedure produced very little keypecking. All subjects were then given one 30-min. background extinction session for each of 5 days. In the last phase of the experiment, subjects were given 20 nonreinforced presentations of the CS during each session. All subjects pecked the key more often in this phase of the experiment than they had in the conditioning phase. The general activity recorded throughout the experiment in the presence of both the context alone and the CS is shown in Fig. 1.4. There is a great deal of context activity in the first phase of the study that extinguishes during the second phase of the study. The

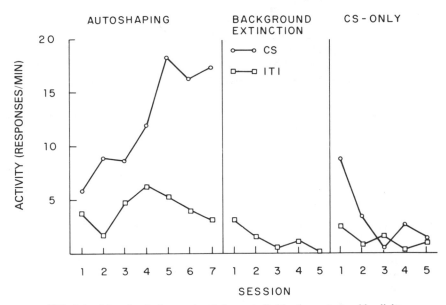

FIG. 1.4. Mean level of general activity controlled by the context and keylight, CS, is shown for each of the experimental phases. The left panel depicts the autoshaping phase in which keylights were paired with grain. The center panel depicts the context extinction phase and the right panel depicts the CS-only phase of the experiment.

general activity in the presence of the CS indicates, in contrast to the keypeck data, that the keylight was a very effective CS. The major point to be made from these experimental results is that context-US associations may interfere with the CR for many reasons. First, examination of the activity data during the conditioning phase shows that in spite of the low level of keypecking observed in this experiment a CS–US association had been formed. The expression of this association in activity might be the result of a weak CS–US association. Equally likely, however, is the possibility that this experimental arrangement may have resulted in CR topographies that are different from the keypeck response that is typically measured in autoshaping experiments as the nominal CR. Secondly, the increase in keypecking following context extinction indicates that the associative value of the test context and, in this case, training context (see Miller & Schachtman, Chapter 7) affects the performance of the CR. Hence, both learning and performance effects may contribute to contextual interference with the CR simultaneously.

Context-US facilitation of the CR

The previous section documents the ability of context-US associations to interfere with CR strength. On the other hand, context-US associations have been shown to be directly related to CR strength in studies that employ a context-shift test, in which subjects are trained under identical conditions and the CS is tested in contexts that differ from the original training context. Generally, when a well-established CS is tested in a context different from the training context, a decrease in CR strength is observed (Archer et al., Chapter 9; Durlach, 1984; Medin & Reynolds, Chapter 12; Miller & Schachtman, Chapter 7; but see Bouton & Bolles, Chapter 6 for an exception). Furthermore, CR strength is greater in a test context associated with the US than in a test context not associated with the US (Durlach, 1984; Gabriel, 1972; McAllister & McAllister, 1965; Rescorla, Durlach, & Grau, Chapter 2).

The inverse relationship between acquisition speed and the associative value of the context described in the preceding section, and the direct relationship between the associative value of the context and CR strength during maintenance, suggest that different contextual functions may dominate performance at different times. For example, early in training, contextual functions that interfere with CR strength such as competition and comparison may dominate, whereas context-US facilitation of performance later in training may result from the later development of summation, retrieval, or occasion-setting functions.

A changing relation between CR strength and context value

There appears to be an inverse relation between context value and CR strength during acquisition but a direct relation between context value and CR strength in maintenance. We have attempted to study this change in the relationship between CR strength and context by simultaneously measuring the behaviors controlled by contextual cues and those controlled by the signal.

Specifically, we have analyzed the relationship between general activity (as a measure of context conditioning) and keypeck strength (as a measure of CS conditioning) across a variety of autoshaping experiments in both pigeons and doves. In the experiments with pigeons all subjects were exposed to an 8-sec illumination of the keylight followed by grain presentation. Each session consisted of 25 of these trials presented every 40 seconds. These experiments lasted for about 7 sessions (175 trials). The Ring Doves, on the other hand, were exposed to an autoshaping procedure that consisted of the 8-sec illumination of a keylight before each grain presentation with a 48-sec ITI. The dove data were collected from several experiments that all consisted of 20 trials per session, but the total number of sessions in each experiment varied between 7 and 28.

Early in training both pigeons and doves show an inverse relationship between general activity and peck strength. The higher the level of general activity, the longer it took subjects to acquire the keypeck response. The correlation between activity and the number of trials to satisfy the criterion of pecks on 3 out of 4 consecutive trials was .25 for doves ($N = 23$) and .38 for pigeons ($N = 15$). The activity during the 10 trials immediately after meeting the acquisition criterion was negatively related to the probability of responding during these trials. The correlation between these measures was −.61 for the doves and −.56 for the pigeons. In both the pigeons and doves these correlations remain negative for at least 150 trials as do the correlations between general activity and peck rates. Because the pigeons were not run for much longer than that, we are forced to examine the effects of extended training on this relationship only in those doves that received a longer exposure to the autoshaping procedure.

Fig. 1.5 shows the daily correlation between general activity and rate of keypecking for 9 doves exposed to the autoshaping procedure for 28 days (560 trials). Although there is a great deal of session to session variability in this measure, the correlations are generally negative for the first 9 days and postivie thereafter. Early in training those subjects that show the most activity peck the least, whereas later in training those subjects that are most active also make the most keypecks. This experiment was done for reasons other than to examine this correlation, and it is unfortunate that the experiment was not continued. It is not clear from Fig. 1.5 that the correlations have reached a stable state in the 28 days of the experiment. The final points in the figure suggest that the relationship between activity and pecking might have become even more positive had training been continued.

There is thus a change in how general activity relates to keypeck strength during the course of an experiment. Initially, there is a negative relation between these two measures that switches over to a positive one with extended training. An implication of this result is that the functional relationship between contextual associations and CR strength may change during the course of training.

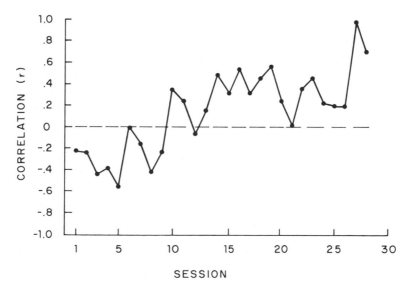

FIG. 1.5.   The daily correlations between general activity level and keypeck rate is shown for a group of Ring Doves exposed to an autoshaping procedure.

Mechanisms of interference and facilitation

The analysis of the influence of contextual cues on the conditioned stimulus has turned out to be a complicated one. On a descriptive level, the context can sometimes interfere with and sometimes facilitate the performance of responses controlled by the CS. In the case of interference it is possible to generate both performance and learning-based explanations of the data. Furthermore, there are two types of learning that might contribute to these effects. The context might modulate the strength of the CS–US association and/or modulate the specific topographies controlled by the CS.

At present we do not have the data necessary to partition context effects into all these classes, and as we have shown these classes need not be mutually exclusive. In addition to the simultaneous operation of various contextual functions, these functions may change over time, For example, one interpretation of the changing correlation between context activity and keypecking is that the nature of the control mechanism is changing. Early in training, cue, context, and US may be processed as separate elements. This may allow for the competition (Rescorla & Wagner, 1972) and/or comparison (Gibbon & Balsam, 1981) functions of context to operate. Later in training, the context, CS, and US may be processed in a more integrated way, such that the CS, US, and context are not represented independently (Medin & Reynolds, Chapter 12; Nadel, Willner, & Kurz, Chapter 14). Hence, later in training there is a positive correlation between the associative value of each of the elements and the strength of the CR. On the basis of this analysis one would expect to find that weakening a context-US association would result in a decrement in the strength of the CR controlled by a CS, and that weakening a CS–US association should decrement the strength of the CR controlled by the context. The former expectation has been verified in the previously described context-shift studies, and the latter expectation has been confirmed in a recent autoshaping study conducted by Rescorla (1984). In that experiment, extinction of a CS in one context resulted in a decrease in the level of general activity controlled by a second context in which that CS had been paired with a US. The evidence is, therefore, consistent with the hypothesis that at least after some training CSs, USs, and contexts are all part of an integrated representation in memory.

One would wish to test this analysis in a number of independent ways, but the basic ideas do a good job of accounting for the changing correlation between activity and keypecking in our experiments and for the differences in the effects of various context manipulations on CR strength when they are done early and late in training.

ORGANIZATION OF THE BOOK

This chapter was designed to provide a brief introduction to the basic issues, concepts, empirical findings, and methods of study in the analysis of the role of context in learning. Each of these topics is developed in greater detail and in more specialized forms in the subsequent chapters of the book. Although many chapters address more than one issue, we have attempted to organize this book thematically. Chapters 2 through 7 analyze the role of contextual cues in excitatory Pavlovian conditioning. These chapters analyze the full range of contextual functions in both appetitive (Rescorla, Durlach, & Grau, Chapter 2; Tomie, Chapter 3; Baker, Singh, & Bindra, Chapter 4) and aversive preparations (Baker, Singh, & Bindra, Chapter 4; Randich & Ross, Chapter 5; Bouton & Bolles, Chapter 6; Miller & Schachtman, Chapter 7). The role of context-US associations in inhibitory learning is demonstrated by Baker, Singh, and Bindra (Chapter 4) and explored in greater detail by both Miller and Schachtman (Chapter 7) and Kaplan and Hearst (Chapter 8).

Chapters 9 through 12 demonstrate how techniques developed for the study of generalization and discrimination can be employed to precisely identify the features of learning environments that become contextual cues. This type of analysis is illustrated for contexts presented simultaneously with cues (Archer, Sjödén, & Nilsson, Chapter 9; Thomas, Chapter 10; Medin & Reynolds, Chapter 12; Overton, Chapter 13), as well as for serially defined contexts (Hulse, Cynx, & Humpal, Chapter 10). Additionally, a formal model of cue-context interactions in a variety of learning paradigms is developed by Medin & Reynolds (Chapter 12).

Chapters 13 and 14 discuss how internal physiological states may serve as contexts or underlie other contextual effects. Overton (Chapter 13) discusses contexts defined by the internal state of an organism and emphasizes the analysis of contextual effects of drugs. Nadel, Willner, and Kurz (Chapter 14) speculate about the neurophysiological basis of spatial contexts.

The chapters of this book explore the role of context in learning with a wide range of procedures. Our hope is that by bringing this work together in one place further debate, analysis, and theoretical integration will be stimulated. The problem of how to conceptualize contexts is one that is germane to many areas of psychology such as human memory, perception, and psycholinguistics. The progress that is made toward understanding the role of context in the conditioning paradigms, that are the major focus of this book may, therefore, contribute significantly to a better understanding and methodology in a wide range of psychological research (see Medin & Reynolds, Chapter 12).

ACKNOWLEDGMENTS

The research reported here was supported in part by NIMH grant MH34759. I thank R. Decker, S. Gonzalez, A. Jim, T. Leung, M. Padilla, J. Rivera, and C. Servetas for assistance with this project.

REFERENCES

Anokhin, P. K. The role of the orienting-exploratory reaction in the formation of the conditioned reflex. In L. G. Voronin, A. N. Leontiev, A. R. Luria, E. N. Sokolov, & O. S. Vinogradova (Eds.), *Orienting reflex and exploratory behavior,* Moscow: Academy of Pedagogical Sciences of RSFSR, 1958.

Baker, A. G., Mercier, P., Gabel, J., & Baker, P. A. Contextual conditioning and the US preexposure effect in conditioned fear. *Journal of Experimental Psychology: Animal Behavior Processes,* 1981, *7,* 109–128.

Balsam, P. D. Bringing the background to the foreground: The role of contextual cues in autoshaping. In M. Commons, R. Herrnstein, & A. R. Wagner (Eds.), *Quantitative analyses of behavior: Volume 3: Acquisition.* Cambridge, Mass.: Ballinger, 1984.

Balsam, P. D. Relative time in trace conditioning. In J. Gibbon & L. Allan (Eds.), *Timing and time perception.* New York: New York Academy of Sciences, in press.

Balsam, P. D. *General activity induced by periodic food presentation is a conditioned response.* Manuscript in preparation.

Balsam, P. D., & Gibbon, J. *Tones paired with food block keylights but not contexts.* Manuscript in preparation.

Balsam, P. D., & Schwartz, A. L. Rapid contextual conditioning in autoshaping. *Journal of Experimental Psychology: Animal Behavior Processes,* 1981, *1,* 382–393.

Durlach, P. Pavlovian learning and performance when CS and US are uncorrelated. In M. Commons, R. Herrnstein, & A. R. Wagner (Eds.), *Quantitative analyses of behavior: Volume 3: Acquisition.* Cambridge, Mass.: Ballinger, 1984.

Estes, W. K. An associative basis for coding and organization in memory. In A. W. Melton & E. Martin (Eds.), *Coding processes in human memory.* Washington, D. C.: Winston, 1972.

Estes, W. K. Structural aspects of associative models for memory. In C. N. Cofer (Ed.), *The structure of human memory.* New York: W. H. Freeman, 1976.

Fanselow, M. S. Signaled shock-free periods and preference for signaled shock. *Journal of Experimental Psychology: Animal Behavior Processes,* 1980, *6,* 65–80.

Fantino, E. Conditioned reinforcement: Choice and information. In W. K. Honig & J. E. R. Staddon (Eds.), *Handbook of operant behavior.* Englewood Cliffs, N. J.: Prentice–Hall, 1977.

Gabriel, M. Incubation of avoidance produced by generalization to stimuli of the conditioning apparatus. In R. Thompson & A. Voss (Eds.), *Topics in learning and performance.* New York: Academic Press, 1972.

Gibbon, J. Scalar expectancy theory and Weber's law in animal timing. *Psychological Review,* 1977, *84,* 279–325.

Gibbon, J. Timing the stimulus and the response in aversive control. In M. D. Zeiler & P. Harzen (Eds.), *Reinforcement and the organization of behavior,* New York: Wiley, 1979.

Gibbon, J., & Church, R. M. Sources of variance in an information processing theory of timing. In H. Roitblat, T. Bever, & H. Terrace (Eds.), *Animal Cognition.* Hillsdale, N.J.: Lawrence Erlbaum Associates, 1984.

Gibbon, J., & Balsam, P. D. The spread of association in time. In C. M. Locurto, H. S. Terrace, & J. G. Gibbon (Eds.), *Autoshaping and conditioning theory.* New York: Academic Press, 1981.

Guthrie, E. R. *The psychology of learning.* New York: Harper & Row, 1935.

Henton, W. W. Kupalov conditioning: Molecular control of response sequences. *The Psychological Record,* 1981, *31,* 489–509.

Holland, P. C. "Occasion-setting" in conditional discriminations. In M. Commons, R. Herrnstein, & A. R. Wagner (Eds.), *Quantitative Analyses of Behavior: Vol.4: Discrimination processes.* New York: Ballinger, 1983.

Hull, C. L. *Principles of behavior.* New York: Appleton–Century–Crofts, 1943.

Jenkins, H. M., & Lambos, W. A. Tests of two explanations of response elimination by noncontingent reinforcement. *Animal Learning & Behavior,* 1983, *11* (3), 302–308.

Killeen, P. On the temporal control of behavior. *Psychological Review,* 1975, *82,* 89–115.

Kohler, W. *Gestalt psychology.* New York: Liveright, 1929.

Konorski, J. *Integrative activity of the brain.* Chicago: University of Chicago Press, 1967.

Konorski, J. Some ideas concerning physiological mechanisms of so-called internal inhibition. In R. A. Boakes & M. S. Halliday (Eds.), *Inhibition and learning.* London: Academic Press, 1972.

Kupalov, P. S. The formation of conditioned place reflexes. In M. Cole & I. Maltzman (Eds.), *A handbook of contemporary Soviet psychology.* New York: Basic Books, 1969.

Lindblom, L. L. & Jenkins, H. M. Responses eliminated by non-contingent or negatively contingent reinforcement recover in extinction. *Journal of Experimental Psychology: Animal Behavior Processes,* 1981, *7,* 175–190.

Locurto, C. M., Travers, T., Terrace, H. S., & Gibbon, J. Physical restraint produces rapid acquisition of the pigeon's keypeck. *Journal of the Experimental Analysis of Behavior,* 1980, *34,* 13–21.

Mackintosh, N. J. Theory of attention. *Psychological Review,* 1975, *72,* 276–298.

Mackintosh, N. J. Stimulus control: Attentional factors. In W. K. Honig & J. E. R. Staddon (Eds.), *Handbook of operant behavior.* Englewood Cliffs, N.J.: Prentice–Hall, 1977.

McAllister, W. R., & McAllister, D. Variables influencing the conditioning and measurement of acquired fear. In W. F. Prokasy (Ed.), *Classical conditioning.* New York: Appleton–Century–Crofts, 1965.

McAllister, W. R., McAllister, D., & Benton, M. M. Measurement of fear of the conditioned stimulus and of situational cues at several stages of two-way avoidance learning. *Learning and Motivation,* 1983, *14,* 92–106.

Odling–Smee, F. J. The role of background stimuli during Pavlovian conditioning. *Quarterly Journal of Experimental Psychology,* 1975, *27,* 201–209.

Patterson, J., & Overmier, J. B. A transfer of control test for contextual associations. *Animal Learning and Behavior,* 1981, *9,* 316–321.

Pavlov, I. P. *Conditioned reflexes.* New York and London: Oxford University Press, 1927.

Randich, A., & LoLordo, V. M. Associative and nonassociative theories of the UCS preexposure phenomenon: Implications for Pavlovian conditioning. *Psychological Bulletin,* 1979, *86,* 523–548.

Rescorla, R. Associations between Pavlovian CSs and context. *Journal of Experimental Psychology: Animal Behavior Processes,* 1984, *10,* 195–204.

Rescorla, R. A., & Wagner, A. R. A theory of Pavlovian conditioning: Variations in the effectiveness of reinforcement and nonreinforcement. In A. H. Black & W. F. Prokasy (Eds.), *Classical conditioning II: Current theory and research.* New York: Appleton–Century–Crofts, 1972.

Skinner, B. F. *The behavior of organisms: An experimental analysis.* Englewood, N. J.: Prentice–Hall, 1938.

Spear, N. E., Smith, G. J., Bryan, R. G., Gordon, W. C., Timmons, R., & Chiszar, D. A. Contextual influences on the interaction between conflicting memories in the rat. *Animal Learning and Behavior,* 1980, *8,* 273–281.

Terrace, H. S. Stimulus Control: In W. K. Honig (Ed.), *Operant behavior: Areas of research and application.* New York: Appleton–Century–Crofts, 1966.

Thorndike, E. L. *Human learning.* New York: Century, 1931. Paperback ed., Cambridge: MIT Press, 1966.

Tomie, A. Interference with autoshaping by prior context conditioning. *Journal of Experimental Psychology: Animal Behavior Processes,* 1976, *2,* 323–334.

Tomie, A. Effects of unpredictable food upon the subsequent acquisition of autoshaping: Analysis of the context blocking hypothesis. In C. M. Locurto, H. S. Terrace, & J. Gibbon (Eds.), *Autoshaping and conditioning theory.* New York: Academic Press, 1981.

2

Contextual Learning in Pavlovian Conditioning

Robert A. Rescorla
Paula J. Durlach
James W. Grau
University of Pennsylvania

Modern discussions of Pavlovian conditioning increasingly acknowledge the importance of the context in which learning and performance occur. This acknowledgment has taken quite a variety of forms that differ in the manner in which they envision context to affect learning about discrete events. One can organize many aspects of available views in terms of two pairs of alternatives: (1) Does the context affect the learning of discrete CS–US associations or performance based on that learning? (2) Is the impact of context based itself on learning or only on its unlearned stimulus properties?

Consider first the potential impact of context on *learning* of CS–US associations. Simply by virtue of its being a stimulus present during a CS–US learning experience, one might anticipate that the context would have an impact on that learning. For instance, contextual stimuli may influence the manner in which the CS or US is perceived, perhaps generating "afferent neural interaction" (Hull, 1943) or a "unique cue" (Rescorla, 1973). A CS presented in one perceptual environment may be seen as different from that same CS presented in other environments; hence the environment would affect how that CS is encoded. Similarly, the environment in which a US is presented may affect its processing. Such primitive stimulus effects of context are widely given informal acknowledgment in discussions of learning.

But context may affect CS–US learning not simply by its presence but rather from its own learned associations with the CS or US. Because the context is present when the CS is paired with the US, many authors have suggested that it too develops an association with that US. Two quite different consequences of context-US associations have been proposed. One possibility is that they compete with the CS–US associations being studied. Competition among discrete stimuli for association with the US is well documented empirically (e.g., Kamin, 1969; Leyland & Mackintosh, 1978) and widely celebrated theoretically (e.g., Mackintosh, 1975; Rescorla & Wagner, 1972) in the modern Pavlovian literature. If one views the context as only an extended CS that, like any CS, becomes associated with the US, then it is natural to think that context-US associations would reduce the strength of CS–US associations. In contrast, Konorski (1967) has suggested that context-US associations might facilitate the formation of CS–US associations. He argued that as a result of its association with the US, the context primarily becomes capable of evoking a motivational state. That motivational state in turn acts to promote the formation of associations between the discrete CS and the US.

Less frequently, it has been suggested that the context might affect CS–US learning by virtue of its association with the CS. For instance, Wagner (1978) has argued that such associations result in a CS of reduced salience, which is consequently more difficult to associate with the US. Certainly the evidence that latent inhibition is sensitive to changes in context agrees with this view (e.g., Channell & Hall, 1981; Dexter & Merrill, 1969; Lubow, Rifkin, & Alek, 1976).

Finally, the context has sometimes been suggested to serve the role of a signal that a particular CS–US relation obtains. Classical "switching" experiments suggest that the organism can learn that different relationships between the same CS and US occur in different contexts (Asratyan, 1965; Kimmel & Ray, 1978; Thomas, 1981). However, the nature of such hierarchical learning has received relatively little analysis.

We may also consider the context's potential impact on *performance* based on a CS–US association. Here too the action may be simply a result of the inherent stimulus properties of the context. Even in the absence of any learning of its own, a context may well control behaviors either by direct elicitation or by providing different degrees of "support" for the behaviors that the CS would normally elicit (e.g., Tolman, 1932). Some behaviors may simply be impossible in the absence of environmental features.

Relatively more theoretical attention has been given to possible performance effects of context that are mediated by its own association with either the CS or US. One possibility for an effect of a context-US association was recently offered by Gibbon and Balsam (1981). According to their view, the relative associative strengths of the CS and context determine performance; regardless of a CS's absolute level of associative strength, manifestation of conditioned responding depends on the CS's conditioned value being substantially greater than the context's conditioned value. Consequently, a context with strong associations to the US would have adverse effects on performance to a CS. Again, Konorski's (1967) theory offers a prediction in contrast to a modern view. He reasoned that the drive that results from associations between context and the US should promote performance to CSs associated with that US. A related notion is that the value of the background can summate with that of a discrete CS, perhaps exposing CS–US associations that are by themselves too weak to be observed.

Less attention has been paid to the potential effects of context-CS associations on CS performance. But Wagner (1978) has argued that they might result in less effective processing of such an associated CS, thus attenuating responding to it.

The present chapter is concerned with some of the ways in which the organism's learning about the context affects Pavlovian conditioning. We discuss three kinds of learning: context-US associations, context-CS associations, and contextual control of a particular CS–US relation. Our discussion of context-US associations is the most extended, for it is there that the most data are currently available. We attempt both to document further the existence of such associations and to examine various ways that they might impact Pavlovian conditioning of discrete CSs. Our discussion of context-CS associations is confined to a demonstration that suggests their existence, and a discussion of a few issues that their existence raises. Finally, we give some preliminary analysis of the possibility that the context signals particular relations between the CS and US.

EVIDENCE FOR CONTEXT-US ASSOCIATIONS

In this section we discuss the most thoroughly studied case of learning about the background, context-US association. We begin with the simple question of whether organisms learn that USs occur in a context. An obvious approach to this question is to present USs in a context for some animals, fail to do so for others, and ask whether the two groups differ in their reaction to the context. The relatively large number of experiments that have used this strategy differ primarily in the particular reaction used as an index of the context's association with the US.

The selection of a behavior to measure in a context is not as simple as it at first may seem. One might select a behavior based on the reactions known to occur to discrete CSs that are paired with that same US. However, considerable recent evidence suggests that the nature of the conditioned response depends on the nature of the CS as well as the US (see Rescorla & Holland, 1982). Even among discrete CSs the decision to observe any particular behavior could seriously mislead one in deciding whether or not that CS was conditioned. That problem may be exacerbated in the case of contextual stimuli, which differ from discrete CSs in begin long-term static, rather than punctate, events. It would hardly be surprising if stimuli differing in this manner showed substantial differences in the form of the CR they elicited.

Experimenters have begun to grapple with this problem for discrete CSs. The procedures adopted have fallen into two classes: those casting a broad behavioral net and those measuring a feature of learning that seems topography-independent. Similar strategies have grown up for measuring learning about contextual stimuli.

One example of the "broad net" strategy has been to construct an apparatus that measures gross motor activity (e.g., Balsam, 1984; Sheffield & Campbell, 1954). The idea is that such an apparatus will be sensitive to a wide range of response forms and hence have a high likelihood of detecting whatever response the context evokes. Although such an approach seems reasonable, the history of general activity devices suggests that one's selection of a particular apparatus importantly affects the kind of activity that is measured (see Bolles, 1967).

Another example of this "broad net" strategy is common in the literature on the interaction between Pavlovian conditioning and instrumental performance. Many Pavlovian fear conditioning experiments measure the strength of CS-shock associations by the ability of the CS to disrupt previously established instrumental behavior. Although the particular instrumental performance established can be narrowly defined (commonly lever-pressing), it is plausible to think that it can be disrupted by any of a broad range of other behaviors that are evoked by the CS. The history of success in using this technique to measure fear conditioning with a wide range of discrete CSs encourages this reasoning. However, there has been less agreement that general suppression of that behavior in the absence of discrete CSs is an adequate measure of any context conditioning (Baker & Mackintosh, 1979; Baker, Singh, & Bindra, this volume).

Two apparently topography-free techniques have been used for assessing conditioning of discrete CSs that evoke different responses. One uses the CS as a reinforcer either for another CS (second-order Pavlovian conditioning) or for an instrumental response (secondary reinforcement). Those procedures have proven to be highly sensitive and theoretically productive for some purposes (see Rescorla, 1980). Context conditioning has sometimes been assessed by an analogous procedure, in which the organism is given an instrumental choice between two contexts with different conditioning histories (e.g., Odling–Smee, 1975, 1978). Different amounts of conditioning are measured by differential preference for one choice over the other.

A second topography-free technique assesses the conditioned strength of a discrete CS by its ability to modulate conditioning of other, concurrently present, stimuli. For instance, Holland (1977) measured conditioning of a light paired with food in terms of its ability to reduce conditioning to a tone when the light-tone compound was subsequently paired with food. Such blocking of conditioning of one stimulus by another is known to depend on its own conditioning history. The analogous procedure has perhaps been the most popular for the detection of context-US associations. Quite a number of authors have reported that presentation of food in a chamber enables that chamber to attenuate conditioning of a discrete CS paired with food in its presence (e.g., Balsam & Schwartz, 1981, Tomie, 1976). Such observations have also been made for other USs (Randich & LoLordo, 1979; Randich & Ross, this volume). It is important to note that this use of the blocking technique involves a theoretical commitment to a particular subset of the ways described earlier, in which context conditioning might interact with CS–US associations. It presumes, for instance, that context-US associations function in the same manner as CS–US associations, a question that one might wish to leave open for empirical investigation.

One particular measure of context-US associations that we have recently come to employ in our laboratory is another example of the "broad net" category. It uses a straightforward, but often tedious, procedure in which videotaped records of the animal's behaviors are analyzed for a range of different responses. Using such an observational procedure has proven highly profitable for coding different response topographies elicited by various discrete CSs (e.g., Holland, 1977). Our hope is that it will prove equally useful in detecting learning about the context.

We describe here an example of using that observational technique. The example is intended both to illustrate the procedure and to provide evidence for context-US associations. Pigeons were given randomly spaced grain deliveries in a particular context and observed for the resulting changes in their behavior patterns in that context. However, because we wished to identify observed changes as due to the fact that the food had occurred in the particular context (rather than to the simple exposure to food and to the context), we used a discrimination procedure. Each animal was exposed to two contexts that bore different relations to food. Initially we studied discriminative acquisition in which food occurred in one context but not the other. Then we examined two procedures for the elimination of that discriminative behavior: removal of food from both contexts and the administration of food in both contexts. Finally, we trained a reversal of the original discrimination. Our intention was to document for context-US associations the occurrence of several standard associative learning phenomena: acquisition, discrimination, extinction, and reversal learning.

The subjects were 16 female Carneaux pigeons, maintained at 75% of their ad lib body weight. Each animal was given daily 30-min exposures to each of two contexts: a standard operant chamber with Plexiglas walls and a similar chamber with all but one wall lined with purple and tan striped poster board; holes cut in the liners allowed access to the food magazine and the response keys (which, however, were inoperative). Each session began with a 5-min period during which the bird received no programmed events but had its behavior monitored and recorded on videotape. For one context the remaining 25 min contained 15 5-sec oprations of the food hopper, variably spaced. The other context contained no events during that time. Subjects were given one session in each context each day, with order of exposure to the two contexts counterbalanced. For half the subjects, the lined chamber served as the reinforced context and the unlined chamber served as the nonreinforced context; the rest received the opposite arrangement. This discrimination treatment continued for 20 days.

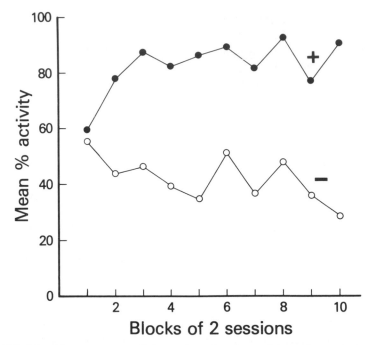

FIG. 2.1.   Mean percentage of observations classed as activity during context discrimination training. In the reinforced context (+) subjects received 15 5-sec food presentations; in the nonreinforced context (−) subjects received no food.

An observer blind to the treatment of the context categorized behavior that occurred during the initial portion of each session. We chose to sample behavior only from the beginning of each session, prior to the delivery of any food, in order to insure that we were measuring only conditioned effects of the context, uncontaminated by any unconditioned effects of receiving food itself. Further, to attenuate the disturbing effects of recent placement into the context, behaviors were scored during only the second 2.5 min of the first 5 min of each session. During this time each bird was observed once every 10 sec, for a total of 15 observations. Behaviors were initially partitioned into several categories; however, for our present purposes, these categories have been grossly collapsed into two: activity (all observations in which any movement was noticed) and inactivity. Interobserver reliability for such judgments was 97%.

Figure 2.1 displays the course of discrimination training, using that measure. It is clear that the birds initially showed a moderate level of activity in both contexts, but that discriminative performance rapidly developed. This consisted both of a decline in activity in the nonreinforced context and an increase in the reinforced context. There seems little doubt that in the 5-min period prior to the daily differential treatment the birds correctly used contextual cues to anticipate that treatment.

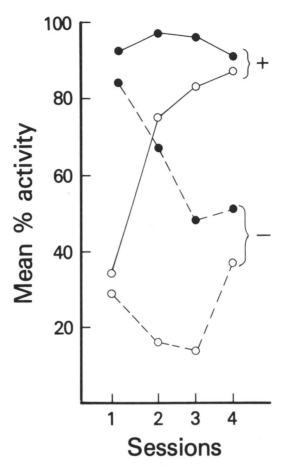

FIG. 2.2.   Mean percentage of observations classed as activity during treatments intended to destroy the previously trained context discrimination. Birds now received the same treatment in both contexts; however, for one group both contexts were reinforced (+), whereas for the other group both contexts were nonreinforced (−). Filled circles show the effect of these treatments on the previously reinforced context; open circles show the effect on the previously nonreinforced context.

The birds were next divided into two groups, matched on their discrimination performance. Both groups received treatments designed to destroy the discrimination. One group was given standard extinction in which no food was presented in either context. The other group received equal numbers of food presentations in each context, in the same manner as had previously been given only in the reinforced context. Aside from these modifications, the treatments of the birds and the manner of their observation were unchanged.

Figure 2.2 shows the consequences of these treatments. Those animals receiving extinction in both contexts (dotted lines) showed a deterioration of the discrimination that took the form of a decline in activity in the previously reinforced context. Those animals receiving undifferentiated reinforcement also showed a deterioration; but it took the form of increased activity in the previously nonreinforced context. Both of these changes were quite rapid, with the effects of the procedures evident during the second session. Subsequently, all animals were returned either to the original discrimination treatment or to its reversal, and all came to display appropriate differential performance once again.

These results are not especially surprising. They indicate in a gross way what any layman knows: that animals can learn that important events occur in one context but not another. But they do provide several important additional pieces of information. First, because of its use of a standard discrimination procedure, this experiment documents the importance of the context/food relation in a manner that allows us to rule out a variety of nonassociative interpretations. Second, this learning about context appears to display phenomena that we are accustomed to seeing in the learning about discrete CSs. The few elementary phenomena examined, acquisition, discrimination, extinction, and reversal, are grossly similar. Third, the course of learning was very rapid. After only a few sessions of the initial discrimination, performance became differential; moreover, the birds adapted equally rapidly when the reinforcement contingencies were changed. These observations agree with those of Balsam (1984) in suggesting that context conditioning is exceedingly rapid.

Finally, we should comment on the form of the response measured. The activity/nonactivity categorization presented in Fig. 2.2 fails to reveal two important features of that behavior. First, the form of the response was widely variable across birds but consistent within a bird. Some birds spent a good deal of time bobbing up and down; others moved back and forth laterally in the area of the food magazine. Such idiosyncratic patterns may thwart more fine-grained topographical analyses; they certainly complicate the task of constructing a satisfactory automated detection device. The second feature is that pecking was an infrequently (less than 5%) observed behavior. That is important because pecking is a dominant behavior to discrete visual (and even auditory) stimuli that precede foor reinforcement. Our observations agree with those of Skinner (1948) in their stereoptypy; they agree with those of Staddon and Simmlehag (1971) in their nature (e.g., interim responses). It is clear that in the present case the form of the response observed to the context was quite different from that which would have been anticipated from the results of standard Pavlovian CSs.

THE EFFECT OF CONTEXT-US ASSOCIATIONS ON LEARNING AND PERFORMANCE

The previous section confirmed the obvious notion that organisms can learn that US occur in particular contexts. Several classes of experiments indicate that this g has a substantial impact on Pavlovian conditioning of discrete CSs. For instance, exposure to the US prior to carrying out CS–US pairings has an adverse effect on conditioning in a wide range of preparations (LoLordo & Randich, 1981; Randich & Ross, this volume; Tomie, 1981). Moreover, part of that US-preexposure effect is apparently attributable to learning about the context, because the decrement in conditioning is partly specific to the context in which the US was previously presented (e.g., Hinson, 1982, Tomie, 1976). Similarly, intermixing exposures to the US with CS–US pairings has been shown to have a substantial negative effect on conditioning of that CS (e.g., Dweck & Wagner, 1970, Gamzu & Williams, 1973, Rescorla, 1968).

These phenomena seem clearly to indicate that conditioning of the context can have a depressive effect on conditioning of a discrete CS. For that reason they are not consistent with the facilitative, motivational mode of operation that Konorski envisioned for context. Instead, they have most commonly received interpretation in terms of the context interfering with learning about the CS (e.g., Rescorla & Wagner, 1972; Tomie, 1981). In fact, however, currently available data offer little basis for choosing between an interpretation in terms of learning and one in terms of performance. A well-conditioned context could either block development of the CS–US association, or it might permit such learning but interfere with its exhibition in performance (e.g., Gibbon & Balsam, 1981).

The experiments reported in this section attempted to separate those alternatives. They followed two parallel strategies in which each animal was exposed to three easily discriminable experimental contexts. In one procedure a CS was conditioned in one context and then tested in two novel contexts, otherwise arranged to have different associative strengths. In the converse procedure, the CS was conditioned in one of two contexts that had different values and then was tested in a third context of common strength. With these designs, one can separate the associative strength of the training context from that of the testing context so as to evaluate separately their impact. Moreover, one can make the evaluation in a manner independent of any impact of changing the context per se. As noted previously, responding to a CS may decrease simply from changing the stimulus properties of the context. With the present three-context procedures we can make all assessments in a shifted context so as to identify the impact of the value of the context separately from the impact of changing its stimulus properties.

The use of these procedures is illustrated for two different kinds of discrete CSs. First, we describe results from CSs given standard discriminative Pavlovian conditioning. This allows us to examine the impact of context on both reinforced and nonreinforced stimuli. Second, we report results from a class of CSs that has become important to modern theories of conditioning: those uncorrelated with the US.

Discriminative CSs

Recently, Grau and Rescorla (in press) completed a discriminative autoshaping experiment that used both of the previously described procedures. The first half of the experiment trained pecking to one stimulus (CS+) but not to another (CS−) in one experimental context; it then tested performance to each stimulus in two other contexts, one of high associative strength and one of low strength. The second half of the experiment conducted excitatory conditioning of CS− in either the high or low valued context and tested performance in the original context.

Initially, all 32 birds received 6 sessions of discriminative autoshaping in a standard operant chamber. Each session contained 15 5-sec presentations each of two discriminably different color-dot pattern keylight stimuli. One stimulus (CS+) was regularly followed by food; the other (CS−) was nonreinforced. Over the next 14 days each bird received 30-min daily exposures to two other contexts, given one context per day in counterbalanced order. The contexts were the striped chamber used in the previous experiment and a similar chamber lined with marbled white poster board. As in the previous experiment, the first 5 min of each exposure were without programmed events. Observations were again made in the 2.5-min period beginning 2.5 min after the start of the session. In the remaining 25 min one context contained 15 randomly spaced unsignaled hopper presentations; the other contained no events.

On each of the next 2 days, the birds received nonreinforced test presentations of CS+ and CS− in the two lined contexts. The first 5 min of each test session was again without programmed events; the remaining 25 min contained 6 presentations each of CS+ and CS−. Order of testing the two contexts was balanced across animals.

The left-hand side of Fig. 2.3 shows the course of discriminative autoshaping in the original context; by the end of conditioning the response rates to CS+ and CS− were quite different. Training of the contexts also proceeded smoothly. The mean percentage of observations classed as activity in the reinforced and nonreinforced contexts during the measuring period of the final two sessions were 89.6 and 52.3, respectively.

The data of primary interest, from the first day of testing of responding to CS+ and CS− in the two differentially treated contexts, are shown in the right-hand panel of Fig. 2.3. The most obvious feature of these data is the relatively small impact that testing context had on performance to the CS. In both contexts, responding to CS+ continued at a high level, whereas that to CS− was relatively low. However, there is some indication of superior discriminative performance in the higher valued context during the first block of test trials. Responding was higher to CS+ and lower to CS− in the better conditioned context. Although the impact of context value on CS+ is consistent with Konorski's (1967) view and that on CS− can be accounted for by Gibbon and Balsam (1981), neither theory can deal with the complete data pattern. Nor does either anticipate that the effect of context value on performance should be so small in magnitude. One possible alternative view is that the conditioned value of the context acts as part of the stimulus complex in which discriminative conditioning took place. Deterioration

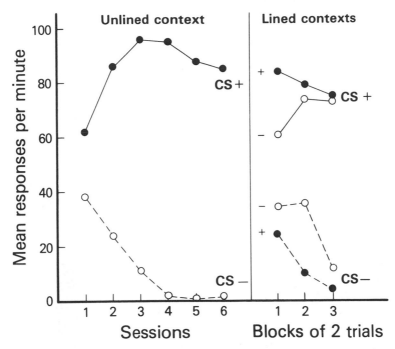

FIG. 2.3.   The left panel shows the mean rate of responding during the course of discriminative autoshaping of CS+ and CS− in the unlined context. The right panel shows mean rate of responding to CS+ and CS− when they were subsequently tested in the lined contexts. Subjects had had discrimination training with the lined contexts such that one had been previously reinforced (filled circles, +), whereas the other had been previously nonreinforced (open circles, −).

of discriminative performance in the nonreinforced context could then be attributable to the absence of that stimulus.

Behavioral observations during the initial part of the test sessions indicated that the contexts controlled quite different levels of activity. Consequently, the data from the first part of this experiment indicate that contexts of substantially different conditioned value have relatively little impact on performance to the discrete CS.

The second portion of the experiment examined the effect of conducting conditioning in differently valued contexts and testing in a common context. Following the preceding test sessions all animals were given 6 more days of differential treatment of their contexts, and then the CS− keylight was paired with food in either the reinforced or nonreinforced context. All birds received a single session that contained six reinforced presentations of CS−; for half the birds those trials occurred in the previously reinforced context, whereas for the other half they occurred in the previously nonreinforced context. Finally, all birds were tested for performance to that previous CS− in the original, unlined

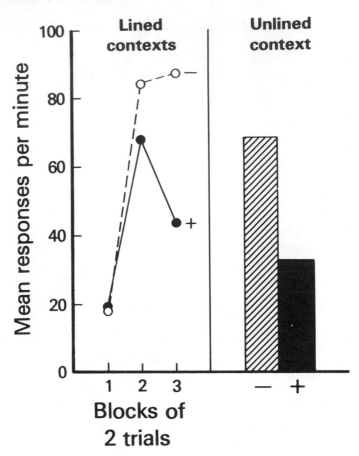

FIG. 2.4. The left panel shows mean rate of responding to CS− during its reinforcement in either the previously reinforced (filled circles, +) or the previously nonreinforced (open circles, −) context. The right panel shows mean rate of responding to CS− when it was tested back in the unlined context, separated according to whether it had been trained in the previously reinforced (filled bar, +) or previously nonreinforced (hatched bar, −) context.

context. The question of interest was whether conditioning to CS− would be differentially successful depending on the value of the context in which its reinforcement took place.

The left-hand panel of Fig. 2.4 shows the course of the development of responding to the previous CS− during its reinforcement in the two differently valued contexts. Performance developed at different rates, being more rapid in the previously nonreinforced context. However, because this performance occurred in contexts known to have different values, its implication is ambiguous. It is possible that CS− acquired a greater associative strength when reinforced in the low-valued context. Alternatively it may be that CS− acquired similar associative strength whatever its reinforcement locus, but that the two contexts differentially modulated exhibition of that strength. The results shown in the right-hand panel of Fig. 2.4 help decide the issue. That panel shows nonreinforced test responding to CS− in the initial unlined context. Presumably the value of *that* context is similar in the two groups, despite the fact that CS− has been differentially treated elsewhere. The results suggest that indeed the stimulus reinforced in the low-value context had gained a stronger association with the US. That conclusion agrees with the usual interpretation of the US-preexposure effect but is here based on a procedure that separates effects on learning from those on performance.

The principle conclusion from this experiment is that conditioning of a context has a substantial negative impact on the conditioning of discrete CSs in its presence, but it has only a small facilitative effect on the exhibition of that conditioning (see also Kaplan & Hearst, this volume). When a fixed-valued CS was tested in contexts of different value, the performance was similar; however, a stimulus conditioned in contexts having different strength exhibited different levels of performance when it was tested in a fixed-value context.

CSs uncorrelated with the US

A finding of major importance in the modern understanding of Pavlovian conditioning has emerged from procedures that arrange for the CS and US to occur in an uncorrelated fashion. By adding a sufficient number of US presentations at times other than the CS, so that the CS and US become uncorrelated, one can convert an otherwise effective Pavlovian procedure into one in which the CS fails to become conditioned. Such procedures suggest that simple CS/US contiguities are insufficient for conditioning; instead some more sophisticated relation, such as CS/US contingency, seems implicated.

These findings have received interpretation from two classes of molecular theories, both of which give a primary role to the conditioning of context. One set of theories suggests that the ''extra'' USs adversely affect learning about the CS, because their presence insures that the CS is reinforced in the presence of well-conditioned contextual stimuli. Such a ''blocking'' interpretation parallels that for the US preexposure effect. This learning interpretation can be made from any contemporary theory of blocking but has been given in most detail by Rescorla and Wagner (1972).

Alternatively, one can view the extra USs as having little impact on the learning of the CS–US association but adversely affecting performance to that CS. This result would be anticipated, for instance, by the Gibbon and Balsam (1981) model, in which performance elicited by a CS depends on its associative strength relative to that of the context in which it is presented. According to this view the extra USs, which make the CS and US uncorrelated, sharply raise the associative strength of the context, reducing the ratio of CS strength to context strength and so reducing performance to the CS. A similar view was given less formally by Estes (1969).

Recently Durlach (1983) has conducted a series of experiments intended to evaluate the merits of these alternatives. The impetus for these experiments was a prediction from models emphasizing the impact of the extra USs on learning about the CS. Just as those models claim that a well-conditioned context can block conditioning of a discrete CS, so they suggest that a well-conditioned CS could block conditioning of the context. Consequently, the ability of the extra USs to condition the context could be substantially reduced simply by preceding each by another discrete CS that itself has a history of conditioning. Additional USs that are well signaled should only poorly condition contextual cues and so should have a reduced adverse impact on conditioning of the original CS. However, this deduction depends on the context and discrete CSs competing for associative strength. A model, such as that of Gibbon and Balsam, that sees the CS and context as independently acquiring associative strength with the US, would not anticipate any change in context conditioning as a result of this manipulation. Consequently, it would still expect poor performance to the original CS (see Baker, Singh, & Bindra, this volume, and Randich & Ross, this volume, for similar deductions concerning US preexposure and conditioned inhibition).

A sample outcome of such a signaling manipulation is shown in Fig. 2.5. That figure displays the results of an autoshaping experiment containing three groups of birds. One group received simple Pavlovian conditioning with a 10-sec keylight terminating in food on 25% of its occasions. A second group (Unsignaled) was treated identically except that they received sufficient additional unsignaled food deliveries to make their CS uncorrelated with food. The third (Signaled) group was treated like Group Unsignaled except that all the extra food deliveries were preceded by a 10-sec tone that had a history of extensive pairing with food.

It is clear that Group 25 rapidly acquired the autoshaped response, but that the additional USs in Group Unsignaled dramatically attenuated pecking. That, of course, is the primary detrimental effect of additional USs that the various accounts attempt to explain. Of most interest, preceding those additional USs by a well-conditioned tone in Group Signaled attenuated that detrimental effect. In agreement with theories that view the context and CS as competing for association with the US, signaling had an important impact.

However, these data do not have a unique interpretation in terms of the context affecting learning about the CS. One could easily construct a performance theory in which unsignaled intertrial USs better condition the context than signaled intertrial USs, therefore producing more attenuation of performance to the original CS. According to such a view, the original CS might be highly conditioned in both the signaled and unsignaled groups but be responded to at different levels because of differences in context conditioning.

That possibility can readily be evaluated using procedures like those em-

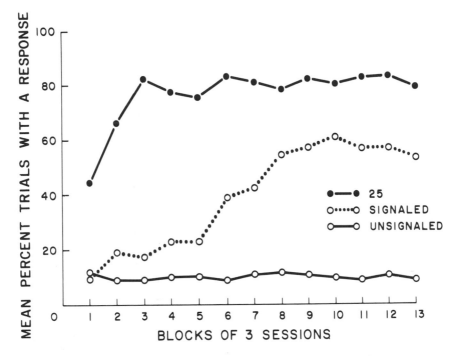

FIG. 2.5.   Mean percentage trials with a response to a CS that was reinforced on 25% of its occasions. Group 25 (filled circles, solid lines) received no intertrial events; however both Groups Signaled and Unsignaled received intertrial foods such that the CS and the food US were uncorrelated. For Group Signaled (open circles, dotted lines), those intertrial foods were signaled by a tone; for Group Unsignaled (open circles, solid lines), they were unsignaled. (From Durlach, P. J., Effect of signaling intertrial unconditioned stimuli in autoshaping. *Journal of Experimental Psychology: Animal Behavior Processes,* 1983, *9,* 374–389. Copyright 1983 by the American Psychological Association. Reprinted by permission of the publisher and author.)

ployed in the previous experiment. For this purpose, Durlach (1983) ran another experiment in which two groups of pigeons received the signaled and unsignaled additional US procedure. Both groups then received test presentations of the CS in each of two contexts having widely different values. By examining performance within a testing context, we can determine whether the two conditions of signaling additional USs resulted in different degrees of learning. By examining performance for either the signaled or unsignaled conditions across the two testing contexts, we can evaluate the impact of different context strengths on performance.

Four groups of 8 pigeons each were initially exposed to uncorrelated presentations of a keylight (a black X on a white background) and food. Food followed the 10-sec X on 25% of its occasions and was additionally given between Xs with sufficient frequency to generate the uncorrelated schedule. Overall, the rate of

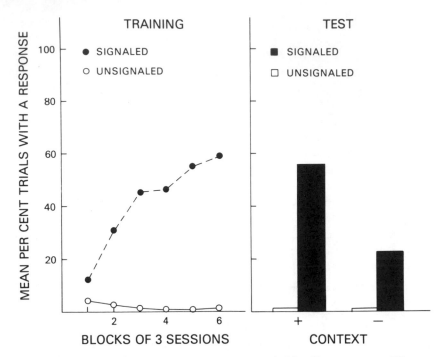

FIG. 2.6.   The left panel shows mean percentage of trials with a response to a CS that was uncorrelated with the food US. For Groups Signaled (filled circles, dashed lines), those foods that did not co-occur with the CS were signaled by a different stimulus; however for Group Unsignaled (open circles, solid lines), those foods were unsignaled. The right panel shows responding to the CS in Groups Signaled (filled bars) and Unsignaled (open bars) when it was transferred to either a previously reinforced (+) or a previously nonreinforced (−) context. (From Durlach, 1983. Copyright by the American Psychological Association. Reprinted by permission of the publisher and author.)

food delivery in the 40-min session was 1 per minute. For half the birds the additional food deliveries were signaled by a 10-sec blue keylight with which all birds had a history of reinforcement. The left-hand side of Fig. 2.6 shows the responding that these schedules produced to the X stimulus. As expected, the depressive effects of the additional foods on responding to X were less in the signaled animals.

All birds were then exposed to each of the two lined contexts (stripes and marbling), with food delivered at a rate of 2 per min in one context but never presented in the other. The intention was to create contexts that differed in rate of food both from each other and from the original training context. After 12 sessions in each treatment context, their differential conditioning was readily apparent, as measured by behavioral observations during the second half of the initial 5-min period of each session. On the final day of this treatment 92.5% of the observations were classified as "active" in the reinforced context and 52% as "active" in the nonreinforced context.

On the next day, half the birds in Group Signaled and half in Group Unsignaled received nonreinforced test presentations of X in each context. The results of that test are shown in the right-hand side of Fig. 2.6, separated according to the training procedure for X and the value of the context in which it was tested. It is clear that there was virtually no responding to X in the unsignaled groups. That was true whether the test took place in a context of high value or one of minimal value. By contrast, there was substantial responding to X in the signaled groups, whichever the test context. However, there was also some evidence that performance to X in the signaled groups was superior in the high-valued context.

These data provide strong support for the proposition that signaling the extra USs affects learning about the target CS. Whatever the value of the test context, responding was greater to a CS trained in the signaled condition. Moreover, there was no evidence of any performance to the CS from the unsignaled condition in either of the testing contexts. By contrast, there is little to support the notion that low levels of context conditioning, whether produced by nonreinforcement or by signaled reinforcement, facilitate performance to the target CS. Indeed, performance to the CS was superior when it was tested in the well-conditioned context. This observation is in agreement with the small performance effect shown in Fig. 2.4. In the present instance it may be interpreted as support for either a stimulus or a motivational role of anticipating food.

The data in this section thus strongly suggest that a primary role of context conditioning is to modulate the effect of USs in conditioning discrete CSs. What little support they offer for an effect of context on performance is more consistent with the kind of motivational role envisioned by Konorski than with the comparison mechanism described by Gibbon and Balsam.

However, there is one worrisome exception to this conclusion about the action of additional USs. Lindblom and Jenkins (1981) found that intertrial USs had a detrimental impact on performance to a keylight CS, apparently without affecting the associative strength of that CS. They found that once autoshaping had been established, adding USs at a high rate in the intertrial interval produced a profound response decrement; yet when all USs were subsequently deleted, responding recovered to near its previous level. It is not clear to what extent these results involve the unconditioned properties of USs as distinct from context conditioning. The rapidity of the recovery suggests an involvement of unlearned US properties. It is also possible that a high rate of US occurrence itself serves as a conditional cue, like that found by Neely and Wagner (1974) and discussed later. But the results of Lindblom and Jenkins suggest that under some circumstances intertrial USs can adversely affect performance.

Before leaving this discussion of context-US associations, we should note that it shares with previous discussions an emphasis on "excitatory" associations.

But modern theories of Pavlovian conditioning envision discrete CSs as also capable of entering into inhibitory associations with USs. One might then consider a similar possibility for contextual stimuli. For instance, the consistent non-reinforcement of an excitatory CS that takes place during extinction might endow contextual stimuli with inhibitory power (see Rescorla, 1979).

Current conceptions of inhibition are relatively response free, assuming that a conditioned inhibitor reduces the excitation elicited by a CS without eliciting any response of its own. Consequently, when an inhibitor is presented in conjunction with an excitor, one anticipates reduction in the likelihood of whatever response that excitor elicits. It follows from this conception that, if a CS were presented in an inhibitory context, the net associative strength present would be reduced and, hence, compared with a neutral context, CS performance would be less.

Yet our discussion of the effect of context-US associations on performance has not emphasized the symmetrical possibility that an excitatory context might (through summation) augment performance. That asymmetry arises because current theories are not prepared to specify the performance combination rules for several excitatory CSs that elicit different responses as a result of their pairing with the same US. Although their associative strengths may summate (and hence affect subsequent learning), it is not clear how that summation should affect performance of the various responses. The present performance results might be interpreted as evidence for the occurrence of such summation. However, it is clear that we need more formal performance rules based on a broader range of data before applying a summation interpretation generally.

ASSOCIATIONS BETWEEN CONTEXT AND CS

Standard studies of Pavlovian conditioning concentrate on the association that a stimulus might have with the US. Relatively less attention has been given to associations that a stimulus might have with other CSs. Similarly, studies of contextual learning have emphasized its associations with the US rather than with the various CSs that occur in its presence.

The main results suggesting that the organism does form associations between a context and CSs come from the study of latent inhibition. This term refers to the loss in associability that a stimulus undergoes as a result of its simple repeated presentation in a context. One interpretation of that finding is that presenting a potential CS in a context leads to a context-CS association that in turn makes the CS less trainable (e.g., Wagner, 1978). Two empirical outcomes have been taken as giving support to that interpretation.

First, the loss in associability is partially context specific. Repeated presentation of a CS reduces its associability most in the context of that presentation and less in other contexts. However, such results actually only demonstrate that the organism recognizes the CS to be different in the two contexts. Such a recognition could readily occur by mechanisms other than context-CS associations. For instance, each context might change the perception of the CS in different ways, perhaps generating a unique or configural cue.

The second line of evidence is more convincing. Wagner (1978) has reported that previously established latent inhibition can be attenuated by repeated presentation of the context without the CS. That outcome would be expected if separate context presentation without the CS resulted in extinction of the context-CS association. But interpretation of this finding as evidence for context-CS associations depends on acceptance of a particular theory of latent inhibition.

In this section, we present what we take to be more straightforward evidence for context-CS associations. We then point to some implications of their existence for thinking about how contexts function. The experiment was modeled after the first reported in this chapter, except that differentially conditioned CSs replaced USs as the events presented in the contexts. It can be seen as an attempt to accomplish second-order conditioning of a context by having it contain a keylight with a history of pairing with the food US.

Sixteen pigeons were run in the three contexts used earlier. Initially they were given discriminative autoshaping in the unlined chamber. This training consisted of 12 presentations each of S+ and S− on each of 9 days. For the first 4 days each S+ terminated in 5 sec of grain whereas all S− trials were nonreinforced; on the next 5 days only 25% of the S+ trials terminated in food. After autoshaping had become asymptotic, the animals received nonreinforced exposure to the two lined contexts (stripes and marbling). Each day they received 30 min of exposure to one context without any programmed events, until they had been exposed to each 6 times.

Over the next 8 days, all animals received conditioning of their lined chambers using S+ and S− as the reinforcers. On each day, the animals were exposed to each chamber for 10 min, during the last 5 min of which either S+ or S− was presented 3 times without reinforcement. Half the animals received S+ in the striped chamber and S− in the marbled chamber; half had the reverse relation. A single "refresher" day on the original discrimination was administered between Days 4 and 5 of context conditioning. The behavior of each animal was monitored during the event-free intial 5 min of each session, as in previous experiments. The issue was whether we would observe greater activity in the context that contained S+ than in that which contained S−.

Figure 2.7 shows activity in the two chambers over the course of conditioning. Although initially there was little activity in either context, the animals gradually became more active in the context containing S+. After 4 days of differential treatment, there was substantially more responding in the initial observation period of the S+ context ($T = 17.5$, $N = 16$; $p < .01$). Clearly differential second-order conditioning of the contexts occurred. In that sense the animals had knowledge of which CS occurred in which context.

Rescorla (1984) has extended these results to show that the organism also forms associations between a CS and its context when that CS is either neutral or currently undergoing Pavlovian conditioning. Consequently, one must anticipate

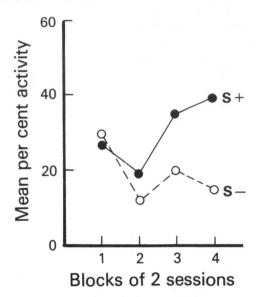

FIG. 2.7.   Mean percentage of observations classed as activity in contexts in which either an S+ (filled circles) or an S− (open circles) had been presented. (From Rescorla, R. A., Associations between Pavlovian CSs and context. *Journal of Experimental Psychology: Animal Behavior Processes*, 1984. Copyright by the American Psychological Association. Reprinted by permission of the publisher and author.)

that standard Pavlovian conditioning experiments will result in the context becoming associated with both the CS and the US. Moreover, both those associations are likely to affect the behavior that we observe to the context itself. This greatly complicates interpretation of contextual conditioning in situations which contain both CSs and USs.

One especially bothersome example of those complications arises in experiments, like those of Durlach described above, with uncorrelated CSs and USs. In those experiments we attempted to modulate the strength of context-US associations by providing a previously conditioned discrete signal for all the extra intertrial USs. But the very signals that were inserted to block conditioning of the context by the US might themselves act to second-order condition the context. Consequently, the signaling manipulation may be considerably less powerful in modifying the total level of background conditioning than we had anticipated. Indeed, in a recent experiment we have found evidence that conditioning to a CS can be attenuated by presentation of a (nonreinforced) first-order excitor in the intertrial interval. One interpretation is that intertrial conditioned excitors condition the background in the same manner as do USs, thereby interfering with conditioning of other discrete CSs.

It seems possible that attention to second-order conditioning might help make sense out of two findings that are otherwise anomolous from the point of view of learning interpretations of the uncorrelated condition. The first is a feature of the results shown in Fig. 2.5 and 2.6 that we have not yet discussed. Those figures show the overall power of the signaling manipulation in restoring conditioning of the original CS. But they also show that this restoration was quite slow to emerge. Despite the fact that the signal itself was previously well conditioned, it took many conditioning sessions before substantial responding occurred to the CS in the signaled condition. Yet learning interpretations would anticipate an immediate ability of the signal to block background conditioning.

One possiblity, of course, is simply that blocking is not as substantial in this conditioning preparation as it is in others (cf. Jenkins, Barnes, & Barrera, 1981). Moreover, any incompleteness of blocking might be especially noticeable with stimuli that are highly salient, a property attributed to background stimuli by some (e.g., Balsam & Schwartz, 1981). Under such circumstances, the effect of the extra USs would be initial conditioning of background cues, whether they are signaled or not. An effect of signaling would only emerge as the value of the background declined due to the organism's subsequent discrimination, a process that might be slow.

But the results shown in Fig. 2.7 suggest another interpretation, that the ability of the signal to block context-US associations is partly compensated for by its own second-order conditioning of the context. Hence, at least in initial conditioning, the signal may be a mixed blessing with regard to inducing differences in background conditioning between the two experimental conditions.

The second anomolous feature of previous experimental outcomes has yet to be mentioned. When one conducts signaling experiments such as those described previously, he infers the differences in conditioning of the context indirectly, by its impact on conditioning of discrete stimuli. However, we have at hand a more direct measurement of the context value—the activity that the organism exhibits in its presence. If the previous arguments are correct, the differential background conditioning induced by signaling the intertrial USs should also be detectable in terms of different levels of general activity. There should be less activity in a context in which the extra USs were signaled. However, the data do not support that conclusion. For instance, Balsam (1984) has reported no difference in general activity (measured by a mechanical device) in birds receiving signaled versus unsignaled food deliveries.

Similarly, we have recently found that, although signaling the intertrial foods in a situation with uncorrelated CS and foods did engender keypecking to the CS, it did not produce a difference in activity to the context. In an experiment similar to that previously described, birds were exposed to either the Signaled or Unsignaled condition; however, additionally, both groups received training in a second context (distinguished by liners) in which they received 25% reinforcement with a different keylight CS, but no intertrial USs. The groups responded similarly in this no-intertrial US condition, both in responding to the keylight CS and in activity (as measured at the beginning of each session). The results of primary interest, keypecking and activity for the signaled and unsignaled intertrial US

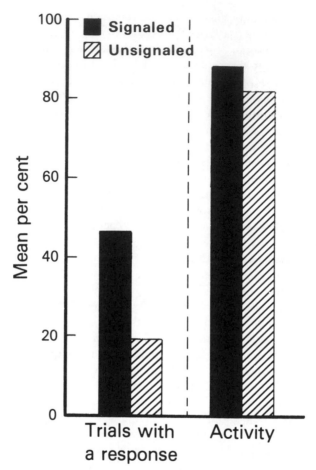

FIG. 2.8.   The left panel shows mean percentage trials with a response to a CS that had been trained in the presence of signaled (filled bars) or unsignaled (open bars) intertrial foods. The right panel shows mean percentage of observations classed as Activity as measured during the second 2.5 min of the signaled (filled) and unsignaled (open) conditions.

conditions, are illustrated in Fig. 2.8. Group Signaled responded to the CS substantially more than Group Unsignaled ($U = 36$, $N1 = N2 = 12$; $p < .05$), replicating the previously described effect of signaling (left panel). However, as illustrated in the right panel of Fig. 2.8, there was no evidence that signaling the additional USs affected the activity levels; both groups were more active in the intertrial US condition than the no-intertrial US condition, but they did not differ from one another.

Results such as these create a paradox. On the one hand, differences in pecking at the target CS in the intertrial US condition suggest differences in background conditioning as a function of whether or not those intertrial USs are signaled. On the other hand, the more direct activity observations suggest that there is no such difference. One possible interpretation is that activity differences are not an especially sensitive index of differences in context conditioning. However, another resolution of that paradox appeals to second-order conditioning of the background by the signal. The activity may reflect different sources of conditioning in the different groups. The unsignaled group may form context-US associations, whereas the signaled groups may have those associations partially blocked but instead form context-signal associations. Although both kinds of learning may be reflected in general activity, both may not equally block CS–US associations. In order for blocking to occur, the context may have to predict the very same outcome as does the CS whose conditioning it is intended to block; that is, the context-signal associations in the signaled group may generate activity but be less effective in blocking the CS–US associations responsible for pecking at the target CS. Moreover, it may only be with extensive conditioning that the organism clearly learns that the target CS and the context are paired with different positive events (the US and the signal, respectively). Only when that learning occurs can conditioning take place to the target CS.

In any case, there may be a considerable amount of both first- and second-order conditioning of context occurring in the course of standard Pavlovian procedures. Animals learn not only what USs but also what CSs occur in a context. Appreciating that richness of contextual learning should give us pause in applying some of our highly simplified theories.

ASSOCIATIONS BETWEEN CONTEXT AND CS/US RELATIONS

The previous sections have documented the occurrence of associations between the context and each of the component events in a standard Pavlovian conditioning experiment. But there is also evidence that organisms learn the relation between the context and the associative relations that obtain between those events. Contexts can become signals that one, rather than another, relation between the CS and US is in force. The classic case is the "switching" experiment, most extensively studied by Asratyan (1965) but also recently conducted by Thomas (1981, this volume) and Kimmel and Ray (1978). In one of its most complete forms, a switching experiment exposes animals to two contexts, each of which contain the same US and the same two signals of that US. However, in one context the US follows one signal and not the other, whereas in the other context the reinforcement contingencies are reversed. The finding of primary interest is that animals can use the context to provide this kind of conditional information so as to behave appropriately to the CSs depending on the context.

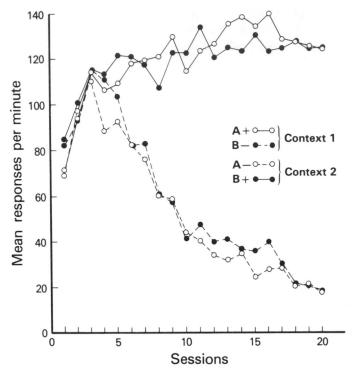

FIG. 2.9.   Mean rate of responding to two CSs, A and B (see text), separated according to the context in which they were presented. In Context 1, A was reinforced (open circles, solid lines) and B was nonreinforced (filled circles, dashed lines); in Context 2, A was nonreinforced (open circles, dashed lines) and B was reinforced (filled circles, solid lines). For half the birds, Context 1 was striped and Context 2 was marbled; the rest received the opposite arrangement.

An example of data from such an experiment, recently conducted in our laboratory, is shown in Fig. 2.9. That figure displays responding from birds run each day in both the marbled and the striped contexts used earlier. All birds received training in both contexts with 2 keylight CSs, a grid of white diagonal lines on a black background, slanted −45 degrees from the vertical (A), and a grid of black diagonal lines on a white background, slanted +45 degrees from the vertical (B). In one context, A was followed by food but B was not. In the other context these reinforcement contingencies were reversed. The identities of the contexts were counterbalanced with this treatment. Figure 2.9 illustrates that the birds readily solved this complex problem. Even though both contexts contained all the same individual CSs and USs, the birds were sensitive to the different relations among those events as conditional upon the context.

Although this is an impressive accomplishment, it turns out to be useful for analytic purposes to use a somewhat reduced form of this discrimination. Recently, we have been exploring the manner in which a contextual stimulus could control one aspect of the discrimination—that a CS signals reinforcement in the presence of that context but not in its absence. Such a relation appears in a variety of learning paradigms. For instance, an operant discriminative stimulus can be thought of as indicating when a response will be paired with a reinforcer. Moreover, drive states can be thought of as stimuli indicating when CSs or responses will result in reinforcers of value. And, of course, any experimental chamber may indicate not only the occurrence of the individual events but also their positive relation. We have adopted the term "facilitation" to apply to cases of this sort.

In analyzing such facilitation we have decided to use "artificial" contexts consisting of nonlocalized auditory and visual events of limited duration. There are two important aspects to this decision. First, our contexts are not physical locations but the occurrence of manipulable stimuli in those locations. This permits us more easily to initiate and terminate multiple contexts and events within a session. The analytic advantages are obvious, but we have sacrificed a naturalness to achieve those advantages. Second, we have selected diffuse events to play the role of these contexts, because we know that any associations that they develop directly with food will not normally promote directed keypecking. Consequently, when the bird pecks to a keylight in the presence of those stimuli, there is no doubt the keylight CS is eliciting the response.

Figure 2.10 shows the results of one recent experiment designed to provide some initial information on this kind of paradigm. The left-hand side of the figure shows results from acquisition. Each bird received two "contextual" facilitating stimuli, each 15 sec long, a white noise and a flashing on and off of the normally illuminated houselight. During one context a yellow stimulus projected on the right-hand side of a response key was followed by food; during the other a horizontal stripe pattern projected on the left-hand side of the key was followed by food. Both types of trials were presented 12 times in each session. In addition, the birds received 12 nonreinforced presentations each of yellow and horizontal given in the absence of any facilitator. Consequently, the houselight and the noise each served as signals that a particular keylight would be reinforced. In order to prevent the absence of these contexts from becoming a general predictor of nonreinforcement, all animals additionally received 12 reinforced presentations of a blue keylight each session. The figure shows the responding to the keylight in the presence and absence of each facilitating diffuse stimulus. The birds initially came to peck at the keylights in both the presence and absence of the diffuse stimuli. However, they rapidly learned the facilitative relation, so as to respond primarily during the contextual stimuli.

The right panel of the figure shows responding during a transfer test session in which each keylight was presented alone and in combination with each contextual stimulus. The results have been separated according to whether or not the animal had previously had experience with the particular context-keylight com-

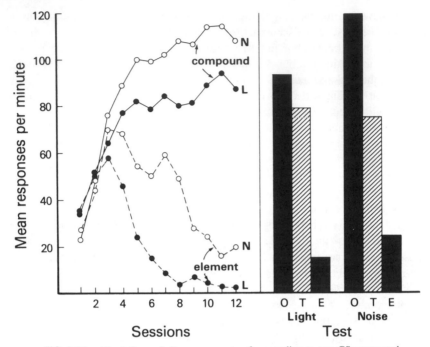

FIG. 2.10.   The left panel shows mean rate of responding to two CSs presented either in the presence (Compound) or absence (Element) of a diffuse noise (open circles) or flashing light (filled circles) "facilitator." Each CS was consistently presented with only one of the facilitators; each was reinforced in the facilitator's presence, but nonreinforced in its absence. The right panel shows mean rate of responding to those CSs, separated according to whether its facilitator was the light or the noise. The CSs were tested either with the original facilitator (O), in transfer with the alternate facilitator (T), or alone (E).

pound. It is clear that the ability of each diffuse stimulus to facilitate performance transfrred to the keylight other than the one with which it had been trained. Despite the fact that the keylights were selected to be easily distinguishable, a hue and a line pattern, and the facilitators were chosen to be in different modalities, there was substantial transfer of facilitation to novel combinations. However, that transfer was incomplete, suggesting some learning about the particular combinations used in training.

The problem of theoretical interest is to characterize the learning that supports this facilitation. In many ways the problem here is analogous to that of characterizing conditioned inhibition. Indeed, the most popular procedure for establishing a conditioned inhibitor (A+/AB−) is the mirror image of the facilitation procedure (A−/AB+). For this purpose, it is convenient to think of the diffuse stimulus as acting on the keylight-food (B–US) association; the issue is then where in the chain of events that allows a keylight to evoke pecking does the facilitator have its impact. Conventionally, three steps in the chain have been identified. The first is activation of some representation of the CS by the illumination of the keylight. That "recognition" of the CS is followed by the second step, activation of its associations. Such associations may be represented as sets of sequential and parallel connections to some representation of the US. If those associations are sufficiently strong, their activation leads to the third step, activation of US representation, which in turn provokes the response. We have argued elsewhere that conditioned inhibitors could in principle reduce responding to a CS by acting at any of these points: the CS, the US, or their association. The same arguments may be applied to facilitators, and we briefly consider each alternative.

CS Activation.   A facilitator could modulate the ability of an external stimulus to activate the CS representation in a variety of ways. A popular account is that it produces a qualitative change in the perception of the stimulus. As noted earlier, the same nominal CS presented in different contexts might well be perceived differently; in that case, the animal's task would be one of discriminating between two relatively similar stimuli, the CS alone and the CS as modified by the facilitator. In many classical studies of switching this possibility has obvious physical bases, because the acoustic and visual properties of discrete stimuli surely are physically affected by the chambers in which they are presented. However, such physical modification seems unlikely in the case of the results in Fig. 2.10, because the keylight stimuli were generated by the same projectors, in the same chambers, whether in the presence of the facilitator or not.

But even if the stimulus is unlikely to be physically different, its processing may be modified by the concurrent presence of the contexts. That idea has received various elaborations, ranging from the Gestalt notion of a configural cue (Gulliksen & Wolfe, 1938), to Hull's (1943) afferent neural interaction, to Spence's (1956) unique cue, to Medin's (1975; Medin & Reynolds, this volume) more recent and sophisticated mathematical treatment.

Such possibilities are difficult to rule out, but again the analogy with conditioned inhibition may prove useful. Several authors (e.g., Konorski, 1967; Brown & Jenkins, 1967) have noted that a B trained in an A+/AB− paradigm can modify the response not only to A but also to other excitors paired with the same US. That observation suggests that B has some power of its own, other than the ability to modify a particular A perceptually. The data in the right panel of Fig. 2.10 suggest that facilitators have a comparable ability. They indicate that the facilitation transferred is substantial, but reduced, for a keylight with which it had never previously been presented. The gross dissimilarities between the two facilitators and between the two keylights make it unlikely that the two facilitators produce comparable perceptual modifications. Consequently, a major portion of the facilitator's power does not seem attributable to perceptual modification.

Finally, the facilitator might produce a quantitative change in the processing of the CS. It might, for instance, increase the animal's attention to the keylight, so as to encourage learning and performance that is superior to that in its absence. Indeed, attentional changes might be responsible for the performance effects of context-US associations described earlier. Although such processes might contribute to the present facilitating effect, they seem inapplicable to more complex switching experiments (such as that illustrated in Fig. 2.9). Simply increased attention to the discrete keylight in a context would not promote the differential performance observed.

Activation of the US Representation.   The facilitator might alternatively act at the other end of the chain, on the activation of the US representation. It is here that modern theories localize the action of conditioned inhibition. One can distinguish two views of how inhibitors act on the US representation, each with a potential analog for the action of a facilitator.

One possibility is that inhibitors and excitors produce effects of the same kind but opposite sign. The consequence of their joint presentation is a summated output. By analogy, facilitators might bring a level of excitation that summates with that of the discrete CS so that the two jointly produce a response. This veiw has been popular as an account of various effects attributed to context (e.g., Bouton & Bolles, 1979). There is no question that combination with another excitor often better exposes a weak level of conditioning, although it is not clear what summation results to expect when the excitors evoke different or even competing responses.

However, several recent experiments in our laboratory suggest that facilitators are not simply weak excitors. The conditions for establishing and removing the facilitatory power of a stimulus differ substantially from those necessary to create or extinguish excitors. In one experiment on acquisition of facilitation, pigeons received concurrent training with a flashing houselight and a white noise. For some animals the noise served as a facilitator for an orange keylight that was reinforced in its presence; but the flashing houselight simply signaled food. The training procedure was otherwise like that described earlier. Each day the animals received 12 trials each of the orange keylight nonreinforced alone, of the orange light reinforced during the noise, and of the houselight followed by food. In addition, they received 12 reinforced trials with a white key. The diffuse stimuli were 15 sec long and the keylights 5 sec long. For other animals the roles of the houselight and the noise were interchanged. The left-hand side of Fig. 2.11 shows that the birds rapidly came to respond to the orange keylight, but only when it was presented during the facilitator. There was no keypecking during either the facilitator alone or the diffuse signal for food. The right-hand side of that figure displays responding during a test session during which the animal received nonreinforced occurrences of the orange keylight alone, as well as in compound with the facilitator and in compound with the simple signal for

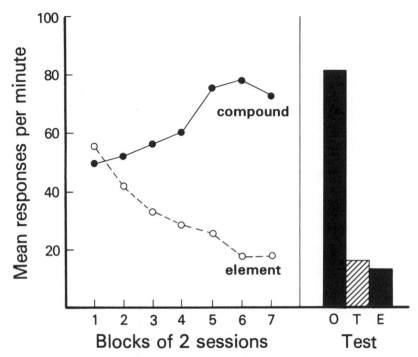

FIG. 2.11.   The left panel shows mean rate of responding to the orange keylight either in the presence of a diffuse facilitator (Compound) or alone (Element). The right panel shows mean rate of responding to the orange keylight CS when it was tested in the presence of its facilitator (O), in the presence of a diffuse simple Pavlovian CS + (T), or alone (E).

food. It is clear that responding to orange occurred primarily during the stimulus trained as a facilitator. The stimulus trained as a simple Pavlovian signal for food did not promote keypecking, even to a discrete keylight that had a history of being in the facilitative relation to another stimulus. Those results suggest that a facilitator and an excitor require different conditions for their establishment. They also suggest that whatever summation rules eventually prove appropriate to performance during compounds whose elements evoke disparate responses, directed keypecking is not generated simply by the animal receiving a signal for food in the presence of a partially trained keylight.

Another recent experiment found a facilitator, once established, not to extinguish in the manner of an excitor. Figure 2.12 shows the results of testing two facilitators, a flashing houselight and a noise, in conjunction with the same keylight CS. For all animals, both diffuse stimuli had been trained as facilitators for that keylight; but each animal then received repeated separate nonreinforced presentations of one facilitator prior to this test. As may be seen, those repeated presentations had no detectable effect on the facilitative ability of the stimulus.

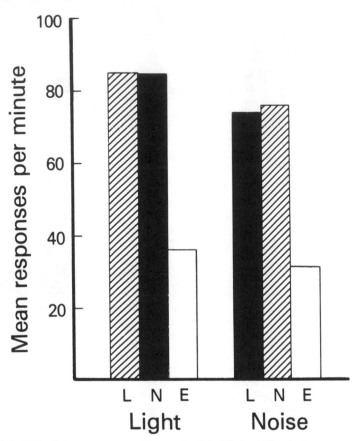

FIG. 2.12.   Mean rate or responding to a keylight CS alone (E) or in the presence of two facilitators, a light (L) or a noise (N). Each subject had received repeated nonreinforced presentations of one of those facilitators (cross hatched) between training and subsequent testing. The data are separated according to whether that nonreinforced facilitator had been the light (left) or the noise (right).

Consequently, the conditions for extinction of facilitation also differ from those of conditioned excitation. It seems unlikely, therefore, that the functioning of a facilitator is attributable to its being simply a conditioned excitor.

    The second popular view of conditioned inhibition rejects the symmetry of conditioned inhibition with conditioned excitation. Instead, some authors (e.g., Konorski, 1948; Rescorla, 1979) have proposed that inhibitors simply raise the threshold for the action of excitors on the US, without themselves eliciting an opposing tendency. Facilitators might likewise lower that threshold but have no excitatory power of their own. Two results have encouraged this view of inhibition. The first is that separately presented inhibitors seldom elicit measureable responses of their own; the exposure of their inhibitory power typically requires the concurrent presence of an excitor (e.g., Rescorla, 1969). The second is that separate presentations of an inhibitor do not seem to extinguish its power (e.g., Zimmer–Hart & Rescorla, 1974). Facilitators prove to have the same two properties. We have already seen that their separate exposure does not lead to their extinction. In a recent experiment we carried out direct behavioral observations of facilitators and could identify no regular pattern that they elicited. These parallels between facilitation and inhibition encourage the view that facilitators may act on the threshold for activation of the US representation. Indeed, it may be that it is inhibitors and facilitators, rather than inhibitors and excitors, that are symmetrical opposites.

Nevertheless, it is clear that action on the threshold of the US representation will not account for the full range of results in switching experiments. In many of those experiments (like the example given at the beginning of this section) two contexts act as facilitators for different discrete stimuli, such that one of the stimuli predicts the US in one context and the other stimulus predicts it in the other context. Such cases of stimulus-specific conditional control demand that the context act on the CS–US pair, not on one of the elements of that pair.

Action on the CS–US Association.   This last observation raises the final possibility, that the facilitator may act on the association between the CS and US representations. Discussion of this, the most interesting of the possibilities, has labored under two disadvantages. First, the empirical results taken as supporting this alternative typically take the form of ruling out the more elementary modes of action on the CS and US individually. Because of the success of associative theory in dealing with learning relations between pairs of events, there has been a natural reluctance to consider more complex relations before the pair-wise alternatives are thoroughly eliminated. Second, this hierarchical possibility has not received very detailed theoretical exposition. Although various hierarchical structures have been proposed (e.g., Estes, 1973), it has not been obvious how to provide evidence for any one such structure in particular. Subsequent research must attempt to further elaborate this notion of a stimulus being associated with a relation between two other stimuli. It may be that the analysis of how context operates provides the best occasion for such an elaboration.

CONCLUSION

This chapter has identified three kinds of learning about context that occur in Pavlovian experiments that pair a CS with a US: associations between the context and the US, those between the context and the CS, and those between the context and the CS–US relation. Following others, we have discussed most extensively the context-US learning. Using a straightforward observational technique, we have found such learning to be rapid and to follow many of the rules of standard Pavlovian conditioning. Separating the effects of context-US associations on learning and performance, we found them to have an adverse effect on the learning of discrete Pavlovian CS–US relations but to promote the performance of those relations that are learned. We presented evidence that the organism also learns what CSs occur in a context and discussed some of the theoretical implications of that evidence. Finally, we reviewed evidence that organisms learn not only what individual events but also what relations among those events occur in a context. We began an analysis of that kind of hierarchical learning. It is clear that organisms learn a variety of things about contextual stimuli and those learnings affect standard Pavlovian conditioning in multiple ways. The theoretical challenge is to characterize such learning in the framework of general accounts of Pavlovian conditioning.

REFERENCES

Asratyan, E. A. *Compensatory adaptations, reflex activity, and the brain.* New York: Pergamon Press, 1965.

Baker, A. G., & Mackintosh, N. J. Preexposure to the CS alone, the US alone, or CS and US uncorrelated: Latent inhibition, blocking by context or learned irrelevance? *Learning and Motivation,* 1979, *10,* 278–294.

Balsam, P. D. Bringing the background to the foreground: The role of contextual cues in autoshaping. In M. Commons, R. Herrnstein, & A. R. Wagner (Eds.), *Quantitative analyses of behavior: Volume 3: Acquisition.* Cambridge, Mass.: Ballinger, 1984.

Balsam, P. D., & Schwartz, A. Rapid background conditioning in autoshaping. *Journal of Experimental Psychology: Animal Behavior Processes,* 1981, *1,* 382–393.

Bolles, R. C. *Theory of motivation.* New York: Harper & Row, 1967.

Bouton, M. E., & Bolles, R. C. Role of conditioned stimuli in reinstatement of extinguished fear. *Journal of Experimental Psychology: Animal Behavior Processes,* 1979, *5,* 368–378.

Brown, P. L., & Jenkins, H. M. Conditioned inhibition and excitation in operant discrimination learning. *Journal of Experimental Psychology,* 1967, *75,* 255–266.

Channell, S. & Hall, G. Facilitation and retardation of discrimination learning after exposure to the stimuli. *Journal of Experimental Psychology: Animal Behavior Processes,* 1981, *7,* 437–446.

Dexter, W. R., & Merrill, H. K. Role of contextual discrimination in fear conditioning. *Journal of Comparative and Physiological Psychology,* 1969, *69,* 677–681.

Durlach, P. J. Effect of signaling intertrial unconditioned stimuli in autoshaping. *Journal of Experimental Psychology: Animal Behavior Processes,* 1983, *9,* 374–389.

Dweck, C. S., & Wagner, A. R. Situational cues and correlation between CS and US as determinants of the conditioned emotional response. *Psychonomic Science,* 1970, *18,* 145–147.

Estes, W. K. New perspectives on some old issues in association theory. In N. J. Mackintosh & W. K. Honig (Eds.), *Fundamental issues in associative learning.* Halifax: Dalhousie University Press, 1969.

Estes, W. K. Memory and conditioning. In F. J. McGuigan & D. B. Lumsden (Eds.), *Contemporary approaches to conditioning and learning.* New York: Wiley, 1973.

Gamzu, E. R., & Williams, D. R. Associative factors underlying the pigeon's key pecking in autoshaping procedures. *Journal of Experimental Analysis of Behavior,* 1973, *19,* 225–232.

Gibbon, J., & Balsam, P. Spreading association in time. In L. C. Locurto, H. S. Terrace, & J. Gibbon (Eds.), *Autoshaping and conditioning theory.* New York: Academic Press, 1981.

Grau, J. W., & Rescorla, R. A. The role of context in autoshaping. *Journal of Experimental Psychology: Animal Behavior Processes,* in press.

Gulliksen, H., & Wolfe, H. L. A theory of learning and transfer: I. *Psychometrika*, 1938, *3*, 127–149.

Hinson, R. E. Effects of UCS preexposure on excitatory and inhibitory rabbit eyelid conditioning: An associative effect of conditioned contextual stimuli. *Journal of Experimental Psychology: Animal Behavior Processes*, 1982, *8*, 49–61.

Holland, P. C. Conditioned stimulus as a determinant of the form for the Pavlovian conditioned response. *Journal of Experimental Psychology: Animal Behavior Processes*, 1977, *3*, 77–104.

Hull, C. L. *Principles of behavior*. New York: Appleton–Century–Crofts, 1943.

Jenkins, H. M., Barnes, R. A., & Barrera, F. J. Why autoshaping depends on trial spacing. In L. C. Locurto, H. S. Terrace, & J. Gibbon (Eds.), *Autoshaping and conditioning theory*. New York: Academic Press, 1981.

Kamin, L. J. Predictability, surprise, attention and conditioning. In B. A. Campbell & R. M. Church (Eds.), *Punishment and aversive behavior*. New York: Appleton–Century–Crofts, 1969.

Kimmel, H. D., & Ray, R. L. Transswitching: Conditioning with tonic and phasic stimuli. *Journal of Experimental Psychology: General*. 1978, *107*, 187–205.

Konorski, J. *Conditioned reflexes and neuron organization*. Cambridge: Mass. Cambridge University Press, 1948.

Konorski, J. *Integrative activity of the brain*. Chicago: University of Chicago Press, 1967.

Leyland, C. M., & Mackintosh, N. J. Blocking of first- and second-order autoshaping in pigeons. *Animal Learning and Behavior*, 1978, *6*, 391–394.

Lindblom, L. L., & Jenkins, H. M. Responses eliminated by noncontingent or negatively contingent reinforcement recover in extinction. *Journal of Experimental Psychology: Animal Behavior Processes*, 1981, *7*, 175–190.

LoLordo, V. M., & Randich, A. Effects of experience of electric shock upon subsequent conditioning of an emotional response: Associative and non-associative accounts. In P. Harzem & M. H. Zeiler (Eds.), *Predictability, correlation, and contiguity*. New York: Wiley, 1981.

Lubow, R. E., Rifkin, B., & Alek, M. The context effect: The relationship between stimulus preexposure and environmental preexposure determines subsequent learning. *Journal of Experimental Psychology: Animal Behavior Processes*, 1976, *2*, 38–47.

Mackintosh, N. J. A theory of attention: Variations in the associability of stimuli with reinforcements. *Psychological Review*, 1975, *82*, 276–298.

Medin, D. L. A theory of context in discrimination learning. In G. H. Bower (Ed.), *The psychology of learning and motivation* (Vol. 9). New York: Academic Press, 1975.

Neely, J. H., & Wagner, A. R. Attenuation of blocking with shifts in reward: The involvement of schedule-generated contextual cues. *Journal of Experimental Psychology*, 1974, *102*, 751–763.

Odling–Smee, F. J. The role of background stimuli during Pavlovian conditioning. *Quarterly Journal of Experimental Psychology*, 1975, *27*, 201–209.

Odling–Smee, F. J. The overshadowing of background stimuli by an informative CS in aversive Pavlovian conditioning with rats. *Animal Learning and Behavior*, 1978, *6*, 43–51.

Randich, A., & LoLordo, V. M. Preconditioning to the unconditioned stimulus affects the acquisition of a conditioned emotional response. *Learning and Motivation*, 1979, *10*, 245–277.

Rescorla, R. A. Probability of shock in the presence and absence of CS in fear conditioning. *Journal of Comparative and Physiological Psychology*, 1968, *66*, 1–5.

Rescorla, R. A. Pavlovian conditioned inhibition. *Psychological Bulletin*, 1969, *72*, 77–94.

Rescorla, R. A. Evidence for "unique stimulus" account of configural conditioning. *Journal of Comparative and Physiological Psychology*, 1973, *85*, 331–338.

Rescorla, R. A. Conditioned inhibition and extinction. In A. Dickinson & R. A. Boakes (Eds.), *Mechanisms of learning and motivation: A memorial volume to Jerzy Konorski*. Hillsdale, N.J.: Lawrence Erlbaum Associates, 1979.

Rescorla, R. A. *Pavlovian second-order conditioning: Studies in associative learning*. Hillsdale, N.J.: Lawrence Erlbaum Associates, 1980.

Rescorla, R. A. Associations between Pavlovian CSs and context. *Journal of Experimental Psychology: Animal Behavior Processes*, 1984, *10*, 195–204.

Rescorla, R. A., & Holland, P. C. Behavioral studies of associative learning in animals. *Annual Review of Psychology*, 1982, *33*, 265–308.

Rescorla, R. A., & Wagner, A. R. A theory of Pavlovian conditioning: Variations in the effectiveness of reinforcement and nonreinforcement. In A. H. Black & W. F. Prokasy (Eds.), *Classical conditioning II: Current theory and research*. New York: Appleton–Century–Crofts, 1972.

Sheffield, F. D., & Campbell, B. A. The role of experience in the "spontaneous" activity of hungry rats. *Journal of Comparative and Physiological Psychology*, 1954, *47*, 97–100.

Skinner, B. F. Superstition in the pigeon. *Journal of Experimental Psychology*, 1948, *38*, 168–172.

Spence, K. W. *Behavior theory and conditioning*. New Haven: Yale University Press, 1956.

Staddon, J. E. R., & Simmelhag, V. L. The "superstition" experiment: A reexamination of its implications for the principles of adaptive behavior. *Psychological Review*, 1971, *78*, 3–43.

Thomas, D. R. Studies of long-term memory in the pigeon. In N. E. Spear & R. R. Miller (Eds.), *Information processing in animals: Memory mechanisms*. Hillsdale, N.J.: Lawrence Erlbaum Associates, 1981.

Tolman, E. C. *Purposive behavior in animals and men*. New York: Century, 1932.

Tomie, A. Retardation of autoshaping: Control by contextual stimuli. *Science*, 1976, *192*, 1244–1246.

Tomie, A. Effect of unpredictable food on the subsequent acquisition of autoshaping: Analysis of the context-blocking hypothesis. In L. C. Locurto, H. S. Terrace, & J. Gibbon (Eds.), *Autoshaping and conditioning theory*. New York: Academic Press, 1981.

Trapold, M. A., & Overmier, J. B. The second learning process in instrumental learning. In A. H. Black & W. F. Prokasy (Eds.), *Classical conditioning II: Current research and theory*. New York: Appleton–Century–Crofts, 1972.

Wagner, A. R. Expectancies and the priming of STM. In S. H. Hulse, H. Fowler, & W. K. Honig (Eds.), *Cognitive processes in animal behavior*. Hillsdale, N.J.: Lawrence Erlbaum Associates, 1978.

Zimmer–Hart, C. L., & Rescorla, R. A. Extinction of Pavlovian conditioned inhibition. *Journal of Comparative and Physiological Psychology*, 1974, *86*, 837–845.

3

Effects of Test Context on the Acquisition of Autoshaping to a Formerly Random Keylight or a Formerly Contextual Keylight

Arthur Tomie
Rutgers, The State University

Contemporary theoretical treatments of Pavlovian conditioning have accorded increasingly well-defined and central roles to contextual stimuli (cf. Gibbon & Balsam, 1981; Rescorla & Wagner, 1972; Wagner, 1978). These theoretical analyses uniformly view contextual stimuli as CSs extended in time with associative properties similar to those of discrete CS events. A contextual stimulus is present throughout the duration of the experimental session. Its presence does not covary with the presentation of the US, and, in this sense, it can be said that contextual stimuli are "unpredictive" of the US. The context may be viewed as "correlated with" or "predictive of" the US only by expanding the boundaries such that the original context is no longer contextual. Contextual stimuli are necessarily unpredictive of the US within the session because contextual stimuli are always present within this time frame. There is, of course, another class of stimuli that may also be described as "unpredictive" of the US within the session—discrete, punctate stimuli whose presentation is randomly related to the presence of the US. Will a contextual stimulus, which is present at all times during experimental sessions wherein intermittent unsignaled US presentations occur, emerge with associative properties similar to those of a discrete CS that is presented randomly during such sessions? This chapter describes a series of experiments that compare the acquisition (Experiments 1 and 3) or reacquisition (Experiments 2 and 4) of the keypecking CR to a keylight CS (in a standard autoshaping procedure with food US), following pretraining with unpredictable US presentations. During pretraining the green keylight stimulus that would later be employed as the autoshaping CS was presented either randomly as a discrete CS (Experiments 1 and 2) or continuously as a pretraining contextual feature (Experiments 3 and 4).

Experiment 1

Tomie, Murphy, Fath, and Jackson (1980, Experiment 2) investigated the effects of "learned irrelevance" pretraining, consisting of random presentations of the green keylight CS and food US, on the subsequent acquisition of autoshaping to the green keylight CS. In that study, 8 groups of pigeons ($n = 12$) were tested for the acquisition of autoshaping to a green keylight CS (7.5 sec duration), which was followed by a response-independent presentation of food (5.0 sec duration). Sixty such autoshaping trials per session (for each of 8 test sessions) were programmed to occur according to a variable-time (VT) 45-sec schedule. The groups were differentiated on the basis of the type of pretraining administered. The subjects in the US-ONLY condition received 30 daily pretraining sessions consisting of 60 presentations of 5 sec access to a tray of mixed pigeon grain (US), programmed according to a VT 45-sec schedule. The subjects in the GREEN KEYLIGHT TRC condition received similar training; however, in addition to the US presentations, each daily session provided for a comparable number of illuminations of the pecking key by a light of 555 nm for 7.5 sec (CS). The CS and US presentations were arranged to occur randomly with respect to one another. The subjects in the GREEN KEYLIGHT CS-ONLY condition received 30 daily sessions of training consisting of 60 CS presentations (555 nm illumination of response key for 7.5 sec), programmed according to a VT 45-sec schedule. The subjects in the ORIGINAL LEARNING CONTROL condition did not receive any extended pretraining but, rather, were tested for the acquisition of autoshaping when each subject attained a hopper-training criterion of feeding for five consecutive presentations of the hopper. The four groups of subjects in the CONTEXT CHANGE condition were administered their pretraining in a ¼ inch brown masonite liner built to fit the full inside dimensions of the chamber, whereas the four groups of subjects in the NO CONTEXT CHANGE condition were administered their pretraining in the normal unlined chamber. Testing for autoshaping was conducted in the unlined chamber.

The mean autoshaping acquisition functions for the first two test sessions are presented in Fig. 3.1. Note that the subjects in the GREEN KEYLIGHT TRC/NO CONTEXT CHANGE group are severely retarded in acquiring the keypecking response, showing virtually no responding on the first test session. The subjects in the US ONLY/NO CONTEXT CHANGE group are also retarded, although to a notably lesser degree. The remaining groups acquire the keypecking CR much more rapidly and do not differ from one another on a number of acquisition analyses (see Tomie et al., 1980, Experiment 2, for a more detailed treatment of the data).

The US ONLY/NO CONTEXT CHANGE group is retarded in the acquisition of autoshaping; whereas, the US ONLY/CONTEXT CHANGE group is not. This type of result has been extensively documented in the autoshaping literature (cf. Balsam & Schwartz, 1981; Tomie, 1976a, b, 1981), as well as in other

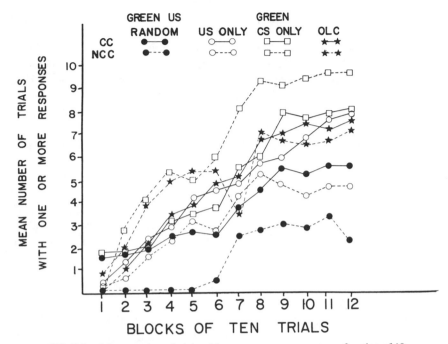

FIG. 3.1.   Mean number of trials with one or more responses as a function of 10 trial blocks for the 8 groups of Experiment 1. Groups tested in the pretraining context (i.e., NO CONTEXT CHANGE) are represented by the broken (- - -) lines. Groups tested in the novel context (i.e., CONTEXT CHANGE) are represented by the solid (——) lines. The GREEN US RANDOM groups (i.e., GREEN KEYLIGHT TRC treatment) are represented by the filled circles. The US ONLY groups are represented by the open circles. The GREEN CS ONLY groups (i.e., GREEN KEYLIGHT CS-ONLY treatment) are represented by the open squares. The OLC (i.e., Original Learning Control) groups are represented by the filled stars.

Pavlovian conditioning procedures (cf. Archer, Sjödén, & Nilsson, this volume; Baker, Singh, & Bindra, this volume; Hinson, 1982; Randich & Ross, this volume; Siegel & Domjan, 1971; Taylor, 1956), and has been widely interpreted as a blocking effect of the contextual stimuli present during the test that have been conditioned by their pairing with the US during pretraining (see Randich & LoLordo, 1979 and Tomie, 1981 for more complete discussions of the context-blocking hypothesis). The retarding effect of the GREEN KEYLIGHT TRC treatment is also attenuated by the context change manipulation (i.e., the GREEN KEYLIGHT TRC/NO CONTEXT CHANGE group is retarded relative to the GREEN KEYLIGHT TRC/CONTEXT CHANGE group); whereas, the effects of the remaining treatments (GREEN KEYLIGHT CS-ONLY and ORIGINAL LEARNING CONTROL) are not. This pattern of results implies that when contextual stimuli are paired with the US during pretraining they become excitatory (and therefore capable of exerting a blocking influence), even though their presence during the session is uncorrelated with the presentation of the US.

If the background contextual stimuli become excitatory during pretraining, other stimuli equally unpredictive of US presentations (such as the randomly illuminated green keylight) might also be expected to become excitatory. There is considerable evidence that despite being uncorrelated with the US, there are circumstances under which the TRC stimulus may become excitatory. Ayres, Benedict, and Witcher (1975) have shown that in the CER procedure the TRC stimulus suppresses barpressing if CS–US pairings occur early during training. If, on the other hand, early US presentations are isolated from the presentation of the CS, later CS–US pairings are not effective in conditioning the random CS. Extended exposure to TRC procedures has been shown to minimize the effects of early CS–US pairings, producing a random CS that is neutral (Keller, Ayres, & Mahoney, 1977). Although comparable analyses of the TRC procedure in auto-shaping have not been reported, there is some evidence that the random keylight is excitatory in that it maintains or enhances previously established keypecking (cf. Brandon, 1981; Farley, 1980; Williams, 1976).

In the procedures utilized here an excitatory green keylight would be expected to facilitate the acquisition of autoshaping. Note, however, that the GREEN KEYLIGHT TRC groups are retarded rather than facilitated relative to the other treatment groups in their respective context change conditions. Of course, it is conceivable that the green keylight TRC stimulus is associated with food, but that its excitatory status is not reflected in superior keypeck performance (i.e., the excitatory strength of the green keylight CS may be too low to be transcribed into overt keypeck performance). It is also possible that the green TRC keylight stimulus is excitatory and would facilitate keypecking; however, its effects on keypecking may be countered by cognitive transfer-of-training influences (i.e., ''learned irrelevance,'' see Baker, Singh, & Bindra, this volume) engendered by this type of pretraining.

The presumption that the excitatory keylight's association with food can only facilitate keypecking may be sanguine. It is clear that in pigeons CR topographies other than keypecking are conditioned to stimuli paired with food (cf. Balsam, 1984; Balsam, this volume; Durlach, 1982; Rescorla, Durlach, & Grau, this volume; Staddon & Simmelhag, 1971). The specific topography of the nonkeypecking CR seems to be idiosyncratic (i.e., varying from subject to subject) and is usually measured as an increase in activity. Recently, Balsam (this volume) in both ring doves and pigeons, has found a negative between-subjects correlation between activity level (conditioned to context) and the speed of acquisition of autoshaping, indicating that subjects that exhibit strong activity CRs are retarded in acquiring the keypecking CR. Moreover, Balsam (this volume) has found that the activity CR is conditioned to keylight CSs whose predictiveness of the US is too weak to support autoshaping acquisition. These recent empirical observations compel reevaluation of the data from the present experiment; in particular, we should recognize the possibility that retardation effects over and above those attributable to context blocking (as were observed in this experiment) may reflect the excitatory properties of the keylight CS.

Experiment 2

Because there is some evidence in the autoshaping literature that the random keylight maintains (i.e., increases resistance to extinction) (cf. Brandon, 1981) or enhances keypecking (i.e., produces behavioral contrast effects) (cf. Farley, 1980; Williams, 1976) in subjects who have previously acquired the keypecking CR, the associative status of the TRC stimulus was evaluated in Experiment 2 in a reacquisition test. Following the acquisition of autoshaping to a vertical line CS, two matched groups of pigeons were administered either CS-ONLY or TRC training. The CS during this phase was the green keylight stimulus to be employed in the reacquisition of autoshaping test. In many respects, the results obtained from reacquisition tests have been similar to those of the retardation test used in Experiment 1. Reacquisition has been shown to be retarded following US-ONLY training or TRC training with a CS other than the reacquisition CS (Tomie, Hayden, & Biehl, 1980, Exp. 1), the degree of retardation is directly related to the amount of training with unpredictable food (Tomie, Hayden, & Biehl, 1980, Exp. 2), and the retardation of reacquisition is context-specific (Tomie, Rhor–Stafford, & Schwam, 1981, Exp. 2). If the TRC stimulus has an effect upon the production of keypecking, the reacquisiton test may provide a more sensitive appraisal, because the subjects have previously acquired the autoshaping CR (albeit to a different keylight CS) and have been matched on that basis.

Twenty-six pigeons were administered 11 daily autoshaping acquisition sessions. The CS was the illumination of the response key for 6 sec by a vertical white line that bisected an otherwise dark response key. The US was the presentation of grain for 4 sec. Sixty trials per session were programmed to occur according to a VT 30 sec schedule. The number of trials to attain a criterion of responding for 5 consecutive trials and the number of trials with 1 or more responses on Day 11 were used to create 2 matched groups of subjects ($n = 13$). On the day following the last acquisition session, the groups received the first of 5 daily response elimination sessions. For both groups, trials were programmed according to the same VT 30-sec schedule used in acquisition. The CS-ONLY/ CONTEXT CHANGE group was given 60 nonreinforced presentations of a green keylight CS per session and at the end of each session received the amount of grain equivalent to 60 US presentations while in their home cages. The TRC/CONTEXT CHANGE group received similar treatment, except that 60 US presentations were programmed to occur randomly with respect to the green keylight CS during each session. Both groups were administered their response elimination treatments in the brown masonite liners. On the day following the

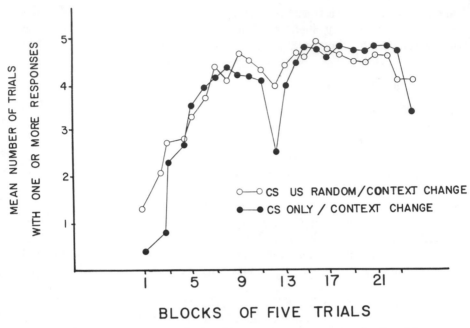

FIG. 3.2.   Mean number of trails with one or more responses as a function of 5
trial blocks for the CS–US RANDOM/CONTEXT CHANGE (i.e., TRC treatment) groups and the CS ONLY/CONTEXT CHANGE group.

last response elimination session, both groups were given the first of two daily
reacquisition sessions identical to those of original acquisition except that the CS
was the green keylight rather than the vertical line stimulus.

As is typically the case when the response elimination phase is accompanied
by the context change manipulation, virtually no responding was observed by
subjects in either group. The mean reacquisition functions for each of the two
groups are presented in Fig. 3.2. The TRC/CONTEXT CHANGE group responded somewhat more on the first 10 trials; however, comparable levels of
responding were observed thereafter. Analysis of variance revealed no reliable
effect of treatment and no reliable treatment by blocks interaction ($p > .05$). In
order to determine if the TRC/CONTEXT CHANGE group responded at a
higher level during the early reacquisition test trials (blocks 1 and 2), the data
were subjected to Fisher's LSD tests, which revealed that the observed group
differences are not reliable ($p > .05$). These data indicate that following TRC
training the green keylight CS does elicit somewhat more keypecking on early
test trials; however, the effect is short-lived and not statistically reliable.

These results are consistent with those observed in Experiment 1 and provide
support for the conclusion that the TRC stimulus is not strongly excitatory. Note
that the reacquisition test is less likely to be contaminated by activity CR to-

pographies incompatible with keypecking, because the keypeck CR is explicitly conditioned during the initial phase of training, and moreover subjects that exhibit CRs that interfere with the performance of stable and reliable keypecking are discarded. In addition, the possible contaminating effect of transfer-of-training cognitions (i.e., "learned irrelevance") seems less feasible in a reacquisition test, because TRC training is preceded by experience with keylight contingent presentations of food, which, ostensibly, would provide for "immunization" against "learned irrelevance."

The results of the first two experiments reveal that contextual stimuli exert a blocking influence, presumably mediated by their excitatory status, whereas, on the other hand, the discrete keylight TRC stimulus exerts no discernible excitatory characteristics in a keypeck production test. The results may be taken to indicate that contextual stimuli are more excitatory than are TRC stimuli, or, alternatively, that the excitatory properties of stimuli are more readily transcribed into a blocking influence than into a consistent effect on keypecking. In the next two experiments, the excitatory status of a contextual stimulus is evaluated in a keypeck production test.

Experiment 3

The third experiment was similar to Experiment 1, except that during pretraining the green keylight was a contextual stimulus rather than a randomly presented CS. Eight groups of pigeons ($n = 10$) were tested for the acquisition of autoshaping to a green keylight CS (5.0-sec duration), which was followed by the response-independent presentation of food (4.0-sec duration). Sixty such autoshaping trials per session (for each of 8 test sessions) were programmed to occur according to a VT 30-sec schedule. The groups were differentiated on the basis of the type of pretraining administered. The subjects in the VERTICAL LINE condition received 20 daily pretraining sessions consisting of 60 presentations of 4-sec access to a tray of mixed pigeon grain (US), programmed according to a VT 30-sec schedule. During the entire duration of the experimental session, the keylight was illuminated by a white vertical line that bisected an otherwise dark response key (i.e., this group is analogous to the US-ONLY group of Exp. 1). The subjects in the GREEN condition received similar training except that the keylight was constantly illuminated by the 555 nm green stimulus to be used in the autoshaping test (i.e., this group is analogous to the TRC group of Exp. 1). The subjects in the GREEN CS-ONLY condition received 20 daily ½-hr sessions of pretraining, during which time the green keylight was constantly illuminated but the food hopper was not presented. The subjects in the ORIGINAL LEARNING CONTROL condition did not receive extended pretraining but, rather, were tested for the acquisition of autoshaping the day after they were successfully hopper trained. As in the first experiment, the ¼ inch brown masonite liners were used during pretraining in the CONTEXT CHANGE groups, and, addi-

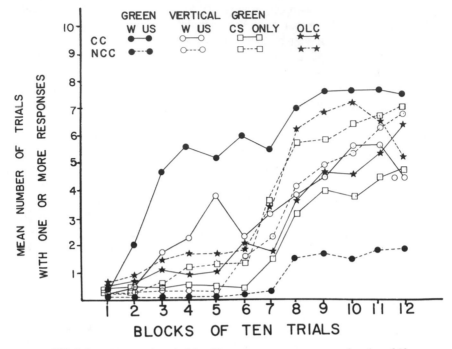

FIG. 3.3.   Mean number of trials with one or more responses as a function of 10 trial blocks for the 8 groups of Experiment 3. Groups tested in the pretraining context (i.e., NO CONTEXT CHANGE) are represented by the broken (- - -) lines. Groups tested in the novel context (i.e., CONTEXT CHANGE) are represented by the solid (———) lines. The GREEN W US groups (i.e., GREEN pretreatment) are represented by the solid circles. The VERTICAL W US groups (i.e., VERTICAL LINE pretreatment) are represented by the open circles. The GREEN CS ONLY groups are represented by the open squares. The OLC (i.e., Original Learning Control) groups are represented by the filled stars.

tionally, an auditory context feature (87 dB of white masking noise) was used only in conjunction with the unlined chambers (i.e., during pretraining for the NO CONTEXT CHANGE groups and during testing for all groups).

The mean autoshaping acquisition functions for the first two test sessions are presented in Fig. 3.3. As in the first experiment, the subjects in the GREEN/NO CONTEXT CHANGE group are severely retarded in acquiring the keypecking response, exhibiting virtually no responding on the first test session. However, in contrast to the results of the first experiment, the subjects in the GREEN/ CONTEXT CHANGE groups acquired the keypecking response very rapidly; the majority of the subjects responded on the first test session. The VERTICAL LINE/NO CONTEXT CHANGE group is retarded relative to the VERTICAL LINE/CONTEXT CHANGE group only early in testing, and, as in Experiment 1, effects of changing the context are not observed in either the GREEN CS-ONLY or ORIGINAL LEARNING CONTROL groups.

In summary, the results of Experiments 1 and 3 are similar in many respects despite a number of differences in procedures. Most notably, the GREEN KEY-LIGHT TRC/NO CONTEXT CHANGE group (Exp. 1) and the GREEN/NO CONTEXT CHANGE group (Exp. 3) are both retarded beyond the degree attributable to pretraining experience with the US alone (i.e., relative to the US ONLY/NO CONTEXT CHANGE and the VERTICAL LINE/NO CONTEXT CHANGE groups, respectively). Furthermore, because in neither experiment was there a suggestion of retardation in the CS ONLY/NO CONTEXT CHANGE groups, this additional retardation is not attributable to the deleterious effects of "latent inhibition."

The results of the two experiments differ most notably in that the GREEN/CONTEXT CHANGE group (Exp. 3) acquired the keypecking CR very rapidly, whereas the GREEN KEYLIGHT TRC/CONTEXT CHANGE group (Exp. 1) exhibited no such facilitation. Facilitation of keypeck production provides rather compelling support for the notion that the contextual green keylight is excitatory. If the GREEN pretreatment produces an excitatory association between the green keylight CS and the food US, this association is transcribed into keypeck production only in the CONTEXT CHANGE condition. When the test context is excitatory (i.e., in the NO CONTEXT CHANGE condition), the excitatory keylight is retarded in keypeck production beyond the degree attributable to context blocking.

Clearly, the effect of an excitatory keylight stimulus depends on the test context. Perhaps, the topography of the CR controlled by the keylight CS depends on the topography of the CR controlled by the context; that is, perhaps during pretraining the keylight CS becomes associated with food, although not to the degree required to engender keypecking. Balsam's data (this volume) suggests that the CR will be an increase in activity. The activity CR controlled by context appears to interfere with the acquisition of keypecking. Perhaps presenting the keylight CS in an excitatory context wherein activity CRs already predominate encourages the production of the activity CR controlled by the keylight CS, rather than the production of the keypecking CR that might otherwise develop. The context shift manipulation would effectively eliminate the activity CR controlled by context from the test situation and thereby provide the opportunity for the keylight-food association to express itself in an alternative response topography (i.e., keypecking). Unfortunately, because activity CRs controlled by keylight or context were not measured in any of the present experiments, this interpretation is highly speculative. This interpretation does, however, provide a relatively complete account of these data and is consistent with the observations of contextual-mediated activity CRs recently reported by other autoshaping investigators. These data are very different from those reported by Rescorla, Durlach, & Grau (this volume), who found that performance to CS+ was not substantially affected by the associative value of the test context (as measured by the activity CR). In their experiment, the keypecking CR to that CS+ was established prior to the test for context mediation, whereas in the present study the keypecking CR was yet to be acquired. This pattern of results suggests that the activity CR controlled by the test context interferes with the acquisition but not with the maintenance of keypecking.

Experiment 4

The results of the previous experiment indicate that even in a keypeck production test a contextual keylight CS appears to be excitatory. This would imply that a contextual keylight CS is more strongly excitatory than is a discrete random CS, in as much as in Experiment 1 the random CS did not facilitate the acquisition of keypecking. Because Experiments 1 and 3 differed in a number of respects (most notably the US density during pretraining and the intertrial interval during testing), the results of the two experiments are not directly comparable. Experiment 4 is analogous to Experiment 2 (reacquisition test following TRC training) and was undertaken to allow a more direct comparison of contextual and random keylights. Note that in this experiment the keylight was constantly illuminated during the response elimination phase, and response elimination treatments were evaluated in both CONTEXT CHANGE and NO CONTEXT CHANGE conditions within-subjects. To facilitate comparisons, all other aspects of the procedures of this experiment were identical to those of Experiment 2.

Eighteen pigeons were administered 8 daily autoshaping acquisition sessions identical to those of the original acquisition phase of Experiment 2. Two groups of subjects ($n = 9$) were matched as described in Experiment 2. The original acquisition phase was followed by 10 daily sessions of response elimination treatment, which were similar to those described in Experiment 2 except that the key was constantly illuminated by the green light. The CS-ONLY group did not receive US presentations during this phase, whereas the CS AND US group was administered 60 US presentations according to a VT 30-sec schedule. As in Experiment 2, this response elimination phase was conducted in the masonite liners (i.e., CONTEXT CHANGE). On the day following the last response elimination session, both groups were given the first of five daily reacquisition sessions identical (i.e., in the unlined chambers) to those of Experiment 2. The first reacquisition test was followed by another response elimination phase, which was identical to the first response elimination phase except that the keylight was constantly illuminated by a red (606 nm) stimulus and the masonite liners were not used (i.e., NO CONTEXT CHANGE). This response elimination phase was followed by a second reacquisition test, which was identical to the first reacquisition test except that the keylight CS was red rather than green.

The mean reacquisition functions for each of the two groups following response elimination in the liners are presented in Fig. 3.4. The CS AND US/CONTEXT CHANGE group is *facilitated* in the reacquisition of autoshaping relative to the CS-ONLY/CONTEXT CHANGE group, an effect that is consistent with that observed in Experiment 2. The mean reacquisition functions

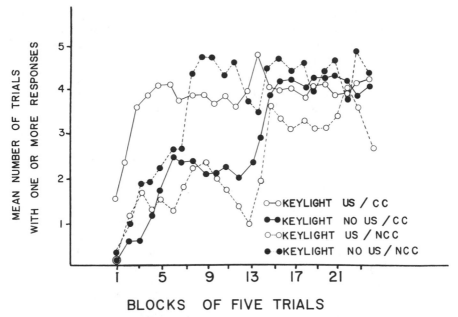

FIG. 3.4.   Mean number of trails with one or more responses as a function of 5 trail blocks for the 2 groups of Experiment 4. The solid lines (——) represent the data from the first reacquisition test (i.e., CONTEXT CHANGE), whereas the broken (- - -) lines represent the data from the second reacquisition test (i.e., NO CONTEXT CHANGE). The KEYLIGHT US (i.e., CS and US treatment) group is represented by the open circles. The KEYLIGHT NO US (i.e., CS ONLY) group is represented by the filled circles. The subjects in the KEYLIGHT US/CC group are those in the KEYLIGHT US/NCC group. The subjects in the KEYLIGHT NO UC/CC group are those in the KEYLIGHT NO US/NCC group.

following the second response elimination phase (conducted without liners) are presented in Fig. 3.5. The CS AND US/NO CONTEXT CHANGE group is *retarded* relative to the CS-ONLY/NO CONTEXT CHANGE group, an effect that is consistent with that observed in Experiments 1 and 3. Note that the group of subjects that reacquired faster in the first test is that which reacquired slower in the second test.

These effects replicate those observed in Experiment 3 and indicate that in a keypeck production test the effects of a contextual keylight depend on the test context, even in subjects for whom the keypecking CR has been previously established. Moreover, because these procedures are analogous to those of Experiment 2, the data may be taken to indicate that the context keylight is more excitatory (as measured in a keypeck production test) than is the discrete random keylight CS.

In summary, the data from these experiments indicate that a randomly presented discrete keylight stimulus that is intermittently presented during the administration of unpredictable food (i.e., TRC procedure) is not subsequently facilitated in either acquisition or reacquisition of autoshaping when testing is conducted in a novel environment. This implies that such pretraining does not establish a strong excitatory association between the keylight stimulus and the food US. If, on the other hand, the test for the acquisition of autoshaping is conducted in the pretraining environment, the formerly random CS is severely retarded in promoting the development of keypecking, an effect that has been attributed to the operation of a ''learned irrelevance'' cognition (cf. Mackintosh, 1973).

On the other hand, a contextual keylight stimulus that is present during the administration of unpredictable food is subsequently facilitated in both the acquisition and reacquisition of autoshaping if the test is administered in a novel context. This implies that such pretraining establishes an excitatory association between the keylight stimulus and the food US, which, in turn, implies that following this type of pretraining contextual stimuli are more excitatory than are random stimuli. If the test for the acquisition or reacquisition of autoshaping is conducted in the pretraining environment, the contextual keylight CS is not facilitated but, rather, is severely retarded in promoting the development of keypecking. Whereas this retardation may, again, be taken to reflect the operation of a ''learned irrelevance'' cognition, the excitatory status of the keylight stimulus seems incompatible with this type of explanation.

The results of these experiments indicate that, following pretraining with unpredictable presentations of food, the contextual keylight is more excitatory than is the random discrete keylight. There are several properties of a contextual keylight, as opposed to a discrete keylight, that may mediate this difference. The contextual keylight is present during all US presentations, thus maximizing the number of context-US pairings, and, presumably, the conditioning of the context. On the other hand, context is also present at all times when the US is not presented, thus maximizing the number of context extinction trials, and, presumably, the extinction of the context-US association. These data may indicate that the increment in associative value accrued during the additional reinforced trials outweighs the decrement in associative value accrued during the additional nonreinforced trials.

There is another characteristic of context that may enhance its tendency to condition relative to random CSs. Context is never absent when the US is presented. The association of other stimuli with the US, therefore, can never be strengthened without the opportunity for the context to also benefit. A randomly presented discrete CS, on the other hand, will be absent during many US presentations and, consequently, will not have the opportunity to gain associative strength while alternative stimuli are being conditioned. To the degree that conditioning of alternative (i.e., contextual) stimuli will interfere with the conditioning of the random CS, the phasic characteristic of the random CS will serve to reduce its conditioning. There is considerable evidence that random and contextual stimuli interact in this fashion. A number of investigators using aversive Pavlovian-conditioning procedures have shown that the conditioning of a randomly presented discrete CS is modulated (i.e., blocked) by the conditioning of the contextual cues (cf. Ayres, Benedict, & Witcher, 1975; Keller, Ayres, & Mahoney, 1977; Kremer, 1974; Odling–Smee, 1975; Witcher & Ayres, 1975).

The difference in the associative strength of the random and contextual keylight is not readily reconciled with contemporary theoretical treatments of Pavlovian conditioning. The Rescorla–Wagner (1972) model predicts that contextual stimuli will more likely become excitatory than random stimuli; however, the Rescorla–Wagner model also predicts that the type of extended pretraining utilized here will produce contextual and random stimuli with associatively neutral properties. Scalar-expectance theory (Gibbon & Balsam, 1981) predicts that the relative rate of reinforcement of either the random or the contextual keylight will be compared to the relative rate of reinforcement of the nonkeylight context, and the ratio of this comparison will determine CR strength. During pretraining, both ratios should approximate 1.0 and no keypecking to either stimulus should be observed. The data are in accord with the prediction. The theory predicts, however, that during the autoshaping test the random and contextual keylight should be equally facilitated in promoting keypecking, and, moreover, facilitation should be observed in both the pretraining and the novel context, and, furthermore the facilitation effect should be greater in the novel context than in the pretraining context. The random and contextual keylights were not equally effective in facilitating keypecking, and both exercised a retarding rather than a facilitative effect in the pretraining context. This raises another question. If one accepts the premise that the contextual keylight CS emerges with excitatory properties, why is this manifested only in the novel test context? One possibility is that keypecking CR performance is based on the ratio of the associative value of the CS and the context (cf. Gibbon & Balsam, 1981). The keylight CS is excitatory but this association is not transcribed into keypeck performance because of the low CS/context ratio. This analysis does not account for the *retardation* effects observed. If one presumes that these *retardation* effects are attributable to the excitatory keylight, one must accept the notion that the topography of the CR elicited by the keylight CS depends on the associative value of the test context. In an excitatory context, the topography of the keylight CR would be incompatible with keypecking, whereas in a novel context, the topography of that CR would be so as to facilitate the acquisition of keypecking.

Note that the activity CR apparently has no effect on the maintenance of the previously established keypecking CR (Rescorla, Durlach, & Grau, this volume), indicating that context mediated keylight CR topography only when the keylight CS has not previously been conditioned sufficiently so as to have previously elicited keypecking. When keypecking has been previously established, the excitatory context seems to exert no effect on a well-conditioned keylight CS (Rescorla, Durlach, & Grau, this volume), or a slightly facilitory effect on a weakly conditioned keylight CS (Durlach, 1982). When the keylight CS is novel (as in studies employing US-only preexposure) the acquisition of autoshaping is retarded by an excitatory test context (cf. Balsam & Schwartz, 1981; Tomie, 1976b, 1981), and when the keylight CS is excitatory but not sufficiently so as to have elicited keypecking (but presumably so as to have elicited activity), the acquisition of autoshaping in the excitatory test context is still more retarded.

Finally, it should be acknowledged that these results may be specific to the kind of Pavlovian-conditioning procedures utilized here. Note that in autoshaping the activity CR controlled by context and the keypecking CR controlled by the autoshaping CS are topographically dissimilar, and, apparently, incompatible with one another (cf. Balsam, this volume). The associative value of the context would, therefore, be expected to diminish the keypecking CR but not necessarily eliminate the CR-eliciting properties of the keylight. In a situation where high levels of activity are conditioned to nonkeylight contextual stimuli, the keylight may elicit an activity CR that summates with the contextual CR. On the other hand, in a situation where activity is not controlled by nonkeylight contextual stimuli (i.e., in a novel context), the CR elicited by the keylight is not directed to nonkeylight contextual stimuli, and CS-directed keypecking is facilitated. In alternative Pavlovian-conditioning procedures, the CR controlled by the discrete CS is typically not CS directed and is often measured in the same fashion as is the CR controlled by the context (e.g., CER; see Baker, Singh, & Bindra, Bouton & Bolles, Miller & Schachtman, all in this volume). In those types of Pavlovian procedures one might observe consistent facilitation effects in experiments such as these, regardless of the history of the test context. Indeed, it is precisely the CS-directed nature of the autoshaping CR that has made it an intriguing preparation for the evaluation of context-cue interactions, and which has encouraged the type of comparator analysis advocated by Gibbon and Balsam (1981). Clearly the relationship between cues and context will depend on the interaction of the specific CR topographies controlled by keylight and context. These interactions obviously need to be evaluated more directly in much greater detail.

ACKNOWLEDGMENTS

This research was supported by NIMH grant MH 37517–01, Rutgers Research Council grants, Biomedical Research Support Grant (administered by Rutgers University), and Charles and Johanna Busch Bequest Grant (administered by Rutgers University) awarded to the author. The author thanks Ines Stafford, Eric Loukas, Kathleen Schwam, and Steven Leichter for their assistance with the running of subjects.

REFERENCES

Ayres, J. J. B., Benedict, J. O., & Witcher, E. S. Systematic manipulation of individual events in a truly random control in rats. *Journal of Comparative and Physiological Psychology,* 1975, *88,* 97–103.

Balsam, P. D. Bringing the background to the foreground: The role of contextual cues in autoshaping. In M. Commons, R. Herrnstein, & A. R. Wagner (Eds.), *Quantitative analyses of behavior: Volume 3: Acquisition.* Cambridge, Mass.: Ballinger, 1984.

Balsam, P. D., & Schwartz, A. L. Rapid contextual conditioning in autoshaping. *Journal of Experimental Psychology: Animal Behavior Processes,* 1981, *7,* 382–393.

Brandon, S. E. Key-light-specific associations and factors determining keypecking in noncontingent schedules. *Journal of Experimental Psychology: Animal Behavior Processes,* 1981, *7,* 348–361.

Durlach, P. J. Direct measurement of context conditioning in the pigeon. *Proceedings of the 53rd Annual meeting of the Eastern Psychological Association,* Baltimore, April, 1982.

Farley, J. Automaintenance, contrast, and contingencies: Effects of local vs overall and prior vs impending reinforcement context. *Learning and Motivation,* 1980, *11,* 19–48.

Gibbon, J., & Balsam, P. D. Spreading association in time. In C. M. Locurto, H. S. Terrace, & J. Gibbon (Eds.), *Autoshaping and conditioning theory.* New York: Academic Press, 1981.

Hinson, R. E. Effects of UCS preexposure on excitatory and inhibitory rabbit eyelid conditioning: An associative effect of conditioned contextual stimuli. *Journal of Experimental Psychology: Animal Behavior Processes,* 1982, *8,* 49–61.

Keller, R. J., Ayres, J. J. B., & Mahoney, W. J. Brief versus extended exposure to truly random control procedures. *Journal of Experimental Psychology: Animal Behavior Processes,* 1977, *3,* 53–65.

Kremer, E. F. The truly random control procedure: Conditioning to the static cues. *Journal of Comparative and Physiological Psychology,* 1974, *86,* 700–707.

Mackintosh, N. J. Stimulus selection: Learning to ignore stimuli that predict no change in reinforcement. In R. A. Hinde & J. Stevenson–Hinde (Eds.), *Constraints on learning.* New York: Academic Press, 1973.

Odling–Smee, F. J. The role of background stimuli during Pavlovian conditioning. *Quarterly Journal of Experimental Psychology,* 1975, *27,* 201–209.

Randich, A., & LoLordo, V. M. Associative and nonassociative theories of the UCS preexposure phenomenon: Implications for Pavlovian conditioning. *Psychology Bulletin,* 1979, *86,* 523–548.

Rescorla, R. A., & Wagner, A. R. A theory of Pavlovian conditioning: Variations in the effectiveness of reinforcement and nonreinforcement. In A. H. Black & W. F. Prokasy (Eds.), *Classical conditioning II: Current theory and research.* New York: Appleton-Century-Crofts, 1972.

Siegel, S., & Domjan, M. Backward conditioning as an inhibitory procedure. *Learning and Motivation,* 1971, *2,* 1–11.

Staddon, J. E. R., & Simmelhag, V. L. The "Superstition experiment": A reexamination of its implications for the principles of adaptive behavior. *Psychological Review,* 1971, *78,* 3–43.

Taylor, J. A. Level of conditioning and intensity of the adaptation stimulus. *Journal of Experimental Psychology,* 1956, *51,* 127–130.

Tomie, A. Retardation of autoshaping: Control by contextual stimuli, *Science,* 1976, *192,* 1244–1246. (a)

Tomie, A. Interference with autoshaping by prior context conditioning. *Journal of Experimental Psychology: Animal Behavior Processes,* 1976, *2,* 323–334. (b)

Tomie, A. Effects of unpredictable food upon the subsequent acquisition of autoshaping: Analysis of the context blocking hypothesis. In C. M. Locurto, H. S. Terrace, & J. Gibbon (Eds.), *Autoshaping and conditioning theory.* New York: Academic Press, 1981.

Tomie, A., Hayden, M., & Biehl, D. Effects of response elimination procedures upon the subsequent reacquisition of autoshaping. *Animal Learning & Behavior,* 1980, *8,* 237–244.

Tomie, A., Murphy, A. L., Fath, S., & Jackson, R. L. Retardation of autoshaping following pretraining with unpredictable food: Effects of changing the context between pretraining and testing. *Learning and Motivation,* 1980, *11,* 117–134.

Tomie, A., Rhor–Stafford, I., & Schwam, K. I. The retarding effect of the TRC response-elimination procedure upon the subsequent reacquisition of autoshaping: Comparison of between- and within-subjects assessment procedures and the evaluation of the role of background contextual stimuli. *Animal Learning & Behavior,* 1981, *9,* 230–238.

Wagner, A. R. Expectancies and the priming of STM. In S. Hulse, H. Fowler, & W. K. Honig (Eds.), *Cognitive processes in animal behavior*. Hillsdale, N. J.: Lawrence Erlbaum Associates, 1978.

Williams, B. A. Elicited response to signals for reinforcement: The effects of overall versus local changes in reinforcement. *Journal of the Experimental Analysis of Behavior*, 1976, *26*, 213–220.

Witcher, E. S., & Ayres, J. J. B. Effect of removing background white noise during CS presentation on conditioning in the truly random control procedure. *Bulletin of the Psychonomic Society*, 1975, *6*, 25–27.

4 Some Effects of Contextual Conditioning and US Predictability on Pavlovian Conditioning

A. G. Baker
Maharaj Singh
Dalbir Bindra
McGill University

Conditioning has usually been described in associative terms. A stimulus is paired with an important event and over time an association is said to form between these two events. Although this pairing of a conditional stimulus (CS) and an unconditional stimulus (US) does not occur in a vacuum but in the presence of other "contextual" stimuli, there has been little effort to place contextual stimuli in a consistent theoretical setting with the CS and the US. In fact, it has only been with the revolution in the theoretical analysis of conditioning that was brought about by the findings of Kamin (1969), Wagner, Logan, Haberlandt, and Price, (1968), and Rescorla (1966), that a strong analytical framework for the analysis of the experimental context's role in classical conditioning has emerged.

Kamin's (1969) work is typical of these results and is of the most immediate relevance to the experiments that we discuss here. In a typical experiment using the conditioned emotional response (CER or conditioned suppression) paradigm, he paired a compound of two stimuli (AB) with a shock US and found that the animals conditioned to both A and B after a few pairings. This finding by itself was quite consistent with the traditional associative view that the amount of conditioning to a stimulus was a consequence of the number of times that that stimulus was paired with the US. However, his more important finding was in certain groups in which one of the stimuli (say A) was paired with the US a number of times prior to the pairings of the AB compound with the US. When B was later tested for conditioning it was found to elicit relatively little suppression when compared to procedures that involved no prior experience with A. Kamin had found that the formation of an association between A and the US could subsequently reduce the ability of B to take part in an association with the US.

This phenomenon is called blocking because prior conditioning to A blocks conditioning to B.

Blocking and related phenomena (e.g., Rescorla, 1966, Wagner, et al., 1968) formed the empirical basis of Rescorla and Wagner's (1972) model of conditioning. This model was essentially a model of compound conditioning and it included one major novel assumption. Like Hull (1943), they assumed that the US was only capable of supporting a finite amount of conditioning (associative strength) at any one time. They added the assumption that if several stimuli were paired in compound with the US, they would compete for and ultimately "share" this limited amount of conditioning. In blocking, A acquires considerable associative strength before compound conditioning, and subsequently there is little associative strength left for B to "share" in.

The theoretical analysis aside, blocking provides an interesting empirical setting for considering the role of the experimental context in the formation of associations between the CS and the US. As we have stated, a CS is never presented alone but always in compound with a number of, usually undefined, stimuli that as a group we refer to as the experimental context. Thus, all conditioning is really a form of compound conditioning, and, as Kamin has shown, any conditioning that accrues to one member of the compound should influence what accrues to the other. Even in the simplest conditioning experiment the contextual stimuli may influence conditioning to the CS.

This framework implies that within certain limits the experimental context acts in a manner that is identical to that of our traditional light, tone, bell, and buzzer CSs. Throughout this chapter we take the position that there is nothing special about the context, and that its role in conditioning can be analyzed in much the same manner as any other CS.

Before discussing the first example of our attempts to analyze the role of the context in conditioning, it is worth discussing one mechanism that may mask the power of the context to control behavior and influence conditioning. Using discrete stimuli, Rescorla (1966) demonstrated that, if the CS and the US are presented randomly within a session, associations between them are unlikely to form. In most conditioning preparations the CS and the US are presented several times during the session and often at irregular intervals to prevent temporal conditioning. During these presentations and in their absence the contextual stimuli are always present. Thus, the temporal relation between the context and the US can be conceptualized as random or at least uncorrelated, and this state of affairs would be expected to minimize contextual conditioning and its influence on the formation of associations between the CS and US. Therefore it is likely that the role of the context as a CS might be masked by many of our traditional experimental procedures.

However, it should be possible to increase the potential effectiveness of the context as a CS in spite of this handicap. Subsequent studies of Rescorla's random procedure have found that in many instances associations do form between the CS and US when they are presented randomly (e.g., Benedict & Ayres, 1972; Kremer, 1971; Quinsey, 1971). It has been most often the case that these associations have formed early in conditioning or when fairly dense schedules of presentation of the CS and US have been used. If our analysis of the context as a "random CS" is appropriate, it would seem that, if one wished to optimize the conditions for context-US associations to form, it would seem necessary to use a fairly dense schedule of US presentations and/or a fairly intense US because of its strong reinforcing properties.

The notion that the context and the US are uncorrelated in conditioning procedures may be unnecessarily naive. Although this is true within a session, it is certainly not true if the animal's entire day is considered. Experimental sessions last about an hour a day and during this one hour all experience with the US occurs. Hence, in almost any experiment there is a strong correlation between the contextual cues and the US. So in this wider spectrum it might not be surprising if the context played an important role in providing the animal with information about the US. In fact, the argument about the random procedure may be turned around. It is quite possible that with dense schedules of CS and US presentation the CS comes more and more to approximate contextual stimuli. After all, the limiting case of a "dense" schedule of CS presentations occurs when the CS is always on and is thus one of the contextual stimuli. It is altogether possible that demonstrations of excitatory conditioning following dense schedules of random CS and US presentations are actually demonstrations of contextual conditioning in which the animals are sensitive to the overall daily correlation between the context and the US. In these instances the dominant contextual stimulus is the CS itself. With less-dense schedules the actual contextual stimuli are less likely to be "overshadowed" by the much less-frequent CS.

The Context as a CS in Conditioned Inhibition

An experiment that was designed to investigate the role of the context in conditional inhibition illustrates the power of the use of the context as a CS in the analysis of conditioning (Baker, 1977).

A conditioned inhibitor is a CS that takes on motivational properties opposite to those of a conditioned excitor. In the case of CER conditioning a conditioned inhibitor would inhibit or reduce suppression. Conditioned inhibition develops when the animal is faced with a situation in which the CS predicts the absence of an otherwise expected US (cf. Hearst, 1969; Rescorla, 1969). In CER conditioning a conditioned inhibitor (CI) is a safety signal.

If a stimulus is suspected of being a CI, there are two tests that it must pass to verify that it is one (cf. Rescorla, 1969; however see also Baker & Baker, in press). Because a CI reduces fear, if it is paired with an excitatory CS in a "summation test" it should be able to reduce fear of that CS. Because a CI has the opposite motivational properties to an excitatory CS, it should acquire excitatory properties relatively slowly if it is paired with a US. Thus an animal should condition slowly if in a ''retardation test'' the CI is paired with the US.

Rescorla (1969) found that the negative correlation procedure produced quite strong conditioned inhibition. According to this procedure the US occurs randomly throughout the session unless the CI occurs. When the CI occurs it signals a shock-free period. Although the CI does provide information about the US, such a finding presents problems for associative accounts of conditioning. If learning involves associations between events, just what are the two events that become associated in this procedure?

Wagner and Rescorla (1972) solved this problem by describing a general process by which stimuli become conditioned inhibitors. According to them, a stimulus will become a CI if it regularly occurs in the presence of a conditioned excitor and if this compound is not followed by the US. Their model may be thought of as a formalization of Kamin's (1969) notion that the association that forms in conditioning is between the CS and the surprise produced by an unexpected US. They extended Kamin's assumptions by assuming that, in conditioned inhibition, the association that forms is between the surprise produced by the nonoccurrence of the expected shock and the CI. This surprise occurs contiguous with the CI and hence the requirements for a temporal association are met.

The problem with Rescorla's finding that the negative correlation procedure produces conditioned inhibition is that there was no discrete excitatory CS to produce the necessary expectation of shock so that the animal could feel relieved that the shock did not occur. Wagner and Rescorla (1972) solved this dilemma by arguing that during exposure to negatively correlated presentations of the CI and US the context becomes conditioned. Hence, whenever the CI is presented it may be considered as being part of a compound containing it and the excitatory context. Because the US never occurs during this compound, the necessary conditions for conditioned inhibition are met. The animal comes to expect shock in the experimental context but is ''surprised'' when these expected shocks never occur during the context-CI compound. Thus this ''surprise'' causes the CI to become inhibitory.

Although this explanation is in accord with the data, it was clearly post hoc. It is, however, open to empirical test. The present experiment used a procedure similar to Rescorla's that also produced conditioned inhibition. If a shock US is presented several times one day and a stimulus is presented several times the next day and this sequence is repeated five or six times, it will become a strong CI. This finding is also consistent with Wagner and Rescorla's explanation of conditioned inhibition. On the shock-exposure days the context might become excitatory, and on the CI-exposure days this excitatory context would be paired with the CI in the absence of shock.

If the conditioned inhibition in Rescorla's and the present procedure occurred because the context was excitatory, and, if we could reduce conditioning to the context, we should also be able to reduce the strength of any conditioned inhibition. The empirical results of Kamin (1969) suggest a way that we could reduce conditioning to the context following our between-days negative correlation procedure. As we have mentioned, Kamin's data suggest that compound conditioning is competitive. The more conditioning that is acquired by one member of the compound, the less will be acquired by another. In addition, other results suggest that the most efficient and/or salient stimulus present will tend to control the most conditioning. It follows from this that it should be possible to reduce conditioning to the context by blocking or overshadowing (cf. Pavlov, 1927) it with a more salient stimulus.

In the present experiment, this was done by signaling each shock presentation on the shock days with a short discrete stimulus. According to the associative account of inhibition, the light stimulus should become strongly conditioned and therefore, through competition, should reduce conditioning to the context. On the alternate days on which the potential CI was presented, the context would control relatively little expectation of shock, and thus there would be little surprise to be associated with this stimulus. Hence signaling the shocks should reduce the amount of conditioned inhibition produced by the between-days procedure.

The specific details of the crucial experiment are straightforward. Rats were trained to press a lever for food on a variable interval schedule. Following this, the levers were removed from the conditioning chambers for an inhibitory conditioning phase of the experiment that lasted for 10 sessions. For the remainder of the experiment the rats were divided into 4 groups. Two groups were subjected to the between-sessions negative correlation procedure; that is, they received 5 blocks of 2 alternating days in which they received either 6 shocks per day or 6 clickers per day. The other 2 groups of animals received exactly the same schedule of shocks and clickers except that all the shocks were signaled by a discrete CS. This CS was a light in 1 group and a tone in the other.

Following the inhibition phase the levers were returned to the chambers and the rats were allowed to resume responding for food. In this test phase of the experiment one of the groups that received the between-days negative correlation and the group for which the shocks were signaled by a light received a retardation test for inhibition. This test continued for 5 days. On each day the animals received two excitatory conditioning trials in which the clicker was paired with shock.

The other two groups received a summation test for inhibition. This test consisted of two phases. In the first excitatory conditioning phase the light was made excitatory by pairing it with shock (remember that during inhibition training this signaled group received a tone rather than the light as the signal). The subsequent summation test proper lasted for 3 days. The animals received one light and one clicker-light compound trial each day. The second and third light presentations were followed by shock, whereas the first light trial and the com-

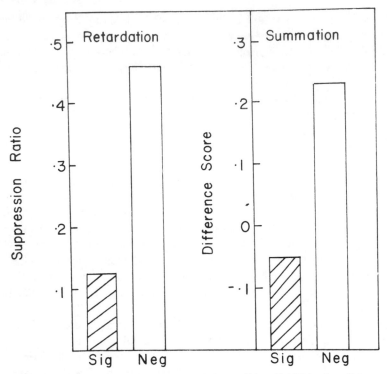

FIG. 4.1.   Retardation and summation tests for conditioned inhibition from Baker (1977), Experiments 3 and 4. Neg = Between-sessions negative correlation group; Sig = Signaled shock group.

pound trials were not reinforced. The purpose of this test was to determine if the clicker would inhibit fear of the excitatory light.

The results of this experiment are shown in Fig. 4.1. The left panel shows results from the fifth test day of the retardation test. The measure used in this panel is Kamin's suppression ratio (cf. Annau & Kamin, 1961), where the conditioned response during the CS is measured by suppression of the food-reinforced lever pressing. According to this measure, low ratios represent strong suppression, whereas higher ratios represent less relative suppression to the CS (a ratio of .5 represents no relative suppression). This figure shows that the animals receiving the between-sessions negative correlation procedure (Neg) developed little suppression to the clicker even after five sessions of conditioning, indicating that the clicker was quite inhibitory. On the other hand, the animals that had received the same treatment except that the shocks had been signaled developed quite strong fear of the clicker during the 5 days of conditioning, and, in fact, these animals conditioned no more slowly to the clicker than a control group that received no shocks during the inhibitory conditioning phase. Thus it can be concluded that signaling the shocks during the inhibitory training reduced conditioned inhibition as measured by a retardation test.

The results of the summation test are shown in the right-hand panel of the figure. The measure reported here is a difference score for inhibition, which is calculated by subtracting each animal's suppression ratio to the excitatory light from its suppression ratio to the compound of the supposedly inhibitory clicker and the light. If the clicker were inhibitory it would reduce suppression to the light and one would expect positive difference scores. Following the between-sessions negative correlation procedure the clicker was quite effective in inhibiting fear of the light, but in the group in which the shocks had been signaled the clicker showed little evidence of inhibiting fear of the light.

The results of this experiment are clearly consistent with the associative account of conditioned inhibition, and taken at face value they suggest that conditioned inhibition can be accounted for quite parsimoniously using simple assumptions. The results have further implications for the analysis of inhibitory processes. It has often been suggested that simple discrimination learning involves not only the development of excitation to the reinforced stimulus but inhibition to the nonreinforced stimulus as well (e.g., Schwartz, 1978). Wagner and Rescorla's (1972) analysis of inhibition suggests that this inhibition may be a special case and not the rule. According to them, inhibition will occur when an excitor and the inhibitor are paired and not reinforced. This analysis suggests that any inhibition to the negative stimulus in a discrimination is often transient and occurs because early in conditioning the context may control some excitation. If conditioning is allowed to reach asymptote with most parameters, the positive stimulus will control all the excitation and the context and the nonreinforced stimulus will become neutral. Our experiment involved a discrimination and the results of it are quite consistent with Wagner and Rescorla's view. There are of course many cases in which the nonreinforced stimulus becomes inhibitory (e.g., Kaplan & Hearst, this volume). Rescorla and Wagner's model, however, would argue that the inhibition that accrues in these cases would do so because the context remains excitatory. The nonreinforced stimulus would be expected to acquire inhibitory properties in much the same manner as described earlier for Rescorla's negative correlation procedure and our own between-days procedure.

The Context and Conditioning: A Tautology?

The experiment that we have just described is quite compelling. The results are clearly consistent with the associative model of conditioning. However, the demonstration does suffer from at least one weakness, and we intend to argue that this weakness is crucial.

Contextual conditioning is an important intervening variable in explaining a wide range of phenomena, but, as we have seen in this experiment, contextual conditioning was only inferred and not directly demonstrated. In our experiment a treatment that was supposed to modify contextual conditioning also influenced inhibition, thereby confirming a prediction of the model. However, although the model and other experiments (e.g., Odling–Smee, 1975a, b) suggest that signaling the shocks should have reduced contextual conditioning, we had no independent means of verifying this. The only way we could argue that we had modified contextual conditioning was to point out that we had reduced inhibition. But what if we had not managed to reduce inhibition? How would we know whether the associative model was wrong or whether we had simply failed to modify contextual conditioning?

This suggests that unless we can independently verify that any supposed manipulation of contextual conditioning actually reduces this conditioning, the theory is in danger of becoming a tautology. The theory makes clear predictions concerning the consequence of manipulations of contextual conditioning on other phenomena. However, if the only way that we can verify that the manipulations are successful is by their effect on the phenomena of interest, then we can never determine whether any failure to get the predicted results is a failure of the model or of contextual conditioning.

Measuring Contextual Conditioning

Although many investigations of the effects of possible contextual conditioning have either used paradigms such as autoshaping, in which it is difficult to measure such conditioning (e.g., Tomie, 1976a, b), or have failed to provide particularly compelling evidence for such conditioning (e.g., Baker & Mackintosh, 1979; Randich & LoLordo, 1979b), it is conceptually quite easy to measure such conditioning. For instance, Odling–Smee (1975a, b, 1978) has provided good evidence that fear of the context can be both measured and manipulated.

In our lab we have recently completed a series of experiments (Baker & Mercier, 1982; Baker, Mercier, Gabel, & Baker, 1981) in which we have simultaneously investigated the effectiveness of a number of manipulations of contextual conditioning and their effect on the US preexposure phenomenon.

The US preexposure phenomenon is the observation that, if animals have been exposed to the US prior to conditioning, they will condition more slowly than nonpreexposed controls. Associative explanations of this phenomenon would claim that it is an instance of blocking involving the context (cf. Randich & LoLordo, 1979a). According to this explanation the context becomes conditioned during preexposure to the US, and later conditioning to the discrete CS is blocked by this contextual conditioning.

The theory makes predictions that are analogous to those concerning the mechanism of conditioned inhibition. If we are able to reduce the contextual conditioning arising from exposure, we should also be able to reduce the US preexposure effect. Baker and Mackintosh (1979) have reported an experiment that demonstrated that signaling the CS during exposure, which should eliminate contextual conditioning, also eliminated the US preexposure effect. Although Randich and LoLordo (1979b) initially failed to replicate this finding, it should be pointed out that they used milder shocks and a less-dense schedule of exposure to the US. As we have mentioned such parameters should reduce contextual conditioning. As well, Randich (1981) has subsequently replicated this basic result. However none of these experiments provided compelling independent evidence of contextual conditioning.

These experiments all used the CER paradigm in which a CS is paired with shock. In these experiments conditioning was assessed by monitoring suppression of food-motivated lever pressing during the CS. If during exposure to the US (shocks), the context is conditioned and if, as we have claimed earlier, the context acts in a manner similar to other CSs, it should also produce suppression of lever-press responding. If this is true, then why have experiments like those that we have just described not provided regular evidence of contextual conditioning?

There are two possible explanations of this paradox. The first involves the general mechanism of performance in conditioning. Gibbon, Terrace, and their associates (Gibbon, Baldock, Locurto, Gold, & Terrace, 1977; Terrace, Gibbon, Farrell, & Baldock, 1975) have demonstrated that, all other things being equal, the conditioned response is strongest if the CS is shorter. Compared to the CS the contextual stimuli are certainly quite long. In addition and, in retrospect, more important in the present case is the problem of measurement. Conditioned fear of the CS is usually measured by ratio scores, such as suppression ratios, and this is no chance occurrence. Although an individual animal's bar press rates on VI schedules are quite consistent, there are usually marked differences in absolute rates between animals. For example it is not unusual for animals in the same group to have response rates varying from 10 to 50 responses per minute. With such high variability it is generally true that even quite large absolute changes in lever press rates do not differ reliably, so most experiments use relative measures of fear such as suppression ratios. Experimenters use ratio scores to get statistically consistent data on conditioning to the CS, so it is surprising that they usually assess suppression to the context by comparing absolute response rates (e.g., Randich & LoLordo, 1979b).

In our CER experiments we were able to get reliable and consistent measures of contextual conditioning (as inferred by suppression of baseline responding), because we used quite a dense schedule of exposure to a fairly intense US and because we developed a ratio measure of conditioning to the context. This measure, called the Baseline Suppression Ratio (cf. Baker et al., 1981), was calculated by comparing an estimate of responding that was taken on the last day before exposure to the US with estimates of response rates taken during the various postexposure days. This ratio has the same properties as Kamin's suppression ratio; that is, low ratios indicate strong relative baseline suppression, whereas ratios of around .5 indicate little relative suppression. Because this measure gave us regular evidence of conditioned suppression following exposure to the US, we were in a good position to see whether this suppression could be blocked, overshadowed, extinguished, or otherwise reduced by our associative manipulations.

Our initial experiments using the baseline suppression ratio to measure fear of the context indicated that our schedule of exposure to the shocks produced readily measurable contextual fear, and that this fear is specific to the exposure context (note the Other Box procedure that is discussed shortly). We were thus in a position to make a fairly direct test of the blocking by context explanation of the US preexposure effect. This explanation predicts quite clearly that the interference with conditioning caused by exposure to the US is the result of contextual fear, and that if we could reduce this contextual fear before conditioning we should also be able to reduce the interference. The theory makes the further prediction that the reduction in interference should be proportional to the magnitude of the reduction of fear.

We used several procedures that should reduce fear of the context during the test phase of the experiment. The first of these involved signaling the US during exposure with a discrete stimulus. This is the same manipulation described in both our conditioned inhibition and in our previous US preexposure experiment (Baker, 1977; Baker & Mackintosh, 1979). It would be expected that the signal would overshadow the contextual cues and hence reduce fear of the context.

In two other procedures we modified the contextual cues between exposure and conditioning. To the extent that the cues during exposure and the test are discriminably different, contextual fear acquired during the exposure period should not generalize to the test period and therefore interference with future conditioning should be reduced. The first procedure that we used had much in common with our signaled shock procedure. We changed the context by presenting a session-long tone during the exposure phase (Group CS/Sh) and then during the test phase we removed the tone. The long and presumably salient tone should have acted as one of the multiple contextual stimuli during exposure and competed with the other contextual stimuli for conditioning. When this stimulus was removed during the test, this should have weakened the total fear of the context during the test and thereby reduced the interference with conditioning caused by exposure to the US. In other words, like the discrete light, the session-long tone should at least partially block or overshadow the context and hence reduce interference. Alternatively the removal of the tone could reduce contextual conditioning by generalization decrement. The exact mechanism of any reduction in conditioning of the context is, of course, of secondary interest to us here. The important feature of these procedures is that they reliably modify contextual conditioning.

The second treatment that we used to modify the context between exposure and the test involved exposing the animals to the shocks in a different physical context to that used in the test. Such a procedure should, to the extent that the other context was discriminably different from the test context, reduce contextual fear and interference during the test.

A final procedure that we used to reduce fear of the context prior to conditioning involved an extinction manipulation. If the context is like other cues, it should be possible to reduce conditioning to it by presenting it in the absence of reinforcement. We did this by placing animals in the shock context for a number of sessions between the shock exposure and the test phase of the experiment. Such a procedure should reduce fear of the context in the test phase and thereby reduce interference with conditioning.

The specific details of these experiments were very similar to those we described earlier. All animals were trained to press a lever for food on a variable interval reinforcement schedule. Following this VI training the levers were removed and the animals received 8 shock presentations on each of the next 5 or 6 days. The standard US preexposure group (Sh) received only these unsignaled shocks. The signaled shock groups (Groups CS–Sh) received the same sequences of shocks except that they were signaled by a 1-min change in overhead illumination. The animals for which the exposure context was to be modified received a session-long 2000 Hz tone or a light during these 5 sessions (Group CS/Sh). The groups that were exposed in a different context (Group O.B., Other Boxes) received the same schedule of shock preexposure in chambers that were somewhat similar to the conditioning chambers but were located in different isolating shells (wood vs. metal), with different ventilating systems (fans vs. no fans), and different lighting conditions (houselight vs. no houselight). Finally, the extinction group received the same basic schedule of preexposure as the shock-only groups, but following this they received five more sessions in the chambers with the levers out before they received the recovery and conditioning phases of the experiment.

Following the exposure phase of these experiments the levers were returned to the chambers and the animals were allowed either 0, 1, or 2 days to recover VI responding for food prior to the conditioning phase of the experiment. On each conditioning day the animals received 4 presentations of the clicker, 2 of which were followed by shock (50% partial reinforcement).

On each recovery day and conditioning day the animals' fear of the context was assessed by calculating baseline suppression ratios that compared the animals' rate of responding in the absence of the clicker CS, with their rate on the last training day before the exposure phase. As well, on each conditioning day the animals' fear of the clicker was assessed using standard suppression ratios.

Figure 4.2 shows the effect of the various treatments that we have described on fear of the context measured on the first day that the lever was returned to the chambers. The first thing that is clear from this figure is that exposure to the US produced considerable fear of the exposure context as compared to untreated controls. A second conclusion that can be drawn is that each of the associative

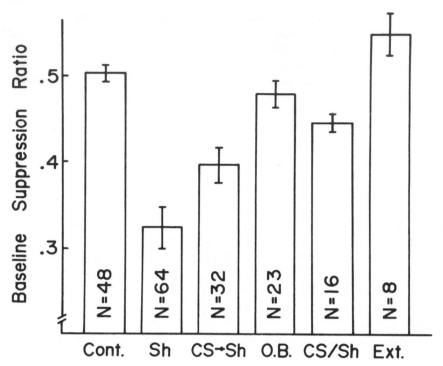

FIG. 4.2.   Baseline suppression data on the first recovery day of Baker et al. (1981) and Baker and Mercier (1982). Cont. = Nonpreexposed controls; Sh = Unsignaled shock in the test context; CS–Sh = Signaled shock; O.B. = Unsignaled shock in the other context; CS/Sh = Session long CS during exposure; Ext = Extinction of the context.

manipulations that was intended to reduce fear of the context was successful in reducing suppression. In fact, some of these treatments produced no measurable fear of the test context. One final point that may be made is that, within the limits of this analysis, the treatment that was least effective in reducing fear of the context was signaling the shocks. However this conclusion is weakened by the fact that the analysis represents an amalgamation of groups from several experiments run over a period of several years.

It should also be mentioned that arguments have been made against relying entirely on baseline suppression as a measure of contextual conditioning (cf. Randich & Ross, this volume). We have, however, regularly used a second measure of fear of the context, latency to the first response of each session, and this measure has agreed well with our measures of baseline suppression (the two are, of course not independent). Others (e.g., Randich & Ross, this volume) have failed to provide much evidence of baseline suppression in their experiments. This is most likely due to parametric differences, particularly in shock density. We have typically exposed animals to more than nine shocks per hour, whereas Randich and Ross often use less than two per hour.

The data that we have shown here comes from the first recovery day of the various experiments. These data show clearly that our manipulations of the context during exposure did reduce baseline suppression, and such evidence is necessary in order to test the blocking by contextual conditioning account of the US preexposure effect. We have elsewhere (e.g., Baker et al., 1981) reported the baseline suppression data for the subsequent recovery and test days. In general, these data indicated that during conditioning there was little evidence of the consistent differential baseline suppression that we have described here for the first recovery day. It becomes apparent that this weakens our claim that we are providing a strong test of the associative account of the US preexposure effect. For the present we ignore this problem save to mention that if these manipulations that do not differentially modify conditioning of the context during conditioning do differentially modify the US preexposure effect, this weakens the argument that the unitary cause of the interference is differential contextual conditioning. In fact, such a result would provide some support for our own cognitive explanation that is outlined later.

Baker and Mackintosh (1979) had previously shown that signaling shocks during exposure would reduce the US interference effect. This result was consistent with the notion that the cause of the interference was blocking by the experimental context, although we had reported relatively little data to show that the context was actually conditioned. The finding from Fig. 4.2 that signaling the shocks reduced baseline suppression certainly supports the blocking by context notion. Furthermore, the results concerning baseline suppression force a clear prediction from the context-blocking model. The model claims that the US preexposure effect is a consequence of conditioning to the context. Moreover, the amount of interference produced by exposure should be proportional to the level of contextual conditioning. Therefore each of our associative manipulations should reduce the US preexposure effect at least as much as signaling the shocks, because we found that all our associative manipulations reduced baseline suppression at least as much as signaling the shocks. Naturally, this assumes that in the present experiments we were able to replicate Baker and Mackintosh's (1979) results.

The next few days of each of these experiments, following VI recovery, comprised the test phase in which the clicker CS was followed by shock. Typical results of these experiments are shown in Fig. 4.3. Each of the panels shows the results from a typical manipulation and includes data from a control group that was not exposed to shocks, a group that was exposed to shocks, and a group that received one of the treatments designed to reduce contextual conditioning. In each of the eight experiments summarized here, the animals exposed to unsignaled shocks (Group Sh) conditioned more slowly than nonpreexposed controls. Further, just as Baker and Mackintosh had already found, signaling the shocks

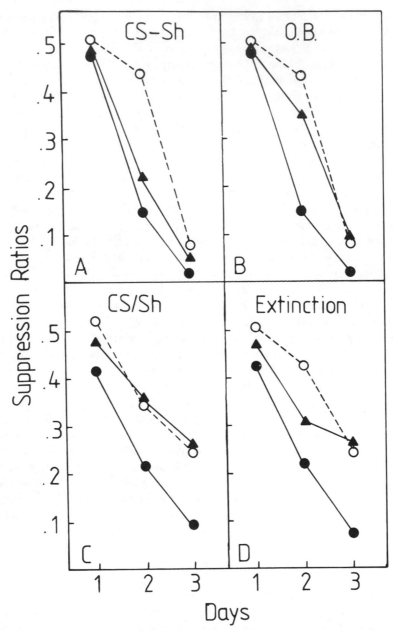

FIG. 4.3.   Data from the first 3 conditioning days of typical experiments follow-ing each associative manipulation of Fig. 4.2. In each panel closed circles repre-sent nonpreexposed controls, open circles represent exposure to unsignaled shocks, and closed triangles represent the associative manipulation of that panel.

during exposure reduced the interference (see Panel A, see also Randich, 1981). This includes one experiment in which the signaled shocks occurred in a different context than the test context (the failure of the other box procedure to reduce interference, Fig. 4.3, panel B, indicates that it is the signaling and not the context change that is responsible for the reduction in interference in this group).

The remainder of the results are not so congenial to the blocking by context explanation. A clear prediction from the baseline conditioning results was that each of the other associative manipulations should have been at least as effective in reducing interference as signaling the shocks. As Fig. 4.3 shows, none of these treatments was as effective in reducing the interference as signaling the shocks with a discrete stimulus. In fact in each of the six individual experiments in which we compared one or more of these treatments with nonpreexposed control groups, we found reliable interference with conditioning (see panels B, C, and D). Furthermore, in only one instance did these treatments reliably reduce interference when compared with animals exposed to unsignaled shocks in the experimental context. The one exception was the extinction procedure that reliably reduced interference on the second test day but not on subsequent test days. This rather small and transient reduction in interference is reminiscent of one of Randich's (1981) results, which also involved the CER procedure and in which he used a relatively diffuse preexposure schedule that produced little evidence of baseline suppression in the nonextinguished but preexposed controls.

The results of these experiments illustrate that the blocking by context argument consists of two hypotheses. The first of these is that during exposure the context acts as a CS and is susceptible to overshadowing and extinction just like any other CS. The second hypothesis, which requires that the first be true, is that the US preexposure effect is a direct consequence of the absolute magnitude of this conditioning.

Our results give strong support to the first of these hypotheses. We found strong conditioned suppression to the experimental context when the rats were exposed to shocks in the experimental context. Further, we found that signaling the shocks would reduce this suppression. We also found that this conditioning was context specific; there was little transfer of the suppression from one set of boxes to the other. As well, it was demonstrated that one contextual stimulus could overshadow another when the two stimuli were presented in compound; that is, the session-long CS reduced the ability of the context to control suppression when it was presented in compound with the context during exposure but removed during the test. Finally, we demonstrated that contextual conditioning was sensitive to extinction just as most other conditioning procedures are. Thus, our results show that the context is susceptible to traditional conditioning manipulations.

Although the experiments provided quite good evidence of contextual conditioning, there was little evidence of any monotonic relation between it and the US preexposure effect. This certainly suggests that the mechanism of the interference is not blocking by the context. Although our results are not consistent with the blocking by contextual conditioning account, we believe it is possible to draw an empirical generalization from them. An important feature of the shocks given during the preexposure phase of a US preexposure experiment is that they are unpredictable. Although exposing the animals in a different context than the test context or changing the context between exposure and test does reduce contextual conditioning, neither of these procedures changes the predictability of the shocks during the exposure sessions. However, although signaling the US with a discrete stimulus also reduces contextual conditioning, it changes the predictability of the shocks during exposure as well. It is hence possible that it is this unpredictability that is the important determinant of the interference produced by exposure to the US. We have suggested that during exposure the animals learn that the shocks are unpredictable, and this knowledge interferes proactively with subsequent conditioning when the shocks are later made predictable (e.g., Baker et al., 1981). Changing the context between exposure and test did not prevent the animals from learning that the shocks were unpredictable, and thus the interference was not reduced. Whereas, when they were signaled, the shocks were not unpredictable and consequently little interference with future conditioning occurred.

We must acknowledge that there is a body of evidence that shows that manipulations such as context change and extinction of the context do reduce the US preexposure effect (e.g., Tomie, 1976a, b, 1981). Three points can be made about these data, however. First, the experimenters generally have not provided much independent evidence that these manipulations actually reduced contextual conditioning. Second, manipulations that change the context or extinguish it tend also to "isolate" the exposure phase from the test phase. To the extent that animals treat these phases as very different for their "analysis" of the predictability of the US, they might be expected to reduce interference in a manner that is consistent with our proposed cognitive mechanism. Finally, if it is granted that these experiments do demonstrate that conditioning to the context can block or overshadow conditioning to a discrete CS, this is certainly consistent with our claim that the context acts like any other CS. We have, after all, just reported evidence that a discrete CS or a session-long CS can block or overshadow conditioning to the context. Our claim is that the mechanism for *all* these effects may not be associative in the sense of the Rescorla–Wagner model. These other data demonstrate that mechanisms like those of Rescorla and Wagner may be operative, but in addition animals are able to learn about the "predictability" of stimuli.

This assumption that the rats could learn that the shocks are unpredictable is reminiscent of the learned-helplessness hypothesis (cf. Maier & Seligman, 1976), in which it is claimed that when faced with inescapable shocks animals learn that these shocks are inescapable, and this interferes with their ability to learn to escape the shocks when they are later made escapable. Maier and

Seligman (1976) have claimed that for this learned-helplessness hypothesis to be true it is crucial to demonstrate that only exposure to inescapable shocks will produce the level of interference that they found. To this end they developed the triadic design in which animals were exposed to either escapable shocks, inescapable shocks, or no shocks. It was found that in these experiments the animals exposed to inescapable shocks learned to escape future shocks quite slowly, whereas the animals exposed to escapable shocks learned to escape no more slowly than the nonpreexposed control group.

A parallel argument could be made concerning the hypothesis that an important variable in the US preexposure effect is the unpredictability of the shocks during exposure. If it is the unpredictability that is important, we should be able to demonstrate this using a triadic design that is similar to that used in the learned-helplessness experiments. When presented this way it is quite clear that our tests of the context-blocking hypothesis were also tests of the unpredictability hypothesis. Neither presenting shocks in another context nor signaling them with a session-long CS does much to reduce their predictabiltiy during exposure, although both treatments reliably reduce contextual conditioning. However, signaling the shocks with a discrete CS does change the predictability, and this was the only treatment that strongly and reliably reduced interference.

Although we have not conducted any experiments to test this, it is possible that our earlier results concerning conditioned inhibition could be explained by a similar mechanism. In the between-days inhibition procedure the shocks are unpredictable and the rats attempt to learn about them, but the only reliable information about them comes from the context and the inhibitor. Hence the animals become afraid of the context and learn that the CI signals safety. When we signaled the shocks, however, the signal was a perfectly good predictor of shocks and the context, in the absence of the US, was a good predictor of safety and thus the temporally isolated CI was not learned about. It is important to point out that we are not simply restating the associative explanation of conditioned inhibition. The associative explanation claims that animals form associations as a result of information that is embedded in the conditioning preparation. We are claiming, much as Tolman (1948) did, that animals form representations of the relationships between events, and these representations are influential in producing the conditioned response and perhaps even in forming associations.

Our results concerning the extinction procedure would seem inconsistent with this cognitive representational model. The extinction procedure should do nothing to change the representation of the shocks as unpredictable, yet we have found that extinction not only reduces fear of the context but also reduces interference (Baker & Mercier, 1984). However, it is possible to reconcile these results with the model if the extinction data is considered more closely.

If the animal's representation of the shocks as unpredictable is to interfere with future conditioning, it must be active during this conditioning. One possible role of extinction aside from reducing fear of the context may be to isolate the experience with unpredictable shocks from the conditioning phase of the experiment. If extinction did this, it would be expected to reduce the interference caused by unsignaled shocks. The reduction in interference produced by extinction was rather small and transient. It appeared on the second conditioning day and by the third was gone. On the last three conditioning days the animals in the extinguished group were as suppressed as the two preexposed but nonextinguished control groups. These results are consistent with our argument that the extinction procedure does not affect the animals' representation of unpredictability but simply isolates it from conditioning. The results further imply that the representation of unpredictability becomes active again during conditioning. It should also be noted that in the signaled shock groups the results were very different from this. In these groups the reduction in interference was long lasting, and if anything the signaled shock groups became more like the nonpreexposed groups over time rather than less like them. Again this suggests that the mechanism for the reduction in interference may have been quite different in the extinction group than in the signaled shock groups.

Unpredictable USs and the Context: An Appetitive Paradigm

The experiments that we have described up to this point have indicated that contextual conditioning can be easily measured, and, as well, it seems to obey many of the rules of traditional conditioning procedures that use discrete stimuli. Our failure to provide strong evidence for the blocking by context explanation of the US preexposure effect does not weaken this conclusion, but it does imply that the mechanism of conditioning in general may involve more complex cognitive representations.

The main virtue of our CER experiments is that we have been able to directly assess contextual conditioning. Unfortunately, in order to do this these experiments used quite a dense schedule of shock preexposure. Such parameters ensured that the animals would be afraid of the context but as well ensured that the animals were in a high state of arousal or anxiety during the test. This anxiety may easily have influenced our results for a number of nonassociative reasons (See Baker et al., 1981 for a discussion of an alternative to the cognitive interpretation of these results), and it is also possible that our results are peculiar to the CER. Finally, and most important, because of the fairly intense shocks and the necessity of indirectly assessing conditioned fear using suppression of lever pressing, we felt that it was necessary to carry out our experiments off baseline in order to minimize any possible associations between the shocks and the lever press response or the food (counter-conditioning). Thus we were unable to assess contextual conditioning while it was occurring, or for that matter assess the role of unsignaled shocks and contextual conditioning during conditioning to the discrete CS.

In order to assess the role of unsignaled USs on simultaneous conditioning, we began a series of experiments that used a conditioned licking paradigm (cf., Baker & Mackintosh, 1977). In this procedure thirsty rats are placed in a conditioning chamber that contains a drinking tube. Occasionally water is presented through this tube by a parastaltic pump. These water presentations are signaled by a 30-sec tone that precedes the water presentation by 10 sec and continues for the entire 20-sec duration of the water presentation. Licks on the tube are recorded using standard contact sensors (drinkometers). After a number of tone–water pairings the animals develop a pattern of anticipatory licking, in which they come to lick at the tube during the tone presentations prior to the appearance of the water. This conditioning is measured either by difference scores in which the number of licks during the 10 sec immediately prior to the tone (PreCS scores) is subtracted from the number of licks during the first 10 sec of the tone (CS scores), or by ratio scores in which these scores are compared using the same formula as Kamin's suppression ratio (CS/(CS+PreCS)). With the latter measure high ratios approaching 1 represent strong conditioning, whereas ratios around .5 represent no conditioning to the CS.

These experiments were designed to investigate not only the role of unsignaled USs in contextual conditioning but also the role of unsignaled USs in degrading the contingency between the CS and US in conditioning. The contingency or correlation between the CS and the US can be varied in several ways: (1) Extra unpaired presentations of the US may be added; (2) extra unpaired presentations of the CS may be added; and (3) the interval between paired presentations may be varied. The first two of these points are self-explanatory but the third needs some discussion.

The most important point to be remembered about the term correlation, as we apply it to conditioning, is that it implies a temporal correlation. In addition, it is important to remember that conditioning is competitive. As we have already stated, if the animal is presented with a number of CS–US pairings, these pairings also involved pairings of the context and the US. The context will compete with the CS for control of conditioning and, to the extent that it is a valid predictor of the US, it may reduce conditioning to the CS. If the interval between CS–US pairings is increased, this will increase the amount of time that the context is presented in the absence of the US and hence reduce its validity as a predictor of the US. Thus, increasing the intertrial interval should increase conditioning to the CS. The opposite will occur if the interval between pairings is decreased (cf. Gibbon et al., 1977).

Thus four types of events influence the contingency between the CS and US. These events are CS–US pairings, US presentations, CS presentations, and periods of time in which neither the CS nor the US occur (we call this latter case nonevents). In a conditioning experiment, with constant CS and US duration, the first three types of events are straightforward, but the fourth type, nonevents, is rather ambiguous. If 5 minutes elapse without an event occurring, does this mean

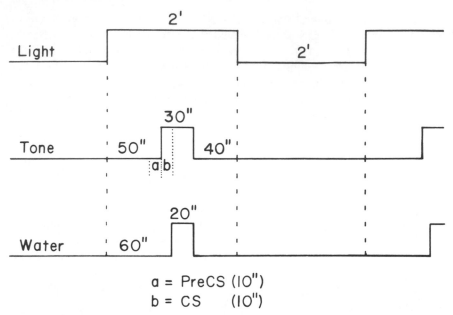

$a = PreCS (10'')$
$b = CS \quad (10'')$

FIG. 4.4.   Temporal relation among the marker stimulus (light), the CS (tone), and the US (water) in the first three conditioned licking experiments. Each session consisted of 20 repetitions of this basic cycle.

that 1 nonevent has occurred, or 5 or 10? The same analysis can, of course, be made for CS and US duration. For the sake of simplicity, however, we assume that these stimuli have been cleverly chosen so that the animal perceives each as a single discrete entity. The present experiments were designed with a rather special context so that it would be more obvious when a nonevent had occurred. We did this by signaling the period in the session during which an event or nonevent could occur. When this signal came on, a pairing, a CS, a US, or no event could occur.

The basic design of these experiments is illustrated in Fig. 4.4. During each session 20 trials were programmed to occur. Each trial was marked by a 2-min light stimulus that alternated with a 2-min period of darkness. Each trial was programmed as a nonevent trial during which neither the tone nor the water occurred, a tone trial in which the 30-sec tone commenced 50 sec after the light began, a water trial during which the 20-sec water presentation commenced 60 sec after the light, or a tone–water pairing in which both the tone and the light were programmed to occur.

Table 4.1 illustrates the design of the first experiment. The experiment included 5 groups but only 4 are relevant to this discussion. Group 10T+ received 10 pairings and 10 nonevents each session. Group 10T+10W received 10 pairings and 10 water presentations each session. Group 5T+5W5T− received 5 presentations of each type of event each session. The fourth group, Group 10W, received 10 water presentations and 10 nonevents each session.

TABLE 4.1
The Number of Occurences of Each of the Four Possible Types of
Event During the 20 Daily Cycles of the Marker Stimulus of the First
Conditioned Licking Experiment

Groups	Daily Number of Trials				
	CS–US	US-alone	CS-alone	Nonevent	Total
10T+	10	0	0	10	20
10T+, 10W	10	10	0	0	20
5T+5W5T−	5	5	5	5	20
10W	0	10	0	10	20

The absolute rates of licking during the PreCS and the CS periods, and the difference scores for the four groups are plotted in Fig. 4.5. For all groups, the PreCS rates were taken from the 10-sec PreCS time period of all the trials regardless of whether a CS occurred or not (i.e., recording began on the 40th second of each light presentation). For Group 10W the CS score was calculated for the time when the CS was normally presented (i.e., during the 10 seconds beginning on the 50th second of each light presentation). These scores are plotted

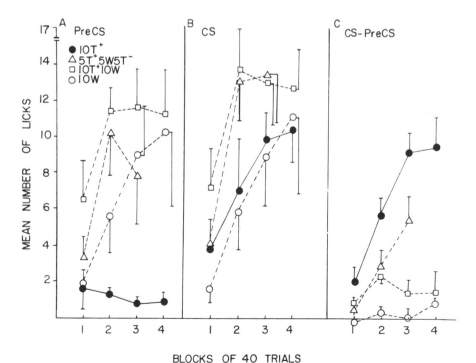

FIG. 4.5.   Mean number of licks per stimulus presentation for the first conditioned licking experiment. The bars represent standard errors of the mean.

in blocks of 40 pairings for each group. Hence they represent 4-day blocks for all groups except Group 5T+5W5T− for which they represent 8-day blocks. There are only 3 blocks of trials for this group because these animals received only 24 days of conditioning and thus, because of the widely spaced conditioning schedule, they only received 120 pairings.

The conditioning results to the CS are plotted in the right-hand panel of this figure and they are quite straightforward. The animals in Group 10T+ reached a high level of conditioning. Group 5T+5W5T− also showed reliable conditioning, but it is clear that the interpolation of unsignaled water presentations, unpaired tones, and the decrease in the number of nonevents reduced the level of conditioned licking. Group 10W showed little evidence of any conditioning following 160 water presentations and thus represents a good control for temporal conditioning. If any of these results were particularly surprising, it was the fact that Group 10T+10W, which on first analysis would seem to have had the absolute contingency between tone and water no more degraded than Group 5T+5W5T−, showed little evidence of any control of licking by the tone.

The left-hand panel of the figure shows the level of responding during the PreCS periods that represents the level of responding controlled by the context or, more accurately, the compound of the context and the light. The most interesting feature of these results concerns the level of licking in Group 10T+. In this group the level of licking during the PreCS was quite low. In fact it is quite clear from inspection of the absolute rate of licking during the CS that the strong level of conditioned licking in this group is a consequence of suppression or inhibition of licking in the presence of the light compared to the other groups, and not stronger excitation during the CS itself. Further there is some, less-convincing, evidence to suggest that the surprisingly low difference scores in Group 10T+10W are due to relatively high rates of responding during the light.

Data from the period before the onset of the light would be of interest here in order to determine whether it or some other aspect of the context controlled this differential licking. Unfortunately lick rates in the absence of the light were not collected for the first two experiments. These data were collected for the third experiment, and, as Fig. 4.7 shows, these data confirmed that the light comes to control differential licking; that is, there was little licking in the absence of the light.

These results indicate that the light context may be quite important in the control of responding by the tone CS. In Group 10T+ the tone was the most valid predictor of the water presentations. Each tone was followed by water and only 50% of the light presentations signaled water. In addition the tone was a much shorter stimulus than the light and therefore, all other things being equal, would have a higher temporal contiguity with the water and be a better CS (cf. Gibbon et al., 1977). Therefore in this group the tone came to control licking and little licking occurred during the light. In each of the other groups the water occurred in the presence of the light alone a number of times. In each of these groups the light came to control considerable licking. However in Group 5T+5W5T− the tone still came to control reliably more licking than the light. This control by the light was present even though every water presentation occurred in the presence of the light, half the water presentations occurred in the absence of the tone, and half the tone presentations did not signal water. In Group 10T+10W it would appear that the tone was at least as good a predictor of the water as it was in Group 5T+5W5T−; yet there was little evidence of any control by the tone. The main feature of this group that separates it from any of the other groups in this experiment is that the light was a perfect although not highly contiguous predictor of the water. By low temporal contiguity we refer to the fact that the onset of the light occurred 60 seconds before the water presentations, and its offset occurred 40 seconds after the water presentations. These values are compared to the more contiguous tone that commenced 10 seconds before the water and coterminated with the water. Thus, it would seem that in Group 5T+5W5T− the light was unable to overshadow the tone, probably because of the light's low temporal contiguity with water, but in Group 10T+10W in which the light was prefectly correlated with water it was able to overshadow the tone.

The most surprising feature of Group 10T+10W was the low level of conditioning found in this group as compared to Group 5T+5W5T−. We have claimed that Group 10T+10W had such a low rate of conditioning because of the perfect correlation that existed between the light and water in this group. However, the first experiment contained no appropriate control group with which to compare the baseline response rates. An appropriate control group would have had no tone−water pairings but would have had a perfect correlation between light and water. Further, although we used Group 5T+5W5T− to compare the level of conditioned licking to the tone, this group may not have been appropriate because it had received extra tone alone presentations and had not received the same number of conditioning trials as Group 10T+10W.

The design of a second experiment that we carried out that incorporated the appropriate control groups is shown in Table 4.2. The experiment included 4

TABLE 4.2
The Number of Occurrences of Each Event During the 20 Daily
Cycles of the Marker Stimulus of the Second
Conditioned Licking Experiment

	Daily Number of Trials				
Groups	CS-US	US-alone	CS-alone	Non-event	Total
10T+10W	10	10	0	0	20
5T+5W	5	5	0	10	20
10W	0	10	0	10	20
20W	0	20	0	0	20

groups that are relevant to the present discussion. Two groups were run for 16 days and received 20 water presentations, 1 for each light onset, each day. For Group 20W all the water presentations were unsignaled, whereas Group 10T+10W received 10 tone–water pairings and 10 water presentations each day. The other groups each received 10 water presentations and 10 nonevent trials each day for 32 days. For Group 10W none of the water presentations was signaled, whereas Group 5T+5W received 5 tone–water pairings and 5 unsignaled water presentations each day.

Figure 4.6 shows the absolute licking rates during the CS and the PreCS periods and the difference scores for the four groups. The difference scores indicate quite clearly that only in Group 5T+5W did the tone show much relative control of licking. Again in this experiment Group 10T+10W that experienced a perfect correlation between the light and water showed relatively little control of licking by the tone, in spite of the fact that for this group the tone signaled the same proportion of water presentations as it did in Group 5T+5W. These data certainly suggest that the perfect correlation between light and water over-shadowed control of licking by the tone. The low conditioning scores in Group 10T+10W were again due to a high level of responding during the PreCS, even when these scores are compared with Group 20W that also received 20 light–

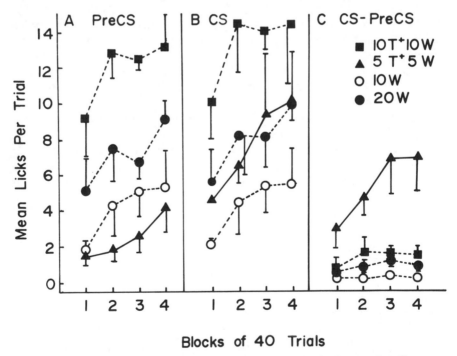

FIG. 4.6.   Mean number of licks per stimulus presentation for the second conditioned licking experiment. The bars represent standard errors of the mean.

water pairings per day. It appears that, even though it developed no relative control of responding, the tone may have had some general facilitory effect on responding.

Our second experiment replicated the results of the first experiment concerning the low level of conditioning to the tone found in Group 10T+10W and gave support to the notion that in this particular group the light overshadowed the tone. However, in this second experiment Group 10T+10W received twice as dense a schedule of water presentations as did Group 5T+5W. In order to rule out the possibility that this difference in density of exposure was the important variable and also to directly test the importance of the light in blocking control of responding by the tone, we carried out another experiment.

This experiment included two groups. One of these groups (Group Marker) received exactly the same treatment that Group 10T+10W received in the previous experiments. The second group (Group No-Marker) received the same schedule of tone–water pairings and unsignaled water presentations as this group, except that the light stimulus was left on for the entire session so that it did not mark the trials. Presumably if the light onset was overshadowing the tone in the 10T+10W treatment, Group Marker should show reliably less control of responding by the tone than Group No-Marker.

In this experiment we collected data to calculate conditioning scores for the light as well as the tone. To do this we recorded the level of licking during the first 40 sec of the light and during the last 40 sec of the dark period between lights and calculated our standard difference and ratio measures of conditioning. For Group No-Marker we collected data from equivalent time periods although the light was on for the entire session. Figure 4.7 shows the ratio conditioning scores for the tone and light for the two groups. We also calculated absolute and difference scores for both measures and they agree well with the ratio scores. We choose to report the ratios in this instance simply to allow a more concise comparison of the light and tone. This figure clearly shows that the tone conditioned reliably more in Group No-Marker than in Group Marker. On the other hand, it is also clear that the light developed considerably more control of conditioning in Group Marker than did the equivalent temporal cues in Group No-Marker.

The first three experiments that we have discussed have shown that the periodic light stimulus could overshadow the more contiguous tone when the light was a better predictor of the water. As well, the absolute level of conditioning in Groups 5T+5W5T−, 5T+5W, and No-Marker was lower than in Group 10T+, which suggests that, even without a perfect correlation between the marker stimulus and the water, unsignaled water presentations would act to reduce control by the tone.

In order to further investigate the effect of unsignaled water presentations and to confirm our analysis of the periodic light stimulus as a contextual cue, we carried out a conditioned licking experiment that did not include a marker stim-

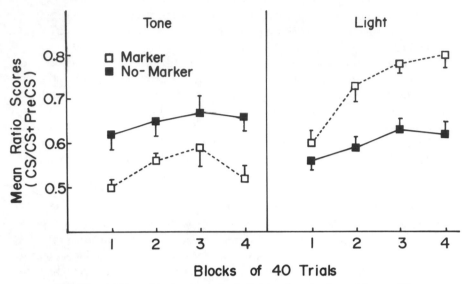

FIG. 4.7.   Ratio conditioning scores for the light marker stimulus and the tone CS from the third conditioned licking experiment. The bars represent standard errors of the mean.

ulus as part of the context. This experiment was designed to show that interpolated water presentation would reduce control of conditioning by a discrete CS. The experiment included three groups. Group T+ received 10 tone–water pairings per session. Group T+W received 10 tone-water pairings and 10 unsignaled water presentations per session. The third and final group was run to demonstrate that any differences in conditioning between Groups T+ and T+W were not due to differences in the density of water presentations between these groups, and to provide an analogue to the signaled shock groups in our US preexposure experiments. Thus Group T+L+ received 10 tone–water and 10 light–water pairings each session.

In this experiment both the tone and the light stimulus were of 30-sec duration. The water stimulus was 20-sec long and on pairing trials the CS onset preceded water onset by 10 sec. The intertrial interval varied from 60 to 120 seconds and averaged 90 sec for Group T+L+. Groups T+W and T+ received the same schedule of events as this group, except that the light or the light–water pairings were omitted, respectively.

Figure 4.8 shows the rate of licking during the PreCS and tone periods as well as difference scores to the tone for this experiment. Figure 4.8 shows quite clearly that interpolated unsignaled water presentations reduced control of licking by the tone. The results of Group T+L+ indicate that this difference is not due to differences in the density of water presentations but to the unsignaled nature of the extra water presentations. The PreCS and CS scores indicate that

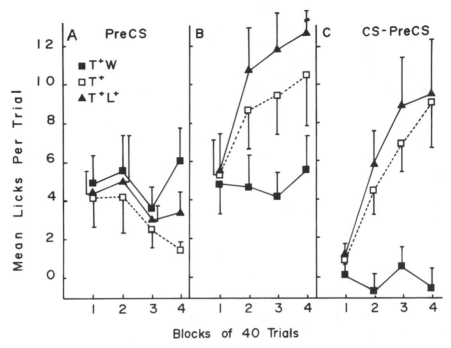

FIG. 4.8.   Mean number of licks per stimulus presentation for the fourth and final conditioned licking experiment. The bars represent standard errors of the mean.

unlike our earlier experiments the differences in control of licking by the tone are largely a consequence of different rates of licking during the CS and not during the PreCS periods. These results concerning conditioning are very similar to some from the autoshaping paradigm that are reported elsewhere in this volume (cf. Rescorla, Durlach, & Grau). The similarity of the two sets of data implies considerable generality in these findings.

One interesting feature of this experiment involves the PreCS rates. It can be seen that, as we would predict and in confirmation of the results of Rescorla et al., the context ultimately came to control more conditioning in Group T+W. This difference was reliable, however, on only the last block of trials. The differences in conditioning to the tone emerged on the second block of trials and appeared to reach asymptote before the differences in baseline conditioning emerged. Again, our data imply that the blocking by context hypothesis is not a unitary explanation of the interference with conditioning produced by unsignaled USs. It is clear that traditional conditioning manipulations, such as overshadowing, affect the control of responding by the context. The finding that the interference with conditioning caused by interpolation of unsignaled USs sometimes is not accompanied by parallel changes in contextual conditioning weakens the claim that this interference is a simple consequence of contextual conditioning.

Perhaps a more conservative claim is that unsignaled USs cause the context to become conditioned and also degrade the predictability of the US by discrete CSs. This conclusion is consistent with our earlier claim that animals can represent the predictability of events as well as represent associations between them.

We have argued that, because contextual conditioning does not always occur either simultaneously with or before the interference, contextual conditioning cannot be the only cause of interference with conditioning. This argument requires assumptions concerning performance rules in conditioning. The differences in conditioning that we are referring to are measured by differences in performance. Thus if the performance rules for responding to long CSs such as the context are different than those for shorter stimuli such as the CS, finding inconsistencies in the order of these empirical effects and the order predicted by theory, as we have here, may tell us little about the possible "causal" relationships between them.

The Context and Predictability of the US

The experiments that we have just described allow us to draw several conclusions concerning the role of the context in conditioning. The CER experiments showed that the context was conditionable, and that it was also sensitive to extinction and overshadowing by a more discrete stimulus. As well, in spite of the sensitivity of contextual conditioning to these manipulations, the experiments indicate that with our parameters at least more complex cognitive representations may be involved in conditioning.

The conditioned licking experiments allow us to extend our conclusions concerning the role of the context in overshadowing. Whereas our CER experiments indicated that a discrete CS can overshadow the context, they provided little evidence that the context could overshadow or compete in other ways with the CS for control of conditioning. However the conditioned licking experiments indicate that the context can overshadow the more discrete CS if it is a much better predictor of the US, as in the case of our experiments using the light as a periodic contextual stimulus. Our final experiment that contained no marker stimulus showed that an invariant context could overshadow a discrete CS.

Much of the data that we have reported here is consistent with the associative framework that is typified by Rescorla and Wagner's (1972) model. The context is readily conditionable and some of our manipulations that modified contextual conditioning modified CS conditioning in a reciprocal manner just as a competitive theory would predict. However, although these particular results are consistent with an associative account, it is true that the vast majority of the data are consistent with a Tolmanian representational view of conditioning.

The only associative manipulation that modified the US preexposure effect in the CER was altering the predictability of the US during exposure, which altered both contextual conditioning and the interference. Other manipulations that were quite effective in modifying this conditioning had little effect on the interference. Although we have no data comparing these procedures, it is interesting to note that the manipulation that we used in our conditioned inhibition and our licking experiments was also signaling the US. Further, although we have made much of the role of the light in overshadowing the context in our conditioned licking experiments, the interpolation of unsignaled water presentations reduced conditioning beyond that. Although the dense schedule of events in Group 10T+10W reduced conditioning markedly when the light was present, even when the light was removed there was considerable interference with conditioning compared with the various perfect correlation groups such as Groups 10T+ and T+. In fact the overall level of conditioning in Group No-Marker was quite similar to that in Groups 5T+5W and 5T+5W5T−. This indicates that the unpredictable water presentations may well have reduced conditioning through their effect on the representation of the unpredictability of the water, rather than their role in conditioning the context. In the past we have provided some independent evidence that such cognitive representational variables may be active in conditioning involving discrete stimuli (e.g., Baker, 1976; Baker & Mackintosh, 1979; Mackintosh, 1973), so perhaps it is not surprising that similar variables influence contextual conditioning.

In closing it should be emphasized that in spite of our rather enthusiastic stewardship of the cognitive representational position, the associative position still has much merit in its testability and in its inherent parsimony. The cognitive position that we espouse is really only an unelaborated alternative to this traditional position and has little in the way of predictive power. Some of the data that we have discussed present a challenge to all associative accounts of conditioning, but they also challenge the cognitive theorist to outline a clear and testable account of such phenomena. In addition, it is clear from the description of our experiments that much work must be done to test and hopefully to increase the generality of our conclusions concerning the role of the context in the cognitive representation of conditioning events.

REFERENCES

Annau, A., & Kamin, L. J. The conditioned emotional response as a function of the intensity of the US. *Journal of Comparative and Physiological Psychology,* 1961, *54,* 428–432.

Baker, A. G. Learned irrelevance and learned helplessness: rats learn that stimuli, reinforcers, and responses are uncorrelated. *Journal of Experimental Psychology: Animal Behavior Processes,* 1976, *2,* 130–141.

Baker, A. G. Conditioned inhibition arising from a between session negative correlation. *Journal of Experimental Psychology: Animal Behavior Processes,* 1977, *3,* 144–155.

Baker, A. G., & Baker, P. A. Does inhibition differ from excitation? In R. R. Miller & N. E. Spear (Eds.), *Information processing in animals: Conditioned inhibition.* Hillsdale, N. J.: Lawrence Erlbaum Associates, in press.

Baker, A. G., & Mackintosh, N. J. Excitatory and inhibitory conditioning following uncorrelated presentations of CS and UCS. *Animal Learning and Behavior*, 1977, *5*, 315–319.

Baker, A. G., & Mackintosh, N. J. Preexposure to the CS alone, the US alone or CS and US uncorrelated: Latent inhibition, blocking by context or learned irrelevance? *Learning and Motivation*, 1979, *10*, 278–294.

Baker, A. G., & Mercier, P. Manipulation of the apparatus and response context may reduce the US preexposure interference effect. *Quarterly Journal of Experimental Psychology*, 1982, *34B*, 221–234.

Baker, A. G., & Mercier, P. Prior experience with the conditioning events: Evidence for a rich cognitive representation. In M. Commons, R. Herrnstein, & A. R. Wagner (Eds.), *Quantitative analyses of behavior: Volume 3: Acquisition*. Cambridge, Mass.: Ballinger, 1984.

Baker, A. G., Mercier, P., Gabel, J., & Baker, P. A. Contextual conditioning and the US preexposure effect in conditioned fear. *Journal of Experimental Psychology: Animal Behavior Processes*, 1981, *7*, 109–128.

Benedict, J. O., & Ayres, J. J. B. Factors effecting conditioning in the truly random control procedure in the rat. *Journal of Comparative and Physiological Psychology*, 1972, *78*, 323–330.

Gibbon, J., Baldock, M. D., Locurto, C., Gold, L., & Terrace, H. S. Trial and intertrial durations in autoshaping. *Journal of Experimental Psychology: Animal Behavior Processes*, 1977, *3*, 264–284.

Hearst, E. Extinction, inhibition and discrimination learning. In N. J. Mackintosh & W. K Honig (Eds.), *Fundamental issues in associative learning*, 1969, 1–41.

Hull, C. L. *Principles of behavior*. New York: Appleton-Century-Crofts, 1943.

Kamin, L. J. Predictability, surprise, attention, and conditioning. In B. A. Campbell & R. M. Church (Eds.), *Punishment and aversive behavior*. New York: Appleton-Century-Crofts, 1969.

Kremer, E. F. Truly random and traditional control procedures in CER conditioning in the rat. *Journal of Comparative and Physiological Psychology*, 1971, *76*, 441–448.

Mackintosh, N. J. Stimulus selection: Learning to ignore stimuli that predict no change in reinforcement. In R. A. Hinde & J. Stevenson–Hinde (Eds.), *Constraints on learning*. London/New York: Academic Press, 1973.

Maier, S. F., & Seligman, M. E. P. Learned helplessness: Theory and evidence. *Journal of Experimental Psychology: General*, 1976, *105*, 3–46.

Odling–Smee, F. J. The role of background stimuli during Pavlovian conditioning. *Quarterly Journal of Experimental Psychology*, 1975, *27*, 201–209. (a)

Odling–Smee, F. J. Background stimuli and the interstimulus interval during Pavlovian conditioning. *Quarterly Journal of Experimental Psychology*, 1975, *27*, 387–392. (b)

Odling–Smee, F. J. The overshadowing of background stimuli by an informative stimulus in aversive Pavlovian conditioning. *Animal Learning and Behavior*, 1978, *6*, 43–51.

Pavlov, I. P. *Conditioned reflexes*. London: Clarendon Press, 1927.

Quinsey, V. L. Conditioned suppression with no CS-US contingency in the rat. *Canadian Journal of Psychology*, 1971, *25*, 69–82.

Randich, A. The US preexposure effect in the conditioning suppression paradigm: A role for conditioned situational stimuli. *Learning and Motivation*, 1981, *12*, 321–341.

Randich, A. & LoLordo, V. M. Associative and nonassociative theories of the UCS preexposure phenomenon: Implications for Pavlovian conditioning. *Psychological Bulletin*, 1979, *86*, 523–548. (a)

Randich, A., & LoLordo, V. M. Preconditioning exposure to the unconditioned stimulus effects the acquisition of a conditioned emotional response. *Learning and Motivation*, 1979, *10*, 245–277. (b)

Rescorla, R. A. Predictability and the number of pairings in Pavlovian fear conditioning. *Psychonomic Science*, 1966, *4*, 383–384.

Rescorla, R. A. Pavlovian conditioned inhibition. *Psychological Bulletin*, 1969, *72*, 77–94.

Rescorla, R. A., & Wagner, A. R. A theory of Pavlovian conditioning: Variations in the effectiveness of reinforcement and non reinforcement. In A. H. Black & W. F. Prokasy (Eds.), *Classical conditioning II: Current research and theory*. New York: Appleton–Century–Crofts, 1972.

Schwartz, B. *Psychology of learning and behavior*. New York: Norton, 1978.

Terrace, H. S., Gibbon, J., Farrell, L., & Baldock, M. D. Temporal factors influencing the acquisition and maintenance of an autoshaped keypeck. *Animal Learning and Behavior*, 1975, *3*, 53–62.

Tolman, E. C. Cognitive maps in rats and men. *Psychological Review*, 1948, *55*, 189–208.

Tomie, A. Interference with autoshaping by prior context conditioning. *Journal of Experimental Psychology: Animal Behavior Processes*, 1976, *2*, 323–334. (a)

Tomie, A. Retardation of autoshaping: Control of contextual stimuli. *Science*, 1976, *192*, 1244–1246. (b)

Tomie, A. Effect of unpredictable food on subsequent acquisition of autoshaping: Analysis of the context blocking hypothesis. In L. C. Locurto, H. S. Terrace, & J. Gibbon (Eds.), *Autoshaping and conditioning theory*. New York: Academic Press, 1981.

Wagner, A. R., & Rescorla, R. A. Inhibition in Pavlovian conditioning: Application of a theory. In R. A. Boakes & M. S. Halliday (Eds.), *Inhibition and learning*. London: Academic Press, 1972.

Wagner, A. R., Logan, F. A., Haberlandt, K., & Price, T. Stimulus selection in animal discrimination learning. *Journal of Experimental Psychology*, 1968, *76*, 171–180.

5
Contextual Stimuli Mediate the Effects of Pre- and Postexposure to the Unconditioned Stimulus on Conditioned Suppression

Alan Randich
Robert T. Ross
The University of Iowa

In a typical Pavlovian conditioning experiment, an organism receives pairings of a discrete conditioned stimulus (CS) and an unconditioned stimulus (US) in the presence of other stimuli intrinsic to the experimental environment. These latter stimuli are commonly referred to as contextual stimuli, and by distinguishing between discrete (phasic) and contextual (static) stimuli the attempt is made to more fully characterize the stimulus antecedents of behavior. Virtually all investigators of Pavlovian conditioning have recognized that contextual stimuli could exert powerful control of behavior, but historically there have been few detailed analyses of the role of contextual stimuli in the normal conditioning process (although see Asratyan, 1965; Konorski, 1948, 1967). In part, this may have been a consequence of the primary interest in delineating the laws of conditioning for discrete CSs, as well as the difficulty in experimentally defining, controlling, and measuring responses evoked by contextual stimuli. However, it is also the case that many investigators were of the opinion that contextual stimuli exerted little if any control of behavior once a conditioned response (CR) was firmly established to a discrete CS. For instance, Pavlov (1927) observed that the whole experimental environment at first acquired conditioned excitatory properties during initial pairings of a discrete CS and US, which he termed *a conditioned reflex to the environment*. However, Pavlov also noted that when a conditioned reflex was firmly established to the discrete CS the conditioned reflex to the environment lost significance, perhaps on the basis of internal inhibition. In this sense, Pavlov did not believe contextual stimuli to be neutral, but rather neutralized through inhibition. Perhaps for these reasons, the analysis of the role of contextual stimuli in the normal conditioning process has remained dormant until recent years.

Renewed interest in contextual stimuli resulted from several innovative characterizations of the necessary conditions for associative learning (Gibbon & Balsam, 1981; Prokasy, 1965; Rescorla, 1967; Rescorla & Wagner, 1972) and experimental protocols in which CS presentation was uncoupled from US presentation (e.g., truly random control procedures, explicitly unpaired procedures, and US-alone procedures). Traditionally, these procedures were viewed as appropriate controls for assessing nonassociative contributions to responding, but the new theories suggested that US presentation in the absence of strict temporal contiguity with CS presentation would have associative effects; one possible effect was conditioning of contextual stimuli. The models also provided mechanisms by which the response conditioned to contextual stimuli could influence both the acquisition and performance of CRs to discrete CSs occurring in their presence. There can be little doubt that specifying a role for contextual stimuli in these models of conditioning has facilitated the analysis of a diverse range of conditioning phenomena. On the other hand, there has been a corresponding failure to specify what would constitute a nonassociative influence on responding and the appropriate procedures to control for such influences.

At the present stage of analysis, it may be inappropriate to attribute special properties to contextual stimuli that are not shared by discrete CSs, although some preliminary data suggest this may be the case (Nadel & Willner, 1980; Nadel, Willner, & Kurz, this volume). Contextual stimuli are present at the time of US occurrence regardless of the presence of a discrete CS and are differentially reinforced with respect to other stimuli in the organism's life (e.g., home cage stimuli). Therefore, the conditions are present for learning about contextual stimuli, and it should be possible to determine the nature of this learning using techniques borrowed from our analysis of conditioning of discrete CSs. Thus, we would argue that there is no need to make any special assumptions about contextual stimuli, beyond those already provided by existing theories, until empirical data suggest a change in perspective is necessary. The present chapter considers these issues and theories by examining the role of contextual stimuli in mediating the effects of preexposure and postexposure to the US on both the acquisition and retention of conditioned suppression of instrumental responding.

DOMAIN OF THE PRESENT CHAPTER

All the studies presented in this chapter involved the use of US-alone procedures. Specifically, they examined the effects of exposure to an electric grid shock US alone on either the acquisition or retention of conditioned suppression of responding maintained by food reinforcers. The effects of US-alone procedures have been interpreted within both nonassociative and associative perspectives (cf. LoLordo & Randich, 1981; Randich & LoLordo, 1979a for reviews). In general, nonassociative perspectives assert that exposure to the US alone could alter the organism's response to the US, such that responding to either a discrete CS entering into an association with that US or a discrete CS previously associated with that US will be correspondingly altered. Such an alteration in responding to the US may reflect habituation or sensitization (Thompson & Spencer, 1966) or the formation of an opponent b-process (Solomon & Corbit, 1974). These nonassociative phenomena have been traditionally applied only to the unconditioned response (UR) evoked by the US, but it is plausible to assume that the "UR" on a "US trial" reflects the responses to all stimuli present (i.e., the US and contextual stimuli). Thus, contextual stimuli could well affect behavior through a nonassociative mechanism. For example, if exposure to the US alone in a given context results in marked habituation of the response evoked by the US and contextual stimuli, a change in contextual stimuli, but not the US (e.g., a context-shift manipulation), may dishabituate the response evoked by contextual stimuli and produce an alteration in conditioning that would not have occurred had conditioning procceded in the original training context. Although most investigators would interpret this outcome in an associative framework, we feel that the nonassociative account provided previously merits some consideration (see Tomie, 1981).

The primary associative perspective asserts that exposure to the US alone results in conditioning of a response to contextual stimuli present at the time of US occurrence, with little or no change in the UR to the US. Although the laws governing the conditioning of contextual stimuli are still a matter of debate, the models of Rescorla and Wagner (1972) and Gibbon and Balsam (1981) will be used as theoretical frameworks for the associative perspective in the present chapter, because they provide the most precise statements about conditioning of contextual stimuli and the mechanisms through which such conditioning is revealed in behavior. Baker, Singh, and Bindra (this volume) discuss cognitive interpretations of US-alone procedures.

In the formulation of Rescorla and Wagner (1972), the US is postulated to support a limited amount of associative strength, λ. The associative strength of each stimulus present at the time of US occurrence is increased by a constant proportion of the difference between λ and the combined associative strengths of all stimuli present on the trial. In this manner, contextual stimuli will compete with discrete CSs for the associative strength that a US can support. The formulation of Gibbon and Balsam (1981) asserts that the US can support a given amount of expectancy or Hope (H). Expectancy is spread uniformly and independently over both the trial and interreinforcement interval at the time of US occurrence. Thus, expectancy values for contextual stimuli and discrete stimuli will be inversely proportional to their stimulus durations, and these stimuli do not compete for associative strength. Response strength is then determined by the value of the ratio formed by discrete CS and contextual stimuli expectancies (i.e., responding is directly related to the value of this ratio). In summary, the model of Rescorla and Wagner (1972) argues that contextual stimuli and discrete CSs compete for a limited amount of associative strength, and responding is determined by the absolute value of the associative strength of each stimulus. The model of Gibbon and Balsam (1981) argues that contextual stimuli and discrete CSs acquire expectance independently of one another, and responding is determined by the value of the ratio formed by their individual expectancies. Each of these views is considered in the following studies assessing the effects of exposure to a shock US alone on the acquisition and retention of conditioned suppression of responding.

US PREEXPOSURE AND THE ACQUISITION OF CONDITIONED SUPPRESSION

Basic Phenomena

The first series of experiments examined the basic effects of exposure to an electric shock US upon the subsequent acquisition of conditioned suppression evoked by a discrete CS paired with a shock US. Experiment 1 examined the effects of preexposure to varying numbers of sessions of shock presentations upon the acquisition of conditioned suppression (Randich & LoLordo, 1979b). Five groups of rats were initially food deprived and trained to depress a lever to obtain food reinforcers on a variable interval 1-min (VI 1-min) schedule of reinforcement. Following this initial baseline training phase, groups of rats were preexposed to unsignaled shock USs for 0 (no shock preexposure control), 1, 3, or 10 sessions. Shocks were nominally 0.8-mA in intensity and 0.5-sec in duration. Three shocks were presented during each 1.5-hr session under off-baseline conditions (i.e., the response levers were removed from the chambers and the VI 1-min schedule was not in effect). Twenty-four hours after the last shock preexposure session, the response levers were reinserted into the chambers and the groups received conditioned suppression training. No baseline recovery period was used. Conditioned suppression training involved repeated presentations of a 3-min noise CS that terminated with the presentation of the 0.8-mA, 0.5-sec shock US. Three CS–US pairings occurred in each 1.5-hr session.

Figure 5.1 presents trial-by-trial mean suppression ratios for the groups during the five sessions of conditioned suppression training. Suppression ratios were calculated as $B/(A + B)$, where B is the number of responses emitted during the 3-min noise CS, and A is the number of responses emitted during the 3-min period immediately preceding that CS presentation (Annau & Kamin, 1961). This figure indicates that the acquisition of conditioned suppression is non-monotonically related to the number of prior sessions of exposure to shock alone. One session of exposure to shock alone facilitated the acquisition of conditioned suppression compared to the control group during the first session of training (Trials 1–3), whereas repeated sessions of exposure to shock alone progressively

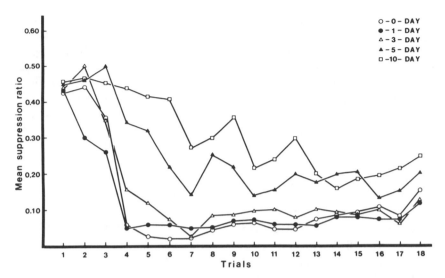

FIG. 5.1.   Trial-by-trial mean suppression ratios for the groups of Experiment 1 preexposed to 0, 1, 3, 5, or 10 days of unsignaled shocks.

retarded the acquisition of conditioned suppression compared to the control group. There were significant between-groups differences in baseline rates of responding during conditioning Days 1–4, but this was due to high rates of responding in the 3-Day group which does not pose interpretative problems. More importantly, there were no significant changes in baseline rates of responding in any group between the last day of baseline training and the first day of conditioned suppression training (see discussion of this issue at end of section).

The facilitation effect observed in Group 1-Day is quite reliable and other data (LoLordo & Randich, 1981) indicate that the magnitude of the facilitation effect produced by a single session of exposure to shock alone is directly related to the intensity of those shocks. However, because additional data regarding this facilitation effect have not been collected, it is not discussed further.

The primary data that bear upon the role of contextual stimuli in the conditioning process are represented by the retardation effects observed in the 3-Day, 5-Day, and 10-Day groups. These retardation effects are formally similar to those obtained in other studies of US preexposure involving conditioning of the eyelid response in humans (Hobson, 1968; Kimble & Dufort, 1956; Taylor, 1956), nictitating membrane response in rabbits (Hinson, 1982; Mis & Moore, 1973; Siegel & Domjan, 1971), taste aversion in rats (cf. Cannon, Berman, Baker, & Atkinson, 1975), and the autoshaped keypeck response in pigeons (Balsam, this volume; Tomie, this volume). At least some of these studies have provided indirect evidence that contextual stimuli are conditioned during exposure to the US alone, and that in some manner they interfere with the acquisition of an excitatory response to the discrete CS paired with that US. Thus, it may be the case that the present retardation effects are due to "blocking" by conditioned contextual stimuli. The model of Rescorla and Wagner (1972) predicts this outcome based upon the view that conditioning of contextual stimuli should occur during exposure to shock alone and should reduce the amount of associative strength available for conditioning of the discrete noise CS during conditioned suppression training. The model of Gibbon and Balsam (1981) also predicts these outcomes based upon the view that conditioning of contextual stimuli during exposure to shock alone will reduce the value of the ratio formed by the discrete CS and contextual stimuli expectancies at the start of conditioned suppression training.

An alternative nonassociative interpretation of these outcomes might assert that repeated preexposure to shock alone reduced the excitatory impact of the shock US and, hence, its effectiveness to serve as a conditioning agent during conditioned suppression training. This could be due to habituation (Thompson & Spencer, 1966), the formation of an opponent b-process (Solomon & Corbit, 1974), or a reduction in the strength of the US representation (Rescorla, 1974). In fact, some evidence for a reduction in the excitatory impact of the shock US following preexposure was obtained in the form of reduced postshock suppression of responding during conditioned suppression training in the 3-, 5-, and 10-session groups. However, it cannot be determined whether these reductions truly reflect a nonassociative influence or an associative action of conditioned contextual stimuli not specified by theory.

In order to more fully characterize the effects of repeated preexposure to shock alone on conditioned suppression, Experiment 2 manipulated the variable of shock intensity during the preexposure phase (Randich, 1981). In a previous experiment of Randich and LoLordo (1979b), this manipulation resulted in retardation effects whose magnitudes were related in an inverted U-shaped fashion to the intensity of preexposed shocks (i.e., the largest retardation effect occurred in a group both preexposed and conditioned with the same intensity shock). However, the latter experiment used rather weak shock intensities (0.5-mA to 1.3-mA), and informal data of Baker and Mackintosh (1979; Baker et al., this volume) suggested that conditioning of contextual stimuli was more likely to occur with stronger shock intensities. Hence, in view of the latter findings and consistent with the theme of this volume, the following experiment represents a replication of the experiment of Randich and LoLordo (1979b), but with the use of shock intensities ranging from 0.5-mA to 2.0-mA. The design of this experiment was identical to that described for the 10-Day group of Experiment 1, except that shock intensity was manipulated during the preexposure phase. Specifically, four groups of rats were preexposed to unsignaled shocks of 0.0-mA (no shock preexposure control), 0.5-mA, 1.0-mA, and 2.0-mA for 10 sessions. Following the preexposure phase, all groups received conditioned suppression training in which the 3-min noise CS was paired with the 1.0-mA shock US.

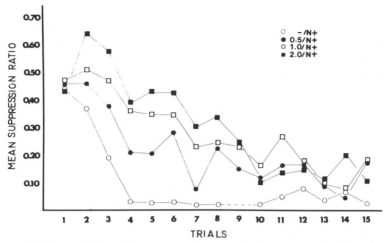

FIG. 5.2.   Trial-by-trial mean suppression ratios for the groups of Experiment 2 preexposed to 0.0-, 0.5-, 1.0-, or 2.0-mA unsignaled shocks and conditioned with the intermediate 1.0-mA shock.

Figure 5.2 presents trial-by-trial mean suppression ratios for the groups of Experiment 2 during the course of conditioned suppression training. All groups preexposed to shock alone showed retardation in the acquisition of conditioned suppression compared to the no shock control group ($-$/N+), but the magnitude of the retardation effect was directly related to the intensity of shock used during the preexposure phase. Baseline rates of responding on the VI 1-min schedule did differ between groups, but it is unlikely that they contributed substantially to the observed group differences in acquisition of conditioned suppression, because the lowest baseline rates of responding were manifested by Group $-$/N+; the group not preexposed to shock.

Thus, not only are there two primary effects of preexposure to an electric shock US upon acquisition of conditioned suppression (i.e., facilitation and retardation depending on the number of sessions of preexposure to shock), but also the magnitude of the retardation effect resulting from repeated sessions of preexposure to shock may be differentially affected by shock intensity. The retardation effects of Randich and LoLordo (1979b) were an inverted U-shaped function of preexposure shock intensity when a range of relatively weak shock intensities were used, but in the present experiment they were a direct function of preexposure shock intensity when the range included a relatively strong shock. A direct relationship between the intensity or concentration of the preexposed US and the retardation of excitatory conditioning is clearly the most common outcome reported in the literature and has been obtained with conditioning of the eyelid response in humans (Taylor, 1956), nictitating membrane response in rabbits (Mis & Moore, 1973), and conditioning of a taste aversion in rats (Cannon et al., 1975). The direct relationship obtained in the present experiment and those noted previously are consistent with the assumptions that: (1) Contextual stimuli are conditioned during exposure to shock alone; (2) the degree of conditioning of contextual stimuli is directly related to the intensity of shock; and (3) the magnitude of the retardation in the acquisition of conditioned suppression is related to the degree of conditioning of contextual stimuli.

If repeated exposure to shock alone results in conditioning of a response to contextual stimuli, it should be possible to extinguish that response through repeated nonshocked presentations of those stimuli. If this extinction treatment reduces conditioning of contextual stimuli to a near zero value, little or no retardation in the acquisition of conditioned suppression should occur. Experiment 3 examined this issue by preexposing groups of rats to 10 sessions of unsignaled shock (1.0-mA, 0.8-sec) as reported in Experiment 2 (Randich, 1981). One group of rats (Group +/N+) then received conditioned suppression training 24 hrs after the last preexposure session to establish the normal retardation function. A group of rats (Group +/OC/N+) was preexposed to shock, then received 10 sessions of nonshocked exposures to the contextual stimuli provided by the operant chambers and the handling procedure used during the preexposure phase. Each session was 1.5 hr in duration. The purpose of this extinction treatment was to eliminate any response that was conditioned to these contextual stimuli during the preexposure phase. The remaining group of rats preexposed to shock (Group +/HC/N+) were kept in their home cages for a 10-day delay interval. These rats were handled only once during this delay interval to minimize the likelihood of extinguishing any response that may have been conditioned to handling stimuli. These latter two groups and a nonshocked preexposure control group (−/N+) then received conditioned suppression training involving normal pairings of the 3-min noise CS and the 1.0-mA shock US.

Figure 5.3 presents trial-by-trial mean suppression ratios for the groups of Experiment 3. This figure reveals that a substantial retardation effect was manifested by Group +/N+, and it did not significantly differ from the function of Group +/HC/N+. Thus, there was no significant loss of the retardation in the acquisition of conditioned suppression when a 10-day delay interval intervenes between preexposure and conditioning phases. However, Group +/OC/N+ showed a loss in the retardation effect compared to Group +/N+, although still demonstrating some retardation in conditioning compared to Group −/N+ on Trials 4–6. These outcomes were not confounded by any between-groups differences in baseline rates of responding.

These outcomes are consistent with an associative interpretation of the US preexposure effect. Nonassociative accounts would generally hold that a 10-day delay interval should be sufficient for recovery of any habituated UR to the US, thereby resulting in a loss of the retardation effect in Group +/OC/N+ due to a restoration of the excitatory impact of the shock US. Although Group +/OC/N+ did show some retardation in conditioning despite a total of 10 sessions (15 hrs)

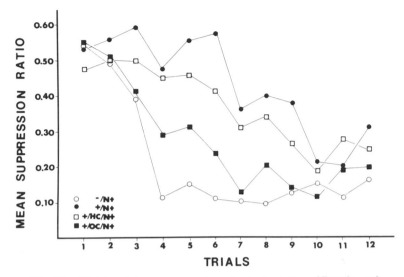

FIG. 5.3. Trial-by-trial mean suppression ratios for the groups of Experiment 3. Group $-$/N+ is the control group; Group $+$/N+ establishes the normal retardation function; Group $+$/HC/N+ remained in the home cages during a 10-day delay between preexposure and conditioning; and Group $+$/OC/N+ received nonshocked placements in the chambers between preexposure and conditioning.

of nonshocked exposures to contextual stimuli, this outcome could be interpreted to mean that either the extinction treatment was incomplete or that a residual nonassociative influence was present and persisted across the delay interval. If such a nonassociative influence was present, it should act in concert with conditioning of contextual stimuli to retard acquisition of conditioned suppression.

A final indirect means of establishing a role for contextual stimuli in mediating these retardation effects involves the use of a "signaled" preexposure manipulation. Specifically, a discrete nontarget CS is used to signal the occurrence of shock USs during the preexposure phase, and conditioned suppression training is then carried out with a different target CS. This manipulation is interesting because the two associative models described earlier predict different outcomes. The model of Rescorla and Wagner (1972) suggests that, to the degree that the discrete nontarget CS overshadows (Pavlov, 1927) contextual stimuli, there will be a corresponding reduction in conditioning of contextual stimuli compared to an unsignaled US procedure. A reduction in the degree of conditioning of contextual stimuli would then be reflected in a reduction in the magnitude of retardation in the acquisition of conditioned suppression. In contrast, the model of Gibbon and Balsam (1981) asserts that contextual stimuli are conditioned independently of discrete CSs. Thus, the degree of conditioning of contextual stimuli should be equivalent with both signaled and unsignaled preexposure treatments and be reflected in equivalent retardation in the acquisition of conditioned sup-

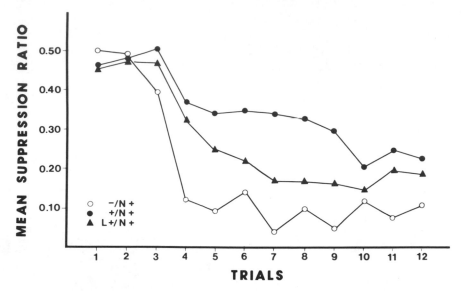

FIG. 5.4.   Trial-by-trial mean suppression ratios for the groups of Experiment 4 preexposed to either signaled or unsignaled shocks.

pression. In Experiment 4, two groups of rats were preexposed to 10 sessions of shock presentations (1.0-mA, 0.8-sec) as generally described for the 10-session groups of preceding experiments (Randich, 1981). One of these groups received unsignaled shock presentations, whereas the second group received each shock preceded by the presentation of a 3-min light stimulus. A third group of rats received no preexposure to shock. All groups then received conditioned suppression training in which a 3-min noise CS was repeatedly paired with the shock US.

Figure 5.4 presents trial-by-trial mean suppression ratios for the various groups of Experiment 4. This figure indicates that groups preexposed to shock showed significant retardation in the acquisition of conditioned suppression compared to the no shock control groups, but that the signaled preexposure procedure was effective in reducing the magnitude of the retardation effect compared to the unsignaled condition. Thus, these outcomes are consistent with predictions based upon the Rescorla and Wagner (1972) model and inconsistent with the model of Gibbon and Balsam (1981). However, there was a residual retardation effect in the signaled preexposure condition. This might reflect the failure of the light CS to completely overshadow contextual stimuli or, as noted previously, a residual nonassociative reduction in the effectiveness of the shock US.

In summary, the preceding experiments examining the effects of the number of sessions of preexposure to shock, shock intensity, an extinction treatment, and a signaled preexposure treatment are all consistent with the view that contextual stimuli are conditioned during US preexposure and interfere with subsequent acquisition of conditioned suppression to a discrete CS paired with a US. However, these experiments provided no direct evidence that contextual stimuli were conditioned during the US preexposure manipulations. Excitatory conditioning of contextual stimuli was inferred on the basis that manipulations that would be expected to influence the degree of conditioning of contextual stimuli affected the subsequent acquisition of conditioned suppression in a systematic fashion (see Balsam, this volume).

Baker, Mercier, Gabel, and Baker (1981; Baker et al., this volume) have argued that evidence for context conditioning in conditioned suppression experiments can be obtained in the form of reduced baseline rates of responding on the schedule of reinforcement following exposure to shock alone. In the present experiments there were no systematic changes in baseline rates of responding on the VI 1-min schedule of reinforcement following preexposure to shock, nor did groups preexposed to shock manifest lower baseline rates of responding than nonshocked controls. Moreover, we would argue that there are two major reasons why reductions in baseline rates of responding cannot be used as independent evidence of context conditioning when the target response involves conditioned suppression of instrumental responding. First, it has been repeatedly demonstrated that the rate of acquisition of conditioned suppression is directly related to the baseline rate of instrumental responding even when reinforcement rate is held *constant* (Blackman, 1968; Randich, Jacobs, LoLordo, & Sutterer, 1978). Thus, decreases in baseline rates of responding could retard acquisition of conditioned suppression independently of any contribution of contextual stimuli. Second, the use of changes in baseline rates as a response measure of context conditioning is not independent of the response measure used during conditioned suppression training (i.e., changes in baseline rates). If one chooses to index conditioning of contextual stimuli through the retardation in the acquisition of conditioned suppression (which is reflected by less suppression of baseline rates), then independent evidence of context conditioning requires a response measure other than reductions in baseline rates to avoid circularity and provide proper anchoring (Hull, 1943). Balsam (this volume) reviews various techniques that have been used to address these issues.

In light of the preceding considerations and the outcomes of the initial experiments suggesting that context conditioning was produced by preexposure to shock alone, the following experiments attempted to: (1) provide an independent demonstration of conditioning of contextual stimuli during preexposure to shock alone by using a response (running or escape) that differed from the response used during subsequent conditioned suppression training (bar pressing); and (2) incorporate shifts in contextual stimuli either prior to or following conditioning of the discrete target CS to specify the mechanism by which contextual stimuli retard acquisition of conditioned suppression.

Measurement of Context Conditioning and
Mechanisms of Context Blocking

Experiment 5 assessed whether a change in contextual stimuli prior to conditioned suppression training would reduce or eliminate the normal retardation in
the acquisition of conditioned suppression obtained when context are identical
during US preexposure and conditioned suppression phases (Baker et al., 1981).
In Experiment 5, groups of rats were trained to bar press for food reinforcers in
two different contexts on alternate days. Context 1 was defined by having: (1) no
houselight; (2) no stripes on the walls; (3) ventilating fan noise; and (4) no odor
of Pine-Sol; whereas Context 2 was defined by having: (1) a houselight; (2) black
and white stripes on the wall; (3) no ventilating fan noise; and (4) the odor of
Pine-Sol.

Groups of rats then received repeated exposure to either unsignaled shock USs
(1.5-mA, 0.8-sec) or no shock in Context 1 for 10 sessions. Prior to each of these
off-baseline preexposure sessions, the latency to escape from the distinctive
context into a temporary holding apparatus fitted into the door of the operant
chamber was recorded. An escape response was defined as placement of all four
paws in the escape chamber. The rat was immediately returned to the transport
cages following either an escape response or a failure to complete an escape
response within 60 sec. Following the preexposure phase, all groups received
conditioned suppression training in which a discrete 3-min noise CS was repeatedly paired with the 1.5-mA, 0.8-sec shock US. For half the rats (Groups
+C1/C1 and −C1/C1), conditioned suppression training occurred in Context 1,
whereas the remaining rats (Groups +C1/C2 and −C1/C2) received conditioned
suppression training in Context 2. Thus, Group +C1/C1 was both preexposed
and conditioned in Context 1; Group +C1/C2 was preexposed in Context 1 and
conditioned in Context 2; Group −C1/C1 was preexposed to Context 1 with no
shock and conditioned in Context 1; and Group −C1/C2 was preexposed to
Context 1 with no shock and conditioned in Context 2. Latencies to escape from
these conditioning chambers into the escape chamber were recorded for all
groups prior to each conditioned suppression session.

The left panel of Fig. 5.5 shows that rats preexposed to unsignaled shock USs
in Context 1 manifested significant decreases in the mean latency to escape into
the holding apparatus, whereas rats not preexposed to shock did not acquire the
escape response. These data provide independent evidence that contextual stimuli were associated with shock during the preexposure phase.

Figure 5.6 presents mean trial-by-trial suppression ratios for each group during the conditioned suppression phase. Groups not preexposed to shock,
−C1/C1 and −C1/C2, show rapid and equivalent rates of acquisition of conditioned suppression. The group both preexposed to shock and conditioned in
Context 1, Group +C1/C1, showed significant retardation in the acquisition of
conditioned suppression compared to the two control groups. Finally, Group

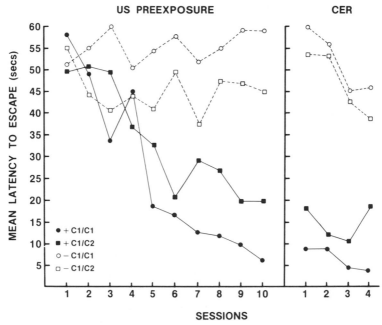

FIG. 5.5. Mean escape response latencies (sec) for each group during the preexposure (left) and conditioned suppression (right) phases in Experiment 5.

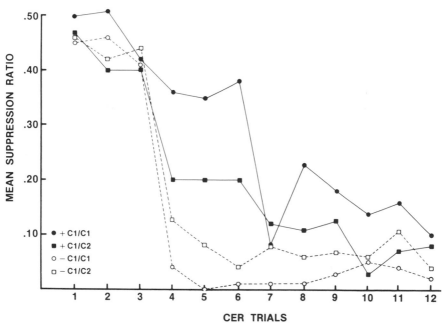

FIG. 5.6. Mean trial-by-trial suppression ratios for each group during the conditioned suppression phase in Experiment 5.

+C1/C2, which received preexposure to shock in Context 1 and conditioned suppression training in Context 2, showed a significant loss of the retardation effect compared to Group +C1/C1 and did not significantly differ from the two control groups.

Overall rates of responding during the 3-min intervals preceding each conditioned suppression trial did differ significantly between groups. Specifically, groups preexposed to shock showed higher rates of responding than groups not preexposed to shock, which poses no serious interpretive problems. However, an inspection of the right panel of Fig. 5.5 reveals that the group of rats preexposed to shock and receiving a context shift (Group +C1/C2) failed to discriminate the two contexts. Specifically, there was no significant increase in the latency to escape from Context 2 during the context test prior to the first conditioned suppression session in this group. It is possible, therefore, that the stimulus controlling escape was not a unique feature of Context 1, but rather either the handling procedure or some stimulus feature common to both contexts (e.g., the shock grid configuration), although the conditioned suppression data indicate that the rats did discriminate contexts.

Thus, Experiment 5 demonstrates two important points. First, it is possible to obtain an independent measure of context conditioning using the acquisition of escape responses from contextual stimuli previously paired with shock. Second, a shift in contextual stimuli following preexposure to shock and prior to conditioned suppression training eliminates the normal retardation in the acquisition of conditioned suppression (Baker et al., 1981). This latter finding is consistent with predictions derived from the models of both Rescorla and Wagner (1972) and Gibbon and Balsam (1981). However, the escape measure of this experiment failed to demonstrate that the animals were able to discriminate contexts during conditioned suppression training, and the experiment also failed to provide information about the mechanisms by which contextual stimuli block conditioning of the discrete CS during conditioned suppression training.

The purpose of Experiment 6 was to assess the mechanisms of context blocking provided by the models of Rescorla and Wagner (1972) and Gibbon and Balsam (1981) using context shift manipulations either prior to or following conditioned suppression training (Randich & Ross, 1984). In addition, a discrimination procedure was used during the preexposure phase to maximize chances of maintaining differentiation between the two contexts during conditioned suppression training (see Rescorla, Durlach, & Grau, this volume). Initially, groups of rats were trained to bar press for food reinforcers in both Contexts 1 and 2 on alternate days (Contexts 1 and 2 refer to those described in Experiment 5 but were counterbalanced within groups). Four groups of rats then received a discrimination preexposure phase in which unsignaled shock presentation (1.5-mA, 0.8-sec) occurred in Context 1, but no shock presentations occurred in Context 2. A total of 20 sessions of discrimination training were administered (3 shocks per session) and the order of shock versus no-shock sessions was quasi-randomly determined with the restrictions that no more than 2 days of a given treatment could occur on consecutive days, and the total number of shock versus no-shock sessions was equivalent. Two remaining groups of rats received an identical sequence of exposure to Contexts 1 and 2 but never received shock presentations in either context.

On the day following completion of the preexposure discrimination phase, all groups received a single session of conditioned suppression training. Two groups of rats receiving preexposure to shock, Groups +C1/+C1 and +C1/−C2, were conditioned in Context 1 and the remaining two groups of rats receiving preexposure to shock, Groups −C2/−C2 and −C2/+C1, received conditioned suppression training in Context 2. For the two groups of rats not preexposed to shock, Groups NS/no shift and NS/shift, four rats in each group received conditioned suppression training in Context 1 and the remaining rats received conditioned suppression training in Context 2. Four pairings of a 3-min noise stimulus with a 1.5-mA, 0.8-sec shock US occurred during the single session of conditioned suppression training. The + and − designations refer only to whether the context was shocked or nonshocked during preexposure.

On the following day, all groups received three extinction test trials of the noise CS. Groups +C1/+C1 and −C2/+C1 received those trials in Context 1 and Groups −C2/−C2 and +C1/−C2 received those trials in Context 2. Group NS/no shift received the noise extinction trials in the same context used during conditioned suppression training, whereas Group NS/shift received the noise extinction trials in the context not present during conditioned suppression training.

According to the associative model of Rescorla and Wagner (1972), the groups receiving both repeated preexposure to shock and conditioned suppression training in Context 1 should show approximately equivalent levels of conditioned suppression to the noise CS when it is subsequently tested in either the excitatory Context 1 (Group +C1/+C1) or the neutral Context 2 (Group +C1/−C2). This model also predicts that groups receiving repeated preexposure to shock in Context 1 and conditioned suppression training in Context 2 should show more conditioned suppression to the noise CS when it is subsequently tested in the excitatory Context 1 (Group −C2/+C1) than in the neutral Context 2 (Group −C2/−C2). These predictions are based upon the assumptions that contextual and discrete stimuli compete for the limited amount of associative strength that the shock US can support and that performance of conditioned suppression reflects the absolute associative strength of stimuli present.

In contrast, the associative model of Gibbon and Balsam (1981) predicts that Group +C1/+C1 should show less-conditioned suppression than Group +C1/−C2 during testing, and that Group −C2/+C1 should show less-conditioned suppression than Group −C2/−C2 during testing. These predictions are based upon the assumptions that contextual and discrete stimuli do not compete for a limited amount of associative strength, and that performance of conditioned

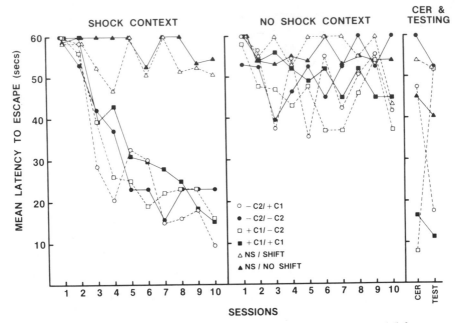

FIG. 5.7.   Mean escape response latencies (sec) for each group in context 1 (left, shocked context) and context 2 (middle, nonshocked context) during discriminative preexposure and for the conditioned suppression and extinction test sessions (right) in Experiment 6.

suppression is determined by the ratio formed by the discrete stimulus and contextual stimuli expectancies.

The left panel of Fig. 5.7 presents mean latencies to escape from Context 1 (shocked context for shock preexposed groups and a nonshocked context for nonpreexposed groups), and the middle panel of Fig. 5.7 presents mean latencies to escape from Context 2 (nonshocked context for shock preexposed groups and a nonshocked context for nonpreexposed groups). In general, groups preexposed to shock during the discrimination preexposure phase readily learned to escape from Context 1 but did not escape from Context 2. Groups not preexposed to shock failed to escape from either Context 1 or Context 2. Thus, the groups preexposed to shock successfully acquired the discrimination.

Figure 5.8 presents mean suppression ratios obtained during conditioned suppression training (left panel) and extinction testing (right panel) for all groups. There were no significant between-groups differences as a function of either prior history of exposure to shock or conditioning in Contexts 1 and 2 on the last trial of conditioned suppression training (Trial 4). The critical data obtained during extinction testing are presented in the right panel of Fig. 5.8. Blocking was evidenced by significantly larger suppression ratios in Group $+C1/-C2$ than the appropriate control comparison Group NS/shift. No blocking occurred

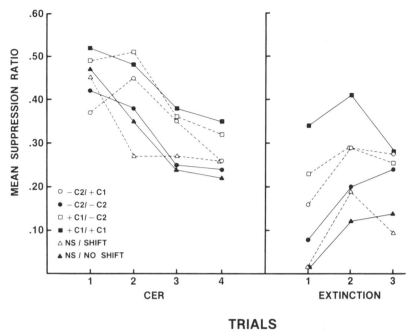

FIG. 5.8.   Mean trial-by-trial suppression ratios for each group during the conditioned suppression (left) and extinction test sessions (right) in Experiment 6.

when conditioned suppression training occurred in the nonshocked Context 2; Group $-C2/-C2$ did not significantly differ from Group NS/no shift. However, testing in the excitatory context did tend to reduce performance of conditioned suppression (compare Group $+C1/+C1$ versus Group $+C1/-C2$, and Group $-C2/-C2$ versus $-C2/+C1$, but neither of these trends was significant).

In addition, the right panel of Fig. 5.7 (escape latency data) shows that the discrimination between Contexts 1 and 2 was maintained during both conditioned suppression training and extinction testing. Thus, the escape measures provide independent evidence of the associative strengths of Contexts 1 and 2.

In summary, Experiment 6 demonstrates that blocking, as indexed by the retardation in the acquisition of conditioned suppression of responding following preexposure to shock alone, occurs only when conditioned suppression training is performed in the context in which shock presentations occurred during the preexposure phase. Blocking is evident even when testing is carried out in a context that is not excitatory (Group $+C1/-C2$). These outcomes support the conditioning assumptions of the model of Rescorla and Wagner (1972) that contextual and discrete stimuli compete for a limited amount of associative strength that the US can support. However, the failure to detect summation of the excitatory strengths of contextual and discrete stimuli in performance of conditioned suppression (Group $-C2/+C1$) and, indeed, the tendency to observe a reduction in conditioned suppression when the discrete noise CS was tested in an excitatory context lends some credence to the performance assumptions of the model of Gibbon and Balsam (1981).

SUMMARY OF US PREEXPOSURE EFFECTS

The preceding studies have demonstrated that preexposure to shock alone retards the subsequent acquisition of conditioned suppression. Experiments 1 and 2 showed that the magnitude of this retardation effect increases both as a function of the number of sessions of preexposure to shock and as a function of the shock intensity. Experiments 3 and 4 also suggested that contextual stimuli were conditioned during preexposure to shock and contributed to these retardation effects, because both an extinction treatment and a signaled preexposure treatment were effective in reducing the magnitude of the retardation effects. Finally, Experiments 5 and 6 provided evidence that contextual stimuli are conditioned during exposure to shock alone. The context shift manipulations of the latter study also provide evidence concerning the mechanisms by which excitatory contextual stimuli block the conditioning of a discrete CS paired with a US in their presence. Specifically, these data suggest that contextual and discrete stimuli compete for a limited amount of associative strength that the US can support, as outlined by the model of Rescorla and Wagner (1972), rather than being conditioned independently of one another, as suggested by the model of Gibbon and Balsam (1981). However, performance of conditioned suppression to a discrete CS was somewhat attenuated when testing occurred in the presence of excitatory contextual stimuli. The nature of this effect is in accord with the performance assumptions of the model of Gibbon and Balsam (1981) and is not consistent with summation performance rules that can be derived from the model of Rescorla and Wagner (1972).

US POSTEXPOSURE AND RETENTION OF CONDITIONED SUPPRESSION

Basic Phenomena

The second series of experiments examined the effects of repeated exposure (postexposure) to an electric shock US upon retention of conditioned suppression evoked by a discrete CS previously paired with a shock US. The US postexposure paradigm is particularly useful in providing converging lines of evidence about the role of contextual stimuli in mediating the effects of US-alone procedures, because the associative models of Rescorla and Wagner (1972) and Gibbon and Balsam (1981) make distinctly different predictions in this situation.

The model of Rescorla and Wagner (1972) asserts that associative strength conditioned to contextual stimuli during postexposure to shock alone should summate with that of an established discrete CS during a retention test, to either augment conditioned suppression (if conditioning of the discrete CS is not asymptotic) or to produce no change in the level of conditioned suppression (if conditioning of the discrete CS is asymptotic). Summation has been demonstrated when two separately conditioned discrete CSs are presented in compound (Hendersen, 1975; Pavlov, 1927; Van Houten, O'Leary, & Weiss, 1970). In contrast, the model of Gibbon and Balsam (1981) predicts that increasing the expectancy value of contextual stimuli through postexposure to shock alone should decrement performance of conditioned suppression by decreasing the value of the ratio formed by trial and contextual stimuli expectancies. The only condition under which this outcome would not occur is when original conditioning of the discrete CS and contextual stimuli is asymptotic prior to US postexposure. Indeed, the performance data described in Experiment 6 already provide some support for the performance assumption of this model.

Experiment 7 represents the postexposure analog of the preexposure shock session manipulation of Experiment 1 (Randich & Haggard, 1983). Four groups of rats initially received baseline training on the VI 1-min schedule of reinforcement. Baseline training was followed by two sessions of conditioned suppression training in which the 3-min noise CS was repeatedly paired with a 1.0-mA, 0.8-sec electric shock US. Three CS–US pairings were administered during each 1.5-hr session, resulting in a total of six conditioning trials. Following conditioned suppression training, the groups were matched to insure that there were no significant between-groups differences in the degree of conditioned suppression. In the shock postexposure phase, groups of rats received exposure to unsignaled shocks for 0 (no shock postexposure control), 1, 5, or 10 sessions. Three shocks were presented in each 1.5-hr session and all shock postexposure was off-baseline. Shocks were 1.0-mA and 0.8-sec as during conditioned suppression training. Twenty-four hrs after the last postexposure session, the on-baseline conditions were reinstated and all groups received extinction testing of the noise CS. This involved three nonreinforced presentations of the noise CS while responding on the VI 1-min baseline.

Figure 5.9 presents trial-by-trial median suppression ratios during the three noise extinction test trials. Median suppression ratios were used because typically one rat in each group showed a markedly deviant suppression ratio. This figure indicates that postexposure to shock alone resulted in a significant loss of conditioned suppression in the 10-Day group, but this decrement attained significance only during the first two extinction test trials. Groups 1-Day and 5-Day did not differ significantly from Group 0-Day, although it might be noted that there is an orderly decrement in retention of conditioned suppression as a function of the number of postexposure sessions among groups postexposed to shock alone. These results were not confounded by any between-groups differences in base-

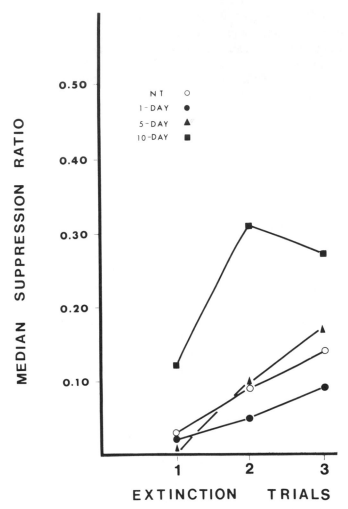

FIG. 5.9.   Trial-by-trial median suppression ratios for the groups of Experiment 7 postexposed to 0, 1, 5, or 10 days of unsignaled shocks.

line rates of responding during the retention tests. Finally, it is useful to note that the 5-Day and 10-Day groups showed substantial retardation in the acquisition of conditioned suppression during a subsequent test phase involving pairings of a 3-min light CS with the 1.0-mA shock US.

The decrement produced by repeated postexposure to shock alone in the 10-Day group is similar to the outcome obtained in Experiment 6, when comparing Group $-C2/+C1$ and Group NS/shift. The experimental protocols for these groups of Experiment 6 and the 10-Day group of Experiment 7 are formally similar, except that the order of exposure to shock alone and conditioned suppression training was reversed. Colby and Smith (1978) obtained similar outcomes in the conditioned taste-aversion paradigm. In that experiment, an aversion established to saccharin through pairings with a LiCl US was decremented following either 5 or 10 postexposures to LiCl alone, but not by a single postexposure to LiCl. However, they were able to detect such decrements only

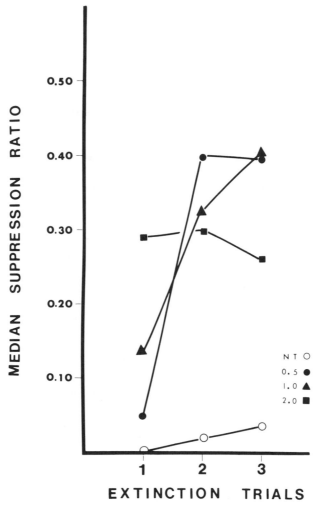

FIG. 5.10   Trial-by-trial median suppression ratios for the groups of Experiment 8 postexposed to 0.0-, 0.5-, 1.0-, or 2.0-mA unsignaled shocks following original conditioning with the intermediate 1.0-mA shock.

with repeated test trials. In the present experiments, such decrements were obtained only during the initial test trials.

These outcomes tentatively suggest that if conditioning of contextual stimuli takes place during postexposure to shock alone, such conditioning does not summate with the associative strength of the discrete CS but rather attenuates performance of conditioned suppression (Gibbon & Balsam, 1981). However, this attenuation of conditioned suppression did not persist for more than two extinction test trials, and one might expect an associative influence based upon conditioning of contextual stimuli to be relatively enduring. Although a non-associative influence might be operative (e.g., habituation) in the absence of direct evidence concerning both the saliences (alphas) of contextual and discrete stimuli, and the learning rate parameter (beta) for extinction, such an assertion remains very tentative.

To more fully characterize the effects of postexposure to shock alone on retention of conditioned suppression, Experiment 8 was conducted as the postexposure analog to the shock intensity manipulation of Experiment 2 (Randich & Haggard, 1983). The procedure was similar to that used for the 10-Day group of Experiment 7, except that during the postexposure phase groups were exposed to no shock (Group NT), 0.5-mA, 1.0-mA, or 2.0-mA shocks. Original conditioned suppression training was with the intermediate shock of 1.0-mA. All groups then received extinction testing of the noise CS as described previously.

Figure 5.10 presents trial-by-trial median suppression ratios for the groups of Experiment 8. This figure indicates that all groups receiving 10 sessions of postexposure to shock alone showed a decrement in retention of conditioned suppression compared to the nonshocked control group. On the first extinction test trial, the magnitude of this decrement was directly related to shock intensity. However, after this trial the shock postexposed groups converged and did not significantly differ from one another. Thus, any orderly effect of these shock intensity manipulations did not persist for more than a single test trial.

SUMMARY OF US POSTEXPOSURE EFFECTS

The outcomes of these preliminary postexposure experiments indicate that repeated exposure to shock alone is required to decrement the retention of conditioned suppression. The decremental effect of postexposure to shock alone is also directly related to the intensity of shock, but this outcome was observed only on the first extinction test trial. Additional studies carried out in our laboratory (Randich & Haggard, 1983) indicate further that a larger decremental effect is obtained when the extinction tests are carried out immediately after the last postexposure to shock (i.e., 10 min after shock), rather than 24 hrs after shock as in Experiments 7 and 8.

GENERAL DISCUSSION

The first researchers to demonstrate the effects of exposure to the US alone on the acquisition and performance of excitatory CRs interpreted their outcomes in nonassociative terms (Kamin, 1961; Kimble & Dufort, 1956; Pavlov, 1927; Taylor, 1956). However, the development of strong associative theories of Pavlovian conditioning (Gibbon & Balsam, 1981; Rescorla & Wagner, 1972) and their provisions for contextual stimuli in the conditioning process provided an alternative and attractive means of accounting for these effects. The preceding experiments have addressed these issues by examining some of the basic effects of exposure to shock alone on the acquisition and retention of conditioned suppression and also have provided some preliminary analyses of the role of contextual stimuli in mediating these phenomena. The purpose of the following sections is to consider these outcomes in light of associative and nonassociative theories with specific emphasis on contextual stimuli.

The model of Rescorla and Wagner (1972) bears upon the outcomes of the present studies because it assumes that: (1) Exposure to shock alone should result in conditioning of contextual stimuli; and (2) conditioned contextual stimuli will interact with both the acquisition and performance of CRs to discrete CSs in their presence. In general, conditioning of contextual stimuli during exposure to shock alone would be expected to: (1) retard the acquisition of conditioned suppression because the high level of associative strength established to contextual stimuli will limit (block) the extent to which the discrete CS can acquire associative strength; and (2) augment or produce no change in retention of conditioned suppression because of summation of associative strengths of contextual stimuli and the discrete CS. Although it is possible to question why repeated preexposure to shock alone should retard rather than facilitate acquisition of conditioned suppression (due to summation of associative strengths of contextual stimuli and the discrete CS), it should be recalled that the discrete CS must have some associative strength before summation can occur. Clearly, this condition is not present at the start of conditioned suppression training. This issue was raised by Baker and Mackintosh (1979), who noted that when the "blocking" analysis is applied to studies of US preexposure it assumes that the discrete target CS is assessed in the presence of neutral contextual stimuli. Thus, contextual stimuli are purported not only to block conditioning of the discrete target CS, but also to provide an excitatory background in which assessment takes place. This perspective raises the possibility that summation could be occurring simultaneously with blocking resulting in an underestimation of the true magnitude of the retardation effect. However, the treatment used in Experiment 6, in which the strength of conditioning of the discrete CS was tested in either an excitatory or a neutral context following a few CS–US pairings (compare Groups +C1/+C1 and +C1/−C2), indicates that summation is not occurring simultaneously with blocking, and there may be an overestimation of the true blocking effect.

These factors not withstanding, the outcomes of the conditioning aspects of all the preexposure studies were in accord with the general predictions of the model of Rescorla and Wagner (1972). Of primary interest are the data obtained in Experiments 5 and 6 in which independent evidence of context conditioning was demonstrated. In these experiments, blocking was only observed when conditioned suppression training was conducted in the presence of excitatory contextual stimuli. In this situation, however, blocking was manifested when testing of the discrete target CS occurred in the presence of either excitatory or neutral contextual stimuli. These outcomes are consistent with the view that contextual stimuli and discrete CSs compete for a limited amount of associative strength in producing context blocking effects in the conditioned suppression paradigm.

Finally, it is worthwhile to note that this model predicts that preexposure to shock alone should facilitate the acquisition of an inhibitory CR, as might be established with a backward conditioning procedure. Hinson (1982) and Kaplan and Hearst (this volume) have obtained this outcome in the rabbit nictitating membrane preparation and in the autoshaped key peck procedure, respectively. We (LoLordo, personal communication; Randich, 1978) have attempted four experiments examining this issue in the conditioned suppression paradigm. In each experiment, we have failed to convincingly demonstrate either facilitation or retardation in the acquisition of conditioned inhibition following preexposure to 10 sessions of shock alone, although demonstrating that a backward conditioning procedure is effective in establishing an inhibitory CS. At the present time, we are at a loss to explain our failures in producing this effect.

The associative model of Gibbon and Balsam (1981) also bears upon the effects of these shock alone procedures, although it must be recalled that this model was formulated only on the basis of data collected in the autoshaping paradigm and has not been fully developed. The unique assumption of this model is that expectancy is "spread" uniformly and independently over both trial and interreinforcement intervals at the time of US occurrence. Response strength is then determined by the value of the ratio formed by trial stimulus and contextual stimuli expectancies. In this fashion, the model predicts that conditioning of contextual stimuli will occur during normal pairings of a discrete CS and US, as well as during US-alone presentations. However, the conditioning of contextual stimuli that takes place during shock-alone presentations in the present circumstances would be expected to: (1) retard the acquisition of conditioned suppression by inflating the value of the denominator of the performance ratio at the start of conditioned suppression training; and (2) decrement the retention of conditioned suppression training by inflating the value of the denominator of the performance ratio relative to its value at the termination of original conditioned suppression training.

Clearly, the outcomes of Experiment 6 indicate that the conditioning aspects of this model do not apply to context blocking obtained in the conditioned suppression paradigm. Specifically, the data indicate that contextual and discrete stimuli are not conditioned independently of one another but compete for associative strength. The outcomes of the signaled preexposure treatment of Experiment 4 are also inconsistent with the conditioning assumptions of this model (cf. Baker & Mackintosh, 1979; Baker et al., 1981; Baker et al., this volume; but see also Balsam, this volume, for differences obtained in the autoshaping paradigm).

However, the performance data obtained in the preexposure study of Experiment 6 and the postexposure studies of Experiments 7 and 8 are consistent with the performance assumptions of the model of Gibbon and Balsam (1981). Specifically, performance of conditioned suppression to a discrete target CS was reduced to a minor extent when tested in the presence of excitatory contextual stimuli, as independently verified by the latency to escape measure. In no circumstances have we observed summation of the excitatory strength of contextual stimuli with the excitatory strength of a discrete CS, as suggested by the model of Rescorla and Wagner (1972) and known to occur when two discrete CSs are presented in compound. This suggests the possibility that there are important differences between the function of discrete CSs and contextual stimuli in the performance of conditioned behaviors. At a more general level, the present data indicate that incorporating the conditioning assumptions of the Rescorla and Wagner (1972) model and the performance assumptions of the Gibbon and Balsam (1981) model provide the most parsimonius explanation of interactions between contextual and discrete stimuli obtained in the conditioned suppression paradigm.

We have alluded to the notion that repeated exposure to shock alone may also bring about a nonassociative reduction in the effectiveness of shock as a conditioning agent. Some of the nonassociative accounts offered to explain the effects of US-alone procedures include: (1) central habituation of the emotional response to the US (Kamin, 1961; Mis & Moore, 1973; Taylor, 1956); (2) physiological tolerance in the case of drug USs (Riley, Jacobs, & LoLordo, 1976); (3) the formation of an opponent b-process (Randich & LoLordo, 1979b; Solomon & Corbit, 1974); (4) emotional exhaustion similar to that posited in learned-helplessness models (Baker et al., 1981); and (5) changes in the strength of the US representation (Randich & Rescorla, 1981; Rescorla, 1974). It is our opinion that the effects of these shock-alone procedures may reflect a combination of associative and nonassociative factors, although no evidence was provided to definitively support this assumption. In particular, we have been concerned about possible nonassociative contributions to the deficits observed when the discrete CS is tested following repeated US postexposure. Specifically, these deficits were not robust and relatively short-lived (1–2 test trials), which makes them difficult to accommodate within as associative perspective. In this regard, we have been struck by the similarities between these effects of US-alone procedures and the phenomenon of external inhibition. Pavlov (1927), in his "New Interpretations" section, also noted this similarity in his studies of US-alone procedures. Perhaps we should consider the possibility that external inhibition serves as the mechanism through which the performance effects of contextual stimuli are manifested in behavior. In this view, exposure to the US alone may result in associative conditioning of contextual stimuli, which not only can block conditioning of a discrete CS but also can disrupt performance of conditioned suppression to a discrete CS through nonassociative external inhibition (i.e., conditioned contextual stimuli may operate as conditioned distractors although undergoing initial conditioning according to the laws specified by the model of Rescorla and Wagner, 1972). This type of notion allows one to capture the stimulus competition assumption of the model of Rescorla and Wagner (1972) and some semblance of the intentions of the performance notions of the model of Gibbon and Balsam (1981). Further, it may provide a resolution to the paradox that US-alone presentations decrement the retention of excitatory CRs (perhaps as a result of external inhibition produced by excitatory contextual stimuli) but "reinstate" responding to a CS subjected to an extinction treatment (perhaps as a result of disinhibition produced by excitatory contextual stimuli; see Bouton & Bolles, this volume).

ACKNOWLEDGMENTS

This research was supported by a N.I.M.H. Biomedical Research grant, a N.I.M.H. grant (MH35716), and a N.I.H. grant (R23 NS18341) to A. Randich. Portions of this research were conducted by A. Randich as a Killam predoctoral fellow at Dalhousie University, Halifax, Nova Scotia, Canada. R. T. Ross was supported by a N.I.H. postdoctoral fellowship (#MH15773). The secretarial assistance of Ms. M. Bowersox is gratefully acknowledged.

REFERENCES

Annau, A., & Kamin, L. J. The conditioned emotional response as a function of intensity of the US. *Journal of Comparative and Physiological Psychology,* 1961, *54,* 428–432.

Asratyan, E. A. *Compensatory adaptations, reflex activity, and the brain.* Oxford: Pergamon Press, 1965.

Baker, A. G., & Mackintosh, N. J. Preexposure to the CS alone, US alone or CS and US uncorrelated: Latent inhibition, blocking by context or learned irrelevance? *Learning and Motivation,* 1979, *10,* 278–294.

Baker, A. G., Mercier, P., Gabel, J., & Baker, P. A. Contextual conditioning and the US preexposure effect in conditioned fear. *Journal of Experimental Psychology: Animal Behavior Processes,* 1981, *7,* 109–128.

Blackman, D. E. Response rate, reinforcement frequency, and conditioned suppression. *Journal of the Experimental Analysis of Behavior,* 1968, *11,* 503–516.

Cannon, D. S., Berman, R. F., Baker, T. B., & Atkinson, C. A. Effect of preconditioning unconditioned stimulus experience on learned taste aversions. *Journal of Experimental Psychology: Animal Behavior Processes,* 1975, *104,* 270–284.

Colby, J. J., & Smith, N. F. The effect of three procedures for eliminating a conditioned taste aversion in the rat. *Learning and Motivation,* 1978, *8,* 404–413.

Gibbon, J., & Balsam, P. D. Spreading association in time. In C. M. Locurto, H. S. Terrace, & J. Gibbon (Eds.), *Autoshaping and conditioning theory.* New York: Academic Press, 1981.

Hendersen, R. W. Compounds of conditioned fear stimuli. *Learning and Motivation,*1975, *6,* 28–42.

Hinson, R. E. Effects of UCS preexposure on excitatory and inhibitory rabbit eyelid conditioning: An associative effect of conditioned contextual stimuli. *Journal of Experimental Psychology: Animal Behavior Processes,* 1982, *8,* 49–61.

Hobson, G. N. Effects of UCS adaptation upon conditioning in low and high anxiety men and women. *Journal of Experimental Psychology,* 1968, *76,* 360–363.

Hull, C. L. *Principles of behavior.* New York: Appleton–Century–Crofts, 1943.

Kamin, L. J. Apparent adaptation effects in the acquisition of a conditioned emotional response. *Canadian Journal of Psychology,* 1961, *15,* 176–188.

Kimble, G. A., & Dufort, R. H. The associative factor in eyelid conditioning. *Journal of Experimental Psychology,* 1956, *52,* 386–391.

Konorski, J. *Conditioned reflexes and neuron organization.* New York: Cambridge University Press, 1948.

Konorski, J. *Integrative activity of the brain.* Chicago: University of Chicago Press, 1967.

LoLordo, V. M., & Randich, A. Effects of experience of electric shock upon subsequent conditioning of an emotional response: Associative and nonassociative accounts. In P. Harzem & M. H. Zeiler (Eds.), *Advance in analysis of behavior: Predictability, correlation, and contiguity* (Vol. 2). Sussex, England: Wiley, 1981.

Mis, R. W., & Moore, J. W. Effects of preacquisition UCS exposure on classical conditioning of the rabbit's nictitating membrane response. *Learning and Motivation,* 1973, *4,* 108–114.

Nadel, L., & Willner, J. Context and conditioning: A place for space. *Physiological Psychology,* 1980, *8,* 218–228.

Pavlov, I. P. *Conditioned reflexes.* London: Oxford, 1927. (Reprinted, New York: Dover, 1960).

Prokasy, W. F. Classical eyelid conditioning: Experimenter operations, task demands, and response shaping. In W. F. Prokasy (Ed.), *Classical conditioning: A symposium.* New York: Appleton–Century–Crofts, 1965.

Randich, A. *Facilitation and attenuation of the acquisition of a conditioned emotional response by prior exposure to the unconditioned stimulus: An explanation based upon the opponent-process theory of acquired motivation.* Unpublished doctoral dissertation, Dalhousie University, 1978.

Randich, A. The US preexposure phenomenon in the conditioned suppression paradigm: A role for conditioned situational stimuli. *Learning and Motivation,* 1981, *12,* 321–341.

Randich, A., & Haggard, D. Exposure to the unconditioned stimulus alone: Effects upon retention and acquisition of conditioned suppression. *Journal of Experimental Psychology: Animal Behavior Processes,* 1983, *9,* 147–159.

Randich, A., Jacobs, W. J., LoLordo, V. M., & Sutterer, J. R. Conditioned suppression of DRL responding: Effect of UCS intensity, schedule parameter and schedule context. *Quarterly Journal of Experimental Psychology,* 1978, *30,* 141–150.

Randich, A., & LoLordo, V. M. Associative and nonassociative theories of the UCS preexposure phenomenon: Implications for Pavlovian conditioning. *Psychological Bulletin,* 1979, *86,* 523–548. (a)

Randich, A., & LoLordo, V. M. Preconditioning exposure to the unconditioned stimulus affects the acquisition of a conditioned emotional response. *Learning and Motivation,* 1979, *10,* 245–277. (b)

Randich, A., & Rescorla, R. A. The effects of separate presentations of the US on conditioned suppression. *Animal Learning & Behavior,* 1981, *9,* 56–64.

Randich, A., & Ross, R. T. Mechanisms of blocking by contextual stimuli. *Learning and Motivation,* 1984, *15,* 106–117.

Rescorla, R. A. Pavlovian conditioning and its proper control procedures. *Psychological Review*, 1967, *74*, 71–80.

Rescorla, R. A. Effect of inflation of the unconditioned stimulus value following conditioning. *Journal of Comparative and Physiological Psychology*, 1974, *86*, 101–106.

Rescorla, R. A., & Wagner, A. R. A theory of Pavlovian conditioning: Variations in the effectiveness of reinforcement and nonreinforcement. In A. H. Black & W. F. Prokasy (Eds.), *Classical conditioning II: Current theory and research*. New York: Appleton–Century–Crofts, 1972.

Riley, A. L., Jacobs, W. J., & LoLordo, V. M. Drug exposure and the acquisition and retention of a conditioned taste aversion. *Journal of Comparative and Physiological Psychology*, 1976, *90*, 799–807.

Siegel, S., & Domjan, M. Backward conditioning as an inhibitory procedure. *Learning and Motivation*, 1971, *2*, 1–11.

Solomon, R. L., & Corbit, J. D. An opponent-process theory of motivation: I. Temporal dynamics of affect. *Psychological Review*, 1974, *81*, 119–145.

Taylor, J. A. Level of conditioning and intensity of the adaptation stimulus. *Journal of Experimental Psychology*, 1956, *51*, 127–130.

Thompson, R. F., & Spencer, W. A. Habituation: A model phenomenon for the study of neuronal substrates of behavior. *Psychological Review*, 1966, *73*, 16–43.

Tomie, A. Effect of unpredictable food on the subsequent acquisition of autoshaping: Analysis of the context blocking hypothesis. In C. M. Locurto, H. S. Terrace, & J. Gibbon (Eds.), *Autoshaping and conditioning theory*. New York: Academic Press, 1981.

Van Houten, R., O'Leary, K. D., & Weiss, S. J. Summation of conditioned suppression. *Journal of the Experimental Analysis of Behavior*, 1970, *13*, 75–81.

6

Contexts, Event-Memories, and Extinction

Mark E. Bouton
University of Vermont

Robert C. Bolles
University of Washington

The focus of this chapter is the question of how contexts control performance in the presence of fear-evoking conditioned stimuli (CSs). Although some alternative answers to this question are available (e.g., Estes, 1973; Medin & Reynolds, this volume; Nadel, Willner, & Kurz, this volume), many major theories of conditioning have assumed that contexts control performance at least partly through their own associations with the unconditioned stimulus (US). The Rescorla–Wagner model (Rescorla & Wagner, 1972; Wagner & Rescorla, 1972; see also Frey & Sears, 1978; Mackintosh, 1975a), for example, uses context to explain a variety of Pavlovian-conditioning phenomena by simply assuming that the context is a second CS that is present in compound with the target CS. As with ordinary nominal CSs, the context's excitatory or inhibitory associations with the US (its "associative strength") are assumed to summate with those of the CS when the context controls behavior. This sort of assumption is consistent with traditional associationistic notions about the structure or composition of learning.

We will argue that this question about context becomes especially important when one considers another question, namely, how to interpret extinction. Most current views of extinction assume that the loss of the conditioned response reflects some loss of original learning. The Rescorla–Wagner model and its competitors (e.g., Frey & Sears, 1978; Mackintosh, 1975a; but see Pearce & Hall, 1980) suppose that the associative strength of a CS declines, and approaches an asymptote of zero, over a series of extinction trials. In effect, the CS–US association is assumed to be "unlearned" during extinction. This assumption provides a convenient framework for understanding inhibition (e.g.,

Wagner & Rescorla, 1972). But it immediately confronts a problem, because there is ample evidence that the CS can retain considerable associative strength following extinction, even when the conditioned response no longer occurs (e.g., Frey & Butler, 1977; Hendry, 1982; Konorski & Szwejkowska, 1950, 1952; Reberg, 1972; Rescorla & Heth, 1975). The problem is to reconcile such findings with the assumption that the CS loses its associative strength in extinction.

One possibility is that a CS may retain some associative strength, but be behaviorally "silent" because its strength lies below some behavioral threshold. Few models assume that the associative strength of a CS is linearly mapped onto behavior. The context may also be important in maintaining the conditioned response. Because responding to the CS is assumed to be a function of the combined associative strengths of the CS and context, which summate, behavior could conceivably collapse through the loss of associative value of the context, while the CS–US association remains at least partially intact.

A quite different approach is also possible. The fact that associative strength remains to an extinguished CS has, historically, suggested the operation of some nonassociative mechanism, such as a loss of drive, to explain the loss of behavior in extinction (e.g., Spence, 1966). A nonassociative mechanism of this sort is suggested by Rescorla's event-memory model of Pavlovian conditioning (e.g., Rescorla, 1973, 1974). According to the event-memory model, conditioning involves both the formation of an association between the CS and US, and the construction of memories about those events themselves. The model suggests that the strength of the response evoked by the CS is determined by both the strength of the CS–US association and the animal's memory of the US. The response may be lost during extinction if presenting the CS without the US weakens the memory of the US (e.g., Rescorla & Heth, 1975). Here again we find the assumption that some component of the original learning, namely the strength of the memory of the US, is lost in extinction. But because the event-memory model emphasizes the loss of the memory of the US instead of the CS–US association, it can account for the apparent integrity of the association following extinction.

In what follows we discuss some experiments that are relevant to each of these views of context and extinction. These studies show that contextual cues may indeed play a role in extinction, even in some of the paradigms that seem to support the event-memory model's account of extinction. We consider some studies suggesting that a context can sometimes modulate fear of a CS in the manner proposed by the Rescorla–Wagner model, through summation of its associative strength with that of the CS. But we also present results suggesting that associative strength in a context is neither necessary nor sufficient for a context to control conditioned fear. Further, we present evidence suggesting that contexts are most likely to affect fear of CSs that have had a history of both reinforcement and nonreinforcement, as is the case with a CS that has undergone extinction.[1] We suggest that the rat does not forget in extinction what it originally learned. In the presence of an extinguished CS, the rat might well remember that the CS has sometimes been paired with the US and sometimes not. After extinction, the meaning of the CS is ambiguous. And the context might then be used to resolve the ambiguity of the information provided by the CS.

The Contextual Control of Extinction: The Renewal Effect

We begin by describing the results of some experiments indicating that contextual cues can modulate the rat's fear of an extinguished CS. In one experiment (Bouton & Bolles, 1979a, Experiment 1), rats received pairings of a tone and shock in a black plywood box that we refer to as the "conditioning context." After receiving a series of extinction trials, the rats eventually received further tests of the tone in this context. Fear conditioning was indexed by the ability of the tone to evoke freezing, a characteristic response of the rat to stimuli that have been associated with shock (e.g., Bouton & Bolles, 1980). One group received extinction trials in the conditioning context. Another group received the same number of extinction trials in a different context, a discriminably different Skinner box in which the animals had been trained to bar press for food.

When extinction of the tone was complete in both groups (as evidenced by the loss of its ability to evoke freezing in the conditioning context and the loss of conditioned suppression in the Skinner box), the rats were returned to the conditioning context and tested there for fear of the tone. Shock was never presented during testing. Even though the group extinguished in the Skinner box had shown complete extinction of fear in that context, when the tone was introduced back into the conditioning context, there was a substantial renewal of fear of the tone. The nonshifted group showed no such evidence of renewed fear. Extinction of the CS in the Skinner box was apparently specific to that context. Here was new evidence that the excitatory strength of a CS can survive extinction (cf. Frey & Butler, 1977; Hendry, 1982; Konorski & Szwejkowska, 1950, 1952; Reberg, 1972; Rescorla & Heth, 1975).

The basic fear-renewing effect of shifting the context after extinction is consistent with the results that have been obtained with other conditioning paradigms. Archer, Sjödén, Nilsson, and Carter (1979; 1980; see also Archer &

---

[1]Back in the old days, it was responses that were learned. And it was responses that were extinguished. Some of us who can remember the old days recall telling our students that one does not extinguish the rat, only its response. That was part of the old language, which we took very seriously. But now we live in a new era in which responses are not learned, S–S relationships are. If we can now reinforce a stimulus, then surely we can also extinguish it. Hence we speak about extinguishing the CS in this chapter.

Sjödén, 1981, and Archer, Sjödén, & Nilsson, this volume) found that an extinguished taste aversion is similarly renewed after extinction in a different context when it is tested in the context where it was originally conditioned. Cunningham (1979) reported that conditioned suppression is renewed when the CS is tested while the rats are in the original "sober" state after extinction under the influence of alcohol. There is also complementary evidence from operant conditioning research (Welker & McAulcy, 1978). The renewal effect thus appears to have some generality.

There are several possible approaches to accounting for this general result. One approach would emphasize the associative status of the contextual cues present during the renewal test. In these experiments, testing was conducted in the context where the CS was originally conditioned. If the stimuli of the conditioning context had gained associative strength when the CS was originally conditioned in their presence, associative strength of the context could summate with the undetected associative strength that evidently remains to the CS after extinction. Alternatively, configural stimuli arising from the CS-context compound could have been conditioned during the conditioning phase, and the renewal effect could have resulted from the reinstatement of these configural stimuli during testing.

We examined these possibilities in another experiment (Bouton & Bolles, 1979a, Experiment 3). Rats received fear conditioning of a tone in a third context before receiving CS-extinction trials in either of the two contexts that had been used in the original study. When extinction appeared complete in both contexts, half the animals were shifted to the other, nonconditioning context and tested there for renewed fear of the tone. Because the contexts used in the test phase of this experiment had never been directly associated with shock, this procedure would seem to eliminate the possibility that the renewal effect was due just to the associative strength of the test context. And because the test and extinction contexts were counterbalanced, it would be difficult to argue that fear was renewed during testing because the two contexts, when used for testing, were nearer to the conditioning context on some hypothetical generalization gradient than when they were used for extinction. We should also note that this design allowed us to examine the renewal effect both with the conventional suppression of an operant baseline and with our freezing measure as indices of fear. Both indices gave the same pattern of results: The groups that received a context shift following extinction showed more fear of the tone than the control groups that were not shifted. Thus, the renewal of fear following extinction does not seem to require that the animals be tested in the context in which fear had been originally conditioned. This result appeared to eliminate associative strength of the context, and the configuring of CS and context, as necessary conditions for the renewal effect.

A further possible account of the renewal effect is based on the idea that, when a CS is presented without reinforcement in extinction, the entire CS-context compound is nonreinforced. When extinction is conducted in a context that differs from the conditioning context, as it was in our experiments, it falls into the familiar A+, AX— conditioned-inhibition paradigm. Thus, it may be possible that stimuli of the extinction context became inhibitory because they were presented in nonreinforced compound with the excitatory CS (see Cunningham, 1979; Rescorla, 1979; and Rescorla & Cunningham, 1978, for related discussions). Such contextual inhibition could result in decreased fear in the presence of the CS through CS-context summation. In this way, extinction could be accounted for with primary reference to the associative status of the context. And the presence of inhibition in extinction could theoretically "protect" the CS from total associative loss (see Chorazyna, 1962), allowing the CS to retain enough associative strength to evoke fear when tested in the presence of an associatively neutral context.

Bouton and King (1983) have recently examined the possibility of contextual inhibition during extinction. Two discriminably different contexts were provided by two sets of Skinner boxes that differed visually (one set was metal, the other striped clear Plexiglas), in the composition of the grid floor (thin vs. fat rods), the size and relative positions of the operant manipulanda, the type of food pellets used to reinforce the bar-pressing baseline, odor (vinegar vs. Vick's VapoRub), and spatial location (different rooms in the laboratory). The contexts were counterbalanced, so that half the animals in any group received the appropriate treatment in each type of box.

In one experiment (Bouton & King, 1983, Experiment 1), rats were first trained to bar press on a VI 90-sec reinforcement schedule in both contexts, and then received pairings of a 60-sec illumination of the houselight with shock, and pairings of a 60-sec tone with shock. All fear conditioning took place in the same context (counterbalanced across animals), which can be designated as Context A. Following conditioning, the rats were divided into three groups. Group Ext-A received 20 extinction presentations of the tone distributed over five 90-min daily sessions in Context A, the conditioning context. Group Ext-B received the same tone extinction trials in Context B, the alternative context. Group NE (no extinction) received no tone-extinction trials but instead was allowed to bar press for the same number of 90-min sessions in Context B.

Following extinction, two kinds of tests were run. The first was a summation test to assess whether inhibition had been conditioned to Context B in Group Ext-B. In this test, all groups were allowed to bar press in Context B and were given 4 nonreinforced presentations of the light, which had not undergone extinction. If contextual inhibition had been conditioned during extinction of the tone in Group Ext-B, then it should be revealed by attenuated suppression to the light. There was, however, no evidence of contextual inhibition. Suppression to the CS was expressed in terms of the familiar B/(A+B) suppression ratio (Annau & Kamin, 1961); a ratio of 0 indicates maximal suppression to the CS, whereas .5 indicates none. The mean suppression ratios during the light-alone trials in

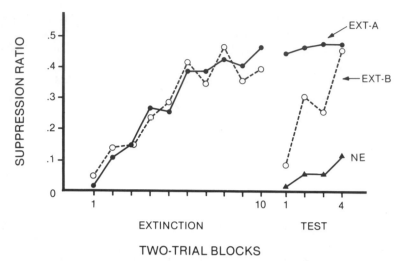

FIG. 6.1. Mean suppression to the tone CS during the extinction and renewal testing phases of the experiment of Bouton and King (1983, Experiment 1). During extinction, Group Ext-A received the tone in the conditioning context; Group Ext-B received it in the alternative context. Renewal testing occurred in the conditioning context. Group NE received no extinction during the extinction phase. (From Bouton, M. E., & King, D. A. Contextual control of the extinction of conditioned fear: Tests for the associative value of the context. *Journal of Experimental Psychology: Animal Behavior Processes,* 1983, *9,* 248–265. Copyright 1983 by the American Psychological Association. Reproduced by permission of the publisher.)

Context B were .24, .22, and .36 for Groups Ext-B, NE, and Ext-A, respectively. These values were not reliably different. Thus, there was no evidence of inhibition to Context B in Group Ext-B, the group for which that context had been nonreinforced in compound with the excitatory tone during extinction. And perhaps not surprisingly, summation tests in a subsequent experiment also revealed no evidence of contextual inhibition when extinction occurred in the conditioning context (i.e., Context A; Bouton & King, 1983, Experiment 4). With these procedures, there is no evidence of contextual inhibition developing in extinction.

Following summation testing in Context B, all the groups in the target experiment were returned to Context A and tested for the renewal of suppression to the extinguished tone. Four nonreinforced presentations of the tone were superimposed on VI-90 responding on each of 2 days. The results of renewal testing, along with the results of the tone-extinction phase, are shown in Fig. 6.1. Clear differences in suppression to the tone emerged during renewal testing in Context A. Group Ext-B showed a robust renewal of fear, as was expected based on our previous results. We may note that Group Ext-B's suppression to the CS was not as powerful as that of Group NE, the group that was not given extinction exposure to the tone prior to renewal testing. Thus, there appears to be some transfer of extinction from Context B to Context A. But the extinction evident in Context B for Group Ext-B clearly did not prevent the CS from producing a great deal of suppression in Context A.

Throughout the experiment, Bouton and King assessed contextual fear by allowing the rat to choose between the interior of the Skinner box itself (where it could earn food pellets) or a small side box that was made accessible when the experimenter opened a door. If a rat is afraid of the Skinner box, it chooses to sit in the side box rather than the Skinner box (cf. Odling–Smee, 1975). Preference for the Skinner box or side box was assessed with a time-sampling observational technique during the first 6 min of each session. Access to the side box was otherwise prevented. During the preference test at the start of the first session of renewal testing, Groups Ext-A, Ext-B, and NE were observed an average of 18.1, 16.1, and 18.6 times in the Skinner box (out of 30 possible observations). These "context preference scores" did not differ reliably. And context preference was not reliably correlated with suppression to the CS. The same results were obtained when Bouton and King examined other indices of contextual fear that could be derived from baseline response rates. Thus, within the limits of the sensitivity of these measures of contextual fear, the differences in fear of the tone that were apparent during renewal testing were not related to differences in the excitatory strength of the renewal context. Moreover, in another experiment (Experiment 3), Bouton and King (1983) again obtained the renewal effect in spite of extinction exposure to the renewal context prior to being tested there. The renewal of suppression in Group Ext-B appears to be independent of demonstrable contextual fear at the time of testing, as well as contextual inhibition during extinction.

There remains the possibility that Group Ext-B's renewal of fear in Context A was due to the reinstatement of a tone-Context A configural stimulus that was conditioned during the original conditioning. But it is curious that the absence of such a configural cue during extinction in Context B did not produce relatively rapid extinction in Group Ext-B. As the data from the extinction phase shown in Fig. 6.1 suggest, the group extinguished in the context that differed from the conditioning context (Ext-B) showed suppression comparable to that of the group extinguished in the conditioning context (Ext-A). This result is not consistent with reports that a context shift following conditioning can decrease the rat's fear of a CS (Balaz, Capra, Hartl, & Miller, 1981; Balaz, Capra, Kasprow, & Miller, 1982). Yet Bouton and King (1983) obtained no such effect in any of their published experiments, as well as several additional unpublished experiments, even though there was ample opportunity for the effect to occur and ample evidence that the animals could discriminate between the two contexts. In addition to the obvious effect of shifting the context following extinction, Groups Ext-A and Ext-B differed in their fear of the two contexts (as judged by context-preference tests) during a baseline-recovery session that occurred just prior to extinction. Bouton and King's results clearly indicate that a context shift follow-ing conditioning does not inevitably lead to a decrement in fear of the CS.

The data obtained by Bouton and King (1983) raise a number of questions. At present, we would emphasize that they make it difficult to justify an account of the renewal effect based purely on the associative status of contextual cues. Contextual stimuli may be able to control extinction performance independently of their demonstrable inhibitory or excitatory power during extinction and re-newal testing.

Latent Inhibition

In our original report of the renewal effect (Bouton & Bolles, 1979a), we pre-sented other evidence arguing for what appears to be some nonassociative func-tion of contextual stimuli. We found that contextual stimuli could attenuate suppression to a CS in a latent inhibition paradigm. Two groups of rats received four exposures to the CS prior to conditioning. One group received its CS preexposure in the test context (Skinner box); the other group received its preex-posure in the black plywood boxes that served as the conditioning context. We can refer to these groups as Groups TC (for preexposure in the test context) and

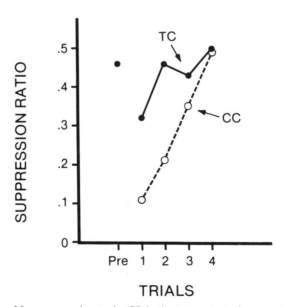

FIG. 6.2.   Mean suppression to the CS in the test context after nonreinforced preexposure to the CS in either the test context (Group TC) or the conditioning context (Group CC) prior to conditioning. For both groups, conditioning had occurred in the conditioning context. Suppression to the CS during the last preex-posure trial for Group TC is shown at left. Adapted from Bouton and Bolles (1979a, Experiment 4).

CC (for preexposure in the conditioning context). Exposure to the two contexts themselves was equated in the two groups. Following the preexposure phase, both groups received 15 CS-shock pairings in the conditioning context. Conditioned suppression was then tested during extinction trials conducted in the alternative, test context.

As Fig. 6.2 indicates, the group that had been preexposed in the test context showed less suppression during testing in the test context than did the group that had received an equal amount of CS preexposure in the conditioning context. Prior exposure to the CS alone in the test context was evidently sufficient to reduce subsequent suppression by the CS there. This example of the contextual control of CS fear is not consistent with the Rescorla–Wagner model, which does not predict the associative value of the test context to differ between the two groups. A similar result has been reported by Dexter and Merrill (1969; see also Anderson, O'Farrell, Formica, & Caponigri, 1969; Anderson, Wolf, & Sullivan, 1969).

Some recent models of latent inhibition predict that the effect will be specific to a particular context (Nadel & Willner, 1980; Nadel, Willner, & Kurz, this volume; Wagner, 1976). Although our results (and those of Dexter and Merrill and Anderson and his colleagues) do suggest some role of the context in the latent inhibition paradigm, it is interesting to observe that the results are actually quite different from what these models would predict. According to the views of Nadel and Willner and Wagner, a preexposed CS should show retarded conditioning only if the preexposure and conditioning phases of the experiment are conducted in the same context. Group CC's treatment satisfied that condition; that group's CS should have therefore acquired less-associative strength during conditioning. But note that Group CC showed *more* fear of its CS than did the group that received preexposure and conditioning in different contexts. The context effect evident in Fig. 6.2 is not predicted by any current treatment of latent inhibition.

The key feature of this study (see also Dexter & Merrill, 1969; Anderson, O'Farrell, Formica, & Caponigri, 1969; Anderson Wolf, & Sullivan, 1969) appears to be that testing occurred in the context in which Group TC had been preexposed. The weaker fear in this group might suggest that Group TC learned that the CS could occur without the US in the preexposure context. In a sense, the preexposure context inhibited fear of the CS in Group TC. But that "inhibition" developed in the absence of the conditions that would be required for inhibition by current models of inhibition (Wagner & Rescorla, 1972); the context in which the CS was preexposed could not have become a conditioned inhibitor because there had been no prior excitatory conditioning of the CS. This point complements the one made in the preceding section. Neither demonstrable associative strength in a context (Bouton & King, 1983) nor predictable associative strength in a context (Fig. 6.2) appears to be necessary for the context to control conditioned fear. Some alternative view of how contexts work is necessary to account for the overall pattern of our results.

Reinstatement of Extinguished Fear

There is evidence that contextual stimuli are involved in other extinction phenomena, such as the reinstatement effect, which was first studied systematically
by Rescorla and Heth (1975). A CS is first paired with shock and then extinguished. When the US is then presented a few times independently of the CS
after extinction, the CS regains some of its ability to evoke conditioned fear; that
is, the CS's response-evoking power is reinstated by presentation of the US
alone. This phenomenon has been widely obtained in conditioned suppression
experiments (e.g., Bouton, 1984; Bouton & Bolles, 1979b; Bouton & King,
1983; Hoffman, 1965; Quinsey & Ayres, 1969; Rescorla & Cunningham, 1977,
1978; Rescorla & Heth, 1975), even though its empirical status in other paradigms is less certain (Bouton, 1982).

The reinstatement phenomenon has often been explained in terms of the
event-memory model (e.g., Rescorla & Heth, 1975). The model proposes that in
extinction, when the CS occurs without the US, the memory of the US is
weakened. Presentation of the US following extinction reinstates the weakened
memory of the US and thus restores the conditioned responding that was lost in
extinction. Indeed, the reinstatement phenomenon is the primary evidence for the
event-memory model's account of extinction (see also Rescorla & Cunningham,
1977,1978).

However, it is possible to explain reinstatement in somewhat different terms.
When a shock US is presented following extinction, it may condition fear to the
contextual stimuli that are present at that time. When the CS is subsequently
tested for reinstated fear in the presence of those contextual cues, contextual fear
may summate with the undetected associative strength that appears to remain to
the CS following extinction. Thus, reinstatement may be a result of CS-context
summation. This account is consistent with the results of studies that have found
that extinguished CSs can show excitatory properties when they are tested in
compound with other excitatory nominal CSs. Reberg (1972) found that an
extinguished CS still elicited a measurable amount of fear when it was compounded with another excitatory CS. Hendry (1982) found that when two individually extinguished CSs (that were behaviorally "silent" by themselves) were
compounded and tested together, the compound elicited reliable conditioned
suppression. Thus, it is possible that an extinguished CS and a context can
combine to produce marked conditioned suppression, even though either stimulus alone does not.

We have explored this account of reinstatement in several experiments. In our
earliest investigation (Bouton & Bolles, 1979b, Experiment 1), we reasoned that
if reinstatement results from the conditioning of contextual stimuli, it should
occur only when the CS is tested in the context made dangerous by presentation
of the US. We should find relatively little reinstatement if the CS is tested in a
different context. Rats initially received tone–shock pairings in the conditioning

context (the same black plywood boxes). They were then given daily extinction presentations of the tone while they bar pressed in the Skinner box (the test context). When fear of the tone had been completely extinguished, each rat received four presentations of the US that had been used during conditioning. Each of these reinstatement presentations was signaled by a second CS. One group of animals received the shocks while they bar pressed in the test context. Another group received the same shocks back in the conditioning context. Beginning 24 hours later, reinstated fear of the tone was assessed in the test context. Note that animals in both groups were reminded about shock; their memories of the US were presumably reinstated. But only the group that received the shocks in the test context had the opportunity to learn that the test context was dangerous. These animals showed a strong reinstatement of fear of the tone. In contrast, the rats that received the same shocks back in the conditioning context showed no discernible reinstatement of fear.

This basic result was replicated in two other experiments (Bouton & Bolles, 1979b). In one study (Experiment 2), we were able to abolish reinstated fear following US presentations in the test context by giving the animals nonreinforced exposure to the test context between shocking and testing. Such exposure to the context in the absence of the US presumably extinguished contextual fear (cf. Bouton, 1984; Dweck & Wagner, 1970; Fanselow, 1980a; Sheafor, 1975; Tomie, 1976).

These experiments suggest that contextual stimuli have an important role in reinstatement. They indicate that the mere reminder of shock after extinction is not sufficient to produce reinstatement, as the event-memory model would suggest. The event-memory model might account for our results if it were modified to include the idea that the representation of the US is context-specific (e.g., that remembering the US depends on retrieval by the contextual cues with which it is associated). However, it is not necessary to invoke the concept of a US-memory to account for these results; the data can be parsimoniously explained by merely noting that contexts and CSs may summate in much the way that nominal CSs are expected to (e.g., Rescorla & Wagner, 1972). The mechanism through which CSs and contexts arouse fear could be left to any model, provided that the model allowed CSs and contexts to summate. It is not necessary to suppose that reinstatement depends on the strengthening of the US-memory, nor is it necessary to suppose that such a memory is ever lost during extinction. The reinstatement phenomenon does not require either conclusion.

Researchers sometimes attempt to minimize or rule out the contribution of context conditioning by signaling shocks with neutral or excitatory CSs (Bouton & Bolles,1979b; Rescorla & Cunningham, 1977, 1978; Rescorla & Heth, 1975). Theoretically, the signal could overshadow or block conditioning to the context, and there is good evidence from fear-conditioning situations suggesting that such a treatment can do so at least partially (e.g., Baker, Mercier, Gabel, & Baker, 1981; Bouton, 1984; Odling–Smee, 1975; Seligman, 1968). However, to our knowledge there is currently no evidence that the conditioning of contextual cues can be completely overshadowed or blocked by a nominal CS (see Balsam, 1984). And there has never been any assurance that the conditioning of the CS that signals the reinstatement shocks is asymptotic, which would be a necessary condition for complete blocking (Kamin, 1968). Moreover, because some evidence suggests that blocking and overshadowing may be multiple-trial phenomena (e.g., Mackintosh, 1975b), it is possible that the number of US presentations that have been used in reinstatement studies may not be sufficient to produce complete interference with context conditioning. Studies that have demonstrated the partial overshadowing of contextual fear have studied the effects of a number of shocks that far exceeds the number typically used in reinstatement studies.

The context-conditioning account of reinstatement would be strengthened by independent evidence of contextual fear during reinstatement testing. Bouton has recently addressed this issue in his laboratory. Consider again the experiment described earlier (Bouton & King, 1983, Experiment 1), in which two groups received fear conditioning in Context A and subsequent extinction in either that same context (Group Ext-A) or in Context B (Group Ext-B). After being tested for contextual inhibition and renewed fear of the tone CS, the animals went into a reinstatement phase. They were tested for reinstatement of tone fear in the contexts in which extinction had been carried out. On the day following the conclusion of renewal testing, Groups Ext-A and Ext-B were each divided into two subgroups that received four reinstating shocks (.5-sec, 1-mA) while they bar pressed in either the context in which testing was to occur, or the alternative context. The design of this new experiment (Bouton & King, 1983, Experiment 2) thus provided animals that were shocked in the same context in which testing occurred (Group Same) and animals that were shocked in the different context (Group Diff), with half the animals in each of these new groups originating in Groups Ext-A and Ext-B. The boxes were counterbalanced. Four nonreinforced reinstatement tests of the tone CS were conducted in the appropriate context during a 90-min session 24 hours later. A 6-min test of the animals' preference for the interior of the Skinner box over the side box was conducted at the start of this session.

The results of each reinstatement test trial, along with the mean suppression ratios from the last nonreinforced test of the tone in the extinction context, are shown in Fig. 6.3. The data are consistent with our previous results (Bouton & Bolles, 1979b). The figure shows the mean of the animals from Groups Same and Diff collapsed over Groups Ext-A and Ext-B. Groups Same and Diff differed marginally during the last extinction trial ($p < .10$). This unfortunate consequence of random assignment was not detected until all the data were collected. However, because Group Same appeared to show less suppression during the "pre" trial, the trend biases the reinstatement test conservatively against the hypothesis that Group Same would show greater suppression during reinstate-

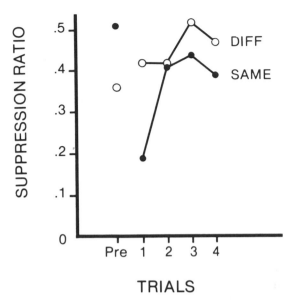

TRIALS

FIG. 6.3. Mean suppression to the CS on each trial of reinstatement testing in the experiment of Bouton and King (1983, Experiment 2). Group Same had received the US in the context where reinstatement was tested; Group Diff received the US in the alternative context. The last preceding nonreinforced test of the CS in the reinstatement test context is shown at left ("pre"). (From Bouton, M. E., & King, D. A. Contextual control of the extinction of conditioned fear: Tests for the associative value of the context. *Journal of Experimental Psychology: Animal Behavior Processes*, 1983, *9*, 248–265. Copyright 1983 by the American Psychological Association. Reproduced by permission of the publisher.)

ment testing than Group Diff. And an analysis of variance on the data from the first test trial still revealed reliably more suppression in Group Same than in Group Diff. This effect did not depend on the group from which the animals had originally come (interaction $F < 1$). And the animals that originally came from Groups Ext-A and Ext-B did not differ reliably ($F < 1$).

During the context preference test conducted at the start of the reinstatement test session, the rats in Group Same had a mean context preference score (the number of time-sampled observations of the rat in the Skinner box out of a possible 30) of 5.1; the rats in Group Diff had a score of 16.6. These values differed reliably. Furthermore, the overall correlation between suppression ratios on the first reinstatement test trial and the context preference scores was reliable, $r(14) = +.63$, $p < .01$. Among the animals in Group Same, this correlation also appeared to hold, $r(6) = +.64$, $p < .05$ (one-tailed). Bouton (1984) obtained similar results when reinstatement was produced by either four .5-mA USs or four 3-mA USs. These data attest to the utility of the context-preference measure of contextual fear. They strongly suggest that reinstatement is related to, and can be predicted from, demonstrable contextual fear under a reasonable range of conditions. Together with Bouton and King's (1983) lack of evidence of contextual inhibition arising in extinction, they are not consistent with the hypothesis that reinstatement occurs because presenting the US returns an inhibitory extinction context back to associative neutrality (cf. Rescorla & Cunningham, 1978). The evidence suggests that reinstatement results from contextual excitation produced by presenting the US.

It may be appropriate to note that the context-conditioning account of reinstatement can provide a reasonable explanation of another reinstatement phenomenon. Rescorla and Cunningham (1977, 1978) have "erased" reinstatement by interposing extinction trials of a second CS between presentation of the US and reinstatement testing. The Rescorla–Wagner model predicts that associative loss to a CS may be enhanced if it is nonreinforced in compound with another excitatory CS (Wagner, Saavedra, & Lehmann, in Wagner, 1969). Nonreinforcement of a CS in compound with excitatory contextual cues may thus enhance the extinction of the context and thereby eliminate the basis of reinstatement.

The evidence currently suggests that reinstatement results from the conditioning of excitatory strength to contextual stimuli when the US is presented following extinction. It is not necessary to suppose that reinstatement results from a strengthening of the US-memory following extinction. In fact, we may well wonder whether there is any loss in strength of the US representation during extinction. Recall that Bouton and King (1983) found that the extinction of one CS produced no decrease in responding to a second CS associated with the same US (see also Kasprow, Schachtman, Cacheiro, & Miller, 1982; Richards & Sargent, 1983). This finding is not consistent with the event-memory model, because the extinction of the first CS should weaken the strength of the memory activated by the second CS (cf. Rescorla & Cunningham, 1977, 1978). We must begin to question whether the event-memory model provides an adequate account of either extinction or reinstatement.

Two Effects of Retaining the US in Extinction

Another extinction phenomenon that is related to reinstatement, and appears to be well documented in the aversive conditioning literature, is the facilatory effect upon responding of retaining the US in extinction. If the US is retained (but not paired with the CS) during extinction, then the response to the CS tends to disappear more slowly (e.g., Frey & Butler, 1977; Spence, 1966). This effect is, of course, consistent with the event-memory model. Presentation of the US during extinction should maintain the strength of the US-memory, which otherwise weakens during extinction.

Once again, however, it is possible that presentations of the US in extinction might increase the associative strength of contextual cues, which then summate with the CS to enhance responding to the CS. Bouton (1980) tested this possibility by presenting the US during extinction in a different context from the one in which the CS was extinguished. The notion that the extinction-retarding effect of retaining the US in extinction is a result of context-conditioning requires that the CS and US be presented in the same context; in its present form, the event-memory model makes no such requirement.

In Bouton's (1980) experiment, several groups of rats initially received conditioning of a tone in the conditioning context, the set of black plywood boxes that we had used before (Bouton & Bolles, 1979a, b). The groups were then given extinction presentations of the CS alone in the Skinner box (the test context) during 15-min sessions conducted on every odd-numbered day. The groups differed in their treatment on even-numbered days. One group, Group NSh (no shock), spent its even-numbered sessions bar pressing in the test context; no shock was presented to this group during extinction. The other groups each received presentation of a single unsignaled US (.5-sec, 1-mA) during each of the even-numbered days. One of these groups, Group TC (test context), received its "extinction shocks" in the test context. Another group, Group CC (conditioning context), received the same shocks back in the conditioning context. A final group, Group BC (backward conditioning), received shocks in the test context, but had originally received backward conditioning of the CS, which was not expected to produce strong excitation to the CS.

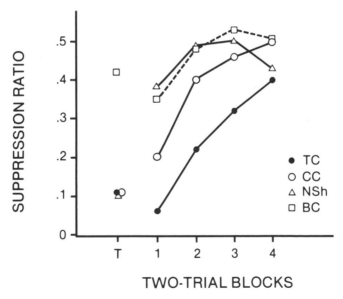

FIG. 6.4.   Mean suppression to the CS during extinction in the test context in the Bouton (1980) experiment. Group NSh received no shock during extinction. Groups TC and CC received shocks in the test and conditioning context, respectively. Group BC had received backward conditioning of the CS. The first extinction trial, which preceded extinction exposure to shock, is shown at left.

Figure 6.4 shows suppression of the groups to the tone over two-trial blocks during extinction. (The first trial, which occurred prior to extinction presentation of the US, is shown separately on the left.) As in our previous experiments with comparable procedures, extinction was quite rapid when no shock was presented during extinction (Group NSh). The two-trial blocks tend to obscure the extinction curve of Group NSh, which had mean suppression ratios of .11, .29, and .48 during the first three extinction trials, including the initial test trial. In distinct contrast, if shock was presented occasionally in the context in which extinction was taking place (Group TC), the loss of CS fear was profoundly retarded. The strong suppression observed in Group TC appeared to depend on prior forward conditioning of the CS: Animals in Group BC showed less suppression to the tone, even though they received equivalent shock in the test context.

The forward-conditioning group that received the extinction shocks in a different context during extinction (Group CC) is of most interest. Although there appears to have been some extinction-retarding effect of presenting the US in the different context for Group CC ($.05 < p < .10$), it is apparent that the effect was smaller than that obtained when the US was presented in the test context (Group TC). The difference in suppression between Groups TC and CC was reliable and is consistent with the notion that fear of the context can contribute to the extinction - retarding effect of retaining the US in extinction.

Retaining the US during extinction is known to have another effect in addition to retarding the loss of the CR. When compared with a condition in which the US is simply omitted during extinction, an extinction procedure in which the US is retained appears to produce a more durable or effective associative loss to the CS. The reacquisition of the CR is slower when the US has been retained in extinction, which suggests that less associative strength has been "saved" during extinction (Frey & Butler, 1977; Rescorla & Cunningham, 1977). Moreover, fear is more difficult to reinstate to the CS if the US, or its memory, has been retained in some manner during extinction (cf. Rescorla & Cunningham, 1977, 1978; see also Uhl, 1973; Uhl & Garcia, 1969). Because reinstatement depends partly on some undetected associative strength remaining to the CS, this result could also be consistent with the view that the CS has sustained a more substantial associative loss when the US has been retained during extinction.

The event-memory model provides a simple account of this second effect of retaining the US in extinction. Because presentation of the US would serve to maintain the strength of the US-memory, the weakening of which ordinarily accounts for extinction, the loss of responding that does eventually occur when the US is retained might reflect a true loss of the CS–US association. However, once again an alternative explanation is possible. The Rescorla–Wagner model predicts that associative loss to a CS will be proportional to the combined associative strengths of all stimuli present during nonreinforcement (Wagner, Saavedra, & Lehmann, in Wagner, 1969). If presenting the US during extinction conditions contextual stimuli, nonreinforcement of the CS in compound with those stimuli should produce a relatively large associative decrement to the CS on each trial. By the end of extinction, this would result in relatively little undetected associative strength remaining to the CS. In Bouton's experiment, the Rescorla–Wagner model predicts that relatively little associative strength would remain to the CS in Group TC by the end of extinction, because that group received nonreinforcement of the CS in a context that was made excitatory by presentations of the US.

Bouton obtained evidence that appears to be consistent with this prediciton. Following extinction, each group in the study received four reinstatement shocks in the test context. The Rescorla–Wagner model suggests that this treatment would begin to equate the groups for contextual fear in the test context. When the CS was subsequently tested for reinstatement in the presence of those contextual cues, any differences in associative strength to the CS that remained following the various extinction treatments might then be revealed, because the model predicts (and our results suggest) that reinstatement depends on contextual fear summating with associative strength that remains to the extinguished CS.

The results of the reinstatement test are shown in Fig. 6.5. A final extinction test of the CS that served as a "pretest" prior to reinstatement shocking is shown on the left. As the figure suggests, only two of the groups (NSh and CC) gave evidence of reinstated suppression to the CS. Both of these groups had received extinction of the CS in a context that was not excitatory. In contrast, the group

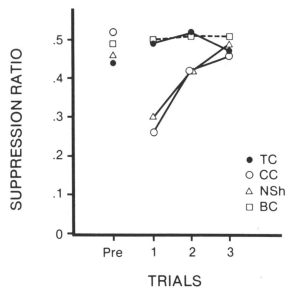

FIG. 6.5 Mean suppression to the CS during each reinstatement test trial in the Bouton (1980) experiment. Group designations are the same as in Fig. 6.4. All groups received exposure to the US in the test context prior to reinstatement testing. The last preceding nonreinforced test of the CS is shown at left.

for which extinction had been conducted in a theoretically excitatory context (Group TC) gave little evidence of reinstated fear.

These results once again suggest the importance of contextual cues in extinction. They are consistent with some rather subtle predictions that can be derived from the Rescorla–Wagner model. That model appears to provide a fairly powerful framework for understanding the effects of presenting the US during or following extinction. Like reinstatement, the effects of retaining the US in extinction can be accounted for by considering the associative status of contextual cues. But we now turn to other evidence that does not entirely fit this framework.

Inflation of the US Value Following Conditioning

The event-memory model's general account of conditioning (which can be considered independently of its account of extinction) gains some support from studies that inflate the value of the US following conditioning. Rescorla (1974, Experiment 2) first conditioned fear to a tone by pairing it with a .5-sec, .5-mA footshock. Following conditioning, different groups were then exposed to 24 .5-sec shocks of either .5-, 1-, or 1-mA. A control group was not exposed to these additional shocks. Then, fear of the tone was tested over the course of eight extinction trials. Even though the tone had been paired only with the .5-mA shock in each of the groups, the overall difference among the groups was reliable during testing. The fear of the tone appeared to be enhanced, or "inflated," by exposure to shocks that were stronger than .5-mA. Rescorla suggested that the tone now evoked the memory of the stronger shock (see also Sherman, 1978).

There is of course an obvious alternative explanation of the inflation effect. Exposure to shock following conditioning might condition additional associative strength to contextual stimuli that are present at the time. If the tone is subsequently presented in the presence of those contextual cues, as it was in Rescorla's and Sherman's experiments, we might expect inflated fear of the tone as a result of CS-context summation. This account of inflation is consistent with our data on the effects of exposure to shocks during or following extinction; perhaps all we need to assume is that fear of a nonextinguished CS, like that of an extinguished CS, is influenced by CS-context summation.

Bouton (1984) has recently investigated the role of CS-context summation in the inflation paradigm. In one experiment (Experiment 1), he compared the effects of inflation shocks delivered in the context in which conditioning and testing were conducted with the effects of shocks that were delivered in a different context. The idea that inflation results from CS-context summation clearly requires that the US presentations and testing occur in the same context. The details of the procedure, including the shock parameters and number of conditioning and inflation shock trials, were like those used by Rescorla (1974). There were 3 groups. Initially all groups received 12 pairings of a tone with a .5-sec, .5-mA shock. In the next 3 sessions, the animals received different treatments. Two of the groups received 24 unsignaled presentations of a .5-sec, 3-mA shock. One of these groups (Group Same) received the shocks in the context in which conditioning had occurred and where testing was to be conducted. The other shocked group (Group Diff) received the same shocks in the alternative context. (The actual boxes in which the various phases were conducted were counterbalanced.) The third group (Group NSh) received no further shock after conditioning; this group merely spent an equal amount of time in the context in which conditioning and testing occurred as did Group Same. Two baseline-recovery days followed the shock exposure phase. Finally, there were two sessions in which fear of the tone was tested.

During the 6-min context-preference tests conducted at the start of the two test sessions, Groups Same, Diff, and NSh had mean context preference scores (the number of observations scored as in the Skinner box out of a possible 30) of 13.8, 19.3, and 22.0, respectively. Pairwise comparisons revealed that Group Same showed reliably more contextual fear than both Groups Diff and NSh, which did not differ from one another. These differences in contextual fear were not detected by baseline bar-press rates, which suggests that baseline rate is insensitive to levels of contextual fear that are measurable with the context-preference technique (see also Bouton & King, 1983). The more sensitive context-preference measure indicated that the 3-mA shocks delivered in the test context produced a reliable amount of contextual fear that was present during testing, and that the same shocks delivered in the alternative context (Group Diff) did not. Thus, it is apparent that the animals could discriminate between the two contexts, a fact that is also supported by our other research with the apparatus (e.g., Bouton & King, 1983). If the inflation effect results from additional contextual fear, the differences found in contextual fear must predict that Group Same would show significantly inflated fear to the tone, whereas Group Diff would not. However, that is not what was found; the prediction was strikingly disconfirmed.

The suppression ratio data from the tests of the tone are shown in Fig. 6.6. Quite surprisingly, the data indicate that 3-mA shocks delivered in *either* context produced enhanced suppression to the tone. Pairwise comparisons of the groups' suppression ratios revealed that Groups Same and Diff differed reliably from Group NSh, and that Groups Same and Diff did not differ. Thus, the 3-mA shocks produced an inflation effect that did not depend on the context in which the shocks were given. The inflation effect evident in Group Diff was not related to contextual fear. In contrast with our results with reinstatement, context preference was not reliably correlated with suppression to the CS.

These results, together with further research reported by Bouton (1984), suggest that contextual fear is not a necessary condition for producing the inflation effect. Consider the results shown in Fig. 6.7 (Bouton, 1984, Experiment 2). In this experiment, each of the groups received conditioning of the tone with the .5-mA shock. Two of the groups (Sh and Sh-E) then received 24 exposures

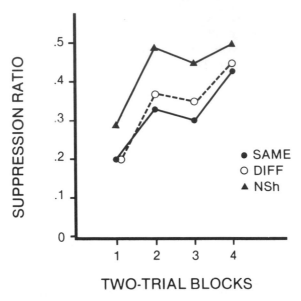

FIG. 6.6   Mean suppression to the CS during inflation testing (Bouton, 1984, Experiment 1). Groups Same and Diff had received inflation presentations of the US prior to testing. For Group Diff, those presentations had occurred in a different context. Group NSh received no inflation USs. (From Bouton, M. E. Differential control by context in the inflation and reinstatement paradigms. *Journal of Experimental Psychology: Animal Behavior Processes,* 1984, *10,* 56–74. Copyright 1984 by the American Psychological Association. Reproduced by permission of the publisher.)

to the 3-mA shock in the context where testing was to occur, whereas the other two groups (NSh and NSh-E) received no further shock. Following these shocks, Group Sh-E received four additional 90-minute sessions bar pressing in the context, which were expected to extinguish contextual fear. One of the non-shocked groups, Group NSh-E, received the same treatment. (The remaining groups received no exposure to the context, but an equal amount of handling.) Context-preference tests conducted at the start of the test sessions that followed revealed that context exposure had virtually abolished contextual fear in Group Sh-E, which had a mean context-preference score of 19.8 during testing. The nonshocked groups had scores of 19.0 and 21.0, which did not differ from each other or from Group Sh-E. Group Sh's score (9.4) was significantly lower than those of each of the other groups. But as Fig. 6.7 clearly indicates, these rather substantial differences in contextual fear were not reflected in fear of the CS. Whereas context exposure had apparently eliminated contextual fear as indexed by the context-preference tests, it did not appreciably attenuate the strength of the inflation effect. The inflation effect does not appear to depend on the presence of demonstrable contextual fear.

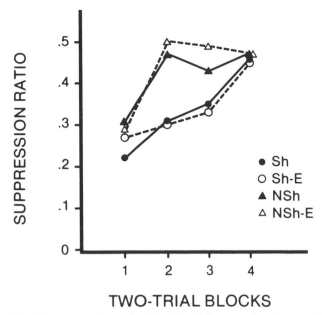

TWO-TRIAL BLOCKS

FIG. 6.7   Mean suppression to the CS during inflation testing (Bouton, 1984, Experiment 2). Groups Sh and Sh-E had received inflation presentations of the US following conditioning; Groups NSh and NSh-E had not. Groups Sh-E and NSh-E had then received extinction exposure to the context prior to testing. (From Bouton, M.E. Differential control by context in the inflation and reinstatement paradigms. *Journal of Experimental Psychology: Animal Behavior Processes*, 1984, *10*, 56–74. Copyright 1984 by the American Psychological Association. Reproduced by permission of the publisher.)

The most interesting and important feature of these results is that measurable amounts of contextual fear appeared to contribute so little to the animals' fear of the CS. As Fig. 6.6 and 6.7 suggest, demonstrably more contextual fear in some groups added almost nothing to the rats' fear of the CS. It is as if there was no evidence of CS-context summation in these experiments. This interpretation of the data is actually quite consistent with results that have been reported in related paradigms. First, following fear conditioning, several experimenters have exposed rats to additional shocks of the intensity used during conditioning (Ayres & Benedict, 1973; Randich & Haggard, 1983; Randich & Rescorla, 1981; Rescorla, 1974; Sherman, 1978; see also Randich & Ross, this volume). Although such shock exposure might be expected to condition contextual fear, none of these investigators found enhanced fear of the CS following those shocks. Bouton (1984, Experiment 4) has obtained similar results; fear of a CS was not reliably enhanced by postconditioning exposure to the US, even though that exposure was shown, via context-preference tests, to have conditioned reliable contextual fear. Second, it is well known that exposure to the US *prior to* conditioning retards the subsequent conditioning of fear to the CS (see Randich & LoLordo, 1979). This effect is often attributed to blocking produced by associative strength conditioned to the context (e.g., Randich, 1981). But if we consider the CS-context summation rule carefully, this effect constitutes something of a paradox. If the associative strength of the context were to summate with that of the CS, we might expect enhanced fear of the CS once the CS acquires some associative strength. This is in fact the opposite of what is usually observed. Thus, the results with the inflation paradigm, together with those of these related procedures, begin to suggest the conclusion that, by itself, excitatory strength conditioned to the context is not always sufficient to enhance the animal's fear of a nominal CS.

Inflation and Reinstatement Compared

This conclusion stands in sharp contrast to the reinstatement results we described earlier. In reinstatement, US presentations condition fear to the context, which then appears to augment fear of the CS. On the other hand, US presentations in the inflation and related paradigms appear to produce contextual fear that has no augmenting effect on fear of the CS. One difference between the two types of paradigms may be the extinction procedure itself. Perhaps CSs that have undergone extinction, like those involved in reinstatement, are more susceptible to the influence of context than are CSs that have never been extinguished.

This possibility is consistent with the differential role of context in the inflation and reinstatement paradigms. (It is also consistent, interestingly enough, with Bouton and King's (1983) finding that, whereas a context-shift following extinction often changed the rat's fear of a CS, a similar shift following conditioning did not.) But there are obvious problems with comparing extinguished and nonextinguished CSs. For one thing, they evoke different amounts of fear; it is possible that the effects of context are simply more detectable in the range of the high suppression ratios usually evident after extinction. The reinstatement paradigm has also typically differed from the other paradigms in the amount of US exposure the rat receives independently of the CS. Consequently, levels of contextual fear present during testing, among other things, might differ between the two types of paradigms. To compare the influence of contextual fear on fear of extinguished and nonextinguished CSs, it would be desirable to equate different groups tested with such CSs on: (1) contextual fear present during testing; and (2) fear of the two types of CSs as they entered testing.

Bouton (1984, Experiment 5) has attempted to arrange such a comparison. The design of the experiment is illustrated in Table 6.1. Two of the groups received a reinstatement treatment (which involves extinction before exposure to the US) and two received an inflation treatment (which does not involve any extinction before exposure to the US). To equate the contextual fear present during reinstatement and inflation testing, all rats received identical US-exposure

TABLE 6.1
Inflation and Reinstatement Compared

	Group	Conditioning	Extinction	US-Exposure	Test
Reinstatement	R-Same	4 AT-3mA	12 AT-	4 A-3mA	AT-
	R-Diff	4 AT-3mA	12 AT-	4 B-3mA	AT-
Inflation	I-Same	4 AT-0.3mA	—	4 A-3mA	AT-
	I-Diff	4 AT-0.3mA	—	4 B-3mA	AT-

Note: A and B refer to different contexts (counterbalanced); T refers to a tone CS; 3mA and 0.3mA describe the intensity of the .5-sec US. From Bouton (1984, Experiment 5).

during the US-exposure phase. One group in each condition received the USs in Context A, where testing was to occur; the other group received them in Context B, the different context (counterbalanced). To equate the groups on fear of the CS prior to the US-exposure phase, the groups in the reinstatement condition received a number of extinction trials that did not completely extinguish fear, whereas the inflation groups merely received conditioning on the day before the US-exposure treatment with parameters that pilot work indicated would condition reliable and comparable suppression to the CS.

The results of the test session are presented in Fig. 6.8. At left, the figure shows the results of the usual 6-min context-preference test that was conducted at the outset of the test session. Exposure to the US produced substantial contextual fear provided that it occurred in the context in which testing was to occur. This effect did not interact with the reinstatement and inflation conditions: The groups shocked in the test context (R-Same and I-Same) were comparably afraid of the context and the groups shocked in the different context (R-Diff and I-Diff) were not. Suppression to the CS is shown at right. The groups' fear of the CS did not differ on the last trial prior to US exposure ("pre"), when the suppression ratios were significantly lower than a hypothetical population mean of .50. But it is clear that CS fear differed dramatically among the groups following US exposure. At that time, fear of the CS in the reinstated groups was related to contextual fear. In contrast, fear of the CS in the "inflated" groups was not: The substantial amount of contextual fear present in Group I-Same was evidently not sufficient to enhance fear of the CS. Fear of the extinguished CS tested in the reinstatement paradigm appears to be more readily affected by an excitatory context than is fear of the nonextinguished CS tested in the inflation paradigm.

Because the study was reasonably successful at equating contextual fear during testing and CS fear prior to testing across the inflation and reinstatement procedures, we cannot attribute the difference in our results with inflation and reinstatement to simple scaling effects. We may note that the design did confound the intensity of the US used during conditioning with treatment condition (it is necessary to do so if one wants to equate the US-exposure parameters and still retain the US-intensity characteristics of the two paradigms). But this does

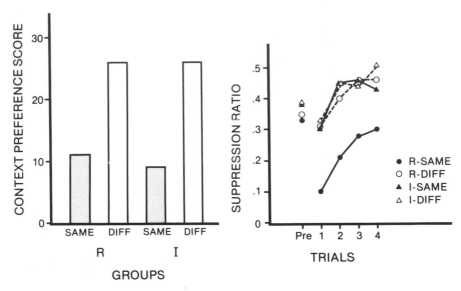

FIG. 6.8   Mean context preference scores (left) and suppression to the CS (right) of the groups during the test session of the experiment comparing inflation and reinstatement (Bouton, 1984, Experiment 5). "Pre" indicates suppression to the CS on the last trial preceding US exposure. Table 6.1 describes the groups' treatments. (From Bouton, M. E. Differential control by context in the inflation and reinstatement paradigms. *Journal of Experimental Psychology: Animal Behavior Processes*, 1984, *10*, 56–74. Copyright 1984 by the American Psychological Association. Reproduced by permission of the publisher.)

not interfere with the principal conclusion to be drawn from the study, which is that CSs that evoke comparable amounts of fear following conditioning or extinction may have very different properties. This conclusion contradicts the independence-of-path assumption often made by models of conditioning (e.g., Rescorla & Wagner, 1972). The properties of conditioned stimuli that control similar amounts of fear depend critically on how the stimuli achieved that degree of control. Extinguished and nonextinguished CSs may differ in the extent to which fear evoked by them depends on the excitatory strength of the context.

Summary

The experiments we have discussed here suggest that the context may often be a powerful determinant of how the rat responds to a nominal CS. But quite significantly, it is not always so. The data fall into an interesting general pattern. Namely, manipulations of the context appear to control the animal's fear of the CS most readily if that CS has been reinforced in some experimental episodes and nonreinforced in others. When we present animals with a CS that has never been nonreinforced (as in, for example, the inflation procedure), we find surprisingly little evidence that demonstrable excitation in the context has any effect on

CS fear. Similarly, we find relatively little change in the rat's fear of the CS when the context is shifted immediately following conditioning (Bouton & King, 1983). But when we shift the context following *extinction,* we often find changes in the rat's fear of the CS (Bouton & Bolles, 1979a; Bouton & King, 1983). Postextinction exposure to the US (i.e., the reinstatement procedure) also changes the rat's fear of the CS in a manner that is related to context, as does retaining the US during extinction. And though we have less evidence on this point, we may note that when the rat receives nonreinforced exposure to the CS prior to conditioning in the latent inhibition paradigm, we have also found some degree of contextual control. The data begin to suggest that the context is especially important in affecting the behavior evoked by CSs that have been reinforced in some experimental episodes and nonreinforced in others.

When the context does control conditioned responding, is that control mediated by the context's associative strength? In the reinstatement and US-retention paradigms, the answer currently appears to be "yes." But in contrast, the renewal effect cannot presently be attributed to independently demonstrable inhibition in the extinction context, or excitation present in the renewal context (Bouton & King, 1983). In addition, our work with the latent inhibition paradigm suggests that contexts may control conditioned fear even when current models of conditioning cannot point to any associative basis for such an effect.

We see two threads emerging. Contexts appear to modulate fear of the CS most readily following extinction, or when the CS has been presented with the US in some experimental episodes and without the US in others.[2] And the context's control over CS fear may not always be related to the context's demonstrable excitatory or inhibitory associations with the US.

GENERAL DISCUSSION

Let us consider the implications of the results we have reviewed here for various theories of context and extinction. We first consider two popular views and then begin to construct one of our own.

---

[2]The distinction we are drawing here may turn out to be one of degree, rather than kind. Data from Miller's laboratory (Balaz et al., 1981, 1982; reviewed by Miller & Schachtman, this volume) suggest that under some conditions the associative strength of a context might summate with that of a CS that has never been nonreinforced. However, Miller and Schachtman (this volume) have suggested that this result might be restricted to the fairly unusual procedure in which the subject is placed in the context with the CS already present during testing. Some investigators have also observed decrements in responding to a Pavlovian CS when the context is changed immediately following conditioning (Balaz et al., 1981, 1982; see also Archer et al., this volume). (Most of the other data that are available on the effects of context shifts involve a context shift following treatments other than simple Pavlovian conditioning.) Our own failures to observe this effect in the presence of evidence that the animals had discriminated between the contexts (e.g., Bouton & King, 1983) suggest that the effect is not as robust as that of the context shift following extinction (see also data reported by Archer & Sjödén, 1981; Archer et al., this volume).

The Rescorla–Wagner Model

In this model, and other essentially associationistic models of conditioning, the associative strength of the CS (i.e., the strength of the CS–US association) is assumed to be "unlearned" to some extent during extinction. Although some of the evidence reported here does suggest that the CS loses some of its power during extinction (compare Groups Ext-B and NE in Fig. 6.1), our results with the renewal and reinstatement paradigms join with results from other paradigms in suggesting that the CS may still retain considerable excitatory power following extinction. We have considered one mechanism that the Rescorla–Wagner model provides to account for this ubiquitous finding: The CR is assumed to depend jointly on the associative strengths of the CS and context, which summate. If the context becomes inhibitory during extinction, such contextual inhibition could inhibit (and therefore mask) fear of the CS during extinction and further protect the CS from total associative loss. Alternatively, residual associative strength that merely goes undetected by our response measures could summate with any excitatory strength of the context that may be present during the various tests of the CS that suggest that fear of the CS has survived extinction.

The Rescorla–Wagner model can "explain" a variety of interesting effects in Pavlovian conditioning by attributing some associative value to the context (e.g., Baker, 1977; Dweck & Wagner, 1970; Fanselow, 1980a, b; Randich, 1981; Rescorla, 1972). However, if this device is to be confirmed, the associative strength of the context must be verified independently of the effects it is supposed to explain. Often, experimenters have merely intervened with manipulations that the model suggests should affect the associative value of the context. Then, when the phenomenon under study changes in a manner that is predicted by the model, the role of the associative value of the context is inferred. We have recently begun to assess the associative strength of the context independently of the phenomena we have studied and have found that, consistent with the model, reinstatement is related to independently demonstrable excitation present in the context. However, the renewal effect does not presently appear to be related to independently demonstrable excitation in the renewal context or inhibition in the extinction context (Bouton & King, 1983).

The core of the Rescorla–Wagner model's treatment of context is its assumption that the context is merely a second CS that is present in compound with the target CS. There is little question that contextual cues can in fact behave like other CSs and exert associative control over behavior (e.g., Blanchard & Blanchard, 1969; Bolles & Collier, 1976; Fanselow, 1980c; Siegel, 1977). Our new findings with the context-preference testing technique provide further evidence of associative control by contexts. Contextual fear looks much like CS fear; it depends on pairing of the context with shock, and it appears to be subject to extinction. Moreover, in at least some cases, the associative strength of the context appears to interact with that of the CS in predictable ways. When shocks are signaled by a nominal CS, less associative strength is conditioned to the context (e.g., Baker et al., 1981; Bouton, 1984; Odling–Smee, 1975; Seligman, 1968). And in the reinstatement paradigm, the evidence suggests that the associative strengths of CSs and contexts can summate. Thus, there is a sense in which contextual stimuli are just like any other stimuli.

However, there is also evidence that poses a challenge for the Rescorla–Wagner model and for its simplifying assumption that contextual stimuli act just like nominal CSs. The problem is basically that the strength of the response evoked by the CS is not always related to the associative strength of the context. The studies by Bouton and King (1983) on the renewal effect (Fig. 6.1) suggest that contexts can control CS fear in the absence of measurable contextual excitation or inhibition. Our data on latent inhibition (Fig. 6.2) further suggest that the context can attenuate or "inhibit" CS fear in the absence of conditions that are required if the context is to acquire inhibitory strength. Moreover, Bouton's (1984) work with the inflation paradigm (e.g., Fig. 6.6, 6.7, and 6.8) suggests that the presence of measurable contextual excitation may sometimes have very little effect on the rat's fear of a CS. Taken together, the data suggest that associative strength conditioned to the context may be neither a necessary nor a sufficient condition for the context to affect the response to the CS.

Memory Models and Mechanisms

There is abundant evidence from the literature on both human and animal memory to suggest that contexts can work as retrieval cues (e.g., Medin & Reynolds, this volume; Miller & Schachtman, this volume; Overton, this volume; Smith, 1979; Spear, 1973). The event-memory model, of course, emphasizes the importance of memory in conditioning and extinction. The CS acts like a retrieval cue to evoke the US-memory, which then evokes fear. A natural extension of the event-memory model would be to suppose that contexts work the same way. Thus, the strength of the US-memory might depend on retrieval by context. As we have previously noted, such an extension of the event-memory model might account for the context-specificity of reinstatement, and also the effects of retaining the US in extinction. We might also note the possible contribution of contextual inhibition to the model's proposition that the US-memory weakens during extinction. Such inhibition could suppress the US-memory, because it has been argued that conditioned inhibitors may suppress the US-memory evoked by excitatory CSs (Rescorla & Holland, 1977). This extension of the event-memory model might thus predict that extinction would be relatively specific to its context, as the renewal effect suggests.

However, the extension fails us exactly where we would expect it to: at those points where the evidence suggests that the context is not just another CS. Bouton and King's tests of one CS following the extinction of another CS revealed no evidence of contextual inhibition arising in extinction, and, more generally, no evidence that the strength of the US-memory had become weakened in extinction (see also Kasprow et al., 1982; Richards & Sargent, 1983). We have also observed renewal in contexts that do not have associations with the US and would therefore presumably not retrieve the memory of the US. In general, we have found so little evidence that would unequivocally support the event-memory model's account of extinction that we must question the utility of adding new mechanisms to it to patch it up.

The memory model outlined by Estes (1973; see also Medin, 1976) attributes a somewhat different role to contexts that might provide the starting point for another account of some of the context effects that we have reviewed here. Estes has suggested that the context might retrieve or activate a memory node that, loosely defined, represents something like the relationship between the CS and US, rather than either of these events themselves. We might suppose that contextual cues present at the time of conditioning might later retrieve the memory of the fact that the CS and US have been paired. Similarly, cues present at the time of extinction might later retrieve the memory of the fact that the CS has occurred alone. Each of these different types of memories might exist in a long-term store; contextual cues might provide access to either of them. In effect, contextual cues might retrieve memories of acquisiton and extinction episodes.

This approach differs from an event-memory kind of model in several important respects. Most fundamentally, it would imply that fear aroused by a CS does not depend on the retrieval of a representation of the US, but rather on the retrieval of some representation of the CS in either an acquisition or an extinction episode. If the context retrieves the memory of the CS in extinction, there will be little fear of the CS. But if, instead, the context retrieves the memory of the CS in acquisition, there will be fear of the CS. This approach might predict extinction to be relatively specific to its context, because there would be a failure to retrieve the memory of extinction concomitant with a shift of context.

We might also attempt to account for reinstatement and the effects of retaining the US in extinction with this kind of analysis. Because the US was an important feature of acquisition, its presentation during or following extinction might itself serve to activate the memory of acquisition. To account for the durable associative loss that appears to occur to the CS when the US is retained during extinction (e.g., Fig. 6.5), we might further presume that the repeated activation of the memory of acquisition while the CS is actually being nonreinforced might dispose the animal toward restructuring its memory of acquisition in some way. However, one problem for this otherwise appealing approach is our finding that the effects of presenting the US during or following extinction are specific to their contexts. This finding would appear to require the additional assumption that the memory of acquisition that is activated by the US is itself specific to the context in which it is activated.

One other thing should be emphasized about this kind of analysis. Our data suggest that there may be an asymmetry between the memories of acquisition and extinction episodes. When the context is shifted following extinction, we often obtain evidence that is consistent with the notion that the animal has failed to retrieve the memory of extinction. By contrast, Bouton and King have repeatedly found little forgetting about acquisition when, immediately following acquisition, the context is similarly shifted. It is possible that extinction memories are more dependent on contextual retrieval than are acquisition memories. On the other hand, we might wonder whether the rat's memory is as easily disrupted by a change of context as the present analysis would assume.

We would not deny that contexts can serve as retrieval cues; the phenomenon has been well documented (e.g., Spear, 1973). But it may be noted that even when memory deficits result from a change of context, a good deal of learned material can often still be retrieved. For example, in the human memory studies reported by Smith (1979), subjects that received a context shift following learning still remembered approximately 70% as much as subjects that received no such shift. Outside of the dentist's office, we can remember that the dentist has hurt us. But note that there is still an effect of the context here. Even though the memory of this painful US can be retrieved when we are in a different context, we are not afraid. Thus, there is a sense in which contexts help us to evaluate memories that have already been retrieved.

Contexts and the Resolution of Ambiguity

It seems possible that the rat remembers much more than it is usually given credit for. Is it unreasonable to suppose that, in extinction, the rat may still remember the US, that the CS and US have been paired, and that the CS has sometimes occurred without the US? Such a notion would be consistent with the ease with which the effects of extinction can often be reversed. In extinction, the problem may not be the fallibility of the subject's memory but, indeed, that the subject may remember too much.

We have previously noted that the various results we have reviewed here fall into a pattern. Contextual cues are critical in supporting the renewal effect, the reinstatement effect, and the effects of retaining the US in extinction. In each case, the CS has been extinguished at some point in the procedure. And, of course, the CS has also been conditioned at some earlier point. In other words, in each of these experimental procedures, prior to the key manipulation of the context, the animal is exposed at one time to CS–US pairings and at another time to the CS alone. If the rat were capable of remembering both types of episodes, the CS, by itself, would convey a mixed message; it would be ambiguous. Perhaps this is also true of the latent inhibition procedure, in which the CS is first presented alone and then later presented with shock. In situations in which we have observed a role of the context, the CS has been made ambiguous by being both presented alone and paired with shock.

The central feature of ambiguous stimuli is that their meaning cannot be resolved without reference to their contexts. Suppose that you are asked to define an ambiguous word, such as "bear." You might be inclined to think of a large mammal, particularly if you were provided with an additional word that provides a context: "grizzly bear." But suppose instead that you are presented with "bear" in a different context: "bear fruit." Here, of course, the meaning of the target stimulus is entirely different. So too with the word "fire" in the movie theater and the shooting gallery. Although our responses to verbal stimuli are probably always influenced by context, appropriate responses to stimuli with double meanings are almost by definition dependent on context.

This notion suggests an account of the overall pattern of our results. We suggest that the animal might be capable of remembering some sense of the history of a CS's reinforcement and nonreinforcement, and that whatever memories this capability requires are all activated by the CS. When a CS with a history of both reinforcement and nonreinforcement episodes is presented, the animal therefore appreciates, in some sense, the ambiguity of the information provided by the CS. And as we have illustrated above, contexts might be expected to be especially important in determining the response to such an ambiguous CS. When confronted with a CS that conveys ambiguous information, the animal responds in terms of what the context signals. With a stimulus that is not ambiguous, the context is less critical. One function of the context is to resolve the ambiguity of ambiguous conditioned stimuli.

Are the signaling properties of the context "associative"? Certainly they can be, as our results with the reinstatement paradigm suggest. But our results with the renewal effect suggest that they may not need to be. Terms like *excitation* and *inhibition* are so deeply entrenched in the associationistic data language of learning theory that it is difficult to think of nonassociative signaling properties. But there appears to be a sense in which a context can provide a signal about whether or not a CS will be followed by a US that is independent of its excitatory or inhibitory associations with the US (see also Rescorla, Durlach, & Grau, this volume). Perhaps the contexts in our experiments provided a superordinate signal about whether the animal was in an acquisition or an extinction episode. The present analysis suggests, however, that such a signal would have provided information with which active memories were evaluated, instead of serving as a retrieval cue.

Conclusion

Jenkins (1974) has distinguished between the views of the associationist and the "contextualist" in the analysis of human memory. The associationist assumes that memory (or, perhaps, behavior) can be understood by an analysis into basic units (stimuli or responses) that are related to one another by a set of basic relations (such as excitatory and inhibitory associations) that concatenate to form the structure underlying complex behaviors. The contextualist, by contrast, understands behavior in terms of psychologically fused events, which derive their meaning from contexts. The contextualist position does more than point to the role of apparatus cues in the control of behavior; it supposes that events "sheer away" into other and larger contexts, such as the subject's prior experience. It is a view that has rarely been taken in animal learning theory. Yet, some of the hypotheses that we have discussed in the latter portions of this chapter are decidedly contextualistic. Thus we have found it useful to speak of acquisition and extinction episodes as if these phases of our experiments were fused as events in the mind of the animal. And perhaps more fundamentally, we have found it useful to think of the animal's momentary reaction to the CS within the larger context of the animal's overall history of experience with the CS.

ACKNOWLEDGMENT

Preparation of the manuscript, and most of the recent research reported here, were supported by National Science Foundation Grant BNS 81–05401 to M.E.B.

REFERENCES

Anderson, D. C., O'Farrell, T., Formica, R., & Caponigri, V. Preconditioning CS exposure: Variation in place of conditioning and of presentation. *Psychonomic Science,* 1969, *15,* 54–55.

Anderson, D. C., Wolf, D., & Sullivan, P. Preconditioning exposures to the CS: Variation in place of testing. *Psychonomic Science,* 1969, *14,* 233–235.

Annau, Z., & Kamin, L. J. The conditioned emotional response as a function of intensity of the US. *Journal of Comparative and Physiological Psychology,* 1961, *54,* 428–432.

Archer, T., & Sjödén, P.-O. Environment-dependent taste aversion extinction: A question of stimulus novelty at conditioning. *Physiological Psychology,* 1981, *9,* 102–108.

Archer, T., Sjödén, P.-O., Nilsson, L. G., & Carter, N. Role of exteroceptive background context in taste-aversion conditioning and extinction. *Animal Learning & Behavior,* 1979, *7,* 17–22.

Archer, T., Sjödén, P.-O., Nilsson, L. G., & Carter, N. Exteroceptive context in taste-aversion conditioning and extinction: Odour, cage, and bottle stimuli. *Quarterly Journal of Experimental Psychology,* 1980, *32,* 197–214.

Ayres, J. J. B., & Benedict, J. O. US-alone presentations as an extinction procedure. *Animal Learning & Behavior,* 1973, *1,* 5–8.

Baker, A. G. Conditioned inhibition arising from a between-sessions negative correlation. *Journal of Experimental Psychology: Animal Behavior Processes,* 1977, *3,* 144–155.

Baker, A. G., Mercier, P., Gabel, J., & Baker, P. A. Contextual conditioning and the US preexposure effect in conditioned fear. *Journal of Experimental Psychology: Animal Behavior Processes,* 1981, *7,* 109–128.

Balaz, M. A., Capra, S., Hartl, P., & Miller, R. R. Contextual potentiation of acquired behavior after devaluing direct context-US associations. *Learning and Motivation,* 1981, *12,* 383–397.

Balaz, M. A., Capra, S., Kasprow, W. J., & Miller, R. R. Latent inhibition of the conditioning context: Further evidence of contextual potentiation of retrieval in the absence of appreciable context-US associations. *Animal Learning & Behavior*, 1982, *10*, 242–248.

Balsam, P. D. Bringing the background to the foreground: The role of contextual cues in autoshaping. In M. Commons, R. Herrnstein, & A. R. Wagner (Eds.), *Quantitative analyses of behavior: Volume 3: Acquisition*. Cambridge, Mass.: Ballinger, 1984.

Blanchard, R. J., & Blanchard, D. C. Crouching as an index of fear. *Journal of Comparative and Physiological Psychology*, 1969, *67*, 370–375.

Bolles, R. C., & Collier, A. C. The effect of predictive cues on freezing in rats. *Animal Learning & Behavior*, 1976, *4*, 6–8.

Bouton, M. E. *Role of conditioned contextual stimuli in two effects of retaining the unconditioned stimulus during extinction*. Unpublished doctoral dissertation, University of Washington, 1980.

Bouton, M. E. Lack of reinstatement of an extinguished taste aversion. *Animal Learning & Behavior*, 1982, *10*, 233–241.

Bouton, M. E. Differential control by context in the inflation and reinstatement paradigms. *Journal of Experimental Psychology: Animal Behavior Processes*, 1984, *10*, 56–74.

Bouton, M. E., & Bolles, R. C. Contextual control of the extinction of conditioned fear. *Learning and Motivation*, 1979, *10*, 445–466. (a)

Bouton, M. E., & Bolles, R. C. Role of conditioned contextual stimuli in reinstatement of extinguished fear. *Journal of Experimental Psychology: Animal Behavior Processes*, 1979, *5*, 368–378. (b)

Bouton, M. E., & Bolles, R. C. Conditioned fear assessed by freezing and by the suppression of three different baselines. *Animal Learning & Behavior*, 1980, *8*, 429–434.

Bouton, M. E., & King, D. A. Contextual control of the extinction of conditioned fear: Tests for the associative value of the context. *Journal of Experimental Psychology: Animal Behavior Processes*, 1983, *9*, 248–265.

Chorazyna, H. Some properties of conditioned inhibition. *Acta Biologiae Experimentalis*, 1962, *22*, 5–13.

Cunningham, C. L. Alcohol as a cue for extinction: State dependency produced by conditioned inhibition. *Animal Learning & Behavior*, 1979, *7*, 45–52.

Dexter, W. R., & Merrill, H. K. Role of contextual discrimination in fear conditioning. *Journal of Comparative and Physiological Psychology*, 1969, *69*, 677–681.

Dweck, C. S., & Wagner, A. R. Situational cues and correlation between CS and US as determinants of the conditioned emotional response. *Psychonomic Science*, 1970, *18*, 145–147.

Estes, W. K. Memory and conditioning. In F. J. McGuigan & D. B. Lumsden (Eds.), *Contemporary approaches to conditioning and learning*. Washington, D. C.: Winston, 1973.

Fanselow, M. S. Extinction of contextual fear and preference for signaled shock. *Bulletin of the Psychonomic Society*, 1980, *16*, 458–460. (a)

Fanselow, M. S. Signaled shock-free periods and preference for signaled shock. *Journal of Experimental Psychology: Animal Behavior Processes*, 1980, *6*, 65–80. (b)

Fanselow, M. S. Conditional and unconditional components of post-shock freezing. *Pavlovian Journal of Biological Science*, 1980, *15*, 177–182. (c)

Frey, P. W., & Butler, C. S. Extinction after aversive conditioning: An associative or nonassociative process? *Learning and Motivation*, 1977, *8*, 1–17.

Frey, P. W., & Sears, R. J. Model of conditioning incorporating the Rescorla–Wagner associative axiom, a dynamic attention process, and a catastrophe rule. *Psychological Review*, 1978, *85*, 321–340.

Hendry, J. Summation of undetected excitation following extinction of the CER. *Animal Learning & Behavior*, 1982, *10*, 476–482.

Hoffman, H. S. The stimulus generalization of conditioned suppression. In D. I. Mostofsky (Ed.), *Stimulus generalization*. Stanford, Calif.: Stanford University Press, 1965.

Jenkins, J. J. Remember that old theory of memory? Well, forget it! *American Psychologist*, 1974, *29*, 785–795.

Kamin, L. J. "Attention-like" processes in classical conditioning. In M. R. Jones (Ed.), *Miami Symposium on the prediction of behavior, 1967: Aversive stimulation.* Coral Gables: University of Miami Press, 1968.

Kasprow, W. J., Schachtman, T., Cacheiro, H., & Miller, R. R. *Extinction does not depend upon degradation of event memories.* Unpublished manuscript, 1982.

Konorski, J., & Szwejkowska, G. Chronic extinction and restoration of conditioned reflexes. I. Extinction against the excitatory background. *Acta Biologiae Experimentalis,* 1950, *15,* 155–170.

Konorski, J., & Szwejkowska, G. Chronic extinction and restoration of conditioned reflexes. III. Defensive motor reflexes. *Acta Biologiae Experimentalis,* 1952, *16,* 91–94.

Mackintosh, N. J. A theory of attention: Variations in the associability of stimuli with reinforcement. *Psychological Review,* 1975, *82,* 276–298. (a)

Mackintosh, N. J. Blocking of conditioned suppression: Role of the first compound trial. *Journal of Experimental Psychology: Animal Behavior Processes,* 1975, *1,* 335–345. (b)

Medin, D. L. Animal models and memory models. In D. L. Medin, W. A. Roberts, & R. T. Davis (Eds.), *Processes of animal memory.* Hillsdale, N. J.: Lawrence Erlbaum Associates, 1976.

Nadel, L., & Willner, J. Context and conditioning: A place for space. *Physiological Psychology,* 1980, *8,* 218–228.

Odling–Smee, F. J. The role of background stimuli during Pavlovian conditioning. *Quarterly Journal of Experimental Psychology,* 1975, *27,* 201–209.

Pearce, J. M., & Hall, G. A model for Pavlovian learning: Variations in the effectiveness of conditioned but not of unconditioned stimuli. *Psychological Review,* 1980, *87,* 532–552.

Quinsey, V. L., & Ayres, J. J. B. Shock-induced facilitation of a partially extinguished CER. *Psychonomic Science,* 1969, *14,* 213–214.

Randich, A. The US preexposure phenomenon in the conditioned suppression paradigm: A role for conditioned situational stimuli. *Learning and Motivation,* 1981, *12,* 321–341.

Randich, A., & Haggard, D. Exposure to the unconditioned stimulus alone: Effects on retention and acquisition of conditioned suppression. *Journal of Experimental Psychology: Animal Behavior Processes,* 1983, *9,* 147–159.

Randich, A., & LoLordo, V. M. Associative and nonassociative theories of the UCS preexposure phenomenon: Implications for Pavlovian conditioning. *Psychological Bulletin,* 1979, *86,* 523–548.

Randich, A., & Rescorla, R. A. The effects of separate presentations of the US on conditioned suppresion. *Animal Learning & Behavior,* 1981, *9,* 56–64.

Reberg, D. Compound tests for excitation in early acquisition and after prolonged extinction of conditioned suppression. *Learning and Motivation,* 1972, *3,* 246–258.

Rescorla, R. A. Information variables in Pavlovian conditioning. In G. H. Bower (Ed.), *The psychology of learning and motivation* (Vol. 6). New York: Academic Press, 1972.

Rescorla, R. A. Effects of US habituation following conditioning. *Journal of Comparative and Physiological Psychology,* 1973, *82,* 137–143.

Rescorla, R. A. Effect of inflation of the unconditioned stimulus value following conditioning. *Journal of Comparative and Physiological Psychology,* 1974, *86,* 101–106.

Rescorla, R. A. Conditioned inhibition and extinction. In A. Dickinson & R. A. Boakes (Eds.), *Mechanisms of learning and motivation: A memorial volume to Jerzy Konorski.* Hillsdale, N. J.: Lawrence Erlbaum Associates, 1979.

Rescorla, R. A., & Cunningham, C. L. The erasure of reinstated fear. *Animal Learning & Behavior,* 1977, *5,* 386–394.

Rescorla, R. A., & Cunningham, C. L. Recovery of the US representation over time during extinction. *Learning and Motivation,* 1978, *9,* 373–391.

Rescorla, R. A., & Heth, C. D. Reinstatement of fear to an extinguished conditioned stimulus. *Journal of Experimental Psychology: Animal Behavior Processes,* 1975, *1,* 88–96.

Rescorla, R. A., & Holland, P. C. Associations in Pavlovian inhibition. *Learning and Motivation,* 1977, *8,* 429–447.

Rescorla, R. A., & Wagner, A. R. A theory of Pavlovian conditioning: Variations in the effectiveness of reinforcement and nonreinforcement. In A. Black & W. F. Prokasy (Eds.), *Classical conditioning II.* New York: Appleton–Century–Crofts, 1972.

Richards, R. W., & Sargent, D. M. The order of presentation of conditioned stimuli during extinction. *Animal Learning & Behavior,* 1983, *11,* 229–236.

Seligman, M. E. P. Chronic fear produced by unpredictable electric shock. *Journal of Comparative and Physiological Psychology,* 1968, *66,* 402–411.

Sheafor, P. J. "Pseudoconditioned" jaw movements of the rabbit reflect associations conditioned to contextual background cues. *Journal of Experimental Psychology: Animal Behavior Processes,* 1975, *1,* 245–260.

Sherman, J. E. US inflation with trace and simultaneous fear conditioning. *Animal Learning & Behavior,* 1978, *6,* 463–468.

Siegel, S. Morphine tolerance acquisition as an associative process. *Journal of Experimental Psychology: Animal Behavior Processes,* 1977, *3,* 1–13.

Smith, S. M. Remembering in and out of context. *Journal of Experimental Psychology: Human Learning and Memory,* 1979, *5,* 460–471.

Spear, N. E. Retrieval of memory in animals. *Psychological Review,* 1973, *80,* 163–194.

Spence, K. W. Extinction of the human eyelid CR as a function of presence or absence of the UCS during extinction. *Journal of Experimental Psychology,* 1966, *71,* 642–648.

Tomie, A. Interference with autoshaping by prior context conditioning. *Journal of Experimental Psychology: Animal Behavior Processes,* 1976, *2,* 323–334.

Uhl, C. N. Eliminating behavior with omission and extinction after varying amounts of training. *Animal Learning & Behavior,* 1973, *1,* 237–240.

Uhl, C. N., & Garcia, E. E. Comparison of omission with extinction in response elimination in rats. *Journal of Comparative and Physiological Psychology,* 1969, *69,* 554–562.

Wagner, A. R. Stimulus selection and a "modified continuity theory." In G. H. Bower & J. T. Spence (Eds.), *The psychology of learning and motivation* (Vol. 3). New York: Academic Press, 1969.

Wagner, A. R. Priming in STM: An information-processing mechanism for self-generated or retrieval-generated depression in performance. In T. J. Tighe & R. N. Leaton (Eds.), *Habituation: Perspectives from child development, animal behavior, and neurophysiology.* Hillsdale, N. J.: Lawrence Erlbaum Associates, 1976.

Wagner, A. R., & Rescorla, R. A. Inhibition in Pavlovian conditioning: Application of a theory. In R. A. Boakes & M. S. Halliday (Eds.), *Inhibition and learning.* London/New York: Academic Press, 1972.

Welker, R. L., & McAuley, K. Reductions in resistance to extinction and spontaneous recovery as a function of changes in transportational and contextual stimuli. *Animal Learning & Behavior,* 1978, *6,* 451–457.

7 The Several Roles of Context at the Time of Retrieval

Ralph R. Miller
Todd R. Schachtman
State University of New York at Binghamton

Stimulus differences between the locations in which acquisition and testing occurred were long ago found to have a strong and usually detrimental effect upon test performance across a wide variety of species, as well as tasks including both classical conditioning and instrumental learning (e.g., Carr, 1917; Pan, 1926; Smith & Guthrie, 1921; Watson, 1907). We refer to this phenomenon as the *contextual cue effect*. Often it is manifest in stimulus control being demonstrated by seemingly irrelevant aspects of the training context. For example, Riccio, Urda, and Thomas (1966) found that keypecking for grain by pigeons decreased as the angle of the grid floor deviated from that which prevailed at the time of training. Moreover, Bouton and Bolles (1979; this volume) found that the manifest extinction of an association is greatest in the context in which extinction takes place relative to either the training context or a third location. Thus, the contextual cue effect appears to apply to extinction as well as acquisition.

Although the importance of similarity between the test context and acquisition context has been repeatedly demonstrated, efforts to understand the bases of the contextual cue effect were uncommon before 1972. Around that time, several researchers suggested that elements of the training context (i.e., background cues) may act as conditioned stimuli (CSs) during a test trial with associative consequences that *summate* with those of nominal CSs (e.g., Rescorla & Wagner, 1972). A similar view arose among cognitive psychologists except they referred to the CSs as retrieval cues (e.g., Falkenberg, 1972). These investigators substantiated the long-held belief (e.g., Estes, 1950; Pavlov, 1927) that, despite the experimenter's best efforts to make the subject attend exclusively to the nominal controlling stimuli, the test context influenced behavior through direct associations between it and any reinforcers that had previously been presented there. Recent interest in context effects has stimulated research indicating that the summation hypothesis is valid but not a complete explanation of the complex effects of context at the time of retrieval. This chapter reviews some of the associative roles played by the training and test contexts at the time of testing. First, factors contributing to the contextual cue effect are discussed. Then we discuss the comparator hypothesis, which is an additional associative effect that appears to influence the manifestation of acquired associations and has profound implications for the way in which conditioned inhibition might be conceptualized.

As our intention is to focus on associative consequences of context during testing, we do not dwell on nonassociative contributions to the contextual cue effect that arise from both sensory adaptation to the test context and habituation of unconditioned responses elicited by the test context (Randich & Ross, this volume; Randich & LoLordo, 1979). However, if these unconditioned effects are incompatible with the target response and are less prevalent in the training context when it is used for testing than in an alternative test context, unconditioned responses will differentially compete with the target behavior in the two contexts to the detriment of the target performance in the nonacquisition context. This effect of unconditioned competing responses can be considerable and should not be neglected. Owing to our present interest in the associative effects of context, the differential contribution of unconditioned response competition to different groups in the present experiments from our laboratory was minimized by equating contextual novelty and counterbalancing within groups which enclosure was used for testing.

For purposes of presentation, we refer to the contextual cues constituting any one location as if they were fully configured as "context," rather than their being processed as a collection of separate background stimuli. However, the roles of context that are discussed here do not depend in any major way on whether the background cues are processed as separate elements or configured as "context." Total configuring is obviously an oversimplification, but a common assumption due to our present ignorance concerning both the actual extent of configuring and the degree to which configuring varies both over time with respect to a single context and between different contexts. Furthermore, total configuring of each context may be a fairly accurate description in that elements of a context ordinarily share a common onset and offset history, as well as a common reinforcement history from which the animal's experience departs only to the extent that attention may not be uniformly distributed to all contextual attributes.

The Summation Hypothesis

By far the most common explanation of the contextual cue effect is that contexts become associated to reinforcers just as nominal CSs do, and the associative strength of the test context is apt to summate (although not necessarily in a purely algebraic fashion) with that of the nominal CSs, thereby influencing the observed test performance. Indirect evidence supportive of summation has been available at least since Pavlov (1927) observed that his previously conditioned dogs increased their rate of salivation immediately upon being strapped into their harnesses (i.e., prior to the day's first presentation of the CS). Several of the other chapters in this volume (e.g., Baker et al.; Medin & Reynolds; Randich & Ross; Rescorla, Durlach, & Grau) describe and analyze specific instances of associative summation; thus, our description of the phenomenon is abbreviated, our purpose being to outline the various consequences of associative summation so that its interaction with the other roles of test context can be fully appreciated.

Although direct associations between the context and the unconditioned stimulus (US) are assumed to follow the same rules as those between nominal CSs and the US, the spatial–temporal characteristics of the context are ordinarily quite different from those of a nominal CS. Specifically, the typical nominal CS is highly localized in space and time (i.e., discrete), whereas the typical context is far more prolonged in time and diffuse in space. These distinctions have numerous consequences. For example, the continuing presence of the context during a training session should permit substantial extinction to the context between trials (but see Gibbon & Balsam, 1981, for an alternative view). Thus, summative contributions by the context to the contextual cue effect can be expected to be greater with short intertrial intervals than with long intertrial intervals. However, data consistent with this prediction are rarely seen due to context-US pairings usually occurring concurrently with the conditioning of discrete CSs. Because of the apparent competition for associative strength that frequently results from compound conditioning of discrete CSs and context (Rescorla & Wagner, 1972; but see Gibbon & Balsam, 1981), the associative weakness of the context produced by long intertrial intervals is ordinarily accompanied by effectively stronger associations to the discrete CSs. Therefore, this hypothesized superiority of context-US associations produced by short as opposed to long intertrial intervals should be evident only when test conditions favor manifestation of direct associations to the context (see later), *and* when differences in associations to discrete CSs have been corrected for or eliminated. Additionally, nonassociative effects of US-alone presentations would have to be taken into consideration (Randich & Ross, this volume).

Beneficial and Detrimental Effects of Direct Associations to the Test Context. In an animal's natural habitat, the more similar a context is to a previously encountered context, the more likely it is that the reinforcement contingencies in force will be the same as those that prevailed in the previous context. Thus, the greater "expectation" of reinforcement that results from testing in contexts similar to that of training is often consistent with the actual reinforcement contingencies. In other words, direct associations between the context and the reinforcer appear to augment "expectation" of the reinforcer in just those situations in which reinforcement is most apt to occur, an effect that normally increases the correlation between an animal's "expectations" and subsequent events. Presumably this increased correlation is advantageous to the animal in dealing with environmental problems. Put in more molecular terms, stimulus generalization between similar contexts is ordinarily advantageous for much the same reasons that stimulus generalization between discrete stimuli is ordinarily advantageous.

Direct context-reinforcer associations have frequently been proposed to account for the contextual cue effect, but only in a few instances has the context-US strength been directly manipulated to support the validity of this position. In one such study, Pearce and Hall (1979) found that rats shaped to leverpress for food decreased their rate of leverpressing if prior to the test they were exposed to the experimental context with the lever absent. This appears to demonstrate the partial extinction of direct associations to the context and, hence, the existence of such associations.

Although direct associations to the context ordinarily enhance test performance when testing occurs in the acquisition context, performance can be impaired when the context has direct associations to memories inconsistent with the target memory. For instance, Spear, Smith, Bryan, Gordon, Timmons, and Chiszar (1980) demonstrated the occurrence of such interference effects using rats trained on active and passive avoidance in the presence of different contextual cues. When subjects were tested on one type of task in the presence of the contextual cues associated with the other task, performance was distinctly impaired. Thus compared to a "neutral" test context, direct associations to the context can either facilitate or impair test performance as a function of the degree to which the test context is directly associated to the target memory or an incompatible memory. However, given the relative consistency of reinforcement contingencies within a given environment, facilitation is probably far more common a consequence of direct context-reinforcer associations than is impairment. In fact impairment may be largely a laboratory phenomenon, for behavioral researchers are far more apt to change contingencies in a given environment than is Mother Nature.

Competition Between Discrete CSs and the Conditioning Context During Acquisition. Although we have described the summation-induced superior performance of animals *tested* with similar training and test contexts (relative to those trained in dissimilar contexts) as enhancement in the "similar context" condition, there is reason to think that this difference can be better conceptualized as an impairment in the "different context" condition. Seemingly deficient acquisition with respect to a discrete CS is often seen when *training* occurs in the presence of a better correlated or more salient stimulus (i.e., blocking or overshadowing). Whatever the underlying processes (e.g., Mackintosh, 1975; Pearce & Hall, 1980; Rescorla & Wagner, 1972), these deficits speak for some kind of effective limit on the total associative strength accrued by all the stimuli (context included) present during conditioning to a common US. Thus, the training context can be regarded as competing with the nominal CSs for effective associative strength. Relatively strong contextual associations, usually at the expense of accrument of behavioral control by the discrete CSs, have been observed when there are a few conditioning trials, a high density of trials (i.e., a short intertrial interval), a distinctive or novel context, a low saliency discrete CS, or a strong US (e.g., Imada, Yamazaki, & Morishita, 1981; Odling–Smee, 1978). One consequence of this competition is that the reactivation of the US representation resulting from the summated associative strength of the nominal CSs and the conditioning context is no greater than that resulting from the CSs alone if the conditioning context had accrued no associative strength. Consequently, that part of the performance difference seen between testing in the conditioning context and testing in some other context, which arises from direct associations between the conditioning context and the US, can be viewed as a deficit relative to the effective associative strength of the discrete CSs had there been "no context" present during acquisition.

Thus we see that direct context-US associations, although behaviorally summative with the discrete CS–US associations at the time of testing, often compete with these same associations during acquisition. This trade-off between the conditioning context and discrete CSs during training is a major tenet of several conditioning theories (e.g., Pearce & Hall, 1980; Rescorla & Wagner, 1972; Wagner, 1978) and has been used to explain a number of common phenomena in conditioning. For example, sequential overshadowing of the CS by the context has been proposed as the basis of the superiority of delay conditioning over trace conditioning (Marlin, 1981). Notably, testing in the conditioning context does not always result in associative summation completely compensating for the loss of behavioral control by the discrete CS due to competition during acquisition; summation appears to occur only under select test conditions even when the test context has considerable associative strength. The particular test conditions that favor CS-context summation are discussed later.

Context-CS Associations.   Although our analysis of direct associations to the context has emphasized context-US relations, under select circumstances the formation of context-CS associations could be expected. Wagner (1978) has proposed that such associations are responsible for the phenomenon of latent inhibition and long-term habituation. Empirical analyses of Wagner's proposals have found them wanting (Baker & Mercier, 1982; Marlin & Miller, 1981). However, under certain conditions context-CS associations appear able to support second-order conditioning (Marlin, 1982; Rescorla, Durlach, & Grau, this volume). As we cannot constructively add to the comments of Rescorla et al. concerning the role of context-CS associations, we merely acknowledge their existence and note that such associations appear to act like CS_1–CS_2 associations. Hence, the summation hypothesis appears to hold as readily for them as for context-US associations (i.e., a context can function in all respects like a discrete CS with associative consequences that summate with discrete CSs just as the associative consequences of diverse discrete CSs summate).

Contextual Potentiation of Retrieval of Nominal CS–US Associations

Despite the available evidence for direct context-US associations summating with CS–US associations during testing, some investigators have argued for a second means by which the conditioning context can facilitate test performance. Konorski (1967) proposed that the conditioning context could enhance the behavioral control of nominal CSs, and Estes (1973), Medin (1975; Medin & Reynolds, this volume), and Spear (1973) were more explicit in suggesting that the conditioning context acts as a retrieval cue for associations between nominal CSs and the US. In a similar vein, Nadel and Willner (1980; Nadel et al., this volume) have suggested that a hierarchical relationship exists in which the conditioning context predicts CS–US associations (i.e., the context "sets the occasion" for the CS–US association, see Holland, in press), or alternatively stated, the context is in some sense a conditional discriminative stimulus.

Evidence for Potentiated Retrieval of CS–US Associations by the Acquisition Context. Although introspection and anecdote tended to support the need, in addition to direct context-US associations, for some sort of facilitated retrieval of CS–US associations in the presence of the conditioning context, until recently there was little direct evidence bearing on the issue. Over the last few years our laboratory has pursued a research program of looking for the contextual cue effect under various circumstances that minimized the contribution of context-US associations. As it turned out, the problem was not in eliminating context-US associations, but in documenting that we had done so completely. Without such evidence, any remaining contextual cue effect could have been explained by residual context-US associations that were too small to be seen in their own right (i.e., below some behavioral threshold) but were sufficient to summate with the associative strength of the discrete target CS during testing. Thus, we required a behavioral measure that would be sensitive to potential subthreshold residual context-US associations. This need was met by a summation test in which the associative strength of the conditioning context with respect to the US was compared to that of a distinctly different neutral context, in the presence of an excitatory nontarget CS that had previously been paired with the US in a third context quite dissimilar to both the conditioning and neutral contexts used in testing. The nontarget CS conditioning parameters were selected to yield lick suppression similar to that induced by the target CS in the neutral test context. Consequently, any residual association between the conditioning context and US should have equal impact on the target CS and nontarget CS. Each of the following experiments employed this strategy while measuring lick suppression in rats. To avoid ceiling effects that might have obscured important differences between groups, a maximum suppression latency of 3600 sec to complete 50 licks was permitted before a test trial was terminated.

In our first experiment, following the suggestions of Imada, Yamazaki, and Morishita (1981) and Odling–Smee (1978), a relatively large number of conditioning trials was used in conjunction with a low-intensity footshock (US) in an effort to minimize direct associations between the acquisition context and the US (Balaz, Capra, Hartl, & Miller, 1981, Experiment 1). First, all subjects were water deprived and shaped to drink water (lick) in two enclosures, designated Y and Z. (The physical enclosures identified as Y and Z were counterbalanced within each group.) Next, each rat was exposed to click–footshock pairings in a third enclosure, X. Then all subjects received pairings of the target stimulus (tone) with footshock in Enclosure Y. Notably, Enclosure X, Y, and Z had been selected to be distinctly different along numerous dimensions including shape, size, floor texture, odor, and background illumination. Moreover, our click stimulus had previously been found not to generalize appreciably to the tone. The subjects were then divided into four groups, two of which were tested for suppression to the tone (T) and two of which were tested for suppression to the click (C), both relative to ongoing preCS lick rates of 6–8 licks per second (i.e., .85 log sec for 50 licks). One group from each of these test conditions was tested in Enclosure Y (i.e., the tone-conditioning location), and the remaining two groups were tested in Enclosure Z (i.e., a location in which footshock had never been given). In order to maximize associative summation between the test CS (click or tone) and test context during the test session, the CS was present from the moment a subject was placed in its test context. The treatments and results are illustrated in Table 7.1. Because we could not be certain that the tone and clicks were of equivalent saliency, comparisons were made only between subjects tested with the same CS.

TABLE 7.1
Experiment 1[a]

Group	Stage 1	Stage 2	Test Condition	Test Suppression[b]
CY	CX+	TY+	CY	2.45 ± .28
CZ	CX+	TY+	CZ	2.30 ± .19
TY	CX+	TY+	TY	2.84 ± .10
TZ	CX+	TY+	TZ	1.63 ± .25

[a]C = clicks; T = tone; X, Y, and Z = three distinctly different contexts; + = footshock.

[b]Mean latency to complete 50 licks ± standard error (log sec). Compare .85 log sec to emit 50 licks in either context in the absence of a CS.

A comparison between subjects tested for suppression to the nontarget CS (C) in conditioning context (Y) and nonconditioning context (Z) (i.e., Groups CY and CZ) found no difference in suppression scores, which is indicative of our having succeeded in minimizing associations between the conditioning context and the US. Nonetheless, Group TY displayed far greater suppression to the tone than Group TZ, despite the two groups having received identical conditioning to the tone. This difference documents the occurrence of the contextual cue effect in the absence of any demonstrable association between the test context in which conditioning had occurred (Enclosure Y) and the US. Thus, although direct context-US associations when present may contribute to the contextual cue effect, they are not the sole source of the effect.

In two further studies, conditioning parameters that permitted the formation of context-US associations were employed. Both studies included the same basic four groups as were employed in the previous experiment, except that now half the subjects in each group received some further treatment to degrade the context-US associations.

In one study (Balaz, Capra, Hartl, & Miller, 1981, Experiment 2), associations to the conditioning context were created by increasing the shock intensity and decreasing the number of trials relative to the preceding experiment. (The effectiveness of these modifications was demonstrated by their behavioral consequences.) Then the effects of direct context-US associations were eliminated in half the animals through contextual extinction (E) occurring between conditioning and testing (i.e., prolonged exposure to Enclosures Y and Z in the absence of discrete CS or US presentations). The group treatments and results of this experiment are depicted in Table 7.2. Group CY displayed more suppression than Group CZ, which is indicative of direct associations between Enclosure Y (the

TABLE 7.2
Experiment 2[a]

Group	Stage 1	Stage 2	Stage 3[b]	Test Condition	Test Suppression[c]
CY	CX+	TY+	—	CY	3.20 ± .08
CZ	CX+	TY+	—	CZ	2.65 ± .13
TY	CX+	TY+	—	TY	3.14 ± .14
TZ	CX+	TY+	—	TZ	2.29 ± .29
CYE	CX+	TY+	Y, Z	CY	1.74 ± .36
CZE	CX+	TY+	Y, Z	CZ	1.60 ± .29
TYE	CX+	TY+	Y, Z	TY	2.56 ± .31
TZE	CX+	TY+	Y, Z	TZ	1.40 ± .18

[a]C = clicks; T = tone; X, Y, and Z = three distinctly different contexts; E = extinction to Enclosures Y and Z; + = footshock.
[b]Four 30-min exposures to both Enclosures Y and Z (Extinction).
[c]Mean latency to complete 50 licks ± standard error (log sec). Compare to .85 log sec to emit 50 licks in either context in the absence of a CS.

site of tone conditioning) and footshock. Consistent with the conventional contextual cue effect, Group TY yielded greater suppression than Group TZ. The effectiveness of extinction to Enclosures Y and Z is evident in the similarity of Groups CYE and CZE, relative to the pronounced difference between Groups CY and CZ. The extinction-induced decreases in latency seen across both CSs and both test contexts indicate that the extinction manipulation attenuated both associative and nonassociative reluctance to drink in Contexts Y and Z. More importantly, Group TYE showed more suppression than Group TZE despite the lack of context-US associations in these groups that can be inferred from Groups CYE and CZE. Thus, context-US associations when present are seen to contribute to the contextual cue effect, but the effect appears to remain even after associations between the conditioning context and the US have been effectively extinguished.

In a third experiment, latent inhibition to Enclosures Y and Z was employed to prevent the formation of context-US associations (Balaz, Capra, Kasprow, & Miller, 1982). Specifically, the same eight groups were included as were used in our second study except that, in place of postconditioning contextual exposure (extinction), half the groups received extensive preconditioning exposure (latent inhibition treatment) to both Enclosures Y and Z (Y being the conditioning enclosure for all animals). The treatments and suppression scores from this experiment are illustrated in Table 7.3. The superior suppression of Group SHCY relative to Group SHCZ speaks for the existence of context-US associations in animals that did not receive latent inhibition treatment. The conventional contextual cue effect can be seen in the greater suppression of Group SHTY relative to Group SHTZ. The effectiveness of our latent inhibition treatment is

TABLE 7.3
Experiment 3[a]

Group	Latent Inhibition[b]	Click Conditioning	Tone Conditioning	Test Condition	Test Suppression[c]
SHCY	—	CX+	TY+	CY	3.10 ± .08
SHCZ	—	CX+	TZ+	CY	2.19 ± .29
SHTY	—	CX+	TY+	TY	3.17 ± .10
SHTZ	—	CX+	TZ+	TY	2.75 ± .07
LICY	Y, Z	CX+	TY+	CY	1.53 ± .27
LICZ	Y, Z	CX+	TZ+	CY	1.62 ± .24
LITY	Y, Z	CX+	TY+	TY	2.77 ± .14
LITZ	Y, Z	CX+	TZ+	TY	1.67 ± .25

[a]C = clicks; T = tone; X, Y, Z = three distinctly different contexts; LI = latent inhibition to Enclosures Y and Z; + = footshock.

[b]Six 1-hr exposures to Enclosure Y and Enclosure Z (one session after lick shaping on each of Days 1–4, one after Click Conditioning on Day 5, and one prior to Tone Conditioning on Day 6).

[c]Mean latency to complete 50 licks ± standard error (log sec). Compare to .85 log sec to emit 50 licks in either context in the absence of a CS.

evident in the highly similar scores of Groups LICY and LICZ. Yet, despite the effectiveness of the preconditioning exposures to Enclosures Y and Z in preventing direct context-US associations, the contextual cue effect is still to be observed in the greater suppression of Group LITY relative to Group LITZ. As in the last experiment, we see that context-US associations, when present, contribute to the superior test performance that ordinarily occurs in the conditioning context compared to testing outside of it. However, this contribution is obviously not essential for the occurrence of a contextual cue effect.

Each of our three experiments demonstrate the occurrence of contextual potentiation of retrieval of an acquired association. Adding to the generality of these observations, Bouton and Bolles (1979) report that extinction of a nominal CS is specific to the location in which extinction occurred relative to either the training context or a neutral context. Moreover, they found that the extinction context had not become a conditioned inhibitor. Thus, their context effect was apparently not due to direct associations to the extinction context. Instead, it apparently arose from contextual potentiation of extinction of associations between the nominal CS and the US.

Contextual potentiation ordinarily enhances target performance because it is precisely the retrieval of the target CS–US association that is potentiated by the conditioning context. However, to the extent that potentially competing nontarget CS–US associations were acquired prior to testing in the test context where target conditioning did not occur, contextual potentiation of the competing associations could contribute to the observed contextual cue effect. Although this explanation cannot be categorically rejected, the extensive exposure that all extinction groups in Experiment 2 and all latent inhibition groups in Experiment 3 received to the nonconditioning test context (Z) in addition to the conditioning context (Y) makes it unlikely that any such interfering associations could have appreciably contributed to the potentiation effect observed between Groups TYE and TZE in Experiment 2 and Groups LITY and LITZ in Experiment 3.

Possible Mechanisms Underlying Contextual Potentiation. All three of these experiments demonstrate that, even in the absence of appreciable conditioning context-US associations, responding to the nominal CS is better in the acquisition context than outside of it. Moreover, with our experimental parameters this contextual potentiation effect was as strong (Experiments 2 and 3) or stronger (Experiment 1) than the behavioral contribution of direct associations to the conditioning context. This suggests that the contextual potentiation effect is not only real but contributes substantially to the contextual cue effect. However, our studies to date do not fully illuminate the mechanisms responsible for contextual potentiation of CS–US associations in the absence of direct context-US associations.

One possible explanation of the potentiating effect of the training context is suggested by the similarity between the paradigm for the contextual cue effect and that for conditional discriminations in which the conditional discriminative stimuli inform the animal of which set of reinforcement contingencies is immediately in effect. Within this framework, contextual potentiation can be viewed as a conditional discrimination with the contextual cues playing the role of conditional discriminative stimuli (see Medin & Reynolds, Rescorla, Durlach, & Grau, this volume). The basis of conditional discrimination has not yet been definitively identified although a number of explanations have been proposed (e.g., Asratian, 1972; Carter & Werner, 1978). Nonetheless, it is possible that the same underlying processes are responsible for conditional discriminations and the potentiating effect of the training context. However, two distinctions between conditional discriminations and the contextual potentiation effect argue against such a common mechanism. First, conventional conditional discrimination training includes discrete S^- trials, whereas contextual potentiation does not. And second, conditional discriminations usually require many training trials, whereas, judging from our own experiments, contextual potentiation effects can be acquired with relatively few trials. If discrete S^- trials and large numbers of training trials are not essential for the establishment of a conditional discrimination, there would be little reason to assume that contextual potentiation is other than a special case of conditional discrimination. If this is true, increases in the quality of the conditional discrimination achieved through discrete S^- trials outside of the conditioning context and the concomitant increase in the total number of S^+/S^- discrimination trials (training in one context and extinction in another context) should be evident in stronger contextual potentiation. Bouton and Bolles (this volume) present data consistent with these expectations. Specifically, they found superior contextual potentiation (i.e., contextual control of responding to S, devoid of context-US associations, following extinction of S in Context B than following only acquisition in Context A). Unfortunately they sought and observed only contextual potentiation of extinction; the conditioned discrimination viewpoint posits that extinction of S in Context B would also enhance contextual potentiation of the excitatory value of S in Context A[1]. Future research is needed to test this possibility. However, even if conditional discrimination and contextual potentiation prove to arise from the same mechanism, our understanding of contextual potentiation would be wanting due to our incomplete knowledge of the processes responsible for conditional discriminations.

A second explanation of contextual potentiation, that may ultimately prove more illuminating than equating it with conditional discrimination, hypothesizes that the conditioning context somehow facilitates retrieval of associations be-

---

[1]In fact, Bouton and Bolles (this volume) report *no* contextual cue effect after acquisition alone despite the numerous reports in the literature, ours and others, to the contrary. We do not find this surprising, as we have no trouble finding training parameters that minimized direct context-US associations and test conditions that minimize contextual potentiation (see text).

tween the nominal CS and US. This position, as originally developed by Estes (1973), Medin (1975), and Spear (1973), speaks of the context as an attribute of the overall target memory system but is not explicit as to how the conditioning context ultimately facilitates retrieval of the critical CS–US association; however, a process akin to "spreading activation" (Collins & Loftus, 1975) is implied. A seemingly similar mechanism is suggested by Rescorla, Durlach, and Grau (this volume) in their suggestion that associations can link associations as well as stimulus events. In this case, their concern is with associations between the context and the CS–US relation. Rescorla et al. refer to the presumably enhanced performance that results when the subject is tested on the discrete CS in the conditioning context as "facilitation" of the CS–US association. Rescorla et al.'s "facilitation" appears similar if not identical to our concept of contextual "potentiation" of retrieval of the CS–US association. This similarity becomes all the more evident with Rescorla et al.'s suggestion that associations between context and CS–US relations may obey different rules than ordinary CS–US relations. Rescorla's proposal is consistent with our finding that extinction and latent inhibition of context-US associations do little to attenuate the role of the conditioning context as a potentiator. Unfortunately, Rescorla et al.'s proposed associations between context and CS–US relations are offered without specific suggestions as to how or why such associations differ from conventional CS–US associations. This criticism is obviously equally applicable to our concept of contextual potentiation. Although the potentiated retrieval viewpoint has yet to be fully developed, it has considerable intuitive appeal and may ultimately provide an explanation not only of contextual potentiation, but also of conditional discrimination (see Medin & Reynolds, this volume).

One apparent distinction between our "potentiation" and Rescorla et al.'s "facilitation" is that our data and theorizing suggest a lack of transfer of potentiation between CSs, whereas Rescorla et al. present data suggesting at least partial transfer. The absence of transfer of contextual potentiation to a CS conditioned in another context is most apparent in our first experiment (see Table 7.1). In this case Context Y was seen to act as contextual potentiator for the tone that was conditioned in Y (Group TY vs. Group TZ), but not for the clicks that were conditioned in Context X (Group CY vs. Group CZ). We cannot at this time fully explain this apparent discrepancy. However, it should be noted that Rescorla et al.'s transfer effects were far from complete. Moreover, Holland (personal communication, 1983) has recently obtained data indicating that transfer of potentiation/facilitation depends on the subject having prior discrimination training on the transferred cue. This suggestion is consistent with the outcome of both our studies and those of Rescorla et al. given the procedures used in each laboratory. Although Holland has begun to illuminate the conditions for transfer of contextual potentiation across CSs associated to the same US, to our knowledge no research has been performed addressing the possibility of transfer across dissimilar CSs and USs with a common CR. Answers to these questions may ultimately help us in understanding the processes underlying contextual potentiation. Further research on the limitations and implications of transfer of contextual potentiation is clearly needed.

A third explanation of contextual potentiation, one far more mundane than the conditional discriminations or facilitation of retrieval mentioned previously, hinges upon stimulus generalization decrement. Specifically, the physical nature of nominal CSs may change as the context is altered. For instance a tone may sound somewhat different in one context as opposed to another because of the different acoustical properties of the two contexts. Thus, the stimulus perceived in the training context will be a better retrieval cue than the modified stimulus perceived in a different context. It is important to recognize that this explanation presumes that the contribution of contextual potentiation to the contextual cue effect actually arises not from representationally mediated potentiation of the nominal CS–US associations by the training context, but from the physical inferiority of the retrieval cue in a nontraining context. This change in the retrieval cues brought about by variance in the test context relative to the training context is a change not originating in the animal, but in the physical stimuli impinging upon the animal. Consequently, the stimulus generalization decrement explanation would predict no contextual potentiation of retrieval despite large, perceived changes in the contexts between training and testing, provided these changes do not alter the physical nature of the retrieval cues. This hypothesis could readily be tested by restricting the modification of the context to stimulus modalities other than that of the nominal CS. For example, if a tone were to serve as the CS, the illumination and odor of the test context could be changed from that of training without incidentally altering the auditory characteristics of the tone; however, changes in the shape of the walls or texture of the floor can possibly influence the acoustic nature of the context and consequently the physical characteristics of the tone. Admittedly this stimulus generalization decrement mechanism is less dramatic than either conditional discrimination or contextual modulation of retrieval of CS–US associations given the physically identical CS in the training and testing context. However, the stimulus generalization decrement hypothesis rests upon established processes, whereas we currently lack clearly understood mechanisms for the other explanations. In practice the acoustical properties of our Contexts Y and Z were sufficiently similar that the human ear could not differentiate the tone in Context Y from the tone in Context Z. Nevertheless, the generalization decrement hypothesis cannot be categorically rejected until it is further tested.

Configuring of the training context and the nominal CS in principle provides yet another explanation of the contextual potentiation effect. This hypothesis also uses stimulus generalization decrement to explain the lesser test performance in the nontraining context relative to the training context; however, the stimulus from which the subject is generalizing is quite different. In the configural view, changes in context are assumed to modify the CS-context configured stimulus, whereas, in the previous generalization explanation, changes in the context were hypothesized to alter the physical nature of the nominal CS. Although this factor could appreciably contribute to contextual potentiation under certain circumstances such as simultaneous presentation and termination of the training context and nominal CS during all phases of the study prior to testing (Rescorla & Durlach, 1981), the vast majority of the experiments demonstrating the contextual cue effect and all the studies reported in this chapter used parameters that would have made context-CS configuring extremely unlikely. For instance, subjects ordinarily received extensive exposure to the training context prior to the first CS–US presentation. Additionally, Kamin and Idrobo (1978), varying the number of conditioning trials, have demonstrated how changes in conditioned suppression to stimulus elements relative to their compound, which had previously been taken as evidence of configuring, can be better explained in terms of changes in the associative strength of the elements without recourse to configuring. Thus, there appear to be no data demonstrating configuring of the context and discrete CS in situations such as ours or even reason to expect that this sort of configuring occurs. In summary, given the available evidence we believe that the most likely explanation of the contextual potentiation observed in our studies is facilitated retrieval of the target CS–US association in the training context.

Durability of the Contextual Cue Effect.   Does the contextual cue effect last as long as the target association? Unpublished data from our laboratory suggest that the contextual cue effect, at least under certain circumstances, fades in as short a time as 72 hours after acquisition, whereas the target CS–US association is substantially more robust. This observation is consistent with reports by Perkins and Weyant (1958) and Steinman (1967). For example, Steinman observed rats running in a maze and found that similarity of maze illumination between training and testing benefitted performance soon after training but not following a retention interval of several days. Assuming the validity of this rapid decay of the contextual cue effect, we might ask which contributions to the overall contextual cue effect are responsible for this fading. Although conventional CS–US associations have been found to be highly resistant to fading (Spear, 1978), there is a slim but consistent literature suggesting that context-US associations, and consequently their contribution to the contextual cue effect, are more prone to decay. Connelly, Connelly, and Timmons (1979) and McAllister and McAllister (1968) both report a decrease over days in behavioral control by the training context in the absence of the nominal CS. On the other hand, our own data demonstrating a fading of the contextual cue effect as well as those of Perkins and Weyant (1958) and Steinman (1967) took the form of *improved* responding in the nontraining context (e.g., Steinman's animals tested with maze illumination different from that of training were deficient with a short retention interval but not with a long one, whereas animals tested with the same illumination as that of training performed equally well at both retention intervals). Moreover, our training and nontraining contexts were sufficiently different from one another to render implausible the possibility that the generalization gradient around the training context broadened sufficiently with time to appreciably benefit performance in the nontraining context through generalization of direct associations between the training context and the US. Both of these factors suggest that it was the potentiated retrieval seen soon after training in the training context relative to the nontraining context that was now influencing behavior in both the training and nontraining contexts. Assuming a facilitated retrieval explanation of contextual potentiation, this broadening of the generalization gradient for the conditioning context could result in subjects forgetting not the central attributes of the conditioning context (e.g., "different from home cage"), but those finer attributes of context that would change with switches in test context. Such differential forgetting of select attributes from a larger memory is well documented in the human memory literature (Bower, 1967; Underwood, 1969).

Context as a Comparator

The preceding comments concerning the contributions of the test context to the contextual cue effect are based upon a relatively large number of independent studies. Thus, contextual summation and potentiation effects, if not their explanations, must be considered seriously; the major empirical questions about these phenomena that are yet to be answered concern not reliability, but the generality, power, and processes underlying these phenomena. The data base supporting the third role of context that we now discuss is smaller. We describe what evidence currently exists, but further research concerning reliability and generality is clearly necessary and is in progress. However, the importance of the related phenomena is sufficient to justify its incorporation in this review of the associative effects of context that influence retrieval and performance.

In the late 1960s, a number of studies found that asymptotic conditioned responding depended not only on the percentage of instances in which the CS was immediately followed by the US (i.e., contiguity), but also on the percentage of instances in which the absence of the CS ($\overline{CS}$) was immediately followed by the US (i.e., contingency, see Rescorla, 1967). For analytic purposes, the CS periods were divided into intervals of time equal to the duration of a CS presentation (which was constant for the sake of simplicity). Rescorla (1968) summarized this approach in terms of probabilities of the US by stating that the CS would become an exciter when the probability of the US given the CS is greater than the probability of the US in the absence of the CS [i.e., when $P(US/CS) > P(US/\overline{CS})$]. Moreover, the CS will be an inhibitor when $P(US/CS) < P(US/\overline{CS})$ and neither an exciter nor an inhibitor when $P(US/CS) = P(US/\overline{CS})$.

Rescorla presumed that at the time of conditioning these comparisons were effective in determining whether a CS would be an exciter or an inhibitor (i.e., CS referred to the time *during conditioning* that the CS was absent). However, in recent years we have come to recognize the importance of information processing that occurs at the time of retrieval. For example, a number of associative performance deficits that initially had been regarded as acquisition failures have been recognized as actually arising from the failure of retrieval cues to reactivate the target information during testing (i.e., the information in question had been acquired and under appropriate circumstances [typically a postconditioning "reminder" treatment that excluded relevant new learning] could be demonstrated to have been originally encoded within the subject. (See Miller & Kasprow, 1983; Miller & Springer, 1973; Spear, 1973). Specific cases of this include blocking (Balaz, Gutsin, Cacheiro, & Miller, 1982) and overshadowing (Kasprow, Cacheiro, Balaz, & Miller, 1982). The restorative treatments in these cases consisted of either CS-alone or US-alone exposures given outside of the apparatus used for conditioning and testing.

In light of such instances of behavior depending on differential information processing at the time of testing, we felt that Rescorla's initial assumptions had to be empirically examined. The first question was whether the conditioning context or the test context serves as the comparator baseline. If it is the test context, the comparison necessarily could not occur until the time of testing. But if it is the conditioning context that serves as the comparator baseline, the probability of responding to the CS on a test trial, P(CR/CS), could reflect a comparison of the associative strength based on P(US/CS) to the associative strength of the conditioning context either at the time of conditioning or at the time of testing (even if testing occurred outside of the conditioning context). These latter two possibilities can be differentiated by postconditioning inflation and deflation of the conditioning context. It should be noted that all of these possibilities result in the same value of P(CR/CS) if testing occurs in the conditioning context without associative inflation or deflation of the conditioning context during the retention interval, as was consistently the case in the initial experiments addressing these issues (e.g., Rescorla, 1967, 1968). However, if P(CR/CS) is not calculated until the time of testing and/or the test context differs from that of conditioning, questions arise as to whether P(US/$\overline{CS}$) represents the nonsignaled US density in the conditioning context or the test context, and if the former is true, whether P(US/$\overline{CS}$) is that of the conditioning context at the time of conditioning or at the time of testing.

Evidence for the Conditioning Context as a Comparator.   Toward answering these questions, we recently performed a series of studies with rats as subjects in which two distinctly different environmental enclosures, A and B, were available for conditioning and testing. The physical enclosures corresponding to A and B were counterbalanced in each group of subjects. In all studies, water-deprived rats were first shaped to drink in both A and B.

In our first set of experiments, we merely wanted to determine if our preparation, given a single value of P(US/CS), would yield both excitation and inhibition as a function of the value of $P(US/\overline{CS})$ in Context A, which was used for both conditioning and testing in these two experiments.

Inhibition training consisted of pairing 2 out of 6 30-sec CS (white noise) presentations with the US (footshock) on each of 4 conditioning days (i.e., $P(US/CS) = .33$). These 6 30-sec CS exposures were pseudorandomly interspersed among 34 30-sec $\overline{CS}$ intervals. During 23 out of these 34 30-sec $\overline{CS}$ intervals, footshock was delivered 25 sec into the interval (i.e., $P(US/\overline{CS}) = .67$). Additionally, for purposes of summation testing, interspersed between the 4 conditioning days were several days on which all subjects were placed in an enclosure dissimilar to Contexts A and B and given a total of 8 out of 8 click trains paired with footshock. During lick suppression testing, half the animals received the click alone and half received the click and white noise simultaneously (i.e., a summation test was performed). It is important to note that in this and in all subsequent experiments in this series, the test CSs were presented after 25 licks had been emitted, which allowed the animals to acclimate (*not* extinguish) to any existing fear of the test context, thereby preventing direct context-US associations from appreciably summating with suppression to the discrete test CSs. (This issue is discussed in the next section.) On the summation test, significantly more suppression was seen to the click alone than the click-plus-white noise compound, suggesting that the procedure had made the noise into a conditioned inhibitor. A parallel study using the identical treatment conditions as well as additional control groups found that the white noise, when subsequently paired consistently with shock, also passed a retardation test for conditioned inhibition.

Excitation training also consisted of giving 6 CS presentations and 2 US presentations. For the excitation group, the 2 footshocks were paired with 2 of the 6 noise presentations (i.e., $P(US/CS) = .33$; $P(US/\overline{CS}) = 0$) and for the explicitly unpaired group they were not (i.e., $P(US/CS) = 0$, $P(US/\overline{CS}) = .06$). Although a summation test was not used for these two groups, to maintain comparability with the inhibition groups, all subjects received the same 8 click–shock pairings as were used in the last experiment's summation test for conditioned inhibition. Testing for lick suppression to the white noise, more suppression was observed in the excitation group than the explicitly unpaired group. Thus, with $P(US/CS) = .33$, the CS acted as either a conditioned inhibitor or an exciter as a function of whether $P(US/\overline{CS}) = .67$ or 0, respectively. These two observations are highly consistent with those of Rescorla (1967).

In our second set of experiments, we varied both the context in which unsignaled shock was given and the context in which testing occurred. As before, $P(US/CS) = .33$ for all groups; moreover, every subject received the 8 click–footshock pairings.

In the first study, on the target conditioning days, half the animals experienced 23 shocks during the 34 $\overline{CS}$ intervals, (i.e., $P(US/\overline{CS}) = .67$), whereas the remaining animals received no unsignaled shocks (i.e., $P(US/\overline{CS}) = 0$). All these CSs and USs were delivered in Context A; none were administered in Context B. Half the subjects were tested for lick suppression to the white noise in Context A and half were similarly tested in Context B. Hence, the study consisted of four groups that differed as to whether or not unsignaled shocks occurred in Context A, and whether testing occurred in Context A or Context B. Based upon the results reported previously, we expected the white noise tested in Context A to produce less suppression in the group that received unsignaled shocks than in the group that received no unsignaled shocks. However, the focal question addressed by the study concerned the effect of test context on the two groups given identical training with unsignaled shocks. Specifically, if the test context is the critical comparator baseline, animals trained with unsignaled shocks in Context A should manifest less fear when tested in Context A than when tested in Context B, where no unsignaled shocks occurred. Alternatively, if the conditioning context serves as the critical comparator baseline, the location of testing should have no effect on performance. As can be seen in Fig. 7.1, regardless of

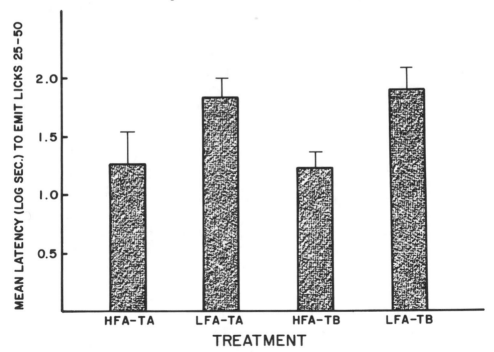

FIG. 7.1.   Mean latency (log sec) to emit 25 licks in the presence of the white noise CS as a function of the probability of unsignaled shock in Context A (the conditioning context) and the location of testing. For all groups P(US/white noise) = .33 in Context A. For the contextual high-fear groups (HFA), P(US/Context A) = .67; for the contextual low-fear groups (LFA), P(US/Context A) = 0. TA groups were tested in Context A, and TB groups were tested in Context B. During conditioning no CSs or USs were presented in Context B.

the test location, subjects for whom P(US/conditioning context) = 0.67 showed far less suppression than subjects for whom P(US/conditioning context) = 0. Moreover, with the same P(US/conditioning context) no difference in suppression was seen as a function of test location, a result quite consistent with one reported by Rescorla, Durlach, & Grau (this volume).

In the next study the procedure was similar te the last experiment except that the unsignaled shocks were given not in Context A (where the reinforced and nonreinforced white noise presentations occurred), but in Context B (where the white noise was not presented during conditioning) (i.e., $P(US/\overline{CS})_A = 0$, $P(US/\overline{CS})_B = .67$ or 0). As can be seen in Fig. 7.2, this time suppression was uniformly high across both test contexts and different values of P(US/Context B). Because these last two studies are paramount to the comparator hypothesis, we recently replicated these experiments eliminating minor procedural dif-

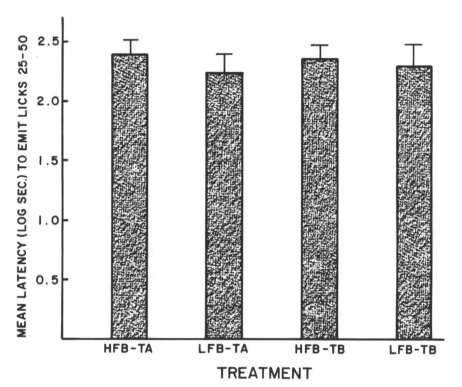

FIG. 7.2.   Mean latency (log sec) to emit 25 licks in the presence of the white noise CS as a function of the probability of unsignaled shock in Context B and the location of testing. For all groups P(US/white noise) = .33 in Context A. For the context high-fear groups (HFB), P(US/Context B) = .67; for the contextual low-fear (LFB), P(US/Context B) = 0. TA groups were tested in Context A and TB groups were tested in Context B. During conditioning, no CSs were presented in Context B and no unsignaled USs were presented in Context A.

ferences between the two studies and running the groups from both studies simultaneously. This experiment corroborated our previous findings. Collectively these studies indicate that performance is dependent on a comparison of the association reflecting P(US/CS) with the association reflecting P(US/conditioning context) independent of where testing takes place.

The contextual comparator effect that we found to modulate responding to the white noise should also have influenced responding to the clicks, for which P(US/clicks) equalled unity. If the comparator baseline had proven to be the test context, differential Ps(US/test context) would have influenced responding to the clicks as well as the white noise, rather than the clicks contributing an equal amount of suppression to each group tested with the compounded white noise and clicks. For this reason in the previously described summation test for conditioned inhibition, all subjects were tested in a common context of uniform associative strength. However, once we had established that the context in which the discrete CS was conditioned rather than the test context served as the associative comparator in modulating responding, further studies using white noise plus clicks were not subject to this constraint. With respect to such summation tests, it is important to note that in these studies all subjects had equal exposure to the context in which the clicks were conditioned; moreover, there were never any unsignaled shocks administered in this context (i.e., $P(US/\overline{clicks}) = 0$, $P(US/clicks) = 1$).

Two additional experiments were conducted to determine if the comparator baseline is the associative strength of the conditioning context (the enclosure used for conditioning the discrete CS) at the time of conditioning or at the time of testing. In the first of these two experiments, the critical manipulation was postconditioning deflation of the conditioning context. Following lick shaping in Contexts A and B, the white noise was made a conditioned inhibitor in Context A (i.e., $P(US/noise) = .33$, $P(US/\overline{noise}) = .67$). Interspersed among these conditioning days, the click trains were paired with shock on 8 out of 8 presentations in a context highly dissimilar to both Contexts A and B. Then half the animals received extensive exposure to Context A in the absence of any CS or US presentations (i.e., associations between Context A and the US were extinguished). Finally, using the clicks and white noise concurrently, both groups were given a summation test for lick suppression. The test was given in Context B to minimize the potential of any direct associations between Context A and unsignaled footshock delivered in Context A during conditioning (residual in the case of extinguished animals) from summating with the associative strength of the white noise. During testing, more suppression was observed in the animals that had received extinction to the conditioning context than those that had not. This counterintuitive finding, that conditioned responding (suppression in this case) could be enhanced by mere exposure to the conditioning apparatus in the absence of both the CS and the US, suggests that *the comparator baseline is the associative strength of the conditioning context (not necessarily the same as the test context) at the time of testing, rather than at the time of conditioning.* Put in other words, these data indicate that test trial responding to a CS reflects the momentary change in US expectation announced by the CS relative to the *current* value of the context in which CS conditioning occurred, not the context in which testing occurs unless it just happens to also have been the conditioning context.

In the second study, the conditioning context was inflated rather than deflated after conditioning of the CS. Following initial lick shaping in both Contexts A and B, subjects received excitatory conditioning in Context A (i.e., $P(US/noise)$ = .33, $P(US/\overline{noise})$ = 0). For purposes of equating experience with the prior study, all animals also received click–shock pairings in a third context, although a summation test was not used in this case. Following conditioning to the white noise and the clicks, half the subjects received a number of sessions in Context A in which no CSs were presented but a large number of unsignaled shocks were administered (i.e., $P(US/\overline{noise})$ = .67). When tested for suppression to the white noise in Context B, the animals that had received the unsignaled shocks in Context A exhibited fear highly similar to the animals that had not received the unsignaled shocks. Thus, in contrast to the preceding study, these results suggest that the comparator baseline is the associative strength of the conditioning context at the time of conditioning. We are currently repeating this study with a more extensive inflation treatment, but it should be noted that Kaplan and Hearst (this volume) also found a loss of CS inhibitory strength following postconditioning contextual deflation without a corresponding loss of CS excitatory strength following postconditioning contextual inflation.

Despite the inability of contextual inflation to influence responding in these studies, the deflation data alone demand that $P(CR/CS)$ not be computed by the subject until the time of testing. Thus, the associations maintained during the retention interval are necessarily direct reflections of $P(US/CS)$ and $P(US/\overline{CS})$ rather than a response tendency with respect to the CS [i.e., $P(CR/CS)$]. In the case of contextual inflation, it currently appears as if the subject at the time of testing is comparing the association based on $P(US/CS)$ to the associative strength of the conditioning context at the time of conditioning. This use of a previous associative strength of the context is consistent with Bottjer's (1982) observation that a novel stimulus at the time of testing can temporarily negate deflation of the conditioning context that occurred during the retention interval (i.e., external disinhibition); clearly her animals had available both the current and past associative strengths of the context.

Both our deflation and inflation data are consonant with several studies reported by other laboratories. For example, Kaplan and Hearst (1981, this volume), using an appetitive US with pigeons, observed that extinction of the conditioning context attenuated conditioned inhibition. However, they employed the same context for conditioning and testing and consequently did not address the relative comparative values of the conditioning and testing contexts. In another study, Fowler and Lysle (1982), using an aversive US with rats, found that following A+, AX− trials the manifest inhibitory strength of X could be decreased by extinguishing A. However, extinction to A occurred in the same context that was used for both conditioning and testing. Consequently, the critical manipulation may not have been extinction of A, but rather extinction of the test context [i.e., a reduction in $P(US/\overline{CS})$]. Supporting this interpretation, a control group that was placed in the context but not presented with A during the extinction phase of the study also exhibited a decrement in the inhibitory strength of X. On the other hand, A may constitute an important component of the comparator term for X following AX conditioning. Our studies to date have intentionally avoided compound conditioning of discrete CSs. It has yet to be determined if stimuli conditioned in compound obey the same comparator principle as stimuli that are conditioned alone in the presence of their background cues.

Competition Between the Comparator Role of the Conditioning Context and Contextual Summation.   The comparator hypothesis posits that the effective excitatory value of a CS decreases as $P(US/\overline{CS})$ for the conditioning context increases because the contrast between the association reflecting $P(US/CS)$ and the association reflecting $P(US/\overline{CS})$ is reduced. On the other hand, we previously described data attesting to the occurrence of direct associations to the conditioning context that summate with associations to the discrete CSs and consequently enhance performance when testing occurs in the conditioning context. This poses a contradiction in that the association to the context [i.e., $P(US/\overline{CS})$] cannot simultaneously enhance and attenuate responding. Are the two factors really in competition, and, if so, which one will predominate? (Potentiated retrieval of the association between the discrete CS and US by the conditioning context doesn't enter into this issue because our studies have found this effect not to depend on $P(US/CS)$.)

There are several points that may contribute to the resolution of these questions. First, we have been presuming that the comparator hypothesis depends on associations reflecting $P(US/\overline{CS})$, which is the probability of the US in the absence of the CS, whereas summation apparently depends on associations reflecting $P(US/context)$, a quantity that can depart appreciably from $P(US/\overline{CS})$. The difference between these two probabilities will depend on the amount of conditioning to the context that occurs during CS–US pairings. This in turn will hinge upon the degree to which the discrete CSs overshadow the context, which itself will be a function of both the specific CS and context in question, as well as the genetic and experiential history of the subject. Experimenters in the Rescorla–Wagner (1972) tradition have generally studied rats in a suppression task and have observed strong overshadowing of the context, whereas those researchers who stress timing of events have usually employed pigeons in autoshaping situations and have found little overshadowing of context (e.g., Gibbon & Balsam, 1981; Jenkins, Barnes, & Barrera, 1981). However, despite the importance of the distinction between $P(US/\overline{CS})$ and $P(US/conditioning context)$, this distinction may be inadequate to resolve the dilemma. The reason is that although we have repeatedly referred to P(US/$\overline{CS}$) when discussing the comparator role of the conditioning context, we do not believe that adequate research has been done to determine if P(US/CS) is actually compared to P(US/$\overline{CS}$) or P(US/conditioning context). In fact, we tentatively favor P(US/conditioning context) as the critical measure and have been using P(US/$\overline{CS}$) only for the sake of consistency with Rescorla (1968). The reason for this preference is that the conditioning context (a real, concrete, impinging stimulus), as opposed to $\overline{CS}$ (an abstract stimulus embodying the absence of a concrete stimulus), is ordinarily the effective stimulus just prior to CS presentations. Depending on parameters, discrete stimuli immediately preceding the US may or may not overshadow or block associations to the context. If, as we suspect, P(US/conditioning context) plays the comparator role as well as summates with associations between discrete CSs and the US, the issue of competition between the comparator hypothesis and summation is not resolved by noting that P(US/$\overline{CS}$) need not equal P(US/conditioning context).

A second and likely superior resolution of the competition question arises from differences in time of onset of the context and of the nominal CSs on test trials conducted in the conditioning context. Assuming the validity of both the summation and comparator hypotheses, the question becomes *which effect will predominate*. To the extent that on a test trial the subject is in the conditioning context for a relatively long period of time prior to presentation of the target CS (but not so long as to cause extinction of the context), the CS will announce a change in US expectation relative to that signaled by the conditioning context alone. However, if CS onset is roughly simultaneous with placement of the subject in the conditioning context (as was the case in the experiments of Balaz, Capra, Hartl, & Miller, 1982), the observed response will reflect the summation of US expectation based upon both the CS relative to the conditioning context and the conditioning context relative to the environment that the animal was in immediately before placement in the conditioning context during acquisition of context-US associations. This position appears to be consistent with pilot data recently gathered in our laboratory but must be regarded as speculative until further research is performed. In any case, it should be recognized that ordinarily the comparator effect will *diminish* the size of the contextual cue effect rather than enhance it as summation and potentiation often do.

Implications of the Comparator Hypothesis.   If the comparator hypothesis is valid as a response generation rule, a number of important consequences follow. First, manifest conditioned inhibition will occur when P(US/CS) < P(US/conditioning context). Thus, there is no need to hypothesize negative associations between a CS and a US. All associations can be regarded as excitatory, consistent with P(US/CS) and P(US/conditioning context) both necessarily being positive numbers between 0 and 1. Conditioned inhibition is not a property of a CS per se; rather it is the manifestation of a *relationship* between a CS and the conditioning context. Second, the manifest excitation or inhibition produced by a CS can be altered as readily by changing the associative value of the conditioning context as by changing the associative value of the nominal CS. Such changes can occur prior to, during, or following conditioning of the discrete CS. For example, we have shown that an "excitatory" CS can be made less excitatory and perhaps even inhibitory by increasing P(US/conditioning context), i.e., by presenting the US in the absence of the CS during the conditioning of the discrete CS. Similarly, an "inhibitory" CS can be rendered less inhibitory and perhaps even excitatory simply by reducing P(US/conditioning context), i.e., by extinguishing the conditioning context. This latter effect when produced following CS conditioning is particularly intriguing in that it confirms a counterintuitive prediction (i.e., making an "inhibitory" CS "excitatory" without exposing the animal to either the CS or US). Additionally, because the association reflecting P(US/CS) is *learned* absolutely rather than relative to any given context, the failure of a subject to respond to a CS when P(US/CS) = P(US/$\overline{CS}$) must be viewed as a performance failure as opposed to an acquisition failure.

Rescorla (1968) first suggested that both associative strength and consequent response strength depend on contingency [i.e., some relationship of P(US/CS) and P(US/$\overline{CS}$)], rather than contiguity (i.e., P(US/CS) alone), primarily to account for the phenomenon of conditioned inhibition. Implicit in his model was a comparison of P(US/CS) and P(US/$\overline{CS}$) during or immediately following acquisition that yielded the likelihood of responding to the CS during later testing. Our model differs in that associations reflecting P(US/CS) and P(US/conditioning context) are presumed to be retained independently and not compared to produce effective response strength until the time of testing. (Obviously such comparisons would have to occur on each conditioning trial to determine the CR for that trial, but the effective comparison for each trial appears to occur at the time of that trial.) Moreover, the comparator probability is P(US/conditioning context) rather than P(US/test context), a distinction that Rescorla did not address as he used the same context for training and testing.

The idea that associations reflecting P(US/CS) and P(US/conditioning context) are independently retained does not necessarily mean that they are independently acquired. Overshadowing and blocking of CS of conditioning context could readily occur and still result in independent associations to each. Independence of acquisition of context and CS associations is consistent with the apparent lack of blocking and overshadowing between the context and the CS, described in a number of autoshaping situations by Gibbon and Balsam (1981) and Jenkins, Barnes, and Barrera (1981). Conversely, several researchers have presented data that appear to demonstrate blocking or overshadowing by the context. For example, as previously mentioned Marlin (1981) showed that the inferiority of trace conditioning with respect to delay conditioning could be attributed in part to overshadowing of the CS by the context. Although her rats spent considerable time in the conditioning context prior to each CS onset, the offset of the CS in her trace conditioning group may have effectively amounted to a new presentation of the context just before US delivery that would favor associative competition between the CS and context during acquisition rather than independent acquisition of P(US/CS) and P(US/context). For present purposes, the point to be made is that *the comparator hypothesis is concerned with response generation* and is neutral concerning the conditions that will yield overshadowing and blocking.

The phenomenon of direct responding to the conditioning context in the absence of a discrete CS (e.g., Pearce & Hall, 1979) poses a seeming problem for the comparator hypothesis, as the comparator baseline in this case obviously cannot be the conditioning context itself. This issue also arises, although in a less-conspicuous form, when the associative strength of a discrete CS summates with the test context; the comparator hypothesis states that the test context must have its own comparator baseline in order for responding directly to the context to occur. Resolution of this apparent paradox lies in recognizing that, in responding to context-US associations, the context is acting as an eliciting stimulus, and the comparative role is likely played by the context in which the subject was residing immediately prior to being placed in the target context at the time of context-US acquisition.

The comparator hypothesis proposed here is quite similar to the models of Rescorla (1968), Fantino (1969), and Jenkins et al. (1981), except that they imply that the comparison occurs during acquisition rather than testing. On the other hand, Gibbon and Balsam (1981) explicitly state that: "the strength of associative responding evoked by the signal is directly related to the degree to which expectancy in the signal exceeds the overall or background reinforcement expectancy" (p. 225). However, these last researchers did not consider the predictions generated by this hypothesis with respect to postacquisition changes in the associative strength of the conditioning context, nor its implications for conditioned inhibition.

One of the more discomforting aspects of our model arises from the evaluation of $P(US/\overline{CS})$ depending on the dissection of the CS intervals into temporal units equal to that of the CS duration. Not only is this somewhat arbitrary, but it introduces ambiguities if the CS duration is changed. A possible resolution of this problem appears to exist in Scalar Expectancy Theory (Gibbon, 1977; Gibbon, 1981; Gibbon & Balsam, 1981) and the Relative Waiting Time Hypothesis (Jenkins et al., 1981), which depend on the average interval between USs to determine P(US/context) independently of CS duration; however, these models have problems of their own (e.g., an inability to predict trace conditioning).

Summary

We have described three different associative roles of context during testing. The first is the well-established principle of direct context-US associations. The second is the recently observed potentiation of retrieval of associations between the nominal CS and US when testing occurs in the conditioning context. And the third is the comparator hypothesis that views responding to the CS as a function of the discrepancy between the expectation of the US raised by the CS and that raised by the conditioning context regardless of where testing occurs. This last factor leads to the prediction of manifest conditioned inhibition without the need for negative associations, thus removing a major obstacle to the otherwise simplifying assumption that all associations are positive. Finally, it is important to recognize that these three roles of context are not mutually exclusive. Specific training and test conditions will determine the relative impact of each upon acquired behavior.

ACKNOWLEDGMENTS

The research described in this chapter was supported in part by NIMH Grant 33881. We are grateful to Andrea Brown, Wesley J. Kasprow, and Joe Serwatka for their comments on a preliminary version of the chapter.

REFERENCES

Asratian, E. A. Genesis and localization of conditioned inhibition. In R. A. Boakes & M. S. Halliday (Eds.), *Inhibition and learning*. London: Academic Press, 1972.

Baker, A. G., & Mercier, P. Extinction of the context and latent inhibition. *Learning and Motivation*, 1982, *13*, 391–416.

Balaz, M. A., Capra, S., Hartl, P., & Miller, R. R. Contextual potentiation of acquired behavior after devaluing direct context-US associations. *Learning and Motivation*, 1981, *12*, 383–397.

Balaz, M. A., Capra, S., Kasprow, W. J., & Miller, R. R. Latent inhibition of the conditioning context: Further evidence of contextual potentiation of retrieval in the absence of context-US associations. *Animal Learning and Behavior*, 1982, *10*, 242–248.

Balaz, M. A., Gutsin, P., Cacheiro, H., & Miller, R. R. Blocking as a retrieval failure: Reactivation of associations to a blocked stimulus. *Quarterly Journal of Experimental Psychology*, 1982, *34B*, 99–113.

Bottjer, S. W. Conditioned approach and withdrawal behavior in pigeons: Effects of a novel extraneous stimulus during acquisition and extinction. *Learning and Motivation*, 1982, *13*, 44–67.

Bouton, M. E., & Bolles, R. C. Contextual control of the extinction of conditioned fear. *Learning and Motivation*, 1979, *10*, 445–466.

Bower, G. H. A multicomponent theory of the memory trace. In K. W. Spence & J. T. Spence (Eds.), *The psychology of learning and motivation* (Vol. 1). New York: Academic Press, 1967.

Carr, H. Maze studies with the white rat. I. Normal animals. *Journal of Animal Behavior*, 1917, *7*, 259–275.

Carter, P. E., & Werner, T. J. Complex learning and information processing by pigeons: A critical analysis. *Journal of the Experimental Analysis of Behavior*, 1978, *29*, 565–601.

Collins, A. M., & Loftus, E. F. A spreading activation theory of semantic processing. *Psychological Review*, 1975, *82*, 407–428.

Connelly, J. F., Connelly, J. M., & Timmons, J. K. Disruption of drug-dependent learning (memory retrieval) using an ethanol drug state: A replication. *Psychopharmacology*, 1979, *65*, 319–320.

Estes, W. K. Toward a statistical theory of learning. *Psychological Review,* 1950, *57,* 94–107.

Estes, W. K. Memory and conditioning. In F. J. McGuigan & D. B. Lumsden (Eds.), *Contemporary approaches to conditioning and learning.* Washington, D.C.: Winston, 1973.

Falkenberg, P. R. Recall improves in short-term memory the more recall context resembles learning. *Journal of Experimental Psychology,* 1972, *75,* 39–47.

Fantino, E. Choice and rate of reinforcement. *Journal of the Experimental Analysis of Behavior,* 1969, *12,* 723–730.

Fowler, H., & Lysle, D. T. *Internal inhibition as a "slave" process: Deactivation of conditioned excitation.* Paper presented at Eastern Psychological Association Meeting, Baltimore, 1982.

Gibbon, J. Scalar expectancy theory and Weber's Law in animal timing. *Psychological Review,* 1977, *84,* 279–325.

Gibbon, J. The contingency problem in autoshaping. In C. M. Locurto, H. S. Terrace, & J. Gibbon (Eds.), *Autoshaping and conditioning theory.* New York: Academic Press, 1981.

Gibbon, J., & Balsam, P. Spreading association in time. In C. M. Locurto, H. S. Terrace, & J. Gibbon (Eds.), *Autoshaping and conditioning theory.* New York: Academic Press, 1981.

Holland, P. C. "Occasion-setting" in conditional discrimination. In M. L. Commons, R. J. Herrnstein, & A. R. Wagner (Eds.), *Quantitative analyses of behavior: Vol. 4: Discrimination processes.* Cambridge, Mass.: Ballinger, 1983.

Imada, I., Yamazaki, A., & Morishita, M. The effects of signal intensity upon conditioned suppression: Effects upon responding during signals and intersignal intervals. *Animal Learning and Behavior,* 1981, *9,* 269–274.

Jenkins, H. M., Barnes, R. A., & Barrera, F. J. Why autoshaping depends on trial spacing. In C. M. Locurto, H. S. Terrace, & J. Gibbon (Eds.), *Autoshaping and conditioning theory.* New York: Academic Press, 1981.

Kamin, L. J., & Idrobo, F. Configural conditioning in the CER: A possible artifact. *Animal Learning and Behavior,* 1978, *6,* 290–293.

Kaplan, P., & Hearst, E. *Excitation, inhibition, and context: Studies of extinction and reinstatement.* Paper presented at Eastern Psychological Meeting, New York, 1981.

Kasprow, W. J., Cacheiro, H., Balaz, M. A., & Miller, R. R. Reminder-induced recovery of associations to an overshadowed stimulus. *Learning and Motivation,* 1982, *13,* 155–166.

Konorski, J. *Integrative activity of the brain: An interdisciplinary approach.* Chicago: University of Chicago Press, 1967.

Mackintosh, N. J. A theory of attention: Variations in the associability of stimuli with reinforcement. *Psychological Review,* 1975, *82,* 276–298.

Marlin, N. A. Contextual associations in trace conditioning. *Animal Learning and Behavior,* 1981, *9,* 519–523.

Marlin, N. A. Within-compound associations between the context and the conditioned stimulus. *Learning and Motivation,* 1982, *13,* 526–541.

Marlin, N. A., & Miller, R. R. Associations to contextual stimuli as a determinant of long-term habituation. *Journal of Experimental Psychology: Animal Behavior Processes,* 1981, *7,* 313–333.

McAllister, D. E., & McAllister, W. R. Forgetting of acquired fear. *Journal of Comparative and Physiological Psychology,* 1968, *65,* 352–355.

Medin, D. L. A theory of context in discrimination learning. In G. H. Bower (Ed.), *The psychology of learning and motivation* (Vol. 9). New York: Academic Press, 1975.

Miller, R. R., & Kasprow, W. J. *Retrieval variability: Psychobiological sources and consequences.* Manuscript under review, 1983.

Miller, R. R., & Springer, A. D. Amnesia, consolidation, and retrieval. *Psychological Review,* 1973, *80,* 69–79.

Nadel, L., & Willner, J. Context and conditioning: A place for space. *Physiological Psychology,* 1980, *8,* 218–228.

Odling–Smee, F. J. The overshadowing of background stimuli: Some effects of varying amounts of training and UCS duration. *Quarterly Journal of Experimental Psychology,* 1978, *30,* 737–746.

Pan, S. The influence of context upon learning and recall. *Journal of Experimental Psychology,* 1926, *9,* 468–491.

Pavlov, I. P. *Conditioned reflexes.* Oxford: Oxford University Press, 1927.

Pearce, J. M., & Hall, G. The influence of context-reinforcer associations on instrumental performance. *Animal Learning and Behavior,* 1979, *7,* 504–508.

Pearce, J. M., & Hall, G. A model for Pavlovian learning: Variations in the effectiveness of conditioned but not of unconditioned stimuli. *Psychological Review,* 1980, *87,* 532–552.

Perkins, C. C., Jr., & Weyant, R. G. The interval between training and test trials as a determiner of the slope of generalization gradients. *Journal of Comparative and Physiological Psychology,* 1958, *51,* 596–600.

Randich, A., & LoLordo, V. M. Associative and nonassociative theories of the UCS preexposure phenomenon: Implications for Pavlovian conditioning. *Psychological Bulletin,* 1979, *86,* 523–548.

Rescorla, R. A. Pavlovian conditioning and its proper control procedures. *Psychological Review,* 1967, *74,* 71–80.

Rescorla, R. A. Probability of shock in the presence and absence of CS in fear conditioning. *Journal of Comparative and Physiological Psychology,* 1968, *66,* 1–5.

Rescorla, R. A., & Durlach, P. J. Within-event learning in Pavlovian conditioning. In N. E. Spear & R. R. Miller (Eds.), *Information processing in animals: Memory mechanisms.* Hillsdale, N.J.: Lawrence Erlbaum Associates, 1981.

Rescorla, R. A., & Wagner, A. R. A theory of Pavlovian conditioning: Variations in the effectiveness of reinforcement and nonreinforcement. In A. H. Black & W. F. Prokasy (Eds.), *Classical conditioning* (II): *Current research and theory.* New York: Appleton–Century–Crofts, 1972.

Riccio, D. C. Urda, M., & Thomas, D. R. Stimulus control in pigeons based on proprioceptive stimuli from floor inclination. *Science,* 1966, *153,* 434–436.

Smith, S., & Guthrie, E. R. *General psychology in terms of behavior.* New York: Appleton–Century–Crofts, 1921.

Spear, N. E. Retrieval of memory in animals. *Psychological Review,* 1973, *80,* 163–194.

Spear, N. E. *The processing of memories: Forgetting and retention.* Hillsdale, N.J.: Lawrence Erlbaum Associates, 1978.

Spear, N. E., Smith, G. J., Bryan, R. G., Gordon, W. C., Timmons, R., & Chiszar, D. A. Contextual influences on the interaction between conflicting memories in rats. *Animal Learning and Behavior,* 1980, *8,* 273–281.

Steinman, F. Retention of alley brightness in the rat. *Journal of Comparative and Physiological Psychology,* 1967, *64,* 105–109.

Underwood, B. J. Attributes of memory. *Psychological Review,* 1969, *76,* 559–573.

Wagner, A. R. Expectancies and the priming of STM. In S. H. Hulse, H. Fowler, & W. K. Honig (Eds.), *Cognitive processes in animal behavior.* Hillsdale, N.J.: Lawrence Erlbaum Associates, 1978.

Watson, J. B. Kinaesthetic and organic sensations; their role in the reactions of the white rat to the maze. *Psychological Monographs,* 1907, *8* (whole No. 33).

8

Contextual Control and Excitatory Versus Inhibitory Learning: Studies of Extinction, Reinstatement, and Interference

Peter S. Kaplan
Eliot Hearst
Indiana University

Pavlovian conditioned excitors (CEs) and conditioned inhibitors (CIs) are usually defined in parallel but opposite fashion: A CE signals a greater likelihood of US occurrence than in its absence, whereas a CI signals a lower likelihood of US occurrence than in its absence. However, even though the circumstances of their separate establishment may appear symmetrical (e.g., positive vs. negative contingency), the question remains as to whether the two types of learning are controlled by basically similar associative mechanisms and performance laws. Several authors have suggested that conditioned excitation and conditioned inhibition are not simple counterparts of one another; instead, the acquisition and behavioral expression of conditioned inhibition are viewed as somehow subordinate to or dependent on prior and current levels of excitatory conditioning (see the discussions in Baker, 1974; Konorski, 1948, 1967; and Rescorla, 1979).

Unfortunately, little research has been performed to compare the effects of various experimental manipulations on properties of CEs and CIs: their rates of acquisition; their control by prevailing contextual cues; their extinguishability when USs are eliminated from the situation and their possible subsequent reinstatement by restoration of USs; their permanence over time; their susceptibility to disruption by novel stimuli and changes in drive states; their sensitivity to interference by exposure to different prior or subsequent CS–US relations; and so on. The scarcity of such comparisons is partially due to conceptual and definitional problems, but methodological considerations seem to have played an especially significant role; it is easy to obtain measures of CRs to CEs on every trial of an experiment but difficult to secure analogous data for CIs. In fact, despite his earlier (Rescorla, 1969) characterization of conditioned inhibition as involving a response tendency opposed to conditioned excitation, Rescorla has more recently described CIs as producing no behavioral effects of their own, but simply acting to modulate CRs to CEs (Rescorla, 1979).

On the other hand, for about 10 years we and some of our colleagues have been using the approach and withdrawal responses of pigeons—with respect to localized signals of food or no food—as overt behavioral indexes of conditioned excitation and conditioned inhibition, respectively (for general descriptions, evaluations, and justifications of these measures, see Hearst & Jenkins, 1974; Wasserman, Franklin, & Hearst, 1974). Unlike more popular but relatively indirect and brief postconditioning assays of conditioned inhibition, such as summation or retardation tests, our sign-tracking arrangement allows trial-by-trial, seemingly parallel measurement of the growth of both approach and withdrawal responses—from the initiation of conditioning until asymptotic performance has been reached. Thus a definite response is produced by presumptive CIs on our procedure (cf. Cunningham, Fitzgerald, & Francisco, 1977; Yadin & Thomas, 1981), and overall findings based on this "tracer" of momentary changes in CI strength appear to correlate well with results obtained from standard summation, generalization, and reconditioning (retardation) assays in sign-tracking, CER, and other arrangements. (For detailed discussions of these correlations see Bottjer, 1982; Gaffan & Hart, 1981; Hearst, Bottjer, & Walker, 1980; Hearst & Franklin, 1977; and Wasserman et al., 1974.) However, one must be careful not to conclude—just as in the excitatory case—that the failure to perform the target (withdrawal) response necessarily implies the absence of underlying inhibitory associations. In other words, the learning–performance distinction is relevant to both excitatory and inhibitory conditioning. Considerable evidence already exists showing that: (1) Failure to observe an overt CR during original acquisition does not necessarily imply the absence of learning; various indirect techniques are available to reveal that learning (see Balsam, 1984; Hearst, 1984; Rescorla, 1980); and (2) positive CS–US associations are not eradicated by extinction or uncorrelated training, despite the disappearance of CRs to the CE (see Bouton & Bolles, this volume; Lindblom & Jenkins, 1981).

In this chapter we focus on analysis of relationships between excitatory versus inhibitory learning and the type of control exerted by the experimental context in which these conditioning experiences are embedded. According to the Rescorla–Wagner (1972) model of Pavlovian conditioning, the growth of conditioned inhibition to a CS negatively correlated with the US is mediated by the development of strong excitation to the general context (cf. Baker et al., this volume), whereas the growth of conditioned excitation to a CS positively correlated with the US leads to a context that possesses little or no excitatory strength. After asymptotic levels of conditioned inhibition have been reached, mere exposure of subjects to the original experimental context, without CSs or USs, should greatly reduce or remove contextual excitation; and we wondered whether subsequent presentation of the old CI in that context would still lead to evocation of its former CRs (that is, withdrawal responses). Rescorla (1979) has suggested that the expression of CIs in performance requires some kind of excitatory background, implying that evidence of conditioned inhibition would no longer be detectable. On the other hand, mere exposure to the original context should have minor, if any, effects on the power of old CEs; that context would remain relatively neutral and approach responses should be immediately exhibited on re-presentation of CSs.

Our first three experiments therefore explored the issue of whether a background of excitation is necessary for the expression of conditioned inhibition, and, symmetrically, whether a neutral or inhibitory background is necessary for the expression of conditioned excitation. These experiments assessed effects on asymptotic CIs and CEs of various manipulations designed to increase, decrease, or maintain levels of background conditioning. And if some of these manipulations lead to the elimination of CRs, can those CRs be reinstated when background strength is restored to near original levels? Our fourth experiment examined the impact of various context manipulations on CIs that had previously been either CEs or random CSs. This work addressed the questions of the fate of old associations, and their retrievability when background cues are appropriately manipulated. Finally, we briefly mention a few experiments, performed in our laboratory by Sarah Bottjer and Michael Owren, which are relevant to Zimmer–Hart and Rescorla's (1974) conclusion that conditioned inhibition does not extinguish when USs are no longer presented in sessions containing preestablished CIs. Zimmer–Hart and Rescorla's findings, which are contrary to the prediction of the Rescorla–Wagner (1972) model that nonreinforced presentations of a CI should reduce its inhibitory associative strength, remain one of the major embarrassments suffered by that version of the model.

Besides their empirical value and their potential implications for current models of conditioning, the studies of extinction, reinstatement, and interference reported here may help isolate reasonable criteria for defining and characterizing what a "context" is and how it controls the effectiveness of discrete stimuli occurring in its presence—the major issues addressed by other contributors to this volume.

GENERAL METHOD

Our basic procedure for obtaining overt, antagonistic CRs to CEs and CIs in the sign-tracking (autoshaping) situation was originally devised by Edward Wasserman and Stanley Franklin at Indiana University. A CS (brief illumination of a key) could appear on either side of the front wall of a standard pigeon chamber, and the subject's position in relation to the keylight was monitored by a teeter-totter floor. Pigeons approach and peck the CS when it predicts an increased likelihood of food US and withdraw from the same stimulus when it predicts a decreased likelihood of food US. The most important aspects of our overall method are outlined in the following; the interested reader should consult Kaplan and Hearst (1982) and Wasserman et al. (1974) for specific details.

Experimentally naive female White Carneaux pigeons, maintained at 75% of their free-feeding weights, served as subjects. At the beginning of an experiment, all birds received magazine training for 2 successive days, on each of which 20 3-sec grain presentations were delivered. Initial placement on CE, CI, random, or discrimination acquisition procedures always began on the following day.

The chambers were standard commercially built boxes fitted with special floors to enable measurement of whether the bird was standing on the left or the right side of the chamber. Single response keys, which could be illuminated by various colors, were located on the left and right sides of the front panel, equidistant from the grain magazine that was centered near the bottom of the panel. A continuously illuminated white houselight was positioned near the top center of the panel.

All key pecks were automatically recorded, but our main dependent measure involved an index of approach–withdrawal toward the illuminated key. On a given trial, either the left or right key was lit; the exact order of left versus right key illuminations varied irregularly from trial to trial. The total amount of time that a bird spent on the same side of the chamber as the illuminated key was recorded during each session, and this number was divided by the total amount of session time that the key light was on; the computation yielded an *approach–withdrawal ratio*. A ratio near 1.00 indicates strong approach toward the lit key and is generally accompanied by key pecking. A ratio near .00 signifies strong withdrawal from the lit key, whereas a ratio near .50 means that the bird's position in the chamber is not systematically controlled by the location of the keylight.

EXPERIMENT 1: EFFECTS OF SEPARATE CONTEXT EXTINCTION OR REINFORCEMENT ON PREESTABLISHED CEs AND CIs

In our initial experiment we first established strong, asymptotic approach or withdrawal to a CS in two different groups of birds and then exposed them to the original context in the absence of any CS presentations. If notions like those of Konorski (1948) and Rescorla (1979) are correct in their claim that some background of excitation is necessary for the expression of conditioned inhibition, exposure to the original context without US presentations should lead to little or no persisting withdrawal behavior when the presumptive CI is finally retested without USs in that setting—as compared to subjects kept in their home cages during the interpolated phase, or to subjects given the usual USs (but no CSs) in the experimental context during the interpolated phase. In the latter two groups contextual excitation ought to be maintained at close to its earlier levels, and therefore withdrawal behavior should be displayed as soon as the CI is re-introduced. We were also curious whether the probable decline and loss of withdrawal behavior over the course of the final test phase with only CSs indicate mere failure of performance or actual erasure of inhibitory associations. There-fore a few unsignaled USs were delivered when the CR became weak, to deter-mine the ease of reinstating withdrawal to the CS.

Another aspect of the experiment considered the possibility of symmetrical effects with respect to preestablished CEs. If, correspondingly, expression of conditioned excitation to a CS somehow depends on a relatively neutral or even inhibitory background, interpolation of a phase involving exposure to the origi-nal context with unsignaled USs (producing increased contextual excitation, according to the Rescorla–Wagner model) might yield weaker approach when CSs are later reintroduced—compared to a phase of interpolated maintenance in the home cage or exposure to the original context without any USs.

Twelve birds were randomly assigned to each of 2 groups. One group was trained on an explicitly paired (EP) procedure, in which 10-sec presentations of a red keylight were always immediately followed by 3-sec access to grain. The other group received training on an explicitly unpaired (EU) procedure, in which 10-sec presentations of the red keylight occurred at least 30 sec after the last grain delivery and were never followed by grain for at least 43 sec. For both groups the average time between successive food deliveries was 148 sec (range: 43 to 226 sec). Each of the 16 daily acquisition sessions of approximately 97 min comprised 40 keylight and grain presentations.

Figure 8.1 displays the acquisition of conditioned approach and withdrawal behavior for animals in the EP and EU groups, respectively. Birds in the EP condition rapidly acquired strong approach (and key pecking) tendencies, and birds in the EU condition developed clear-cut withdrawal responses. Over the final 10 sessions of this acquisition phase, the mean approach–withdrawal ratio for EP birds was .93 (range: .85 to .96), and for EU birds .33 (range: .21 to .44).

Manipulations of contextual associative strength in the absence of CS presen-tations began on the day following the final acquisition session. Three subgroups ($n = 4$) of birds within each major group were established, matched as closely as possible with respect to approach–withdrawal ratios (and number of key pecks in the EP group). During the next five daily sessions birds from one subgroup of each major group were placed in the original apparatus for a standard 97-min session without any presentations of CSs or USs. This treatment was designed to decrease contextual excitation to minimal levels, and the subgroups are labeled CONTEXT(−). Another pair of subgroups also received no CSs, but 40 periodic unsignaled US presentations occurred while subjects were left in the original apparatus; USs were scheduled according to the same interreinforcement interval as was in force during acquisition. This treatment was intended to maintain

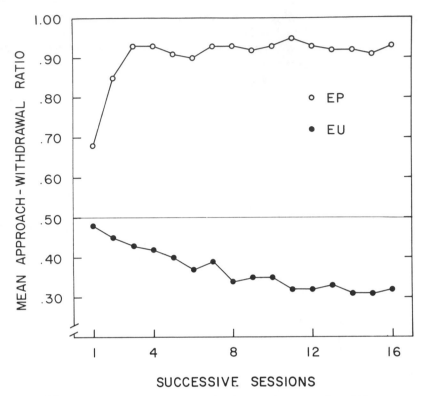

FIG. 8.1.   Mean approach–withdrawal ratios over the course of acquisition to a CS (red keylight) either explicitly paired (EP) or unpaired (EU) with food in different groups. A ratio of .50 represents chance performance (Experiment 1).

(Gibbon & Balsam, 1981) or, for the CE group, even increase (Rescorla & Wagner, 1972) contextual excitation, and the subgroups are labeled CONTEXT(+). Subjects in the final pair of subgroups were confined to their home cages throughout the 5 days of this phase; the associative value of general contextual cues would presumably be unaffected by this treatment, unless some "memory loss" occurs over a 5-day period of no contextual exposure (HOME CAGE groups).

Because CSs were not presented to any subgroup during this phase, data concerning CS approach–withdrawal or key pecking were of course unavailable for those five sessions. However, a rough measure of general activity in the experimental chamber was secured from the context-exposed subgroups (+ and −) via counts of the number of openings and closings of the microswitch beneath the teeter–totter floor ("floor crossings"). We collected these data because changes in activity brought about by CONTEXT (+ and −) manipulations could affect later performance during CS test sessions, and a knowledge of any activity changes would be valuable in the assessment of, for example, the contribution of competing responses to our findings.

All birds given nonreinforced exposure to apparatus cues, CONTEXT($-$), exhibited large decreases in activity over the five sessions. The mean number of floor crossings per min during the final session of acquisition, first session of exposure, and last session of exposure was 14.4, 4.3, and 0.2 for the EP group and 8.1, 2.9, and 0.2 for the EU group, respectively. On the other hand, 3 of the 4 birds in subgroup EP, CONTEXT($+$), and all 4 birds in subgroup EU, CON-TEXT($+$) exhibited increases in activity. Their mean number of floor crossings per min during the final acquisition session, and first and last sessions of exposure, was 11.0, 13.4, and 13.9 (EP) and 8.3, 9.0, and 14.5 (EU).[1]

During the final (test) phase of the experiment, all birds were placed in the original setting and red CSs were reintroduced. After a 15-min warm-up period, in which each bird received its immediately prior treatment (nonreinforced apparatus exposure, unsignaled USs in the apparatus, or home cage confinement), 32 presentations of the keylight occurred on the old variable time (VT) schedule, but no USs were delivered. Each 8-trial block contained an equal number of left and right key illuminations. After the 32nd presentation, a reinstatement procedure was initiated; a block of 8 3-sec USs was given (VT 148 sec) in the absence of any keylights. Then another block of 8 CSs occurred as before, in the absence of food.

The data of primary interest are contained in Fig. 8.2, which displays mean approach–withdrawal ratios during the final acquisition session and the first 16 CS presentations of the test phase for the EU (top panel) and EP (bottom panel) subgroups (examination of these data in smaller blocks of trials leads to the same conclusions). The EU birds given home cage confinement or unsignaled USs (CONTEXT$+$) continued to withdraw from the CS, but birds given nonreinforced exposure to the context exhibited no withdrawal at all. The t-tests comparing mean approach–withdrawal ratios during the final acquisition session to those over the first 16 test trials for each subgroup revealed a significant difference only in subgroup EU, CONTEXT($-$): $t(3) = 3.75$, $p < .05$.

In contrast to the EU findings, none of the experimental manipulations had any significant effect on CS-directed behavior in the EP birds (bottom, Fig. 8.2). Furthermore, the number of key pecks per trial and the percentage of trials with at least one key peck were similarly unaffected in those birds.

---

[1]Balsam (1984) and Rescorla, Durlach, and Grau (this volume) claim that measures of general activity reflect conditioning to contextual cues. Consistent with these claims are the decreases in activity we observed in our CONTEXT($-$) conditions, and increases in our CONTEXT($+$) conditions, here and in later experiments. We do not discuss whether our activity data support predictions derived from the Gibbon–Balsam or Rescorla–Wagner models; but the interested reader can consult the aforementioned citations and examine our activity data along these lines.

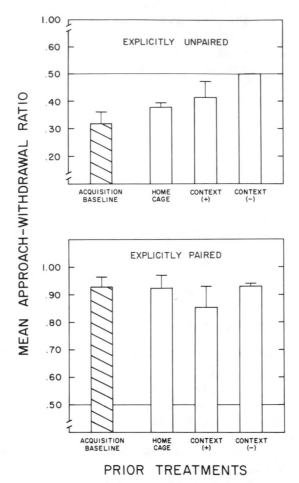

FIG. 8.2.   Mean approach–withdrawal ratios to the CS for birds given either explicitly unpaired (top) or explicitly paired (bottom) training prior to placement for 5 sessions in either (1) their home cages, (2) the original apparatus with reinforcement, CONTEXT(+), or (3) the original apparatus without reinforcement, CONTEXT(−). Performance is displayed for the final session of initial acquisition, and for the first 16 presentations of the CS after the three different interpolated treatments. Marks over each bar show one standard error above the mean (Experiment 1).

The consequences of reintroducing food on subsequent CS withdrawal in EU birds are shown in Fig. 8.3. During the last 16 CS trials before food was reintroduced, the ordering of subgroups remained the same as during the first 16 test trials (Fig. 8.2), although CONTEXT(+) and HOME CAGE birds exhibited weaker withdrawal than before. However, strong withdrawal reappeared in all

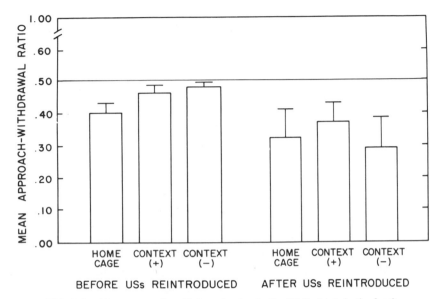

FIG. 8.3.   Mean approach–withdrawal ratios to the CS for birds in the 3 subgroups of the explicitly unpaired condition (1) during the last 16 unreinforced CS test trials before a block of 8 USs was given, and (2) during the 8 trials after that block. Marks over each bar show one standard error above the mean (Experiment 1).

three subgroups after exposure to the separate block of 8 USs. The reinstatement effect shown in Fig. 8.3 did not attain acceptable levels of statistical significance within the individual subgroups, but comparison of approach–withdrawal ratios before and after US reintroduction yielded a significant outcome when all 12 EU subjects were combined, $t(11) = 2.52, p < .05$. Our second experiment, to be described shortly, produced highly significant reinstatement of CS withdrawal in similarly treated separate subgroups.[2]

This experiment demonstrated that the conditioned withdrawal behavior of pigeons to a CS explicitly unpaired with food is eliminated by a period of simple nonreinforced exposure to apparatus cues, whereas pigeons' conditioned approach and key pecking behavior is largely unaffected by either nonreinforced contextual exposure or exposure to unsignaled USs in the apparatus. Furthermore, the loss of conditioned withdrawal behavior after nonreinforced apparatus exposure did not seem to involve a permanent erasure of prior inhibitory learning; withdrawal to the CS returned immediately after an interpolated block of 8 USs. The overall findings are consistent with the view (e.g., see Rescorla, 1979)

---

[2]"Reinstatement" of CS approach after reintroduction of USs in the EP group could not be meaningfully evaluated in this experiment (and Experiment 2), because approach levels remained near their ceiling throughout prior CS-alone trials.

that some background of excitation is necessary for the expression of conditioned inhibition. No support was found for the idea that a neutral or inhibitory background is necessary for the continued expression of conditioned excitation.

EXPERIMENT 2: EFFECTS OF EXTINCTION AND REINFORCEMENT IN NOVEL VERSUS ORIGINAL CONTEXTS

One could argue that the loss of withdrawal behavior to the CS after contextual extinction in Experiment 1 was related either to the inactivity produced by the interpolated phase of nonreinforcement or possibly to the development of inattention to environmental features during that phase; that is, "inactive" behaviors could subsequently have competed with withdrawal tendencies toward the CI; and subjects that are "inattentive" may not have noticed the reoccurrence of red keylights. However, loss of *approach* and key pecking behavior to CS did not occur in the final test phase (see Fig. 8.2) for the EP group, which reached equivalent, very low levels of activity during the last session of exposure to CONTEXT(−); as mentioned earlier, both the EP and EU groups averaged 0.2 floor crossings per min in that session. Data to be mentioned in connection with later experiments in our series of studies (see, e.g., Fig. 8.7) also argue against simple explanations based on inactivity or inattention.

It seemed possible that approach behavior in the EP birds may have been unaffected by exposure to five sessions of unsignaled USs in the original context because the interreinforcement interval was relatively long (VT 148 sec) and remained the same as during original acquisition. According to Gibbon and Balsam's (1981) model, which assumes independence of signal and context conditioning, the density of US presentations would have to be increased during the CONTEXT(+) phase in order to increment background expectancy levels.

Our second experiment bore on these various alternatives and involved two parallel lines of inquiry. The EU subjects all received a CONTEXT(−) treatment, but half the birds were exposed to this period of nonreinforcement in a novel apparatus and half in the original apparatus. The EP subjects all received a CONTEXT(+) treatment in the original apparatus, but half the birds received USs at approximately double the earlier rate and half the birds at approximately four times the earlier rate. The major focus of this and our subsequent experiments was on the EU groups and on whether the loss of CS withdrawal in Experiment 1 was due to mere removal of USs in any kind of standard test chamber, or rather to the elimination of USs in the specific context of original inhibitory training. Our secondary focus was on the effect of different US densities during contextual exposure in the EP groups; we do not pursue that particular issue in later experiments.

The acquisition phase of this experiment was conducted in the same way as in Experiment 1. Eight birds were initially trained on the EP procedure and 8 birds on the EU procedure, and after 16 sessions each major group was divided into 2 matched subgroups ($n = 4$). One EU subgroup, SAME CONTEXT(−), then received nonreinforced exposure to the original apparatus, just as for the CON-TEXT(−) subjects of Experiment 1. The other subgroup, NOVEL CON-TEXT(−), was given nonreinforced exposure to a novel apparatus. The novel context involved several modifications of the standard one: (1) Vertical 3.8-cm black and white striped paper covered the chamber walls, with holes cut for the response keys and grain aperture (even though no food was presented); (2) a red houselight replaced the old white houselight; and (3) the chamber's white noise and ventilating fan were turned off.

For the EP birds the novelty of the context was not varied, but different densities of reinforcement were provided the birds during the SAME CON-TEXT(+) phase. After the 16 acquisition sessions, 1 EP subgroup received 40 daily unsignaled USs on a VT 74-sec schedule (range: 43–83 sec), and the other subgroup obtained the 40 USs on a VT 37-sec schedule (range: 17–57 sec). Session durations lasted approximately 49 min for the former group, and 24 min for the latter—compared to the standard 97-min sessions in force throughout Experiment 1 and the acquisition phase of this experiment.

As in Experiment 1, the test session for all four subgroups took place on the day after the fifth day of interpolated treatment without CSs. The procedure on the test day was identical to the arrangement in Experiment 1, except that no warm-up period was included. Thirty-two CSs were presented on their old schedule in the original context, followed by a block of 8 unsignaled USs and then a final block of 8 more CSs.

Acquisition of approach and withdrawal to the CS proceeded as for the subjects in Fig. 8.1. The mean approach–withdrawal ratio over the final 10 sessions was .90 for the EP birds (range: .74 to .96) and .32 for the EU birds (range: .26 to .37).

During the next (context exposure with no CSs) phase, EU subjects given nonreinforced placement in the original or novel apparatus showed a decrease in activity relative to the final session of acquisition. The mean number of activity counts per min during the final acquisition session, and first and last sessions of the next phase, was 11.7, 8.2, and 0.3 for subgroup EU, SAME CONTEXT(−), and 9.2, 0.6, and 0.4 for subgroup EU, NOVEL CONTEXT(−). Every individual subject in these two groups displayed large activity decreases of this kind. As in Experiment 1, most of the birds in the two EP groups showed an increase in activity rate during this phase; average rates in the VT 74-sec group were 10.1, 12.4, and 16.4 crossings per min, and in the VT 37-sec group 14.4, 18.9, and 22.0 crossings per min during the last acquisition session, first exposure session, and last exposure session, respectively.

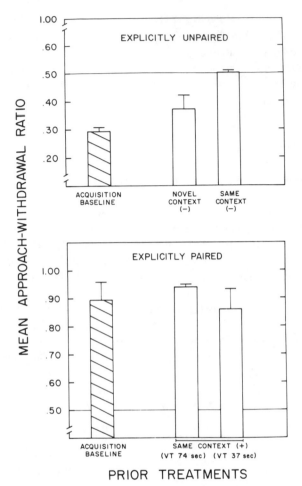

FIG. 8.4.   Mean approach–withdrawal ratios to the CS for birds given either explicitly unpaired (top) or explicitly paired (bottom) training prior to placement for 5 sessions in (1) a novel apparatus without reinforcement, NOVEL CONTEXT(−), (2) the original apparatus without reinforcement, SAME CONTEXT(−), (3) the original apparatus with approximately double the earlier US density, SAME CONTEXT(+), VT 74 sec, or (4) the original apparatus with approximately four times the earlier US density, SAME CONTEXT(+), VT 37 sec. Performance is displayed for the final session of initial acquisition, and for the first 16 presentations of the CS after the different interpolated contextual manipulations. Marks over each bar show one standard error above the mean (Experiment 2).

Approach–withdrawal data over the first 16 CS trials of the test session, when subjects were placed in the original context but given no USs, are summarized in Fig. 8.4 for the EU birds (top panel) and EP birds (bottom panel); conclusions drawn here, as in Experiment 1, would be the same if a smaller number of CS trials had been selected for analysis. The EU data demonstrate a large effect of the type of interpolated, extinguished context on CS withdrawal. Birds that had received nonreinforced exposure to new apparatus cues, NOVEL CONTEXT(−), continued to show withdrawal behavior, whereas birds nonreinforced in the original context, SAME CONTEXT(−), failed to withdraw, just as they had in the same condition of Experiment 1. A comparison of approach–withdrawal ratios to the CS during the final acquisition session with ratios obtained during the initial 16 test trials showed a significant difference only in subgroup EU, SAME CONTEXT(−): $t(3) = 24.98, p < .001$.

The bottom panel of Fig. 8.4 indicates that interpolated exposure of EP birds to the original context—with more frequent but unsignaled USs than before—led to no clear-cut decline in approach behavior to the CS. There were no statistically significant differences between performance during the final acquisition session and the first 16 test trials for either subgroup (p's $> .10$). The number of key pecks per trial and the number of trials with at least one key peck were also not significantly changed by either SAME CONTEXT(+) manipulation. Furthermore, birds in both subgroups continued to approach and peck the CS with undiminished vigor during the last 16 test trials (not shown in Fig. 8.4).

Performance of EU birds during the final 16 CS trials, before USs were reintroduced, along with performance on the 8 CS trials given after the separate block of 8 USs had been delivered, is shown in Fig. 8.5. Little or no withdrawal to the CS was observed in either subgroup during the final 16 regular test trials, but all birds in both subgroups exhibited a reinstatement of withdrawal behavior after the block of 8 USs. The reinstatement effect was statistically significant in each subgroup: $t(3) = 4.85, p < .02$ (SAME CONTEXT), and $t(3) = 4.95, p < .02$ (NOVEL CONTEXT).

The results of this second experiment demonstrate that the disappearance of withdrawal to a CS after nonrewarded exposure to apparatus cues is a context-specific phenomenon. This finding is consistent with the view that an excitatory background is needed for the behavioral expression of conditioned inhibition. Furthermore, conditioned approach to CS seemed largely independent of manipulations that, according to both the Gibbon–Balsam and the Rescorla–Wagner formulations, should have increased the level of excitation to background cues. The rapid reinstatement of conditioned withdrawal in EU groups after delivery of a few unsignaled USs indicated that the inhibitory power of the CS had not been erased by contextual extinction, but that its overt manifestation was simply absent without some background of concurrent excitation. There was no suggestion that the expression of conditioned excitation in the form of CS-approach

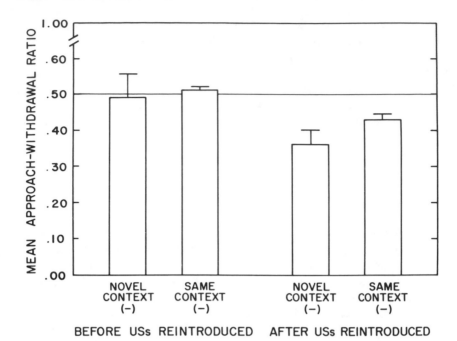

FIG. 8.5. Mean approach–withdrawal ratios to the CS for birds in the 2 sub-groups of the explicitly unpaired condition (1) during the last 16 unreinforced CS test trials before a block of 8 USs was given, and (2) during the 8 trials after that block. Marks over each bar show one standard error above the mean (Experiment 2).

and pecking behavior is affected in a symmetrical way by separate manipulation of background cues.

EXPERIMENT 3: WITHIN-SUBJECT COMPARISONS OF THE EFFECTS OF CONTEXTUAL EXTINCTION ON CE AND CI

Next we examined the consequences of nonreinforced exposure to the same or novel apparatus cues in birds originally trained on a discriminative conditioning procedure, in which one key color signaled food delivery and another color signaled the absence of food. One aim of the experiment was to provide a within-subject replication of the major findings of Experiments 1 and 2. A second aim was to explore further the nature of the "background excitation" required to reinstate the overt performance of an unexpressed CI. Perhaps a series of CS+s could revive or retrieve conditioned withdrawal to an explicitly unpaired CS, as did delivery of USs themselves in the earlier work.

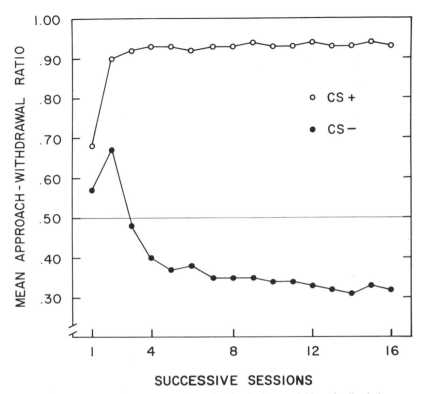

FIG. 8.6.   Mean approach–withdrawal ratios during acquisition of a discrimination between a green keylight (CS+) followed by food and a red keylight (CS−) never followed by food (Experiment 3).

In the first phase of this experiment, 21 birds were trained on a discrimination in which 10-sec presentations of a green keylight (CS+) were always followed immediately by food, and 10-sec red keylights (CS−) by no food. The temporal relation between the red key and food was identical to that between the red key and food on the EU procedure of Experiments 1 and 2, and the temporal relation between the green key and food was identical to that between the red key and food on the earlier EP procedure. Forty green key, red key, and food presentations occurred during each of the 16 acquisition sessions. All other procedural details were the same as those during acquisition phases of the prior work.

As Fig. 8.6 illustrates, birds rapidly acquired the discrimination between green and red keys, although (unlike Fig. 8.1) there was some initial approach to the CS−—presumably due to stimulus generalization of the CS+'s excitatory effects (see also Hearst & Franklin, 1977). At asymptote, levels of approach to the CS+ and withdrawal to the CS− were very close to those in the separate EP and EU groups of Experiments 1 and 2 (cf. Baker et al., this volume; Rescorla & Wagner, 1972). Averaged across the final 10 sessions for all subjects, the mean approach–withdrawal ratio to the CS+ was .93 (range: .88 to .96) and to the CS– was .33 (range: .27 to .41).

After completion of the acquisition phase, two subgroups of birds were established, matched for degree of approach–withdrawal to the CS+ and the CS–, as well as for amount of key pecking to the CS+. Then one subgroup ($n = 11$) received nonreinforced exposure to the original training apparatus, SAME CONTEXT(–), whereas the other subgroup ($n = 10$) was exposed to the different apparatus, NOVEL CONTEXT(–). Details of this exposure phase were the same as in the prior work described in this chapter; no CSs or USs were presented during five 97-min sessions of placement in the appropriate apparatus. General activity decreased for every bird in both subgroups during this phase; the mean number of activity counts per min during the final acquisition session, and the first and last sessions of apparatus exposure was 10.9, 6.4, and 1.3 for the SAME CONTEXT subjects and 8.8, 0.9, and 0.4 for the NOVEL CONTEXT subjects.

During the test session following contextual extinction, each bird was placed in the original training apparatus and tested with both the red key (CS–) and green key (CS+) in the following sequence: (1) 8 nonreinforced presentations of the red key; (2) 8 nonreinforced presentations of the green key; and (3) 4 red and 4 green key presentations that were nonreinforced and randomly intermixed. Then a block of 8 3-sec USs was given, followed by another 8 nonreinforced CS– presentations. All CSs occurred on the same VT schedule as before.

The first two 8-trial test blocks yielded results generally paralleling those in Experiments 1 and 2. Figure 8.7 shows that birds given interpolated, nonreinforced exposure to the original context no longer withdrew from the CS– (top panel, middle set of bars, SAME CONTEXT), whereas birds given interpolated, nonreinforced exposure to the novel context continued to withdraw from the CS–. The middle set of bars in the bottom panel indicates that birds in both subgroups continued to approach the CS+ strongly, but, unlike the corresponding group in Experiment 1 (see Fig. 8.2), the SAME CONTEXT(–) birds exhibited some decrement in approach to the CS+ relative to the final acquisition day. Birds in the SAME CONTEXT subgroup showed a statistically significant decrease in withdrawal to the CS– compared to the final acquisition day, $t(10) = 6.99$, $p < .001$, as well as a significant decrease in approach to the CS+, $t(10) = 3.01$, $p < .02$. Birds in the NOVEL CONTEXT subgroup did not exhibit any significant changes from the acquisition baseline in approach or withdrawal behavior during this pair of test blocks. No decrement in key pecking to the CS+ was observed in either group; we have usually found conditioned approach to be a more sensitive index of behavior than key pecking (e.g., Kaplan & Hearst, 1982).

The right portions of Fig. 8.7 display approach–withdrawal ratios to the CS– and the CS+ during the 8-trial block when presentations of the CS+ and the CS– were intermixed. For the SAME CONTEXT birds, stronger withdrawal to the CS– and stronger approach to the CS+ were produced by the intermixture

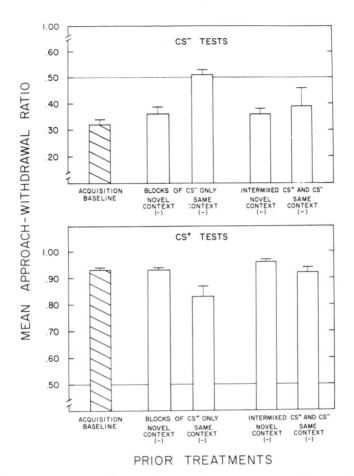

FIG. 8.7.   Mean approach–withdrawal ratios to the CS− (top) and the CS+ (bottom) during the final session of discrimination acquisition and during different blocks of a test session following a phase of unreinforced placement in a novel apparatus, NOVEL CONTEXT(−), or in the original apparatus, SAME CONTEXT(−). See the text for details of stimulus presentations within the different blocks. Marks over each bar show one standard error above the mean (Experiment 3).

procedure. Nine of the 11 individual subjects showed both greater approach and more pronounced withdrawal during this trial block, as compared to their scores during the immediately prior separate blocks of the CS− or the CS+. Birds in the NOVEL CONTEXT subgroup did not display any significant change from their prior levels of approach and withdrawal.

When USs were reintroduced and then removed in the final set of test blocks, 7 of the 11 SAME CONTEXT birds and 6 of the 10 NOVEL CONTEXT birds exhibited even more withdrawal to the CS− than in the intermixture block (the US-reinstatement values are not pictured in Fig. 8.7). This result should be viewed as supportive of the US-reinstatement effects obtained in Experiments 1 and 2, but the complicated sequence of prior test trials prevents strong conclusions along these lines.

Therefore, on the within-subject procedure of this experiment, selective elimination of CS-withdrawal behavior by unreinforced exposure to the original but not a novel context was once again obtained. There was some evidence from this discrimination and testing procedure, however, that approach behavior to a CS+ can be reduced by mere exposure to the original context; further work involving variations of the test sequence (e.g., starting with a block of CS+s) might help isolate the reasons for this apparent difference from Experiment 1 (cf. Rescorla, Durlach, & Grau, this volume, who observed some decrement in key pecking to a CS+ on its first two presentations in a *novel* context in which food had never been delivered). Both withdrawal from the CS− and approach to the CS+ were revived or enhanced in the SAME CONTEXT group when CS− and CS+ presentations were intermixed. Thus actual presentations of the US do not seem necessary to unmask conditioned inhibition; CS+ presentations (or interspersal of the two types of original training trials) were also effective (cf. Konorski, 1967, Chapter VII; and Bottjer's 1979, 1982 work also appears relevant). This finding is consistent with our prior comments on the role of the removal and reinstatement of contextual ''supports'' for conditioned inhibition. A background of excitation can presumably be provided by delivery of USs, or by presentation of CS+s. The latter stimuli may act by producing associatively elicited US representations (see a discussion in Dickinson, 1980).

Taken in combination, our first three experiments demonstrate that nonreinforced exposure to the original training context eliminates the subsequent overt expression of preestablished CIs, but not of CEs—at least so far as our particular measures of withdrawal, approach, and key pecking, and our selection of parametric experimental details, are concerned. On the other hand, reinforced exposure to the original training context has little or no retroactive effect on either preestablished CEs or CIs. Background excitation seems necessary for the manifestation of conditioned inhibition, but from Experiments 1–3 there is no reason to conclude, symmetrically, that the associative value of the background (manipulated in separate sessions without CS presentations) likewise modulates the appearance of conditioned excitation. Despite losses of withdrawal *performance,* there is strong evidence that the inhibitory associative strength of a CS− still remains intact, because the reintroduction of USs or CS+s usually produces an almost immediate recovery of withdrawal behavior to the old CI.

EXPERIMENT 4: PROACTIVE INTERFERENCE AND THE POSSIBLE "RETRIEVAL VALUE" OF CURRENT CONTEXTUAL ASSOCIATIVE STRENGTH

Nonreinforced exposure to the training apparatus eliminates the overt manifestation of CRs to a CI, but those CRs can be immediately reinstated when USs are again "expected" in the situation. Apparently, CIs are not active when their contextual supports are removed. We wondered what would happen if birds that had (1) initially acquired approach behavior to an explicitly paired CS, and then (2) learned to withdraw from the same CS because of its later explicit *unpairing* with US, were subsequently given nonreinforced exposure to the training apparatus. In a final test session, might not such birds show *approach* toward the CS, rather than the unsystematic behavior we have consistently reported in EU birds after SAME CONTEXT(−) experience?

This outcome seems conceivable for two reasons. First, the original excitatory association may be retained after counterconditioning (Lindblom & Jenkins, 1981) but may not be expressed in performance due to suppression or interference by the new inhibitory association. Elimination of the contextual supports for the inhibitory association (through SAME CONTEXT(−) exposure) may neutralize the source of suppression or interference and therefore lead to the renewed expression of the excitatory association. Second, the low levels of background excitation that should exist after nonreinforced exposure to the training apparatus may serve as a "retrieval cue" for the positive CS–US association that had prevailed on prior occasions when the background cues were theoretically neutral (recall that the Rescorla–Wagner model predicts that background cues should be relatively neutral at asymptote on EP procedures, but highly excitatory at asymptote on EU procedures). In other words, when a CS has a mixed conditioning history, animals may use the current associative strength of background cues to guide their behavior toward the CS, just as they apparently use external characteristics of contexts to modulate their behavior under certain circumstances (see Asratian, 1972; Medin & Reynolds, this volume; Thomas, this volume). As a result, previously excitatory but now silent CS–US relations may be unmasked (cf. Bouton & Bolles, this volume; Lindblom & Jenkins, 1981; Weisman & Dodd, 1979). Our next experiment examined these kinds of possibilities.

Thirty-six birds were randomly assigned to two major groups ($n = 18$). One group was first trained on our standard EP procedure, and the other on a random procedure (RAN; see Rescorla, 1967) in which 10-sec red keylights and 3-sec USs occurred on equal but independent VT 148 sec schedules (and therefore chance pairings occasionally happened). After the usual 16 sessions of acquisition, all 36 subjects were switched to the EU procedure described earlier, with the same red keylight serving as the CS. Following 16 sessions of EU training, 3 subgroups of birds ($n = 6$) were created from each of the 2 main groups; these subgroups were matched as closely as possible for EU and prior EP or RAN performance. Then the different subgroups received either the SAME CONTEXT(−), NOVEL CONTEXT(−), or HOME CAGE treatment described earlier in the present chapter. This phase lasted the usual 5 sessions and no CSs or USs occurred in any condition. On the following (test) day 32 CSs were first presented on their old VT schedule in the original context, followed by a block of 8 unsignaled USs and then a final block of 8 more CSs, as in Experiment 2.

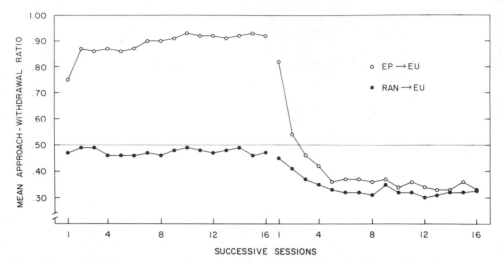

FIG. 8.8.   Mean approach–withdrawal ratios to the CS for two groups of subjects first given either 16 sessions of training with an explicitly paired CS (EP→EU) or a random CS (RAN → EU), and then both placed on an explicitly unpaired (EU) procedure for the final 16 acquisition sessions (Experiment 4).

Figure 8.8 displays acquisition and transfer performance for birds initially given EP training (EP→EU) and birds initially given random training (RAN→EU). The EP birds quickly acquired a strong tendency to approach the red key and their mean approach–withdrawal ratio over the final 10 sessions of EP training was .92 (range: .66 to .97). On the other hand, RAN birds failed to acquire any systematic response tendencies, and their asymptotic approach–withdrawal ratios averaged .48 (range: .43 to .52). When subsequently shifted to the EU procedure, EP → EU birds soon stopped approaching the CS and began to withdraw from it. Birds in the RAN → EU condition also quickly acquired CS-withdrawal behavior. Over the final 10 sessions of the EU phase, approach–withdrawal ratios for EP→EU birds averaged .35 (range: .12 to .45) and for RAN → EU birds .32 (range: .21 to .46). The mean ratios were virtually identical on the final day of this phase.

During the subsequent differential treatment phase, birds in both context-exposure conditions exhibited large decrements in general activity, as had been observed in the SAME CONTEXT(−) and NOVEL CONTEXT(−) subgroups of EU birds in corresponding prior experiments. On the final day of EU training, and the first and last days of exposure, the mean number of activity counts per min was 10.3, 7.1, and 1.8 for the SAME CONTEXT(−), EP → EU birds, and 12.7, 3.2, and 1.5 for the NOVEL CONTEXT(−), EP → EU birds. In the RAN → EU groups the values were 13.4, 7.7, and 0.3 for the SAME CONTEXT birds and 11.8, 1.8, and 0.7 for the NOVEL CONTEXT birds.

Performance during the first eight CS test trials is shown in Fig. 8.9 for all subgroups in the experiment. The bottom panel reveals that RAN → EU birds

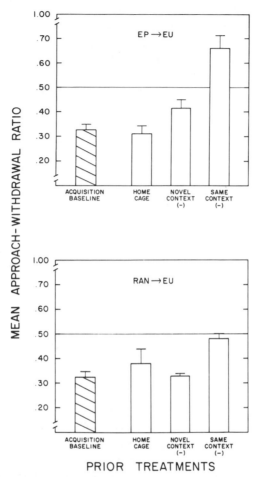

FIG. 8.9.   Mean approach–withdrawal ratios to the CS for birds given either EP → EU (top) or RAN → EU (bottom) training prior to placement for 5 sessions in (1) their home cages, (2) a novel apparatus without reinforcement, NOVEL CONTEXT(−), or (3) the original apparatus without reinforcement, SAME CONTEXT(−). Performance is displayed for the final session of EP → EU or RAN → EU training (see Fig. 8.8), and for the first 8 presentations of the CS after the 3 different interpolated treatments. Marks over each bar show one standard error above the mean (Experiment 4).

performed in a manner similar to birds pretrained only on the EU procedure: Subjects given home cage confinement or nonreinforced exposure to a novel apparatus continued to withdraw, whereas birds that had received nonreinforced exposure to the original apparatus exhibited little or no withdrawal. A comparison of mean performance during the final acquisition (EU) session with mean performance on the first 8 test trials revealed a significant difference only in the SAME CONTEXT(−) subgroup, $t(5) = 6.26$, $p < .002$.

The top panel of Fig. 8.9 indicates that birds given initial EP training followed by EU training, and then either (1) home cage confinement or (2) nonreinforced exposure to a novel apparatus, continued to withdraw from the CS, as in our earlier experiments and in the data displayed in the bottom panel. However, EP → EU birds that received nonreinforced exposure to the original training apparatus actually *approached and pecked* the CS. Birds in this subgroup were the only EP → EU subjects to exhibit a significant change in approach–withdrawal ratios relative to the final session of EU acquisition, $t(5) = 30.11$, $p < .001$. In addition, this subgroup also yielded approach–withdrawal ratios significantly higher than the .50 baseline, $t(5) = 2.87$, $p < .05$.

During the remaining 24 test trials before reintroduction of food, EP → EU birds in the HOME CAGE and NOVEL CONTEXT(−) subgroups displayed weaker withdrawal from the CS than they had during the first eight test trials, and some of these birds actually began to approach the CS during this period—which had almost never happened in corresponding groups of our other experiments (but cf. Lindblom & Jenkins, 1981). The EP → EU, SAME CONTEXT(−) birds started to show weaker approach than before, but most of them continued to produce ratios above .50 throughout the remaining 24 trials. Approach–withdrawal ratios for RAN → EU birds moved toward .50 as testing progressed; no approach behavior was observed in these subgroups.

Subjects in the RAN → EU subgroups yielded overall statistically reliable ($p < .02$) reinstatement of withdrawal during the eight CS trials after USs had been reintroduced. However, the reintroduction of USs failed to produce a significant effect in the EP → EU birds ($p > .10$), although the large majority of individual subjects displayed lower approach–withdrawal ratios.

This experiment showed that old excitatory associations apparently survive their counterconditioning and can be reactivated or retrieved when contextual supports for more recent associations are removed or changed appropriately. Thus, for birds trained on the EP procedure followed by the EU procedure, either approach or withdrawal to the CS could be produced, depending on the presumed "current associative strength" of contextual cues. Perhaps a similar interpretation can be applied to the provocative results of Lindblom and Jenkins (1981), who found that placement on RAN or EU procedures following standard positive autoshaping (like our EP procedure) suppressed signal-directed key pecking—which was, however, strongly reinstated when subjects received CS trials in the total absence of USs (this would involve extinction of contextual excitation, too). At any rate, the results of all our experiments implicate complex relations between CSs and contextual conditioning, and they reiterate the obvious need to distinguish between learning and performance in Pavlovian conditioning. The "path" by which subjects reach equivalent CR levels (say, on the two EU procedures of Experiment 4) must be taken into account in making hypotheses about the form of the underlying associative structures that govern behavior at any given time.

THE "EXTINCTION" OF CONDITIONED INHIBITION

Our experiments have shown that overt CRs to a conditioned inhibitor no longer occur after an interpolated period of simple nonreinforced exposure to the context in which the CI was originally trained. However, this loss of CS-withdrawal behavior apparently represents a performance failure rather than an erasure of the CS → no-US association, because subsequent presentation of a block of US-alone trials led to a sizable recovery of withdrawal when the CS was retested. The term *extinction* can refer to at least two kinds of outcomes in studies of this kind: (1) elimination of some overt CR to the CI; and (2) more or less permanent disappearance of the CI's negative associative strength. Outcome (1) does not necessarily imply outcome (2), a point that has not received sufficient attention in the past, particularly with respect to conditioned inhibition.

Although a detailed analysis is beyond the scope of this chapter and of the present authors' current ability to integrate all the pertinent data, experimental reports of failures to extinguish CIs via their continued presentation in the absence of USs seem relevant to the findings presented previously. Contrary to a clear prediction of the Rescorla–Wagner (1972) model of Pavlovian conditioning—namely, that simple exposure to an established CI without any delivery of USs should extinguish its negative associative strength—Zimmer–Hart and Rescorla (1974) found that such a procedure failed to decrease the inhibitory power of a CI, as measured during subsequent nonreinforced test trials in a CER arrangement (they did not measure any CR during the interpolated CS-exposure period). The Rescorla–Wagner model's symmetrical treatment of conditioned excitation and conditioned inhibition was rendered questionable by this outcome, and Zimmer–Hart and Rescorla (see also Rescorla, 1979) suggested that CIs may be functional only when occurring in the presence of excitatory cues. More specifically, they proposed that CIs raise the behavior-evoking threshold for those cues, rather than triggering some kind of active negative effect. Perhaps nonreinforced presentations of a CI do not alter its inhibitory power because such presentations also involve extinction of background excitation, which we have seen renders the CI inactive. When in an inactive state, the CI may be "protected" from actual changes in its associative strength, and subsequent tests of the CI in conjunction with a discrete CS+ (e.g., summation tests) may lead to renewed expression of the CI (related to the reinstatement effects we observed in Experiments 1–4 earlier).

However, acceptance of such an asymmetrical view of conditioned excitation and conditioned inhibition may be premature, because various experiments (see discussions in Bouton & Bolles, 1979; Bouton & Bolles, this volume; Lindblom & Jenkins, 1981; Reberg, 1972; and Rescorla, 1979) have also been able to detect clear evidence of conditioned *excitation* to a formerly positive CS during assays instituted after many unreinforced CS trials and loss of the established CR to the CS. Thus, performance evoked by *both* CEs and CIs may disappear during

CS-alone presentations, even though the underlying excitatory or inhibitory associations remain relatively intact and can be unmasked by appropriate test procedures (including the technique used in our Experiment 4). Bottjer (1979, 1982) employed the sign-tracking preparation and approach–withdrawal measures stressed in this chapter to measure trial-by-trial behavior to CEs and CIs during their acquisition and during a subsequent period when all USs were removed from the situation. In between-group and within-subject experiments, she found that not only did approach behavior to an explicitly paired CS decline gradually to chance levels over the course of these standard extinction periods, but so did withdrawal behavior. Furthermore, later presentation of a novel visual stimulus reinstated approach and withdrawal responses to their respective CSs; that is, both "extinguished" CEs and CIs were apparently susceptible to reinstatement via a phenomenon akin to Pavlovian disinhibition.

Bottjer's findings, as well as those mentioned earlier indicating survival of excitatory CS–US connections in the face of failures to perform the CR, suggest that the original Rescorla–Wagner model encounters difficulty in handling the persistence of excitatory associative strength following US removal, as well as in handling analogous data from the inhibitory case. Rescorla (e.g., 1979, pp. 107–108) has implied that conditioned excitatory associations are more easily weakened by US removal than are conditioned inhibitory associations. However, empirical substantiation of this view is lacking, especially when one considers the difficulty of equating original strengths of CEs and CIs for an appropriate comparison. This general problem is inherent in our work, too, because acquired levels of withdrawal did not correspond to acquired levels of approach in terms of the magnitude of their distance from the .50 baseline (see Hearst et al., 1980, for additional relevant discussion).

These kinds of difficulties notwithstanding, Owren and Kaplan (1981) performed a systematic replication of the Zimmer–Hart and Rescorla (1974) CER experiment but included for comparison a CE group as well as a CI group. During acquisition the CE rats received nonreinforced presentations of two different auditory stimuli (A−, B−) along with shocked compound trials (AX+); the X stimulus involved houselight illumination. The CI rats received A+, B+, and AX− trials. At the end of acquisition CE subjects showed considerably greater suppression to AX than to A and B, whereas CI subjects showed more suppression to A and B than to AX. Then, to extinguish the CE or CI stimulus (X), half the subjects in each group were only given X-alone trials during six consecutive sessions of lever pressing; the other half of the subjects served as controls and did not receive any stimulus presentations during their corresponding six sessions. By the end of this period no CE rats in the experimental group showed significant suppression to X, and of course neither did their CI counterparts.

Figure 8.10 shows the results of tests involving nonreinforced presentations of A and AX (Test Day 1) and B and BX (Test Day 2) for CI and CE groups. In the

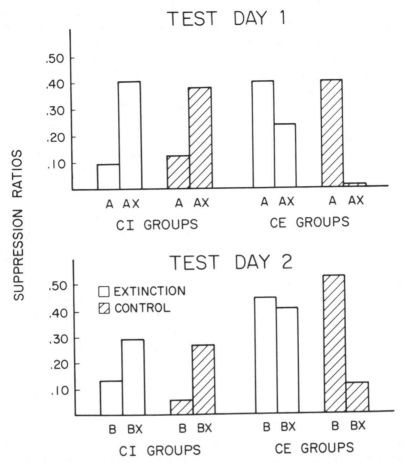

FIG. 8.10.   Mean suppression ratios on test days for subjects that had (open bars) and had not (filled bars) received nonreinforced presentations of X. A ratio of .00 indicates complete suppression, whereas a ratio of .50 indicates no suppression. See text for explanation of labels and group treatments.

CI groups (left panels), nonreinforced presentations of X did not alter its ability to attenuate conditioned suppression; significantly less suppression occurred to the AX and BX compounds than to A and B alone, regardless of whether or not X had been separately nonreinforced; that is, in replication of Zimmer–Hart and Rescorla's major findings, there was no evidence of a loss of the X → no-US association as a result of nonreinforced presentations of the X stimulus. In contrast, nonreinforced presentations of X in the CE group (right panels) *did* alter its ability to produce conditioned suppression. There was significantly less suppression on the compound trials when X had been nonreinforced than when it had not (for AX and BX, compare open and filled bars). In addition, the difference in suppression between A and AX and between B and BX was smaller for animals that had received X-alone trials than for controls. Thus, clear-cut extinction of X's acquired effects was seen in the CE group, but no parallel extinction in the CI group. Nonetheless, it is still possible that an appropriate assay (e.g., ease of reconditioning X) would reveal a strong persisting X → US association in the CE subjects whose performance no longer indicated a powerful effect of X.

Owren and Kaplan pointed out that, although their findings could be used to support Zimmer–Hart and Rescorla's suggestion of an asymmetry between the effective mechanisms of conditioned excitation and conditioned inhibition, an alternative but relatively informal interpretation would consider conditioned excitation and inhibition as basically symmetrical. Perhaps inhibitory associations do not extinguish when the USs are withdrawn, because at no point are the subject's expectancies during X violated by subsequent events (i.e., the CI is still not followed by US). On the other hand, preestablished expectancies of the US during a CE are violated during standard extinction (i.e., the CE is *not* followed by an expected US). The most obvious way to contradict the no-US expectancy generated by a CI would be to follow it consistently by the US during the postacquisition treatment phase. Zimmer–Hart and Rescorla instituted a procedure of this kind in their final experiment and found that, unlike what happens after removal of all USs, the amount of conditioned inhibition shown by X was highly attenuated on the critical test trials. However, even though this procedure removed the overt expression of conditioned inhibition, the possibility remains that decrements in conditioned inhibition observed within this counterconditioning arrangement do not signify erasure of the preestablished CS → no US association—which might be revealed by other assays or in other contexts (cf. our Experiment 4).

According to arguments advanced in Rescorla's (1979) paper, he would attribute the loss of CI-withdrawal behavior in our Experiments 1–4 described earlier, and in Bottjer's (1982) simple extinction (no USs) experiments, to removal of the background excitation required to detect conditioned inhibition. Likewise, Bottjer's evidence for "disinhibition" of extinguished CI performance could be alternatively interpreted as involving disinhibition of extinguished background excitation. A more detailed, direct experimental analysis of relations between actual performance losses and persisting but masked excitatory and inhibitory associative learning seems needed, via application of several different assays for determining the current power of discrete CSs and background factors. Until then, the best overall interpretation of these various findings will probably remain elusive.

We think that our procedures for obtaining trial-by-trial measures of opposing response tendencies to CEs and CIs in the sign-tracking arrangement are helpful in connection with assessing both learning and performance effects and could be extended to situations with aversive USs (see Hearst & Jenkins, 1974; Leclerc & Reberg, 1980). Rescorla's claim that conditioned inhibitors do not produce specific behaviors of their own seems unwarranted, although his argument that the expression of conditioned inhibition requires some kind of excitatory background has received general support from the work summarized in this chapter. Nevertheless, our suspicion that both CEs and CIs are difficult to "extinguish"—when extinction refers not to mere decrements in performance in a particular setting, but to reduction or elimination of learned relations between CSs and USs—appears plausible in view of the many techniques described here and elsewhere that have unmasked or reinstated currently silent excitatory and inhibitory associations.

SOME IMPLICATIONS FOR THE ROLE OF "CONTEXT" IN LEARNING AND PERFORMANCE

As indicated previously, our work involving separate postacquisition manipulation of the associative value of the experimental context could be taken to imply a basic asymmetry between conditioned excitation and inhibition. Whereas performance of asymptotic conditioned excitation appears to be largely unaffected by subsequent increases or decreases in the strength of general apparatus cues, background excitation seems to play a necessary, "supportive" role in the expression of conditioned inhibition. However, circumstances may certainly exist under which separate increases in contextual conditioning would weaken preestablished performance to a CE (cf. Randich & Ross, this volume, whose rats exhibited a transient decrement in conditioned suppression following 10 sessions of postacquisition exposure to unsignaled USs). The difficulties in equating the relative strengths of CIs and CEs have already been noted.

We have left unresolved the issue of how best to characterize the mechanisms by which background excitation controls CI performance, although Rescorla's (1979) threshold notion was judged compatible with much of our data. Another pertinent theoretical possibility derives from the view that losses of CRs in standard extinction studies may largely be due to the deterioration of an animal's US representation, despite survival of the original, learned CS–US relation (see, for example, Rescorla & Heth, 1975). In our studies, loss of CI performance after CONTEXT(−) exposure could have occurred because of a weakened US representation; and reinstatement of withdrawal CRs by a block of USs may be attributable to renewal of the US representation. However, no parallel loss of CRs was observed in the CE counterpart. Furthermore, our experiments suggest that US representations may be more context-specific than suspected in the past, First, nonreinforced exposure to a novel context did not weaken CI performance in Experiments 2–4. Second, our subjects received US (grain) presentations every day in their home cages when fed to maintain deprivation weights. A final relevant point is that actual US presentations were not required to reinstate CI performance, because CS+ presentations (or an intermixture of CS+ and CS−) revived withdrawal behavior in Experiment 3.

Bouton and Bolles (1979; see also Bouton & Bolles, this volume) advanced another alternative: that because animals can discriminate between situations where USs occur and do not occur, they learn to differentiate between episodes of "acquisition" and "extinction" while retaining appropriate memories of prior CS–US relations. Applied to our CI experiments, this formulation suggests that subjects discriminate between the context with USs and without USs. In the latter case, CONTEXT(−), reintroduction of the US may restore one of the most important features of the original training episode and hence reinstate CI performance. But there are problems applying this kind of analysis to our CE results, because approach and key pecking were largely unaffected by the various manipulations we tried.

Our proactive interference study (Experiment 4) raised the interesting possibility that the level of background associative strength can itself serve as a retrieval cue for old associations—like other, more traditional and external characteristics of contexts (see Medin & Reynolds, this volume, and Thomas, this volume). Thus, when a CS has a mixed or complicated conditioning history, the current associative value of the background may modulate the occurrence of "appropriate" behavior. Apparently, attributes of the general context can become associated with, integrated with, or actually signal a given CS–US relation. This possibility is analogous to Bouton and Bolles's (this volume) interpretation of several pertinent findings, as well as to aspects of Asratian's (1972) "switching" experiments (see also Balsam, this volume; Rescorla et al., this volume). Approaches stressing the hierarchical organization and conditional nature of contexts and CSs (Kaplan & Hearst, 1982; Nadel, Willner, & Kurz, this volume) may also provide some parallel insights. In any event, results of our Experiment 4 call into question the independence-of-path assumption of the Rescorla–Wagner model (see Wagner & Rescorla, 1972) and suggest that descriptions of the CSs in that experiment as "possessing" either excitatory or inhibitory associative strength fail to convey the richness of the animal's information-processing capabilities. We think that our techniques will prove valuable tools in the further study of the apparently complex interactions between CSs and attributes of contextual cues in Pavlovian conditioning.

Our chapter has certainly raised more questions than it has answered, and we have not offered any integrated approach encompassing a variety of seemingly related phenomena reported by ourselves and others. However, like most contributors to this volume and current researchers in human learning and memory (see Medin & Reynolds, this volume; Smith, 1979; Smith, Glenberg, & Bjork, 1978), we are convinced that the study of associative learning without consideration of the role of contextual factors would be an incomplete and misguided endeavor.

ACKNOWLEDGMENTS

The research described in this chapter was supported by National Institute of Mental Health Grant MH19300. We thank Sarah W. Bottjer, Dexter Gormley, Michael Owren,

Edda Thiels, and William T. Wolff for valuable advice and assistance. Peter Kaplan is now at the Department of Psychology, University of Colorado, Boulder, Co. 80309.

REFERENCES

Asratian, E. A. Genesis and localization of conditioned inhibition. In R. A. Boakes & M. S. Halliday (Eds.), *Inhibition and learning.* New York: Academic Press, 1972.

Baker, A. G. Conditioned inhibition is not the symmetrical opposite of conditioned excitation: A test of the Rescorla–Wagner model. *Learning and Motivation,* 1974, *5,* 369–379.

Balsam, P. D. Bringing the background to the foreground: The role of contextual cues in autoshaping. In M. Commons, R. Herrnstein, & A. R. Wagner (Eds.), *Quantitative analyses of behavior: Volume 3: Acquisition.* Cambridge, Mass.: Ballinger, 1984.

Bottjer, S. W. *Extinction and "disinhibition" of conditioned excitation and inhibition.* Unpublished doctoral dissertation, Indiana University, 1979.

Bottjer, S. W. Conditioned approach and withdrawal behavior in pigeons: Effects of a novel extraneous stimulus during acquisition and extinction. *Learning and Motivation,* 1982, *13,* 44–67.

Bouton, M. E., & Bolles, R. C. Contextual control of the extinction of conditioned fear. *Learning and Motivation,* 1979, *10,* 445–466.

Cunningham, C. L., Fitzgerald, R. D., & Francisco, D. L. Excitatory and inhibitory consequences of explicitly unpaired and truly random conditioning procedures on heart rate in rats. *Animal Learning and Behavior,* 1977, *5,* 135–142.

Dickinson, A. *Contemporary animal learning theory.* Cambridge, England: Cambridge University Press, 1980.

Gaffan, E., & Hart, M. M. Pigeons' withdrawal from an appetitive conditioned inhibitor under two training procedures. *Quarterly Journal of Experimental Psychology,* 1981, *33B,* 77–94.

Gibbon, J., & Balsam, P. Spreading association in time. In C. M. Locurto, H. S. Terrace, & J. Gibbon (Eds.), *Autoshaping and conditioning theory.* New York: Academic Press, 1981.

Hearst, E. Absence as information: Some implications for learning, performance, and representational processes. In H. L. Roitblat, T. G. Bever, & H. S. Terrace (Eds.), *Animal cognition.* Hillsdale, N.J.: Lawrence Erlbaum Associates, 1984.

Hearst, E., Bottjer, S. W., & Walker, E. Conditioned approach–withdrawal behavior and some signal–food relations in pigeons: Performance and positive vs. negative "associative strength." *Bulletin of the Psychonomic Society,* 1980, *16,* 183–186.

Hearst, E., & Franklin, S. Positive and negative relations between a signal and food: Approach–withdrawal behavior to the signal. *Journal of Experimental Psychology: Animal Behavior Processes,* 1977, *3,* 37–52.

Hearst, E., & Jenkins, H. M. *Sign-tracking: The stimulus–reinforcer relation and directed action.* Austin, Texas: The Psychonomic Society, 1974.

Kaplan, P., & Hearst, E. Bridging temporal gaps between CS and US in autoshaping: Insertion of other stimuli before, during, and after CS. *Journal of Experimental Psychology: Animal Behavior Processes,* 1982, *8,* 187–203.

Konorski, J. *Conditioned reflexes and neuron organization.* Cambridge, England: Cambridge University Press, 1948.

Konorski, J. *Integrative activity of the brain.* Chicago: University of Chicago Press, 1967.

Leclerc, R., & Reberg, D. Sign-tracking in aversive conditioning. *Learning and Motivation,* 1980, *11,* 302–317.

Lindblom, L. L., & Jenkins, H. M. Responses eliminated by noncontingent or negatively contingent reinforcement recover in extinction. *Journal of Experimental Psychology: Animal Behavior Processes,* 1981, *7,* 175–190.

Owren, M. J., & Kaplan, P. S. *On the failure to extinguish Pavlovian conditioned inhibition: A test of a reinstatement hypothesis.* Paper presented at the meeting of the Midwestern Psychological Association, Detroit, April, 1981.

Reberg, D. Compound tests for excitation in early acquisition and after prolonged extinction of conditioned suppression. *Learning and Motivation,* 1972, *3,* 246–258.

Rescorla, R. A. Pavlovian conditioning and its proper control procedures. *Psychological Review,* 1967, *74,* 71–80.

Rescorla, R. A. Pavlovian conditioned inhibition. *Psychological Bulletin,* 1969, *72,* 77–94.

Rescorla, R. A. Conditioned inhibition and extinction. In A. Dickinson & R. A. Boakes (Eds.), *Mechanisms of learning and motivation: A memorial volume to Jerzy Konorski.* Hillsdale, N.J.: Lawrence Erlbaum Associates, 1979.

Rescorla, R. A. *Pavlovian second-order conditioning: Studies in associative learning.* Hillsdale, N.J.: Lawrence Erlbaum Associates, 1980.

Rescorla, R. A., & Heth, C. D. Reinstatement of fear to an extinguished conditioned stimulus. *Journal of Experimental Psychology: Animal Behavior Processes,* 1975, *104,* 88–96.

Rescorla, R. A., & Wagner, A. R. A theory of Pavlovian conditioning: Variations in the effectiveness of reinforcement and nonreinforcement. In A. H. Black & W. F. Prokasy (Eds.), *Classical conditioning II: Current research and theory.* New York: Appleton–Century–Crofts, 1972.

Smith, S. M. Remembering in and out of context. *Journal of Experimental Psychology: Human Learning and Memory,* 1979, *5,* 460–471.

Smith, S. M., Glenberg, A. M., & Bjork, R. A. Environmental context and human memory. *Memory and Cognition,* 1978, *6,* 342–353.

Wagner, A. R., & Rescorla, R. A. Inhibition in Pavlovian conditioning: Application of a theory. In R. A. Boakes & M. S. Halliday (Eds.), *Inhibition and learning.* New York: Academic Press, 1972.

Wasserman, E. A., Franklin, S., & Hearst, E. Pavlovian appetitive contingencies and approach vs. withdrawal to conditioned stimuli in pigeons. *Journal of Comparative and Physiological Psychology,* 1974, *86,* 616–627.

Weisman, R. G., & Dodd, P. W. D. The study of association: Methodology and basic phenomena. In A. Dickinson & R. A. Boakes (Eds.), *Mechanisms of learning and motivation: A memorial volume to Jerzy Konorski.* Hillsdale, N.J.: Lawrence Erlbaum Associates, 1979.

Yadin, E., & Thomas, E. Septal correlates of conditioned inhibition and excitation in rats. *Journal of Comparative and Physiological Psychology,* 1981, *95,* 331–340.

Zimmer–Hart, C. L., & Rescorla, R. A. Extinction of Pavlovian conditioned inhibition. *Journal of Comparative and Physiological Psychology,* 1974, *86,* 837–845.

9 Contextual Control of Taste-Aversion Conditioning and Extinction

Trevor Archer
Astra Chemicals, Södertälje, Sweden

Per–Olow Sjödén
University of Uppsala, Uppsala, Sweden

Lars–Göran Nilsson
University of Umeå, Umeå, Sweden

In the natural environment, organisms must select between various stimulus events in order to survive. The specification of stimulus selection principles has been achieved in the laboratory by investigations of associative learning (Kehoe & Gormezano, 1980; Mackintosh, 1973; Razran, 1971). In such studies, the experimenter arbitrarily defines and purposely presents some stimuli in the array as conditioned stimuli (CSs), others as unconditioned stimuli (USs), whereas the remaining events are not considered at all or are relegated to a class of background or contextual stimuli. Most studies of associative learning up to the 1960s focused solely on relationships between those discrete events that were defined as CSs and USs. The more or less continuously present background stimuli or context in which the discrete events were presented attracted very little interest. The relative neglect of the total context of stimulus presentations can be illustrated by the fact that until recently, only a few works on associative learning have used *background stimuli* or *context* as index terms (e.g., Domjan & Burkhard, 1982; Honig & Staddon, 1977). This is not to say that the topic of contextual influences has been ignored in other works (e.g., Dickinson, 1980; Estes, 1975), but that the topic seems not to have been considered important enough to deserve a special index term. In fact, the observation of conditioning to contextual stimuli in the absence of a specific, formal CS was described already by Pavlov in terms of a "synthetic environmental reflex" (1927). Conditioning involving contextual stimuli is often studied with the traditional overshadowing and blocking procedures (e.g., Mackintosh, 1977) and therefore frequently indexed under these terms.

In fact, there may be good reason why the terms background stimuli and context deserve no special status in the analysis of learning. From the learning organism's point of view, the distinction between background stimuli and discrete CSs and USs may be quite arbitrary. The most apparent differences between CS/USs and contextual stimuli are the following: (1) CSs and USs frequently have a phasic character, whereas contextual stimuli are more or less static features of the environment. (It should be noted that this is a quantitative rather than a qualitative distinction.); (2) CSs and USs are often relatively more novel to the organism than are contextual stimuli. However, to the extent that principles governing learning about novel, phasic stimuli and familiar, static stimuli are similar (cf. Baker et al., this volume), a background stimulus is "just another stimulus" to the organism. On the other hand, learning about contextual stimuli may be different from learning about other sorts of stimuli (cf. Nadel, Willner, & Kurz, this volume) and may therefore require special treatment (see Bouton & Bolles, this volume, for a discussion of this issue). Irrespective of these considerations, the theoretical importance of an analysis of contextual conditioning phenomena can hardly be overestimated (Estes, 1973, 1975; Rescorla & Wagner, 1972; Wagner, 1976; Wagner & Rescorla, 1972).

Contextual Stimuli in Taste-Aversion Learning: Early Notions

Contextual stimuli are often defined as exteroceptive stimuli within the experimental environment that are not purposely correlated with CS and US presentations. Typical examples are lights that illuminate the environment, background noise, odors, and the walls and floor of the test box. When taste substances are employed as CSs, properties of the fluid source (e.g., the bottle) should also be considered. In most early studies of associative learning, these kinds of stimuli were usually not varied systematically with CS and US presentations. This practice was presumably a consequence of the then prevalent assumption that they acquired no control over responding. In spite of its relatively recent nature, the field of taste-aversion learning was dominated by a similar assumption for some time, due mostly to the results of some early studies.

Garcia and Koelling (1966) presented rats with a compound CS composed of taste, auditory, and visual elements, which was paired with either an electric shock or an illness-type US. During subsequent testing, rats that had the compound paired with illness avoided only the taste element, whereas rats that had the compound paired with shock avoided only the auditory–visual element. One of several implications of this result was that of a differential associability of interoceptive (taste) and exteroceptive (auditory, visual) stimuli with illness-type USs. Thus, in rats, associations between exteroceptive stimuli and nausea were considered difficult, if not impossible, to establish, at least in comparison to taste-nausea associations (Garcia, Kimeldorf, & Hunt, 1961; Green, Holmstrom, & Wollman, 1974). In several other studies, where exteroceptive stimuli have been paired with illness, subsequent water intake in the presence of these stimuli has been suppressed very little (Domjan & Wilson, 1972; Garcia & Koelling, 1967; Garcia, McGowan, Ervin, & Koelling, 1968). There are also a large number of subsequent studies in which rats were presented with a taste–auditory–visual compound paired with illness, and which demonstrate that aversions are learned to the taste element but not to the auditory–visual elements (Best, Best, & Mickley, 1973; Garcia, Kovner, & Green, 1970; Hargrave & Bolles, 1971; Larsen & Hyde, 1977; Slotnick, Brown, & Gelhard, 1977; Wilcoxon, Dragoin, & Kral, 1971; Woods, Makous, & Hutton, 1969). On the basis of these findings from experiments in which exteroceptive stimuli were paired with illness either singly or in compound with taste, it was concluded that contextual stimuli in general were of little or no relevance in the taste-aversion learning paradigm. Thus, it was proposed by Revusky and Garcia (1970) that rats "tend to ignore external events" (p. 22) and that, according to Garcia, Hankins, and Rusiniak (1974) "time–space contextual information . . . is dispensed with as unnecessary" (p. 828) in taste-aversion learning. The independence of taste-aversion learning from contextual stimuli was thought to set this form of learning apart from more traditional types of associative conditioning, and a neoevolutionary theoretical framework was proposed to handle this observation (Seligman, 1970). It was proposed that "Rats are prepared, by virtue of their evolutionary history, to associate tastes with malaise. . . . Further, rats are contraprepared to associate exteroceptive events with nausea" (p. 409). This preparedness/contrapreparedness was thought to have originated in the nocturnal feeding habits of rodent species and made sense from an evolutionary point of view, because stimulus qualities of ingested substances seem to be the most reliable predictors of malaise in the natural environment.

Thus, the finding of an unequal associability of taste and visual–auditory CSs with illness and shock USs (the "Garcia effect") seems amply documented. In the preceding studies, the exteroceptive stimuli were mostly presented in compound with taste, and no efforts were made to study the influence of more static features of the environment. This procedural choice was dictated by the main interest of the research: to investigate the relative roles of interoceptive and exteroceptive stimulus events in aversion learning in general. However, the conclusions from this research regarding the role of contextual stimuli in taste-aversion learning were too far ranging in view of the procedures employed. We maintain that the role of static as well as phasic contextual stimuli in taste-aversion learning needs to be examined with other procedures and experimental designs.

Procedural Requirements for Demonstrating Context Effects

The basic taste-aversion learning situation can be defined as follows: An organism ingests some solid food substance or fluid and experiences a gastrointestinal disturbance some time later. The disturbance is usually thought of as malaise, nausea, and/or vomiting, although its precise nature still remains in doubt (Braveman, 1977; Gamzu, 1977), as do the possible commonalities of agents capable of inducing it. In aversion learning with a gastrointestinal US, the animal is faced with the task of finding out what stimulus events caused the subsequent nausea and illness. In any particular situation, there are several classes of stimuli within which possible causes of illness could conceivably be found: visual, auditory, olfactory, gustatory, and kinesthetic. In each class, there is a multitude of events with which the animal could associate the illness. If we confine ourselves to the ingested solid or fluid, there is likewise a range of stimulus classes and a number of events within each class that could be used to predict future nausea episodes: taste, smell, texture, temperature, etc. The central concern in much of the research on aversion learning with gastrointestinal USs has been to delineate whether and to what extent the animal "attributes" the cause of the illness to exteroceptive versus interoceptive CSs. And, as mentioned earlier, the main conclusion has been that, for rats, taste stimuli generally acquire a higher associative strength than stimuli of other classes, and at a faster rate. However, this finding does not address the main issue concerning contextual effects in taste-aversion learning, viz. how the control over aversion strength by taste CSs is affected by contextual stimuli.

A recent concern in the contemporary study of virtually all forms of associative learning has been to investigate the possible influences of contextual stimuli on the learning process (e.g., Dickinson, 1980). In line with this tradition, we wish to define the central problem in the area of contextual influences on taste-aversion learning as follows: Does the presence or absence of contextual stimuli influence whether and to what extent the animal "attributes" the cause of an illness experience to a preceding taste stimulus? In the studies reported, contextual stimuli can be either relatively static (e.g., presented on a 24-hr basis), or of a more phasic character (e.g., presented for 30 min). In some of the experiments, they are relatively uncorrelated with CS and US events. In others, they are correlated with a nominal CS, as when a taste substance (CS) is presented in a specific drinking bottle (contextual stimulus). The inclusion of phasic as well as static stimuli with different temporal relationships to CSs and USs in the contextual category is motivated by the lack of clear topographical and, so far, functional distinctions between them. In accordance with the suggestion by Thomas (this volume), the central concern in the study of contextual stimulus control is the effect of one stimulus on the control of behavior exercised by other stimuli (e.g., nominal CSs). As is discussed later, the definition of contextual stimuli and their temporal relation to CS and US events is more complex in taste-aversion learning than in many other paradigms. For each experiment described in the following pages, the prevailing stimulus characteristics are explicitly stated.

A straightforward way of investigating the influence of contextual stimuli on taste-aversion learning was suggested by Estes' model of memory and conditioning (1973) (i.e., testing of postconditioning aversion strength in the presence and absence of the conditioning background context). Thus, we varied some aspects of contextual stimuli in a systematic fashion during the phases of acquisition and extinction of taste aversions. Our initial experiments studied the role of stimuli pertaining to: (1) the bottle in which the taste CS is presented; (2) the animal housing environment in which the taste CS is consumed; and (3) an odor component. In some of the experiments, we employed a conditioning context consisting of these several components and then studied the extinction of the taste aversion in situations where one or more of the conditioning stimulus components were present. In some experiments, we retested the animals in the conditioning context after their taste aversion was extinguished in contexts characterized by a varying number of conditioning context stimulus components.

The basic design used in these experiments was as follows: Rats were first trained to drink a daily water ration during a 30-min period per day. On the taste-aversion conditioning trials, a 2% saccharin solution was substituted for water and an intraperitoneal .15 M lithium chloride (LiCl) solution (10 ml/kg bodyweight) was administered within 15–20 min of saccharin drinking. Manipulations of contextual stimuli consisting of an animal compartment and an odor element were achieved by presenting this stimulus compound either on a 24-hr basis beginning at the first saccharin-conditioning trial, or only during the 30-min saccharin-drinking periods. Contextual bottle stimuli were always presented only in conjunction with the saccharin presentations. After conditioning, saccharin aversions were extinguished in the presence of either the entire contextual stimulus compound or some or one of its elements. Daily 30-min saccharin-drinking periods constituted extinction trials. A *context-dependent conditioning effect* was said to occur if, during extinction, the saccharin intake of animals drinking in the presence of the same context as during conditioning was less than that of animals not exposed to contextual-conditioning cues. Postextinction saccharin preference tests (one bottle of saccharin vs. one bottle of water) were performed in the presence of the entire conditioning context, and/or the extinction context of each specific group. A *context-dependent extinction effect* was defined as a lower saccharin preference in groups not exposed to conditioning contextual cues during extinction as compared to those that had drunk saccharin in the conditioning context during the extinction phase.

It should be noted that the context-dependent conditioning effect is usually measured by one-bottle tests, whereas extinction effects are measured by a two-bottle procedure. This makes direct comparisons of the magnitude of these effects impossible, because the two-bottle procedure is usually the more sensitive of the two (Grote & Brown, 1971). Moreover, context-dependent extinction effects (measured during preference tests) cannot be considered totally independent of the conditioning effects, because the magnitude of drinking during extinction is both a consequence of events taking place at conditioning and, presumably, determines the intake on the subsequent preference tests. However, one-bottle tests were chosen for the extinction phase in most experiments in order to ensure complete extinction of the aversiveness of relevant stimuli in a small number of trials. Preference tests were selected for the last testing phase to achieve sufficient sensitivity to detect weak aversions.

A Demonstration of Contextual Effects in Taste-Aversion Learning

Our starting point for the first study (Archer, Sjödén, Nilsson, & Carter, 1979b) was the fact that, in some contemporary theories of conditioning (e.g., Estes, 1973; Rescorla & Wagner, 1972), an important role was assigned to the exteroceptive background context in which the CS–US pairing takes place. This notion was in sharp contrast to the prevailing opinion among taste-aversion learning researchers concerning the role of exteroceptive contextual stimuli. On the basis of Estes' model of memory and conditioning (1973), we thus predicted that a change of exteroceptive context from the conditioning to an extinction phase would lead to a weaker conditioned response (CR) than if the conditioning context was maintained. Further, we wished to investigate the effects of extinguishing the CR in a context different from the conditioning context on the CR in the conditioning context. A possible prediction from Estes (1973) would be that extinction is specific to its context (cf. Bouton & Bolles, this volume).

It should be noted that clear evidence implicating contextual stimuli in taste-aversion learning was already available in earlier literature, but was inexplicably overlooked. As an example, Slotnick et al. (1977) monitored water intake by rats at three spatial positions, A, B, and C, of which A was the preferred one. Saccharin (CS) was presented at location A, and apomorphine (US) was injected after its consumption. During subsequent saccharin-aversion tests, the animals avoided saccharin when it was presented at A, but showed considerable preference for it when presented at location B. Because the rats continued to prefer water at location A after conditioning, the authors concluded that a taste aversion, but not a location aversion, was established, ignoring the fact that saccharin was copiously consumed at location B. Our interpretation of these data is that the animals acquired an aversion for saccharin that was specific to location A, and that they acquired an aversion for location A only when saccharin, but not when water, was presented at that location.

In our first demonstration of contextual effects, four groups of rats ($n = 6$) were given two 30-min presentations of a saccharin solution followed either by a

LiCl injection (3 groups), or by a sodium chloride (NaCl) injection (1 group). All animals were placed in an unfamiliar context during a 6-day drinking training period prior to conditioning. The unfamiliar context consisted of a darkened, opaque plastic box, in which a thin layer of menthol-smelling ointment was smeared on one inner wall to give a distinct odor stimulus. In these "contextual compartments," water was presented in "noisy" bottles with metal nozzles that had a 6-mm hole at the tip and contained two small metal balls, which created considerable noise when the animals licked the nozzles. Beginning at the first conditioning trial, the animals were returned to "normal" compartments, consisting of individual Perspex cages with metal grid covers, no explicit odor stimulus, and fluids presented in "silent" standard glass bottles with 2-mm wide metal nozzles. They remained in these cages on a 24-hr basis during conditioning. Thus, cage and odor stimuli were present on a 24-hr basis, whereas the bottles (also considered to be a contextual aspect for taste presentations) were present only during saccharin drinking. The animals had previously experienced the cages during a 2-week period of acclimatization to laboratory conditions.

All animals were given saccharin + LiCl (or saccharin + NaCl) pairings in relatively unfamiliar contexts. Group labels refer to: (1) the number of conditioning trials (viz., 2); and (2) whether they were placed in the same (S) or a different (D) context during saccharin-aversion extinction as during conditioning. In addition, W indicates that water was presented instead of saccharin during the extinction phase, and C (control) alludes to the fact that this group was given NaCl instead of LiCl at conditioning.

The results of this experiment are illustrated in Fig. 9.1. The data from the extinction phase ($E_1 - E_5$) indicate that the background stimuli of the conditioning phase exerted considerable control over the amount of fluid drunk during extinction (Fig. 9.1, left-hand panel). Thus, only Group 2S showed a strong and consistent saccharin aversion in comparison to Groups 2DW (water) and 2DC (saccharin), whereas Group 2D (saccharin) evidenced an aversion only on E_1. A context-specific saccharin aversion is clearly indicated. After the extinction phase, three preference tests were performed, the first two in the conditioning context of all groups ("normal" cages, no odor, "silent" bottles) and the third in the context prevailing during the extinction phase ("contextual" compartments, mentholated odor, "noisy" bottles). The preference test data (Fig. 9.1, right-hand panel) illustrate that extinction of the saccharin aversion in a context different from that of the conditioning trials (Group 2D) did not result in a decrease of the aversion in the conditioning context (T_1 and T_2). However, reinstatement of the extinction context for Group 2D on T_3 yielded no evidence of a saccharin aversion. These observations warrant the conclusion that a context-specific extinction effect was demonstrated. In a second experiment of the same study (Archer et al., 1979b), we switched the background stimuli across conditioning and extinction phases, so that conditioning took place in "contextual" compartments, and extinction in "normal" cages. Also, the effect of

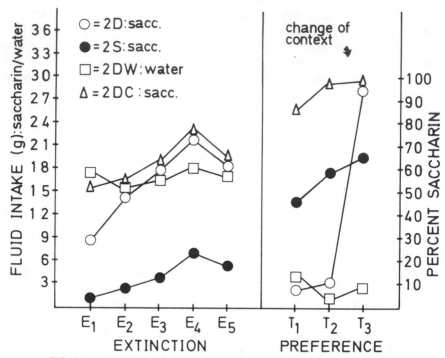

FIG. 9.1.   Fluid intake during extinction phase (left) and percentage saccharin preference on preference tests (right) for Groups 2D, 2S, 2DW, and 2DC. Fluids presented during extinction are indicated in the left-hand panel. (Copyright 1979 Psychonomic Society, Inc. Reprinted by permission of the publisher from T. Archer, P. O. Sjödén, L. G. Nilsson, & N. Carter, Role of exteroceptive background context in taste-aversion conditioning and extinction, *Animal Learning and Behavior*, 1979, 7, 17–22.)

one versus two conditioning trials was investigated. The results were essentially the same, except that a smaller context-dependent conditioning effect was seen after one trial than after two trials.

On the basis of these results, we concluded that the background context of the conditioning trial exerts a major control over the amount of saccharin consumed on subsequent one-bottle tests. In fact, evidence of a saccharin aversion was obtained on a number of the extinction tests only when the background contexts of the conditioning and extinction trials were identical. Moreover, the background context present during the extinction phase largely determined the degree of aversion on subsequent preference tests. Thus, the importance of contextual stimuli was clearly illustrated, whereas the specific stimuli exerting contextual control and the precise nature of this control cannot be decided from the data of the first study.

The background context consisted of a compound of visual, auditory, tactual, and olfactory elements. There are thus several possible stimulus elements that could constitute the basis for the context-dependent effects. For example, the taste of saccharin in the presence of the odor could conceivably be sufficiently different from the taste in the absence of the odor, resulting in a stimulus generalization decrement from conditioning to extinction in the D groups. It should also be noted that the size of the drinking nozzles differed between the contexts employed in the first study, as did the tongue-tactile stimulation arising from the presence of metal balls in one type of nozzles. Nachman, Rauschenberger, and Ashe (1977a, b) have shown that this variable can be used to establish an aversion to a specific drinking bottle in the absence of a taste stimulus.

Aversions to Nongustatory Stimuli

Odor Stimuli.   The interaction of gustatory and olfactory stimuli in feeding and drinking behavior (Barnett, 1963) might lead one to assume that odor stimuli are more relevant to the conditioning of aversions than are stimuli derived from other modalities. However, a serious source of confounding in odor-aversion studies is that airborne olfactory stimuli may be potential sources of stimulation for both olfactory and gustatory receptors (Somjen, 1972). Notwithstanding this complication, a number of studies have demonstrated odor aversions (Booth & Simson, 1971; Domjan, 1973; Garcia & Koelling, 1967; Larue, 1975; Lorden, Kenfield, & Braun, 1970; Lovett, Goodchild, & Booth, 1968; Pain & Booth, 1968; Rudy & Cheatle, 1977; Simson & Booth, 1973; Supak, Macrides, & Chorover, 1971; Taukulis, 1974; Taukulis & Revusky, 1975). In spite of the preceding findings, the importance of odor stimuli in taste-aversion learning has been questioned. In studies where peripherally anosmic rats were utilized (Barnett, Cowan, Randford & Prakash, 1975; Hankins, Garcia, & Rusiniak, 1973), no impairment of taste-aversion learning was found. It has been concluded that when a stimulus compound consisting of taste and odor elements is presented at conditioning, aversions are conditioned to the taste element, and odor is largely ignored (Hankins, Rusiniak, & Garcia, 1976; Hargrave & Bolles, 1971). Still, olfaction apparently exerts some influence on performance in a taste-aversion learning paradigm, and the possibility of taste-odor and odor-taste generalization has been considered (Ader, 1977). In any case, the contribution of the odor element to the observed contextual control of learned taste aversions (Archer et al., 1979b) clearly needs specification.

Tactual Stimuli.   Similarly, there is considerable evidence that tactual or somatosensory stimuli associated with the animal's drinking responses are of importance. In the Nachman et al. (1977a) study it was found that the size of spouts of the fluid containers was an important stimulus in learned aversions. Similarly, Nachman (1970) showed that rats are capable of learning an aversion to the temperature of water. Revusky and Parker (1976) have demonstrated marked aversions to unflavored water presented in a particular drinking cup. Although the consensus of these studies is that somatosensory and, in particular, tongue-tactile stimuli are effective, they are not considered to be equally effective as gustatory stimuli (Nachman et al., 1977a, b) for establishing aversions. In general, aversions to nongustatory stimuli are weaker and require a greater number of acquisition trials compared to aversions to taste stimuli.

Compartment Stimuli. In the absence of an explicit taste stimulus at conditioning, it has been demonstrated that some degree of aversion is established to a distinctive animal compartment after severe illness (Andrews & Cameron, 1960; Arbit, 1959; Garcia, Kimeldorf, & Hunt, 1956, 1961; Martin, 1966; Martin & Ellinwood, 1974; Mitchell, Kirschbaum, & Perry, 1975; Overall & Brown, 1959; Overall, Brown, & Logie, 1960; Overall, Logie, & Brown, 1959; Rozin, 1969). Also, if toxicosis occurs in connection with ingestion of visually distinctive material, rats will form an aversion to those stimuli (Braveman, 1977). Negative findings have been reported (Garcia & Koelling, 1967; Rohles, Overall, & Brown, 1959). Learned aversions to an exteroceptive stimulus (usually a distinctive compartment) in the presence of a taste CS at conditioning have been shown (Cunningham, 1979, 1980; Morrison & Collyer, 1974). Another methodological variation used to illustrate the importance of the environmental context is the Kamin (1969) blocking procedure. This has been employed most widely in the investigation of the "drug preexposure effect" in taste-aversion learning. Typically, presentations of an illness-inducing drug are made in the presence of a particular exteroceptive context, followed by the conditioning of an aversion to a novel taste CS with the identical US. Rudy, Iwens, and Best (1977) found that environmental stimuli associated with illness through preexposure acquired the ability to block the formation of subsequent taste-illness associations. That general finding has since been replicated repeatedly (Batson & Best, 1979; Best & Batson, 1977; Braveman, 1979; Willner, 1978), although the suitability of the blocking explanation has been questioned (Braveman, 1979). Rudy, Rosenberg, and Sandell (1977) also demonstrated the importance of contextual, exteroceptive stimulation for the CS (taste) preexposure phenomenon.

The Relative Importance of Different Contextual Elements. In two studies (Archer, Sjödén, & Carter, 1979a; Archer, Sjödén, Nilsson, & Carter, 1980), we attempted to reach a specification of the relative importance of odor, bottle, and compartment stimuli for the contextual control of learned taste aversions. The main findings are illustrated by results from two of the eight experiments of these studies. The purpose of the first experiment was to compare the degree of control over subsequent saccharin aversion exerted by an odor stimulus (menthol) and by compartment + bottle elements present on a saccharin-aversion conditioning trial. Thus, saccharin and LiCl were paired either in the presence of a novel odor stimulus or of a novel compartment + drinking bottle. During a subsequent extinction phase, saccharin intake was measured in the presence or absence of the particular conditioning context. Compartments and the odor stimulus were presented on a 24-hr basis within each experimental phase, thus constituting relatively static contextual aspects. Bottle stimuli were present only during 30-min periods of saccharin drinking. Two groups were given a saccharin-LiCl pairing in the presence of a distinct mentholated odor, and for one of the groups, the odor was present (Group OP) during subsequent extinction, whereas it was absent (OA) in the other group. Two other groups were conditioned in the presence of novel compartment + bottle stimuli, and for one, compartments + bottles were present (CBP) during extinction, whereas they were absent (CBA) for the other group. In addition, one group was conditioned without any explicit manipulation of contextual stimuli and was given water to drink during the extinction phase (Group NW). When the animals were not exposed to the odor, compartments, or ''noisy'' bottles, they were housed in their home cages and water was presented in standard ''silent'' bottles. After five extinction trials, saccharin-preference tests were performed in the presence of the conditioning context for all groups, in order to investigate possible context-dependent extinction effects.

The main results are illustrated in Fig. 9.2. During the extinction phase, the odor stimulus of the conditioning trial did not control saccharin intake. Thus, the amount of saccharin drunk by the group in the presence of the odor stimulus (OP) did not differ from that drunk by the group removed from the odor (OA) on any of the test days. In contrast, the compartment + bottle contextual compound exerted a major control over saccharin intake. The group given extinction trials in the presence of these elements (CBP) consumed less saccharin on the three first trials (E_1-E_3) than did the group in which these elements were absent during extinction (CBA). The preference-test data illustrate a context-dependent extinction effect for the compartment + bottle elements, but not for the odor elements. Thus, the saccharin aversion had extinguished in both odor groups (OP and OA), irrespective of the presence or absence of the odor during extinction. However, the group in which the compartment + bottle elements were absent during extinction (CBA) showed as strong an aversion as the no-saccharin-extinction control group (NW). This should be contrasted with the virtually nonexistent aversion in Group CBP.

The fact that the odor element was demonstrated not to exert significant control over saccharin intake should not be taken to indicate that odor stimuli are ignored in this situation. In one of the experiments (Archer et al., 1980), we found evidence that rats learn about the mentholated odor as well. In the absence of the taste stimulus during a postconditioning extinction phase, the odor that had been present on the saccharin-aversion conditioning trial did control the amount

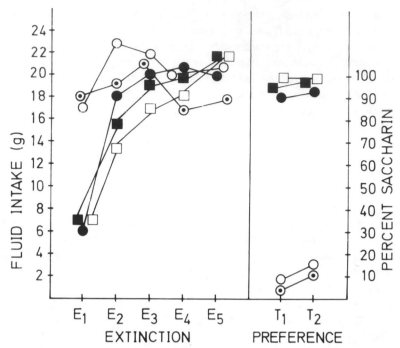

FIG. 9.2. Fluid intake during extinction phase (left) and percentage saccharin preference on preference tests (right) for Groups OP ■, OA ● CBP □, CBA ○, and NW ◉ Fluids presented during extinction are indicated in the text. (Reprinted by permission of the Experimental Psychology Society from T. Archer, P. O. Sjödén, L. G. Nilsson, & N. Carter, Exteroceptive context in taste-aversion conditioning and extinction: Odour, cage, and bottle stimuli, *Quarterly Journal of Experimental Psychology*, 1980, *32*, 197–214.)

of water consumed. On subsequent preference tests, the groups that had consumed water during extinction in the presence of the odor context, evidenced a lesser saccharin aversion than groups not exposed to the odor. It thus seems as if the role of odor as a contextual stimulus in taste-aversion learning is most easily revealed when the taste is absent at testing or during extinction.

To pinpoint more specifically which aspect of the compartment + bottle context controls postconditioning saccharin intake, we varied each of these elements separately in a further experiment. In addition, we altered the temporal relationship of the compartments to the taste CS so that compartments were present only during saccharin drinking. Thus, compartments as well as bottles had approximately the same temporal relationship to saccharin drinking. Four groups of rats were given a saccharin-aversion conditioning trial in the presence of a novel compartment + bottle context. During saccharin-aversion extinction, both compartment + bottle stimuli were present in one group (CBP) and were absent in one group (CBA), only the compartments were present in one group (CP), and only the bottles were present in the last group (BP). Postextinction preference tests were performed in the total conditioning context. The relative influence of the compartments and bottles should be indicated by the degree to which they suppress saccharin drinking during extinction. Moreover, their relative importance should be reflected in context-dependent preference-test results.

The results of this experiment are illustrated in Fig. 9.3. The presence of the compartments + bottles (Group CBP) of conditioning resulted in a lesser saccharin intake during extinction than when these stimuli were absent (CBA). In addition, the results suggest that the presence of the bottle element (BP) also resulted in a suppression of saccharin intake on the first extinction trial (E_1), whereas there was no suppression due to the animal compartment alone (CP). However, the presence of the compartment contributed to the suppression of intake on E_2 in Group CBP as compared to BP. Reinstatement of the total conditioning context during preference tests (CBA) revealed a stronger aversion

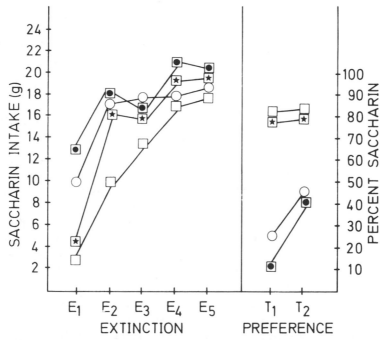

FIG. 9.3. Saccharin intake during extinction phase (left) and percentage saccharin preference on preference tests (right) for Groups CBP □, CBA ○, CP ●, and BP ★ (Reprinted by permission of the Experimental Psychology Society from T. Archer, P. O. Sjödén, L. G. Nilsson, & N. Carter, Exteroceptive context in taste-aversion conditioning and extinction: Odour, cage, and bottle stimuli, *Quarterly Journal of Experimental Psychology*, 1980, *32*, 197–214.)

than that occurring when the conditioning context had been present throughout the extinction phase (CBP). Furthermore, the reinstatement of the bottle element (CP) resulted in a considerable aversion, whereas no aversion was observed when the compartment element was reinstated (BP). In conclusion, the contextual bottle element of the conditioning trial exerts relatively strong control over learned saccharin aversions, whereas the control exerted by the compartment element is much weaker.

The bottle stimulus employed in the present studies provides the animals with contextual elements pertaining to several sensory modalities. Apart from differences of tongue-tactile stimulation arising from the use of nozzles of different sizes, and steel balls in the case of the "noisy" bottles, a difference of auditory stimulation is created by the clicking noise produced when drinking from the "noisy" bottles. In a further study (Archer et al., 1979a), we gave different groups of animals saccharin-aversion extinction trials in the presence of the "noisy" bottle used at conditioning, in its absence, or in the presence of the clicking noise of the "noisy" bottles while drinking from "silent" bottles. Whereas the presence or absence of the conditioning bottle resulted in the previously observed control of saccharin intake during extinction, the auditory element exerted no such control. Neither was there any evidence of an influence of the clicking noise on postextinction preference tests. Thus, tongue-tactile stimuli remain as the likely basis for the contextual bottle control over learned taste aversions.

The evidence cited in favor of context-dependent conditioning and extinction effects produced by stimuli arising from the animal compartment is relatively weak (cf. Archer et al., 1979a). However, the weakness of this evidence may have to do with the inadequacy of the designs employed in the experiments reviewed so far. Thus, in both studies (Archer et al., 1979a, Experiment 1; 1980, Experiment 5), compartment elements were conditioned in compound with previously unfamiliar "noisy" bottles, which raises the possibility that the strong bottle stimulus may have overshadowed (cf. Mackintosh, 1971) stimuli from the animal compartment. In order to investigate the role of compartment stimuli more directly, a study was initiated (Archer & Sjödén, 1981) in which the same bottles were presented to the animals during the preconditioning, conditioning, extinction, and preference-test phases. Thus, the animals already had considerable familiarity with the fluid bottles prior to the conditioning trial. The role of contextual stimulus novelty is discussed further later. At this point, it should be noted that the relative novelty of a contextual stimulus at conditioning is a strong determinant of the degree to which it will control later intake of the taste substance (Archer & Sjödén, 1979a, b, 1980, 1981). Thus, by using familiar bottles, the risk of bottle stimuli overshadowing compartmental stimuli should be considerably reduced.

Two saccharin-LiCl pairings were administered to four groups of rats in the presence of a novel, distinctive compartment, which was presented on a 24-hr basis within each experimental phase. During a subsequent saccharin-aversion extinction phase, saccharin was presented to two groups, either in the same compartment as during conditioning (Group SS = same, saccharin), or in a different environment (DS = different, saccharin). Two groups were offered water in the same (SW = same, water) or in a different (DW = different, water) environmental context. The latter two groups were included to investigate whether contextual control of postconditioning fluid intake was dependent on the presence of the taste stimulus, as found in a previous study (Archer et al., 1980). In that study, a compound consisting of compartment and bottle elements was demonstrated to control postconditioning fluid intake only in the presence of the taste CS.

Postextinction saccharin preference tests were performed in the conditioning environment for all groups. Contextual compartment-based control over fluid intake should be evidenced by a lower intake in Group SS than in Group DS during extinction, and by lower saccharin preference values in Group DS than in Group SS after the extinction phase.

The findings are illustrated in Fig. 9.4. In the extinction data, there was no evidence that the presence (SS and SW) or absence (DS and DW) of the conditioning compartment influenced the amount of fluid drunk during extinction: No context-dependent conditioning effect was observed. In contrast, the preference-test data revealed a context-dependent extinction effect. Group DS showed a significantly lower preference value than did Group SS after extinction. Thus, when rats extinguish their saccharin aversion in an animal compartment different from that present at conditioning, the saccharin aversion in the conditioning compartment remains virtually intact. The absence of a context-dependent conditioning effect based on compartment stimuli alone is in line with our previous conclusion that such stimuli exert relatively weak control over learned taste aversions. However, the context-dependent extinction effect attests to the fact that the animals learn about compartmental stimuli as well as odor, bottle, and taste stimuli on a taste-aversion conditioning trial.

In a recent experiment, we have attempted to use a procedure somewhat different from that employed in earlier studies. The purpose was to further investigate the relative importance of the various contextual elements: odor, compartments, and bottles. The procedure may be designated as a "contextual generalization" experiment. Thus, saccharin and LiCl were paired in the usual manner for all animals and presented in an environmental context consisting of novel "contextual" compartments (Archer et al., 1979b), novel "noisy" bottles, and a novel mentholated odor stimulus (Vick VapoRub). Subsequent saccharin-preference tests (saccharin vs. water) for assessing the degree of generalization of the saccharin aversion were given to different groups of animals ($n = 6$) in different contexts. Group CBO was tested in the presence of compartments, bottles, and the odor of the conditioning trial, Group CB in the presence of compartments and bottles, Group C in the presence of compartments only,

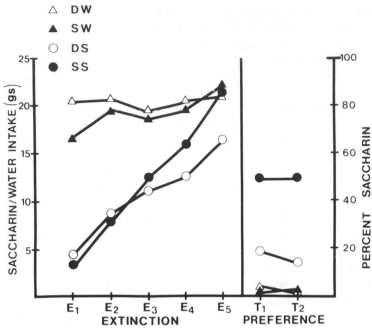

FIG. 9.4.   Fluid intake during extinction phase (left) and percentage saccharin preference on preference tests (right) for Groups DW, SW, DS, and SS. Fluids offered during extinction are indicated in the left-hand panel (second letter W = water, S = saccharin). (Copyright 1981 Psychonomic Society, Inc. Reprinted by permission of the publisher from T. Archer & P. O. Sjödén, Environment-dependent taste-aversion extinction: A question of stimulus novelty at conditioning, *Physiological Psychology*, 1981, *9,* 102–108.)

Group O in the presence of odor alone, and Group NIL was tested in the absence of all three contextual conditioning elements. When groups were not exposed to contextual conditioning elements, home cage and "silent" bottles were used. In this study, compartments and the odor were present on a 24-hour basis.

Nine consecutive, daily, 8-hr preference tests were administered, and the results are illustrated in Fig. 9.5. A split-plot analysis of variance indicated a significant Groups by Tests interaction ($F(32,200) = 3.1, p < .01$). Testing of pairwise between-groups, within-days differences with the Tukey HSD-test (Kirk, 1968) demonstrated that the strength of saccharin aversion was greatest in Groups CBO, CB, and C, where all three contextual elements, compartments + bottles, or compartments alone were present. Significantly weaker aversions were obtained in Groups O and NIL, where the odor stimulus alone or none of the contextual elements were present. (The decrease of saccharin preference on Tests 4 and 9 in Groups O and NIL represents a periodicity of saccharin intake,

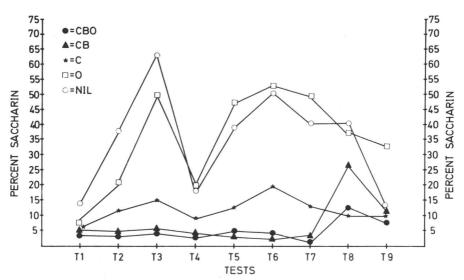

FIG. 9.5. Percentage saccharin preference for Groups CBO, CB, C, O, and NIL during a series of nine preference tests.

which has been routinely observed in our laboratory when a large number of two-bottle (saccharin vs. water) tests is given to animals with relatively high saccharin preference.) These results: (1) illustrate that animal compartments exert significant control over saccharin intake, provided that a more sensitive two-bottle preference test is used (cf. Grote & Brown, 1971); (2) attest to the importance of the bottle element; and (3) confirm our previous conclusions concerning the relative lack of influence from the odor element when presented in conjunction with taste.

The results of this experiment necessitate a revision of our previous conclusion (Archer & Sjödén, 1981) concerning the absence of a generalization decrement when cage or compartment stimuli alone are allowed to vary between conditioning and testing. By replacing the relatively insensitive one-bottle test with a two-bottle preference test of aversion differences, a clear and consistent generalization decrement was observed. It has been proposed that contextual background stimuli present at conditioning in appetitive (e.g., Sheafor, 1975) and aversively motivated paradigms (e.g., McAllister & McAllister, 1971) enter into the associative relationships established. By varying apparatus (McAllister & McAllister, 1963) and extraapparatus background stimuli (McAllister & McAllister, 1965) between shock-based fear conditioning and later hurdle-jumping escape responding, a generalization decrement had been previously demonstrated. Our data on taste-aversion learning demonstrate a similar kind of contextual dependence. And, as stated previously (Archer & Sjödén, 1981), "it seems as if the number and kinds of conditioning compound elements are strong determinants of the extent of contextual control over conditioned taste aversions'' (p. 107).

The Temporal Relationship Between CSs, USs, and Contextual Stimuli

In most paradigms of associative conditioning other than taste-aversion learning, the temporal relationship between the CS and contextual stimuli is comparatively unproblematic. Animals are placed in a certain compartment, a visual or auditory CS is presented, and a shock US follows. All background stimuli remain equally uncorrelated with CS and US presentations throughout. In taste-aversion learning, however, presentation of the taste CS necessitates that the animal is always tactually stimulated (whether CS presentation is accomplished by oral syringe or free drinking from a bottle), and sometimes visually (by the introduction of a bottle) or even auditively stimulated (when ''noisy'' bottles are used). These aspects of background stimulation are necessarily correlated with CS presentations to a greater or lesser extent. Odor and compartment stimuli can be as freely varied in taste-aversion learning as in other paradigms.

When considered in this perspective, our finding that bottle stimuli exert a stronger contextual control over saccharin aversions than odor and compartment stimuli is not surprising. In our first studies (Archer et al., 1979a, b), the bottle stimuli were the single stimuli present only during saccharin drinking at conditioning, extinction as well as during preference tests. The compartment stimuli were present for 24-hr per day during all three phases as was the odor stimulus.

Archer et al. (1980, Exp. IV and V) altered the procedure to achieve an identical temporal relationship between each of the contextual elements and CS presentation. Thus, compartments, odor, and bottle stimuli were present only during the saccharin-drinking periods at conditioning, extinction, and preference tests. This procedure obviously does not create a completely identical temporal relationship between all contextual stimuli and the taste CS. Such a relationship is probably impossible to reach, because each lick requires direct tactual stimulation from the fluid source simultaneously with delivery of the taste substance. A relationship with such close spatial and temporal characteristics as between tongue-tactile and taste stimuli is probably impossible to achieve for any of the other contextual elements.

The taste-aversion conditioning procedure differs from most other associative procedures also with respect to the temporal relation between the US and contextual stimuli. The US in taste-aversion learning mostly consists of the injection of an illness-inducing drug, or exposure to an illness-inducing treatment like irradiation. Whereas the administration of these treatments is easy to define temporally, the ''effective'' US (i.e., the aversive state presumably experienced by the animal) is more difficult to pinpoint in time and, presumably, extends over hours or even longer (e.g., Barker & Smith, 1974; Kalat & Rozin, 1971). This raises the possibility that the contextual stimuli of the CS-presentation period, and the contextual stimuli present after the US-inducing treatment has been administered, may acquire different degrees of contextual control over aversions learned in their presence. It should be noted that different classes of contextual stimulus events are present during the CS- and US-periods, irrespective of whether taste-aversion learning occurs in a laboratory situation or under natural circumstances. Thus, properties of the solid food or fluid source (e.g., odor, texture, temperature, and bottle stimuli) and the surrounding environment (e.g., location, illumination, and auditory stimuli) are present during the CS-period, whereas only the latter type is present during the US-period.

The relative contribution of contextual-events-during-CS and contextual-events-during-US to the contextual control of taste-aversion extinction was investigated in a recent experiment (Archer, Sjödén, & Nilsson, 1984). Because the main purpose of our entire project has been to study what occurs in the standard taste-aversion learning paradigm, we varied the presence/absence of bottles during the CS-presentation and animal compartments during the CS- as well as the US-period according to the pattern specified in the following. Two groups of rats ($n = 6$) were exposed to novel compartments and a novel ("noisy") type of drinking bottle when saccharin (CS) was first introduced during a 30-min drinking period. For Group CS + US, the same compartments were maintained also after the LiCl injection, which was administered approximately 15 min after the end of the saccharin-drinking period. The US period is thus defined as starting 15 min after the termination of saccharin drinking and ending 23¼ hr later. Group CS was moved to previously familiar cages ("normal" cages, ibid.) during the US period. Two other groups were given their first CS presentation in familiar cages and drinking bottles. During the US period, Group US was placed in novel compartments, whereas Group CONTR remained in familiar cages throughout the US period as well. In order to facilitate understanding of the results, the experimental design is specified in further detail in Table 9.1. As should be obvious from Table 9.1, group labels refer to the conditioning periods during which the animals were exposed to novel contextual stimuli consisting of compartments (during CS and US periods alike) and bottles (during CS periods only). Subsequent preference for saccharin was assessed in a series of five consecutive, daily two-bottle tests (saccharin vs. water), performed in the presence of the types of compartments and bottles that were used as novel contextual stimuli at conditioning. All preference tests lasted 8 hr (0800–1600 hrs).

A split-plot analysis of variance of percentage preference scores resulted in the emergence of a significant Group effect ($F(3,20) = 3.2$, $p < .05$). Mean values for each of the groups were: CS + US = 48.3%; CS = 44.8%; US = 67.7%; and CONTR = 70.6%. Pairwise comparisons between all group means (Tukey HSD-test) revealed that Groups CS + US and CS showed significantly ($p < .05$) stronger aversions than Groups US and CONTR, which did not differ

TABLE 9.1
Design of Experiment Aimed at Specifying the Relative Contributions of Contextual Events During CS- and US-periods to Contextual Control of Learned Taste Aversions

| Groups | Preconditioning 18 Days | Conditioning, One Trial | | Extinction |
	Water (Last 4 Days, 30 Min/Day)	CS Period = 30 Min Saccharin	US Period = 23½hr After LiCl Injection	Five Tests × 8 hr Saccharin/Water
CS + US	Normal cages, silent bottles	Novel compartments, noisy bottles	Compartments	Compartments, noisy bottles
CS	Normal cages, silent bottles	Novel compartments, noisy bottles	Normal cages	Compartments, noisy bottles
US	Normal cages, silent bottles	Normal cages, silent bottles	Compartments	Compartments, noisy bottles
CONTR	Normal cages, silent bottles	Normal cages, silent bottles	Normal cages	Compartments, noisy bottles

from each other. In order to outline the implications of this result for the question of what is learned about contextual elements during CS- and US-periods, Table 9.1 should be consulted. A comparison of the scores of Groups CS + US and CS should reveal whether the different treatments received by these groups during the US period has influenced the strength of the aversion. Because the means of these groups are nearly identical, the presence of the same animal compartment during the US period and testing in Group CS + UCS but not in Group CS is obviously of little relevance. The same conclusion emerges from a comparison of Group US and Group CONTR, which received different treatments only during the US period. In contrast, the presence of the same compartment and bottle in Group CS + US during the CS period and during testing, as compared to Group US, where these elements were absent during CS, reveals a strong influence. Similarly, a comparison of Groups CS and CONTR indicates that the presence of compartments and bottles during the CS-period in Group CS resulted in stronger contextual control than in Group US, where these elements were absent (Archer et al., 1984).

The observation that Groups CS + US and CS demonstrated stronger taste aversions than Groups US and CONTR must be interpreted with caution, due to two factors: (1) Bottle stimuli, earlier shown to be the most salient contextual elements for rats in this situation, were present only during CS-periods (as is always the case in taste-aversion learning); (2) The relatively short-lasting, illness-inducing effects of the LiCl injections almost certainly dissipated within 4 hr (cf. Boland, 1973; Domjan & Gregg, 1977). Thus, the contextual stimuli presented during the 23¼ hr US-period may have been paired with the induction of as well as the recovery from illness. With these qualifications in mind, it can be suggested that rats learn more readily about those contextual events that are presented during CS-periods than about those presented during US-periods in the standard taste-aversion learning paradigm. However, analyses of the role of contextual stimuli in autoshaping (e.g., Balsam & Schwartz, 1981; Gibbon & Balsam, 1981; Tomie, 1976) certainly suggest considerable context-US associations, as do our data on second-order conditioned and sensory preconditioned taste aversions in rats (Archer & Sjödén, 1982).

In a second experiment (Archer et al., 1984) the menthol-odor stimulus was included in the contextual events manipulated during CS- and US-periods. Group designations were maintained as in the previous experiment. A split-plot analysis of variance of preference-test data revealed a significant Groups by Tests interaction (F(12,80) = 4.6, $p < .01$), illustrated in Fig. 9.6. Tukey-HSD tests indicated the following differences between groups. On Tests 2 and 3, Groups CS + US and CS showed stronger taste aversions than Groups US and CONTR ($p < .05$). On Tests 4 and 5, Group CS + US showed stronger aversions than the remaining groups ($p < .05$). This result is in general agreement with those of the previous experiment, but differs in one important respect: The saccharin aversion was notably stronger in Group CS + US than in Group CS. Thus, the presence of

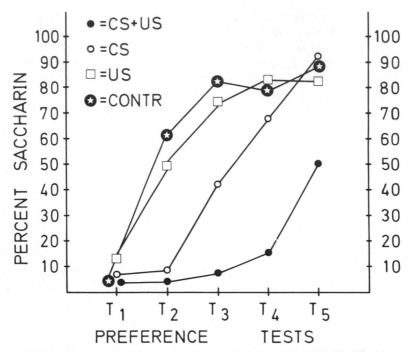

FIG. 9.6.   Percentage saccharin preference for Groups CS + US, CS, US and CONTR. during a series of five preference tests. (Copyright 1984 Almqvist & Wiksell Tryckeri AB. Reprinted by permission of the publisher from T. Archer, P. O. Sjödén & L. G. Nilsson, The importance of contextual events in taste-aversion learning, *Scandinavian Journal of Psychology,* 1984, *25.*)

the odor element during CS- and US-periods in the former group, as compared to only the CS-period in the latter group, seems to have resulted in a context-US association. It may be of some interest to note that the high degree of associative strength achieved by the contextual elements in these two experiments was accomplished in a single conditioning trial. Rapid contextual conditioning has also been shown to be an important feature of background stimuli in autoshaping (e.g., Balsam, 1984; Balsam & Schwartz, 1981).

The Role of Contextual Stimulus Novelty

Novel stimuli typically produce an unconditioned suppression of ongoing behavior (Pavlov, 1927). Barnett (1963) suggested that this effect represents an instinctive survival mechanism, and termed it *neophobia.* The innate avoidance of novel stimuli has been documented in a variety of behavioral situations (Boice, 1970, Jennings & McCutcheon, 1974; Mitchell, Williams, & Sutter, 1974; Rolls & Rolls, 1973), and in several species (e.g., Hebb, 1946). Similarly, food novelty has been observed to suppress ingestion in a variety of animal species including rats (Barnett, 1956; Domjan & Bowman, 1974; Green & Parker, 1975; Nachman & Jones, 1974; Revusky & Bedarf, 1967), birds (Capretta & Bronstein, 1967; Rabinowitch, 1968, 1969), fish (Mackay, 1974; Miller, 1963), and humans (Birch & Marlin, in press; Hollinger & Roberts, 1929). Neophobia has been conceived of as the first stage in the rat's gustatory response when confronted with a novel food (Rzóska, 1954). It has been repeatedly demonstrated that animals initially ingest only small amounts of novel-tasting solutions but increase their intake as they gain familiarity with the flavors (Carroll, Dinc, Levy, & Smith, 1975; Domjan, 1976; Domjan & Gillan, 1976; Siegel, 1974). This gradual increase is not due simply to an increasing level of fluid deprivation (Navarick & Strouthes, 1969; Strouthes, 1971).

The novelty of a taste solution is of considerable importance also for the acquisition of taste aversions. When a novel stimulus is repeatedly presented, it gradually loses its neophobic properties. It has been suggested that prior presentations of a CS not only reduce unconditioned suppression by that stimulus but may also block the acquisition of associative strength by that stimulus (Carlton & Vogel, 1967; Domjan & Siegel, 1971; Lubow, 1965; Lubow & Moore, 1959; Siegel, 1969). Revusky and Bedarf (1967) found that when novel and familiar taste solutions were presented to rats, a much stronger aversion was learned to the novel solution than to the familiar one. This finding has subsequently been replicated in a number of studies (e.g., Ahlers & Best, 1971; Kalat, 1974; Wittlin & Brookshire, 1968).

In view of the importance of CS novelty in taste-aversion learning, it may be expected that the relative novelty of contextual background stimuli plays a similar role. In fact, Mitchell and coworkers (1975) have suggested that the differential associability of interoceptive and exteroceptive stimuli with illness may be due, at least in part, to the fact that familiar exteroceptive stimuli were employed in most studies of this phenomenon. In parallel with this line of reasoning, we have employed a novel set of contextual stimuli during conditioning in most of our studies (Archer et al., 1979a, b, 1980). In our first attempt to demonstrate contextual conditioning effects with familiar background stimuli in the taste-aversion paradigm, we found much weaker effects than when novel stimuli were used (Archer & Sjödén, 1980). The usual procedure for testing contextual control was used, and only a weak context-dependent conditioning effect was obtained during the extinction phase. However, a context-dependent extinction effect was observed during preference testing. This effect was as strong as that obtained with a novel conditioning context in previous studies (Archer et al., 1979a, b, 1980). Thus, although no explicit comparison of the degree of contextual control exerted by a novel versus a familiar conditioning context was made, we concluded that rats learn about a familiar conditioning context as well as a novel one, but that the control acquired by the familiar context is weaker than that acquired by a novel one.

In a subsequent study (Sjödén & Archer, 1981), we provided a within-experi-
ment comparison of the degree of contextual control over postconditioning saccharin intake resulting from a novel as compared to a familiar conditioning
context. Contextual compartments were presented on a 24-hr basis within each
experimental phase and bottles were present only during fluid presentations (30
min). All animals were exposed to "normal" housing conditions (transparent,
individual cages, and standard, "silent" fluid bottles) during a 32-day preconditioning period. Two groups ($n = 5$) were then given two saccharin-LiCl pairings
in "contextual" environments (opaque, dark compartments, and "noisy" bottles). These groups were labeled N–D and N–S, N before dash (–) indicating a
novel conditioning context. Two other groups, F–D and F–S received their
conditioning trials in a familiar (F) context ("normal" housing and "silent"
bottles). After conditioning, one group from each novelty/familiarity condition
was given five saccharin-aversion extinction trials in the same (S) context as
during conditioning (N–S and F–S), whereas the two other groups (N–D and F–
D) were given extinction trials in a different (D) context. Group N–D was given
extinction trials in the "normal" condition, and Group F–D in the "contextual"
condition. Two postconditioning preference tests were then performed in the
conditioning context of the respective groups. A last preference test was performed with the D groups in their extinction context.

The results of the extinction phase (Fig. 9.7, left-hand panel) indicate that the
presence or absence of the exteroceptive conditioning context influenced saccharin intake strongly. This was so over all extinction trials in the case of a novel
conditioning context (N groups), but only for E_2 and E_3 in the case of a familiar
conditioning context (F groups). Thus, the results suggest that a novel conditioning context (N groups) acquires a much stronger control over saccharin intake
during the extinction phase than a familiar one (F groups). The preference-test
data (Fig. 9.7, right-hand panel) show that the S groups that drank saccharin in
the conditioning environment during extinction showed an extinguished aversion
on T_1 and T_2, which were performed in the conditioning context. In contrast, the
D groups demonstrated considerable aversion on T_1 and T_2, but a dramatic
reversal on T_3, when replaced in the extinction context. On the basis of these
data, we conclude that context-dependent conditioning effects are stronger when
a novel conditioning context is employed than when a familiar context is used.
Although direct comparisons of the strength of conditioning and extinction effects are difficult to defend, it seems as if the extinction effects are less dependent on conditioning context novelty.

The importance of contextual stimulus novelty at conditioning is further illustrated in another experiment (Archer & Sjödén, 1981), in which compartment
stimuli alone were used as the context. Saccharin aversions were conditioned
(two trials) in different groups in the presence of either novel or familiar compartments, and extinction was then attempted in the same (as used during condi-

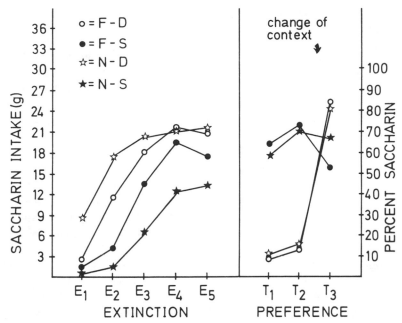

FIG. 9.7.   Saccharin intake during extinction phase (left) and percentage saccharin preference on preference tests (right) for Groups F–D, F–S, N–D, and N–S. (Copyright 1981 Academic Press, Inc. Reprinted by permission of the publisher from P. O. Sjödén & T. Archer, Associative and nonassociative effects of exteroceptive context in taste-aversion conditioning with rats, *Behavioral and Neural Biology*, 1981, *33*, 74–92.)

tioning) or in different compartments. Animals given extinction trials in the same or in different compartments consumed similar amounts of saccharin irrespective of whether novel or familiar conditioning compartments were used. In the preference-test data, however, there was a large and statistically significant difference between the groups given "same" and "different" context during extinction only in the case of a novel conditioning compartment. Thus, the relative novelty of the compartment present at conditioning determined whether or not a context-dependent extinction effect would appear.

In sum, novel contextual stimuli appear to gain significantly more associative strength at a saccharin-aversion conditioning trial than do familiar contextual stimuli. The data from several of our experiments indicate that this is a matter of degree and not an all-or-none affair. Thus, rats learn about a familiar as well as a novel compound consisting of bottle + compartment + odor (Archer & Sjödén, 1980), bottle + compartment (Sjödén & Archer, 1981), or compartments alone (Archer & Sjödén, 1981).

Associative Versus Nonassociative Accounts of Contextual Control

Our discussion regarding contextual effects has implied an associative basis for the phenomenon. However, it may be possible to account for all our findings concerning context-dependent conditioning effects in terms of a nonassociative effect of the *extinction context,* an effect that depends on the relative novelty of that environment. The demonstration of contextual control over saccharin intake during extinction rests upon a comparison of those groups that consumed saccharin in the "same" background context as during conditioning, and those drinking saccharin in a "different" (from conditioning) context. A potential source of confounding here is the fact that the exteroceptive contexts in which the "same" and "different" groups were placed *during extinction* differed also with respect to their relative novelty to the animals. The "same" groups had experienced their extinction context only during the conditioning trials, whereas the "different" groups were placed in a highly familiar context during extinction (usually the preconditioning context). Thus, the large "same" < "different" differences of saccharin intake obtained (e.g., Archer & Sjödén, 1979a, b; Archer et al., 1979a, b, 1980) may have been inflated by the relative novelty of the extinction context. This raises the serious criticism that what we have interpreted as an associative effect is, in fact, mediated by a nonassociative neophobic reaction to the novel extinction context in the "same" context groups.

To differentiate between an associative and the nonassociative account given earlier, five groups of rats ($n = 8$) were included in an experiment in which group labels refer to characteristics of the extinction contexts only: Letters before a slash (/) refer to whether the context used was the same as (S) or different from (D) that used during conditioning. Letters after the slash refer to whether the extinction context was novel (N) or familiar (F) to the animals. The groups were: D/N, placed during extinction in a totally novel context, which differed from the conditioning context in several respects; S/N, placed in the conditioning context during extinction; D/F, placed in a different, familiar context during extinction (the preconditioning environment); S/F, placed in the same context during extinction as during conditioning, but this group had a total of 30 hr preexposure to that context. A fifth group (Control/Novel = C/N) was included, which was given unpaired, backward presentations of LiCl and saccharin, and which was tested in a context previously experienced only on the two saccharin presentations.

The extinction-phase data (Fig. 9.8, left-hand panel) indicate that the "same" context groups (S/N and S/F) showed nearly identical aversions, and the strongest among all the groups; the "different" context groups (D/N and D/F) showed much less aversion; Group C/N showed none at all. Space will not allow a detailed examination of all between-group comparisons relevant to a differentiation between associative and nonassociative accounts (see Sjödén & Archer,

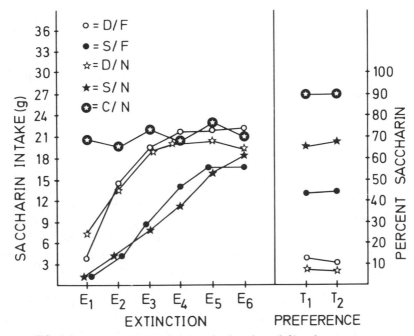

FIG. 9.8. Saccharin intake during extinction phase (left) and percentage saccharin preference on preference tests (right) for Groups D/F, S/F, D/N, S/N, and C/N. (Copyright 1981 Academic Press, Inc. Reprinted by permission of the publisher from P. O. Sjödén & T. Archer, Associative and nonassociative effects of exteroceptive context in taste-aversion conditioning with rats, *Behavioral and Neural Biology*, 1981, *33*, 74–92.)

1981). However, inspection of Fig. 9.8 reveals that extinction context novelty exerted virtually no influence on saccharin intake, whereas the ''same''–''different'' dimension did so to a great extent. Thus, there were no significant differences between Groups D/N and D/F on any of the test days, although the extinction context of Group D/N was much less familiar than that of Group D/F. The same pattern of effects appears in the comparisons of Groups S/N and S/F. In support of an associative interpretation, Groups S/N and S/F drank less saccharin than Group D/N on E_1, less than Groups D/N and D/F throughout E_2-E_4, and less than Group D/F on E_5. This pattern of findings can be used to exclude the relative novelty of the extinction context as an explanation of previously demonstrated context-dependent conditioning effects, favoring instead an associative interpretation. On the preference tests, which were performed in the conditioning context of all groups, the ''different'' context groups showed full-blown aversions, whereas the ''same'' context groups showed only intermediate degrees of aversion (Fig. 9.8, right-hand panel). These data parallel previous findings. It should be noted that the contextual manipulations involved only compartment + bottle elements that were present only during saccharin drinking in this study. This eliminates the possibility that context-US associations may have increased the neophobic response to saccharin in the "same"-context groups, because the relevant contextual stimuli were never paired with the US. Also, these findings illustrate that learning about contextual stimuli takes place during CS presentations.

Potentiation: A Contributor to Contextual Effects in Taste-Aversion Learning

The basis for a discussion of contextual effects in associative conditioning is the concept of stimulus compound. Every conditioning trial harbors a number of potential stimuli to be conditioned, and other stimuli than the nominal CS will acquire associative strength (Rescorla & Wagner, 1972). One of the most widely accepted empirical generalizations concerning compound conditioning is that there will be an inverse relationship between the associative strengths acquired by each of the elements of a reinforced compound (e.g., Rescorla & Wagner, 1972; Sutherland & Mackintosh, 1971). Furthermore, the associative strength achieved by a certain stimulus element is dependent on the relative salience of that element. Under certain circumstances, a less salient element will acquire more associative strength if paired separately with a US than if it is reinforced in compound with a more salient element. This phenomenon has been termed overshadowing of the weaker element by the stronger, and it has been demonstrated in a variety of learning tasks (D'Amato & Fazzaro, 1966; Kamin, 1969; Mackintosh, 1971; Revusky, 1971). If this line of reasoning is applied to our results concerning contextual control of learned taste aversions, it should be expected that a taste element would overshadow other, contextual elements due to its greater salience when an illness-inducing US is employed (Domjan & Wilson, 1972; Garcia & Koelling, 1966; Garcia et al., 1968). On the basis of these and other studies, it can thus be expected that taste stimuli will gain higher associative strength than bottle, compartment, and odor stimuli in single-stimulus as well as in compound conditioning with illness-inducing USs. However, our findings of relatively strong contextual control by bottle and compartment stimuli after taste + context compound conditioning trials render this possibility rather unlikely.

To test for possible overshadowing of bottle by taste elements, the strength of a bottle aversion should be studied under two conditions: (1) when the bottle alone has been paired with LiCl; and (2) when it has been paired in compound with taste. If a stronger bottle aversion is evident after the single-element trial than after the compound trial, an overshadowing account is supported. However, a number of recent studies have suggested another possible outcome of the overshadowing paradigm when taste is compounded with other contextual elements and an illness-inducing US is used. In rats, it has been demonstrated that the presence of a taste element at conditioning increases conditioning to visual (Galef & Osborne, 1978) and odor elements (Durlach & Rescorla, 1980; Rusiniak, Hankins, Garcia, & Brett, 1979). Similar findings have been reported in avian species (Clarke, Westbrook, & Irwin, 1979; Lett, 1980). This phenomenon has been termed potentiation, and represents the opposite of overshadowing (i.e., the presence of a more salient stimulus in a compound increases conditioning to a less salient stimulus as compared to conditioning of the less salient stimulus alone). As illustrated by two recent investigations (Holland, 1983; Mikulka, Pitts, & Philput, 1982), the conditions are not yet known that govern whether potentiation or overshadowing results from compound conditioning. However, in view of our findings of strong contextual control exerted by the bottle stimulus, potentiation seems a more likely candidate than overshadowing in compound taste-aversion conditioning with rats.

In a recent study (Sjödén & Archer, 1983), a series of experiments was performed to investigate whether overshadowing or potentiation of bottle by taste would occur. These experiments demonstrated: (1) that saccharin acquired greater associative strength than the "noisy" bottle after single-stimulus pairings with LiCl; (2) that this phenomenon is of an associative nature; and (3) that the bottle aversion cannot be interpreted as an aversion to water but involves learning about the properties of the bottle itself. When the strength of aversion to the taste alone and to the bottle alone was tested after two compound taste + bottle pairings with LiCl, the bottle aversion was found to have reached a greater strength than the taste aversion. Thus, whereas taste stimuli acquire greater conditioning strength than the bottle stimuli in single-stimulus paradigms with LiCl as the US, it seems that the reverse is true when a taste + bottle compound is used.

In a direct test of the potentiation account, we administered two conditioning trials to three groups of rats ($n = 8$). Group TB–B was given taste + bottle (TB) compound pairings with LiCl, Group B–B was given bottle (B) pairings with LiCl, and Group T–B was given saccharin (T) pairings with LiCl. The purpose of the first two groups was to compare the strength of aversion to the bottle element when conditioned in compound with taste and when conditioned alone. The purpose of Group T–B was to investigate the possibility that the taste aversion generalized to the bottle stimulus. All groups were then given two 30-min one-bottle tests (D5 and D6 in Fig. 9.9) on which the aversion to the bottle (B) element alone was tested.

The results are presented in Figure 9.9, where mean intakes of water from the "noisy" conditioning bottles are illustrated. On D5, Group TB–B drank significantly less water than Group B–B, which, in turn, consumed less than Group T–B. The fact that Group T–B drank more water than the remaining groups on D5 shows that the TB–B < B–B difference cannot be attributed to a generalization of a taste aversion to the bottle element. Therefore, we conclude that the presence of the taste stimulus in compound conditioning potentiated conditioning of a bottle aversion. This means that the stimulus element found to be most salient in

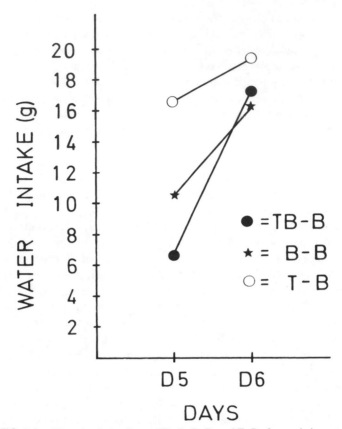

FIG. 9.9.   Water intake by Groups TB–B, B–B, and T–B of potentiation experiment. (Copyright 1983. Reprinted by permission of the publisher from P. O. Sjödén & T. Archer, Potentiation of a bottle aversion by taste in compound conditioning with rats, *Experimental Animal Behaviour*, 1983, 2, 1–18.)

the single-CS paradigm (taste) potentiated conditioning to the less-salient element (bottle) in the compound-CS paradigm. The findings thus stand in direct contradiction to predictions concerning overshadowing and indicate a reversal of the relative strengths of taste and bottle aversions between single-CS and compound-CS aversion conditioning paradigms.

The basis for potentiation effects in associative conditioning is still unknown. Several possibilities have been suggested: (1) The presence of the taste element may have facilitated establishment of a bottle-US association (Rusiniak et al., 1979); (2) An association may have been formed between the bottle and taste elements, based either on unconditioned properties of the taste (e.g., novelty), or on the taste becoming aversive due to pairings with LiCl (Durlach & Rescorla, 1980). As has been pointed out by Durlach and Rescorla (1980), an account of potentiation in terms of within-compound associations opens up the possibility that modern theories of associative conditioning may ultimately be able to handle this phenomenon. However, in recent versions of such theories (e.g., Mackintosh, 1975; Rescorla & Wagner, 1972), no allowance seems to have been made for potentiation of a weaker stimulus by a stronger.

The demonstration of taste stimuli potentiating the conditioning of bottle stimuli in taste-aversion learning is relevant to a discussion of contextual effects. The presence of a taste CS at conditioning may have potentiated the acquisition of associative strength by contextual elements in our previous studies. Thus, taste-based potentiation could contribute to our previously demonstrated contextual effects. On the other hand, an examination of the data in Fig. 9.9 reveals that potentiation effects are confined to the first postconditioning one-bottle test. This indicates that potentiation probably does not account for more than a fraction of the contextual effects demonstrated in our previous studies where marked between-group differences were found on four to five consecutive, daily, one-bottle tests.

Second-Order Conditioning and Sensory Preconditioning of a Saccharin Aversion Based on Contextual Stimuli

The considerable associative strength acquired by contextual stimuli in most of our experiments led us to consider the possibility that they could be used to support higher order conditioning and sensory preconditioning (Archer & Sjödén, 1982). Three separate experiments were performed, in which a conditioning context was employed consisting of "noisy" bottles, opaque compartments, and a mentholated odor. This contextual compound was designated as the CS_1, saccharin served as the CS_2, and a LiCl injection was used as US. In the case of higher order conditioning (H–OC), CS_1 was first paired with the US, and CS_2 and CS_1 were then paired, before testing for an aversion to CS_2. The question of interest is whether the animals will show an aversion to the CS_2 saccharin stimulus, although they have never experienced the toxic effects of the US in connection with the taste—and thus, whether a sufficient condition for a taste aversion is that they are first poisoned in the CS_1 context in which they later drink the taste solution (CS_2). In sensory preconditioning (SPC), CS_2 and CS_1 were paired prior to the CS_1–US pairing, after which an aversion to CS_2 was tested. Again, the point of interest is whether an aversion to the CS_2 taste can be mediated via taste-context and context-illness associations. Rizley and Rescorla (1972) have found that second-order conditioning of a conditioned emotional response (CER) to a tone is unaffected by extinction of the response to the CS_1 upon which it is based, whereas a fear reaction established by SPC is considerably reduced in magnitude by CS_1-extinction. An additional purpose of the present experiments was to investigate whether or not the same "asymmetric" relationship between H–OC and SPC, on the one hand, and the effects of CS_1-extinction trials, on the other, is also true for context-based taste aversion conditioning.

In both of these experiments, group labels refer to whether paired presentations (P), unpaired presentations (U), no trials (N), or extinction trials (E) were given during the four different phases employed. The unpaired condition was achieved by administering the US 24 hr prior to the CS_1 (in the first experimental phase), and the CS_2 24 hr prior to the CS_1 (in the second phase). In the H–OC study, four groups of rats ($n = 6$) labeled PPN, PPE, PUN, and UPN, were given CS_1 + US presentations in Phase I, CS_1 + CS_2 presentations in Phase II, and CS_1 presentations in Phase III according to their group labels. In Phase IV, two-bottle saccharin-preference tests were administered to all groups in the absence of those contextual elements used during Phases I–III. If second-order taste-aversion conditioning can be established by a contextual CS_1 and is mediated by the same mechanisms as is CER conditioning to tone stimuli (Rizley & Rescorla, 1972), only Groups PPN and PPE should show saccharin aversions in Phase IV.

The results of the H–OC experiment are presented in Fig. 9.10. First-order conditioning was evidenced by a decrease of water intake in all the paired groups in Phase I. The same groups showed a lower fluid intake than Group UPN in Phase II, demonstrating an acquisition of aversive properties by CS_1 in Phase I—a finding that provides evidence of context-US associations. Extinction of CS_1 aversiveness was seen in the only group (PPE) placed in the CS_1 context during Phase III, whereas no changes of fluid intake occurred in the remaining groups. On the first test for second-order conditioning (T1 in Phase IV), Groups PPN and PPE showed significantly greater saccharin aversions than the remaining groups. Thus, our prediction concerning a context-mediated saccharin aversion was confirmed. However, there is one aspect of the data that threatens the unequivocal conclusion that second-order conditioning was demonstrated. In Phase II, Groups PPN, PPE, and PUN consumed less fluid than Group UPN, and the same general relationship between the groups remained in the preference data in Phase IV. Thus, Phase IV data may reflect differential habituation of neophobia to the saccharin solution. In order to exclude this possibility, a further experiment was performed, in which fluid intake during Phase II was equalized for all groups. In spite of this, and of the fact that only the "noisy" bottle was employed as a contextual element, Group PPN showed a stronger aversion than Groups PUN and UPN (PPE was not included in this experiment) on both preference tests. These findings illustrate that a contextual compound stimulus (compartment + bottle + odor) as well as the bottle element alone can be used to establish a second-order saccharin aversion in rats. Stimulus generalization between CS_1 and CS_2 can be excluded as an explanation of these findings, because Group PUN showed no aversion. The lack of aversion in Group UPN shows that the CS_1–US pairing is necessary for the effect observed. As in Rizley and Rescorla

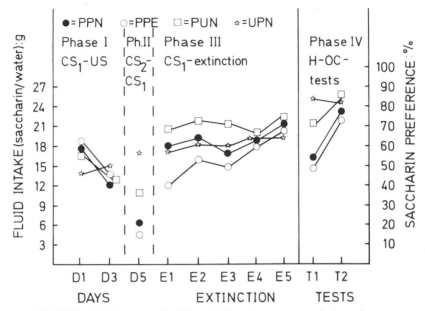

FIG. 9.10. Fluid intake during Phases I–III and percentage saccharin preference
during Phase IV by four groups of rats in higher order conditioning experiment.
Fluids offered are indicated in the text. (Reprinted by permission of the Experimental Psychology Society from T. Archer & P. O. Sjödén, Higher-order conditioning and sensory preconditioning of a taste aversion with an exteroceptive CS_1,
Quarterly Journal of Experimental Psychology, 1982, *34B*, 1–17.)

(1972), extinction of CS_1 aversiveness in Group PPE did not affect the saccharin
aversion on the first preference test.

In the SPC experiment (Archer & Sjödén, 1982) three groups (PPN, PPE, and
PUN) were placed in the compartment + bottle + odor condition during Phase I,
when a CS_2–CS_1 pairing took place. One group (UPN) received an unpaired
CS_2–CS_1 presentation (CS_2 24 h prior to CS_1). Phase II consisted of two CS_1–
US presentations, and Phase III entailed CS_1-extinction trials for Group PPE.
Phase IV consisted of two saccharin-preference tests. If sensory preconditioning
of a taste aversion is similar to sensory preconditioning of a CER (Rizley &
Rescorla, 1972), only Group PPN should show an aversion in Phase IV. Group
PUN controlled for first-order conditioning and Group UPN served to test a CS_1–
CS_2 generalization account of the results.

The findings are presented in Fig. 9.11. In Phase I, Group UPN (water) drank
significantly more than the remaining groups (saccharin). Because all groups
received fluid presentations in the novel contextual condition, this most likely
represents a neophobic response to saccharin. First-order conditioning (CS_1–US)
of aversiveness to the CS_1 context was seen in Phase II, where all groups given

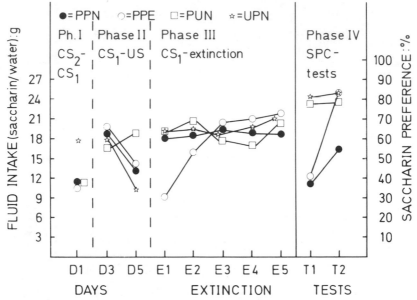

FIG. 9.11. Fluid intake during Phases I–III and percentage saccharin preference during Phase IV by four groups of rats in sensory preconditioning experiment. Fluids offered are indicated in the text. (Reprinted by permission of the Experimental Psychology Society from T. Archer & P. O. Sjödén, Higher-order conditioning and sensory preconditioning of a taste aversion with an exteroceptive CS_1, *Quarterly Journal of Experimental Psychology*, 1982, *34B*, 1–17.)

paired presentations showed a decrease in fluid intake. The successively increasing intake of water by Group PPE during Phase III indicates extinction of the aversive properties of CS_1 with repeated presentations. On the tests for sensory preconditioned saccharin aversion, Groups PPN and PPE showed stronger aversions than remaining groups on T1, whereas only Group PPN showed a greater aversion on T2. Thus, sensory preconditioning of a saccharin aversion, mediated through a set of contextual stimuli as the CS_1, was demonstrated. Only the data from T2 are in full agreement with the prediction that CS_1 extinction trials should abolish associations established via an SPC procedure. However, a weaker aversion was present in Group PPE than in Group PPN, because the former was extinguished by T2.

The previous two experiments have demonstrated that exteroceptive stimuli, which usually serve as contextual elements in taste-aversion learning experiments, can be used to support second-order conditioning as well as sensory preconditioning of a taste aversion. The results strengthen the conclusion that context-US associations can be formed. Furthermore, it is possible that the SPC effects may contribute to long-delay taste-aversion learning. In Table 9.2, the

TABLE 9.2
Summary of Procedures for Sensory Preconditioning (SPC) and
Long-delay Conditioning of a Taste Aversion

Procedure	Phase I	Phase II	Phase III
SPC	Taste (CS_2) presented in novel context (CS_1)	LiCl injection (US) in same context (CS_1)	Taste-aversion test
Long delay	Taste (CS)	LiCl injection (US)	Taste-aversion test

procedures used in long-delay taste-aversion learning and in the present SPC experiment are compared. In the first phase of the SPC procedure, the taste solution was made available in a specific context. This parallels the taste (CS) presentation in long-delay studies. In the second phase, a LiCl-injection was given, and the animals were replaced in the same context. This corresponds to the US presentation in long-delay studies, provided that CS and US exposure takes place in the same context. In the case of SPC, it is assumed that the animals have learned a taste-context association in Phase I, and a context-illness association in Phase II, and, because the contextual stimuli are the same in both phases (but not at the later taste-aversion test), these associations underlie the taste aversion. It is possible that the same set of factors operate in standard long-delay taste-aversion experiments. Thus, an indirect temporal contiguity, not between taste and the onset of illness (cf. Bitterman, 1976), but rather, on the one hand, between taste and context, and on the other, between context and illness may contribute to taste-aversion learning with long CS–US delays. There are, however, some problems with this notion: (1) The interval between exposure to taste and to illness in the SPC experiment was 48 hr, and this is much longer than the intervals over which taste aversions are usually reported; (2) the SPC effect has so far been demonstrated only when the taste stimulus is presented in a novel context in the first phase; and (3) the delay of reinforcement gradient observed in many taste-aversion experiments may be difficult to account for, unless prolonged nonreinforced exposure to the contextual cues during the delay is assumed to result in extinction of context-taste associations. In spite of this, SPC may be a possible artifact in long-delay learning, and, in view of the recent controversy (Garcia, 1978; Mitchell, 1977, 1978; Mitchell, Scott, & Mitchell, 1977; Revusky, 1977b, 1978, 1979; Riley, 1978; Smith, 1978) regarding the role of associative and nonassociative confounding, may be relevant to an assessment of the real status of the long-delay learning effect.

The Analysis of Contextual Effects as a Tool in Studies of Neurochemical Substrates of Selective Attention

At the outset of the present chapter, it was mentioned that the study of associative learning can be used to map stimulus selection principles. Elsewhere (Archer & Sjödén, 1981; Archer et al., 1979a, 1980), we have argued that the procedure for investigating contextual control of taste aversions may be useful when selective attention to various features of the environment is studied. In a recent study (Archer, Cotic, & Järbe, 1982), the experiments were designed to investigate the role of central noradrenergic pathways in the contextual control of taste-aversion conditioning and extinction. A great deal of recent theoretical discussion has centered on the role of noradrenaline (NA) in selective attention (e.g., Mason, 1979a, b; Mason & Iversen, 1979; McNaughton & Mason, 1980). Thus, the selective noradrenaline neurotoxin N-2-chloroethyl-N-ethyl-2-bromobenzyl-amine hydrochloride (DSP 4, cf. Jonsson, Hallman, Ponzio, & Ross, 1981; Ross, 1976) was systemically administered to rats in a dose of 50mg/kg, intra-peritoneally, to cause a severe degeneration of the terminal regions arising from the locus coeruleus. Control rats were given saline (5ml/kg). Following recovery, all DSP 4 and control rats were presented with a novel saccharin solution in novel "noisy" bottles on each of two conditioning trials. Thus, only bottle stimuli were employed as a contextual element. Immediately after the 30-min saccharin presentation, LiCl injections were given to all animals. During the subsequent extinction trials, half the DSP 4 and half the control rats received the saccharin solution in the "noisy" bottles, and the other half received saccharin in "silent" bottles. After a five-trial extinction phase, saccharin/water preference tests were given in the presence of "noisy" bottles to all groups.

Saccharin intake during the extinction phase by Groups DSP4(D), given "silent" bottles during extinction (different context = D), DSP4(S), given "noisy" bottles during extinction (same context = S), CONT(D), and CONT(S) is presented in the left-hand portion of Fig. 9.12. Saccharin preference values are presented in the right-hand panel. Saccharin intake during extinction by the "same" context groups, DSP4(S), and CONT(S) did not differ significantly from that of the different context groups, DSP4(D), and CONT(D). With regard to the control condition, this result is in agreement with an earlier finding (Archer et al., 1979a, Exp. 1) where no differences were found between a "bottle present" and a "bottle absent" condition during extinction. In other studies, however (Archer et al., 1979a, Exp. 1; 1982, Exp. 2), reliable differences between these conditions were demonstrated. It may be that the one-bottle test usually employed during extinction is in the lower range of sensitivity for the detection of contextual bottle control of saccharin intake. During the saccharin-preference tests, Group CONT(D) demonstrated a significantly greater saccharin aversion than Group CONT(S), whereas the difference between Group DSP4(D)

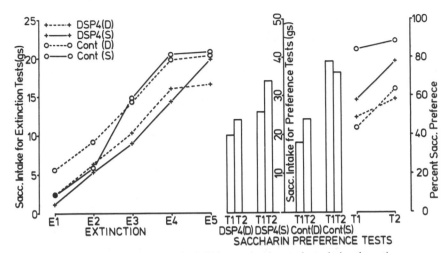

FIG. 9.12.   Saccharin intake by DSP4-treated and control rats during the extinction phase (left) and preference tests (center). Percentage saccharin preference
during preference tests (right) for Groups DSP4(D), DSP4(S), Cont(D), and
Cont(S). (Copyright 1982 Academic Press, Inc. Reprinted by permission of the
publisher from T. Archer, T. Cotic, & T. U. C. Järbe, Attenuation of the context
effect and lack of unconditioned stimulus-preexposure effect in taste-aversion
learning following treatment with DSP4, the selective noradrenaline neurotoxin,
Behavioral and Neural Biology, 1982.)

and DSP4(S), although in the same direction, did not reach statistical significance. Thus, it seems as if the context effect was attenuated in NA-depleted rats,
a finding that does support the notion that the ability of NA-depleted rats to
attend to all aspects of a given stimulus compound is altered to some extent. This
finding, which was confirmed in three subsequent experiments, seems to be in
agreement with data from a recent blocking experiment with noradrenaline-
depleted rats (Lorden, Rickert, Dawson, & Pelleymounter, 1980) in suggesting
that noradrenaline may modulate the selective processing of stimulus information
in associative learning.

In other experiments (Archer & Köhler, unpublished), rats with ibotenic acid
lesions of the medial entorhinal cortex were found also to show an attenuation of
the context effect. Ibotenic acid destroys all cell bodies when microinjected into
a specified region. It should be noted that the entorhinal cortical region has been
implicated as a site where informational input is selectively filtered (cf. Nadel et
al., this volume).These findings illustrate that an analysis of contextual conditioning and extinction effects in taste-aversion learning may be profitable in
mapping the functional role of brain regions and putative neurotransmitters in
stimulus selection.

Contextual Control in Taste-Aversion Conditioning: Context-CS and Context-US Associations

Recent reviewers seem to agree that most taste-aversion learning phenomena can be accounted for by principles of learning common to many forms of conditioning, and that no special principles are required (Dickinson & Mackintosh, 1978; Logue, 1979; Revusky, 1977a). A recent study by Charlton and Ferraro (1982) has provided further empirical evidence in support of this notion.

Before examining the presently reviewed data on contextual effects in relation to the possible uniqueness of taste-aversion learning, a brief summary of the major findings is in order. These are: (1) A contextual compound stimulus consisting of bottles, compartments and an odor element was demonstrated to exert strong control over postconditioning saccharin intake. Context-dependent conditioning as well as context-dependent extinction effects were observed, indicating that rats learn about contextual stimuli both during acquisition and extinction of taste aversions; (2) the relative salience of the contextual elements was demonstrated to be in the order of bottles > compartments > odor, and tongue-tactile bottle stimuli are likely to be the most salient; (3) rats learn more readily about those contextual events that are presented during CS-periods than about those that are presented during US-periods in the standard taste-aversion learning paradigm; (4) novel contextual stimuli were observed to acquire stronger control over subsequent saccharin intake than do familiar contextual stimuli, although familiar stimuli acquired some control as well. The greater salience of novel as compared to familiar stimuli was true for context-dependent conditioning effects but not for context-dependent extinction effects when the compartment + bottle + odor and the compartment + bottle compound was used. When compartments alone were manipulated, the influence of novelty was limited to the context-dependent extinction effect; (5) a nonassociative account of these contextual effects in terms of extinction context novelty was shown to be untenable. Instead, an associative account was favored; (6) one phenomenon possibly contributing to contextual control was demonstrated: Taste stimuli potentiated learning about the bottle element; (7) contextual compartment + bottle + odor stimuli were found to be salient enough to support the establishment of second-order conditioned and sensory preconditioned taste aversions. Context-based sensory preconditioning of a taste aversion may contribute to long-delay taste-aversion learning under certain circumstances, which illustrates the importance of a study of contextual effects in taste-aversion learning.

Although these findings concern a variety of phenomena, we assume that they can be accounted for by reference to a few general principles, applicable to many kinds of learning. The first is the effect of spatial/temporal contiguity between stimuli (Rescorla, 1980, pp. 50–55), and the second is simultaneous or within-compound associations (Durlach & Rescorla, 1980; Rescorla, 1981). The fact that learning about contextual elements takes place in taste-aversion conditioning requires no special explanation. Such learning seems to be a property of all forms of conditioning. The relative salience of contextual elements in the order of bottles < compartments < odor corresponds relatively well with the spatiotemporal arrangement of such stimuli in relation to the taste CS. Thus, tongue-tactile stimuli are perfectly correlated with drops of the taste solution, whereas compartments and odor stimuli are not. The fact that learning about contextual stimuli occurs most readily during the CS presentation may be taken to indicate a further role for temporal contiguity but may likewise illustrate the importance of within-compound associations forming when the CS is presented. The establishment of associations within the compound consisting of contextual stimuli and saccharin should come as no surprise. First, saccharin is an effective reinforcer for operant behavior and may be conceptualized equally well as a CS and a US. In the latter case, learning about contextual elements with saccharin as a US should be expected to occur. The possibility of within-compound associations based on either unconditioned or conditioned properties of the taste stimulus in potentiation studies has already been considered by Durlach and Rescorla (1980). Thus, the principle of within-compound learning may be relevant to contextual effects by accounting both for why contextual learning occurs during CS presentations and for the potentiation phenomenon.

Indeed, Rescorla (1981) has recently reviewed a number of experiments in which the formation of within-compound associations between affectively neutral events is forcefully demonstrated. Such associations seem to be formed equally well when two neutral events are paired in the absence of a subsequent US as when a US follows their pairing. Because virtually all our experiments on contextual effects involve the simultaneous presentation of two or more stimuli, the conditions for establishment of within-compound associations are present. An important implication of this line of reasoning is that the presence of contextual effects in the taste-aversion learning paradigm does not imply that bottle, compartment, and odor stimuli become associated directly with the US. Rather, it may be that contextual stimuli form associations with the taste CS that, in turn, becomes associated with the US (Rescorla, 1981; Rescorla et al., this volume). Thus, context-CS associations may also contribute to the contextual effects observed, although this notion cannot be directly supported by our data.

This is not to say that context-US associations can be disregarded in taste-aversion learning. In fact, some of our findings provide evidence to support the existence of context-US associations as well: (1) the fact that Group CS + US showed a stronger taste aversion than Group CS when compartments + bottles + odor were present during CS- and US-periods in the former, but only during the CS-period in the latter group (Fig. 9.6); (2) the fact that clear evidence of context-US associations was obtained in the higher order conditioning and sensory preconditioning experiments (Fig. 9.10 and 9.11).

ACKNOWLEDGMENTS

Research for this chapter was supported by grants 584/79, 897/80, 422/81, and 424/82 to Per-Olow Sjödén and Trevor Archer from the Swedish Council for Research in the Humanities and Social Sciences, and grants from Astra Läkemedel AB, Södertälje, Sweden.

REFERENCES

Ader, R. A note on the role of olfaction in taste-aversion learning. *Bulletin of the Psychonomic Society*, 1977, *10*, 402–404.

Ahlers, R. H., & Best, P. J. Novelty vs. temporal contiguity in learned taste-aversions. *Psychonomic Science*, 1971, *25*, 34–36.

Andrews, H. L., & Cameron, L. M. Radiation avoidance in the mouse. *Proceedings of the Society for Experimental Biology and Medicine*, 1960, *103*, 565–567.

Arbit, J. Spatial avoidance behavior in the rats as a result of exposure to ionizing radiation. *British Journal of Radiology*, 1959, *32*, 214–218.

Archer, T., Cotic, T., & Järbe, T. U. C. Attenuation of the context effect and lack of unconditioned stimulus-preexposure effect in taste-aversion learning following treatment with DSP4, the selective noradrenaline neurotoxin. *Behavioral and Neural Biology*, 1982, *35*, 159–173.

Archer, T., & Sjödén, P. O. Positive correlation between pre and postconditioning saccharin intake in taste-aversion learning. *Animal Learning and Behavior*, 1979, *7*, 144–148. (a)

Archer, T., & Sjödén, P. O. Neophobia in taste-aversion conditioning: Individual differences and effects of contextual changes. *Physiological Psychology*, 1979, *7*, 364–369. (b)

Archer, T., & Sjödén, P. O. Context-dependent taste-aversion learning with a familiar conditioning context. *Physiological Psychology*, 1980, *8*, 40–46.

Archer, T., & Sjödén, P. O. Environment-dependent taste-aversion extinction: A question of stimulus novelty at conditioning. *Physiological Psychology*, 1981, *9*, 102–108.

Archer, T., & Sjödén, P. O. Higher-order conditioning and sensory preconditioning of a taste aversion with an exteroceptive CS_1. *Quarterly Journal of Experimental Psychology*, 1982, *34B*, 1–17.

Archer, T., Sjödén, P. O., & Carter, N. Control of taste-aversion extinction by exteroceptive cues. *Behavioral and Neural Biology*, 1979, *25*, 217–226.

Archer, T., Sjödén, P. O., & Nilsson, L. G. The importance of contextual events in taste-aversion learning. *Scandinavian Journal of Psychology*, 1984, *25*.

Archer, T., Sjödén, P. O., Nilsson, L. G., & Carter, N. Role of exteroceptive background context in taste-aversion conditioning and extinction. *Animal Learning and Behavior*, 1979, *7*, 17–22.

Archer, T., Sjödén, P. O., Nilsson, L. G., & Carter, N. Exteroceptive context in taste-aversion conditioning and extinction: Odour, cage, and bottle stimuli. *Quarterly Journal of Experimental Psychology*, 1980, *32*, 197–214.

Balsam, P. D. Bringing the background to the foreground: The role of contextual cues in autoshaping. In M. Commons, R. Herrnstein, & A. R. Wagner (Eds.), *Quantitative analyses of behavior: Volume 3: Acquisition*. Cambridge, Mass.: Ballinger, 1984.

Balsam, P. D., & Schwartz, A. L. Rapid contextual conditioning in autoshaping. *Journal of Experimental Psychology: Animal Behavior Processes*, 1981, *7*, 382–393.

Barker, L. M., & Smith, J. C. A comparison of taste-aversions induced by radiation and lithium chloride in CS–US and US–CS paradigms. *Journal of Comparative and Physiological Psychology*, 1974, *87*, 644–654.

Barnett, S. A. Behaviour components in the feeding of wild and laboratory rats. *Behaviour*, 1956, *9*, 24–43.

Barnett, S. A. *The rat: A study in behavior*. Chicago: Aldine Press, 1963.

Barnett, S. A., Cowan, P. E., Randford, G. G., & Prakash, I. Peripheral anosmia and the discrimination of poisoned food by Rattus rattus L. *Behavioral Biology*, 1975, *13*, 183–190.

Batson, J. D., & Best, P. J. Drug-preexposure effects in flavor-aversion learning: Associative interference by conditioned environment stimuli. *Journal of Experimental Psychology; Animal Behavior Processes*, 1979, *5*, 273–287.

Best, M. R., & Batson, J. D. Enhancing the expression of flavor neophobia: Some effects of the ingestion-illness contingency. *Journal of Experimental Psychology: Animal Behavior Processes*, 1977, *3*, 132–143.

Best, P. J., Best, M. R., & Mickley, G. A. Conditioned aversion to distinct environmental stimuli resulting from gastrointestinal distress. *Journal of Comparative and Physiological Psychology*, 1973, *85*, 250–257.

Birch, L. L., & Marlin, D. W. I don't like it, I never tried it; The effects of familiarity on 2-year-olds' food preferences. *Child Development*, in press.

Bitterman, M. E. Technical comment. Flavor aversion studies. *Science*, 1976, *192*, 266–267.

Boice, R. The effect of domestication on avoidance learning in the Norway rat. *Psychonomic Science*, 1970, *18*, 13–14.

Boland, F. J. Saccharin aversions induced by lithium chloride toxicosis in a backward conditioning paradigm. *Annual Learning and Behavior*, 1973, *1*, 3–4.

Booth, D. A., & Simson, P. C. Food preferences acquired by association with variations in aminoacid nutrition. *Quarterly Journal of Experimental Psychology*, 1971, *23*, 135–145.

Braveman, N. S. Visually guided avoidance of poisonous foods in mammals. In L. M. Barker, M. R. Best, & M. Domjan (Eds.), *Learning mechanisms in food selection*. Waco, Texas: Baylor University Press, 1977.

Braveman, N. S. The role of blocking and compensatory conditioning in the treatment preexposure effect. *Psychopharmacology*, 1979, *61*, 177–189.

Capretta, P. J., & Bronstein, P. M. Effects of first food ingestion on later food preferences in chicks. *Proceedings of the 75th Annual Convention of the American Psychological Association*, 1967, *2*, 109–110.

Carlton, P. L., & Vogel, J. R. Habituation and conditioning. *Journal of Comparative and Physiological Psychology*, 1967, *63*, 348–351.

Carroll, M. E., Dinc, H. I., Levy, C. J., & Smith, J. C. Demonstration of neophobia and enhanced neophobia in the albino rat. *Journal of Comparative and Physiological Psychology*, 1975, *89*, 457–467.

Charlton, S. G., & Ferraro, D. P. Effects of deprivation on the differential conditionability of behaviour in Golden Hamsters. *Experimental Animal Behaviour*, 1982, *1*, 18–29.

Clarke, J. C., Westbrook, R. F., & Irwin, J. Potentiation instead of overshadowing in the pigeon. *Behavioral and Neural Biology*, 1979, *25*, 18–29.

Cunningham, C. L. Flavor and location aversions produced by ethanol. *Behavioral and Neural Biology*, 1979, *27*, 362–367.

Cunningham, C. L. Spatial aversion conditioning with ethanol. *Pharmacology, Biochemistry, and Behavior*, 1980, *14*, 263–264.

D'Amato, M. R., & Fazzaro, J. Attention and cue-producing behavior in the monkey. *Journal of Experimental Analysis of Behavior*, 1966, *9*, 469–473.

Dickinson, A. *Contemporary animal learning theory*. Cambridge: Cambridge University Press, 1980.

Dickinson, A., & Mackintosh, N. J. Classical conditioning in animals. *Annual Review of Psychology*, 1978, *29*, 587–612.

Domjan, M. Role of ingestion in odor-toxicosis learning in the rat. *Journal of Comparative and Physiological Psychology,* 1973, *84,* 507–521.

Domjan, M. Determinants of the enhancement of flavored-water intake by prior exposure. *Journal of Experimental Psychology: Animal Behavior Processes,* 1976, *2,* 17–27.

Domjan, M., & Bowman, T. G. Learned safety and the CS–US delay gradient in taste-aversion learning. *Learning and Motivation,* 1974, *5,* 409–423.

Domjan, M., & Burkhard, B. *The principles of learning and behavior.* Monterey, Calif.; Brooks/Cole, 1982.

Domjan, M., & Gillan, D. Role of novelty in the aversion for increasingly concentrated saccharin solutions. *Physiology and Behavior,* 1976, *16,* 537–542.

Domjan, M., & Gregg, B. Long-delay backward taste-aversion conditioning with lithium. *Physiology and Behavior,* 1977, *18,* 59–62.

Domjan, M., & Siegel, S. Conditioned suppression following CS preexposure. *Psychonomic Science,* 1971, *25,* 11–12.

Domjan, M., & Wilson, N. E. Specificity of cue to consequence in aversion learning in the rat. *Psychonomic Science,* 1972, *26,* 143–145.

Durlach, P. J., & Rescorla, R. A. Potentiation rather than overshadowing in flavor-aversion learning: An analysis in terms of within-compound associations. *Journal of Experimental Psychology: Animal Behavior Processes,* 1980, *6,* 175–187.

Estes, W. K. Memory and conditioning. In F. J. McGuigan & D. B. Lumsden (Eds.), *Contemporary approaches to conditioning and learning.* Washington, D.C.: Winston, 1973.

Estes, W. K. (Ed.). *Handbook of learning and cognitive processes* (Vol. 2): *Conditioning and behavior theory.* Hillsdale, N.J.: Lawrence Erlbaum Associates, 1975.

Galef, B. G. Jr., & Osborne, B. Novel taste facilitation of the association of visual cues with toxicosis in rats. *Journal of Comparative and Physiological Psychology,* 1978, *92,* 907–916.

Gamzu, E. The multifaceted nature of taste-aversion inducing agents: Is there a single common factor? In L. M. Barker, M. R. Best, & M. Domjan (Eds.), *Learning mechanisms in food selection.* Waco, Texas: Baylor University Press, 1977.

Garcia, J. Mitchell, Scott, and Mitchell are not supported by their own data. *Animal Learning and Behavior,* 1978, *6,* 116.

Garcia, J., Hankins, W. G., & Rusiniak, K. W. Behavioral regulation of the milieu interne in man and rat. *Science,* 1974, *185,* 823–831.

Garcia, J., Kimeldorf, D. J., & Hunt, E. L. Conditioned responses to manipulative procedures resulting from exposure to gamma radiation. *Radiation Research,* 1956, *5,* 79–87.

Garcia, J., Kimeldorf, D. J., & Hunt, E. L. The use of ionizing radiation as a motivating stimulus. *Psychological Review,* 1961, *68,* 383–395.

Garcia, J., & Koelling, R. A. Relation of cue to consequence in avoidance learning. *Psychonomic Science,* 1966, *4,* 123–124.

Garcia, J., & Koelling, R. A. A comparison of aversions induced by X-rays, toxins, and drugs in the rat. *Radiation Research Supplement,* 1967, *7,* 439–450.

Garcia, J., Kovner, R., & Green, K. F. Cue properties vs. palatability of flavors in avoidance learning. *Psychonomic Science,* 1970, *20,* 313–314.

Garcia, J., McGowan, B. K., Ervin, F. R., & Koelling, R. A. Cues: Their relative effectiveness as a function of the reinforcer. *Science,* 1968, *160,* 794–795.

Gibbon, J., & Balsam, P. D. Spreading association in time. In C. M. Locurto, H. S. Terrace, & J. Gibbon (Eds.), *Autoshaping and conditioning theory.* New York: Academic Press, 1981.

Green, K. F., Holmstrom, L. S., & Wollman, M. A. Relation of cue to consequence in rats: Effect of recuperation from illness. *Behavioral Biology,* 1974, *10,* 491–503.

Green, K. F., & Parker, L. A. Gustatory memory: Incubation and interference. *Behavioral Biology,* 1975, *13,* 359–367.

Grote, F. W., Jr., & Brown, R. T. Conditioned taste aversions: Two-stimulus tests are more sensitive than one-stimulus tests. *Behavior Research Methods and Instrumentation,* 1971, *3,* 311–312.

Hankins, W. G., Garcia, J., & Rusiniak, K. W. Dissociation of odor and taste in bait shyness. *Behavioral Biology,* 1973, *8,* 407–419.

Hankins, W. G., Rusiniak, K. W., & Garcia, J. Dissociation of odor and taste in shock-avoidance learning. *Behavioral Biology,* 1976, *18,* 345–358.

Hargrave, G. E., & Bolles, R. C. Rat's aversion to flavors following induced illness. *Psychonomic Science,* 1971, *23,* 91–92.

Hebb, D. O. On the nature of fear. *Psychological Review,* 1946, *53,* 259–276.

Holland, P. C. Representation-mediated overshadowing and potentiation of conditioned aversions. *Journal of Experimental Psychology: Animal Behavior Processes,* 1983, *9,* 1–13.

Hollinger, M., & Roberts, L. J. Overcoming food dislikes: A study with evaporated milk. *Journal of Home Economics,* 1929, *21,* 358–366.

Honig, W. K., & Staddon, J. E. R. (Eds.). *Handbook of operant behavior.* Englewood Cliffs, N.J.: Prentice–Hall, 1977.

Jennings, W. A., & McCutcheon, L. E. Novel food and novel running wheels. Conditions for inhibition of sucrose intake in rats. *Journal of Comparative and Physiological Psychology,* 1974, *87,* 100–105.

Jonsson, G., Hallman, H., Ponzio, F., & Ross, S. B. DSP4(N-2-chloroethyl-N-ethyl-2-bromobenzylamine)-a useful noradrenaline denervation tool for central and peripheral noradrenaline neurons. *European Journal of Pharmacology,* 1981, *72,* 173–188.

Kalat, J. W. Taste salience depends on novelty, not concentration, in taste-aversion learning in the rat. *Journal of Comparative and Physiological Psychology,* 1974, *86,* 47–50.

Kalat, J. W., & Rozin, P. Role of interference in taste-aversion learning. *Journal of Comparative and Physiological Psychology,* 1971, *77,* 53–58.

Kamin, L. J. Predictability, surprise, attention and conditioning. In B. A. Campbell & R. M. Church (Eds.), *Punishment and aversive behavior.* New York: Appleton–Century–Crofts, 1969.

Kehoe, E. J., & Gormezano, I. Configuration and combination laws in conditioning with compound stimuli. *Psychological Bulletin,* 1980, *87,* 351–378.

Kirk, R. E. *Experimental design: Procedures for the behavioral sciences.* Belmont, Calif.: Brooks/Cole, 1968.

Larsen, J. D., & Hyde, T. S. A comparison of learned aversions to gustatory and exteroceptive cues in the rat. *Animal Learning and Behavior,* 1977, *5,* 17–20.

Larue, C. Comparison des effects de l'anosmie périphérique et de la bulbectomie sur la sequence alimentaire du rat. *Journal de Physiologie (Paris),* 1975, *70,* 299–306.

Lett, B. T. Taste potentiates color-sickness associations in pigeons and quail. *Animal Learning and Behavior,* 1980, *8,* 193–198.

Logue, A. W. Taste aversion and the generality of the laws of learning. *Psychological Bulletin,* 1979, *86,* 276–296.

Lorden, J. F., Kenfield, M., & Braun, J. J. Response suppression to odors paired with toxicosis. *Learning and Motivation,* 1970, *1,* 391–400.

Lorden, J. F., Rickert, E. J., Dawson, R., & Pelleymounter, M. A. Forebrain norepinephrine and the selective processing of information. *Brain Research,* 1980, *190,* 569–573.

Lovett, D., Goodchild, P., & Booth, D. A. Depression of intake of nutrient by association of its odor with effects of insulin. *Psychonomic Science,* 1968, *11,* 27–28.

Lubow, R. E. Latent inhibition: Effects of frequency of nonreinforced preexposure of the CS. *Journal of Comparative and Physiological Psychology,* 1965, *60,* 454–457.

Lubow, R. E., & Moore, A. V. Latent inhibition: The effect of nonreinforced preexposure of the CS. *Journal of Comparative and Physiological Psychology,* 1959, *52,* 415–419.

Mackay, B. Conditioned food aversion produced by toxicosis in Atlantic cod. *Behavioral Biology,* 1974, *12,* 347–355.

Mackintosh, N. J. An analysis of overshadowing and blocking. *Quarterly Journal of Experimental Psychology*, 1971, *23*, 118–125.

Mackintosh, N. J. Stimulus selection: Learning to ignore stimuli that predict no change in reinforcement. In R. A. Hinde & J. Stevenson–Hinde (Eds.), *Constraints on learning*, New York: Academic Press, 1973.

Mackintosh, N. J. A theory of attention: Variations in the associability of stimuli with reinforcement. *Psychological Review*, 1975, *82*, 276–298.

Mackintosh, N. J. Stimulus control: Attentional factors. In W. K. Honig & J. E. R. Staddon (Eds.), *Handbook of operant behavior*. Englewood Cliffs, N.J.: Prentice–Hall, 1977.

Martin, J. C. Spatial avoidance in a paradigm in which ionizing radiation precedes spatial confinement. *Radiation Research*, 1966, *27*, 284–289.

Martin, J. C., & Ellinwood, E. H. Conditioned aversions in spatial paradigms following methamphetamine injections. *Psychopharmacologia*, 1974, *36*, 323–335.

Mason, S. T. Noradrenaline: Reward or extinction? *Neuroscience and Biobehavioral Reviews*, 1979, *3*, 1–10. (a)

Mason, S. T. Dorsal bundle extinction effect: Motivation or attention. *Physiology and Behavior*, 1979, *23*, 43–51. (b)

Mason, S. T., & Iversen, S. D. Theories of the dorsal bundle extinction effect. *Brain Research Review*, 1979, *1*, 107–137.

McAllister, W. R., & McAllister, D. E. Increase over time in the stimulus generalization of acquired fear. *Journal of Experimental Psychology*, 1963, *65*, 576–582.

McAllister W. R., & McAllister, D. E. Variables influencing the conditioning and the measurement of acquired fear. In W. F. Prokasy (Ed.), *Classical conditioning: A symposium*. New York: Appleton–Century–Crofts, 1965.

McAllister, W. R., & McAllister, D. E. Behavioral measurement of conditioned fear. In F. R. Brush (Ed.), *Aversive conditioning and learning*. New York: Academic Press, 1971.

McNaughton, N., & Mason, S. T. The neuropsychology and neuropharmacology of the dorsal ascending noradrenergic bundle—A review. *Progress in Neurobiology*, 1980, *14*, 157–219.

Mikulka, P. J., Pitts, E., & Philput, C. Overshadowing not potentiation in taste-aversion conditioning. *Bulletin of the Psychonomic Society*, 1982, *2*, 101–104.

Miller, N. E. Certain recent developments in experimental psychology. *Proceedings of the Royal Society of Biology*, 1963, *158*, 481–497.

Mitchell, D. Reply to Revusky. *Animal Learning and Behavior*, 1977, *5*, 321–322.

Mitchell, D. The psychological vs. the ethological rat: Two views of the poison avoidance behavior of the rat compared. *Animal Learning and Behavior*, 1978, *6*, 121–124.

Mitchell, D., Kirschbaum, E. H., & Perry, R. L. Effects of neophobia and habituation on the poison-induced avoidance of exteroceptive stimuli in the rat. *Journal of Experimental Psychology: Animal Behavior Processes*, 1975, *104*, 47–55.

Mitchell, D., Scott, D. W., & Mitchell, L. K. Attenuated and enhanced neophobia in the taste-aversion "delay of reinforcement" effect. *Animal Learning and Behavior*, 1977, *5*, 99–102.

Mitchell, D., Williams, K. D., & Sutter, J. Container neophobia as a predictor of preference for earned food by rats. *Bulletin of the Psychonomic Society*, 1974, *4*, 182–184.

Morrison, G. R., & Collyer, R. Taste-mediated conditioned aversion to an exteroceptive stimulus following LiCl poisoning. *Journal of Comparative and Physiological Psychology*, 1974, *86*, 51–55.

Nachman, M. Learned taste and temperature aversions due to lithium chloride sickness after temporal delays. *Journal of Comparative and Physiological Psychology*, 1970, *73*, 31–37.

Nachman, M., & Jones, D. R. Learned taste aversions over long delays in rats: The role of learned safety. *Journal of Comparative and Physiological Psychology*, 1974, *86*, 949–956.

Nachman, M., Rauschenberger, J., & Ashe, J. H. Stimulus characteristics in food aversion learning. In N. W. Milgram, L. Krames, & T. M. Alloway (Eds.), *Food aversion learning*. New York: Plenum Press, 1977. (a)

Nachman, M., Rauschenberger, J., & Ashe, J. H. Studies of learned aversions using nongustatory stimuli. In L. M. Barker, M. R. Best, & M. Domjan (Eds.), *Learning mechanisms in food selection.* Waco, Texas: Baylor University Press, 1977. (b)

Navarick, D. J., & Strouthes, A. Relative intake of saccharin and water on a restricted drinking schedule. *Psychonomic Science*, 1969, *15*, 158–159.

Overall, J. E., & Brown, W. L. Instrumental behavior of albino rats in response to incident X-radiation. *British Journal of Radiology*, 1959, *32*, 411–414.

Overall, J. E., Brown, W. L., & Logie, L. C. The shuttlebox behavior of albino rats during prolonged exposure to moderate level radiation. *Nature*, 1960, *185*, 665–666.

Overall, J. E., Logie, L. C., & Brown, W. L. Changes in shuttlebox behavior in albino rats in response to X-irradiation at 1 r/min. *Radiation Research*, 1959, *11*, 589–599.

Pain, J. F., & Booth, D. A. Toxiphobia for odors. *Psychonomic Science*, 1968, *10*, 363–364.

Pavlov, I. P. *Conditioned reflexes.* Oxford: Oxford University Press, 1927.

Rabinowitch, V. The role of experience in the development of food preferences in gull chicks. *Animal Behavior*, 1968, *16*, 425–428.

Rabinowitch, V. The role of experience in the development and retention of seed preferences in Zebra finches. *Behavior*, 1969, *33*, 222–236.

Razran, G. *Mind in evolution. An east–west synthesis of learned behavior and cognition.* Boston: Houghton Mifflin, 1971.

Rescorla, R. A. Simultaneous and successive associations in sensory preconditioning. *Journal of Experimental Psychology: Animal Behavior Processes*, 1980, *6*, 207–216.

Rescorla, R. A. Simultaneous associations. In P. Harzem & M. D. Zeiler (Eds.), *Predictability, correlation, and contiguity.* New York: Wiley, 1981.

Rescorla, R. A., & Wagner, A. R. A theory of Pavlovian conditioning. Variations in the effectiveness of reinforcement and nonreinforcement. In A. H. Black & W. F. Prokasy (Eds.), *Classical conditioning II: Current research and theory:* New York: Appleton–Century–Crofts, 1972.

Revusky, S. H. The role of interference in association over a delay. In W. K. Honig & P. H. R. James (Eds.), *Animal memory.* New York: Academic Press, 1971.

Revusky, S. Learning as a general process with an emphasis on data from feeding experiments. In N. W. Milgram, L. Krames, & T. M. Alloway (Eds.), *Food aversion learning.* New York: Plenum Press, 1977. (a)

Revusky, S. Correction of a paper by Mitchell, Scott, and Mitchell. *Animal Learning and Behavior*, 1977, *5*, 320. (b)

Revusky, S. Reply to Mitchell. *Animal Learning and Behavior*, 1978, *6*, 119–120.

Revusky, S. More about appropriate controls for taste aversion learning: A reply to Riley. *Animal Learning and Behavior*, 1979, *7*, 562–563.

Revusky, S. H., & Bedarf, E. W. Association of illness with ingestion of novel foods. *Science*, 1967, *155*, 219–220.

Revusky, S., & Garcia, J. Learned associations over long delays. In G. H. Bower & J. T. Spence (Eds.), *The psychology of learning and motivation: Advances in research and theory* (Vol. IV). New Yok: Academic Press, 1970.

Revusky, S., & Parker, L. A. Aversions to unflavored water and cup drinking produced by delayed sickness. *Journal of Experimental Psychology: Animal Behavior Processes*, 1976, *2*, 343–353.

Riley, A. L. In response to and in defense of Mitchell and Revusky: An analysis of nonassociative effects. *Animal Learning and Behavior*, 1978, *6*, 472–473.

Rizley, R. C., & Rescorla, R. A. Associations in second-order conditioning and sensory preconditioning. *Journal of Comparative and Physiological Psychology*, 1972, *81*, 1–11.

Rohles, F. H., Overall, J. E., & Brown, W. L. Attempts to produce spatial avoidance as a result of exposure to X-radiation. *British Journal of Radiology*, 1959, *32*, 244–246.

Rolls, B. J., & Rolls, E. T. Effects of lesions in the basolateral amygdala on fluid intake in the rat. *Journal of Comparative and Physiological Psychology*, 1973, *83*, 240–247.

Ross, S. B. Long-term effects of N(2-chloroethyl)-N-ethyl-2-bromobenzylamine hydrochloride on noradrenergic neurons in the rat brain and heart. *British Journal of Pharmacology*, 1976, *58*, 521–527.

Rozin, P. Central or peripheral mediation of learning with long CS–US intervals in the feeding system. *Journal of Comparative and Physiological Psychology*, 1969, *67*, 421–429.

Rudy, J. W., & Cheatle, M. D. Odor-aversion learning by neonatal rats. *Science*, 1977, *198*, 845–846.

Rudy, J. W., Iwens, J., & Best, P. J. Pairing novel exteroceptive cues and illness reduces illness-induced taste-aversions. *Journal of Experimental Psychology: Animal Behavior Processes*, 1977, *3*, 14–25.

Rudy, J. W., Rosenberg, L., & Sandell, J. H. Disruption of a taste familiarity effect by novel exteroceptive stimulation. *Journal of Experimental Psychology: Animal Behavior Processes*, 1977, *3*, 26–36.

Rusiniak, K. W., Hankins, W. G., Garcia, J., & Brett, L. Flavor-illness aversions. I. Potentiation of odor by taste in rats. *Behavioral and Neural Biology*, 1979, *25*, 1–17.

Rzóska, J. The behavior of white rats towards poison baits. In D. Chitty (Ed.), *Control of rats and mice* (Vol. 2). Oxford: Clarenden Press, 1954.

Seligman, M. E. P. On the generality of the laws of learning. *Psychological Review*, 1970, *77*, 400–418.

Sheafor, P. J. "Pseudoconditioned" jaw movements of the rabbit reflect associations conditioned to contextual background cues. *Journal of Experimental Psychology: Animal Behavioral Processes*, 1975, *104*, 245–260.

Siegel, S. Effect of CS habituation on eyelid conditioning. *Journal of Comparative and Physiological Psychology*, 1969, *68*, 245–248.

Siegel, S. Flavor preexposure and "learned safety." *Journal of Comparative and Physiological Psychology*, 1974, *87*, 1073–1082.

Simson, P. C., & Booth, D. A. Olfactory conditioning by association with histidine-free or balanced amino-acid loads in rats. *Quarterly Journal of Experimental Psychology*, 1973, *25*, 354–359.

Sjödén, P. O., & Archer, T. Associative and nonassociative effects of exteroceptive context in taste-aversion conditioning with rats. *Behavioral and Neural Biology*, 1981, *33*, 74–92.

Sjödén, P. O., & Archer, T. Potentiation of a bottle aversion by taste in compound conditioning with rats. *Experimental Animal Behaviour*, 1983, *2*, 1–18.

Slotnick, B. M., Brown, D. L., & Gelhard, R. Contrasting effects of location and taste-cues in illness-induced aversion. *Physiology and Behavior*, 1977, *18*, 333–335.

Smith, J. C. Comment on paper by Mitchell, Scott, and Mitchell. *Animal Learning and Behavior*, 1978, *6*, 117–118.

Somjen, G. *Sensory coding in the mammalian nervous system*. New York: Appleton–Century–Crofts, 1972.

Strouthes, A. Thirst and saccharin preference in rats. *Physiology and Behavior*, 1971, *6*, 287–292.

Supak, T. D., Macrides, F., & Chorover, S. L. The bait-shyness effect extended to olfactory discrimination. *Communications in Behavioral Biology*, 1971, *5*, 321–324.

Sutherland, N. S., & Mackintosh, N. J. *Mechanisms of animal discrimination learning*. New York: Academic Press, 1971.

Taukulis, H. K. Odor aversions produced over long CS–US delays. *Behavioral Biology*, 1974, *10*, 505–510.

Taukulis, H. K., & Revusky, S. H. Odor as a conditioned inhibitor: Applicability of the Rescorla–Wagner model to feeding behavior. *Learning and Motivation*, 1975, *6*, 11–27.

Tomie, A. Retardation of autoshaping: Control by contextual stimuli. *Science*, 1976, *192*, 1244–1245.

Wagner, A. R. Priming in STM: An information-processing mechanism for self-generated or retrieval-generated depression in performance. In T. J. Tighe & R. N. Leaton (Eds.), *Habituation: Perspectives from child development, animal behavior, and neurophysiology*. Hillsdale, N.J.: Lawrence Erlbaum Associates, 1976.

Wagner, A. R., & Rescorla, R. A. Inhibition in Pavlovian conditioning. Application of a theory. In M. S. Halliday & R. A. Boakes (Eds.), *Inhibition and learning*. London: Academic Press, 1972.

Wilcoxon, H. C., Dragoin, W. B., & Kral, P. A. Illness-induced aversions in rats and quail: Relative salience of visual and gastatory cues. *Science,* 1971, *171,* 826–828.

Willner, J. A. Blocking of a taste aversion by prior pairings of exteroceptive stimuli with illness. *Learning and Motivation,* 1978, *9,* 125–140.

Wittlin, W. A., & Brookshire, K. H. Apomorphine-induced conditioned aversion to a novel food. *Psychonomic Science,* 1968, *12,* 217–218.

Woods, S. C., Makous, W., & Hutton, R. A. Temporal parameters of conditioned hypoglycemia *Journal of Comparative and Physiological Psychology,* 1969, *69,* 301–307.

10 Pitch Context and Pitch Discrimination by Birds

Stewart H. Hulse
Jeffrey Cynx
John Humpal
The Johns Hopkins University

It is both an old and a current truism, as the chapters of this book testify, that learning never occurs in a vacuum. At one level, there is the nature of the *external* stimulus context surrounding the events—whatever they may be—that enter into learning. As we now know, the external context that contains the stimuli that form new relationships in both operant and Pavlovian conditioning helps to determine what will be learned, how it will be learned, and—if it is learned—in what form it will be remembered. But there is another sense in which context can be conceived, and that is the sense, equally important, that the stimulus events themselves that enter into learning—taken as a patterned whole—define an *internally organized, within-stimulus* context with properties that will also determine what is perceived and processed, and so learned and remembered. It is to some aspects of the latter idea—the serial organization of stimulus information, in particular—that this chapter is directed.

We begin with a brief historical discussion of the theory of serial stimulus organization in learning, turn to some applications of that theory to reinforcement processes within animal learning, then examine some recent data that have come from animal perception of serial sequences of acoustic stimuli.

Serial Pattern Learning

The problem of how stimulus collections are organized internally is hardly new. Its roots are buried in the philosophical problem of form versus substance, a problem that nourished Gestalt psychology both in the original form of that approach and in its modern guise (e.g., Garner, 1974). The theory in psychology

273

of the *serial* organization of stimulus information has a strange and curious history, however.

The problem of serial order in behavior had, until 1951, been largely treated theoretically in terms of linear associative chains of stimuli and responses. With a background stimulated no doubt by Ebbinghaus's work on rote serial learning of *verbal* materials by humans, the relevant models were supplied initially by Hull (1931) and Skinner (1934) to describe the serial *motor* behavior of *animals!* Hull's model was developed as a tongue-in-cheek (to the historical eye, at least) account of ''goal-directed thinking'' expressed in the peripheralistic terms of stimulus and response. Skinner's, which was less formally expressed, was also less elegantly adorned. However, these models were applied through the 1930s and 1940s not only to the behavior of animals, but also to the verbal behavior of humans. Maze and memory drum were equated, and the principles governing both the performance of rats at choice points in mazes and the development of human language and memory were assumed to be at least functionally analogous. General process learning theory prevailed.

In 1951, however, Lashley pointed out many instances in which the behavior of humans—*especially* in the organization of their language and complex motor behavior—failed to follow the linear associative chains of stimulus and response espoused by theorists such as Hull. Instead, Lashley argued, behavior seemed in many instances (though not necessarily all, he might have added) to be better described by hierarchical structures that were centrally rather than peripherally controlled. On the surface, behavior might appear linear in time and space, but the underlying structures producing that apparent linearity were, in fact, often stacked upon one another in a very complex fashion.

Lashley's ideas were a primary force that helped to stimulate at least three major developments in psychology. First, for students of behavior save Skinner, the rat and the pigeon were relegated to the animal laboratory as a model and source of theory for complex human learning (to be replaced—for better or worse—by the computer). Second, the field of psycholinguistics appeared, which, in the hands of Chomsky, Deese, Miller, and others, capitalized so productively on the concept of generative structure in the acquisition and management of language. Third, and most significant for present purposes, new, general models began to appear for describing how people—in the broadest sense—organize, encode, and retrieve stimulus material that appears in some temporally defined, serial order. Simon and Kotovsky (1963) were perhaps the first to publish such a formal model, but their work was followed by a spate of theories that further developed and embellished the principles governing human serial pattern learning. Among others, Restle (1970), Vitz and Todd (1969), Bower and Winzenz (1969), and Jones (1974) made major theoretical contributions, and the new theories were applied to data coming from stimulus domains as simple as the order in which a series of lights were turned on or as complex as the serial sequences of sounds in a Bach prelude.

Although the theories differed in detail, their core ideas were similar. Among other things, they assumed that people—confronted with an array of stimulus material arranged in a temporal series—actively sought to organize the bits and pieces of the array into larger units with some overarching formal structure. Predictions were then made and tested about the ease with which pattern learning would progress when, for example, the formal structure of a pattern was simple or complex (compare the number pattern 123234345456 with the pattern 163354452523), or the pattern was parsed or unparsed into "chunks" of stimuli with a coherent internal structure (compare the pattern 123–234–345–456 with the pattern 12–32–343–454–56). Above all, formal structures were studied that departed from the simple linear chains that characterized the older S–R models. Thus, the pattern 123–234–345–456 is defined at its lowest hierarchical level by a simple "next" rule that generates a set of 3-number sequences. On a higher level, however, each 3-number sequence is systematically related to its neighbor by another "next" rule. Of course, there is nothing to prevent people from learning hierarchically organized patterns as if they were linear chains, and a good deal of effort was expended in a search, for example, for bowed serial position curves that would be expected if each stimulus item was learned and remembered as an independent link of such a chain. People proved stubbornly sensitive to formal structure, however. They tended to make recall errors not in the middle of patterns, as a serial-association model would demand, but at any location where a rule changed, and errors were more apt to occur the higher the level of rule change in the pattern's formal structure.

Within the experimental psychology of human behavior, principles of serial pattern learning have now been applied in many domains. Perhaps one of the most interesting is that of human music perception—a serially organized information-processing capacity that is closely related to language in many aspects of its formal structure (Deutsch, 1982). Tantalizingly enough, many Eastern languages (such as Thai) depend on intonation through pitch changes to convey semantic meaning.

Patterned Reinforcement

Reinforcement processes provided the first test of the utility of theoretical models based on human serial pattern learning in accounting for animal learning. In an early experiment in 1973, which set the stage, Hulse showed that the effectiveness of a given quantity of food as a reinforcer for learning a new response was a direct function of the *serial context* in which that food stimulus had appeared in an animal's past history. For example, some rats were trained initially in an operant box in which, at first, a tone was followed automatically a few seconds later by the delivery of a single 45-mg pellet of food. Over daily sessions during the next 2 weeks, however, the *number* of food pellets gradually increased so that the tone was eventually followed by 10 pellets of food. Other rats were trained with food quantities presented in the reverse order, that is, the tone first predicted 10 pellets of food, a quantity that then decreased to one pellet over the ensuing 2 weeks. Still other rats had the *probability* that the tone would be followed by food either increased or decreased from 0.0 to 1.0 or from 1.0 to 0.0, whereas some had *both* the quantity and probability increased or decreased. Then all the animals were trained to lever press in the same operant box for a single pellet of food. The question was: Would the initial training modulate the effectiveness of a food pellet as a reinforcer for acquiring the new response?

The answer was yes. One of the more remarkable results was that if quantity and/or probability of food (especially both) had increased initially, the single food pellet was not very effective as a reward; many of the animals failed to learn at all. On the other hand, if quantity and/or probability had decreased, learning was extraordinarily rapid. These results—which at the time seemed most pertinent for phenomena such as reinforcement contrast effects (albeit in the *acquisition* as compared with the performance of a response)—seem (for better or worse) to have been largely neglected. But they stimulated a lively interest in the more general question of the psychological properties of serial sequences of stimuli, how they were encoded and remembered, and so on.

Hulse and Dorsky (1977) made the first direct application of the theory of human serial pattern learning to animals. They did an experiment in which the formal *complexity* of a series of different quantities of food (14, 7, 3, 1, or 0 pellets) was varied for different groups of rats who ran a closely spaced series of trials in a runway to receive each quantity in order. The prediction (with Restle, 1970) was that the less complex the pattern, the less difficult the pattern would be to learn—as measured by the number of trials required before the rats began to reliably slow their running in anticipation of the smaller quantities of food (especially the 0-pellet quantity). The results of the experiment were in line with prediction. For example, a formally simple pattern whose structure was described by a single "decrease" rule—14–7–3–1–0 pellets—was easier to learn than a formally more complex pattern described by a series of both "decrease" and "increase" rules—14–1–3–7–0 pellets. Ensuing research showed that rats—in close functional parallel to human behavior—could, among other things: (1) generalize a rule structure from one set of food quantities to another (Hulse & Dorsky, 1979); (2) induce a rule structure and use it to extrapolate a pattern by anticipating the size of a novel quantity of reinforcement (Fountain & Hulse, 1981); (3) use a sequence of food quantities to code a series of spatial locations (Hulse & O'Leary, 1982); and (4) respond to a serial pattern of food quantities with greater facility if the pattern were "chunked" into subunits with a coherent as compared with a more haphazard formal structure (Fountain, Henne, & Hulse, 1984). The application of this "rule-learning" approach to animal learning has not been without critics espousing a traditional associative-chaining model (e.g., Capaldi, Nawrocki, & Verry, 1982), but part of the controversy may have arisen because of misconceptions about the nature of a "rule" and the conditions appropriate for application of the "rule-learning" model (Hulse, 1980).

Although the use of different quantities of food as a tool to study rats' capacity to process serial information remains of interest for many reasons, recent research has turned to acoustic stimuli as a source of input for serial pattern learning. There were three main reasons for this change. First, acoustic stimuli offered a much richer selection of dimensions along which stimulus change could take place in constructing serial patterns. Second, simple principles of human music perception offered a ready-made theoretical guide upon which to base initial experimentation. Finally, an understanding of the principles shaping serial sound perception promised a potentially much broader range of application— from the cognitive processing of arbitrary sound structures by animals, to bird-song, and even, perhaps, to the grammatical and syntactic underpinnings of human music and speech perception. We now turn to that newer research.

Comparative Acoustic Perception

How do people (and animals) recognize complex serial patterns of sound stimuli? For people, this question has relevance for many facets of sound perception, among them the perception of music and language. For animals, the question bears on communication among animals of the same species, and for the recognition of animals of other species.

If we examine simple principles of human acoustic perception in greater detail, we find that people have relatively little difficulty identifying familiar sound patterns that maintain some form of constant pitch *relationship* between successive pattern components. This is true in the case of music perception, for example (the same principles would also hold generally for speech), because constant pitch relationships define the *melody* or pitch *contour* of the pattern in question. Thus, once learned, the opening measures of very complex acoustic patterns, like Beethoven's Fifth Symphony, or the song of the wood thrush, are easily recognized. On the other hand, people generally have greater difficulty identifying sound patterns on the basis of any *absolute* properties they may possess, such as the musical key in which a melody is played or the specific frequency with which a wood thrush's song begins. Thus, for example, from one performance to another, few people will notice changes in the pitch of the beginning note of Beethoven's Fifth Symphony.

In theories of human music perception, these observations exemplify the distinction between *tone chroma* and *tone height* (e.g., Deutsch, 1969, 1978, 1982; Shepard, 1965, 1982). Tone chroma refers to the fact that as one moves from octave to octave on, say, the piano keyboard, or a melody changes from key to key (such as from C minor to D minor) on a tempered scale, the frequencies of neighboring notes in the melody maintain a constant *ratio* with respect to each other and, therefore, maintain equal spacing on a *log* scale of sound frequency. People respond to this ratio invariance by perceiving the melody as unchanged. Tone height, on the other hand, refers to the general highness or lowness in pitch, in an absolute sense, of a sound pattern. We shift a melody in tone height when we play it in one octave as compared with another, or when we transpose it to a new key. People are generally far less able to discriminate the absolute pitch changes that occur with shifts in tone height, than the *relative* pitch changes that occur with shifts in tone chroma. Most can certainly distinguish the absolute pitch difference between the top and bottom notes on a piano, and, similarly, the relative note-to-note pitch changes that occur in the shift of a familiar melody from a major to a minor key. But the slight (absolute) frequency shift in tone height that occurs with a key change from C minor to D minor may only be discernible to the average listener if it occurs within seconds.

In theory, identical principles hold for birdsong. However, whereas the relative contribution of tone chroma and tone height has received extensive study in music perception, and researchers are aware at least informally of parallel factors in human speech production, there have been no systematic attempts, so far as we know, to measure relative as compared with absolute properties of birdsong *production*—or, until recently, the ability of birds (or other animals, for that matter) to *perceive* and process serial acoustic information in either the relative or absolute sense outlined by the foregoing analysis. This is true not only for a physical analysis of the signal itself, but also for a functional analysis of the signal for its behavioral significance. Yet the problem is important—especially from a comparative viewpoint—because the ability to process serial acoustic information—with which relative and absolute contexts are closely associated by definition—is essential not only for the production and perception of birdsong and other forms of auditory communication in animals, but also for the production and perception of human music and speech. These considerations prompted the research to which we now turn.

The experimental analysis addressed the following questions: (1) Do animals have the capacity to discriminate sound patterns on the basis of relative pitch? (2) Do animals have the capacity to discriminate sound patterns on the basis of absolute pitch? (3) Does the discrimination generalize over a frequency change, that is, over a change in tone height?

ANALYTIC METHODS

Species

Such an analysis of acoustic perception requires a priori evidence that the species to be studied is not perceptually locked to some narrowly limited set of acoustic signals—such as the calls or communicative sounds of its conspecifics. Furthermore, there should be some richness evident in the signaling system; that is, the species should possess a relatively wide variety of sound patterns in its natural repertoire. Birds come immediately to mind, and, within birds, species that mimic provide good evidence of the ability to attend to and process a wide variety of sound patterns. Accordingly, the European starling (*Sturnus vulgaris*), which is a good mimicker, was selected.

Procedural Strategies

There are two ways, in principle, in which the acoustic information-processing capacity of an animal may be studied. First, in the case of a mimicking species, at any rate, one could try to teach the bird to actually reproduce some sound pattern of theoretical interest (Pepperberg, 1981, 1983). A *production* method of this sort has many attractive features (e.g., one can measure errors), but it promises endless hours of training—perhaps without eventual success. This could happen not because of an inability of the animal to perceive and process the acoustic information in question, but because of physical or other limitations on the animal's ability to produce the relevant sounds.

A *reception* method, on the other hand, avoids many of these handicaps. In this case, the animal listens to two (or more) sound exemplars generated by the experimenter and selects among them through some simple indicator response according to contingencies established by the experimental procedure. The animal's processing capacity can be assessed, on the one hand, by the judicious selection of discriminative stimuli, each designed to test the relevance for accurate perception of some stimulus parameter. On the other hand, transfer tests can be used once a discrimination is learned, each transfer designed to probe for the animal's dependence on some feature of the discriminative stimuli to maintain the discrimination in question. One of the major advantages of the reception method is that the experimenter, not the subject, determines the important relevant characteristics of the stimulus array, such as the order in which stimuli occur. For these reasons, the reception method was selected.

Stimuli

The stimulus patterns selected for initial discrimination training were based on perhaps the simplest principle of pitch discrimination, the ability to distinguish a rising from a falling sequence of pitches (Hulse, Cynx, & Humpal, 1984b). The stimuli were sine waves. They were drawn from a frequency *alphabet*, a set of tones that were both discriminable from one another and ordered from low to high in frequency (Hulse & O'Leary, 1982; Jones, 1974). In particular, the frequencies were selected to provide pitches based on the whole-tone scale, a musical scale that divides an octave into six equal intervals on a log scale of frequency. Four exemplars of both rising and falling 4-tone patterns, were constructed, each beginning on a different pitch within a single octave. As Fig. 10.1 shows, many pitches were common to both rising and falling pattern exemplars, but the sequences were constructed in an effort to minimize the possibility that the discrimination could be solved by attending to any set of single frequencies.

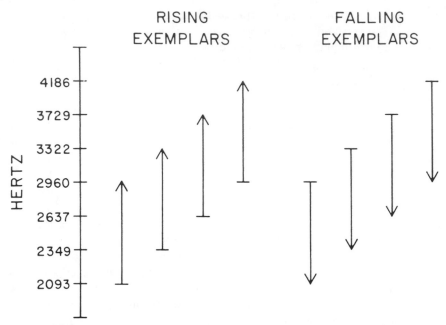

FIG. 10.1.   The frequencies of the rising and falling 4-tone pitch patterns used in baseline discrimination training.

The stimuli were configured temporally into 4-tone groups. This was done in an effort to draw attention to the rising and falling dimension of interest. In baseline training, each tone within a group was on for 100 msec, and each tone was separated from the subsequent tone by 100 msec. Four-tone patterns were separated by an 800-msec interpattern interval. During stimulus presentation, repeating sequences of 4-tone patterns and interpattern intervals proceeded in a continuous train, whose total duration was controlled by other experimental contingencies.

Procedures

The details of the experimental procedures have been described elsewhere (Hulse, Cynx, & Humpal, 1984a; Hulse, Cynx, & Humpal, 1984b). Four starlings (*Sturnus vulgaris*), two males and two females, were tested at 85% to 90% ad lib weight and maintained (and reinforced in the test apparatus) with a standard laboratory diet.

The apparatus was a wire-mesh test cage suspended in an IAC soundproof chamber. The bird faced a panel on one wall containing three keys that could be transilluminated with white light. (The left key was not used.) A loudspeaker was mounted directly over the test cage.

The pure tones were generated with a programmable oscillator. Stimulus loudnesses were set at 70 db ± 5 db; control tests showed that behavior did not vary as a function of stimulus loudness. Stimulus patterns, experimental contingencies, and data collection were managed on-line by a minicomputer.

The birds were first autoshaped to peck a lighted key. They then began discrimination training using a go/no-go procedure. A trial began with the lighting of the center key. A peck on the key turned on either ($p = .50$) a rising or a falling tone pattern for a 4-sec listening period. During this period, pecks had no programmed consequences. Following the listening period, the center key darkened, and the side key was lighted, while the sound pattern continued. If the sound pattern *fell* in pitch, a peck on the side key during a 4-sec response period darkened the key, turned off the sound pattern, and provided 1.5 sec access to the food hopper. A 4-sec intertrial interval then ensued. If the sound pattern *rose* in pitch, a peck on the side key during the ensueing 4-sec response period darkened the key, turned off the sound pattern, and darkened the houselights for 8 sec. The 4-sec intertrial interval then began. If the bird witheld a peck to a rising pattern for the 4-sec response period, the 4-sec intertrial interval then began immediately. The birds were tested for a half hour each test day.

The data of interest were the latencies to peck the side key after the initial 4-sec listening period. Good discrimination performance was reflected by a large difference between the latencies to falling patterns (go trials) and rising patterns (no-go trials). Initial discrimination training continued until the birds had reached a stable asymptote, as measured by visual inspection of daily mean go/no-go latency differences.

BASELINE DISCRIMINATION PERFORMANCE

All birds learned the initial baseline discrimination. The number of test sessions required to reach asymptote ranged from 15 to 42 days. Averaged across birds over 3 days at asymptote, the go/no-go latency differences were 3.1 sec ($p < .01$).

The excellent baseline discrimination between exemplars rising and falling in pitch provides strong evidence that starlings can learn an acoustic discrimination on the basis of relative pitch perception.

ABSOLUTE AND RELATIVE PITCH PERCEPTION

In order to further assess the role of absolute and relative pitch strategies, a transfer test was run in which the birds had to maintain the rising–falling pattern discrimination in the baseline pitch range when the number of tones in a pattern was reduced progressively over days from 4 to 3, 2, and 1 tone, and the birds heard each pattern just once on a trial (see Hulse et al., 1984b, for details). To do this, the standard discrimination procedure (Baseline A) was altered in two ways. First, the 4-sec listening period was eliminated, and the side key lit so the birds could respond (or not) just as soon as they had received enough information to make a go or no-go decision as the pattern repeated on a trial (Baseline B). Following the latter transfer, the birds underwent a series of tests in which a peck on the center key initiated a *single* presentation of a pattern that, over a series of test sessions, was either 3, 2, or 1 tone in length. The 1-tone "patterns" were arbitrarily ($p = 0.5$) determined as rising or falling by the computer and "falling" sequences were reinforced, whereas responses to "rising" sequences produced 8-sec "timeouts" as in baseline training. All possible exemplars were tested at each pattern length, so some of the transfer exemplars for the truncated patterns were novel in that they began on frequencies that had never appeared as the first tone in baseline exemplars—and then rose or fell in pitch from there. Each test with a truncated pattern was followed the next day by a session under standard baseline conditions.

The starlings showed evidence for *both* relative and absolute pitch discrimination when responding to truncated patterns in the context of the baseline pattern frequencies. Figure 10.2 displays the relevant results.

Figure 10.2 shows mean data for the 10–12 observations made for each pattern exemplar at each pattern length. Inspection of the data revealed that the mean data were quite representative of the data obtained during the first tests, so transfer of discrimination performance to the truncated exemplars was rapid.

One major conclusion to be drawn from the data of Fig. 10.2 is that, if serial information was reduced by eliminating the listening period (Baseline B) or by reducing pattern length, the starlings were nevertheless able to maintain the discrimination: The latencies for rising patterns were consistently longer than those for falling patterns regardless of pattern length. This was true even for novel exemplars that began on frequencies never used in baseline training (e.g., the 3-tone falling exemplar beginning on 2637 Hz, or the 2-tone rising exemplar beginning on 3322 Hz). The starlings thus showed a generalizable ability to respond differentially to the *relative* pitch properties of the exemplars (i.e., whether they rose or fell from their initial frequencies).

Figure 10.2 also shows, however, that—regardless of pattern length—the starlings were responding to an *absolute* feature of the pitch patterns. Thus, as the general pitch range of pattern exemplars became higher (that is, as one goes from the bottom to the top of the graph), the "no-go" response latencies to the rising patterns became shorter. The purest demonstration of this fact, in the sense that the data are uncontaminated by relative pitch effects, appears in the data for 1-tone "patterns." There, there was a consistent decrease in latency the higher the frequency of the exemplar.

The source of the differential responding on the basis of absolute pitch no doubt arose from the birds' inherent bias to peck when: (1) faced with insuffi-

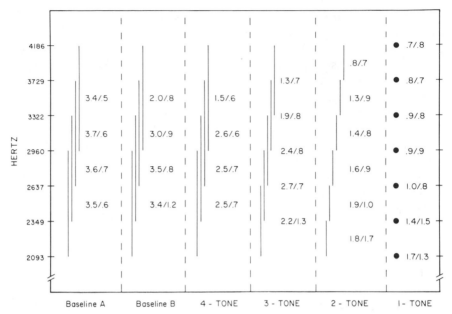

FIG. 10.2. "Go" response latencies (to the right of the slash marks) and "No-go" response latencies (to the left of the slash marks) for 4-tone baseline patterns under initial training conditions (Baseline A), for 4-tone baseline patterns in which the 4-sec listening period was eliminated (Baseline B), and for patterns reduced in length and heard just once. The frequencies spanned by the several exemplars are marked by the vertical lines to the left of each go/no-go latency pair. Pattern discrimination on the basis of the *relative* rising–falling feature of successive tones in the patterns (measured by Go/No-go latency differences) decreases with pattern length. Discrimination also decreases as pitch range of pattern exemplars becomes higher in frequency—reflecting a tendency to respond on the basis of an *absolute* "high" or "low" pitch feature of the patterns.

cient information to make an accurate discrimination; or (2) faced with an exemplar that began in a high-as compared with a low-frequency range. Thus, as best shown by the data for the 1-tone "sequences," the birds reverted to short-latency responses—generally less than a second—when it was impossible to make a discrimination based on relative pitch. Also, baseline training exemplars that fell in pitch—and called for rapid, short-latency "go" responses—generally began on tones that were high in frequency, whereas exemplars that rose in pitch—and called for long-latency "no-go" reactions—generally began on tones that were low in frequency. The joint effect of these two reactions to an *absolute* pitch feature of the exemplars increased the higher the pitch range of the exemplar, and the birds tended to peck with short latencies most characteristic of high-pitch ranges—even on "no-go" trials. It is important to recognize, however, that in spite of the decrease in the go/no-go latency differences with higher pitch ranges, the birds were still able to maintain the discrimination and respond on the basis of the *relative,* rising and falling properties of the pitch patterns as long as relative pitch information was available (i.e., for patterns 2 tones or longer); that is, "no-go" reactions to rising patterns remained consistently longer than "go" responses to falling patterns.

Thus, although the relative and absolute pitch strategies were, in an important sense, competing with each other—it became more difficult, operationally, for the birds to show their capacity to respond relationally the higher the absolute pitch of the tone patterns—there was evidence that the birds were responding on the basis of both. The next logical question was whether comparable results would be obtained after a change of the general pitch range within which the birds had learned the rising–falling pitch discrimination originally—that is, after a change in tone height of the overall pitch context.

CONTEXT CHANGES IN TONE HEIGHT: NOVEL RANGES

All birds were tested for their ability to maintain the discrimination when the pitch context in which the original discrimination had been learned was shifted in tone height by one octave. This was accomplished first by dividing the baseline test frequencies of the patterns in half. The birds remained in the lower frequency context until behavior stabilized there, then returned to the original baseline frequencies to test for recovery of the discrimination in the baseline context. Next, the pitch context was shifted up one octave from the baseline range by doubling the frequency of the baseline exemplars. After behavior stabilized in the higher frequency range, this transfer was also followed by a return to the baseline test range. For one bird, the upward shift occurred before the downward shift. Complete details for these procedures are reported elsewhere (Hulse & Cynx, in preparation).

Downward Shift.   When the frequencies of the rising and falling exemplars were halved, and there was a downward shift of an octave in pitch context, all birds lost the ability to discriminate rising from falling patterns. The primary data for the downward shift, mean go/no-go latency differences averaged over each day's performance, appear in Fig. 10.3 (excluding one bird for whom the downward-shift data are unavailable). Latency differences are close to 0.0 sec on the first day of transfer. Inspection of the "go" and "no-go" latencies taken alone showed that the birds reverted to their inherent bias to peck quickly, and response latencies were short for *both* rising and falling exemplars over all trials of the day.

Although not shown in Fig. 10.3, the discrimination was recovered over succeeding days in the new pitch context—but relatively slowly. There were some savings as measured by number of days to reach a new asymptote relative to original discrimination learning, but recovery was far from an immediate affair—there was no sign of a go/no-go latency difference for any bird on the first day of transfer, for example. On this basis, the data suggest that at least part of the process at work was relearning as opposed to momentary disruption, say,

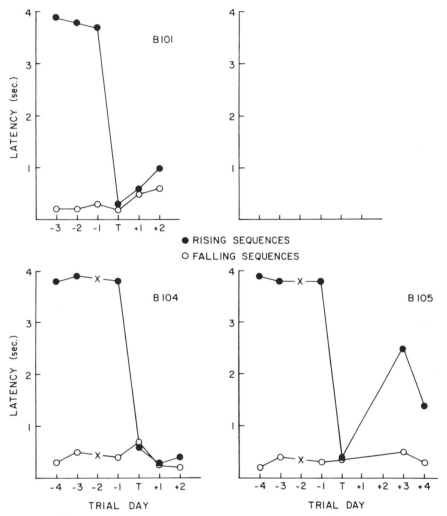

FIG. 10.3.   Mean go/no-go latencies for falling and rising pitch sequences for starlings when the birds were on baseline contingencies and the frequencies of the pattern exemplars were shifted *down* one octave in tone height. The letter T on the abscissa marks the day of the frequency context shift. Transfer resulted in complete loss of the discrimination. Data for one bird (B102) are missing, and *x*s indicate days for which data were lost.

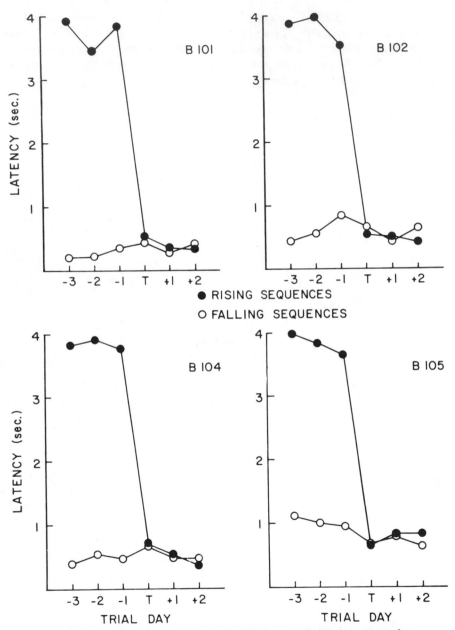

● RISING SEQUENCES

○ FALLING SEQUENCES

FIG. 10.4.   Mean go/no-go latencies for falling and rising pitch sequences for starlings when the birds were on baseline contingencies and the frequencies of the pattern exemplars were shifted *up* one octave in tone height. The letter T on the abscissa marks the day of the frequency context shift. Transfer resulted in complete loss of the discrimination.

of a readily transferred discrimination. Furthermore, recovery to a point such that no-go latencies were three times go latencies required from 3 to 16 days. Also, in two birds, the mean go/no-go latency difference failed to approach that characteristic of baseline discrimination, although the differences were substantial and significantly different from 0.0 for all birds ($ps < .01$).

Return to Baseline.   After the starlings' performance had stabilized in the lower pitch range, they were returned to baseline frequencies to see if accurate performance was retained there. In general, mean go/no-go latency differences reappeared in the tone-height context in which the discrimination was originally learned within the first day.

Upward Shift.   After behavior had reestablished itself on baseline frequencies, the baseline frequencies were doubled, and the starlings were tested when tone height was raised one octave. Again, as Fig. 10.4 shows, the starlings lost the discrimination immediately. Relatively slow recovery of the discrimination requiring much the same time as that following the downward shift suggests they had, in part, to *relearn* the discrimination in the new, higher pitch context. Data for the first days of relearning appear in Fig. 10.4.

Return to Baseline.   After behavior had stabilized in the higher pitch range, the starlings were returned once again to the original baseline pitch range. And once again, discrimination performance reappeared quite rapidly within the first day.

CONTEXT CHANGES IN TONE HEIGHT: ORIGINAL RANGE

The data produced by the foregoing changes in pitch context could suggest that the birds responded predominantly on the basis of an absolute pitch strategy, a strategy based on the acquired ability to identify and accurately "name" specific frequencies. This idea receives support from the birds' remarkable failure to maintain the rising–falling discrimination with a change in tone height either above or below the pitch context in which original training took place. Other data show, however, that the rising–falling discrimination was not based solely on the starlings' ability to recognize frequencies according to absolute pitch. Instead, the bird had to be familiar with a *general* pitch context, and, given this, a relative pitch strategy could emerge.

Proof for this reasoning comes from two sources. First, in the tests with truncated patterns, the birds were able to discriminate rising from falling exemplars when the exemplars began on tones that had never before initiated a pattern.

Second, a transfer was used in which the starlings were presented with 4-tone sequences that contained *novel* frequencies, but the exemplars incorporating the frequencies were within the original, familiar, baseline context. Three rising and three falling 4-tone exemplars were used, each incorporating the formal structure of the usual whole-tone scale. However, the initial frequencies of the exemplars were either higher or lower than the baseline frequencies by one semitone, that is, half a whole tone on a log scale of frequency. The results of this within-range transfer test showed that the birds could maintain the discrimination perfectly. Latencies on "go" trials for falling patterns were approximately 0.5 sec, whereas latencies on "no-go" trials for rising patterns were approximately 3.7 sec— figures that correspond in every way with tests involving baseline frequencies.

A CONCLUSION

The operation of a relative pitch strategy for starlings is tied to an absolute pitch constraint. For relative pitch to be learned and maintained, a familiar context of absolute pitch appears necessary. Within this context, not only can the birds perform on the basis of an absolute pitch strategy, but also phenomena readily appear based on the operation of a relative pitch strategy (e.g., the birds generalize their perception of pitch sequences sharing a common formal structure).

The interaction between the relative pitch strategy and the absolute pitch constraint poses many interesting problems and questions. One or two may be mentioned. First, how broad a pitch context can one establish and still obtain relational pitch effects? The research we have reported here was based on an initial context spanning one octave; suppose the span were reduced by half, or doubled, tripled? Second, what are the true limits on the ability to generalize relational strategies outside the familiar pitch context? The current results suggest the limits are extraordinarily narrow (i.e., that birds may not be able to maintain a relational strategy with virtually *any* shift from the familiar range). If this is so, there are interesting implications for the more general study of stimulus generalization outside the baseline range. One would like to know what would happen, for example, if birds were trained to respond relationally in *two* octave ranges, each separated by an octave in which no training occurred. A transfer test involving exemplars in that intervening, unfamiliar octave should produce interesting data indeed.

In any event, the data have provided answers to the major questions prompting the research initially. Starlings can discriminate rule-based pitch patterns. In so doing, they can respond on the basis of both absolute and relative pitch. However, the use of relative pitch strategies requires familiarity with the absolute pitch context in which relative pitch perception is to take place.

GENERALIZATION ACROSS FREQUENCY IN
RHYTHMIC DISCRIMINATION

To this point, the data suggest that birds are highly constrained by an absolute pitch context in processing relative acoustic information. Although our results are the first to show the interaction between absolute and relative pitch in such detail, they are not, however, the first to suggest that acoustic perception in starlings, at least, may be closely bound to absolute pitch properties of sound stimuli. In fact, Trainer (1946) found in generating an audiogram for the starling that, in contrast to some dozen and a half other bird species, the starling failed to generalize a simple Pavlovian indicator response from one frequency to another. In order to obtain threshold measurements for the audiogram, starlings had to be essentially retrained at each test frequency.

Several questions arise from these considerations. First, it could be that our observations concerning absolute pitch, like those of Trainer, are unique to starlings or, perhaps, mimicking species of birds. Second, it could be that Trainer's results were a special consequence of the Pavlovian conditioning techniques he used. Trainer applied a shock US, and gross bodily movement served as the CR. Only further research will resolve these issues.

Nevertheless, our results and those of Trainer raise an important question: Does the perceptual constraint apparently dictated by absolute pitch for starlings hold universally for all attributes of acoustic stimuli, or, for example, does the constraint hold only for perceptual processes involving pitch itself? Quite obviously, the perception of serial sequences of sound is based on stimulus dimensions other than pitch alone. In this section, we report the results of a shift in frequency of a discrimination between *temporally* organized sound patterns that were either rule based or randomly structured in form. Here, starlings transferred the discrimination across a frequency shift with great facility.

Using the reception principle, the same apparatus, and a discrimination task similar to the one outlined earlier for pitch, Hulse, Humpal, & Cynx (in press) trained starlings on a go-right/go-left discrimination task. The computer generated two temporal patterns. The first was a rule-based, rhythmically structured pattern of four 100-msec, 2000-Hz pure tones, each tone separated from its neighbor by 100 msec. Successive patterns were separated by a 800-msec interpattern interval to generate a continuing train of configured four-tone rhythmic groups. The total duration of the train was determined by other experimental contingencies. The second pattern was a random presentation of tones and intertone intervals whose lengths varied from 30 msec to 300 msec.

Again, a peck on the lighted center key produced one of the two patterns, with $p = .50$, and turned off the center key. The stimulus pattern repeated throughout a 4-sec listening period, during which pecks had no consequence on any key. At the end of the 4-sec period, the right and left keys were illuminated with the sound pattern continuing. A peck on the left key during an arrhythmic pattern produced 1.5-sec access to the food hopper and extinguished the key lights. A peck on the right key during the same pattern caused the key lights to go out, and the houselights to go out for 10 secs. The complementary contingencies held for the structured pattern (i.e., a peck on the right key produced reinforcement, whereas a peck on the left key produced a time out). Test sessions were daily half-hour periods. All birds learned the discrimination within 60 days.

A frequency transfer—analogous to the one for the four birds that learned the relative pitch discrimination described earlier—was then introduced in which the frequency of the pattern tones was changed. Thus there were counterbalanced daily sessions at 1000 Hz and at 4000 Hz, alternating with baseline sessions at the usual 2000-Hz frequency.

The results of the transfer showed that the birds maintained excellent discrimination for transfers to both 1000 Hz and 4000 Hz. The mean percentage correct at the baseline, 2000-Hz frequency was 88% (range 83% to 91%). For the 1000-Hz and 4000-Hz tests, the corresponding data were 72% (range 69% to 77%) and 81% (range 74% to 87%). So, although there was some loss in discrimination performance relative to baseline, the birds performed significantly above chance when the temporal patterns were shifted in pitch.

It follows from these data that the constraint imposed by the absolute pitch range on relative pitch performance in the research described earlier in this chapter cannot be due to some dominating perceptual limitation that makes it impossible for starlings to generalize *all* forms of complex acoustic perception from one frequency context to another. Thus the frequency constraint found in both the relative pitch discrimination experiments described and Trainer's (1946) Pavlovian conditioning to single tones is *not* caused by a fundamental incapacity to transfer all perceptual processing across changes in pitch. Rather the constraint appears to depend on the type of perceptual processing called for by the discrimination task. If pitch is the relevant discriminative attribute, absolute pitch establishes a necessary context for further processing of complex pitch relationships like relative pitch discrimination. However, if time or rhythmic structure is the relevant discriminative attribute, the capacity to make complex relative discriminations (like those involved in rhythm discrimination) is independent of pitch context. Whether this holds for relations among other acoustic attributes remains to be seen. For example, it might be that temporal pattern discriminations are equally locked to the time context in which they are learned. Given a discrimination between two complex, structured temporal patterns, for example, an increase or decrease in the speed with which they were produced (i.e., a change in tempo) might destroy the discrimination—just as an increase or decrease in pitch context destroys a complex relative pitch discrimination. Unfortunately, however, it does not appear that perception is nicely symmetrical in this regard. Hulse, Cynx, and Humpal (1984a) and Hulse, Humpal, and Cynx (in press) have shown that starlings readily generalize a discrimination between two complex temporal patterns outside the time context in which the discrimination was originally learned. Apparently, there are substantial differences in pitch and temporal acoustic processing by starlings, and, presumably, by other species of birds.

The absolute range constraint demonstrated for birds is something for which there are few, if any, reported parallels in human perception. Most people readily perform the relative pitch transfers involved in key or other forms of tone-height change so as to maintain perceptual constancy of a complex acoustic pattern like a melody. However, not everyone does so, and there is good evidence (e.g., Attneave & Olson, 1971; Deutsch, 1982) that musical experience plays a major role in developing such perceptual capacities. It has also been claimed that humans have a predilection to respond to complex stimuli relationally, while animals do not (Premack, 1983). Perhaps, however, the functional relations between absolute and relative pitch perception may be different from those proposed in the past—even for people. Perhaps the two pitch strategies compete in the initial development of pitch perception, and absolute pitch provides the inherent baseline from which relative pitch perception emerges. Experiments with acoustically inexperienced listeners, both human and animal, should provide the relevant data to settle this issue.

BIRDSONG

We close with a speculation or two concerning the implications of this research for the study of birdsong. Recognition and, possibly, learning and production of birdsong—in starlings and other birds—may be tied to the context of an absolute frequency range. Both relative and absolute pitch perception may be operating in allowing a bird to identify, mimic, and learn birdsong, with absolute pitch range providing the context within which relative pitch perception occurs. As far as we know, no one has yet addressed the issue of whether songbirds, for example, identify birdsong on the basis of relative pitch, absolute pitch, or some interaction thereof. Furthermore, if the results of the frequency transfers in the rhythm experiment are any indication, the processing of pitch structures in birdsong may be more constrained than the processing of rhythmic information. These are important observations that clearly invite further investigation.

ACKNOWLEDGMENTS

We thank E. Burroughs, C. Crowder, R. Feuerstein, S. Fisher, J. Freitag, P. Garlinghouse, S. Gucker, L. Rowe, S. V. Hulse, R. Morrison, and T. Park for their invaluable help in maintaining and testing the birds. We also thank T. Green, R. Wurster, and J. Yingling for important technical assistance. Special appreciation goes to Dr. C. Grue of the Patuxent Wildlife Research Center for providing experimental subjects. The research was supported by National Science Foundation Research Grant BNS–801437.

REFERENCES

Attneave, F., & Olson, R. K. Pitch as a medium: A new approach to psychophysical scaling. *American Journal of Psychology*, 1971, *84*, 147–166.

Bower, G. H., & Winzenz, D. Group structure, coding, and memory for serial digits. *Journal of Experimental Psychology Monographs*, 1969, *80*, Part 2, 1–17.

Capaldi, E. J., Nawrocki, T. M., & Verry, D. R. Difficult serial anticipation learning in rats: Rule encoding vs. memory. *Animal Learning and Behavior*, 1982, *10*, 167–170.

Deutsch, D. Music recognition. *Psychological Review*, 1969, *76*, 300–307.

Deutsch, D. The psychology of music. In E. C. Carterette & M. P. Friedman (Eds.), *Handbook of perception* (Vol. 10). New York: Academic Press, 1978.

Deutsch, D. (Ed.). *The psychology of music*. New York: Academic Press, 1982.

Fountain, S. B., Henne, D. R., & Hulse, S. H. Phrasing cues and hierarchical structure in serial pattern learning by rats. *Journal of Experimental Psychology: Animal Behavior Processes*, 1984, *10*, 30–45.

Fountain, S. B., & Hulse, S. H. Extrapolation of serial stimulus patterns by rats. *Animal Learning and Behavior*, 1981, *9*, 381–384.

Garner, W. R. *The processing of information and structure*. Potomac, Md.: Lawrence Erlbaum Associates, 1974.

Hull, C. L. Goal attraction and directing ideas conceived as habit phenomena. *Psychological Review*, 1931, *38*, 487–506.

Hulse, S. H. Patterned reinforcement. In G. Bower (Ed.), *The psychology of learning and motivation* (Vol. 7). New York: Academic Press, 1973.

Hulse, S. H. The case of the missing rule. *Animal Learning and Behavior*, 1980, *8*, 689–690.

Hulse, S. H., & Cynx, J. Effects of shifts in pitch context on serial pitch perception in birds. In preparation.

Hulse, S. H., Cynx, J., & Humpal, J. Cognitive processing of pitch and rhythm structures by birds. In H. L. Roitblat, T. G. Bever, & H. S. Terrace (Eds.), *Animal cognition*. Hillsdale, N.J.: Lawrence Erlbaum Associates, 1984. (a)

Hulse, S. H., Cynx, J., & Humpal, J. Absolute and relative discrimination in serial pitch perception by birds. *Journal of Experimental Psychology: General*, 1984, *113*, 38–54. (b)

Hulse, S. H., & Dorsky, N. P. Structural complexity as a determinant of serial pattern learning. *Learning and Motivation*, 1977, *8*, 488–506.

Hulse, S. H., & Dorsky, N. P. Serial pattern learning by rats: Transfer of a formally defined stimulus relationship and the significance of nonreinforcement. *Animal Learning and Behavior*, 1979, *7*, 211–220.

Hulse, S. H., Humpal, J., & Cynx, J. Discrimination and generalization of rhythmic and arrhythmic sound patterns by European starlings (*Sturnus vulgaris*). *Music Perception*, in press.

Hulse, S. H., & O'Leary, D. K. Serial pattern learning: Teaching an alphabet to rats. *Journal of Experimental Psychology: Animal Behavior Processes*, 1982, *8*, 260–273.

Jones, M. R. Cognitive representations of serial patterns. In B. Kantowitz (Ed.), *Human information processing: Tutorials in performance and cognition*. Hillsdale, N.J.: Lawrence Erlbaum Associates, 1974.

Lashley, K. S. The problem of serial order in behavior. In L. H. Jeffress (Ed.), *Cerebral mechanisms in behavior*. New York: Wiley, 1951.

Pepperberg, I. Functional vocalization by an African Grey parrot (*Psittacus erithacus*). *Zeitschrift für Tierpsychologie*, 1981, *55*, 139–160.

Pepperberg, I. Cognition in the African Grey parrot: Preliminary evidence for comprehension of a class concept. *Animal Learning and Behavior*, 1983, *11*, 179–185.

Premack, D. The codes of man and beast. *The Behavioral and Brain Sciences*, 1983, *6*, 125–167.

Restle, F. Theory of serial pattern learning: Structural trees. *Psychological Review*, 1970, *77*, 481–495.

Shepard, R. Approximation to uniform gradients of generalization by monotone transformations of scale. In D. I. Mostofsky (Ed.), *Stimulus generalization*. Stanford, Calif.: Stanford University Press, 1965.

Shepard, R. Geometrical approximations to the structure of musical pitch. *Psychological Review*, 1982, *89*, 305–333.

Simon, H. A., & Kotovsky, K. Human acquisition of concepts for sequential patterns. *Psychological Review*, 1963, *70*, 534–546.

Skinner, B. F. The extinction of chained reflexes. *Proceedings of the National Academy of Sciences*, 1934, *20*, 234–237.

Trainer, J. E. *The auditory acuity of certain birds*. Unpublished Doctoral Dissertation, Cornell University, 1946.

Vitz, P. C., & Todd, R. C. A coded element model of the perceptual processing of stimuli. *Psychological Review*, 1969, *76*, 433–449.

11 Contextual Stimulus Control of Operant Responding in Pigeons

David R. Thomas
University of Colorado

INTRODUCTION

There are many ways in which stimuli can be categorized. Skinner (1938) attempted a functional description that called attention to the nature of the relationship between the stimulus and operant behavior. According to Skinner, stimuli may have eliciting, discriminative, emotional, and reinforcing functions. A discriminative stimulus is one that ''sets the occasion'' for an operant response (i.e., one in the presence of which the response is more likely than in its absence). The usual way of establishing the discriminative role of a stimulus is for the experimenter to arrange conditions such that an operant is reinforced only when the stimulus is present in the experimental situation. If the stimulus is one to which the subject's sensory systems are attuned, this procedure typically establishes the differential behavior that provides evidence of its discriminative function. We may distinguish, however, between a ''procedural'' definition of a discriminative stimulus (e.g., a stimulus that signifies the availability of reinforcement for a given operant response) and a functional definition (e.g., a stimulus that demonstrably controls the rate of an operant response). The significance of this distinction is twofold. Some physical events will fail to function as discriminative stimuli even with explicit discrimination training, either because the subject is not sensitive to them or they are not readily associated with the response and (or the reinforcer) being employed (cf. LoLordo, 1979). On the other hand some physical events may function as discriminative stimuli without any explicit discrimination training. A few examples illustrate this latter point.

An essential and usually constant feature of any operant conditioning chamber is the floor on which the subject stands while performing the operant response

1966, Riccio, Urda, and Thomas reported a study in which floor tilt provided a stimulus dimension with which discriminative stimulus control was investigated. In Experiment 1, two groups of pigeons received variable interval (VI) training to peck an illuminated key with stimulus-on periods separated by brief blackouts. For one group, the floor was in the normal horizontal (0 deg) position; for the other it was tilted 30 deg counterclockwise. After the completion of training, a generalization test in extinction was performed with the floor tilt adjusted, during blackout periods, to 0 deg, 10 deg, 20 deg, or 30 deg. The result was a decremental gradient of stimulus generalization (in both groups) with maximal responding occurring under the training floor tilt condition.

In an experiment by Perkins and Weyant (1958), rats were trained to traverse a straight alley for food. Throughout training, the floor had a particular texture, rough or smooth. In an extinction test, a change from the training floor texture to the alternative value resulted in generalization decrement.

Both of these examples used generalization gradients (or decrements) as evidence of discriminative control, but we may also use performance in subsequent discrimination training to reveal discriminative control previously acquired. Thus Welker, Tomie, Davitt, and Thomas (1974) trained pigeons to peck at a green key with a particular unchanging physical context present (i.e., houselight and tone [HL T]). Later the birds received explicit discrimination training between the green keylight (S+) and a white vertical line on a dark surround (S−), and the former context was paired with S+ or with S− in two different groups. This produced massive positive transfer in the first instance and negative transfer in the second, indicating that responding was still largely controlled by the previously "contextual" stimuli. In a third group the previous context accompanied both S+ and S−, and these subjects never learned to withhold responding under the S− condition.

These studies indicate that the procedural definition of a discriminative stimulus needs to be broadened. Explicit discrimination training, carried out in the experimental environment, is often unnecessary for environmental stimuli to gain discriminative control over operant responding. Quite possibly this is because environmental stimuli may differentiate the experimental environment from that of the home cage. Thus they signal availability of reinforcement from a molar, though not a molecular perspective. Neither is it necessary that the home cage and the experimental environment differ along the dimension to be tested for discriminative stimulus control. A body of literature exists that shows that training in which one dimension is manipulated may result in enhanced control by other (nonmanipulated) dimensions (cf. Thomas, 1970).

A broadened view of discriminative stimulus control will require a change in the way we think of contextual stimuli. It has been common practice to use the term context to refer to constant (generally unspecified) features of the experimental environment. Until recently the assumption had been made that these stimuli will exert little or no control over behavior, particularly if other stimuli that do change are correlated with the availability of reinforcement. The experiments just described, as well as those in the remainder of this chapter and in all other chapters in this book, testify that this position is no longer tenable. Any stimulus that the animal is capable of perceiving may have acquired discriminative control over operant behavior if it was present during reinforced training, and it would not seem to be fruitful to continue to use the term context to designate stimuli whose discriminative function the experimenter has neglected to measure.

We believe that clarity might be served by thinking of context in terms of an indirect relationship between constant environmental stimuli and behavior, an effect mediated by the direct effect of discriminative stimuli. Just as a statement taken "out of context" has a changed meaning, we propose to use the term context, or, better still, contextual stimulus control to denote a conditional relationship between (environmental) contextual stimuli, discriminative stimuli, and behavior. Thus it is the context that gives "meaning" to discriminative stimuli. Note that just as discriminative stimulus control does not always require explicit discrimination training, we show that contextual stimuli acquire conditional control by virtue of their mere presence during training. Thus contextual stimulus control may be thought of as implicit conditional control. We define a contextual stimulus, as we did a discriminative stimulus, functionally (i.e., in terms of its relationship to operant behavior). A given physical entity (e.g., a houselight or a smooth floor) could be a discriminative stimulus, a contextual stimulus, or both, depending on what we choose to measure. The issue of the relationship between discriminative and contextual stimulus functions is also addressed in several other chapters in this book (cf. Baker, Singh, & Bindra; Rescorla, Durlach, & Grau), and we return to it later.

If the measurement of contextual stimulus control is indirect, we must first make clear what it is that is measured directly. Refer here to the examples already given. All demonstrations of discriminative stimulus control require that a stimulus be changed and a corresponding change in operant behavior noted. Where the stimulus is changed along a specified dimension and reinforcement is either omitted or administered without regard to stimulus value, the procedure is called stimulus generalization testing. Where differential reinforcement is correlated with differing stimulus values, the procedure is known as discrimination training. In the material to follow, we describe many instances of contextual stimulus control in which generalization gradients provide the measure of contextual effects, some in which performance of a discrimination is the dependent variable and at least one in which both measures are used.

Because most research on the role of context uses a measure of response strength to an explicit CS or discriminative cue in order to make inferences about contextual control, a further discussion of how such measures differ from ours is appropriate here. The concept of stimulus control is discussed in most contemporary textbooks on learning, but the term is used in two different ways. One of these, called "excitatory stimulus control" by Hearst, Besley, and Farthing (1970), refers to the extent to which a specified response is more probable in the presence of a stimulus than in its absence. For practical purposes, a measure of response strength (e.g., rate or magnitude) provides an index of excitatory stimulus control. This measure has been used extensively in the study of classical conditioning. Alternatively, "dimensional stimulus control," according to Hearst et al., refers to the slope of a stimulus generalization gradient obtained by varying the training stimulus along some physical continuum (e.g., wavelength or intensity). The measure of relative generalization slope (e.g., the percentage of all responses during the generalization test that occurs to the training stimulus) is frequently used in operant conditioning studies. It has commonly been assumed, either explicitly or implicitly, that excitatory and dimensional stimulus control are two measures of the same learning process (cf. Blough, 1975; Mackintosh, 1975, 1977), but this is an empirical question that has rarely been addressed. Confirmatory evidence would consist of a positive correlation between the two measures and the determination that they are similarly affected by the same controlling variables, that is, amount of training, amount of reinforcement, etc. Not only is such evidence conspicuously lacking, but rather there is a growing body of evidence to the contrary. Several examples follow.

Thomas, Burr, and Eck (1970) gave rats either discrimination training or nondifferential training and tested for control by an incidental (irrelevant) stimulus. They found that discrimination training yielded less responding to the incidental stimulus, which is consistent with the Rescorla and Wagner (1972) formulation, which is concerned only with the measure of excitatory stimulus control. Thomas et al. also measured dimensional stimulus control in this same experiment by comparing responding to the incidental stimulus with that emitted to a variation of that stimulus (a dimmer light), and they found that discrimination training had led to a sharper gradient, that is, greater dimensional control.

Thomas and Lopez (1962) showed that the relative generalization gradients of pigeons trained to respond to a monochromatic stimulus were reliably flatter after a 24-hr delay than in an immediate test, despite the fact that the rate of responding was not measurably reduced. They suggested that the subjects forgot the value of the training stimulus, whereas remembering the key-pecking response. Newlin and Thomas (1982) varied the number of stimulus exposures, the duration of those exposures, and the number of reinforcers obtained in their presence and found that measures of excitatory stimulus control and dimensional stimulus control were affected differently by these manipulations.

It should be clear that the unitary conception of "stimulus control" as a reflection of "signal value" or of what has been learned about a stimulus has outlived its usefulness. On the other hand it is not clear how to best characterize what the two measures reflect about learning. Perhaps dimensional stimulus control tells us how well the subjects know the physical characteristics of the stimulus, whereas excitatory stimulus control tells us about the meaning of the stimulus as a signal for other events or contingencies. In our research we have restricted our interest to dimensional stimulus control, which always involves a comparison between rates of responding to different stimuli. Furthermore we use relative measures of discrimination performance or of stimulus generalization, because the data are more lawful when analyzed in this way. For example, Thomas and King (1959) studied wavelength generalization in pigeons as a function of drive level (i.e., level of food deprivation). Although they found vast individual and group differences in rate of responding and thus in absolute measures of generalization, a comparison of the high-rate and the low-rate responders *within* each drive-level condition yielded no systematic differences in relative generalization slope.

Our treatment of context as a conditional stimulus differs from that of most other investigators in the field and leads us to ask different questions about the way in which context affects behavior. Following the lead of Rescorla and Wagner (1972), many investigators, including Tomie (1976) and Baker et al. (this volume), have treated contextual stimuli just like discrete conditioned stimuli (i.e., as competitors for the limited associative strength supportable by the US). Others, like Kaplan and Hearst (this volume) emphasize the role of context in controlling performance after learning is complete, an approach also favored by Miller and his colleagues (cf. Balaz, Capra, Hartl, & Miller, 1981). A problem for this latter approach is that one can never be certain that context-US associations have been completely extinguished, thus residual associative strength to the context could summate with that to an explicit CS thereby enhancing responding. This is not an issue when context serves a conditional role. What is important then is not the associative strength of the context per se, but rather its unique association with one S–R relationship rather than another. The question that remains, then, is whether contextual stimuli work like other (discrete) conditional stimuli. This issue is raised later in the chapter, and our tentative answer is ''no.''

MASKING BY CONTEXTUAL STIMULI

In studying discriminative stimulus control by compound stimuli, the possibility of interactions among the component stimuli must be considered. One such interaction has been called masking. It refers to a testing effect whereby the control exhibited by one component stimulus is obscured by the presence, during testing, of another component stimulus. An example of masking comes from an experiment reported by Freeman and Thomas (1967). Pigeons were given VI training to peck a stimulus consisting of a white vertical line on a green surround. They were then tested for angularity (i.e., line orientation) generalization with the green background present or a black background substituted for it. Responding was substantially reduced with the removal of the green element of the training compound, but the relative generalization gradient, a typical measure of dimensional stimulus control, was reliably sharpened.

This study is instructive to start with because it clarifies our use of the concepts of discriminative and contextual stimulus control. The vertical line was the discriminative stimulus because the experimenters chose to study angularity generalization. The green background was the context because its (indirect) effect on angularity generalization was studied. The roles of the two elements could have been reversed, but they were not, in this study. Thus the designation discriminative or contextual does not refer to any inherent property of a stimulus but only to its relationship to the behavior being studied. Note also that in this case (and in most cases of masking), the contextual stimulus was discrete and well defined; it was the green surround on the key and nothing more. In their chapter in this volume, Medin and Reynolds also treat as the context one element of a compound training stimulus. More often than not in the literature, discriminative stimuli are localized and contextual stimuli are diffuse, but these are not critical defining characteristics.

The results reported by Freeman and Thomas (1967) have been replicated and extended by others. For example, Newman and Benefield (1968) established a vertical line on a green surround as a conditioned reinforcer by pairing it with food presentations, but without any response requirement. The birds were then tested for response strength (i.e., key pecking) in the presence of various line angles, either with the green background or without it, and, again, the latter condition produced a reliably sharper gradient.

In a study reported by Farthing (1972), two groups of pigeons were trained on a successive discrimination. For one group, a vertical line on a red background served as S+, and a green key light served as S−. For the second group, the color projected onto the key was the same on both positive and negative trials, and the only stimulus correlated with the availability of reinforcement was the presence or absence of the line. After acquisition, generalization tests were given along the angularity dimension, displayed on either a red or a black background. With both training groups, the gradients were significantly flatter when the red background was used, indicating masking. Furthermore, under both test background conditions the group of subjects for which color was a discriminative cue during training yielded flatter angularity gradients. This effect, in which the presence *during training* of one cue reduces the control acquired by another cue, is called overshadowing. The Farthing (1972) experiment is unique in demonstrating, within a single experiment, that the competition between cues for the control of operant behavior can occur at the time of the acquisition of that control (overshadowing), or at the time of its manifestation in behavior (masking).

In a study reported by Thomas, Svinicki, and Svinicki (1970), pigeons were given single stimulus VI training with a white vertical line on either a green or a black background (in different groups). A generalization test along the angularity dimension exposed each subject to both green and black backgrounds during testing. Although background condition during training had no significant effect on generalization slope (i.e., there was no overshadowing), within each training condition the generalization gradients were sharper when the testing background was black than when it was green (see Fig. 11.1). Thus, the study showed that the masking stimulus (the green background) need not itself be a signal for responding; when the green background was novel it still had a masking effect, presumably by serving as a distractor.

The masking of angularity by wavelength is a relatively small effect that has not always been obtained. For example, Baron and Bresnahan (1969) reported a failure to obtain masking under conditions rather similar to those used in successful studies. One procedural difference that seemed potentially important was their use of a houselight in the experimental chamber, whereas we had used none. In a dark chamber, the white line on the pecking key is the only visual stimulus available, and a chromatic surround may compete with the line for control over the subjects' behavior during generalization testing. An illuminated chamber, however, presents a very complex visual array to the bird, such that one additional visual cue (the chromatic field) may make little difference. Thomas, Ernst, and Andry (1971) performed an experiment to test this hypothesis. One group of pigeons was trained to peck a vertical line on a yellow–green surround with the chamber dark; for another group the houselight was present. Both groups were then tested for angularity generalization, in the same houselight condition used in training, in a single test that included both yellow–green and black backgrounds. Masking was found (i.e., the black background gradient was sharper) only for the group trained in the dark chamber. Thus, we replicated Baron and Bresnahan's (1969) results and isolated the factor that accounted for them.

The fact that masking does not always occur and that its effect can be small should not obscure its potential procedural and theoretical significance. In other situations, masking effects can be critical. Consider an experiment by Thomas, Burr, and Eck (1970) in which rats were trained to discriminate between two tone-plus-light compounds in which tone frequency differed but light intensity was held constant. In generalization testing, with different light intensities, it was found that a decremental gradient could be obtained when the lights were presented alone, but not when they were paired with tones or even when tones were alternately presented along with the lights during the same test session. Thus, in the Thomas et al. (1970) study, masking was total, and only when this was recognized could a valid assessment of dimensional stimulus control by light intensity be made. Note that in the Thomas et al. (1970) study the masking stimulus was not contextual (by our definition), because it was varied during training. Whether contextual stimuli could produce that potent a masking effect remains to be determined. At least one major theorist (Mackintosh, 1977) assigns a critical role to masking by context in his interpretation of extradimensional training effects on generalization. He argues that discrimination training with

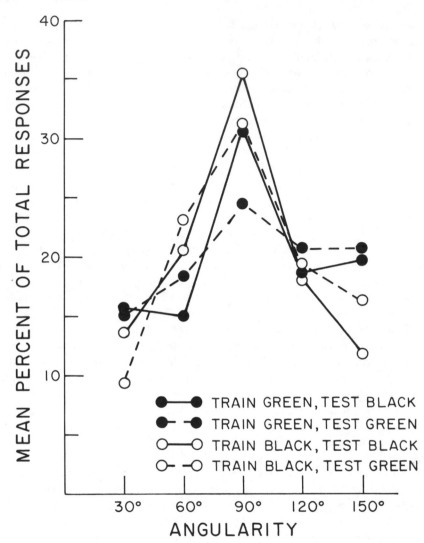

FIG. 11.1.   Mean relative generalization gradients of subjects exposed to four different combinations of training and testing background conditions. (From Thomas, Svinicki, & Svinicki. Copyright 1970 by the American Psychological Association. Reprinted by permission of the publisher.)

two values from one dimension enhances control by a subsequently experienced dimension by neutralizing and thus rendering insignificant contextual cues that are present throughout the experiment. These contextual cues are thus less effective as masking stimuli than are contextual cues following other forms of training, thereby allowing more control to be exercised by the explicit training stimulus.

Before concluding this section on context as a masking stimulus, several points should be made. Generally the masking stimulus is one that was present during training, such that it is also capable of exerting a discriminative stimulus role, but because our interest is elsewhere we generally do not measure its direct effect on behavior. On the other hand a novel stimulus present during testing may also mask the expression of control by a discriminative cue. The latter effect is clearly nonassociative in nature, in the sense that the masking stimulus is not one previously associated with responding, or indeed previously experienced at all. Thus the competition for control over behavior that masking reflects may come about through two entirely different mechanisms. In subsequent sections of this chapter, the effects of contextual stimuli we consider all come about through an associative mechanism.

CONTEXT EFFECTS IN NONSPECIFIC TRANSFER

Nonspecific transfer refers to the effect of discrimination training or nondifferential ("equivalence") training on the rate of acquisition of a subsequent discrimination along an orthogonal stimulus dimension. In our research, successive discrimination training is employed. A multiple reinforcement schedule is used with two stimuli sequentially presented on the pecking key. They occur in a random order with one signaling VI reinforcement and the other signaling extinction. In nondifferential (ND) training, responding to the two sequentially presented stimuli is reinforced on the same or comparable schedules. In one form of nondifferential training, called PD (for "pseudodiscrimination"), half the presentations of each stimulus are paired with VI reinforcement and half with extinction, so that the temporal patterning of reinforcement deliveries is comparable under nondifferential and ("true") discrimination training procedures. A study by Thomas and Wheatley (1974) compared the effects of PD and ND training on generalization slope and found no differences, so these procedures are treated as equivalent in the discussions that follow.

In the first nonspecific transfer study performed in our laboratory, Eck, Noel, and Thomas (1969) trained subjects to respond to one of two line angles (VI reinforced), and then, after acquisition, the birds were transferred to a wavelength discrimination or a brightness discrimination problem. The birds acquired this second discrimination more rapidly than did subjects given either single stimulus training with a single line angle or PD training with two different line angles during the initial phase of training. This finding has been replicated and extended in several ways. Thomas, Miller, and Svinicki (1971) found that TD-trained rats acquired an auditory frequency discrimination faster than either single stimulus (SS) or PD-trained rats, even though the original training has employed visual (houselight brightness) stimuli. Frieman and Goyette (1973) provided evidence of TD facilitation (i.e., positive transfer) in pigeons when the discriminative stimuli changed modalities (from visual to auditory), and the required operant was altered (from key pecking to ring pulling) between the initial and the transfer problem.

Thomas (1970) proposed that nonspecific transfer is attributable to a mechanism called general attention. The notion is that during discrimination training subjects learn about the significance of stimuli in general, as well as learning the values of the current S+ and S−. Such learning is akin to a "learning set" and would be reflected in positive transfer to a new discrimination or in the sharpening of generalization gradients along dimensions not involved in the discrimination training. Switalski, Lyons, and Thomas (1966) used the term extradimensional discrimination training to refer to this paradigm, and the sharpening of gradients following such training has been called, by Mackintosh (1977) and others, the TD enhancement effect.

Mackintosh (1977) asserted that TD enhancement in extradimensional generalization is due to differences in degree of control over behavior by contextual stimuli. This argument can be applied directly to the nonspecific transfer paradigm. In this case the claim would be that contextual stimuli whose control was suppressed by TD training would less effectively *block* acquisition of control by the discriminative stimuli in the transfer phase than would be the case with PD subjects. Subjects given single stimulus training should show transfer performance intermediate between that of TD and PD subjects, because control by context for them should be intermediate between the low level of TD subjects and the high level in PD subjects.

Most nonspecific transfer experiments in which single stimulus control groups have been used have failed to show a reliable difference in the transfer performance of PD and SS subjects; both typically perform more poorly than do TD subjects, but equally so. There is a parallel situation in the extradimensional stimulus generalization literature. Single stimulus control groups have generally produced gradients that are not reliably sharper than those produced by PD groups. On the other hand, Switalski, Lyons, and Thomas (1966), Thomas, Miller, and Hansen (1972), Tomie, Davitt, and Thomas (1973), and many others have demonstrated a reliable flattening of the gradient produced by interdimensional nondifferential training (e.g., equal reinforcement for responding to a green key or one with a white vertical line on a dark surround). Newlin and Thomas (1978) therefore decided to use the interdimensional training paradigm to see if ND training would retard the acquisition of a subsequent discrimination relative to the performance of a single stimulus control group. A major purpose of this experiment was to evaluate the contribution of control by the context to any performance differences that were found. Two groups of pigeons were given ND training with a green keylight and a white vertical line on a dark surround. Two other groups received SS training with the green light only. All groups were then transferred to a green S+ (VI reinforced) and a red S− (extinguished) transfer problem. One ND and one SS group was tested (i.e., exposed to the transfer problem) in the same context as in original training (houselight-off), and one ND and one SS group was tested in a changed context (houselight-on). In both contexts the ND groups performed less well than did the SS groups (i.e., a reliable ND retardation effect was observed). For present purposes, the most interesting results are those concerning the context change. The initial reaction to the change in lighting conditions was a dramatic reduction in rate of key pecking, indicating that contextual cues did, indeed, exert considerable discriminative control over responding. Upon removal of that control, the nominal discriminative stimuli should gain more control, and they did; under both ND and SS

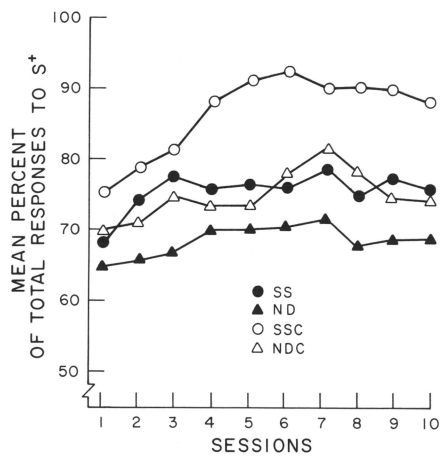

FIG. 11.2. Mean discrimination ratios in a transfer test following either single stimulus (SS) or nondifferential training (ND) in Stage 1. Groups designated SS or ND were tested for transfer in the same context used in Stage 1; Groups SSC and NDC were tested in a changed context. (From Newlin, R. J. & Thomas, D. R. Nondifferential training of pigeons retards acquisition of subsequent discriminations involving other stimuli. *Animal Learning and Behavior,* 1978, *6,* 385–390. Copyright 1978 by the Psychonomic Society, Inc. Reproduced by permission of the publisher.)

conditions, the context change groups had higher discrimination ratios than did the no-context-change groups. However, there was no evidence that the context had more control in the ND than the SS condition (i.e., both groups showed comparable improvements in performance when the context was changed, (see Fig. 11.2).

THE ROLE OF CONTEXT IN BLOCKING THE ACQUISITION OF DIMENSIONAL STIMULUS CONTROL

In the preceding section on nonspecific transfer it was shown that the context present during original SS on ND training could block the acquisition of control by an orthogonal dimension during subsequent discrimination training by merely being present, although uninformative, during that training. Another procedure for producing such blocking that more closely resembles the traditional blocking design is to use contextual stimuli from original training as informative but redundant cues in the learning of a new discrimination. This was done under one condition in an experiment reported by Welker, Tomie, Davitt, and Thomas (1974). In their experimental groups, pigeons received extensive SS training with the response key dark but a houselight and a 1000 Hz tone present. Control subjects did not receive this initial training. Then all subjects learned a successive discrimination with a 555 nm keylight as S+ (VI reinforced) and a white vertical line on a dark surround as S− (extinguished). For one group (S+ context) the houselight and tone were paired with S+, for one (S− context) they were paired with S−, and for one they were paired with both (no-context-change group). For each group, a matched control group experienced the same stimulus configurations without the prior single stimulus training. Then all groups were tested for wavelength generalization. Of the three experimental groups, the S+ context group acquired the discrimination the fastest. This instance of positive transfer was expected, as it reflects discriminative control over responding acquired by the contextual stimuli in Stage 1. Indeed the subjects performed the discrimination almost perfectly on the very first day, suggesting that the S+ wavelength may have played little or no role in performance, at least at first. The S− context group initially showed massive negative transfer with less than 20% of total responses made to S+ during the first 2 days. At asymptote, however, this group performed as well as did the S+ context group. The no-context-change group showed negative transfer (blocking) that was persistent; even after 20 training sessions, these subjects responded less than 80% to the S+ with a discrimination task that is so easy that naive subjects yielded nearly 90% of their responses to S+ on their first training session (see Fig. 11.3).

In this experiment, the degree of control acquired by the wavelength S+ was assessed in wavelength generalization tests in extinction. The tests included trials

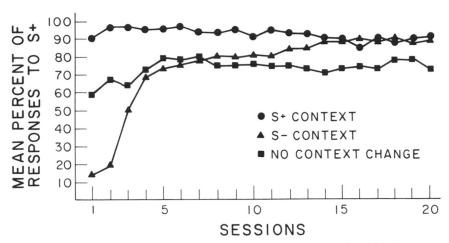

FIG. 11.3.   Mean discrimination ratios in a transfer test for groups for which the S+ was paired with the previous context (i.e., the S+ context group), the S− was paired with the previous context (i.e., the S− context group), or both S+ and S− were paired with the previous context (no-context-change group). (From Welker, Tomie, Davitt, & Thomas. Copyright 1974 by the American Psychological Association. Reprinted by permission of the publisher.)

in which the houselight and tone were present and trials in which they were absent. The generalization gradients were based on data obtained in the context accompanying S+ in Stage 2, because over 90% of all test responses occurred under this condition. In both S+ context and S− context groups, for which the (former) context was an informative cue in Stage 2, the wavelength gradients were reliably and substantially flatter than in their matched control groups (see Fig. 11.4). This finding constitutes blocking, which is defined here as the reduction of the dimensional stimulus control acquired by one stimulus as a consequence of prior training with another stimulus. Blocking of the acquisition of dimensional stimulus control has also been reported in studies by Mackintosh and Honig (1970), Miles (1970), and Vom Saal and Jenkins (1970). The finding of blocking in the S+ context group is consistent with most theoretical accounts of blocking, if we extend those accounts to include the measure of dimensional stimulus control. Note that the Rescorla–Wagner (1972) formulation, however, would make an opposite prediction for the S− context group. When the previous context was paired with S−, superconditioning of S+ might have been expected rather than the blocking that was found. Furthermore, blocking in this group was achieved by the presentation of S+ in the *absence* of the previous context, in violation of the principle (Kamin, 1969) that redundancy of cues is essential to obtain the effect. It is certainly true that in the S− context condition the subjects could use the absence of houselight and tone as a predictor of reinforcement, but they should have been retarded in learning to do so relative to an original learning

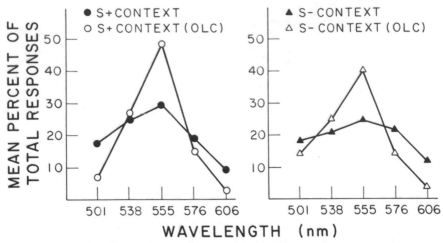

FIG. 11.4.   Mean relative generalization gradients of S+ context and S− context groups compared with original learning control groups exposed to the same stimulus configurations without any prior single stimulus training. (From Welker, Tomie, Davitt, & Thomas. Copyright 1974 by the American Psychological Association. Reprinted by permission of the publisher.)

control group exposed to the same stimulus combinations without prior single stimulus training. The ability of the *absence* of context to block learning about the explicit S+ in discrimination learning is consistent with Fowler's (1978) distinction between the signaling and the affective properties of a stimulus. Apparently the ability of the houselight and tone to signal nonreinforcement (and hence of its absence to signal reinforcement) was enhanced by prior training despite the fact that the affective sign of the stimuli was reversed. One final point worthy of note about this experiment is that the blocking effect seen with both the S+ context and S− context groups is also inconsistent with the claim by Vom Saal and Jenkins (1970) that discrimination training in initial training is essential to produce blocking. Clearly, it is not!

The results of the Welker et al. study contradict so much of what is commonly believed about the blocking phenomenon that the experiment is surely deserving of more attention than it has received. Possibly, blocking by contextual stimuli follows different rules than does blocking by explicit discriminative stimuli. The Rescorla–Wagner (1972) formulation makes the opposite assumption, as do researchers such as Tomie (1976) and Balsam (1984). Alternatively, because we already know that excitatory stimulus control and dimensional stimulus control reflect different processes, it would not be surprising if the difference is response measures is responsible for the discrepancies with most of the published literature on blocking. More research on the blocking of dimensional stimulus control is surely needed before these issues can be resolved.

CONTEXT AS A RETRIEVAL CUE IN MEMORY

Spear (1978) has proposed that an animal's degree of success in retrieving the memory of a training experience is a function of the extent to which the subject notices, during retention testing, ambient contextual stimuli that were present but inconsequential to the target learning task and were stored as attributes of the target memory. In keeping with our view of contextual stimulus control, we measure the effectiveness of a contextual retrieval cue by determining the extent to which it enhances the control over behavior exerted by other (discriminative) stimuli.

Thomas and Lopez (1962) demonstrated the effect of forgetting on the slope of generalization gradients. They trained pigeons to peck at a monochromatic light for VI reinforcement and then tested for wavelength generalization in extinction either immediately after training or after a delay of 24 hr (or longer). They found that the delay between training and testing produced substantially flatter generalization gradients. In many subsequent experiments in our laboratory, the flattening of generalization gradients with the passage of time has constituted the primary measure of long-term forgetting in pigeons.

Thomas and McKelvie (1982a) reported two experiments in which the presence or absence of contextual cues was manipulated in generalization (i.e., retention) testing after a delay interval. In Experiment 1, pigeons were given single stimulus training to peck at a green keylight for VI reinforcement in a particular context, say houselight and tone (HL T). They then received single stimulus training with a horizontal line stimulus in a different context, say no houselight and white noise ($\overline{\text{HL}}$ N). For purposes of retention testing, the birds were divided into two groups, one tested in Context 1 and one tested in Context 2. The generalization tests were conducted, in extinction, one day after the completion of training, and each test included stimuli from both wavelength and line orientation dimensions. Thus, for each bird the test context was consistent with one of the two training problems and inconsistent with the other. The experimental design was within subjects with regard to the assessment of memory for the two training problems, but between subjects with regard to the use of a single test context with each bird. Testing with both dimensions provided a control for any nonassociative effects of the contextual cues because response strength should be greater and the generalization gradient should be sharper only when testing is carried out in the consistent context condition.

The results of this experiment were substantially in accordance with prediction. The subjects responded far more to generalization test stimuli that were consistent with the context than to the test stimuli that were inconsistent with the context. Although the absolute generalization gradients were sharper, along both wavelength and angularity dimensions, in the consistent context condition, these differences did not achieve significance. Furthermore, relative generalization gradients, the common measure of dimensional stimulus control, revealed no differences attributable to the context manipulation.

Thomas and McKelvie (1982a) performed a second experiment in which the training conditions were the same as those used in Experiment 1 but the testing conditions were altered. In an attempt to enhance the effectiveness of the context as a retrieval cue, each subject was tested for the memory of both problems (as before) but in both contexts rather than just one. This procedural modification had the hoped-for consequences. Again, responding was far greater under the consistent context condition and absolute generalization gradients, for both dimensions were now significantly sharper in this condition. In the case of the wavelength problem, though not the line angle problem, the relative generalization gradient was also significantly sharper when the consistent context condition was in effect. Experiment 2 was particularly useful in demonstrating that contextual stimulus control effects may be very subtle and may require a sensitive test to be revealed. The potential for contextual cues to govern generalization slope must have been present in both experiments, because the training conditions were identical. That potential was manifested, however, only when the test condition permitted comparison of the two training contexts.

Because the Thomas and McKelvie (1982a) study compared the effectiveness of consistent and inconsistent contexts as retrieval cues, there was no neutral control condition that would enable us to determine whether the consistent context facilitated retrieval, whether the inconsistent context inhibited retrieval, or whether both of these effects occurred. Because the gradients were very flat in the inconsistent context condition without clear peaks at the training values, it seems clear that the inappropriate context has an inhibiting effect. This suggests that interference effects may profitably be conceptualized as retrieval errors (i.e., the subjects haven't forgotten the target response but rather the text context has produced retrieval of an alternative memory).

The role of contextual retrieval cues was most clearly illustrated in a study designed to maximize the opportunity for interference between memories by training subjects on two diametrically opposed tasks. In this experiment, by Thomas, McKelvie, Ranney, and Moye (1981, Experiment 2), pigeons were first trained to peck a keylight of 538 nm (S+) but not to one of 576 nm (S−). A given context, say HL T, was present during this training, which was carried out for several sessions until a criterion of 90% of total responses to S+ was achieved. On the next day, in a single (extended) session, the birds learned the reversal of this discrimination (i.e., 576 nm was now S+) in the alternative context ($\overline{\mathrm{HL}}$ N). In wavelength generalization testing carried out the next day in extinction, blocks of test stimuli were presented in each of the two contexts and a remarkable degree of contextual stimulus control was revealed. For every subject the gradient peaked sharply at 538 nm in Context 1 and at 576 nm in Context 2. Thus, in this instance, contextual stimulus control was demonstrated in the location of peak responding rather than in differences in gradient slope (see Fig. 11.5).

The results of this experiment resemble those that would be expected if the birds had been extensively trained on an explicit conditional discrimination; for example, when HL and T are present, 538 nm is S+ and 576 nm is S−; when $\overline{HL}$ and N are present, the reverse is true. Note, however, that such conditional discriminations are difficult to establish in pigeons when traditional methods involving repeated alternations of the conditional (superordinate) stimuli are employed. In the present experiment, there was only one alternation *in training* between Context 1 and Context 2, and, furthermore, the association between Context 2 and Problem 2 was formed in a single training session. Richards (1979) reported a study in which a conditional cue, a vertical black line, determined which of two colors was reinforced. In the presence of the line, white was S+ and red was S− (counterbalanced). In the absence of the line, the reverse was true. The four components of this conditional discrimination were successively alternated within sessions. Two of the original 8 birds were dropped from the study for showing no learning after 30 sessions, and only 2 of the

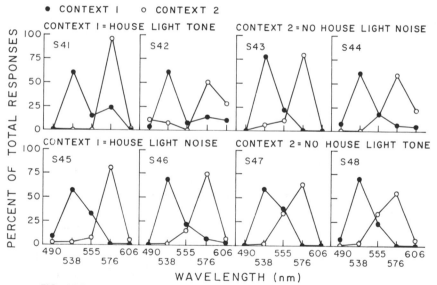

FIG. 11.5. Generalization gradients obtained following original and reversal discrimination training in two different contexts, with the two contexts alternated during the course of generalization testing. (From Thomas, D. R., McKelvie, A. R., Ranney, M., & Moye, T. B. Interference in pigeons' long-term memory viewed as a retrieval problem. *Animal Learning and Behavior*, 1981, *9*, 581–586. Copyright 1981 by the Psychonomic Society, Inc. Reprinted by permission of the publisher.)

remaining 6 birds had achieved a discrimination ratio of greater than 90% of total responses to the S+ values after 75 sessions of training.

The rapidity with which contextual stimulus control is established seems to be one of its distinguishing characteristics. Thus Balsam and Schwartz (1981) showed that as few as eight unsignaled grain presentations significantly retarded subsequent autoshaping carried out in the same environment, presumably because of blocking by contextual stimuli conditioned during those eight presentations (cf. Tomie, 1976).

Subsequent to the Thomas, McKelvie, Ranney, and Moye (1981) study, we have performed several other experiments designed to determine why contextual stimuli gain conditional control so much more rapidly than explicit conditional stimuli typically do. Because the original experiment had employed spaced practice over several sessions for the original problem and massed practice within a single session for the reversal, we replicated the study but used spaced practice to the same discrimination criterion in both phases. Again conditional control over the two discriminations was found in all subjects. We considered the possibility that the generalization test procedure, particularly when both contexts are alternately presented, provides an extremely sensitive test of conditional control. During ordinary conditional discrimination training, the presence of reinforcement may mask control that has actually been acquired by the conditional cues. Another possibility is that on-key stimuli, such as lines and colors, are somehow less capable of acquiring conditional control over operant responding than are diffuse environmental stimuli, such as houselight and tones. Perhaps stimuli at which pecking is directed are therefore more readily treated as discriminative cues than conditional ones.

We have gathered data relevant to each of these possibilities. In one unpublished study by McKelvie and Thomas, the same general procedure used by Thomas et al. (1981) was carried out except that the discrimination was between two line angles and the initial context was the blue surround on the pecking key. During the learning of the reversal, the surround was changed to red. The generalization test, which alternated the two colored surrounds, failed to reveal conditional control by the context. Rather both gradients showed recency, peaking at the S+ of the reversal problem. Thus a very salient on-key stimulus failed to establish conditional control, as indicated by the generalization test measure.

Another difference between the contextual (conditional) cue used by Thomas et al. and that used in explicit conditional discrimination training studies is that a compound audiovisual cue was used rather than simply a visual cue. A study was performed by Thomas, McKelvie, and Mah (in press) to evaluate the contributions of the auditory and visual component to the effectiveness of the entire compound. In Experiment 1 of their study all subjects learned a wavelength discrimination with 555 nm as S+ and 576 nm as S−. The context was $\overline{HL}$ N. Then all subjects learned the reversal in a changed context (i.e., HL T).

For purposes of generalization testing the subjects were divided into six groups, and in each group some or all of the elements of the two contexts were changed after each two blocks of test stimuli. For Group 1 the contextual stimuli were paired as they had been in training, for Group 2 they were repaired so as to be in opposition (i.e., HL N, $\overline{NL}$ T). For Groups 3 and 4, the auditory cue was held constant, at N and T, respectively, whereas $\overline{HL}$ and HL conditions were alternated after every two blocks of wavelength stimuli. For Groups 5 and 6 the houselight condition was held constant, at $\overline{HL}$ and HL, respectively, whereas N and T conditions were alternated after every two blocks.

The results of this experiment were clear. The visual component of the context virtually always determined the locus of maximal responding, whereas the auditory cue never did. This raised the interesting possibility that the presence of the visual cue during training may have overshadowed the development of control by the auditory element. In a second experiment, Thomas, McKelvie, and Mah (in press) used just the visual elements or just the auditory ones as the entire context. In other words the alternative cue (e.g., white noise) was constant throughout and not manipulated in training or in testing. Conditional control was achieved by the visual cues but not by the auditory ones. The fact that the auditory cues failed to gain conditional control cannot be accounted for on the assumption that they went unnoticed. In the group with the auditory context alone, responding was clearly disrupted by the change from T to N at the start of reversal training.

The fact that the houselight gains conditional control whereas key color, in the case of a line angle discrimination, did not raises a basic theoretical question about the nature of conditional discrimination learning. It is often assumed that subjects learn a conditional discrimination by learning a conditional "if-then" rule (e.g., if houselight and tone are present, peck green; if dark and noise are present, peck yellow). The same performance can be achieved, however, without any such rule learning. In its general form, the alternative possibility is that the subjects learn "simple" discriminations between compound stimuli (e.g., S+ = green plus houselight plus tone, S− = green plus dark chamber plus noise). This argument gains additional plausibility in the present case because the green in the S+ compound is presumably not the same green as in the S− compound (i.e., due to brightness contrast with its surround it is dimmer and possibly less saturated, (cf. Blough, 1961). Although it isn't clear how the general form of the stimulus compounding interpretation of conditional discrimination performance can ever be disproven, this specific form seems unlikely to be true. In the dozens of stimulus control studies to use Kodak Wratten filters since they were first employed by Switalski, Lyons, and Thomas (1966), smooth and lawful generalization gradients have been obtained based on wavelength differences despite substantial and unsystematic differences in the intensity and the spectral purity of the stimuli produced by the filters. This makes it highly probable that discrimination performance, even during the reversal phase of our experiments, was based on wavelength differences alone. Nevertheless, it seemed useful to be able to show that the contextual stimuli used in our studies would gain conditional control over discriminations based on stimuli that were not altered in so fundamental a way by changes in the illumination of the experimental chamber. This was accomplished in another experiment reported by Thomas, McKelvie, and Mah (in press). In this experiment the discrimination was between two different angles of a white line on a dark key. The HL T accompanied Problem 1 whereas the reversal, Problem 2, was learned in $\overline{\text{HL}}$ N. In subsequent line angle generalization testing the two contexts were alternated, and each gradient peaked at the appropriate S+ value for each context.

The finding that auditory cues failed to gain conditional control whereas visual cues may is consistent with Foree and LoLordo's (1973) result that visual cues function better than auditory ones as discriminative stimuli for pigeons in an appetitive task. But why should a houselight cue succeed whereas background key color failed? If one chooses to interpret conditional discrimination performance as a case of stimulus compounding, the opposite result would be expected, because the principle of proximity would suggest that a line on the pecking key would be more readily compounded with its colored surround than with the level of ambient illumination. The obtained result is consistent with the view that compounding does not underlie conditional discrimination performance, but rather that it discourages the learning of the if-then conditional rules that do underlie that performance.

THE RELATIONSHIP BETWEEN CONTEXTUAL (I.E., CONDITIONAL) AND DISCRIMINATIVE FUNCTIONS OF STIMULI

Consider the standard conditional discrimination-learning paradigm. Pigeons are trained to peck at blue but not red when a vertical line is present, but to peck at red and not blue when the line is horizontal. Stated in this fashion, the line angle is the conditional cue informing the subject of the consequences of responding to the color (discriminative) stimuli. But does the pigeon view the world in this way? The designations of conditional and discriminative cues are entirely arbitrary. We might as easily conceptualize the problem as to peck at the vertical line when the background is blue but to peck at the horizontal line when the background is red. Thomas and McKelvie (1982b) have obtained evidence that pigeons learn both problems (i.e., that both the colors and the lines serve as both conditional and discriminative cues in this paradigm). They trained their birds as described previously and tested for generalization in extinction with many combinations of line angles and wavelengths. When the background was blue, angularity gradients peaked at vertical; when the line was vertical, the wavelength gradients peaked at blue; the same was true for the horizontal-red combination. Perhaps this result will surprise no one. After all, in training the two dimensions were symmetrically or reciprocally related. We wondered whether the reciprocal relation between the two functions of the stimuli was dependent on this fact. In a second experiment, birds were again trained to peck at blue when the vertical line was present and to peck at red when the line was horizontal; however, the two line angles were never presented within a session. On odd sessions, the vertical line was used; on even sessions the horizontal line was used. Furthermore, to make the analogy with ambient contextual stimuli more complete, the appropriate line angle remained on the key constantly, even during "blackouts" when neither color was present. Again, in generalization testing various combinations of colors and line angles were used.

In view of the studies on contextual stimulus control described previously, it was no surprise that the wavelength gradients peaked at blue or red, depending on whether the vertical or horizontal line was present. It was very surprising, however, that the lines served equally well as discriminative cues (i.e., when the background was blue the angularity gradients peaked at vertical; when it was red, horizontal was preferred). Certainly the design of this experiment did not encourage the birds to treat the two dimensions equally, with the colors changing every minute, whereas the lines changed only between sessions. Nevertheless, the relations learned were reciprocal ones (see Fig. 11.6). We need to determine the conditions under which such symmetry develops. One way to approach this question is to determine whether the minimal conditions for achieving contextual stimulus control suffice in establishing symmetry. We knew from the Thomas, McKelvie, Ranney, and Moye (1981) study that contextual stimulus control could be established with just one alternation between two contexts (across sessions) during training. Furthermore, we knew that the houselight alone could serve as an effective contextual cue in this paradigm. Thus, in a study reported by Thomas and McKelvie (1982b) we replicated the Thomas et al. (1981) training procedure with the houselight alone as context and then tested for generalization with the different wavelengths on the key used in combination with different intensities of houselight. The houselight used as a training context was the intermediate intensity value. In the presence of the houselight-on or-off condition, the wavelength gradients peaked at the appropriate (training) values. Testing with different houselight intensities indicated that the subjects treated the houselight intensity as a dichotomy, rather than a continuum. When the S+ wavelength appropriate to the houselight-on context was used, subjects responded very little in the dark chamber but they responded a great deal (and comparably) to the three light intensities. When the S+ wavelength appropriate to the houselight-off context was used, response rate was low to all houselight intensity values and high in the dark. Thus the minimal condition that results in conditional control by the context (i.e., one alternation of the contexts in train-

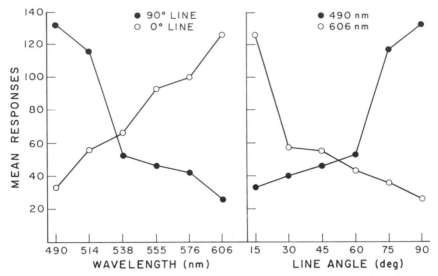

FIG. 11.6.   Mean relative generalization gradients obtained along angularity and wavelength dimensions with the value from the alternative dimension held constant as indicated. Gradients comparable to these were obtained when the two line angles appeared on alternate days in conditional discrimination training (from Thomas & McKelvie, 1982b).

ing) is sufficient to produce symmetry in the relation between conditional and discriminative stimulus functions.

Surely the relationship between conditional and discriminative stimulus functions cannot always be reciprocal. Sidman and Tailby (1982) and Sidman, Rauzin, Lazar, Cunningham, Tailby, and Carrigan (1982) have reported a number of experiments with the symbolic matching to sample paradigm where symmetry or reciprocity between comparison and sample stimulus functions did not develop. In those studies, subjects of various species were trained that Comparison Stimulus B was the correct symbolic match to Sample Stimulus A. When subsequently tested with B as a sample stimulus, they showed no tendency to select A when it was available as a comparison stimulus. Although it is possible that a more sensitive test, such as a generalization test in extinction, might have revealed such reciprocal relationships, it seems most unlikely. Because of the temporal sequence of events inherent in the matching paradigm, the sample (i.e., conditional) stimulus must always be presented first. If the problem the bird must learn is: "If the sample stimulus is a vertical line, peck the blue (comparison) stimulus," the bird will have no opportunity to learn the reciprocal rule because the blue will never be presented first. In the paradigms we have used, "conditional" and "discriminative" cues are always presented concurrently, and this would appear to be the critical factor.

When symmetrical relations between conditional and discriminative stimulus functions are obtained, as in the present series of experiments, one possible interpretation is that if-then rules are indeed learned in both directions. An alternative interpretation, discussed earlier in this chapter, would deny that rule learning is involved at all. The same generalization test results would obtain as a reflection of multidimensional stimulus control by the training stimulus compound, say vertical line on a green surround. Following training to respond to this stimulus, one could test for generalization along both wavelength and angularity dimensions with the expectation that each gradient would peak at the appropriate training value. Because of this, the fact that symmetry is obtained is noncommital on the issue of whether or not rule learning underlies conditional discrimination performance. The situation that Sidman and his associates have employed (i.e., symbolic matching to sample) would seem, on the basis of temporal factors, to favor a rule learning rather than a stimulus compounding interpretation, yet there was no symmetry. On the other hand with our procedures, symmetry attains whenever conditional discrimination performance is obtained but that performance is more difficult to obtain with stimuli that, theoretically, should lend themselves to rapid and easy compounding. It is probably an oversimplification to assume, as we have implicitly done, that conditional discrimination performance is an either-or proposition. Perhaps when it is rapidly acquired, as when the houselight serves as context, it is subserved by rule learning (which is, in fact, bidirectional), whereas when it requires extensive training, as with lines on colored backgrounds, stimulus compound learning comes into play. It may prove more profitable to ask under what circumstances the two processes manifest themselves than to continue to ask which one explanation of conditional discrimination performance is correct.

A final word may be in order about the relationship between contextual and (other) conditional stimuli. Throughout this chapter we have considered the issue of whether contextual stimulus control and conditional stimulus control are one and the same. Indeed we defined contextual stimulus control as implicit conditional stimulus control. There do seem to be some important differences, however. Contextual control develops without the context being manipulated during training, and it occurs much more rapidly than does explicit conditional control. Furthermore contextual control is facilitated by the use of diffuse environmental stimuli rather than discrete localized ones. Perhaps research will reveal that conditional control by context involves rule learning, whereas conditional control by explicit discrete and localized conditional cues does not. The need for further research on this and other unsettled issues raised in this chapter should be readily apparent.

SUMMARY

Until quite recently, ambient environmental stimuli that were uninformative but merely present during the learning of an operant response were ignored in the analysis of the stimulus control of behavior. This is no longer the case. Theorists such as Rescorla and Wagner (1972) and Mackintosh (1977) argue that the conditioning of environmental cues may prevent or reduce the subsequent conditioning of explicitly manipulated stimuli. In our laboratory we have demonstrated dimensional stimulus control over pigeons' responding by varying, during generalization testing in extinction, a previously constant feature of the training environment such as the angle of the floor on which the animal stands. Because dimensional stimulus control constitutes evidence for the discriminative function of a stimulus, we cannot continue to distinguish between contextual and discriminative stimuli on the basis of physical characteristics of the stimuli or the need for discrimination training to establish their effectiveness.

It is here proposed that the concept of contextual stimulus control be employed to denote indirect or conditional effects of environmental stimuli. Contextual stimulus control refers to the effect of contextual stimuli on the control acquired or manifested by discriminative stimuli.

Contextual stimulus control is illustrated by the phenomenon of masking. If pigeons are trained to respond to a vertical line on a green surround, they yield flatter angularity generalization gradients when the green surround is present during testing than when it is removed. Several masking experiments performed in our laboratory and elsewhere are described in this chapter.

A study by Newlin and Thomas (1978) illustrated a role of contextual stimuli from single stimulus or nondifferential training in blocking the acquisition of a subsequent discrimination along an orthogonal dimension. Contrary to predictions based upon Mackintosh's (1977) theory, however, there was no evidence of greater control by context under the nondifferential training condition.

A study by Welker et al. (1974) employed a more traditional blocking design by making the previous context redundant to either the S+ or S− in a new discrimination. This had the expected effects on performance of the discrimination (i.e., when paired with S+ it facilitated performance), when paired with S− it initially inhibited it. In both cases, however, generalization testing along the wavelength dimension (that of the S+) revealed blocking (i.e., reduction) in the control acquired by this stimulus. The blocking of the acquisition of dimensional stimulus control by pairing the previous context with S− is a fascinating anomaly that is inconsistent with much of the published literature on blocking. Whether this is because the rules governing blocking are different for contextual and discriminative stimuli, or because they are different for measures of excitatory versus dimensional stimulus control, remain to be determined.

Studies by Thomas and McKelvie (1982a) and by Thomas, McKelvie, Ranney, and Moye (1981) demonstrate that contextual cues can serve as retrieval cues in memory. In the Thomas and McKelvie (1982a) experiment subjects learned to peck at a color in one context and at a line in another. Subsequent generalization tests revealed higher and sharper gradients when testing was under the appropriate context. In the Thomas et al. (1981) experiment, subjects learned a wavelength discrimination in one context and its reversal in another. When generalization testing included both contexts, the gradients peaked at the appropriate training value for each. Both of these experiments indicate that implicit conditional control over operant behavior may be established by context very quickly and without explicit conditional discrimination training.

In subsequent experiments by Thomas, McKelvie, and Mah (in press), we have determined that it is the visual element of the context (i.e., the houselight) that exercises conditional control, whereas the auditory element serves no apparent role. This is not due to overshadowing, because the auditory stimuli when used alone in training fail to gain conditional control. Furthermore the conditional control gained by the houselight is not dependent on the use of colors as discriminative stimuli, because the same result is obtained with line angle discriminative cues.

Not all visual cues so readily gain conditional control over operant discriminations. For example, a colored background on the key during line angle discrimination training does not gain conditional control, whereas the houselight (on or off) does. This finding seems inconsistent with a stimulus compounding interpretation of conditional discrimination performance.

Additional experiments by Thomas and McKelvie (1982b) have illustrated a symmetrical relationship between conditional and discriminative stimulus functions. Pigeons given explicit conditional discrimination training to respond to one of two colors depending on the angle of line also present yield angularity gradients, when tested with each of the colors present, which peak at the appropriate line angle. This symmetry occurs even when the two line angles had never been experienced in the same training session. Another experiment revealed that symmetry did not require the use of explicit conditional discrimination training procedures. The procedures used by Thomas, McKelvie, Ranney, and Moye (1981) involving one reversal of a wavelength discrimination in a changed houselight intensity yielded symmetry between the wavelength and houselight intensity dimensions.

The finding of symmetry is silent on the issue of whether conditional discrimination performance reflects an underlying process of if-then rule learning or a simpler phenomenon of multidimensional stimulus control by compound S+s and S−s. The ease with which that performance arises in some experimental situations versus the difficulty with which it arises in others suggests both explanations may be applicable at different times.

REFERENCES

Balaz, M. S., Capra, S., Hartl, P., & Miller, R. R. Contextual potentiation of acquired behavior after devaluing direct context-US associations. *Learning and Motivation*, 1981, *12*, 383–397.

Balsam, P. D. Bringing the background to the foreground: The role of contextual cues in autoshaping. In M. Commons, R. Herrnstein, & A. R. Wagner (Eds.), *Quantitative analyses of behavior: Volume 3: Acquisition.* Cambridge, Mass.: Ballinger, 1984

Balsam, P., & Schwartz, A. Rapid background conditioning in autoshaping. *Journal of Experimental Psychology: Animal Behavior Processes*, 1981, *1*, 382–393.

Baron, M. R., & Bresnahan, E. L. Effect of chromatic surround during nondifferential training and generalization test upon generalization along the angularity dimension in pigeons. *Psychonomic Science*, 1969, *17*, 187–188.

Blough, D. S. Animal psychophysics. *Scientific American*, 1961, *205*, 113–122.

Blough, D. S. Steady state data and a quantitative model of operant generalization and discrimination. *Journal of Experimental Psychology: Animal Behavior Processes*, 1975, *104*, 3–21.

Eck, K. O., Noel, R. C., & Thomas, D. R. Discrimination learning as a function of prior discrimination and nondifferential training. *Journal of Experimental Psychology*, 1969, *82*, 156–162.

Farthing, G. W. Overshadowing in the discrimination of successive compound stimuli. *Psychonomic Science*, 1972, *28*, 29–32.

Foree, D. D., & LoLordo, V. M. Attention in the pigeon: The differential effects of food-getting vs shock-avoidance procedures. *Journal of Comparative and Physiological Psychology*, 1973, *85*, 551–558.

Fowler, H. Cognitive associations as evident in the blocking effects of response-contingent CSs. In S. H. Hulse, H. Fowler, & W. K. Honig (Eds.), *Cognitive processes in animal behavior*. Hillsdale, N.J.: Lawrence Erlbaum Associates, 1978.

Freeman, F., & Thomas, D. R. *Attention vs cue utilization in generalization testing*. Paper presented at the meeting of the Midwestern Psychological Association, Chicago, May, 1967.

Frieman, J., & Goyette, C. H. Transfer of training across stimulus modality and response class. *Journal of Experimental Psychology*, 1973, *97*, 235–241.

Hearst, E., Besley, S., & Farthing, G. W. Inhibition and the stimulus control of operant behavior. *Journal of the Experimental Analysis of Behavior*, 1970, *14*, 373–409.

Kamin, L. J. Predictability, surprise, attention and conditioning. In R. Church & B. Campbell (Eds.), *Punishment and aversive behavior*. New York: Appleton–Century–Crofts, 1969.

LoLordo, V. M. Selective associations. In A. Dickinson & R. A. Boakes (Eds.), *Mechanisms of learning and motivation: A memorial to Jerzy Konorski*. Hillsdale, N.J.: Lawrence Erlbaum Associates, 1979.

Mackintosh, N. J. A theory of attention: Variations in the associability of stimuli with reinforcement. *Psychological Review*, 1975, *82*, 276–298.

Mackintosh, N. J. Stimulus control: Attentional factors. In W. K. Honig & J. E. R. Staddon (Eds.), *Handbook of operant behavior*. Englewood Cliffs, N.J.: Prentice–Hall, 1977.

Mackintosh, N. J., & Honig, W. K. Blocking and attentional enhancement in pigeons. *Journal of Comparative and Physiological Psychology*, 1970, *73*, 78–85.

Miles, C. G. Blocking the acquisition of control by an auditory stimulus with pretraining on brightness. *Psychonomic Science*, 1970, *19*, 133–134.

Newlin, R. J., & Thomas, D. R. Nondifferential training of pigeons retards acquisition of subsequent discriminations involving other stimuli. *Animal Learning and Behavior*, 1978, *6*, 385–390.

Newlin, R. J., & Thomas, D. R. On the acquisition and measurement of stimulus control in pigeons. *Animal Learning and Behavior*, 1982, *10*, 194–200.

Newman, F. L., & Benefield, R. L. Stimulus control, cue utilization, and attention: Effects of discrimination training. *Journal of Comparative and Physiological Psychology*, 1968, *66*, 101–104.

Perkins, C. C., Jr., & Weyant, R. G. The interval between training and test trials as a determiner of the slope of generalization gradients. *Journal of Comparative and Physiological Psychology*, 1958, *51*, 596–600.

Rescorla, R. A., & Wagner, A. R. A theory of Pavlovian conditioning: Variations in the effectiveness of reinforcement and nonreinforcement. In A. H. Black & W. F. Prokasy (Eds.), *Classical conditioning II. Current research and theory*. New York: Appleton–Century–Crofts, 1972.

Riccio, D. C., Urda, M., & Thomas, D. R. Stimulus control in pigeons based on proprioceptive stimuli from floor inclination. *Science,* 1966, *153,* 434–436.

Richards, R. W. Stimulus control following training on a conditional discrimination. *Animal Learning and Behavior,* 1979, *7,* 309–312.

Sidman, M., Rauzin, R., Lazar, R., Cunningham, S., Tailby, W., & Carrigan, P. A search for symmetry in the conditional discrimination of rhesus monkeys, baboons, and children. *Journal of the Experimental Analysis of Behavior,* 1982, *37,* 23–44.

Sidman, M., & Tailby, W. Conditional discrimination vs matching to sample: An expansion of the testing paradigm. *Journal of the Experimental Analysis of Behavior,* 1982, *37,* 5–22.

Skinner, B. F. *The behavior of organisms.* New York: Appleton–Century–Crofts, 1938.

Spear, N. E. *The processing of memories: Forgetting and retention.* Hillsdale, N.J.: Lawrence Erlbaum Associates, 1978.

Switalski, R. W., Lyons, J., & Thomas, D. R. The effects of interdimensional training on stimulus generalization. *Journal of Experimental Psychology,* 1966, *72,* 661–666.

Thomas, D. R. Stimulus selection, attention, and related matters. In J. H. Reynierse (Ed.), *Current issues In animal learning.* Lincoln: University of Nebraska Press, 1970.

Thomas, D. R., Burr, D. E. S., & Eck, K. O. Stimulus selection in animal discrimination learning: An alternative interpretation. *Journal of Experimental Psychology,* 1970, *86,* 53–62.

Thomas, D. R., Ernst, A. J., & Andry, D. K. More on masking of stimulus control during generalization testing. *Psychonomic Science,* 1971, *23,* 85–86.

Thomas, D. R., & King, R. A. Stimulus generalization as a function of the level of motivation. *Journal of Experimental Psychology,* 1959, *57,* 323–328.

Thomas, D. R., & Lopez, L. J. The effect of delayed testing on generalization slope. *Journal of Comparative and Physiological Psychology,* 1962, *64,* 77–80.

Thomas, D. R., & McKelvie, A. R. Retrieval of memory in the pigeon by context manipulations. *Animal Learning and Behavior,* 1982, *10,* 1–6. (a)

Thomas, D. R., & McKelvie, A. R. *Symmetry in conditional discriminations.* Paper presented at the meeting of the Psychonomic Society, Minneapolis, November, 1982. (b)

Thomas, D. R., McKelvie, A. R., & Mah, W. The context as a conditional cue in operant discrimination reversal learning. *Journal of Experimental Psychology: Animal Behavior Processes,* in press.

Thomas, D. R., McKelvie, A. R., Ranney, M., & Moye, T. B. Interference in pigeons' long-term memory viewed as a retrieval problem. *Animal Learning and Behavior,* 1981, *9,* 581–586.

Thomas, D. R., Miller, J. T., & Hansen, G. The role of stimulus comparison in equivalence training. *Journal of Experimental Psychology,* 1972, *96,* 297–300.

Thomas, D. R., Miller, J. T., & Svinicki, J. G. Nonspecific transfer effects of discrimination training in the rat. *Journal of Comparative and Physiological Psychology,* 1971, *74,* 96–101.

Thomas, D. R., Svinicki, M. D., & Svinicki, J. G. Masking of stimulus control during generalization testing. *Journal of Experimental Psychology,* 1970, *84,* 479–482.

Thomas, D. R., & Wheatley, K. L. Effects of interdimensional training on stimulus generalization: An extension. *Journal of Experimental Psychology,* 1974, *103,* 1080–1085.

Tomie, A. Interference with autoshaping by prior context conditioning. *Journal of Experimental Psychology: Animal Behavior Processes,* 1976, *2,* 323–334.

Tomie, A., Davitt, G. A., & Thomas, D. R. The role of stimulus similarity in equivalence training. *Journal of Experimental Psychology,* 1973, *101,* 146–150.

Welker, R. I., Tomie, A., Davitt, G. A., & Thomas, D. R. Contextual stimulus control over operant responding in pigeons. *Journal of Comparative and Physiological Psychology,* 1974, *86,* 549–562.

Vom Saal, W., & Jenkins, H. M. Blocking the development of stimulus control. *Learning and Motivation,* 1970, *1,* 52–64.

12

Cue-Context Interactions in Discrimination, Categorization, and Memory

Douglas L. Medin
University of Illinois

Thomas J. Reynolds
Ayerst Laboratories, Inc.

INTRODUCTION

Historically, the status of *context* in theoretical analyses of learning and memory is like the setting for the staging of a play. Occasionally striking effects are produced, but almost always the setting serves as "background" for the real action in the drama. Similarly, it is well known that changes in context can alter performance in learning and memory tasks. Such observations, however, are usually assigned to the catch-all category of "generalization decrement," and context effects rarely are represented formally in theories. In many cases context is treated as just one of those variables that one has to "control for."

When not being treated as a confounding, context effects have often been viewed as imposing limitations on an organism. For example, one might think that monkeys are smarter than pigeons because they readily show transfer to changed situations, whereas pigeons appear to be more "context-bound."

These attitudes are not the only way to view context. As Wickens (1982) notes, context also is defined as that which disambiguates or gives meaning. Thus, one complains of being misunderstood because they have been "quoted out of context." As is seen in this chapter in this respect context can be viewed as essential.

The present chapter describes work where context is afforded a central status and where context effects are manifest as strengths as well as limitations. We aim to show that analyses of context can provide insights into some key problems associated with learning and memory research.

Our approach to context is sufficiently different from common practice that it may be in order to provide a brief overview. Once one decides to address context effects, an immediate question arises—how should one treat the relationship between context and the traditional "stimuli" or "cues" upon which the experimenter has chosen to focus? Do cue and context exert independent influences on performance, or do they interact in some way? We think this question is but one instance of the more general problem of element–compound or part–whole relationships. Therefore, our theoretical efforts have been concentrated on element–compound relationships. As the following sections show, we have been led to an unusual definition, where it is assumed that an element of a compound acts both as a cue and as context with respect to other elements (see also the chapter by Thomas, this volume). The core of this chapter describes this theoretical approach and evidence bearing on it.

The organization of this chapter is as follows: The first section considers the proper relationship among units of analysis in learning and memory research, focusing on relationships between elements or components and compounds. The section describes critical problems that arise when theories either ignore context or give it an auxiliary status. The second section outlines one theoretical treatment of context that has guided much of our research over the last few years. The third section briefly reviews some of this work, with examples drawn from discrimination learning, memory, and classification learning. Research in this section serves to point out that context effects may facilitate, rather than impair, abstraction and generalization. The final section outlines some further problems and issues associated with context effects in learning and memory.

UNITS OF ANALYSIS

Element–Compound Relationships

British Associationism.   The tradition of viewing complex concepts or compounds in terms of their elements or components can be traced directly back to the British associationists. In his 1829 book *Analysis of the Phenomenon of the Human Mind,* James Mill argued that complex ideas should be thought of as the *sum* of their constituents:

Where two or more ideas have been often repeated together, and the association has become very strong, they sometimes spring up in such close combination as not to be distinguishable. Some cases of sensation are analogous. For example, when a wheel, on the seven parts of which the seven prismatic colours are respectively painted, is made to revolve rapidly, it appears not of seven colours, but of one uniform colour, white. By the rapidity of the succession, the several sensations cease to be distinguishable; they run, as it were, together, and a new sensation, compounded of all seven, but apparently a simple one, is the result. Ideas, also which have been so often conjoined, that whenever one exists in the mind, the others immediately exist along with it, seem to run into one another, to coalesce, as it were, and out of many to form one idea; which idea, however in reality complex, appears to be no less simple, than any one of those of which it is compounded.

John Stuart Mill proposed that his father's *mental composition* be replaced with *mental chemistry*. The contrast is apparent in this quote from John Stuart Mill's *A System of Logic* of 1843:

Reverting to the distinction which occupies so prominent a place in the theory of induction, the laws of the phenomena of mind are sometimes analogous to mechanical, but sometimes also to chemical laws. When many impressions or ideas are operating in the mind together, there sometimes takes place a process of a similar kind to chemical combination. When impressions have been so often experienced in conjunction that each of them calls up readily and instantaneously the ideas of the whole group, those ideas sometimes melt and coalesce into one another, and appear not several ideas, but one in the same manner, as when the seven prismatic colours are presented to the eye in rapid succession the sensation produced is that of white. But as in this last case it is correct to say that the seven colours when they rapidly follow one another *generate* white, but not that they actually *are* white; so it appears to me that the Complex Idea, formed by the blending together of several simpler ones, should, when it really appears simple, (that is, when the separate elements are not consciously distinguishable in it), be said to *result from,* or *be generated by,* the simple ideas, not to *consist* of them. Our idea of an orange really *consists* of the simple ideas of a certain colour, a certain form, a certain taste and smell, &c., because we can, by interrogating our consciousness, perceive all these elements in the idea. But we cannot perceive, in so apparently simple a feeling as our perception of the shape of an object by the eye, all that multitude of ideas derived from other senses, without which it is well ascertained that no such visual perception would ever have had existence; nor, in our idea of Extension, can we discover those elementary ideas of resistance derived from our muscular frame in which it has been conclusively shown that the idea originates. These, therefore, are cases of mental chemistry, in which it is proper to say that the simple ideas generate, rather than that they compose, the complex ones.

A key aspect of this mental chemistry is that properties of compounds may not be deducible from properties of their components in any transparent manner. A compound is not the same as the sum of its components.

Learning Theory.   Learning theorists have tended to follow the view of James Mill rather than his son. The consensus has been that complex ideas or compounds can be thought of simply as a sum of component aspects. This assumption is implicit in Thorndike's "identical elements theory of transfer" and explicit in formal analyses of discrimination learning and generalization. For example, Spence's (1936) theory of discrimination learning assumed that acquisition and generalization could be directly represented by the number of components in common between pairs of stimuli. Components acquire and maintain associative information in a completely additive and independent manner. If 10 units of strength are associated with *white* when it appears as part of a large white triangle in some context, then *white* would continue to have 10 units of strength even if it appeared as part of a new compound differing in size, shape, and experimental context. Note that in following James Mill's mental composition one is crediting organisms with tremendous powers of abstraction and transfer.

Not surprisingly, the practice of treating component associations as additive and independent runs into difficulties. One major problem with Spence's theory is that it predicted that certain solvable discrimination problems would be impossible to solve. For example, if a response to the left is correct when two black circles are presented and a response to the right is correct when two white squares are presented (a successive discrimination), each of the components left, right, black, white, circle, square is rewarded equally often and all the compounds should have equivalent associative strengths. Thus none should be preferred in any test and the problem should be impossible to solve.

There are ways of getting around this difficulty (such as Hull's 1943 assumption of afferent neural interaction), just as there are ways of dealing with context effects; however, they have pretty uniformly been viewed as auxiliary aspects of theoretical analyses. (For an exception see the pattern and mixed models of Atkinson & Estes, 1963; Estes & Hopkins, 1961.)

The Problem of Direct Associations to Elements

The idea that performance is determined by independent, simple associations between stimulus elements and events leads to several problems. Consider, for example, Wyrwicka's (1956) studies of the relation between conditioned responses trained in two different situations. Situation A was a conditioning chamber with a dog placed on the stand and fed from a feeder; Situation B was a second room with the dog standing on the floor and having bread pieces tossed to him by the experimenter. The dog was trained to make Movement A to Stimulus A in Situation A and to make movement B to Stimulus B in Situation B. Then the dog was tested with Stimulus A in Situation B and Stimulus B in Situation A. The responses of the dogs were controlled by the situations: They made Movement B to Stimulus A in Situation B and Movement A to Stimulus B in Situation A. Adding a nonrewarded Stimulus A' to Situation A to force differentiation between Stimulus A and Stimulus A' did not change the pattern of results. Dogs made Movement B to Stimulus A in Situation B and made no response to Stimulus A' in Situation B. It is not clear how a simple associative theory could handle Wyrwicka's results.

A related problem is that control of performance by some cue can be modulated by other cues. For example, monkeys can readily master discrimination problems where the correct stimulus of a pair depends on the color of the food tray on which the stimulus objects are presented (see French, 1965, for a review). For example, a triangular form might be correct and a circular form incorrect when the food tray is yellow, but the circular form is correct when the food tray is green. To address these results, one would have to make additional assumptions (such as that the discriminative cues and the conditional cues [food tray color] came to act as compound stimuli), assumptions that are not in the spirit of direct associations to elements.

The preceding problems are neither new nor devastating to a simple associative theory. As the number of patches needed to bring an existing theory into line with experimental results increases, however, the idea that a reevaluation of its basic assumptions is necessary becomes more viable.

The remainder of this chapter is focused on a theory that does not assume that information associated with stimulus components is stored and retrieved in an independent manner. In this sense the theory follows John Stuart Mill's mental chemistry rather than his father's mental composition. Although it does not imply any special compounding or configurational process (such as gestalt theories do), it does give important weight to the role of context in the retrieval of associative information. Context continues to play out its role as background, but it functions in our theory in a manner that emphasizes its disambiguating properties (see also Bouton & Bolles, this volume).

CONTEXT MODEL OF LEARNING, MEMORY, AND CATEGORIZATION

Relationship Between Cue and Context

A typical distinction between stimuli or cues and context might be to say that cues are those aspects of a situation that the experimenter varies and to which it is assumed subjects respond, whereas context refers to those relatively invariant aspects of a situation in which a response occurs. A distinctly different view, adopted in the context model under consideration here, is that a particular stimulus may function both as a cue *and* as context for other cues (again, see the chapter by Thomas in this volume for a closely related idea). Elements of a compound stimulus are assumed to have both a cue function and a context function. The mechanism for addressing context effects is precisely the same as the mechanism for addressing element–compound relationships.

Consider a situation where a blue square is presented and some event (e.g., reward) occurs. Individual stimulus components, such as blue or square, are not assumed to be directly and independently associated with the event. Instead, information concerning the cue, the context, and the event are assumed to be stored together in memory. For the representation of the event to be retrieved, both cue and context must be activated simultaneously. A change in either the

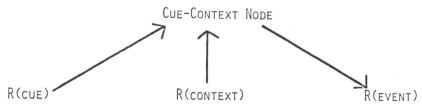

FIG 12.1.   A cue-context node depicting the interactive influence of cue and context. R(cue), R(context), and R(event) refer to the representation of the cue, context, and event or outcome, respectively.

cue or the context can reduce the accessibility of information associated with both.

This idea is depicted in Fig. 12.1. R(cue), R(context), and R(event) refer to the representation of the cue, context, and event, respectively. Event retrieval is linked to the combined activation of cue and context. In our example, blue is part of the context in which square appears and vice versa. As a result, transfer along the form dimension is not independent of color. This nonindependence or interactive coding represents an important constraint on the accessibility of stored information.

The assumptions regarding cues and context just discussed are closely related to the assumptions of the Estes hierarchical association model (Estes, 1972, 1973, 1976). The cue-context node corresponds to what Estes refers to as a "control-element," and it is used here to underline the assumptions that cue and context interact dynamically.

These interactive assumptions resolve many of the difficulties associated with independent learning models. Consider again Wyrwicka's experimental results. Predictions from the context model, which is presented more formally in the next section, depend on the similarity of Stimulus A to Stimulus B and the similarity of Situation A to Situation B. If the two stimuli are more similar than the two situations, the cue-context node that is activated depends mainly on the situation in which the dog is placed. In this case performance would be controlled more by the situations than the stimuli, as Wyrwicka found. In fact, there should be no unusual difficulty for the special case where Stimulus A and Stimulus B are identical, because activation of the cue-context node depends both on cues and on context.

Specific Assumptions

The following assumptions formalize the preceding proposal that cue changes and context changes combine in an interactive manner.

1. The similarity of two cues along a dimension can be represented by a similarity parameter ranging in value between 0 and 1, with 1 corresponding to maximum similarity (identity) and 0 to total lack of similarity. Similarity of cues

along a dimension depends not only on their physical properties, but also on attention. Specifically, effective similarity of two cues along some dimension is less when that dimension is attended to than when it is not.

2. Cue and context dimensions combine in an interactive, specifically multiplicative, manner to determine overall similarity.

3. Probe stimuli act as retrieval cues to access information associated with stimuli similar to the probe. Just what is retrieved depends on the overall similarity of the stored stimuli to the probe.

4. Performance is based on the information retrieved. The precise rule mapping accessed information onto responding has varied depending on the domain of application, as is indicated in subsequent sections.

To illustrate these assumptions, consider the analysis of a blue square and a red triangle. According to the first assumption, color similarity of these two objects can be represented by a parameter c, and form similarity by a parameter f. It is expected that c would be larger for the colors orange and red versus blue and red, because presumably orange is more similar to red than is blue to red. The second assumption of our model specifies that the overall similarity of the blue square to the red triangle is computed from the product of c and f or cf. One immediate implication of this multiplicative rule is that, if differences along any single dimension are large (i.e., similarity parameter $= 0$), variations in any or all other dimensions will not alter performance. Finally, our representation of selective attention is much weaker than that of most attention theories (e.g., Sutherland & Mackintosh, 1971), which typically assume no generalization along dimensions not observed (i.e., similarity parameter given attention $= 0$, similarity parameter given absence of attention $= 1$). The present assumption allows attention to control generalization but only proposes that generalization gradients will be sharper along observed dimensions.

The basic assumptions of the context model have been applied and tested in experiments on discrimination learning, memory, and classification. The next section provides a review of this work to indicate how the model functions and to illustrate the different ways in which context may enter into performance. Where appropriate, contrasts with additive models are made.

EXPERIMENTAL APPLICATIONS OF THE CONTEXT MODEL

Discrimination Learning

The application of the context model to discrimination learning requires the addition of learning and choice assumptions (see Medin, 1975, for greater detail). For present purposes an abbreviated algebraic version of the context model is described, in order to illustrate and to derive qualitative predictions.

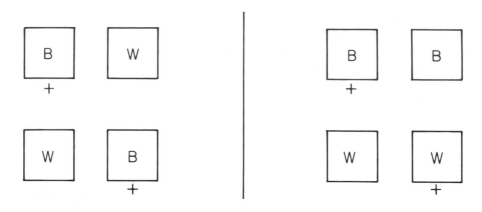

Simultaneous   Successive

FIG. 12.2.   The simultaneous and successive discrimination paradigms. The
"+" sign refers to the rewarded stimulus for each of the two settings of a
problem.

Algebraic Version.   To see how the algebraic version of the context model
works, consider the simultaneous discrimination problem shown in the left half
of Fig. 12.2. Informally, the solution is "choose black." We assume that when a
response is made to a stimulus the outcome information (reward or nonreward) is
associated with the chosen stimulus but also tends to generalize to other stimuli
of the problem. The amount of this generalization is determined by overall
similarity derived from the multiplicative combination of component differences.

The similarity values for the various problem stimuli are shown in Table 12.1.
Because black on the left (B_L) differs from white on the right along both bright-

TABLE 12.1
Similarity Matrix for the Stimuli in
Fig. 12.2. The Letters p and b are
Parameters for Position and Brightness
Similarity, Respectively. B_L, B_R, W_L, and
W_R Stand for Black on the Left, Black on
the Right, White on the Left, and White
on the Right

	B_L	B_R	W_L	W_R
B_L	1	p	b	bp
B_R	p	1	bp	b
W_L	b	bp	1	p
W_R	bp	b	p	1

ness and position, their similarity is represented by b (brightness similarity) times p (position similarity). This table can be used to describe generalization of outcome information from any one stimulus to any other.

Let the information acquired from a response to a stimulus be designated by I_R when followed by reward and by I_N when followed by nonreward. In the simultaneous discrimination of Fig. 12.2, let us assume that the two trial settings ($B_L - W_R$, $W_L - B_R$) are randomly intermixed and, for illustrative purposes, focus on $B_L - W_R$ information differences resulting from trials on the two settings. On a $B_L - W_R$ trial when B_L is chosen, the reward will be associated with B_L and other stimuli, depending on their similarity to B_L. If information in an amount I_R is associated with B_L, a reduced amount bpI_R (remember that b and p are constrained to be between 0 and 1) will be associated with W_R and the net difference in information will be $I_R(1 - bp)$. If W_R is chosen, nonreward will be associated with W_R and to a lesser extent with B_L. The net difference in nonreward information (B_L minus W_R) would be $I_N(bp - 1)$. The total information that would be favorable toward choosing a stimulus will be represented by I_R minus I_N, and with this equation the net difference in information (ΔI) from a rewarded response to B_L and a nonrewarded response to W_R would be ($I_R + I_N)(1 - bp)$.

Now consider the effects of $W_L - B_R$ trials on the $B_L - W_R$ information difference. When B_R is chosen, both B_L and W_R may be associated with reward, the generalization to B_L being diminished by a position difference, p, and generalization to W_R by a difference in brightness, b. Continuing this line of development, following one rewarded response to B_R and one nonrewarded response to W_L, the value for B_L would be $pI_R - bI_N$ and for W_R would be $bI_R - pI_N$. The net difference for B_L and W_R would be ($I_R + I_N)(p - b)$. From this we can see that $W_L - B_R$ trials will facilitate performance on $B_L - W_R$ trials when $b < p$ (i.e., brightness less similar than position).

Combining trials on the two settings the overall information difference for $B_L - W_R$ trials would be ($I_R + I_N)(1 - bp + p - b)$. Assuming that $I_R + I_N$ remains constant across settings, and arbitrarily assigning their sum to 1, the overall information gain from a trial on each setting can be factored to yield:

$$\Delta I = (1 + p)(1 - b). \tag{1}$$

From equation (1) we can derive the intuitive predictions that simultaneous discriminations will be solved more rapidly the greater the distinctiveness of the brightness cue (the smaller b) and the greater the similarity of the positional cues (the larger p).

The algebraic version of the context model is a convenient oversimplification that can be used to derive qualitative predictions. Without specific learning and choice assumptions, however, it is not clear how information differences map onto performance. One set of detailed assumptions was spelled out in the original presentation of the context model (Medin, 1975), and any predictions discussed here are consistent with that full model. The relationship between the algebraic and more formal versions of the context model is that qualitatively the predictions of the algebraic version are correct, and that whenever the difference in information is greater than zero the formal version of the context model will predict that a discrimination problem can be solved.

One can develop the analogous equation for the successive discrimination problem shown in the right half of Fig. 12.2,

$$\Delta I = (1 - p)(1 - b). \tag{2}$$

Equation (2) predicts that performance on successive discriminations will improve with both position and brightness distinctiveness. Analogous equations for an additive model would yield $\Delta I = 0$, indicating that a successive discrimination cannot be solved (recall Spence's model). Of course, successive discriminations are solvable.

Because greater information differences yield more correct choices and hence easier discriminations, one can compare equations (1) and (2) and derive the prediction that simultaneous discriminations will be easier than successive discriminations (except when $p = 0$). One might also expect that if one reward is associated exclusively with one position and a distinct reward is associated with another position, simultaneous discriminations will be slowed and successive discriminations will be speeded up due to decreased position similarity. Shepp (1962, 1964) demonstrated both these effects using retarded children as subjects. (See also Peterson, Wheeler, & Trapold, 1980, for related work using animals.)

The context model makes a variety of predictions concerning the difficulty, solvability, and the varied effects of dimensional similarity that generally have been supported (Medin, 1975). In the next few paragraphs we highlight phenomena that distinguish the context model from alternative discrimination learning models, particularly those that assume that stimulus components are independently conditioned.

Solvability. Figure 12.3 shows a conditional successive discrimination learning problem. Informally, it can be described as "for large stimuli, black—go left, white—go right; for small stimuli, black—go right, white—go left." As mentioned earlier, a theory based on independent conditioning of stimulus components (e.g., Spence, 1936) predicts that successive discriminations cannot be solved. The conditional successive problem is of particular interest, because a modification of Spence's theory that predicts that successive discriminations can be solved (Spiker, 1970) nonetheless predicts that a conditional successive discrimination cannot be solved by inarticulate organisms. Flagg (1974) tested monkeys on a conditional successive discrimination and found that the problem, although difficult, could be solved.

The appropriate equation for Fig. 12.3 from the algebraic version of the context model is

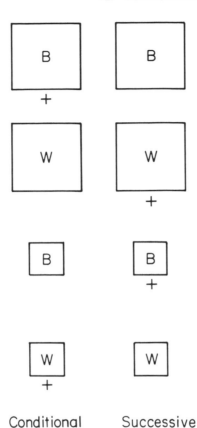

Conditional   Successive

FIG. 12.3.   The conditional successive discrimination paradigm.

$$\Delta I = (1 - p)(1 - s)(1 - b), \tag{3}$$

where s represents size similarity. Unless p, s, or b is 1, ΔI will be greater than 0 and the problem should be solvable. As far as we know, this prediction is unique to the context model.

Configural Versus Component Learning.   One issue in discrimination-learning research concerns how discriminations are learned, an issue that frequently is evaluated by means of transfer tests. Consider the paradigm shown in Fig. 12.4 used to evaluate component versus configural learning. R, Y, B, and W stand for red, yellow, black, and white. After training on the top problem, subjects are given transfer tests on both stimulus arrangements. The argument is that, if subjects continue to select the same rewarded stimuli (red and white), they have learned about stimulus components. Responses to yellow and black are taken as evidence that subjects have learned which response (left or right) is appropriate

Training

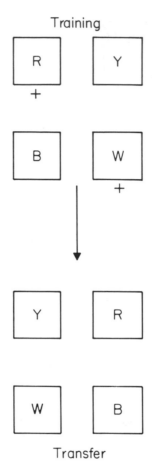

FIG. 12.4.   Paradigm used to evaluate configural versus component learning.

for the entire stimulus configuration (e.g., for the red and yellow setting—go left).

The context model does not assume that there are distinctive styles of learning and interprets transfer in terms of stimulus similarity. To develop transfer predictions, we let c_w equal within-setting color similarity and c_b equal between-setting color similarity. (For simplicity, we assume that red and yellow are equally similar to black and to white, and that red and yellow are as similar to each other as are black and white.) On the transfer test the difference in reward information between Y_L and $R_R(Y_L - R_R)$ would be:

$$\Delta I = c_w + pc_b - p - c_b. \tag{4}$$

From Equation (4) one can predict that a "configural" response pattern will increase with within-setting color similarity, decrease with between-setting color similarity, and decrease with position similarity (see White & Spiker, 1960, for experimental support). If the within-setting similarity varies in the two settings, it is possible that one might observe "configural responding" for one transfer pair and "component responding" for the other transfer pair. This outcome can be observed (Campione, McGrath, & Rabinowitz, 1971; Liu & Zeiler, 1968), suggesting that one is indeed observing stimulus similarity effects rather than distinct styles of learning.

Constant Irrelevant Cues.   Constant irrelevant cues can be thought of as contextual cues and the context theory predicts that constant irrelevant cues will have a substantial effect on transfer responding. Other theories either assume that constant irrelevant cues never influence choices (e.g., Fisher & Zeaman, 1972) or that their influence diminishes in the course of learning. These theories have in common the assumption that relevant and irrelevant features are processed independently.

To evaluate this independence assumption (rejected by the context model), Flagg and Medin (1973) trained monkeys on two concurrent discrimination problems, one having color relevant and form constant irrelevant, and the other having form relevant and color constant and irrelevant. Transfer tests gave choices among the two previously rewarded objects, a new object formed by combining the relevant color and form cues, and a new object formed by combining the constant irrelevant color and form cues. Subjects consistently chose the previously rewarded objects during transfer, rather than new objects combining both relevant features. Theories assuming that relevant and irrelevant features are independent cannot handle these results, because they predict that model choices should be of the stimulus-combining relevant features.

One response to this result is to argue that subjects had attended to compound cues and continued to respond to these compound cues during transfer. Of course, attempting to preserve the assumption of component independence by redefining the unit of analysis is not a very graceful solution, but this interpretation does have at least one testable consequence. Consider the concurrent object discrimination task shown in Fig. 12.5. For two of the problems color is relevant and form is constant and irrelevant, and for the other two problems the roles of color and form are reversed. In addition, one color and one form discrimination differ from the other two problems in both size and orientation (e.g., the large stimuli were upright whereas the small stimuli were flat).

Pigtailed monkeys were trained on the problem shown in Fig. 12.5 and then given a variety of transfer tests. The comparison of greatest interest involves choices of stimuli comprised of previously relevant features in relation to between-problem similarity. For example, consider a test between a blue triangle combining relevant color and form features and a yellow triangle combining the same relevant features. The context model predicts that the blue triangle will be preferred because the strength associated with blue will be reduced only by the

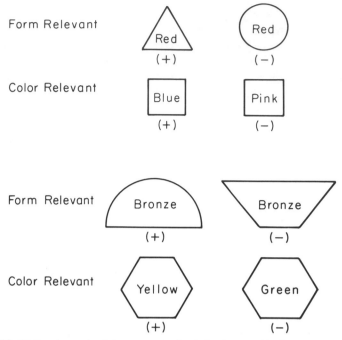

FIG. 12.5.   A sample of the concurrent discriminations used in the compounding study. The large stimuli were presented in a vertical position and the small stimuli were presented horizontally (flat). Only one of the two settings for each simultaneous discrimination is shown.

form difference from the training stimulus (blue square), whereas the strength associated with yellow will be diminished by the form difference and the size and orientation difference between the yellow triangle and the yellow hexagon. There is no basis for expecting a difference in choices on such tests if the monkeys had simply learned to attend to compounds, and component information is assumed to be independent of the compound from which it was derived. The results were consistent with the context model—choices of new stimuli were related to the overall similarity of these objects to the stimuli from which they were constructed.

Transverse Patterning.   In the transverse patterning problem, three trial settings are presented with each of three stimuli correct in one pair and incorrect in another. If we denote the three stimuli as A, B, and C, then $A+B-$, $B+C-$, and $C+A-$ trials are randomly intermixed. The context model in its simplest form predicts such problems to be impossible to solve but can predict solvability if a distinction is made between within-setting and between-setting transfer. In that event,

$$\Delta I = (1 - f)(1 - s_b), \tag{5}$$

where f refers to object similarity and s_b refers to context similarity between settings. As equation (5) would predict, decreasing the similarity of between-setting cues facilitates transverse pattern learning (Birch & Israel, 1971).

Consideration of the transverse patterning problem makes an interesting point. One often speaks of overcoming effects of context—yet paying attention to contextual cues associated with between-setting changes holds the key to solving transverse pattern problems. This is one clear example of a situation where context provides or conveys meaning.

Discrimination Shifts.   Attention to a dimension in the context model works by means of reducing the effective similarity of cues on that dimension. Because, in general, similarity of irrelevant cues facilitates and similarity of relevant cues impairs learning, intradimensional shifts (new problem same relevant dimensions) should be easier than extradimensional shifts (new problem, different relevant dimensions) because the relevant dimension is more likely to be observed at the time of transfer. (There is a variety of processing assumptions that will work to insure that relevant dimensions are more likely to be attended than irrelevant dimensions; again see Medin, 1975, for details.)

The context model can account for a variety of selective attention effects (see Medin, 1975). In contrast with many other attention models, the context model predicts that intra and extradimensional shift differences may interact with salience of dimensions in such a way that an extradimensional shift to a dimension with large cue differences (i.e., salient) may be learned faster than an intradimensional shift to a less-salient dimension. This can occur if the similarity of cues along a salient dimension when it is not directly attended is less than the similarity of cues along a less-salient dimension when it is observed. Most other attention models do not predict this effect because they assume no generalization for attended dimensions and complete generalization for dimensions not attended. The interaction of shifts with cue salience has been observed often (e.g., Campione, 1969; Mackintosh & Little, 1969).

It is also the case that subjects trained on a simultaneous discrimination subsequently learn a successive discrimination more rapidly when the same stimulus dimension is relevant in both tasks than when the relevant dimensions are shifted between the first and second problem (e.g., Mumma & Warren, 1968). The context model predicts such a result, but it is difficult to see how other attention theories would handle this finding; that is, if successive discriminations can be solved only by attending to compound dimensions (as these theories almost always assume), it is hard to see what one should predict for simultaneous discriminations, which presumably are solved on the basis of attention to component dimensions.

Summary.   The context model adequately describes learning and transfer performance in a variety of discrimination paradigms and situations. Of particular interest is the observation that a direct benefit of representing the effects of context directly is that the difficulty and solvability of various discrimination problems are described accurately. This is in contrast with independent conditioning models that do not address context effects directly. Much of the success of the context model derives from the assumption that components of a compound stimulus function both as cues and as context for other cues.

The next section of this chapter presents evidence bearing more directly on the idea that a probe stimulus acts as a retrieval cue to access information associated with similar stimuli. The paradigms to be considered are quite different but the basic ideas of the context model are preserved.

Memory

Retroactive Interference and Facilitation.   Although stimulus similarity has long been assumed to play a major role in retroactive interference (e.g., Osgood, 1953), theoretical treatments in animal memory research have given similarity little status and instead assumed that interfering stimuli primarily alter performance indirectly by reducing or eliminating rehearsal of the to-be-remembered information in short-term memory (e.g., Roberts & Grant, 1978). A recent series of experiments in our laboratory (Medin, Reynolds, & Parkinson, 1980) showed clear stimulus similarity effects and also indicated that the to-be-remembered sample and an interpolated stimulus cannot be treated as independent events.

The design of one experiment is shown in Fig. 12.6. Monkeys were tested on delayed matching to sample problems where an interpolated stimulus might be presented either 6 or 12 seconds after the sample. If the sample had been rewarded it was correct on the test; if the sample was not rewarded the alternative choice stimulus was correct. The interpolated stimulus always matched the sample stimulus on the irrelevant dimension. If the sample was a red triangle, for example, and the choice test was to be between the red triangle and a red square, the interpolated stimulus might be a red circle. Finally, the interpolated stimulus either had the same outcome as the sample stimulus (same trials $\pm$ and $\pm$) or a different outcome (different trials $\pm$ and $\mp$).

If interpolated stimuli simply interfere with short-term memory processing, control trial performance should be uniformly better than interference trials. If the interpolated stimulus influences performance solely in terms of generalization to the test stimuli, interpolated stimuli should not help and might impair performance.

If, on the other hand, an interpolated stimulus is viewed as a retrieval cue, it could provide the opportunity for additional processing of the initial sample and its associated outcome. On Same trials this should only be beneficial, but on Different trials the memory representation for the sample stimulus may be modi-

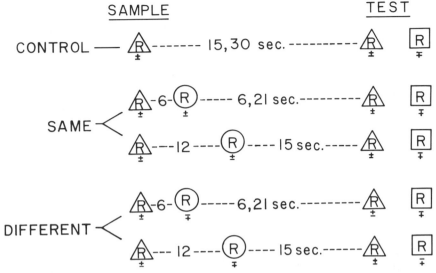

FIG. 12.6. The basic trial types used in the Medin, Reynolds, and Parkinson study. The ± refers to the fact that sample and interpolated stimuli might either be rewarded or nonrewarded and the same versus different conditions were defined in terms of whether the sample and interpolated stimulus had the same (++ or −−) or different (+− or −+) reward status. The correct and rewarded stimulus depended on whether or not the sample was rewarded.

fied by the (different) outcome associated with the interpolated stimulus. This would interfere with performance.

Compared to the control condition, the interpolated stimuli had a dramatic effect for both interstimulus intervals. On Different trials retroactive *interference* was strong; on Same trials, however, retroactive *facilitation* was observed. This pattern of results is exactly that predicted when it is assumed that the initial sample and interpolated stimuli do not act as independent events. Instead, the results suggest that the interpolated stimulus acted as a retrieval cue to access and lead to further processing of the sample stimulus.

A follow-up experiment replicated these results and indicated that the effects of the interpolated stimulus depend on the specific similarity of the sample and interpolated stimulus. Facilitation and interference effects were greater when the sample and interpolated stimulus differed in color alone than when they differed in color and form. This rules out the interpretation that interference derives from same versus different outcomes independent of stimulus similarity.

These and other results reported by Medin et al. (1980) are inconsistent with the idea that sample and potentially interfering stimuli are encoded independently, and that any pattern of interferences or facilitation can be described in terms of a simple, additive function of generalization along component stimulus dimensions. The results further suggest that the underlying mechanisms producing nonindependence of stimulus events are closely tied to retrieval and rehearsal processes. The next section presents a formal model for retrieval processes in delayed-matching-to-sample.

Proactive Interference.   In many memory theories proactive interference is strictly a function of temporal parameters; that is, memory strength is assumed to decrease with time and interference is produced by response competition at the time of recall.

The idea that a probe stimulus may act as a retrieval cue leads one to expect that processes other than time may be instrumental in forgetting. In particular, the context model predicts major effects of stimulus similarity on proactive interference. Consider the between-trials interference design shown in Fig. 12.7, in which color is relevant and form is constant and irrelevant within, and variable

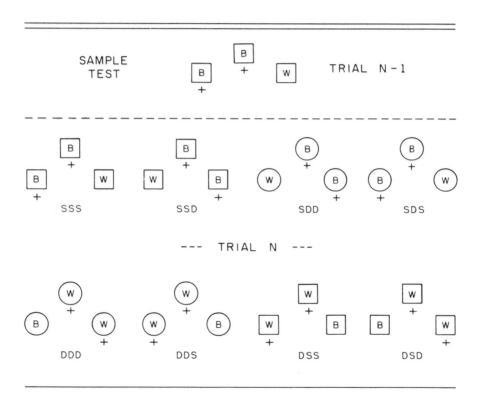

FIG. 12.7.   Relations between consecutive trials in the Reynolds and Medin study. (In Trials SSS, SSD, etc., S = same and D = Different; each set of letters indicates color, form, and position in that order. B = black; W = white.)

between, trials. Conditions are described in terms of the relations between trials. In the figure the preceding matching to sample trial consisted of a black square appearing as the sample and then being presented on the left for the choice test. For any pair of trials, the correct color may be same or different, the form may either remain the same or be different, and the position of the rewarded object may be the same or different. Thus an SSS trial is an exact repetition of the preceding trial; SSD refers to a trial in which the same color is correct, the same forms are used, but the position of the correct object shifts between trials.

Of course all theories would expect condition SSS to yield better performance than DSD because the test conditions are the same on consecutive trials, but for DSD the reward conditions have been reversed. This prediction follows from the context theory because high between-trial similarity increases the likelihood that the preceding trial will be recalled when the current trial cues and context are presented. In condition SSS, influence of the preceding trial will improve performance, whereas in condition DSD prior trial recall will favor the incorrect choice, shortly we describe assumptions concerning specifically how a preceding trial alters performance on a current trial, and the reader is referred to Reynolds and Medin (1981) for additional details. Different predictions arise on SSS versus SDS trials, however. According to the context theory, the change in form associated with condition SDS should decrease the likelihood that the representation associated with the preceding trial will influence performance. Because responding on the basis of information from the preceding trial should facilitate performance in this case, condition SDS is predicted to produce lower performance than condition SSS, which is not associated with a change in form.

If components of a compound are processed independently, there is no basis for predicting condition SSS to be better than SDS. Both conditions should be helped by positive transfer from the preceding test along the relevant dimension, and because SSS also matches the prior and current stimuli along the irrelevant (form) dimension, a constant amount of additional generalization would be added to both objects. This should work to impair performance on SSS trials.

Although one might formulate a choice rule to predict SSS trials to be better than SDS trials (e.g., by adding similarity from each dimension to compute overall prior trial effects), it is still possible to contrast the context model with independent conditioning models. Any such rules that predict SSS superior to SDS would also predict DSD trials to be better than DDD trials. The context model predicts DDD trials to be easier than DSD trials, because changing form between trials in condition DDD will reduce the (detremental) influence of the prior trial.

To evaluate these and related predictions we (Reynolds & Medin, 1981) ran monkeys on the DMTS paradigm shown in Fig. 12.7. Rhesus monkeys were given a raisin reward for responding to a sample presented over the center foodwell of a three-well formboard. Following a variable delay, a choice was given between the sample and a second stimulus differing in color but not form,

TABLE 12.2
Mean Proportion Correct for Each Between-Trial Condition as a
Function of Delay

Condition[a]			Delay		
Color	Form	Position	6 sec	12 sec	24 sec
S	S	S	.92	.92	.90
S	S	D	.90	.90	.80
S	D	D	.87	.88	.81
S	D	S	.90	.89	.72
D	D	D	.87	.76	.69
D	D	S	.88	.76	.67
D	S	S	.75	.61	.58
D	S	D	.56	.46	.42

[a]S = Same
D = Different

presented over the side foodwells. A response to the sample was rewarded with a raisin. The main results are shown in Table 12.2. At all delay intervals, condition SSS was better than SDS and condition DDD was better than DSD. These results are consistent with the context model's interactive assumptions and inconsistent with the idea of independent component processing.

A quantitative version of the context model was developed and applied to these data. It was assumed that the representation of the sample from the current trial and the representation of the immediately preceding choice test influence performance on the basis of their similarity to the current test cues and context. The probability of control by the sample or the preceding test was computed directly from the overall similarity of the presented test cues and context to the previous sample and test events, according to the multiplicative rule. Time was treated as acting like any other dimension, with the temporal similarity of the current test to the current sample presumably greater than the temporal similarity of the current test to the preceding test. An additional parameter was used to represent the similarity of the single sample context to the test context (see Reynolds & Medin, 1981, for further details).

It was assumed that if the test retrieved only the current sample or only the preceding test, whichever was retrieved would control performance. If neither was retrieved, monkeys were assumed to guess randomly. Finally, if both the current sample and preceding test were retrieved, it was assumed that the monkey was equally likely to use either event as the basis of responding.

The similarity parameters were estimated by a grid search procedure to find values that minimized the mean squared deviation of predicted and observed proportions. The data were collapsed across delay intervals to yield the eight basic trial types. The context model produced excellent fits to the data—the

TABLE 12.3
Mean Proportion Correct for Each Between-Trial Condition. Predicted
Values Derived from the Context Model are in Parentheses

Condition[a]			Expt I	Expt II	
Color	Form	Position		Close	Far
S	S	S	.92(.92)	.82(.83)	.82(.85)
S	S	D	.86(.86)	.78(.77)	.60(.62)
S	D	D	.85(.83)	.79(.79)	.64(.64)
S	D	S	.84(.85)	.81(.81)	.74(.75)
D	D	D	.77(.76)	.65(.66)	.48(.48)
D	D	S	.77(.79)	.75(.73)	.71(.66)
D	S	S	.65(.64)	.65(.65)	.66(.66)
D	S	D	.48(.48)	.48(.48)	.27(.30)

[a]S = Same
D = Different

average absolute deviation of predicted and observed values was less than .01, and the model accounted for 99% of the variance (see Table 12.3). A quantitative version of an independent component model could account for only 63% of the variance.

An important implication of the model is that proactive interference is not solely time dependent but is also similarity dependent. According to the parameter estimates, the probability that the preceding trial was influential in performance ranged from .09 on SDD and DDS trials to .78 on SSS and DSD trials.

The quantitative model also leads to further qualitative predictions. Recall that the model posits a similarity parameter associated with the difference in context between sample and test settings. Increasing this similarity should facilitate performance. In a second experiment relations between the sample and the test setting were varied by changing the separation of the foodwells and the color of the formboard. For the Close condition, the foodwells were moved close together and the entire formboard was painted a neutral tan. For the Far condition, the foodwells were widely separated, and the background surrounding the center (sample) foodwell was painted tan, the background of one choice site was red, and that of the other was green.

The context model predicts the Close condition to yield better performance than the Far condition, because the current sample should be more likely to control performance than the preceding tests. This prediction is not very intuitive, and, indeed, we thought that the Close condition might be the more difficult.

The results, shown on the right side of Table 12.3, were that the Close condition led to better performance than the Far condition, especially on those trial types where control by the preceding test trial should lower performance (e.g., DSD). Predicted values from the context model for these conditions are also shown in Table 12.3. The model accounted for 99% of the variance in the Close condition and 98% of the variance in the Far condition. The parameter estimates suggest that the sample was 26% less likely to be retrieved in the Far condition than in the close condition. The estimated similarity parameter for position was also much larger in the Close than in the Far condition, as one might expect.

These studies make a case against the practice of treating proactive interference solely in terms of processes linked to time. Similarity along both relevant and irrelevant stimulus dimensions, as well as contextual similarity, contributed importantly to memory performance.

As in the studies of discrimination learning, the memory experiments suggest that components of stimulus compounds and context are not processed independently but rather combine in an interactive manner. The next section of this chapter reviews research on a seemingly very different topic—human classification learning—but again a major contrast is drawn between independent and interactive component processing.

Human Classification Learning

Recently there has been a substantial shift in psychologists' thinking about the structure of natural categories such as *fruit, furniture,* or *mammal.* The old view is that all natural concepts are characterized by simple sets of defining features that are singly necessary and jointly sufficient to determine category membership (Katz & Postal, 1964). Each exemplar of the concept must possess these defining features, and, therefore, each exemplar is equally representative of the concept. Concepts containing singly necessary and jointly sufficient features are said to be well-defined concepts.

In contrast, the current consensus is that most natural concepts are not well defined but rather are based on relationships that are only generally true. Individual exemplars may vary in the number of characteristic features they possess, and, consequently, some exemplars may be more representative or more typical of a concept than others. For example, cows may be better examples of the concept *mammal* than are whales. Instances are neither arbitrarily associated with categories nor strictly linked by defining features, but rather instances reflect more nearly a "family resemblance" structure (Rosch & Mervis, 1975).

If many natural categories do not have simple sets of defining features, how do people acquire and use them? Posner and Keele (1968) proposed that people form an impression of the central tendency of a category as a result of experience with exemplars, and that categorical judgments come to be based on this central tendency or prototype. An eagle, for example, would be judged to be a bird and not a mammal because it is more similar to the bird prototype than to the mammal prototype.

Prototype theory is one instance of a class of categorization theories known as independent cue theories. These theories assume that the information entering into category judgments (overall similarity, distance, or validity) can be derived from an additive combination of the information from component attributes (Franks & Bransford, 1971; Reed, 1972). In other words, the more characteristic attributes an exemplar has, the easier it should be to learn and classify. These theories, like Spence's (1936) discrimination theory, assume that the components of a compound stimulus are learned about in an independent manner.

The context model, which as we have seen does not assume component independence, can account for many of the observations that have been taken as support for prototype theory (see Medin & Schaffer, 1978, for details). The additional assumptions needed to apply the context model to classification are;

1. Category judgments are based on the retrieval of specific item information; no categorical information is assumed to enter into the judgments independent of specific item information.

2. The probability of classifying exemplar i into category j is an increasing function of the similarity of exemplar i to stored category j exemplars and a decreasing function of the similarity of exemplar i to stored exemplars associated with alternative categories where overall similarities are found via the multiplicative rule for components. Specifically, it is assumed that the probability of a category j response to probe i is determined by a ratio rule, where the sum of the similarities of probe i to the stored j exemplars is divided by the sum of the similarities of probe i to all stored exemplars. It is assumed that the probability of a j response is equal to the evidence favoring a j classification. The key that distinguished the context model from additive models is the multiplicative rule for stimulus components.

Note that the model does not seem to assume that abstraction takes place—performance is assumed to be controlled by the retrieval of specific exemplar information. Actually this is a bit misleading. To handle certain discrimination-learning results, the context model assumes that selective attention may alter the effective similarity of two cues along a dimension. In an analogous way, the context model would represent the effects of learning strategies or testing hypotheses in terms of changes in the similarity parameters. As a consequence there may not be a distinct representation for each exemplar. The key difference from a prototype model is that the context model assumes that information is combined in an interactive rather than an independent fashion.

Even though we have strayed from simple discrimination tasks, to memory, to classification involving ill-defined concepts, certain issues remain the same. In particular, the question of independent versus interactive components arises in all three settings. The next few paragraphs describe some of our recent classification experiments bearing on this issue.

Density Versus Distance.   Because components are assumed to combine in a multiplicative manner, the context model has as an implication that an exemplar may be classified more efficiently if it is highly similar to one instance and dissimilar to a second than if it has medium similarity to two instances of a category. Hence it predicts that categorization performance will vary with the number of stored exemplars similar to the test item. Independent-cue models are insensitive to such density effects. In a series of four experiments, Medin and Schaffer (1978) obtained clear support for the context model. Data from original learning transfer and speeded classification were in each case more in line with the context model than with a generalized independent-cue model. In addition, a mathematical version of the context model gave an excellent quantitative account of classification performance on transfer tests involving new and old instances.

Strategies.   One response to the preceding results is to question their generality, particularly with respect to the issue of strategies. One could argue that there was something about the Medin and Schaffer (1978) items, or some detail of the experimental situation, that discouraged people from developing the type of category representation appropriate to independent-cue theories, like a prototype model. If people had been instructed, say, to form a prototype, the results might well have been different.

In a second series of experiments (Medin & Smith, 1981) we attempted to induce strategy variations by means of instructions. The task involved two fuzzy categories; that is, no individual cue was perfectly valid and associated with members of one category but not the other. In one condition people were asked to use a rule-plus-exception strategy; in a second people were asked to learn the central tendency, or prototypes, of the categories; in the third people were given no special instructions. Our aim was to see if the model could handle learning and transfer data from these three distinct conditions solely in terms of differences in the similarity parameters associated with the attributes.

The basic design of the experiments is shown in Table 12.4. The items were Brunswik faces varying in eye height (EH), eye separation (ES), nose length (NL), and mouth height (MH). There were two possible values for each attribute, which are represented in the table in terms of a binary notation. For example, the value 1 on the attribute of nose length might correspond to a long nose, the value 0 to a short nose. Categories A and B differ with respect to what is generally true; that is, on each attribute Category A exemplars tend to have the value 1 and Category B exemplars the value 0, although there is at least one exception for each attribute in each category.

A good guidepost for distinguishing the context model from independent-cue models is the comparison of Face 4 and Face 7 (see Table 12.4). Because the central tendency, or modal prototype, for Category A is 1111, Face 4 must be at least as close to the prototype as Face 7 regardless of how the attributes are weighted. Thus all independent-cue models predict that Face 4 will be easier to

TABLE 12.4
Attribute Structure of Categories used in the
Medin and Smith Experiment 5

Face no.	Attribute Value			
	EH	ES	NL	MH
	Training items A exemplars			
4	1	1	1	0
7	1	0	1	0
15	1	0	1	1
13	1	1	0	1
5	0	1	1	1
	B exemplars			
12	1	1	0	0
2	0	1	1	0
14	0	0	0	1
10	0	0	0	0
	New transfer items			
1	1	0	0	1
3	1	0	0	0
6	1	1	1	1
8	0	0	1	0
9	0	1	0	1
11	0	0	1	1
16	0	1	0	0

Note: EH = eye height; ES = eye separation; NL = nose length; MH = mouth height. See the text for explanation of binary notation.

learn and more accurately classified than Face 7 because, for the only dimension where the two differ, Face 4 has the typical or characteristic value and Face 7 the atypical value. In contrast, the context model predicts Face 7 should be easier because the number of highly similar patterns is the most important factor in performance. Although one would not want to assume all dimensions are equally salient, for convenience we call two faces highly similar if they differ in value along only one dimension. Face 7 is highly similar (differs on only one attribute) to two other faces in Category A (4 and 15) but is not highly similar to any face in Category B. Face 4, on the other hand, is highly similar to one face in Category A (7) and to two in Category 2 (2 and 12); it should be more difficult to classify.

The main results are easy to describe. The instructional variations produced large differences in the pattern of errors, reaction time, and transfer performance. There were strong interactions of instructional conditions with particular faces.

Yet certain relationships in the data held across all conditions, relationships that were accurately described by the context model. For example, in each condition Face 7 was easier to learn and more accurately classified than Face 4. Despite the variations in performance for each of the instructional conditions, performance was more in line with interactive-cue models than with models that assume that information is combined in an additive and independent manner.

Linear Separability.   What does prototype theory imply about the structure of categories? The main constraint is that categorizing on the basis of similarity to a prototype will work only if all members of a category are more similar to the prototype for their category than to the prototype for any contrasting category. If, by some quirk of fate, robins were mammals rather than birds, a prototype process would not work, because robins have many characteristic features of birds and few characteristic features of mammals.

One way of thinking about classifying stimuli on the basis of similarity to prototypes is that it involves a summing of evidence (e.g., characteristic features) against some criterion. The more typical a category member is, the more quickly this criterion would be exceeded. Therefore, it would not be surprising to find that people categorize robins as birds more rapidly than they categorize penguins as birds (see Mervis & Rosch, 1981, for a review). The key constraint is that the choice rule based on a summing of evidence (or, alternatively, similarity to prototype) accept members and exclude nonmembers of a category.

The formal term for the preceding constraint is that categories be *linearly separable* or separable by a linear discriminant function (Sebestyen, 1962). Linearly separable categories are categories that can be partitioned on the basis of weighted, additive combination of component information. For geometric forms differing in color, form, size, and position, the component information would be derived from the values a stimulus had on each of these four dimensions. If two categories are linearly separable, their members could be classified correctly on the basis of similarity to the respective prototypes.

To evaluate the importance of linear separability in human classification, we (Medin & Schwanenflugel, 1981) set up two categorization tasks similar in major respects, except that in one task the categories were linearly separable and in the other they were not. A clear implication of independent-cue models is that the task involving linearly separable categories should be easier to master than the task not conforming to this constraint; that is, the idea is to see if it is important that categories be separable by an additive combination of component information. The context model does not imply that this constraint is important. Instead, similarity of exemplars to each other is assumed to be the major factor controlling classification.

The first experiment compared linearly separable (LS) and nonlinearly separable (NLS) tasks using geometric forms as stimuli and holding constant all other variables thought to be important. No differences in task difficulty were found.

The second experiment held average between-category similarity constant and pitted linear separability against number of cases of high between-category similarity. The NLS classification task proved to be easier than the LS task both when instructions focused on individual stimuli and when they urged subjects to form category generalizations.

The third experiment introduced a number of modifications designed to more closely approximate natural categories. Photographs of faces were used and the number of potential category members was unlimited. In addition, variable irrelevant attributes were present and the relevant attributes were themselves abstractions (e.g., long hair). Again, linear separability was pitted against high similarity of individual face types. The NLS task led to fewer errors than the LS task, though the differences fell short of statistical reliability.

The fourth experiment also used photographs of faces and reduced the number of relevant dimensions from four to three. Although this change allowed perhaps the most straightforward summation rule (two out of three), the LS task was no easier than the NLS task.

Despite our varied attempts, we were unable to find any evidence that linear separability is a factor in classification learning.

Correlated Attributes.   One difference between independent-cue and interactive-cue theories is their sensitivity to correlated attributes. For example, a prototype based on central tendency has no way of representing the fact that small birds are more likely to sing than large birds.

We studied people's sensitivity to correlated attributes, or configural information, in a simulated medical problem-solving task (Medin, Altom, Edelson, & Freko, 1982). Subjects learned about a fictitious disease or diseases from hypothetical case studies of patients having the disease. The case studies included descriptions of symptoms that tended to be characteristic of the disease. Some symptoms were correlated with each other, whereas others were independent. After subjects studied the descriptions, they were presented with pairs of new cases and asked to judge which was more likely to have the disease based on what they had learned from the earlier case studies. A second medical diagnosis task involved case studies from two contrasting hypothetical diseases, and again some symptoms were correlated and others were not. Following an initial learning phase, subjects were required to diagnose new cases. Across four experiments, the principal question that was investigated concerned the extent to which subjects' diagnoses of new cases were sensitive to the correlations between symptoms.

The context model provides a process model that assumes that people are sensitive to the configural information provided by correlated attributes when they make classification judgments. Sensitivity to correlated attributes is an indirect result of memory retrieval processes. Because similarity of an item's attributes to those of the memory representations of the category exemplar are combined in a multiplicative fashion, cases that preserve a correlation between attributes should be more likely to retrieve exemplars represented in memory than cases that do not preserve the correlation.

The first experiment used two groups of subjects, one given training with cases that included a correlation between two symptoms and the other given training with cases in which the symptoms were all independent. During an initial training phase, subjects were presented with nine different case studies of the fictitious disease, burlosis. A given patient could have from one to four symptoms, and each symptom appeared in six of the nine patient descriptions.

The basic design of the learning cases for the correlated case study condition is depicted in Table 12.5. An abstract notation of 1's and 0's is used to represent presence or absence of each symptom, respectively. For example, the code 1100 would represent presence of the first two symptoms and absence of the last two symptoms. Two symptoms were perfectly correlated in that a given patient either had both symptoms or neither symptom. For example, in Table 12.5, discolored gums and nosebleeds were perfectly correlated symptoms. Assignment of symptoms to the correlation condition was counterbalanced across subjects.

Following the learning phase, subjects received a series of pairs of cases. In each pair, subjects were instructed to choose the case that was more likely to have burlosis. In general both independent- and interactive-cue models predict that the case with the greater number of symptoms will be chosen as the one more likely to have burlosis. However, models differ in their predictions on cases that do and do not preserve the correlation between symptoms. Suppose the test pits a patient with a symptom pattern 1101 against a patient with a pattern 0111. The

TABLE 12.5
Learning Cases Represented in Abstract Notation for the Correlated
Symptom Condition

| Case Study | Symptoms of Burlosis-Correlated Condition | | | |
	Swollen Eyelids	Splotches On Ears	Discolored Gums	Nosebleed
1. R.C.	1	1	1	1
2. R.M.	1	1	1	1
3. J.J.	0	1	0	0
4. L.F.	1	1	1	1
5. A.M.	1	0	1	1
6. J.S.	1	1	0	0
7. S.T.	0	1	1	1
8. S.E.	1	0	0	0
9. E.M.	0	0	1	1

context model predicts that subjects should judge that the latter patient (where the correlation is preserved) is more likely to have burlosis than the former patient. Independent-cue models could predict a difference if more weight were given to the third and fourth symptoms than to the first two symptoms. In practice, however, symptoms were counterbalanced, so that there is no a priori basis for expecting differential weighting. Even with differential weighting of the two correlated symptoms, other tests distinguish independent-cue models from the context model. For example, differential weighting would lead one to expect that a patient with a symptom pattern 1010 is more likely to have burlosis than a patient with a symptom pattern 1100. The context model leads to the opposite prediction.

The results were clear-cut. Subjects did not behave in accord with independent-cue models in that they consistently indicated that patient descriptions preserving the correlation between symptoms were more likely to have the disease than patient descriptions that did not preserve the correlation. The results cannot be explained by the suggestion that the correlated symptoms independently became salient, because the partial information test descriptions with different values (one present, one absent) on Symptoms 3 and 4, which had been correlated, were judged as less likely to have burlosis than descriptions with different values on Symptoms 1 and 2.

This pattern of results held across each of four experiments. For example, where tests pitted cases maintaining the correlation versus cases having more typical symptoms, subjects tended to choose the case that maintained the correlation.

Sensitivity to correlations may be a very beneficial property for organisms to have. As we have seen, processing components of compounds in an independent manner *precludes* correlational information. In like fashion there may be correlation among cues and contextual stimuli that have functional predictive value for organisms. This underlines the point that context should not be considered solely as a limitation in the information-processing life of organisms.

One benefit of categorization is that it allows one to go beyond the information given and draw useful inferences. Thus, for example, one can predict with virtual certainty that an animal identified as a bird, is small, is seen on a branch, and has the potential to fly, and with at least some confidence that it can sing. It may be that categories are organized to exploit correlations among properties or attributes and thereby to permit predictions and inferences from partial information to be maximized.

Summary.   Our experiments on human categorization converge on the conclusion that organisms encode information in an interactive rather than an independent manner. The success of the context model in addressing classification data can be traced directly to its multiplicative (interactive) similarity function.

SUMMARY AND FURTHER ISSUES

Context and Element/Compound Relationships

To briefly recapitulate the main theme of this chapter: The role of context is seen as central to the understanding of learning and memory processes. When context is given formal consideration rather than auxiliary status, it can be seen as associated with other key problems, such as the relationship between elements and compounds.

This chapter has described the application of one representation of context in learning, memory, and classification. The key idea is that a given stimulus component acts both as a cue and as context for other cues. Thus cue and context are interactive rather than independent. This assumption blurs the distinction between cue and context but allows the model to predict a number of phenomena that pose problems for models assuming independent conditioning of elements.

This has been a somewhat one sided and oversimplified presentation. Some problems and issues associated with cue and context as well as element/compound associations are considered next.

Further Issues

Belongingness.   Although our experiments suggest that people are sensitive to correlated attributes, that may be only part of the story. Within the category bird there is a correlation between type of feather and whether or not the feet are webbed. But this is not a raw correlation that just happens to emerge; that is, adjusting to an aquatic environment may bring out a number of adjustments (e.g., webbed feet, water repellant feathers) that would manifest themselves as correlated attributes. In our simulated medical problem-solving experiments, people not only noticed that certain symptoms were correlated, but they also offered numerous explanations as to *why*. They also seemed more likely to notice correlations that were "related" than those that were not. By "related" we mean that a participant offered some form of explanation linking particular symptoms. For example, if eye condition and blood pressure were correlated, a participant might claim particular job demands that would produce both effects.

Similarly, in conditioning and learning experiments one might imagine that some components are more readily associated than others. For example, a compound of red and triangle may be linked more tightly than a compound of a light and a tone. Rescorla and Durlach (1981) recently presented evidence that associations develop between elements of a compound (e.g., flavor plus smell), and that these associations can dramatically modify blocking and overshadowing effects. In addition, we have evidence that for a given category structure classification learning is increased by increasing the spatial proximity of components.

It is clear that various factors may alter intercomponent associations and independence. There is no reason to think that stimulus and context will not interact in a similar way. This is one issue that remains relatively unexplored.

Status of Time.   In the analysis of proactive interference, time was given no special status, being simply treated as an additional dimension along which similarity could be measured. This was a simplifying assumption that may be worth considering in greater detail. Currently we are trying to determine whether changes in time alter the similarity parameters associated with other stimulus dimensions. One possibility is that as forgetting proceeds (as a function of time), the similarity parameters for other dimensions tend to increase; the alternative possibility is that they remain constant. The Reynolds and Medin (1981) analysis assumed that other similarity parameters remained constant as time changed, but the reported experiments did not provide direct evidence on this issue.

The other main aspect of treating time as a dimension of similarity is that it raises a question about principles of association. The early British Associatiionists assumed that both temporal contiguity and similarity influenced the formation of associations. Later on, it was proposed that temporal contiguity was the main principle and that similarity was influential only to the extent that it confounded or was part of temporal contiguity. It is interesting to consider the reverse argument: It may be that similarity controls associative learning and that temporal contiguity is just a special (or not so special) case of temporal similarity. In other words, time is simply a continuous dimension along which events occurring closer together are more similar than events that are temporally distinct.

Units.   The treatment of elements, context, and compounds presented here implicitly assumes, at least to a first approximation, that one can specify the basic units of analysis. There are several ways in which this analysis may be a gross oversimplification.

It has been argued that when a stimulus is presented in some context, it acts as a retrieval cue to access information similar to the probe. Presumably this happens all the time and not just when it is convenient for our analysis (e.g., the retroactive interference studies). This means that one should represent the status of retrieved information not only during transfer tests but also during learning (see Honig, 1978, for further relevant arguments).

A second problem is that we have pretty much ignored sequential and overlapping events. For many purposes it may prove useful to treat a light and tone having simultaneous onset and offset as a single compound, but what about the cases when their on and off times only overlap partially? One might also expect that sometimes sequential events become integrated to form a single, higher order unit (see Estes, 1976, for one application).

Finally, it is possible that the proper units of analysis change as a function of the organism's preceding experiences. This has long been a question of interest in studies of child development (e.g., Shepp, 1978), but this possibility has not received much attention in either animal or adult human learning and memory literature.

Final Comment

The reader could readily add to the preceding list of issues. The collection of chapters in this volume represents some of the first attempts to give context central status in analyses of learning and memory. Although the final status of context is far from obvious, it is clear that context is not a set of props for the play—it is an integral part of the drama.

REFERENCES

Atkinson, R. C., & Estes, W. K. Stimulus sampling theory. In R. D. Luce, R. R. Bush, & E. Galanter (Eds.), *Handbook of mathematical psychology*. New York: Wiley, 1963.

Birch, D. B., & Israel, M. Solution of the transverse patterning problem: Response to cue–cue relations. *Psychonomic Science*, 1971, *23*, 383–384.

Campione, J. E. Intra and extradimensional shifts in retardates as a function of dimensional preference. *American Journal of Psychology*, 1969, *82*, 212–220.

Campione, J. C., McGrath, M., & Rabinowitz, F. M. Component and configurational learning in children: Additional data. *Journal of Experimental Psychology*, 1971, *88*, 137–139.

Estes, W. K. An associative basis for coding and organization in memory. In A. W. Melton & E. Martin (Eds.) *Coding processes in human memory*. Washington, D.C.: Winston, 1972.

Estes, W. K. Memory and conditioning. In F. J. McGuigan & D. B. Lumsden (Eds.), *Contemporary approaches to conditioning and learning*. New York: Wiley, 1973.

Estes, W. K. Structural aspects of associative models for memory. In C. N. Cofer (Ed.), *The structure of human memory*. New York: W. H. Freeman, 1976.

Estes, W. K., & Hopkins, B. L. Acquisition and transfer in pattern vs. component discrimination learning. *Journal of Experimental Psychology*, 1961, *61*, 322–328.

Fisher, M. A., & Zeaman, D. An attention-retention theory of retardate discrimination learning. In N. R. Ellis (Ed.), *International review of research in mental retardation* (Vol. 6). New York: Academic Press, 1972.

Flagg, S. F. Learning of the insoluble conditional reaction problem by rhesus monkeys. *Animal Learning and Behavior*, 1974, *2*, 181–184.

Flagg, S. F. & Medin, D. L. Constant irrelevant cues and stimulus generalization in monkeys. *Journal of Comparative and Physiological Psychology*, 1973, *85*, 339–345.

Franks, J. J., & Bransford, J. D. Abstraction of visual patterns. *Journal of Experimental Psychology*, 1971, *90*, 65–74.

French, G. M. Associative problems. In A. M. Schrier, H. F. Harlow, & F. Stollnitz (Eds.), *Behavior of nonhuman primates* (Vol. 1). New York: Academic Press, 1965.

Honig, W. K. Studies of working memory in the pigeon. In S. H. Hulse, H. Fowler, & W. K. Honig (Eds.), *Cognitive processes in animal behavior*. Hillsdale, N.J.: Lawrence Erlbaum Associates, 1978.

Hull, C. L. *Principles of behavior*. New York: Appleton–Century–Crofts, 1943.

Katz, J. J., & Postal, P. M. *An integrated theory of linguistic descriptions*. Cambridge, Mass.: MIT Press, 1964.

Liu, S. W., & Zeiler, M. D. Independence of concurrent discriminations. *Journal of Comparative and Physiological Psychology*, 1968, *65*, 61–65.

Mackintosh, N. J., & Little, L. Intradimensional and extradimensional shift learning by pigeons. *Psychonomic Science*, 1969, *14*, 5–6.

Medin, D. L. A theory of context in discrimination learning. In G. H. Bower (Ed.), *The psychology of learning and motivation* (Vol. 9). New York: Academic Press, 1975.

Medin, D. L., Altom, M. W., Edelson, S. M., & Freko, D. Correlated symptoms and simulated medical classification. *Journal of Experimental Psychology: Learning, Memory, and Cognition*, 1982, *8*, 37–50.

Medin, D. L., Reynolds, T. J., & Parkinson, J. K. Stimulus similarity and retroactive interference and facilitation in monkey short-term memory. *Journal of Experimental Psychology: Animal Behavior Processes*, 1980, *6*(2), 112–125.

Medin, D. L., & Schaffer, M. M. Context theory of classification learning. *Psychological Review*, 1978, *85*, 207–238.

Medin, D. L., & Schwanenflugel, P. J. Linear separability in classification learning. *Journal of Experimental Psychology: Human Learning and Memory*, 1981, *7*, 355–368.

Medin, D. L., & Smith, E. E. Strategies and classification learning. *Journal of Experimental Psychology: Human Learning and Memory*, 1981, *7*, 241–253.

Mervis, C. B., & Rosch, E. Categorization of natural objects. In M. R. Rosenzweig & L. W. Porter (Eds.), *Annual Review of Psychology*, 1981, *32*, 89–115.

Mill, J. *Analysis of the Phenomena of the Human Mind*. London: Longmans, Green, Reoder, and Dyer, 1869 (Originally published 1829).

Mill, J. S. *On the Logic of the Moral Sciences*. New York: Bobbs-Merrill, 1965 (Originally published 1843).

Mumma, R., & Warren, J. M. Two-cue discrimination learning by cats. *Journal of Comparative and Physiological Psychology*, 1968, *66*, 116–122.

Osgood, C. E. *Method and theory in experimental psychology*. London and New York: Oxford University Press, 1953.

Peterson, G. B., Wheeler, R. L., & Trapold, M. Enhancement of pigeons' conditional discrimination performance by expectancies of reinforcement and nonreinforcement. *Animal Learning and Behavior*, 1980, *8*, 22–30.

Posner, M. I., & Keele, S. W. On the genesis of abstract ideas. *Journal of Experimental Psychology*, 1968, *77*, 353–363.

Reed, S. K. Pattern recognition and categorization. *Cognitive Psychology*, 1972, *3*, 382–407.

Rescorla, R. A., & Durlach, P. J. Within-event learning in Pavlovian conditioning. In N. E. Spear & R. R. Miller (Eds.), *Information processing in animals: Memory mechanisms*. Hillsdale, N.J.: Lawrence Erlbaum Associates, 1981.

Reynolds, T. J., & Medin, D. L. Stimulus interaction and between-trials proactive interference in monkeys. *Journal of Experimental Psychology: Animal Behavior Processes*, 1981, *7*, 334–347.

Roberts, W. A., & Grant, D. S. An analysis of light-induced retroactive inhibition in pigeon short-term memory. *Journal of Experimental Psychology: Animal Behavior Processes*, 1978, *4*, 219–236.

Rosch, E., & Mervis, C. B. Family resemblances: Studies in the internal structure of categories. *Cognitive Psychology*, 1975, *7*, 573–605.

Sebestyen, G. S. *Decision-making processes in pattern recognition*. New York: Macmillan, 1962.

Shepp, B. E. Some cue properties of anticipated rewards in discrimination learning of retardates. *Journal of Comparative and Physiological Psychology*, 1962, *59*, 856–856.

Shepp, B. E. Some cue properties of rewards in simultaneous object discriminations of retardates. *Child Development*, 1964, *35*, 587–592.

Shepp, B. E. From perceived similarity to dimensional structure: A new hypothesis about perceptual development. In E. Rosch & B. B. Lloyd (Eds.), *Cognition and categorization*. Hillsdale, N.J.: Lawrence Erlbaum Associates, 1978.

Spence, K. W. The nature of discrimination learning in animals. *Psychological Review*, 1936, *43*, 427–449.

Spiker, C. C. An extension of Hull–Spence discrimination learning theory. *Psychological Review*, 1970, *77*, 496–515.

Sutherland, N. S., & Mackintosh, N. J. *Mechanisms of animal discrimination learning*. New York: Academic Press, 1971.

White, B. N., & Spiker, C. C. The effect of stimulus similarity on amount of cue-position patterning in discrimination problems. *Journal of Experimental Psychology*, 1960, *59*, 141–136.

Wickens, D. D. *The dual meaning of context in both human and animal research*. Unpublished manuscript, 1982.

Wyrwicka, W. Studies of motor conditioned reflexes. VI. On the effect of experimental situation upon the course of motor conditioned reflexes. *Acta Biologiae Experimentalis*, 1956, *17*, 189–203.

13

Contextual Stimulus Effects of Drugs and Internal States

Donald A. Overton
Departments of Psychiatry and Psychology
Temple University

> Dr. Abel informed me of an Irish porter to a warehouse, who forgot, when sober, what he had done when drunk; but being drunk, again recollected the transactions of his former state of intoxication. On one occasion, being drunk, he had lost a parcel of some value, and in his sober moments could give no account of it. Next time he was intoxicated, he recollected that he had left the parcel at a certain house, and there being no address on it, it had remained there safely, and was got on his calling for it (Combe, 1835, p. 389).

Thus Combe described a phenomenon now called state dependent learning (SDL), which is produced by several centrally acting drugs as well as by certain nonpharmacological manipulations. Although the mechanism responsible for SDL is not definitely known, it is quite likely that the SDL effects of drugs are mediated by drug-induced sensory events. The exact nature of these drug-induced stimuli is unknown. Some may result from drug-induced changes in visual, auditory, or gustatory sensory input. More commonly, they are assumed to be interoceptive (internal) and to result from changes in arousal, drive states, affects, etc. In any case, changes in internal state can produce impairments in memory retrieval similar to those produced by changes in exteroceptive sensory context, and the SDL phenomenon can be viewed as an instance of contextual stimulus control. This chapter reviews the major phenomena observed in SDL experiments, interpreting them as properties of contextual control.

357

EXPERIMENTAL DESIGNS USED TO STUDY SDL

Symmetrical SDL

Drug-induced SDL is commonly investigated by use of the 2 × 2 experimental design shown in Table 13.1A. Four groups of rats are trained and subsequently tested for retention of the learned response. Sessions are conducted either while the animals are drugged (D), or while they are in the no-drug (N) condition. If symmetrical SDL occurs, control level performance (C) is observed during testing in the N−−>N and D−−>D groups, whereas impaired performance (-) is observed in the N−−>D and D−−>N groups during testing. It is considered that the imposition or removal of a drug state in the N−−>D and D−−>N groups, respectively, produces a significant change in the contextual stimulus

TABLE 13.1
Experimental Designs Used to Study State Dependent Learning and
Drug Discriminations

A. The 2 × 2 SDL Design

Group #	Drug condition during training	Drug condition during testing	Performance during testing
1	N	N	C
2	N	D	—
3	D	N	—
4	D	D	C

B. The Two-Response SDL Design

Group #	Drug condition and correct response during first training session	Drug condition and correct response during second training session	Drug conditions and expected response during test sessions		
			Test 1	Test 2	Test 3
1	N-R1	D-R2	N-R1	D-R2	N-R1
2	D-R1	N-R2	D-R1	N-R2	D-R1
3	N-R2	D-R1	N-R2	D-R1	N-R2
4	D-R2	N-R1	D-R2	N-R1	D-R2

C. Two-Response Drug Versus No Drug Discrimination Training

Day	Drug condition and reinforced response in Group 1	Drug condition and reinforced response in Group 2
1	N-R1	N-R2
2	D-R2	D-R1
3	N-R1	N-R2
4	D-R2	D-R1
etc.		

environment of the animals, and that this accounts for the poor test session performance observed in these two groups. Note that the rate, frequency, or vigor of responding is taken as an index of the efficiency of memory retrieval in this paradigm, as in other paradigms in this volume (Bouton & Bolles, Medin & Reynolds, Miller & Schachtman). Because drugs can directly influence rate or vigor of responding via a number of mechanisms other than SDL, the results obtained in 2 × 2 experiments are often difficult to interpret (Deutsch & Roll, 1973; Overton, 1974; Swanson & Kinsbourne, 1978, 1979). Despite this difficulty, the 2 × 2 design has been used in the majority of published SDL studies.

The so-called two-response design, occasionally used in SDL studies, is diagrammed in Table 13.1B. This design requires the use of a behavioral task in which two different behavioral responses (R1 and R2) are possible. Ideally, the rate at which these two responses are performed should be equally influenced by drug effects such as muscular weakness and impairment of memorization, and symmetrical tasks such as a T-maze or an operant compartment containing two levers meet this requirement. Group 1 in Table 13.1B illustrates the design. These animals first learn to perform R1 while undrugged. Then they learn to perform R2 while drugged. Subsequently they are tested while undrugged and while drugged. If SDL occurs, R1 will occur during N test sessions and R2 will occur during D test sessions. A complete experimental design can include 2, 4, or even more groups, depending on how carefully one wishes to balance the assignment of drug conditions to responses, and the order of occurrence of drug conditions. The two-response design appears to have advantages for the study of SDL, because behaviorally depressant drug effects may block the occurrence of either or both responses but will not systematically predispose the animal to make the "other" response (Overton, 1974, 1982b). Nonetheless, this design has been used in only a few reported SDL studies.

Drug Discriminations

Drugs are also used to control responding in drug discrimination (DD) paradigms. Table 13.1C diagrams a typical D versus N discrimination training procedure carried out in an apparatus in which two responses (R1 and R2) are possible (e.g., an operant training compartment with two levers). During sessions 1, 3, 5, responses on lever 1 are reinforced and responses on lever 2 have no programmed consequence (i.e., are extinguished). During sessions 2, 4, 6, responses on lever 2 are reinforced and responses on lever 1 are extinguished. The drug is, therefore, a contextual cue, present throughout the session, that is correlated with the reinforced response choice across days. The accuracy with which the animal selects the reinforced response on the basis of the imposed drug state is determined by noting the response performed at the beginning of each training session (before reinforcement has been delivered). With most centrally acting drugs, differential responding occurs after 10 to 60 sessions of discrimination training. The asymptotic accuracy of response selection after prolonged training varies depending on the behavioral task, drug, and dosage that is utilized. In ''good'' drug discrimination tasks, accuracies exceeding 90% can often be obtained (Colpaert & Rosecrans, 1978; Ho, Richards, & Chute, 1978; Lal, 1977).

Many variants of this training procedure are possible. Animals may be trained to discriminate between two different drugs (D1 vs. D2), or to discriminate two different dosages of a single drug (high dose vs. low dose). In compartments allowing a single behavioral response, subjects may learn go/no-go discriminations or may experience a different schedule of reinforcement in each drug condition (e.g., DRL vs. FR10). Three or more different drug conditions (e.g., D1 vs. D2 vs. D3) may be employed in compartments allowing three or more responses (R1 vs. R2 vs. R3).

After DD training is completed (i.e., after asymptotic accuracy has been achieved), subjects are often subjected to ''substitution tests'' prior to which novel drugs are injected. A substitution test may last only a few seconds, during which responses on either lever are reinforced. The imposed drug condition may either be a novel dose of the same drug used during training, or a different drug not previously experienced by the subject. During such tests, subjects may fail to respond, respond exclusively on lever 1, respond exclusively on lever 2, or exhibit mixed responding on both levers. In recent years, the results obtained during substitution tests have been increasingly viewed by pharmacologists as providing useful information about the pharmacologically significant actions of drugs (Colpaert & Slangen, 1982).

For a variety of reasons, many more DD than SDL studies have been published. Also, the DD procedure gives more stable and reliable results than does the 2×2 SDL design. Hence, most knowledge presently available regarding the parametric properties of drug stimuli has been obtained in DD rather than in SDL studies. For this reason, throughout this chapter we refer frequently to data obtained in DD studies in order to elucidate the nature of the stimulus properties of drugs and their ability to function as contextual cues.

PROPERTIES OF CONTEXTUAL CONTROL BY DRUG STATES

Relative Strength of Contextual Control by Drugs and by Stimuli

SDL can be, under certain conditions, a very strong effect causing an apparently complete amnesia for responses learned under drug conditions different than those present during testing (Bliss, Sledjeski, & Leiman, 1971; Overton, 1964; Sachs, Weingarten, & Klein, 1966). However SDL is more frequently either a weak effect, or unmeasurably small (i.e., obscured by noise or by other drug effects, Eich, 1980; Overton, 1968a 1971). If one considers the entire literature of reported studies using designs in which SDL might reasonably be observed, it appears as a significant effect in less than half of these reports. The strength of SDL effects is markedly dependent on the drug and dosage employed (Mayse & DeVietti, 1971; Overton, 1982a). Hence an explicit comparison of the degree of impairment of memory retrieval produced by changes in drug state and by changes in sensory context is almost impossible. A few studies have attempted this comparison and, depending on the parameters employed, have observed that response control by drug stimuli was either stronger than or weaker than response control by sensory stimuli (Balster, 1970; Kilbey, Harris, & Aigner, 1971; Overton, 1968b, 1971; Spear, Smith, Bryan, Gordon, Timmons, & Chiszar, 1980). In general it appears that the strength of drug SDL effects can be considered comparable to that of the effects of contextual stimuli on memory retrieval.

Comparison of Thresholds for SDL and for DDs

Suppose that one starts with a task, drug, and dosage, with which both SDL and DDs can be obtained. If SDL and DD experiments are iteratively repeated using increasingly reduced dosages, the SDL effects will disappear first. Then, at lower doses, discriminative control will also be lost. Although only a few explicit comparisons of the threshold dose adequate to produce SDL and DDs have been reported (Overton, 1979, 1982b; Zenick & Goldsmith, 1981), the total literature on these phenomena clearly support the generalization just stated. SDL is only produced by some drugs at the highest doses compatible with sustained behavioral responding. In contrast, DDs can be maintained by intermediate doses of the same drugs and by a variety of other drugs that are unable to produce measurable SDL effects at any usable dose. The difference in threshold dosage for SDL and DDs strongly supports a sensory interpretation of SDL and DDs, because such a result is discordant with the predictions of most neurological models for SDL (see later) but compatible with sensory mediation models.

Effect of Overtraining on SDL

Overtraining abolishes SDL retrieval deficits. In other words, a well-learned response will generalize successfully across changes in drug state that will disrupt performance of a response that is not overtrained. Most studies demonstrating this effect have varied the amount of training carried out before a state change occurred (Eich & Birnbaum, 1982; Iwahara & Noguchi, 1972, 1974; Modrow, Salm, & Bliss, 1982). Additionally, it has been shown that if two responses of unequal difficulty are learned by an animal before a state change occurs, the easier (long since learned) response will generalize, whereas the more difficult (recently mastered) response will fail to generalize across the change in drug state (Bliss, 1973). In the entire literature reporting SDL effects, all positive findings involve recently mastered responses; there are no reports in which well-established, overly trained habits failed to generalize across a change in drug state.

Interactions between Exteroceptive Contextual Change and Drug State Change

If a change in drug state and a change in sensory context occur simultaneously, both changes will affect retrieval; it is unclear whether the effects of these two manipulations simply summate, or whether some more complex interaction occurs. In an animal preparation, Duncan (1979) found that the SDL effects of ethanol were insignificant if retrieval testing occurred in the same compartment where the animals had been trained, but were obvious if the animals were tested in a different compartment. In this study, the change in contextual cues apparently acted to unmask an SDL effect that was too weak to be seen in animals tested without a concurrent environmental contextual change (also see Connelly, Connelly, & Epps, 1973; Connelly, Connelly, & Nevitt, 1977; Connelly, Connelly, & Phifer, 1975). In human subjects, a number of studies have shown that "category cues" could abolish SDL. In these experiments, subjects learned a list of words (red, green, daffodil, chrysanthemum). If a simple test for retrieval was performed after a drug state change, SDL effects were observed. However if category cues were provided at the time of retrieval ("Name the flowers that you recall"), SDL did not occur. One can argue that this was an artefact caused by a "ceiling effect," with the category cues sufficiently improving retrieval so that residual differences caused by SDL effects were insignificantly small. However the actual data from some of these experiments does not suggest that such a ceiling was present; even with category cues available, retrieval was still relatively poor. Hence it may be that category cues truly do abolish SDL (Eich, 1977, 1980; Eich & Birnbaum, 1982; Petersen, 1977).

The interactions between changes in sensory contextual cues and drug-induced SDL, as well as the abolishment of SDL by overtraining, serve to emphasize the general conclusion that drug-induced SDL is usually a relatively weak effect, notwithstanding a few reports in which it appears very robust (Bliss et al., 1971; Overton, 1964).

Effect of Prior Exposure to Drug

In several conditioning paradigms, prior exposure to the conditioned or discriminative stimulus has been observed to impede the subsequent acquisition of conditioning or discriminative control, presumably by habituating the animal to the to-be-conditioned stimulus. However, this effect has not been observed in connection with drug stimuli. Investigators have exposed animals to drugs on several occasions before commencing D versus N training. Such prior exposure to drug has neither facilitated nor impaired the subsequent acquisition of DDs (Hinderliter, 1978; Jarbe & Henriksson, 1973; Jarbe & Holmgren, 1977; Kilbey et al., 1971; McKim, 1976; Overton, 1972). One could also inquire whether prior exposure to drug would reduce or enhance the strength of SDL effects in 2 × 2 experiments; such studies have not been reported.

Learning Set Phenomena in DD and SDL Experiments

In a T-maze DD task, Overton (1971) demonstrated that light versus dark discriminations could be more rapidly learned if rats had previously mastered an ethanol versus N discrimination in the same task. This suggests that a learning set established by DD training can facilitate subsequent acquisition of sensory discriminations.

Bliss (1974) required monkeys to learn a series of visual discriminations while drugged. Each individual discrimination failed to generalize out of the drug state, but after several had been learned the resulting learning set did generalize to the no-drug condition. This result is somewhat counterintuitive, because it is usually argued that simple types of learning should generalize more easily across changes in drug state than would be the case for complex tasks. However Bliss' data suggest the opposite—the learning set generalized even though the individual component discriminations failed to generalize. Modrow et al. (1982) have obtained similar results. Further studies on the interactions between changes in drug state and learning set phenomena might be profitable.

Symmetrical Versus Asymmetrical SDL

Thus far in this chpater we have considered only symmetrical SDL effects, instances in which D− −>N and N− −>D state changes produce equally large impairments in the retrieval of a learned response. However in many experiments impaired retrieval is observed only after D− −>N state changes and not after N− −>D state changes (Barnhart & Abbott, 1967; Berger & Stein, 1969a, b; Eich et al., 1975; Holloway, 1972). In other studies, retrieval deficits are observed after both D− −>N and N− −>D state changes but are larger after D− −>N transitions. The term *asymmetrical SDL* has been used to describe such results in which retrieval deficits were observed, primarily in the D− −>N group (Overton, 1968a).

Because of our theoretical presuppositions about SDL, asymmetrical SDL has been a neglected phenomenon. The original stimulus models for SDL predicted symmetrical SDL, and most subsequently elaborated hypothetical mechanisms for SDL have also been developed to explain symmetrical SDL (Overton, 1973, 1978b). Even the statistical methods most commonly used to test for the occurrence of SDL pool results in the D− −>N and N− −>D groups and do not identify whether both N− −>D and D− −>N transitions have produced re-trieval deficits. However, it appears that both symmetrical and asymmetrical SDL do exist as bona fide phenomena. In the majority of reported SDL studies some degree of asymmetry is present, and in a substantial percentage of SDL reports impairment if retrieval is entirely lacking in the N− −>D group. Data from DD studies do not elucidate this issue; apparently the training procedures used in DD studies always produce symmetrical generalization gradients irre-spective of whether symmetrical gradients may have existed prior to discrimina-tion training. We return later to a consideration of the theoretical formulations used to explain SDL, and the predictions of various formulations as regards symmetrical versus nonsymmetrical SDL.

Width of Generalization Gradients—Quantitative Specificity

In DD experiments, rather broad generalization gradients are obtained along the intensity (dosage) continuum. After D versus N training using a particular drug and dosage, substitution tests may be conducted with various doses of the train-ing drug. Usually the drug response generalizes to doses significantly higher and lower than the training dose, with an appreciable percentage of drug responses occurring with doses down to about 30% of the training dose (Colpaert & Slangen, 1982; Overton, 1966). In a few instances, sharp gradients have been obtained, and the particular factors that caused such steep gradients have not been determined. In the very few 2 × 2 SDL studies where dosage has been parametrically varied, a similar pattern of results has been observed (Holmgren, 1964). To some degree this result may be artifactual, because the actual levels of drug in the brain vary somewhat during the training session(s) as the result of drug excretion, redistribution in body tissues, etc. However even if this source of artefact were controlled, which has not been done in any published studies, it appears likely that rather broad dosage generalization gradients would be obtained.

Width of Generalization Gradients—Qualitative Specificity

After D versus N DD training with a particular drug and dose, tests may be conducted using drugs that differ pharmacologically from the training drug. Such tests reveal very sharp generalization gradients. Typically the drug state response will not occur during tests with any novel drugs except those that produce pharmacological effects similar to those of the training drug. The effect is quite striking, and the results are analogous to those that one might expect if animals were trained using a visual discriminative stimulus and were then tested with the visual stimulus absent and auditory stimuli substituted for it. This type of experiment has been repeated over and over using a different training drug in each successive group of animals; sharp generalization gradients have been obtained irrespective of the training drug employed (Overton, 1971, 1972, 1978a). The trained animals are said to exhibit high qualitative specificity and can be used as an assay to detect the presence or absence of the actions of the training drug and of its close pharmacological relatives. Indeed, the high qualitative specificity produced by D versus N training is the primary property that has made DD training a useful psychopharmacological assay procedure (Barry, 1974; Colpaert & Slangen, 1982; Lal, 1977). Because a high degree of qualitative specificity has been observed in a variety of DD training paradigms, it appears to reflect some intrinsic property of drug-induced stimuli rather than a characteristic induced by the particular training paradigm employed. Only a few 2 × 2 SDL studies have examined the consequences of testing with drugs different than the training drug; these reports suggest that a high degree of qualitative specificity can be observed in 2 × 2 SDL studies as well as in DD paradigms (Sachs et al., 1966).

Masking Apparently Does Not Occur

The term *masking* is used here to convey the same meaning that it denotes in sensory psychophysics: A situation in which one stimulus prevents the perception of a second concurrently presented stimulus. After D versus N DD training, rats frequently have been tested while simultaneously drugged with the training drug and with another drug; such tests have usually been performed to identify antagonists of the training drug. In most data thus far reported, the only occasions when a second drug prevents the rat from detecting the presence of the training drug (and performing the drug response) are those in which the second drug pharmacologically antagonizes or blocks the effects of the training drug so that its discriminable effects are not present (Browne, 1981; Browne & Ho, 1975; Browne & Weissman, 1981; Hernandez, Holohean, & Appel, 1978; Hirschhorn & Rosecrans, 1974a, b; Jarbe, 1977; Jarbe & Ohlin, 1977; Romano, Goldstein, & Jewell, 1981; Rosecrans, 1979; Shearman & Lal, 1981; Silverman & Ho, 1980). Thus the results of these experiments suggest that masking seldom if ever occurs.

However, the conclusion that masking does not occur between drug stimuli must be regarded as only tentatively established, because experimental designs can be envisaged that might be considerably more sensitive to masking than are any of the "accidental" tests for its occurrence presently in the literature. Apparently, masking will be most likely if a rapidly discriminated drug (with strong sensory effects) is used to mask a training drug with weak, slowly discriminated effects. Additionally, if the sensory literature is a useful guide, it may be that drugs producing "similar" sensory effects (effects in the same "modality"?) will mask one another more effectively than do drugs that produce markedly dissimilar effects. Tests using such combinations of drugs have not been performed. Additionally, there are a few reported data in which masking may have occurred (Browne, 1981; Browne & Weissman, 1981). Possibly these reports include instances of masking, and if so they constitute a first step toward enumerating the conditions under which masking will in fact occur. Notwithstanding these occasional instances of possible masking, it appears that most drugs do not mask the effects of most other drugs in DD preparations (Overton, 1984), and this is an interesting property of drug stimuli congruent with the idea that pharmacologically dissimilar drugs can be regarded as producing stimuli in a variety of nonoverlapping "modalities." There are no data available regarding the question of whether drugs will mask one another's SDL effects.

Interchangeability of Drug-induced and Other Interoceptive Stimuli

If drugs truly achieve contextual and discriminative control via the mechanism of drug-induced stimuli, it may be possible through appropriate manipulations of the internal or external milieu to duplicate the stimulus conditions produced by drugs. Successful identification of interoceptive or exteroceptive manipulations that could mimic the sensory effects of drugs would be extremely important for two reasons. First, such results would identify the specific sensory actions responsible for SDL and DDs, at least for the specific drug in question, thus providing a more rational basis than presently is available for evaluating the results of DD experiments conducted with that drug. More importantly, successful identification of sensory mediators for SDL and DDs would establish the general principle that such effects can be mediated by sensory drug effects—a principle presently supported only by indirect evidence.

There are at least three different general types of sensory effects that drugs apparently can produce, any or all of which might be responsible for SDL and DDs: (1) Some drugs directly induce changes in peripheral organs, and these changes produce altered sensory input returning to the brain via the classical afferent pathways. For example, antimuscarinics reduce the flow of saliva and produce sensations of "dry mouth." Sedative drugs such as ethanol produce ataxia and the associated altered proprioceptive feedback. (2) Other drugs may modify the processing and perception of interoceptive or exteroceptive stimuli. Blurred or double vision is one example of such a drug-induced modification in sensory processing. Analgesia produced by narcotics provides a second example. (3) Finally, some drugs may directly induce central "sensory" effects by altering the organism's emotions, drive states, or arousal level. It is clear that drugs do produce such effects; there is some question as to whether these actions should be regarded as "sensory."

The first type of hypothesis—that drugs produce changes in peripheral organs that cause altered sensory feedback responsible for SDL and DDs—has been tested on several occasions with negative results. For example, antimuscarinic drugs produce SDL and DDs and cause altered functioning in a variety of organs enervated by the autonomic nervous system. Tertiary antimuscarinic drugs act at both central and peripheral sites, whereas quaternary antimuscarinics cross the blood-brain barrier less easily and thus act only at peripheral sites. After D versus N DD training with scopolamine hydrobromide (which produces both central and peripheral actions), animals fail to generalize the D response to quaternary scopolamine compounds that produce only peripheral actions. Hence it appears that the peripheral actions of scopolamine are not responsible for its discriminable and SDL actions (Overton, 1977). Similarly, after D versus N DD training with pentobarbital, the D response fails to appear during tests with gallamine, a curare-type drug that produces muscular weakness and uncoordination vaguely reminiscent of the ataxic actions of pentobarbital (Overton, 1964). Other tests of this type have also been reported, with negative results (Downey, 1975; Hazell, Peterson, & Laverty, 1978). In general, it has been found that drugs that act only on peripheral organs do not produce SDL and are discriminated only with difficulty, whereas centrally acting drugs are more likely to produce SDL and are more readily discriminated (Miksic, Shearman, & Lal, 1980; Overton, 1971). This has discouraged further attempts to identify specific peripheral sites where SDL and DDs might be mediated.

The possibility that drug-induced alterations in sensory processing might mediate SDL and DDs has also been tested. For example, Overton (1968b) hypothesized that blurred vision might mediate the discriminable effects of pentobarbital. To test this possibility, he first blinded rats and then required them to learn a D versus N discrimination in a T-maze. This discrimination was learned as rapidly by blind as by sighted rats, indicating that drug-induced alterations in visual stimuli were not a prerequisite for the establishment of the discrimination. In another experiment, sighted rats were required to discriminate pentobarbital versus N; these rats were then blinded, and training was continued. Only a transient disruption in discriminative control was noted at the time of blinding, suggesting that even in sighted rats alterations in visual perception do not mediate discriminative control. In a similar vein, Overton bypothesized that pentobarbital versus N discriminations in a shock-escape T-maze task might be mediated by drug-induced analgesia, or at least by a drug-induced insensitivity to some of the consequences of electric shock. However two pieces of evidence contradicted this hypothesis. First, after D versus N training with high shock levels, undrugged rats could not be induced to make D choices by the application of low (less painful) shock intensities (Overton, 1968b). Secondly, after D versus N training with pentobarbital, the D response did not occur during tests with morphine or other narcotic analgesics. We should note that all data relevant to the first two types of hypotheses regarding the sensory mediation of drug action have been obtained in DD experiments; 2×2 SDL designs have not been used.

The third type of hypothesis regarding possible sensory mediation of SDL and DDs essentially asserts that altered states of the central nervous system can have contextual and discriminative effects analogous to those of drugs. Two questions follow: First, which altered CNS states, if any, produce contextual and/or discriminative effects?; second, do any of the altered CNS states that can be induced by nonpharmacological manipulations produce sensory effects equivalent to those induced by drugs? Regarding the first question, electroconvulsive shock (ECS) produces SDL, and ECS versus no ECS discriminations are robust (McIntyre & Reichert, 1971; Overton, Ercole, & Dutta, 1976). Alterations in hunger or thirst are discriminable and produce SDL (Bolles, 1958; Peck & Ader, 1974). Electrical brain stimulation is discriminable (Colpaert, 1977). REM-sleep deprivation can produce SDL (Joy & Prinz, 1969), and learning that occurs during REM sleep is state dependent (Evans, 1972). All these studies, discussed in more detail later, show that alterations in CNS activity can be discriminated and/or produce SDL. With regard to the second issue, there is only one study (never fully reported) that we can cite. Huang (1973) trained rats to press one lever after normal sleep and the second lever after REM-deprivation. This discrimination was learned, and subsequent tests showed that amphetamine would cause some REM-deprivation responses in rats that had slept normally. Conversely, pentobarbital would cause some responses on the normal-sleep lever in REM-deprived rats. Although the drugs did not completely antagonize (or mimic) the sleep manipulations, these results suggest that the ''sensory'' effects of REM deprivation and normal sleep were to some degree overlapped by the ''sensory'' effects of pentobarbital and/or amphetamine. Presumably both the REM-deprivation manipulation and the drugs moved the animals along some dimension of arousal level that provided the basis for discriminative control.

Overall, our knowledge about the specific sensory consequences of drug actions that are responsible for SDL and DDs is very small. Most studies designed to investigate this issue have failed to yield positive results. The one study that yielded positive results has never been followed up. The assertion that drug-induced SDL and DDs are based on the sensory consequences of drug action remains an assertion. Although many formal similarities exist between the rules describing properties of SDL and those describing the properties of contextual stimulus control, there is only indirect evidence indicating that sensory events mediate SDL and DDs.

SDL PRODUCED BY NONPHARMACOLOGICAL MANIPULATIONS

Drugs are not the only manipulation that can produce SDL. Several naturally occurring internal states such as hunger, fatigue, and depression appear to produce similar effects. Investigation of drug SDL has proceeded in parallel with exploration of SDL produced by nonpharmacological states, and the two areas share similar problems of experimental design, interpretation of results, and identification of mechanism.

Affect or Emotion as a Memory Cue

Bower (1981) recently reviewed a body of evidence testing whether emotions (affects, feelings) could act as retrieval cues, and the evidence points to at least two related phenomena. First, a happy (or sad) mood will facilitate recall of memories about happy (or sad) events (Teasdale & Taylor, 1981). Second, moods can sometimes produce weak SDL-type retrieval deficits such that emotionally neutral materials are best recalled if the current emotional state matches that present when the memories were formed (Bower, Monteiro, & Gilligan, 1978; Leight & Ellis, 1981). In many studies these two effects are inextricably confounded, which makes it difficult to determine their relative strengths, and Bower, Gilligan, and Monteiro (1981) suggested that both reflect operation of the same mechanism. In some experiments, emotional states have been experimentally induced by fear of electric shock (Macht, Spear, & Levis, 1977), by winning or losing a game (Isen, Shalker, Clark, & Karp, 1978), by hypnotic suggestion (Bower, 1981; Bower et al., 1978, 1981), by happy or sad stories (Bartlett & Santrock, 1979), or by reading happy or sad self-referential statements (Teasdale & Fogarty, 1979). In other studies, moods were allowed to spontaneously occur in normal subjects or in manic–depressive patients (Bower, 1981; Weingartner et al., 1977, 1978a, b). The data suggest that the effects of emotional states on memory retrieval are sometimes as large as those induced by drugs or contextual stimuli. It has even been suggested that drug-induced SDL may really be a special instance of mood SDL, with drug-induced changes in mood providing the "sensations" that underlie SDL (Overton, 1978b; Weingartner et al., 1978a).

Mood-induced SDL has interesting ramifications as a factor influencing everyday memory retrieval. Additionally, mood-induced alterations in memory retrieval may aggravate the severity of clinical disorders such as depression, because selective recall of memories congruent with the current mood may aggravate the strength of that mood (Teasdale & Fogarty, 1979).

REM-Sleep SDL

One fascinating series of studies showed that learning could occur during rapid eye movement (REM) sleep, and that subsequent retention was more efficient in the REM-sleep state than in the waking state (Evans, 1972; Evans, Gustafson, O'Connell, Orne, & Shor, 1966, 1969, 1970). The learning task consisted of hearing and remembering one or more verbal commands that instructed the subjects to perform particular motor responses whenever they heard particular stimulus words. The retention test involved presenting the stimulus words and noting whether the motor responses occurred. These SDL studies provide a viable alternative to "repression" and "inadequate formation of engrams," as explanations for the almost universally experienced poor recall of dream content, and for the enhanced dream recall frequently experienced immediately after awakening before one is entirely out of the sleep state.

Retrieval Failures Based on Time of Day

Holloway and his coworkers have published a series of studies indicating that changes in time of day can produce SDL effects (Holloway, 1978; Holloway & Jackson, 1976; Holloway & Sturgis, 1976; Holloway & Wansley, 1973a, b). Curiously, a 12-hour cycle was observed, with optimal retrieval at 12, 24, 36, 48, . . . hours after training and impaired retrieval at 6, 18, 30, 42, . . . hours. Similar effects have also been reported by other laboratories (Elson, Seybert, & Ghiselli, 1977; Stephan & Kovacevic, 1978; Stroebel, 1967), although they have not been universally observed (Caul, Barrett, Thune, & Osborne, 1974). Apparently, the influence of time of day on memory retrieval is relatively weak and hence can only be observed if the training and testing conditions are properly selected. Obviously this phenomenon may be a source of artifact in studies designed to investigate drug effects unless time of testing is adequately controlled. To date, this effect has not been observed in human subjects in classroom situations (Folkard, Monk, Bradbury, & Rosenthal, 1975).

Drives as Contextual Cues

The states produced by food and/or water deprivation can provide a basis for discriminative control (Capaldi & Davidson, 1979) and have been reported to produce SDL effects (Otis, 1956; Peck & Ader, 1974). These effects are sometimes strong (Wickens, Hall, & Reid, 1949), but in most reports response control by drive states has not been as robust as that produced by many of the other manipulations discussed in this review (Bolles, 1958, 1975; Webb, 1955).

SDL Induced by Hormonal Changes

There has been considerable interest in whether changes in the levels of circulating hormones could produce SDL. Stewart, Krebs, and Kaczender (1967) reported that changes in steroid levels were discriminable, but their results apparently reflected pharmacologically induced SDL, because they used doses of progesterone and hydroxydione high enough to produce sedative drug effects. SDL produced by ACTH has been reported by some investigators (Gray, 1975; Levine & Jones, 1965; Nakajima, 1975) but not by others (Barrett, Leith, & Ray, 1971; Overton, 1982a). Only some of a series of studies by Klein and other workers support the hypothesis that the Kamin effect (amnesia 3 to 12 hours after avoidance training) is an SDL effect caused by reduced levels of ACTH in the body at that time (Dunn & Leibmann, 1977; Klein, 1972, 1975; Spear, Klein, & Riley, 1971). Hormonal changes within physiological limits accompanying the estrus cycle have not been found to produce SDL (Gray, 1977). It is difficult to summarize these diverse findings except by saying that there is little evidence indicating that hormones produce *strong* SDL effects, but there is evidence that some hormones may produce weak SDL in some tasks.

SDL Produced by ECS and Kindled Convulsions

Electroconvulsive shock (ECS) and kindled convulsions produce SDL. In rats, learning that occurs during the postictal state immediately following electroconvulsive shock is strongly state dependent, and this effect gradually attenuates over a period of about 60 minutes according to most reports (Gardner, Glick, & Jarvik, 1972; Overton et al., 1976). Equally strong SDL effects have also been observed following kindled convulsions induced by localized electrical brain stimulation (McIntyre & Gunter, 1979; McIntyre & Reichart, 1971; Thompson & Neely, 1970; Wann, 1971). Presumably SDL also occurs in human subjects following ECS, but it appears unlikely that this plays a role in the therapeutic effectiveness of ECS because the duration of ECS's SDL effects in rats is much shorter than the time course of ECS's antidepressant actions in humans (but see DeVietti & Larson, 1971; DeVietti, Mayse, & Morris, 1974).

SDL Produced by Spreading Depression

Cortical spreading depression can produce SDL (Greenwood & Singer, 1974), and two possible mechanisms for this effect have been suggested. According to the "confinement" theory, when unilateral depression is induced, engrams can only be formed in the nondepressed hemisphere and retrieval will subsequently only be possible when that hemisphere is again functional (Nadel, 1971). According to the "stimulus" theory, spreading depression produces stimuli that act as retrieval cues for engrams deposited elsewhere in the brain, thus producing SDL (Schneider, 1966, 1967, 1973). Many reports have demonstrated SDL-like effects that appear to result from memory confinement (e.g., Lehr & Nachman, 1973; Mayes & Cowey, 1973). However other results are difficult to explain on the basis of confinement and suggest that spreading depression can also produce SDL via its "stimulus" effects (Langford, Freedman, & Whitman, 1971; Reed & Trowill, 1969). Interpretation of all spreading depression results is complicated by the intermittent nature of the altered brain state that is induced by spreading depression (Freedman, 1969; Freedman, Pote, Butcher, & Suboski, 1968).

The studies described in this section, which demonstrate SDL effects produced by nonpharmacological manipulations, have been some of the most exciting developments in SDL research in recent years. They have extended the range of conditions under which SDL is known to occur and have a variety of implications for the understanding of memory retrieval phenomena.

THEORETICAL INTERPRETATIONS OF SDL

Nineteenth-Century Theories

The earliest report of SDL that is presently known was by Combe (1835), who devoted a substantial portion of his book *System of Phrenology* to an empirical description of the amnesias associated with changes in internal physiological states, cases of multiple personality, and hypnosis. Embedded in this discussion was the description of drug-induced SDL quoted at the beginning of this chapter. Although Combe, like other writers of his era, devoted substantial attention to a description of episodic disorders of memory retrieval, he did not know what caused these phenomena. He (Combe, 1835) stated: "These facts cannot be accounted for in a satisfactory way; but by communicating a knowledge of their existence, attention will be drawn to them, and future observations and reflection may ultimately throw light upon the subject" (p. 490). Combe's case report of drug-induced SDL was quoted subsequently in other nineteenth-century books on disorders of the nervous system (Elliotson, 1840; Macnish, 1834, 1835; Winslow, 1860), and the phenomenon of SDL was central to the plot of the classic mystery novel *The Moonstone* by Collins (1981/1868). Apparently the existence of drug-induced SDL was an accepted fact in English scientific and literary circles, even if no one knew why it occurred (Siegel, 1982, 1983).

Ribot (1891) proposed the first theoretical explanation for SDL known to this author. He was primarily trying to explain the shifting availability of memories that occurs in cases of multiple personality and somnambulism, and he did so by postulating that "organic sensations" play a critical role in determining the content of consciousness: "The organic sensations proceeding from all the tissues, organs, and movements . . . are in some degree and form represented in the sensorium." The memories available, and the content of consciousness "must vary as they vary, and these variations admit of all possible degrees . . . instances of double personality are but an extreme case" (page 30). Ribot attributed Combe's case of drug-induced SDL to the altered physiological conditions created by ethanol. His theoretical explanation of SDL is not fundamentally different from the more contemporary theoretical formulations discussed elsewhere in this chapter (Ribot, 1882, 1891, 1897).

Neurological Theories for SDL

Although the earliest known theoretical explanation for SDL (Ribot's) involved a hypothesized sensory mechanism, a variety of other explanations have been proposed, many of which have not included sensory mediators. The first such theory known to this author was that proposed by Semon, who postulated that engrams could only be recalled when a pattern of brain activity ("energetic condition") was reestablished that was similar to the one that existed at the time when memorization took place (Semon, 1921/1904, p. 145). More significantly, Girden and Culler (1937), when they first reported an experimental demonstration of drug-induced SDL, postulated that a nonsensory mechanism was responsible for the phenomenon. Specifically, they hypothesized that drug blocked normal functioning of the cortex, and that in undrugged animals the cortex inhibited the subcortex and prevented it from functioning. Hence when conditioning took place in the N state, engrams were laid down only in the cortex and could be subsequently retrieved only when the animal was undrugged and the cortex was functional. Similarly they proposed that D state conditioning created engrams only in subcortical structures, which could be retrieved only when the animal was again drugged and the subcortical structures were released from cortical inhibition. A variety of other mechanisms for SDL have been proposed that also do not involve sensory mediation. These were termed *neurological* models by Bliss, have been adequately reviewed in previous publications (Bliss, 1974; Overton, 1978b), and are outside the scope of the present chapter. We mention them only to point out that it is not universally accepted that SDL and DDs are caused by sensory effects of drugs.

Sensory Theories for SDL

This writer is not familiar with statements regarding the stimulus properties of drugs that may have appeared in the scientific literature between 1890 and 1950. However it is clear that in the mid-1950s the notion that drugs could produce stimulus effects was moderately widespread. Auld (1951) referred to such effects. Conger (1951) reported the first drug discrimination experiment. Miller (1957) proposed the use of the 2×2 design to differentiate SDL effects from other effects of drugs on performance. Heistad (1957) postulated that drug-induced SDL might be a significant side effect produced by the clinical use of psychoactive drugs (also see Barry, Miller, & Tidd, 1962; Barry, Wagner, & Miller, 1962; Heistad & Torres, 1959; Shmavonian, 1956). These writers all expected SDL effects to be symmetrical, with $N--{>}D$ and $D--{>}N$ state changes producing an equal impairment in memory retrieval, and this expectation has persisted up to the present time. Hence the frequent reports of data indicating asymmetrical SDL effects have been problematic, because they appeared to reflect a phenomenon contrary to theoretical expectations (Overton, 1974). However, we will argue that the sensory model for symmetrical SDL that has been accepted by most investigators since the mid-1950s is inconsistent with contemporary notions regarding the operation of contextual cues, and that both symmetrical and asymmetrical SDL are entirely consistent with contemporary notions.

In Table 13.2, Model 1 is the traditional sensory formulation for SDL. In the $N-->N$ and $D-->D$ groups, the same environmental contextual cues (C) and interoceptive cues (N or D cues) are present during training as during the test for retention; hence test session performance is normal. In the $N--->D$ group, learning takes place in the presence of C and N cues; during the retrieval test, N cues are replaced by D cues and hence memory retrieval is impaired. In the $D--->N$ group, training takes place in the presence of C and D cues; during the test, D cues are replaced by N cues and so memory retrieval is impaired here also. The model appears straightforward and has survived for at least 25 years (a full century if we count Ribot's initial description of the theory).

What are N cues? Ribot asserted that they were sensations reflecting the normal functioning of the organs of the body and normal levels of activity in various

TABLE 13.2

Effect of the Degree of Control Exercised by No-Drug Cues on the
Predicted Outcome of 2 × 2 SDL Experiments

Drug Conditions:		Salient Cues:		Performance
During Training	During Test	During Training	During Test	During Test Session
Model 1: D cues replace (eliminate) N cues.				
No Drug	No Drug	C + N	C + N	1.0
No Drug	Drug	C + N	C + D	.5
Drug	No Drug	C + D	C + N	.5
Drug	Drug	C + D	C + D	1.0
Model 2: D cues superimpose on N cues.				
No drug	No Drug	C + N	C + N	1.0
No Drug	Drug	C + N	C + N + D	1.0
Drug	No Drug	C + N + D	C + N	.66
Drug	Drug	C + N + D	C + N + D	1.0
Model 3: D cues (D1, D2) replace some N cues (N1) and superimpose on others (N2, N3).				
No Drug	No Drug	C + N1 + N2 + N3	C + N1 + N2 + N3	1.0
No Drug	Drug	C + N1 + N2 + N3	C + N2 + N3 + D1 + D2	.75
Drug	No Drug	C + N2 + N3 + D1 + D2	C + N1 + N2 + N3	.6
Drug	Drug	C + N2 + N3 + D1 + D2	C + N2 + N3 + D1 + D2	1.0

Notes:
C = Exteroceptive contextual cues (apparatus cues).
N = All salient interoceptive cues present in the no-drug state.
D = All salient drug-induced cues.
N1, N2, N3 = Individual salient interoceptive cues present in the no-drug state.
D1, D2, D3 = Individual salient drug-induced cues.

portions of the brain. Today we might specify that at a particular instant in time N cues reflect the current degree of arousal, hunger, thirst, depression, distention of the stomach, vertigo, ringing in the ears (if any), degree of fatigue, etc. Next consider a question that is crucial; when a moderate dose of a psychoactive drug is administered, how many of these N cues are substantially changed? To this writer it appears that the answer is either "some" or "none," depending on the drug and dose administered. For example, pentobarbital may increase thirst and decrease arousal but may not alter the other interoceptive sensations mentioned. An antihistamine may decrease motion sickness and dry up one's mucosa but will probably have no other effects. Most N cues will still be present in the D state. In addition, drugs may create sensory cues (hallucinations, euphoria) that are superimposed on any preexisting N state cues. Such drug-induced cues (a different set of cues for each type of drug) appear to match what most contemporary DD investigators have in mind when they refer to "drug-induced discriminative stimuli."

Model 2 in Table 13.2 recasts the traditional sensory interpretation of SDL in a more contemporary vein by assuming that drug injection simply adds D cues, whereas N cues are left unchanged. The N−−>N and D−−>D groups experience no change in contextual stimuli between training and testing; hence these groups show unimpaired retrieval. So does the N−−>D group because, although D cues have been added to its internal environment during the test session, both the C and N cues that were present during training are still present during test sessions and allow efficient retrieval. Only the D−−>N group shows a retrieval deficit because D cues were present during training, became associated with the learned response, and are absent during the test for retrieval. It appears that if drug states simply create D cues, without abolishing N cues, then a sensory model for SDL predicts asymmetrical SDL (Barry, 1978; Boyd & Caul, 1979)!

Finally, Model 3 in Table 13.2 portrays an intermediate case in which some N cues are modified by the drug (N1 becomes D1), other N cues are unaffected (N2 and N3 remain), and the drug creates still other sensory input (D2). The effectiveness of memory retrieval during the test session is considered to be proportional to the number of cues that were present during training and are still present during the test session; all cues are assumed to be equally strong and effects are additive. In the N−−>N and D−−>D groups, no cues change and retrieval is normal. In the N−−>D group the C, N2, and N3 cues are still present during testing but N1 is missing, yielding somewhat impaired retrieval; the addition of cues D1 and D2 has no effect. In the D−−>N group, C, N2, and N3 cues are present at the time of retrieval, but both D1 and D2 are missing, yielding a larger impairment in retrieval. The result is a partially asymmetrical SDL effect. Obviously we can manipulate the predicted result by varying the assumed relative strength and number of C, N, and D cues, and by varying the number of N cues that we assume to be modified by the drug. Depending on the assumptions that we make (the drug that we use?), the predicted SDL effect may be symmetrical, partially asymmetrical, or entirely asymmetrical.

The theoretical issues raised in the preceding paragraphs have not been empirically addressed in SDL studies. However the vast majority of published SDL results are at least partially asymmetrical, and thus inconsistent with the traditional sensory model for SDL (Model 1 in Table 13.2). It appears that an experimental appraisal of alternate models might be fruitful.

A parallel theoretical problem exists in the interpretation of the results of DD studies. Early DD investigators sometimes argued that their animals discriminated D cues versus N cues (Brown, Feldman, & Moore, 1968; Browne & Ho, 1975; Jones, Grant, & Vospalek, 1976; Schechter, 1973). However most contemporary investigators believe that animals discriminate presence versus absence of specific drug stimuli (N cues are never mentioned). This formulation is congruent with the common finding that, during tests with novel drugs that are pharmacologically dissimilar to the training drug, the animals invariably perform the N response. Such results are interpreted as showing that because D cues like those of the training drug are absent, the N response is performed (Colpaert, 1978). The change in the nomenclature used to describe DD results has taken place quietly during the past 20 years without any theoretical discussion and appears to have taken place so that DD investigators' theoretical formulations would not be obviously inconsistent with the data that they obtained. However a parallel change in theoretical conceptions has not occurred among SDL investigators, most of whom still accept a theory that predicts symmetrical SDL, use statistical tests that can only properly evaluate the occurrence of SDL if it is symmetrical, and regularly obtain results that are asymmetrical.

SUMMARY

For more than a century it has been believed that changes in an organism's physiological milieu, whether induced by drugs or by other manipulations, could produce profound impairments in memory retrieval. The SDL retrieval deficits produced by changes in drug state are analogous in many respects to those produced by changes in environmental stimuli, and SDL retrieval deficits may indeed be mediated by events that could be termed stimuli. Drugs might appear to provide a very convenient method for manipulating the internal milieu of an animal and investigating the contextual significance of this internal milieu. However there are certain problems associated with the use of drugs to manipulate interoceptive stimuli. The specific effects of drugs that act as sensory cues are entirely unknown. Additionally, theoretical formulations regarding the contextual effects of drug states have developed very little during the past 100 years and do not very accurately fit the available data. Hopefully the current re-emergence of interest in contextual control by exteroceptive stimuli will create a profitable interchange between investigators interested in the external sensory world and those interested in internal sensory events. Drug manipulations do indeed provide a convenient method for manipulating he internal milieu of an organism and may produce phenomena of interest to investigators of contextual control. Conversely, as the properties of contextual control become more precisely defined through experiments in which exteroceptive stimuli are manipulated, our improved understanding of contextual control may allow us to achieve a more precise understanding of the retrieval deficits that can be produced by changes in the pharmacological and physiological state of an organism.

ACKNOWLEDGMENTS

Preparation of this manuscript was supported in part by NIMH grant #MH25136, NIDA grant #DA02403, and BRSG grant #RR05417.

REFERENCES

Auld, F. The effects of tetraethylammonium on a habit motivated by fear. *Journal of Comparative and Physiological Psychology*, 1951, *44*, 565–574.

Balster, R. L. *The effectiveness of external and drug produced internal stimuli in the discriminative control of operant behavior.* Doctoral dissertation, University of Houston, 1970.

Barnhart, S. S., & Abbott, D. W. Dissociation of learning and meprobamate. *Psychological Reports*, 1967, *20*, 520–522.

Barrett, R. J., Leith, N. J., & Ray, O. S. Kamin effect in rats: Index of memory or shock-induced inhibition?. *Journal of Comparative and Physiological Psychology*, 1971, *77*, 234–239.

Barry, H., III. Classification of drugs according to their discriminable effects in rats. *Federation Proceedings*, 1974, *33*, 1814–1824.

Barry, H., III. Stimulus attributes of drugs. In H. Anisman & G. Bignami (Eds.), *Psychopharmacology of aversively motivated behavior.* New York: Plenum Press, 1978, 455–485.

Barry, H. III, Miller, N. E., & Tidd, G. E. Control for stimulus change while testing effects of amobarbital on conflict. *Journal of Comparative and Physiological Psychology*, 1962, *55*, 1071–1074.

Barry, H. III, Wagner, A. R., & Miller, N. E. Effects of alcohol and amobarbital on performance inhibited by experimental extinction. *Journal of Comparative and Physiological Psychology*, 1962, *55*, 464–468.

Bartlett, J. C., & Santrock, J. W. Affect-dependent episodic memory in young children. *Child Development*, 1979, *50*, 513–518.

Berger, B. D., & Stein, L. An analysis of learning deficits produced by scopolamine. *Psychopharmacologia*, 1969, *14*, 271–283. (a)

Berger, B. D., & Stein, L. Asymmetrical dissociation of learning between scopolamine and Wy4036, a new benzodiazepine tranquilizer. *Psychopharmacologia*, 1969, *14*, 351–358. (b)

Bliss, D. K. Dissociated learning and state-dependent retention induced by pentobarbital in rhesus monkeys. *Journal of Comparative and Physiological Psychology*, 1973, *84*, 149–161.

Bliss, D. K. Theoretical explanations of drug-dissociated behaviors. *Federation Proceedings*, 1974, *33*, 1787–1796.

Bliss, D. K., Sledjeski, M., & Leiman, A. State dependent choice behavior in the rhesus monkey. *Neuropsychologia*, 1971, *9*, 51–59.

Bolles, R. C. A replication and further analysis of a study on position reversal learning in hungry and thirsty rats. *Journal of Comparative and Physiological Psychology*, 1958, *51*, 349.

Bolles, R. C. *Theory of motivation*. New York: Harper & Row, 1975.

Bower, G. H. Mood and memory. *American Psychologist*, 1981, *36*, 129–148.

Bower, G. H., Gilligan, S. G., & Monteiro, K. P. Selective learning caused by affective states. *Journal of Experimental Psychology: General*, 1981, *110*, 451–473.

Bower, G. H., Monteiro, K. P., & Gilligan, S. G. Emotional mood as a context for learning and recall. *Journal of Verbal Learning and Verbal Behavior*, 1978, *17*, 573–585.

Boyd, S. C., & Caul, W. F. Evidence of state dependent learning of brightness discrimination in hypothermic mice. *Physiology and Behavior*, 1979, *23*, 147–153.

Brown, A., Feldman, R. S., & Moore, J. W. Conditional discrimination learning based on chlordiazepoxide: Dissociation or cue? *Journal of Comparative and Physiological Psychology*, 1968, *66*, 211–215.

Browne, R. G. Anxiolytics antagonize Yohimbine's discriminative stimulus properties. *Psychopharmacology*, 1981, *74*, 245–249.

Browne, R. G., & Ho, B. T. Role of serotonin in the discriminative stimulus properties of mescaline. *Pharmacology, Biochemistry and Behavior*, 1975, *3*, 429–435.

Browne, R. G., & Weissman, A. Discriminative stimulus properties of delta-9-tetrahydrocannabinol: Mechanistic studies. *Journal of Clinical Pharmacology*, 1981, *21*(8–9, suppl.), 227–234.

Capaldi, E. , & Davidson, T. L. Control of instrumental behavior by deprivation stimuli. *Journal of Experimental Psychology: Animal Behavior Processes*, 1979, *5*, 355–367.

Caul, W. F., Barrett, R. J., Thune, G. E., & Osborne, G. L. Avoidance decrement as a function of training-test interval: Single cycle or multiphasic? *Behavioral Biology*, 1974, *11*, 409–413.

Collins, W. *The moonstone*. New York: Penguin Books, 1981. (Originally published, 1868.)

Colpaert, F. C. Sensitization and desensitization to lateral hypothalamic stimulation. *Archives Internationales de Pharmacodynamie et de Therapie*, 1977, *230*, 319–320.

Colpaert, F. C. Discriminative stimulus properties of narcotic analgesic drugs. *Pharmacology, Biochemistry, and Behavior*, 1978, *9*, 863–887.

Colpaert, F. C., & Rosecrans, J. A. (Eds.). *Stimulus properties of drugs: Ten years of progress*. Amsterdam: Elsevier/North–Holland and Biomedical Press, 1978.

Colpaert, F. C., & Slangen, J. L. (Eds.). *Drug discrimination applications in CNS pharmacology*. Amsterdam: Elsevier Biomedical Press, 1982.

Combe, G. *A system of phrenology* (3rd ed.). Boston: Marsh, Copen, & Lyon, 1835.

Conger, J. J. The effects of alcohol on conflict behavior in the albino rat. *Quarterly Journal of Studies on Alcohol*, 1951, *12*, 1–29.

Connelly, J. F., Connelly, J. M., & Epps, J. O. Disruption of dissociated learning in a discrimination paradigm by emotionally important stimuli. *Psychopharmacologia*, 1973, *30*, 275–282.

Connelly, J. F., Connelly, J. M., & Nevitt, J. R. Effect of foot-shock intensity on amount of memory retrieval in rats by emotionally important stimuli in a drug-dependent learning escape design. *Psychopharmacology*, 1977, *51*, 153–157.

Connelly, J. F, Connelly, J. M., & Phifer, R. Disruption of state-dependent learning (memory retrieval) by emotionally important stimuli. *Psychopharmacologia*, 1975, *41*, 139–143.

Deutsch, J. A., & Roll, S. K. Alcohol and asymmetrical state-dependency: A possible explanation. *Behavioral Biology*, 1973, *8*, 273–278.

DeVietti, T. L., & Larson, R. C. ECS effects: Evidence supporting state-dependent learning in rats. *Journal of Comparative and Physiological Psychology*, 1971, *74*, 407–415.

DeVietti, T. L., Mayse, J. F., & Morris, L. W. Footshock/ECS induced state dependent learning in rats: Parametric evaluation of ECS intensity and time of testing. *Learning and Motivation*, 1974, *5*, 70–79.

Downey, D. J. State-dependent learning with centrally and noncentrally active drugs. *Bulletin of the Psychonomic Society*, 1975, *5*, 281–284.

Duncan, P. M. The effect of external stimulus change on ethanol-produced dissociation. *Pharmacology, Biochemistry and Behavior*, 1979, *11*, 377–381.

Dunn, A. J., & Leibmann, S. The amnestic effect of protein synthesis inhibitors is not due to the inhibition of adrenal corticosteroidogenesis. *Behavioral Biology*, 1977, *19*, 411–416.

Eich, J. E. State-dependent retrieval of information in human episodic memory. In I. M. Birnbaum & E. S. Parker (Eds.), *Alcohol and human memory*. Hillsdale, N.J.: Lawrence Erlbaum Associates, 1977, 141–157.

Eich, J. E. The cue-dependent nature of state-dependent retrieval. *Memory and Cognition*, 1980, *8*, 157–173.

Eich, J. E., & Birnbaum, I. M. Repetition, cuing, and state-dependent memory. *Memory and Cognition*, 1982, *10*, 103–114.

Eich, J. E., Weingartner, H., Stillman, R. C., & Gillin, J. C. State-dependent accessibility of retrieval cues in the retention of a categorized list. *Journal of Verbal Learning and Verbal Behavior*, 1975, *14*, 408–417.

Elliotson, J. *Human physiology* (5th ed.). London: Longman, Orme, Brown, Green, & Longmans, 1840.

Elson, I. J., Seybert, J. A., & Ghiselli, W. B. Retention of aversively motivated behavior: Effects of time of training and associative versus nonassociative processes, *Behavioral Biology*, 1977, *20*, 337–353.

Evans, F. J. Hypnosis and sleep: Techniques for exploring cognitive activity during sleep. In E. Fromm & R. E. Shor (Eds.), *Hypnosis: Research developments and perspectives*. Chicago: Aldine, 1972, 43–83.

Evans, F. J., Gustafson, L. A., O'Connell, D. N., Orne, M. T., & Shor, R. E. Response during sleep with intervening waking amnesia. *Science*, 1966, *152*, 666–667.

Evans, F. J., Gustafson, L. A., O'Connell, D. N., Orne, M. T., & Shor, R. E. Sleep-induced behavioral response. *Journal of Nervous and Mental Disease*, 1969, *148*, 467–476.

Evans, F. J., Gustafson, L. A., O'Connell, D. N., Orne, M. T., & Shor, R. E. Verbally induced behavioral responses during sleep. *Journal of Nervous and Mental Disease*, 1970, *150*, 171–187.

Folkard, S., Monk, T. H., Bradbury, R., & Rosenthal, J. Time of day effects in school children's immediate and delayed recall of meaningful material. *British Journal of Psychology*, 1975, *68*, 45–50.

Freedman, N. L. Recurrent behavioral recovery during spreading depression. *Journal of Comparative and Physiological Psychology*, 1969, *68*, 210–214.

Freedman, N. L., Pote, R., Butcher, R., & Suboski, M. D. Learning and motor activity under spreading depression depending on EEG amplitude. *Physiology and Behavior*, 1968, *3*, 373–376.

Gardner, E. L., Glick, S. D., & Jarvik, M. E. ECS dissociation of learning and one-way cross-dissociation with physostigmine and scopolamine. *Physiology and Behavior*, 1972, *8*, 11–15.

Girden, E., & Culler, E. A. Conditioned responses in curarized striate muscle in dogs. *Journal of Comparative Psychology*, 1937, *23*, 261–274.

Gray, P. Effect of adrenocorticotropic hormone on conditioned avoidance in rats interpreted as state-dependent learning. *Journal of Comparative and Physiological Psychology*, 1975, *88*, 281–284.

Gray, P. Effect of the estrous cycle on conditioned avoidance in mice. *Hormones and Behavior*, 1977, *8*, 235–241.

Greenwood, P. M., & Singer, J. J. Cortical spreading depression induced state dependency. *Behavioral Biology*, 1974, *10*, 345–351.

Hazell, P., Peterson, D. W., & Laverty, R. Inability of hexamethonium to block the discriminative stimulus property of nicotine. *Pharmacology, Biochemistry and Behavior*, 1978, *9*, 137–140.

Heistad, G. T. A bio-psychological approach to somatic treatments in psychiatry. *American Journal of Psychiatry*, 1957, *114*, 540–545.

Heistad, G. T., & Torres, A. A. A mechanism for the effect of a tranquilizing drug on learned emotional responses. *University of Minnesota Medical Bulletin*, 1959, *30*, 518–527.

Hernandez, L. L., Holohean, A. M., & Appel, J. B. Effects of opiates on the discriminative stimulus properties of dopamine agonists. *Pharmacology, Biochemistry and Behavior*, 1978, *9*, 459–463.

Hinderliter, C. F. Hypothermia: Amnesic agent, punisher, and conditions sufficient to attenuate amnesia. *Physiological Psychology*, 1978, *6*, 23–28.

Hirschhorn, I. D., & Rosecrans, J. A. A comparison of the stimulus effects of morphine and lysergic acid diethylamide (LSD). *Pharmacology, Biochemistry and Behavior*, 1974, *2*, 361–366. (a)

Hirschhorn, I. D., & Rosecrans, J. A. Studies on the time course and the effect of cholinergic and adrenergic receptor blockers on the stimulus effect of nicotine. *Psychopharmacologia*, 1974, *40*, 109–120. (b)

Ho, B. T., Richards, D. W., III, & Chute, D. L. *Drug discrimination and state dependent learning*. New York: Academic Press, 1978.

Holloway, F. A. State-dependent effects of ethanol on active and passive avoidance learning. *Psychopharmacologia*, 1972, *25*, 238–261.

Holloway, F. A. State-dependent retrieval based on time of day. In B. T. Ho, D. W. Richards III, and D. L. Chute (Eds.), *Drug discrimination and state dependent learning*. New York: Academic Press, 1978, 319–343.

Holloway, F. A., & Jackson, F. D. Differential operant behavior based on time of day. *Bulletin of the Psychonomic Society*, 1976, *8*, 94–96.

Holloway, F. A., & Sturgis, R. D. Periodic decrements in retrieval of the memory of nonreinforcement as reflected as resistance to extinction. *Journal of Experimental Psychology: Animal Behavior Processes*, 1976, *2*, 335–341.

Holloway, F. A., & Wansley, R. A. Multiple retention deficits at periodic intervals after active and passive avoidance learning. *Behavioral Biology*, 1973, *9*, 1–14. (a)

Holloway, F. A., & Wansley, R. A. Multiphasic retention deficits at periodic intervals after passive-avoidance learning. *Science*, 1973, *180*, 208–210. (b)

Holmgren, B. Nivel de vigilia y reflejos condicionados. *Boletin del Instituto de Investigaciones de la Actividad Nerviosa Superior (Havana)*, 1964, *1*, 33–50.

Huang, J. T. Amphetamine and pentobarbital effects on the discriminative response control by deprivation of rapid eye movement sleep (REMS). *Federation Proceedings*, 1973, *32*, 786.

Isen, A. M., Shalker, T. D., Clark, M., & Karp, L. Affect, accessibility of material in memory and behavior: A cognitive loop? *Journal of Personality and Social Psychology*, 1978, *36*, 1–12.

Iwahara, S., & Noguchi, S. Drug-state dependency as a function of overtraining in rats. *Japanese Psychological Research*, 1972, *14*, 141–144.

Iwahara, S., & Noguchi, S. Effects of overtraining upon drug-state dependency in discrimination learning in white rats. *Japanese Psychological Research*, 1974, *16*, 59–64.

Jarbe, T. U. C. Alcohol-discrimination in gerbils: Interactions with bemegride, DH-524, amphetamine, and delta-9-THC. *Archives Internationales de Pharmacodynamie et Therapie*, 1977, *227*, 118–129.

Jarbe, T. U. C., & Henriksson, B. G. Open-field behavior and acquisition of discriminative response control in delta-9-THC tolerant rats. *Experientia*, 1973, *29*, 1251–1253.

Jarbe, T. U. C., & Holmgren, B. Discriminative properties of pentobarbital after repeated noncontingent exposure in gerbils. *Psychopharmacology*, 1977, *53*, 39–44.

Jarbe, T. U. C., & Ohlin, G. Ch. Stimulus effects of delta-9-THC and its interaction with naltrexone and catecholamine blockers in rats. *Psychopharmacology*, 1977, *54*, 193–195.

Jones, C. N., Grant, L. D., & Vospalek, D. M. Temporal parameters of d-Amphetamine as a discriminative stimulus in the rat. *Psychopharmacologia*, 1976, *46*, 59–64.

Joy, R. M., & Prinz, P. N. The effect of sleep altering environments upon the acquisition and retention of a conditioned avoidance response in the rat. *Physiology and Behavior*, 1969, *4*, 809–814.

Kilbey, M. M., Harris, R. T., & Aigner, T. G. Establishment of equivalent external and internal stimulus control of an operant behavior and its reversal. *Proceedings of the American Psychological Association*, 1971, *6*, 767–768.

Klein, S. B. Adrenal–pituitary influence in reactivation of avoidance-learning memory in the rat after intermediate intervals. *Journal of Comparative and Physiological Psychology*, 1972, *79*, 341–354.

Klein, S. B. ACTH-induced reactivation of prior active-avoidance training after intermediate intervals in hypophysectomized, adrenalectomized, and sham-operated rats. *Physiological Psychology*, 1975, *3*, 395–399.

Lal, H. (Ed.). *Discriminative stimulus properties of drugs: Advances in behavioral biology* (Vol. 22). New York: Plenum, 1977.

Langford, A., Freedman, N., & Whitman, D. Further determinants of interhemispheric transfer under spreading depression. *Physiology and Behavior*, 1971, *7*, 65–71.

Lehr, P. P., & Nachman, M. Lateralization of learned taste aversion by cortical spreading depression. *Physiology and Behavior*, 1973, *10*, 79–83.

Leight, K. A., & Ellis, H. C. Emotional states, strategies, and state dependency in memory. *Journal of Verbal Learning and Verbal Behavior*, 1981, *20*, 251–266.

Levine, S., & Jones, L. E. Adrenocorticotropic hormone (ACTH) and passive avoidance learning. *Journal of Comparative and Physiological Psychology*, 1965, *59*, 357–360.

Macht, M. L., Spear, N. E., & Levis, D. J. State-dependent retention in humans induced by alterations in affective state. *Bulletin of the Psychonomic Society*, 1977, *10*, 415–418.

Macnish, R. *The philosophy of sleep.* New York: Appleton, 1834.

Macnish, R. *The anatomy of drunkenness* (5th ed.). New York: Appleton, 1835.

Mayes, A. R., & Cowey, A. The interhemispheric transfer of avoidance learning: An examination of the stimulus control hypothesis. *Behavioral Biology*, 1973, *8*, 193–205.

Mayse, J. F., & DeVietti, T. L. A comparison of state-dependent learning induced by electroconvulsive shock and pentobarbital. *Physiology and Behavior*, 1971, *7*, 717–721.

McIntyre, D. C., & Gunter, J. L. State-dependent learning induced by low intensity electrical stimulation of the caudate or amygdala nuclei in rats. *Physiology and Behavior*, 1979, *23*, 449–454.

McIntyre, D. C., & Reichart, H. State-dependent learning in rats induced by kindled convulsions. *Physiology and Behavior*, 1971, *7*, 15–20.

McKim, W. A. The effects of preexposure to scopolamine on subsequent drug state discrimination. *Psychopharmacology*, 1976, *47*, 153–155.

Miksic, S., Shearman, G., & Lal, H. Discrimination of the interoceptive stimuli produced by phenyl-quinone. A measure of the affective component of pain in the rat. In E. L. Way (Ed.), *Endogenous Exogenous Opiate Agonists Antagonists, Proceedings of the International Narcotics Research Club Conference, 1979*. Elmsford, N.Y.: Pergamon, 1980, 435–438.

Miller, N. E. Objective techniques for studying motivational effects of drugs on animals. In S. Garattini & V. Ghetti (Eds.), *Psychotropic Drugs, Proceedings of the International Symposium on Psychotropic Drugs*. Amsterdam: Elsevier, 1957, 83–103.

Modrow, H. E., Salm, A., & Bliss, D. K. Transfer of a learning set between drug states in monkeys. *Psychopharmacology*, 1982, *77*, 37–42.

Nadel, L. Interhemispheric transfer—Monocular input and varied sensory conditions. *Physiology and Behavior*, 1971, *6*, 655–661.

Nakajima, S. Amnesic effect of cycloheximide in the mouse mediated by adrenocortical hormones. *Journal of Comparative and Physiological Psychology*, 1975, *88*, 378–385.

Otis, L. S. Drive conditioning: Fear as a response to biogenic drive stimuli previously associated with painful stimuli. *American Psychologist*, 1956, *11*, 397.

Overton, D. A. State-dependent or "dissociated" learning produced with pentobarbital. *Journal of Comparative and Physiological Psychology*, 1964, *57*, 3–12.

Overton, D. A. State-dependent learning produced by depressant and atropine-like drugs. *Psychopharmacologia*, 1966, *10*, 6–31.

Overton, D. A. Dissociated learning in drug states (state-dependent learning). In D. H. Efron, J. O. Cole, J. Levine, & R. Wittenborn (Eds.), *Psychopharmacology, a review of progress, 1957–1967* (U.S. Pub. Health Serv. Pub. No. 1836). Washington, D.C.: U.S. Government Printing Office, 1968, 918–930. (a)

Overton, D. A. Visual cues and shock sensitivity in the control of T-maze choice by drug conditions. *Journal of Comparative and Phsyiological Psychology*, 1968, *66*, 216–219. (b)

Overton, D. A. Discriminative control of behavior by drug states. In T. Thompson & R. Pickens (Eds.), *Stimulus properties of drugs*. New York: Appleton–Century–Crofts, 1971.

Overton, D. A. State-dependent learning produced by alcohol and its relevance to alcoholism. In B. Kissen & H. Begleiter (Eds.), *The biology of alcoholism* (Vol II): *Physiology and behavior*. New York: Plenum Press, 1972.

Overton, D. A. State-dependent learning produced by addicting drugs. In S. Fisher & A. M. Freedman (Eds.), *Opiate addiction: Origins and treatment*. Washington, D.C.: Winston, 1973.

Overton, D. A. Experimental methods for the study of state-dependent learning. *Federation Proceedings*. 1974, *33*, 1800–1813.

Overton, D. A. Discriminable effects of antimuscarinics: Dose response and substitution test studies. *Pharmacology, Biochemistry and Behavior*, 1977, *6*, 659–666.

Overton, D. A. Discriminable effects of antihistamine drugs. *Archives Internationales de Pharmacodynamie et Therapie*, 1978, 232, 221–226. (a)

Overton, D. A. Major theories of state dependent learning. In B. T. Ho, D. W. Richards III, & D. L. Chute (Eds.), *Drug discrimination and state dependent learning*. New York: Academic Press, 1978. (b)

Overton, D. A. Drug discrimination training with progressively lowered doses. *Science*, 1979, *205*, 720–721.

Overton, D. A. Comparison of the degree of discriminability of various drugs using the T-maze drug discrimination paradigm. *Psychopharmacology*, 1982, *76*, 385–395. (a)

Overton, D. A. Memory retrieval failures produced by changes in drug state. In R. L. Isaacson & N. E. Spear (Eds.), *The expression of knowledge, neurobehavioral transformations of information into action*. New York: Plenum Press, 1982, 113–139. (b)

Overton, D. A. State dependent learning and drug discrimination. In L. Iversen, S. D. Iversen, & S. H. Snyder (Eds.), *Handbook of psychopharmacology* (Vol. 18). New York: Plenum Press, 1984, 59–127.

Overton, D. A., Ercole, M. A., & Dutta, P. Discriminability of the postictal state produced by electroconvulsive shock in rats. *Physiological Psychology*, 1976, *4*, 207–212.

Peck, J. H., & Ader, R. Illness-induced taste aversion under states of deprivation and satiation. *Animal Learning and Behavior*, 1974, *2*, 6–8.

Petersen, R. C. Retrieval failures in alcohol state-dependent learning. *Psychopharmacology*, 1977, *55*, 141–146.

Reed, V. G., & Trowill, J. A. Stimulus control value of spreading depression demonstrated without shifting depressed hemispheres. *Journal of Comparative and Physiological Psychology*, 1969, *69*, 40–43.

Ribot, T. *Diseases of memory*. London: Kegan Paul, Trench & Co., 1882.

Ribot, T. *The diseases of the personality*. Chicago: Open Court Pub. Co., 1891.

Ribot, T. *Psychology of the emotions*. New York: Scribner, 1897.

Romano, C., Goldstein, A., & Jewell, N. P. Characterization of the receptor mediating the nicotine discriminative stimulus. *Psychopharmacology*, 1981, *74*, 310–315.

Rosecrans, J. A. Nicotine as a discriminative stimulus to behavior: Its characterization and relevance to smoking behavior. *NIDA Research Monograph*, 1979, *23*, 58–69.

Sachs, E., Weingarten, M., & Klein, N. W., Jr. Effects of chlordiazepoxide on the acquisition of avoidance learning and its transfer to the normal state and other drug conditions. *Psychopharmacologia*, 1966, *9*, 17–30.

Schechter, M. D. Ethanol as a discriminative cue: Reduction following depletion of brain serotonin. *European Journal of Pharmacology*, 1973, *24*, 278–281.

Schneider, A. M. Retention under spreading depression: A generalization decrement phenomenon. *Journal of Comparative and Physiological Psychology*, 1966, *62*, 317–319.

Schneider, A. M. Control of memory by spreading cortical depression: A case for stimulus control, *Psychological Review*, 1967, *74*, 201–215.

Schneider, A. M. Spreading depression: A behavioral analysis. In J. A. Deutsch (Ed.), *The physiological basis of memory*. London: Academic Press, 1973, 269–303.

Semon, R. [*Die Mneme*]. London: George Allen & Unwin, 1921. (Originally published 1904.)

Shearman, G. T., & Lal, H. Discriminative stimulus properties of cocaine related to an anxiogenic action. *Progress in Neuro-psychopharmacology*, 1981, *5*, 57–63.

Shmavonian, B. H. *Effects of serpasil (rauwolfia serpantina) on fear training*. Unpublished master's thesis, University of Washington, 1956.

Siegel, S. Drug dissociation in the nineteenth century. In F. C. Colpaert & J. L. Slangen (Eds.), *Drug discrimination: Applications in CNS pharmacology*. Amsterdam: Elsevier Biomedical Press, 1982, 257–261.

Siegel, S. Wilkie Collins: Victorian novelist as psychopharmacologist. *Journal of the History of Medicine and Allied Sciences*, 1983, *38*, 161–175.

Silverman, P. B., & Ho, B. T. The discriminative stimulus properties of 2,5-Dimethoxy-4-Methylamphetamine (DOM): Differentiation from amphetamine. *Psychopharmacology*, 1980, *68*, 209–215.

Spear, N. E., Klein, S. B., & Riley, E. P. The Kamin effect as "state-dependent learning": Memory retrieval failure in the rat. *Journal of Comparative and Physiological Psychology*, 1971, *74*, 416–425.

Spear, N. E., Smith, G. J., Bryan, R. G., Gordon, W. C., Timmons, R., & Chiszar, D. A. Contextual influences on the interaction between conflicting memories in the rat. *Animal Learning and Behavior*, 1980, *8*, 273–281.

Stephan, F. K., & Kovacevic, N. S. Multiple retention deficit in passive avoidance in rats is eliminated by suprachiasmatic lesions. *Behavioral Biology*, 1978, *22*, 456–462.

Stewart, J., Krebs, W. H., & Kaczender, E. State-dependent learning produced with steroids. *Nature*, 1967, *216*, 1223–1224.

Stroebel, C. F. Behavioral aspects of circadian rhythms. In J. Zubin & H. Hunt (Eds.), *Comparative psychopathology*. New York: Grune & Stratton, 1967, 158–172.

Swanson, J. M., & Kinsbourne, M. The 2 × 2 design reconsidered: Limitations imposed by the statistical model. In F. C. Colpaert & J. A. Rosecrans (Eds.), *Stimulus properties of drugs: Ten years of progress*. Amsterdam: Elsevier/North Holland Biomedical Press, 1978, 467–480.

Swanson, J. M., & Kinsbourne, M. State-dependent learning and retrieval: Methodological cautions and theoretical considerations. In J. F. Kihlstrom & F. J. Evans (Eds.), *Functional disorders of memory*. Hillsdale, N.J.: Lawrence Erlbaum Associates, 1979, 275–299.

Teasdale, J. D., & Fogarty, F. J. Differential effects of induced mood on retrieval of pleasant and unpleasant events from episodic memory. *Journal of Abnormal Psychology*, 1979, *88*, 248–257.

Teasdale, J. D., & Taylor, R. Induced mood and accessibility of memories: An effect of mood state or of induction procedure? *British Journal of Clinical Psychology*, 1981, *20*, 39–48.

Thompson, C. I., & Neely, J. Dissociated learning in rats produced by electroconvulsive shock. *Physiology and Behavior*, 1970, *5*, 783–786.

Wann, P. D. Amnestic and dissociative effects of kindled convulsions in rats. Master's thesis, Carleton University, 1971.

Webb, W. B. Drive stimuli as cues. *Psychological Reports*, 1955, *1*, 287–298.

Weingartner, H., Miller, H., & Murphy, D. L. Mood state-dependent retrieval of verbal associations. *Journal of Abnormal Psychology,* 1977, *86,* 276–284.

Weingartner, H., Murphy, D. L., & Stillman, R. C. Drug and mood state-specific encoding and retrieval of experience. In R. C. Petersen (Ed.), *The international challenge of drug abuse.* Rockville, Md.: NIDA Research Monograph 19, National Institute of Drug Abuse, 1978, 210–223. (a)

Weingartner, H., Murphy, D. L., & Stillman, R. C. Mood state dependent learning. In F. C. Colpaert and J. A. Rosecrans (Eds.), *Stimulus properties of drugs: Ten years of progress.* Amsterdam: Elsevier/North Holland Biomedical Press, 1978, 445–453. (b)

Wickens, D. D., Hall, H., & Reid, L. S. Associative and retroactive inhibition as a function of the drive stimulus. *Journal of Comparative and Physiological Psychology,* 1949, *42,* 398–403.

Winslow, F. *Obscure diseases of the brain and mind.* Philadelphia: Blanchard & Lea, 1860.

Zenick, H., & Goldsmith, M. Drug discrimination learning in lead-exposed rats. *Science,* 1981, *212,* 569–571.

14

Cognitive Maps and Environmental Context

Lynn Nadel
Jeffrey Willner
Elizabeth M. Kurz
Cognitive Sciences Program,
University of California–Irvine (LN and EMK)
University of Virginia (JW)

> *"Your place or mine?"*
>
> —Anonymous

Places convey moods, memories, and more, yet we seem to know so little about them. How are they defined, learned about, and internally represented? How do they mold ongoing behavior in adaptive ways? How do they influence learning about objects and events that occur within their confines?

These questions about places are also questions about environmental contexts and their role in behavior. Based on behavioral and neurophysiological data, O'Keefe and Nadel (1978) argued that the hippocampus plays a central role in creating cognitive maps. Nadel and Willner (1980) subsequently explored some implications of this view for our understanding of environmental context. In this chapter, we attempt a fuller integration of these two sets of ideas by outlining neural processes that could realize the psychological functions we have attributed to cognitive maps. Much of what follows is speculative, in that there is little direct evidence for or against the specific schemes we propose. There is good evidence, however, for many of the component processes on which these schemes are based. Even if specific neural details turn out to be wrong, attempts to show how psychological processes are realized in the nervous system force one to be more explicit about the processes that are being modeled. In the long run, this can only improve psychological theorizing. Supporting evidence is offered where possible.

Our use of the term cognitive map is similar in spirit to that of Tolman (1948), though it is more restricted in that we stress the explicitly spatial content of the representations underlying these maps. These internal models of the world influence learning and performance in several ways. We briefly outline these influences here and expand upon them in the body of the chapter.

1. Maps generate expectations concerning the whereabouts of objects/events, including those that would be confronted if the animal moved through the environment—thereby allowing for the detection of the unexpected.

2. Depending on the animal's current motivational state, these expectations provide information needed for the generation of "place" strategies. These involve direction of behavior toward/away from locations, even distant ones, in a flexible manner (i.e., largely independent of specific stimuli existing at or near any particular locale).

3. The knowledge contained in these representations contributes to the processes, both during and after the event, by virtue of which an organism learns about the causal texture of its environment. In particular, the expected/unexpected nature of stimuli strongly influences what an animal learns about them.

This view of environmental context differs from the traditional notion that it is simply a collection of unrelated cues competing for associative strength.[1] In our earlier paper (Nadel & Willner, 1980) we suggested that the objects/events comprising an environment are internally represented both as individual entities, and as things contained within a spatial framework (i.e., a hierarchical approach to context, cf. Konorski, 1967). The present chapter seeks to flesh out those early speculations, which seem consistent with other recent views (Balsam, 1984; Bouton & Bolles, this volume; Medin & Reynolds, this volume).

O'Keefe and Nadel (1978, 1979) reviewed the data suggesting that there exists a specific brain region/system charged with the function of internally representing the spatial world. They suggested that it does this by linking together a neural ensemble of elements that individually represent things experienced in an environment (see later for details). By virtue of its pattern of interconnection, this ensemble amounts to an internal map, enabling the organism to behave as if it had direct access to a roughly veridical model of the environment. With it, the unseen danger can be avoided, the hidden food recovered; that is, the animal can act at a distance. Indeed, it is difficult to conceive of complex animals functioning adaptively in nature without recourse to something like a cognitive map (Shillito, 1963). We have suggested that the hippocampal formation is a central part of this cognitive mapping system, subserving the representation of environmental contexts (Nadel & Willner, 1980; O'Keefe & Nadel, 1978, 1979; O'Keefe, Nadel, & Willner, 1979).

A variety of evidence attests to the importance of environmental context for a number of learning/performance phenomena. Two rather different sorts of con-

---

[1]The competition was not entirely even. For reasons that are not made explicit, Hull (1943) and Rescorla and Wagner (1972) both attach a 0.2 weighting factor to static background cues in their learning equations. This is justified by asserting that because these cues are constantly present they will have undergone a certain amount of extinction. Whereas this intuition is reasonable, the particular value chosen seems arbitrary. Further, it simply builds in, rather than explains, the relationship between foreground and background cues. Wagner (1981) incorporates a similar weighting factor in his state-transition equations, again without any explicit justification.

text effects have been identified. Early on, it was recognized that animals were capable of directly associating an environment with the reinforcers that occur there (cf. Nadel & Willner, 1980). This raised the possibility that so-called "contextual cues" and nominal CSs might compete for the control of behavior, and this has indeed proven to be the case (see chapters by Thomas, Medin & Reynolds, Bouton & Bolles, Tomie, and Rescorla, Durlach, & Grau). Recently, a more indirect effect of environmental context on learning has been identified. It now appears that much of what an animal learns is referred to the environment where training takes place. For example, "latent inhibition"—the finding that simple exposure to a stimulus can retard later learning involving that stimulus— is now known to be specific to the environment in which stimulus exposure takes place (Channell & Hall, 1983; Lubow, Rifkin, & Alek, 1976). And, a number of studies have demonstrated better performance of a learned response in the training environment than in any other environment (Logan, 1961; Zentall, 1970; earlier noted chapters). This facilitation of conditioned responding cannot be attributed to associations between environmental cues and the US, because the effect is observed even when such associations have been extinguished (Balaz, Capra, Hartl, & Miller, 1981; Balaz, Capra, Kasprow, & Miller, 1982). Environmental context thus exerts both direct and indirect effects on learning and behavior, and a theory of environmental context must account for each. We attempt such a theory in what follows, explicated as a set of themes about the workings of a cognitive map/environmental context system.

Theme I: How Environments Are Represented in Cognitive Maps

Structure.   A cognitive map consists of an interconnected set of neural elements in the hippocampal formation. There appear to be four types of functional elements, organized in stages, that make up this system.[2]

1. The first stage is comprised of cells driven by a precise combination of analyzed inputs from sensory systems acting much like AND-gates; that is, they fire maximally only when the proper spatial conjunction of inputs exists.
2. The second stage is comprised of "place" cells that, driven by a few inputs from first-stage cells, act much like OR-gates, or ALMOST-gates; that is, they fire maximally when any subset of their inputs is present.

---

[2]The functional elements described herein stay close to currently available physiological data. Though recent years have markedly increased our knowledge, we still do not know enough to link our "functional" elements directly to specific neurons. For example, the elements we are labeling *place* and *misplace* cells could be two different kinds of place cell (see O'Keefe, 1979)—the former determined by the summation of excitatory inputs, the latter by the summation of inhibitory inputs. Future results will no doubt alter our understanding of the precise physiological details of the hippocampal system, but they should not radically change the functions we ascribe to its elements.

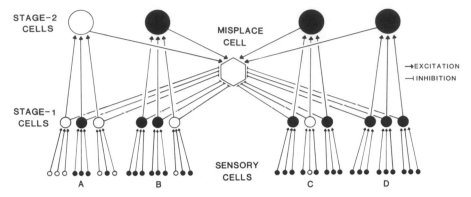

FIG. 14.1.   Schematic buildup of a misplace element. Sensory cells are assumed to transmit information of a highly analyzed, multisensory nature to the stage-1 cells. Refer to the text for a description of the functional requirements of the stage-1, stage-2, and misplace cells. Both stabilized and dynamic aspects of the functioning of a misplace circuit are shown in the figure, with shaded circles representing active cells and unshaded circles inactive ones. Circuits A and D represent stabilized ensembles that would be observed in a familiar environment. In circuit D, the stage-2 place cell is maximally active, driven by its full complement of sensory inputs. The circuit shown in A is not part of the current map and is therefore inactive. Circuits B and C represent the dynamic aspect of misplace unit activity. In each case a particular set of inputs has been deleted. Although the remaining inputs are sufficient to excite the stage-2 cells, generating excitation to the misplace cells, these deletions decrease the amount of inhibitory input to the misplace cells. In this way, change yields increased activation — see the text for some discussion of how this affects behavior. (Note that to avoid contradicting Dale's Law an interneuron would have to be inserted between the stage-1 cells and the misplace cells, mediating the inhibitory effect of the former on the latter.)

3.   The third-stage cells fire maximally when some normally present input is missing, or changed. Figure 14.1 shows how these ''misplace'' cells might act as NAND-gates in this fashion. There are several ways in which this function could be realized—the figure presents one possibility consistent with current physiological data.

4.   The fourth type of element, the theta-cell, comes into play when maps are being written in or read out (see later).

What makes this neural ensemble a functional map is: (1) the way in which it is connected to representational systems outside the hippocampus; and (2) its own internal wiring. It is assumed that reciprocal (though not necessarily monosynaptic) connections exist between (primarily) neocortical sites representing objects and sets of hippocampal cells. A map could be said to contain the addresses of the representations of things, and to interconnect these in a way that captures the spatial relations among these things in an environment. This set of interconnections among representations (or, more properly, addresses of representations) of things that occurred in an environment is the internal map for that place—it is what we mean by the representation of environmental context.

The things represented in a map must include both static and phasic cues— that is, things that are either permanently a part of an environment or that come and go in that environment. It seems most likely that the difference between these two is but one of degree, and that an organism's internal map of an environment represents the most recent state of affairs in all locations in that environment. As we see shortly, it is precisely because the internal mapping system is sensitive to unexpected stimuli that it can fulfill its particular functions. This sensitivity demands a constant updating of the internal model, a continuous mapping about which we unfortunately have very little data at present. We postulate that phasic stimuli are represented such that a given location is "addressed" by two different input sets, one specifying the phasic stimulus, the other an empty place. In this way, the various things that occupy a particular location with any degree of regularity share occupancy of that location in the internal map—the current occupant being that which has been most recently experienced. Habituation reflects the fact that, with repeated exposure to sporadic stimuli in a given location, the switching in and out of alternate input sets becomes easier—a kind of "learning set" develops that enables the organism to rapidly alter the contents of its map. Evidence supporting this speculation is provided by the study of repeated extinction-retraining cycles in an operant learning situation. Intact rats extinguish more rapidly with each successive cycle, but rats with hippocampal lesions fail to show such improvement (Schmaltz & Isaacson, 1967).

Another problem concerns the status of seemingly nonlocalizable stimuli. In what way does a map represent something like a sound that can seem present throughout an environment? We assume that such stimuli are referred to specific locations—their supposed source—even though this source can only be guessed at by the organism. The importance of apparent location (e.g., the speaker from which a sound emanates) has been clearly demonstrated (Buzsaki, Grastyan, Mod, & Winiczai, 1979; Karpicke, Christoph, Peterson, & Hearst, 1977), but we remain largely in the dark concerning the special features, if any, of the representation of these unusual stimuli. For present purposes we need say little more about the way in which cues other than static, well-localized ones are represented in maps.

Construction.   A cognitive map is continuously active, but the process of remapping or constructing a new map occurs only when unexpected stimuli/events trigger orientation and investigation, leading to the acquisition of new information. The construction or updating of a map demands the establishment of functional connections among the appropriate elements in the hippocampus. Which elements are appropriate is determined by their hard-wired connections to the neocortical elements representing those things the animal finds in its investigations. Figure 14.2 shows how this process might be initiated by an interaction between sensory inputs specifying things in the environment, and inputs related to the animal's movements through the environment. (This latter source of information, reflected in the highly characteristic theta activity recorded in the hippocampus, is more fully described elsewhere—see O'Keefe & Nadel, 1978;

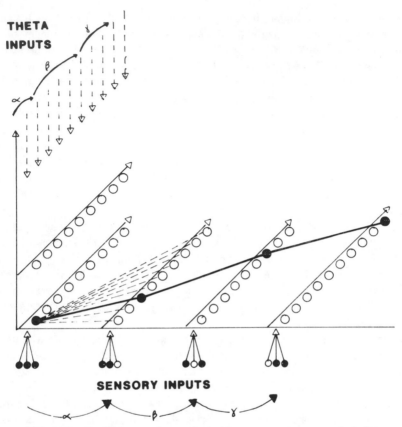

FIG. 14.2.   Establishment of a map in the hippocampus. A sequence ($\alpha > \beta >$ γ) of movements brings the organism into contact with three stimuli, which sequentially elicit activity in specific (neocortical) input channels to the hippocampus. These inputs potentially activate any of a number of neurons in a strip of cells (the diagonal row of circles in the figure). Input from a movement system (theta) reflecting the distances covered between stimuli during exploration interacts with this sequence of inputs to determine which of the potential connections (dotted lines) will be activated. These active cells (indicated by shading) will be linked together into a map (the heavy line).

Robinson, 1980.) As the figure shows, the hippocampal system can form any of a large number of connections among elements representing particular inputs—which connections are actually formed depends on the spatial relations among stimuli in the environment. Allocation of particular stimuli to specific locations in the map depends on the theta activity generated during exploration—this in turn depends on the exact spatial relations existing among things to be explored. Distance in the external world is translated into distance represented in the map by virtue of this mechanism (Morris, Black, & O'Keefe, 1976; O'Keefe & Nadel, 1978).

Internal models are formed within hippocampal circuitry prepared to undergo rapid shifts in synaptic efficacy. In the past decade considerable attention has focused on a phenomenon known as long-term potentiation (LTP), or enhancement. A short burst of high-frequency activity in various parts of the hippocampal circuitry can induce persisting changes in the ease of transmission through those circuits (Bliss & Lomo, 1973; Douglas & Goddard, 1975; Lynch & Schubert, 1980; McNaughton, 1982). We assume that there is a brief "fixation" period, upon exposure to a new environment, or part thereof, during which linkages are being made among map elements connected to just-activated neocortical representations. The fixation of inputs to a set of place and misplace cells, and their interconnection, may be subserved by LTP, driven by several cycles through the reciprocal hippocampal-neocortical circuitry. As we see later, the dynamics of the fixation of this "map" determine the content of the animal's memory for the environment. This newly formed map then serves as a sort of "template," permitting: (1) easy retrieval of associations among things/events experienced in the same environment, thereby strongly influencing performance in that place; and (2) the eventual establishment of stronger connectivity among the neocortical elements representing the various things making up the environment. This aspect of the role of the hippocampal system in long-term "consolidation" of input was considered in Squire, Cohen, and Nadel (1984).

Theme II: Maps in Action

Environment Recognition. Upon entering a previously mapped environment, an organism identifies the place it is in by detecting a small set of things in a particular spatial arrangement. Appropriate spatial arrangements activate enough elements in one particular map ensemble to initiate place recognition. This recognition process involves the activation of a specific set of place cells, ultimately affecting activity within the entire ensemble of neural elements involved in the representation of that environment. This is not to say that all these elements are literally excited—merely that they are in a different state than when the organism is not in that environment. This altered state disposes the organism to interpret or act upon the environment in certain ways, reflecting the "expectations" embodied in the environment-specific activation. Unfamiliar environments activate misplace cells, leading to exploration unless the fear provoked by relatively extensive uncertainty interferes. In the complete absence of the hippocampal system, organisms seem oblivious to the familiarity/unfamiliarity of environments, showing little, if any, "place" fear (e.g., Jarrard, 1968).

Results from single-neuron recording studies in the hippocampus offer support for some of these assertions. O'Keefe and Dostrovsky (1971) provided the initial evidence that some hippocampal neurons are activated whenever the animal is in a particular location. O'Keefe (1976, 1979; O'Keefe & Conway, 1978) and others (Olton, Branch, & Best, 1978; Ranck, 1973) have provided further evidence about, and insight into, these hippocampal place cells. Recently, Kubie and Ranck (1981) recorded from the same hippocampal place neurons in several environments—a large open field, a smaller box put on top of the open field, and an operant chamber also put in the same region of the test area. Many cells were active in two, or all three, of these environments. (Though these cells were part of the map for several environments, they did not map the same part of space in the three situations.) Each cell not only fired maximally when the rat was in the appropriate "place field" in a given environment but also showed an environment-specific background firing rate when outside the place field. This background rate changed from environment to environment. Such results raise the possibility that place cells in the hippocampus identify both environment and location within an environment—the former in terms of specific background firing rates, the latter in terms of brief high-frequency bursts. The specific background rate seen anywhere in an environment outside the place field could be a manifestation of the special state of activation entered into by all the cells representing the animal's current environment.

Subject Location.   The animal's current position within the environment is signaled by activity in particular place cells, triggered into action by the neural elements representing some subset of the cues defining that location. (Remember that place cells function like OR-gates, requiring only a subset of their defining inputs.) We propose that this will occur when the organism is: (1) in the location; (2) predicting that it will be there after a certain, planned movement; or (3) rehearsing or reactivating the appropriate elements.

Within the ensemble of elements comprising the map for an environment, two "active" states are thus defined. First, there is a form of activation associated with merely being in the environment—reflected perhaps in the background firing rates recorded by Kubie and Ranck (1981). Second, there is a form of activation associated with being in (or thinking about) a particular location within the environment—reflected in the bursts of activity first reported for the hippocampal place cells. We refer to these two different states of activation as the "background" and "foreground" states (BS and FS), respectively.

Expectations.   As the animal moves through the world (or imagines itself doing so), a particular kind of "theta" activity occurs in the hippocampus, through the mediation of the theta cells, driven by extrahippocampal sources (the movement programming system).[3] This activity has the effect of eliciting the FS

---

[3]There are two types of theta activity in the hippocampus—a high-frequency type seen during many nonreflexive movements, and a low-frequency type seen during "attention" or the like (Robinson, 1980). Hippocampal ablation does not seem to interfere with the organism's ability to move skillfully through the world, indicating that theta activity cannot be necessary for the generation of movement itself. Further, theta activity is seen quite prominently in sleep, particularly in REM sleep—thus it need not be generated by movements themselves. Rather, it seems to be generated from a central movement planning system, whose output could be inhibited (e.g., during sleep) without interrupting theta.

in those map elements representing locations to be encountered as a result of the movement. This, in turn, activates the neocortical representations of the objects/events to be encountered in these locations. The mapping system thus provides a steady stream of expectations about what will be found in a given location, by activating the appropriate neocortical representations. This is what was meant by the assertion that the mapping system is continuously active.

These expectations are realized through influences upon neocortical and hippocampal representations. Activity in misplace cells increases whenever some part of the original set of defining inputs is changed, thereby removing an inhibitory influence on these cells (remember that misplace cells function as NAND-gates). This increased activity is the neural instantiation of the failure to confirm an expectation and leads to exploration (or withdrawal), because this part of the hippocampal formation (CA1 field) connects to midbrain regions responsible for eliciting these species-typical patterns (cf. Fischette, Komisaruk, Edinger, Feder, & Siegel, 1980). When expectations are not confirmed, thereby causing investigation, the set of inputs to the appropriate place cells is redefined and misplace cell activity is stabilized. In this way the map is updated, and the animal continues on its way.

Place Strategies. Cognitive maps are important for the use of behavioral strategies involving approach to, or withdrawal from, specific locations. The predictive system discussed earlier enables an animal to plan movements toward unseen locations, navigating via whatever routes are available. Perhaps hunger primes neocortical elements, which are then activated as well by inputs reflecting hippocampal BS. This conjunction specifies the location of the desired goal object; appropriate movements toward that location can then be generated.

Animals behave as though they expect particular things in specific locations. Even when such things as food or danger are sporadic and signaled by other things, their occurrence is still predicted by the environment. In other words, we do not see places and nominal cues as simply competing with one another for associative strength. Cues may come to supplant places in terms of behavioral control, but they do not displace the animal's knowledge that an event occurs in a certain locale. Recent evidence from behavioral studies supports this view that the environmental context retains its linkage to a US, even when that US is reliably signaled by a CS (Balsam, 1984). The asymmetry between places and cues reflects the different ways in which they are represented internally by the animal. Places, as the next section attempts to show, lead a double life.

Theme III: The Double Life of a Place

In Nadel and Willner (1980) we argued that places both contained and consisted of cues. This duality derives from the two levels at which environmental context information is represented within the nervous system. In the (largely) neocortical systems, all the cues to be found within an environment are represented simply as things that have certain features, and these representations provide one means by which cues can be associated with each other. Exposure to any stimulus will activate its neocortical representation, and those of its associates (via spreading activation), but will go no further.

Places, on the other hand, are higher order constructs elaborated in the hippocampal system. Here, all the cues in an environment are linked together such that their spatial relations are represented, and such that they can act in concert. In this hippocampal mode, particular cues could be largely interchangeable in their ability to define an environment, or to guide an animal to a distant location. Whereas most authors assume that places are defined by static background cues, the critical research has not yet been done. We are currently investigating how an organism defines an environment—whether all cues are equally important, and, if not, which kinds of cues play a predominant role. By being in a place, then, an animal activates (in some fashion) all the representations of things to be experienced in that environment, even if they are not within its immediate perceptual grasp, and hence are in the BS rather than the FS. From this perspective, places are more than just a set of cues and the sum of their bidirectional associations.

Support for this split-level view of places is provided by two sets of considerations. First, hippocampal dysfunction selectively interferes with place, but not simple cue, learning (Nadel & MacDonald, 1980; O'Keefe, Nadel, Keightley, & Kill, 1976). Second, were places no more than static, distal cues, one might imagine that place learning would be relatively slow. Every indication suggests that this is not the case (Balsam, 1984; Balsam & Schwartz, 1981; Rescorla, Durlach, & Grau, this volume). The rapidity of place learning is one of its more noticeable features and is consistent with the demonstration of highly plastic neural networks within the hippocampus, as discussed previously.

Theme IV: Foreground and Background in Animal Learning

Which Comes First?   Most learning about novel stimuli proceeds more slowly in an unfamiliar environment than in a familiar one (Lubow, Rifkin, & Alek, 1976; but see Kurz & Levitsky, 1982). We assume that this reflects the fact that until the stable background has been explored and internally represented, little learning about the temporal/causal relations among stimuli can occur. As in perception, figure-ground separation seems crucial to learning.

Map Fixation.   Maps will be neither constructed nor corrected in the absence of novelty; that is, activation of misplace cells is a necessary condition in the process by which place fields are defined and place cells are linked together into a map. The mechanisms subserving map fixation include both environmental and neural components. Misplace cell activity triggers exploration aimed at the specific location not ''living up to expectations.'' In conjunction with investigation-generated inputs along sensory channels, misplace cell activity sets in motion a processing "loop," which guarantees the fixation (by LTP) of connections within the map among hippocampal cells driven by just-activated neocortical representations. Several cycles of coherent activation of elements in the neocortical-hippocampal circuitry must be achieved in order for LTP to occur, thereby fixing the map.[4] How is the sustained and coherent activity needed for map fixation maintained within this circuitry?

We consider the entire set of neocortical representations as potential entrants into the processing loop: The most active representations have the greatest chance of entering into, and remaining within, this dynamic representational set. In other words, the formation of a map follows upon sustained activity in a set of reciprocally connected neocortical and hippocampal representations and will be affected by whatever influences the state of activation in these representations. Activity resulting from the excitation of misplace cells, as well as current sensory and motivational inputs, all contribute to determining what an animal learns about in a particular situation.

This is partly so because the rapidly fixed hippocampal map serves as a template for longer-term consolidation of new linkages in neocortical circuits. Early research indicated that the hippocampus exerted an influence upon the formation of connections in the neocortex (Cazard & Buser, 1963). Work with amnesic patients indicates that this influence on the formation of permanent memory remains important for up to several years, and we have recently discussed the reasons for postulating this long-term consolidation process (Squire, Cohen, & Nadel, 1984). The present chapter extends these views about consolidation in the neocortex and couples them with a short-term fixation process in the hippocampal part of the circuitry. Together, these interacting representational systems engage in an ongoing dialectic that strengthens connections among representational elements in neocortical systems and hence alters the content of representations in the hippocampal system as well. We now apply this view of environmental context to several phenomena central to learning.

The Importance of Being Unexpected

We asserted that the mapping system, by generating predictions, provides the basis for detecting the unexpected. Further, the representations activated by such unexpected events can be differentiated from those activated by expected events—the latter lack input from the misplace system. This difference between expected and unexpected events has important consequences for learning. Such a

---

[4]Several investigators have demonstrated that LTP will only be elicited when two or more inputs converge upon a single site (e.g., McNaughton, Douglas, & Goddard, 1978). This restriction confirms the initial intuition of Hebb (1949) and provides the basis for limiting plasticity to a restricted set of synapses receiving adequate inputs.

view of the role of environmental context makes contact with the extensive
literature on stimulus preexposure effects, or "latent inhibition" (henceforth LI;
see Lubow, 1973; Wagner, 1978). Conventional wisdom suggests that familiarity breeds neglect; that is, exposing an animal to a stimulus in a particular
context decreases attention to it in that setting, thereby reducing its ability to
enter into associations with other stimuli (Lubow, Wiener, & Schnur, 1981).
Whereas this appears to be descriptively accurate (however, see Oberdieck &
Tarte, 1981), we entertain the converse possibility—namely, that being unexpected enhances associability. The activation of misplace cells by unexpected
events and the influence of this activation upon representations in both hippocampus and neocortex provide the basis for such an effect. As suggested previously, the detection of unexpected stimuli is essential to the establishment of
place fields in the hippocampus, and to the interconnection of those hippocampal
cells jointly representing an environment. Because hippocampal representations
can influence association formation within the neocortex, this same expected/
unexpected aspect of experience will also influence learning in these circuits.

Recent work has demonstrated several surprising features of LI. First, as
noted already, it appears that LI for a particular stimulus is specific to the
environment in which the stimulus was preexposed (Channell & Hall, 1981,
1983; Lubow, Rifkin, & Alek, 1976; Willner, 1980). Second, any experience
with a stimulus, be it exposure in isolation, in association with a US, or as the
added stimulus in a blocking experiment, leads to LI for that stimulus in the
environment of exposure. The generality of LI led Hall and Pearce (1979) to
assert that any familiarity has a negative impact upon subsequent learning—in
other words, unexpected stimuli preferentially enter into newly forming associations. We are suggesting that LI, rather than being a "loss of associability," is
the absence of the facilitatory effects of being unexpected. This view is supported by the fact that LI fails to develop in the absence of a functioning
hippocampal system (Solomon, 1979; Solomon & Moore, 1975).

A final point concerning LI: The effects of preexposing stimuli must be
interpreted in light of the kind of information an animal is likely to use in solving
the experimental task. If the exposed stimulus plays no role in the learning
required of the animal, LI could pass unnoticed. The value of considering behavioral (e.g., place and cue) strategies in any analysis of LI was brought out in a
study recently done in our laboratory (LN & EMK). The task used a water maze,
designed by Morris (1982), and ideal for the study of place strategies. A 5'
diameter pool, about 18" deep, was filled with milky water. A platform, heavy
and stable, sat beneath the surface of the opaque water, offering a respite from
swimming if located. Invisible from the surface, the platform could only be
found with reference to its location, as defined by various extra-maze stimuli.
The learning of this place task is rapid and depends on the integrity of the
hippocampal system (Morris, Garrud, Rawlins, & O'Keefe, 1982). Rats can also
be trained to find the submerged platform by learning to approach a stimulus

object hung above it. This cue-learning version of the task, in which the platform and its associated cue are moved about from location to location across trials, takes somewhat longer to acquire than the place-learning version.

Our study sought to compare the effects of exposure to places and cues prior to training. One group of rats was given 60 trials with random placements of the platform. On each trial the rat had to find the platform anew. Following this exposure to "random" locations, rats were trained with the platform in a fixed location. Would exposure to a training regime in which places were irrelevant to solution induce slower acquisition in these rats when compared to others not so preexposed? Our preliminary findings indicate that in terms of latencies to find the platform this was indeed the case. Rats exposed to random locations for 60 trials had a more difficult time learning to approach a fixed location than did the rats who had only four such exposures, during their adaptation to the pool prior to training. Another group of rats was given 60 trials in which a cue and the submerged platform, unrelated to one another, were randomly moved about the pool from trial to trial. Following this, they were trained to approach the cue, under which the platform could now consistently be found. These rats were compared to others who received only four preexposure trials. Paradoxically, preexposure to random places and random cues together had the effect of slightly facilitating subsequent cue learning. How could this happen?

Figure 14.3 portrays the behavior of a cue-learning rat in the water-maze over several trials—note how it returned on most trials to the location of the platform on the previous trial. This demonstrates both the rapidity of place learning and the probable predominance of place strategies in this situation. Exposure to

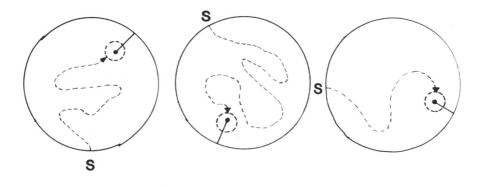

TRIAL 1   **TRIAL 2**   **TRIAL 3**

FIG. 14.3.   Patterns of swimming in three trials in the water tank. On each trial the hidden platform (dashed circle) is located in a new position, but it is always identified by the cue (small filled circle) hanging over the tank. The rat starts (S) from a different location on the edge of the tank each trial—its path is shown in the dashed line. Note the immediate return to the location of the platform on the previous trial.

random goal locations decreased the use of place strategies, accounting for the slower acquisition seen in the place-learning groups. If the use of place strategies interferes with cue learning in naive subjects, latently inhibiting both places and cues could result in more rapid learning, as we observed in the cue-learning group. What we did not do, but should have, is expose a group of rats to random places (but no cues) and then train them on the cue task. If our interpretation of these data is correct, this exposure manipulation should considerably facilitate cue learning. Our exposure conditions probably led to a tradeoff between the effects of exposing places and cues—the former helping cue learning, the latter hindering it. The lesson here is that the effects of preexposure depend heavily on what one subsequently requires of the animal. In all cases unexpected stimuli will be more likely to enter into new associations than will expected stimuli, but the consequences of this difference will depend on the demands of the learning task employed (see Dore, 1981; O'Keefe, Nadel, & Willner, 1979).

Generalization Decrement

It has long been known that performance suffers when the test context differs from the training context (see Medin & Reynolds, this volume). There are two possible ways of conceiving this phenomenon; these rely upon quite different views of environmental context. The traditional view (e.g., Mackintosh, 1975; Rescorla & Wagner, 1972) is that contextual cues, taken as elements or as a compound, enter into associations just as nominal CSs, and their removal by environment shift leads to a loss of associative strength. The other view, implicit in Konorski (1967), and explicit in Nadel and Willner (1980), is that environmental contexts exist both as integrated ensembles (in the hippocampal map) and as collections of individual cues (in the neocortex). We have already discussed some of the implications of this duality.

The effects of CS occurrence upon representational systems in neocortex and hippocampus are shown schematically in Fig. 14.4. "Generalization decrement" resides in the fact that a CS will be less likely to activate the US representation when the animal is out-of-context because of the absence of a preexisting BS induced by being in the training context. Not all learning is dependent on context in this way. Habits and skills, be they perceptual, cognitive, or motor in nature, are typically evidenced with equal facility across a wide range of environments. In organic amnesia, associated with hippocampal dysfunction, it is precisely these context-free forms of learning that are preserved (cf. Squire, Cohen, & Nadel, 1984). Virtually all learning during infancy is similarly independent of context. Nadel and Zola–Morgan (in press) marshall the evidence that relates this context-free learning in the neonate to the delayed maturation of the hippocampal system. The common thread linking these phenomena is the formation of context-free memories whenever the hippocampus is nonfunctional. We expect that learning in the intact adult can also be context-free, if conditions preclude

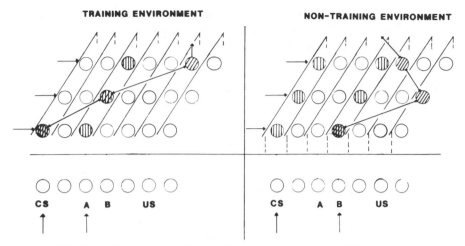

FIG. 14.4.   Schematization of generalization decrement. In the training environment (I): Elements representing things that will occur in this environment (CS,
US, all other stimuli denoted as A) are activated into the background state (BS -
slanted hatching). Inputs along sensory channels (vertical hatching) interact with
this state to yield the increased activity characteristic of the foreground state (FS -
combined hatching). In the nontraining environment (II): Only elements representing things in the nontraining environment, denoted here as B, are activated into the
background state. Thus, when the CS occurs it makes contact with elements not
previously activated. In this way, being in the training environment enables the CS
to elicit greater activation in US representations than it does outside of that
environment.

the participation of the hippocampal system. There are indications that stress
might have such an effect (Jacobs & Nadel, submitted; Micco, McEwen, &
Shein, 1979). Much learning, however, is context-dependent. Thus, latent inhibition (Channell & Hall, 1983; Lubow, Rifkin, & Alek, 1976; Willner, 1980),
habituation (Evans & Hammond, 1983), extinction (Bouton & Bolles, 1979a;
Hanford, Mulvaney, & Kelfer, 1980), reinstatement (Bouton & Bolles, 1979b),
and event-memory (Bouton & Bolles, this volume) are all relatively specific to
the environment in which they occurred.

A hierarchical approach to environmental context was tested directly by Balaz
et al. (1981). They devalued direct environment-US (shock) associations to the
point where the animal did not appear to be afraid in that environment, by a
variety of measures. They then tested for generalization decrement and found it
still present; that is, the CS–US link remained stronger in the training environment than out of it. Yet this could not be accounted for by direct associations
between environmental cues and the US. As the authors point out, these data
support the view that there is an association between the CS–US event and the
overall environmental context, independent of any specific "place-cue"-US
connections. Similar conclusions were reached in another study reported by this

group (Balaz et al., 1982). Thus, we suggest that the potentiation of performance by being "in context" is the result of the activation (to the BS) generated by calling up the map for that environment.

Beyond the Here and Now

Tolman (1932) understood that internal representations of environments could enable an animal to escape from dependence on the immediate stimulating environment. We have seen that maps provide information about unseen things and allow for action at a distance and in advance. What was not so clear in early thinking about cognitive maps was the way in which this freedom from dependence on the immediately given could influence learning as well as performance. Rescorla (1967) argued that animals were sensitive to the contingencies in a Pavlovian task, and not only to temporal contiguity relations. Recent controversy concerning such effects (Gibbon, 1981; Gibbon & Balsam, 1981; Jenkins, Barnes, & Barrera, 1981) does not obscure the fact that animals behave as though comparing some "overall" rate of US occurrence with some "local" rate, presumably defined by a temporal window around a phasic CS (Marlin, 1981).

This overall rate is represented by the animal's expectation of US occurrence in that environment. It reflects, in other words, the strength of a place strategy. We suggest that the results seen when overall and local rates are manipulated reflect the shifting strengths of place and cue strategies induced by particular treatments. This view is supported by the work of Odling–Smee (1975, 1978), which demonstrated how the strengthening of the CS–US bond (by approaching the optimal CS–US interval) diminished the use of a place strategy. We do not believe, however, that this shift in behavioral control reflects a dissipation of the stored information about the US-environment link (see previous discussion of generalization decrement). A similar line of reasoning, pursued in Nadel and Willner (1980), indicates that several other phenomena, such as trace conditioning and some forms of conditioned inhibition, can also be interpreted within this framework (see Kaplan & Hearst, this volume).

A series of experiments by Devenport and his colleagues (1980; Devenport, Devenport, & Holloway, 1981; Devenport & Holloway, 1980) connect these thoughts about places, contingencies, and the hippocampus. The sensitivity of rats with (or without) hippocampal dysfunction to temporal contiguity and to contingency was investigated. They found that in the absence of a functioning hippocampal system rats were no longer sensitive to contingencies (cf. Calderazzo Filho, Moschovakis, & Izquierdo, 1977). Rather, they were entirely at the mercy of temporal contiguity, which had the effect of opening the animal to the development of stereotyped behavior patterns, paradigm examples of "superstition." The existence of such behavioral abnormalities has been well documented (cf. O'Keefe & Nadel, 1978), but our understanding of the conditions leading to their development has heretofore been limited. As Devenport points out, access to information about "contingent" (broad span) relations frees an organism from undue dependence on local contiguity relations in the control of behavior. At the neural level, this freedom translates into an ability to transcend circuits capturing local temporal relations to the acquisition of "associations" based on relations at a temporal and/or spatial remove.

Conclusions

We started by asserting that theories in psychology should be constrained by physiological evidence, and have proposed a model of environmental context effects that reflects such constraints. In addition to constraints vested in the physiological realization of internal representations, one must wonder about the adaptive functions served by these models of the external world. Representational systems in biological organisms do not arise in a vacuum (see Nadel, 1982; Roitblat, 1982). They mirror features of the world that are both relatively stable across long periods of time, and of some importance to the animal. One such feature is spatial extent—organisms move through space, find necessary resources in particular parts of space, and benefit greatly from the ability to remember where things are located. We join Tolman and others (e.g., Jerison, 1973; Wyers, 1976) in supposing that a representational system concerned with spatial mapping evolved under such selective pressures. This leads us to suppose that environmental context is different from other kinds of context, such as temporal context (e.g., time of day) or internal (e.g., drug-state) context.

Each form of contextual information pertains to separate biological problems. There is no good reason to assume that these various kinds of context are all represented within the same processing system. There has been a tendency to adopt this "general context" view (Balsam, 1984; Hirsh, 1974, 1980), much as the notion of a "general learning process" dominated research on learning for many years. Yet the data support neither assertion. Arguments against the notion of a general learning process are now commonplace, and they apply with equal force to the notion of a general context system. Recent ontogenetic data support this view of separate representations for different kinds of contextual information. Infant rats, who become sensitive to environmental context only at about 3 weeks of age (cf. Nadel & Zola–Morgan, in press), are sensitive to time-of-day context by 2 weeks of age (Infurna, 1981). Similarly, there is no a priori reason to assume that the contexts provided by internal state, as manipulated in research on state-dependent learning (see Overton, this volume), are dependent on the system concerned with external contexts. We posit that the differing "contextual" systems reflect the action of separate representational mechanisms, realized within different neural modules.

Representations of environmental context—spatial maps—provide the basis for exploration, place strategies, context specificity of learning, and action-at-a-distance. Because of their special role in maintaining the "connectivity" among elements representing everything occurring in an environment, these maps play an extended role in the dynamic reorganization of memory with the passage of time after an event. Rehearsals, reactivations, and reminders all effect a retrieval of memories that can activate appropriate hippocampal–neocortical circuitry, leading to improved consolidation. In order to specify the precise details of this interaction between hippocampal maps and neocortical associative links, we need more research on the anatomical and physiological machinery. Current work on these systems offers the hope that we might soon be able to provide a detailed model of the mechanisms underlying spatial mapping. At the same time, we need more information about the ways in which organisms treat environmental contexts. How are environments defined? How much change is needed before the animal concludes that it is in a new, rather than a changed, environment? Does any class of cues play a special role in defining environments? These and related questions are the focus of our current research, which will add to a growing body of knowledge concerning the significance of environmental context/cognitive maps.

ACKNOWLEDGMENTS

We would like to acknowledge the people whose ideas and discussions have shaped our thinking on context: J. O'Keefe, J. Ranck, B. McNaughton, C. Barnes, R. Morris, G. Goddard, N. Cohen, W. J. Jacobs, L. Squire, T. Teyler, and S. Zola–Morgan. LN would also like to thank Bolek Srebro, who made invaluable suggestions on what we thought was a finished version of our initial paper on context. Would that he could have brought his Konorskian wisdom to bear on this effort. LN was supported by NINCDS 17712, JW by MH 08527, and EMK by MH 08911.

REFERENCES

Balaz, M. A., Capra, S., Hartl, P., & Miller, R. R. Contextual potentiation of acquired behavior after devaluing direct context-US associations. *Learning and Motivation,* 1981, *12,* 383–397.

Balaz, M. A., Capra, S., Kasprow, W. J., & Miller, R. R. Latent inhibition of the conditioning context: Further evidence of contextual potentiation of retrieval in the absence of appreciable context-US associations. *Animal Learning and Behavior,* 1982, *10,* 242–248.

Balsam, P. D. Bringing the background to the foreground: The role of contextual cues in autoshaping. In M. Commons, R. Herrnstein, & A. R. Wagner (Eds.), *Quantitative analyses of behavior: Volume 3: Acquisition.* Cambridge, Mass.: Ballinger, 1984.

Balsam, P., & Schwartz, A. L. Rapid contextual conditioning in autoshaping. *Journal of Experimental Psychology: Animal Behavior Processes,* 1981, *7,* 382–393.

Bliss, T. V. P., & Lomo, T. Long-lasting potentiation of synaptic transmission in the dentate area of the unanaesthetised rabbit following stimulation of the perforant path. *Journal of Physiology* (London), 1973, *232,* 331–356.

Bouton, M. E., & Bolles, R. C. Contextual control of the extinction of conditioned fear. *Learning and Motivation,* 1979, *10,* 445–466. (a)

Bouton, M. E., & Bolles, R. C. Role of conditioned contextual stimuli in reinstatement of extinguished fear. *Journal of Experimental Psychology: Animal Behavior Processes*, 1979, *5*, 368–378. (b)

Buzsaki, G., Grastyan, E., Mod, L., & Winiczai, Z. Importance of cue location for intact and fimbria-fornix lesioned rats. *Behavioral and Neural Biology*, 1979, *29*, 176–189.

Calderazzo Filho, L. S., Moschovakis, A., & Izquierdo, I. Effect of hippocampal lesions on rat shuttle responses in four different behavioral tests. *Physiology and Behavior*, 1977, *19*, 569–572.

Cazard, P., & Buser, P. Modification des reponses sensorielles corticales par stimulation de l'hippocampe dorsal chez le lapin. *Electroencephalography and Clinical Neurophysiology*, 1963, *15*, 413–425.

Channell, S., & Hall, G. Facilitation and retardation of discrimination learning after exposure to the stimuli. *Journal of Experimental Psychology: Animal Behavior Processes*, 1981, *7*, 437–446.

Channell, S., & Hall, G. Contextual effects in latent inhibition with an appetitive conditioning procedure. *Animal Learning and Behavior*, 1983, *11*, 67–74.

Devenport, L. D. Response-reinforcer relations and the hippocampus. *Behavioral and Neural Biology*, 1980, *24*, 105–110.

Devenport, L. D., Devenport, J. A., & Holloway, F. A. Reward-induced stereotypy: Modulation by the hippocampus. *Science*, 1981, *212*, 1288–1289.

Devenport, L. D., & Holloway, F. A. The rat's resistance to superstition: Role of the hippocampus. *Journal of Comparative and Physiological Psychology*, 1980, *94*, 691–705.

Dore, F. Y. L'effet de la preexposition au SC dans les apprentissages d'evitement bidirectionnel et unidirectionnel. *L'Annee Psychologique*, 1981, *81*, 23–32.

Douglas, R. M., & Goddard, G. V. Long-term potentiation of the perforant path—granule cell synapse in the rat hippocampus. *Brain Research*, 1975, *86*, 123–133.

Evans, J. G. M., & Hammond, G. R. Differential generalization of habituation across contexts; A function of stimulus significance. *Animal Learning and Behavior*, 1983, *11*, 431–434.

Fischette, C. T., Komisaruk, B. R., Edinger, H. M., Feder, H. H., & Siegel, A. Differential fornix ablations and the circadian rhythmicity of adrenal corticosteroid secretion. *Brain Research*, 1980, *195*, 373–387.

Gibbon, J. The contingency problem in autoshaping. In C. M. Locurto, H. S. Terrace, & J. Gibbon (Eds.), *Autoshaping and conditioning theory*. New York: Academic Press, 1981.

Gibbon, J. & Balsam, P. D. Spreading association in time. In C. M. Locurto, H. S. Terrace, & J. Gibbon (Eds.), *Autoshaping and conditioning theory*. New York: Academic Press, 1981.

Hall, G., & Pearce, J. M. Latent inhibition of a CS during CS–US pairings. *Journal of Experimental Psychology: Animal Behavior Processes*, 1979, *5*, 31–42.

Hanford, P. V.. Mulvaney, D. E., & Kelfer, D. A. The effect of novel environments on CS extinction in a conditioned suppression paradigm. *Bulletin of the Psychonomic Society*, 1980, *16*, 341–344.

Hebb, D. O. *The organization of behavior*. New York: Wiley, 1949.

Hirsh, R. The hippocampus and contextual retrieval of information from memory: A theory. *Behavioral Biology*, 1974, *12*, 421–444.

Hirsh, R. The hippocampus, conditional operations, and cognition. *Physiological Psychology*, 1980, *8*, 175–182.

Hull, C. L. *Principles of behavior*. New York: Appleton–Century–Crofts, 1943.

Infurna, R. N. Daily biorhythmicity influences homing behavior, psychopharmacological responsiveness, learning, and retention of suckling rats. *Journal of Comparative and Physiological Psychology*, 1981, *95*, 896–914.

Jacobs, W. J., & Nadel, L. Stress-induced recovery of fears and phobias. *Psychological Review* (submitted).

Jarrard, L. E. Behavior of hippocampal lesioned rats in home cage and novel situations. *Physiology and Behavior*, 1968, *3*, 65–70.

Jenkins, H. M., Barnes, R. A., & Barrera, F. J. Why autoshaping depends on trial spacing. In C. M. Locurto, H. S. Terrace, & J. Gibbon (Eds.), *Autoshaping and conditioning theory*. New York: Academic Press, 1981.

Jerison, H. *Evolution of the brain and intelligence*. New York: Academic Press, 1973.

Karpicke, J., Christoph, G., Peterson, G., & Hearst, E. Signal location and positive versus negative conditioned suppression in the rat. *Journal of Experimental Psychology: Animal Behavior Processes*, 1977, *3*, 105–118.

Konorski, J. *Integrative activity of the brain: An interdisciplinary approach*. Chicago: University of Chicago Press, 1967.

Kubie, J. L., & Ranck, J. B., Jr. Sensory-behavioral correlates in individual hippocampal neurons of the rat across four situations. *Society for Neuroscience Abstracts*, 1981, *7*, 358.

Kurz, E. M., & Levitsky, D. A. Novelty of contextual cues in taste aversion learning. *Animal Learning and Behavior*, 1982, *10*. 229–232.

Logan, F. A. Specificity of discrimination learning to the original context. *Science*, 1961, *133*, 1355–1356.

Lubow, R. E. Latent inhibition. *Psychological Bulletin*, 1973, *79*, 398–407.

Lubow, R. E., Rifkin, B., & Alek, M. The context effect: The relationship between stimulus preexposure and environmental preexposure determines subsequent learning. *Journal of Experimental Psychology: Animal Behavior Processes*, 1976, *2*, 38–47.

Lubow, R. E., Weiner, I., & Schnur, P. Conditioned attention theory. In G. H. Bower (Ed.), *The psychology of learning and motivation* (Vol. 15). New York: Academic Press, 1981.

Lynch, G., & Schubert, P. The use of in vitro brain slices for multidisciplinary studies of synaptic function. *Annual Review of Neuroscience*, 1980, *3*, 1–22.

Mackintosh, N. J. A theory of attention: Variations in the associability of stimuli with reinforcement. *Psychological Bulletin*, 1975, *82*, 276–298.

Marlin, N. A. Contextual associations in trace conditioning. *Animal Learning and Behavior*, 1981, *9*, 519–523.

McNaughton, B. L. Long-term synaptic enhancement and short-term potentiation in rat fascia dentata act through different mechanisms. *Journal of Physiology* (London), 1982, *324*, 249–262.

McNaughton, B. L., Douglas, R. M., & Goddard, G. V. Synaptic enhancement in fascia dentata: Cooperativity among co-active afferents. *Brain Research*, 1978, *157*, 277–293.

Micco, D. J., McEwen, B. S., & Shein, W. Modulation of behavioral inhibition in appetitive extinction following manipulation of adrenal steroids in rats: Implications for involvement of the hippocampus. *Journal of Comparative and Physiological Psychology*, 1979, *93*, 323–329.

Morris, R. G. M. Spatial localization does not require the presence of local cues. *Learning and Motivation*, 1982, *12*, 239–261.

Morris, R. G. M., Black, A. H., & O'Keefe, J. Hippocampal EEG during a ballistic movement (abstract). *Neuroscience Letters*, 1976, *3*, 102.

Morris, R. G. M., Garrud, P., Rawlins, J. N. P., & O'Keefe, J. Place navigation impaired in rats with hippocampal lesions. *Nature*, 1982, *297*, 681–682.

Nadel, L. Some thoughts on the proper foundations for the study of cognition in animals. *The Behavioral and Brain Sciences*, 1982, *5*, 383–384.

Nadel, L., & MacDonald, L. Hippocampus: Cognitive map or working memory? *Behavioral Biology*, 1980, *29*, 405–409.

Nadel, L., & Willner, J. Context and conditioning: A place for space. *Physiological Psychology*, 1980, *8*, 218–228.

Nadel, L., & Zola–Morgan, S. Infantile amnesia: A neurobiological perspective. In M. Moscovitch & S. Soroka (Eds.), *Infant memory*. New York: Plenum Press, in press.

Oberdieck, F., & Tarte, R. D. The effect of shock prod preexposure on conditioned defensive burying. *Bulletin of the Psychonomic Society*, 1981, *17*, 111–112.

Odling–Smee, F. J. Background stimuli and the interstimulus interval during Pavlovian conditioning. *Quarterly Journal of Experimental Psychology,* 1975, *27,* 387–392.

Odling–Smee, F. J. The overshadowing of background stimuli by an informative CS in aversive Pavlovian conditioning with rats. *Animal Learning and Behavior,* 1978, *6,* 43–51.

O'Keefe, J. Place units in the hippocampus of the freely moving rat. *Experimental Neurology,* 1976, *51,* 78–109.

O'Keefe, J. A review of the hippocampal place cells. *Progress in Neurobiology,* 1979, *13,* 419–439.

O'Keefe, J., & Conway, D. H. Hippocampal place units in the freely moving rat: Why they fire where they fire. *Experimental Brain Research,* 1978, *31,* 573–590.

O'Keefe, J., & Dostrovsky, J. The hippocampus as a spatial map. Preliminary evidence from unit activity in the freely moving rat. *Brain Research,* 1971, *34,* 171–175.

O'Keefe, J., & Nadel, L. *The hippocampus as a cognitive map.* Oxford: The Clarendon Press, 1978.

O'Keefe, J., & Nadel, L. Precis of The hippocampus as a cognitive map, and Authors' reply to Commentaries on same. *The Behavioral and Brain Sciences,* 1979, *2,* 487–534.

O'Keefe, J., Nadel, L., Keightley, S., & Kill, D. Fornix lesions selectively abolish place learning in the rat. *Experimental Neurology,* 1976, *48,* 152–166.

O'Keefe, J., Nadel, L., & Willner, J. Tuning out irrelevancy? Comments on Solomon's temporal mapping view of the hippocampus. *Psychological Bulletin,* 1979, *86,* 1280–1289.

Olton, D. S., Branch, M., & Best, P. Spatial correlates of hippocampal unit activity. *Experimental Neurology,* 1978, *58,* 387–409.

Ranck, J. B., Jr. Studies on single neurons in dorsal hippocampal formation and septum in unrestrained rats. *Experimental Neurology,* 1973, *41,* 461–555.

Rescorla, R. A. Pavlovian conditioning and its proper control procedures. *Psychological Review,* 1967, *74,* 71–80.

Rescorla, R. A., & Wagner, A. R. A theory of Pavlovian conditioning: Variations in the effectiveness of reinforcement and nonreinforcement. In A. H. Black & W. F. Prokasy (Eds.), *Classical conditioning II: Current research and theory.* New York: Appleton–Century–Crofts, 1972.

Robinson, T. E. Hippocampal rhythmic slow activity (RSA; Theta): A critical analysis of selected studies and discussion of possible species differences. *Brain Research Reviews,* 1980, *2,* 69–101.

Roitblat, H. L. The meaning of representation in animal memory. *The Behavioral and Brain Sciences,* 1982, *5,* 353–372.

Schmaltz, L. W., & Isaacson, R. L. Effect of bilateral hippocampal destruction on the acquisition and extinction of an operant response. *Physiology and Behavior,* 1967, *2,* 291–298.

Shillito, E. E. Exploratory behavior in the short-tailed vole. *Behaviour,* 1963, *21,* 145–154.

Solomon, P. R. Temporal versus spatial information processing theories of hippocampal function. *Psychological Bulletin,* 1979, *86,* 1272–1279.

Solomon, P. R., & Moore, J. W. Latent inhibition and stimulus generalization of the classically conditioned nictitating membrane response in rabbits (Oryctolagus cuniculus) following dorsal hippocampal ablation. *Journal of Comparative and Physiological Psychology,* 1975, *89,* 1192–1203.

Squire, L. R., Cohen, N. J., & Nadel, L. The medial temporal region and memory consolidation: A new hypothesis. In H. Weingartner & E. Parker (Eds.), *Memory consolidation.* Hillsdale, N.J.: Lawrence Erlbaum Associates, 1984.

Tolman, E. C. *Purposive behavior in rats and men.* New York: Century, 1932.

Tolman, E. C. Cognitive maps in rats and men. *Psychological Review,* 1948, *55,* 189–208.

Wagner, A. R. Expectancies and the priming of STM. In S. H. Hulse, H. Fowler, & W. K. Honig (Eds.), *Cognitive processes in animal behavior.* Hillsdale, N.J.: Lawrence Erlbaum Associates, 1978.

Wagner, A. R. SOP: A model of automatic memory processing in animal behavior. In N. E. Spear & R. R. Miller (Eds.), *Information processing in animals: Memory mechanisms*. Hillsdale, N.J.: Lawrence Erlbaum Associates, 1981.

Willner, J. A. Spatial factors in latent inhibition. *Paper presented at the meetings of the Eastern Psychological Association*, Hartford, Conn., April, 1980.

Wyers, E. J. Learning and evolution. In L. Petrinovich & J. L. McGaugh (Eds.), *Knowing, thinking and believing*. New York: Plenum Press, 1976.

Zentall, T. R. Effects of context change on forgetting in rats. *Journal of Experimental Psychology*, 1970, *86*, 440–448.

Author Index

Numbers in *italics* denote pages with bibliographic information.

A

Abbott, D. W., 363, *377*
Ader, R., 233, *264*, 368, 370, *382*
Ahlers, R. H., 247, *264*
Aigner, T. G., 361, 363, *381*
Alek, M., 24, *55*, 387, 394, 396, 399, *404*
Altom, M. W., 349, *355*
Anderson, D. C., 141, *163*
Andrews, H. L., 234, *264*
Andry, D. K., 301, *321*
Annau, A., 78, *101*, 108, *130*, 137, *163*
Anokhin, P. K., 13, *20*
Appel, J. B., 365, *380*
Arbit, J., 234, *264*
Archer, T., 135, 157, *163*, 230, 231, 232, 233, 234, 236, 237, 238, 239, 240, 242, 243, 244, 245, 246, 247, 248, 249, 250, 251, 253, 254, 255, 257, 258, 259, 260, 261, *264, 270*
Ashe, J. H., 233, 234, *268, 269*
Asratian, E. A., 24, 45, *54*, 105, *130*, 177, *192*, 213, 222, *223*
Atkinson, C. A., 109, 111, 112, *131*
Atkinson, R. C., 326, *354*
Attneave, F., 291, *292*
Auld, F., 373, *377*

B

Ayres, J. J. B., 60, 69, *70, 71, 72*, 75, *102*, 142, 153, *163, 165*

Baker, A. G., 7, *20*, 26, *54*, 75, 78, 80, 81, 82, 84, 85, 88, 89, 90, 91, 101, *101, 102*, 110, 115, 116, 118, 127, 129, *130*, 143, 158, 159, *163*, 171, *192*, 195, *223*
Baker, P. A., 7, *20*, 75, 80, 81, 84, 85, 88, 90, *102*, 115, 116, 118, 129, *130*, 143, 159, *163*
Baker, T. B., 109, 111, 112, *131*
Balaz, M. A., 139, 157, *163*, 173, 174, 175, 182, 189, *192, 193*, 299, *319*, 387, 399, 400, *402*
Baldock, M. D., 81, 91, 94, *102, 103*
Balsam, P. D., 4, 6, 8, 9, 10, 11, 12, 13, 14, 18, *20*, 24, 26, 30, 31, 32, 35, 43, *54*, 57, 58, 60, 69, 70, *71*, 106, 107, 108, 110, 113, 114, 118, 119, 122, 123, 126, 127, 128, 129, 130, *130, 131, 164*, 169, 188, 190, 191, *193*, 200, 201, 204, *223*, 245, 246, *264, 266*, 308, 312, *319, 320*, 386, 393, 394, 400, 401, *402, 403*
Balster, R. L., 361, *377*
Barker, L. M., 243, *264*

407

Barnes, R. A., 43, *55,* 188, 190, 191, *193,* 400, *404*
Barnett, S. A., 233, 246, 247, *265*
Barnhart, S. S., 363, *377*
Baron, M. R., 301, *320*
Barrera, F. J., 43, *55,* 188, 190, 191, *193,* 400, *404*
Barrett, R. J., 370, *377, 378*
Barry, H., III, 365, 373, 375, *377*
Bartlett, J. C., 369, *377*
Batson, J. D., 234, *265*
Bedarf, E. W., 247, *269*
Benedict, J. O., 60, 69, *70,* 75, *102,* 153, *163*
Benefield, R. L., 300, *320*
Benton, M. M., 11, *21*
Berger, B. D., 363, *377*
Berman, R. F., 109, 111, 112, *131*
Besley, S., 298, *320*
Best, M. R., 227, 234, *265*
Best, P., 227, 234, 247, *264, 265, 270,* 391, *405*
Biehl, D., 61, *71*
Birch, D. B., 337, *354*
Birch, L. L., 247, *265*
Birnbaum, I. M., 361, *379*
Bitterman, M. E., 259, *265*
Bjork, R. A., 222, *224*
Black, A. H., 390, *404*
Blackman, D. E., 115, *130*
Blanchard, D. C., 158, *164*
Blanchard, R. J., 158, *164*
Bliss, D. K., 360, 361, 362, 363, 373, *377, 378, 381*
Bliss, T. V. P., 391, *402*
Blough, D. S., 298, 313, *320*
Boice, R., 246, *265*
Boland, F. J., 245, *265*
Bolles, R. C., 26, 50, *54,* 135, 136, 140, 142, 143, 147, 157, 158, *164,* 167, 176, *192,* 217, 221, *223,* 227, 233, *267,* 368, 370, *378,* 399, *402, 403*
Booth, D. A., 233, *265, 267, 269, 270*
Bottjer, S. W., 187, *192,* 196, 212, 218, 220, *223*
Bouton, M. E., 50, *54,* 135, 136, 137, 138, 139, 140, 141, 142, 143, 144, 145, 146, 147, 149, 150, 151, 152, 153, 154, 155, 156, 157, 158, 159, *164,* 167, 176, *192,* 217, 221, *223,* 399, *402, 403*
Bower, G. H., 181, *192,* 274, *292,* 369, *378*
Bowman, T. G., 247, *266*

Boyd, S. C., 375, *378*
Bradbury, R., 370, *379*
Branch, M., 391, *405*
Brandon, S. E., 60, 61, *71*
Bransford, J. D., 345, *354*
Braun, J. J., 233, *267*
Braveman, N. S., 228, 234, *265*
Bresnahan, E. L., 301, *320*
Brett, L., 253, 254, *270*
Bronstein, P. M., 247, *265*
Brookshire, K. H., 247, *271*
Brown, A., 376, *378*
Brown, D. L., 227, 230, *270*
Brown, P. L., 49, *54*
Brown, R. T., 230, 241, *266*
Brown, W. L., 234, *269*
Browne, R. G., 365, 366, 376, *378*
Bryan, R. G., 4, *21,* 170, *194,* 361, *383*
Burkhard, B., 225, *266*
Burr, D. E. S., 298, 301, *321*
Buser, P., 395, *403*
Butcher, R., 371, *379*
Butler, C. S., 134, 135, 146, 148, *164*
Buzsaki, G., 389, *403*

C

Cacheiro, H., 146, 160, *165,* 182, *192, 193*
Calderazzo Filho, L. S., 400, *403*
Cameron, L. M., 234, *264*
Campbell, B. A., 26, *56*
Campione, J. C., 335, 337, *354*
Cannon, D. S., 109, 111, 112, *131*
Capaldi, E. J., 276, *292,* 370, *378*
Caponigri, V., 141, *163*
Capra, S., 139, 157, *163,* 173, 174, 175, 189, *192,* 299, *319,* 387, 399, 400, *402*
Capretta, P. J., 247, *265*
Carlton, P. L., 247, *265*
Carr, H., 167, *192*
Carrigan, P., 316, *321*
Carroll, M. E., 247, *265*
Carter, N., 135, *163,* 230, 231, 232, 233, 234, 236, 237, 238, 239, 242, 247, 250, 260, *264*
Carter, P. E., 177, *192*
Caul, W. F., 370, 375, *378*
Cazard, P., 395, *403*
Channell, S., 24, *54,* 387, 396, 399, *403*
Charlton, S. G., 262, *265*

Cheatle, M. D., 233, *270*
Chiszar, D. A., 4, *21*, 170, *194*, 361, *383*
Chorazyna, H., 137, *164*
Chorover, S. L., 233, *270*
Christoph, G., 389, *404*
Church, R. M., 4, *20*
Chute, D. L., 360, *380*
Clark, M., 369, *380*
Clarke, J. C., 253, *265*
Cohen, N. J., 391, 395, 398, *405*
Colby, J. J., 125, *131*
Collier, A. C., 158, *164*
Collins, A. M., 178, *192*
Collins, W., 372, *378*
Collyer, R., 234, *268*
Colpaert, F. C., 360, 364, 365, 368, 376, *378*
Combe, G., 357, 372, *378*
Conger, J. J., 373, *378*
Connelly, J. F., 180, *192*, 362, *378*
Connelly, J. M., 180, *192*, 362, *378*
Conway, D. H., 391, *405*
Corbit, J. D., 107, 110, 129, *132*
Cotic, T., 260, 261, *264*
Cowan, P. E., 233, *265*
Cowey, A., 371, *381*
Culler, E. A., 373, *379*
Cunningham, C. L., 136, 137, 142, 143, 146, 148, *164, 165*, 196, *223*, 234, *265*
Cunningham, S., 316, *321*
Cynx, J., 279, 280, 284, 289, 290, *292*

D

D'Amato, M. R., 252, *265*
Davidson, T. L., 370, *378*
Davitt, G. A., 296, 304, 306, 307, 308, 318, *321*
Dawson, R., 261, *267*
Deutsch, D., 275, 277, 291, *292*
Deutsch, J. A., 359, *378*
Devenport, J. A., 400, *403*
Devenport, L. D., 400, *403*
DeVietti, T. L., 361, 371, *378, 381*
Dexter, W. R., 24, *54*, 141, *164*
Dickinson, A., 212, *223*, 225, 228, 262, *265*
Dinc, H. I., 247, *265*
Dodd, P. W. D., 213, *224*
Domjan, M., 59, *71*, 109, *132*, 225, 227, 233, 245, 247, 252, *266*
Dore, F. Y., 398, *403*
Dorsky, N. P., 276, *292*

Dostrovsky, J., 391, *405*
Douglas, R. M., 391, 395, *403, 404*
Downey, D. J., 367, *379*
Dragoin, W. B., 227, *271*
Dufort, R. H., 109, 127, *131*
Duncan, P. M., 362, *379*
Dunn, A. J., 371, *379*
Durlach, P. J., 2, 8, 9, 11, 12, 13, 14, 16, *20*, 36, 37, 38, *54*, 60, 70, *71*, 180, *194*, 253, 254, 262, 263, *266*, 352, *355*
Dutta, P., 368, 371, *382*
Dweck, C. S., 31, *54*, 143, 158, *164*

E

Eck, K. O., 298, 301, 303, *320, 321*
Edelson, S. M., 349, *355*
Edinger, H. M., 393, *403*
Eich, J. E., 361, 362, 363, *379*
Ellinwood, E. H., 234, *268*
Elliotson, J., 372, *379*
Ellis, H. C., 369, *381*
Elson, I. J., 370, *379*
Epps, J. O., 362, *378*
Ercole, M. A., 368, 371, *382*
Ernst, A. J., 301, *321*
Ervin, F. R., 227, 252, *266*
Estes, W. K., 1, 2, *20*, 36, 53, *54*, 133, 160, *164*, 167, 172, 178, *193*, 225, 226, 229, 230, *266*, 326, 328, 353, *354*
Evans, F. J., 368, 369, *379*
Evans, J. G. M., *403*

F

Falkenberg, P. R., 167, *193*
Fanselow, M. S., 7, *20*, 143, 158, *164*
Fantino, E., 7, *20*, 191, *193*
Farley, J., 60, 61, *71*
Farrell, L., 81, *103*
Farthing, G. W., 298, 300, *320*
Fath, S., 58, *71*
Fazzaro, J., 252, *265*
Feder, H. H., 393, *403*
Feldman, R. S., 376, *378*
Ferraro, D. P., 262, *265*
Fischette, C. T., 393, *403*
Fisher, M. A., 335, *354*
Fitzgerald, R. D., 196, *223*
Flagg, S. F., 332, 335, *354*
Fogarty, F. J., 369, *383*

Folkard, S., 370, *379*
Foree, D. D., 314, *320*
Formica, R., 141, *163*
Fountain, S. B., 276, *292*
Fowler, H., 187, *193*, 308, *320*
Francisco, D. L., 196, *223*
Franklin, S., 196, 198, 209, *223, 224*
Franks, J. J., 345, *354*
Freedman, N., 371, *379, 381*
Freeman, F., 299, 300, *320*
Freko, D., 349, *354*
French, G. M., 327, *354*
Frey, P. W., 133, 134, 135, 146, 148, *164*
Frieman, J., 303, *320*

G

Gabel, J., 7, *20*, 80, 81, 84, 85, 88, 90, *102*, 115, 116, 118, 129, *130*, 143, 159, *163*
Gabriel, M., 2, 16, *20*
Gaffan, E., 196, *223*
Galef, B. G., Jr., 253, *266*
Gamzu, E. R., 31, *54*, 228, *266*
Garcia, E. E., 148, *166*
Garcia, J., 226, 227, 233, 234, 252, 253, 254, 259, *266, 267, 269, 270*
Gardner, E. L., 371, *379*
Garner, W. R., 273, *292*
Garrud, P., 396, *404*
Gelhard, R., 227, 230, *270*
Ghiselli, W. B., 370, *379*
Gibbon, J., 4, 6, 11, 12, 13, 18, *20, 21*, 24, 31, 32, 35, *54*, 57, 69, 70, *71*, 81, 91, 94, *102, 103*, 106, 107, 108, 110, 113, 114, 118, 119, 122, 123, 126, 127, 128, 129, 130, *131*, 169, 188, 190, 191, *193*, 200, 204, *223*, 245, *266*, 400, *403*
Gillan, D., 247, *266*
Gilligan, S. G., 369, *378*
Gillin, J. C., 363, *379*
Girden, E., 373, *379*
Glenberg, A. M., 222, *224*
Glick, S. D., 371, *379*
Goddard, G. V., 391, 395, *403, 404*
Gold, L., 81, 91, 94, *102*
Goldsmith, M., 361, *384*
Goldstein, A., 365, *382*
Goodchild, P., 233, *267*
Gordon, W. C., 4, *21*, 170, *194*, 361, *383*
Gormezano, I., 225, *267*
Goyette, C. H., 303, *320*

Grant, L. D., 376, *380*
Grant, D. S., 338, *355*
Grastyan, E., 389, *403*
Grau, J. W., 31, *54*
Gray, P., 370, 371, *379*
Green, K. F., 227, 247, *266*
Greenwood, P. M., 371, *379*
Gregg, B., 245, *266*
Grote, F. W., Jr., 230, 241, *266*
Gulliksen, H., 49, *55*
Gunter, J. L., 371, *381*
Gustafson, L. A., 369, *379*
Guthrie, E. R., 1, *20*, 167, *194*
Gutsin, P., 182, *192*

H

Haberlandt, K., 73, 74, *103*
Haggard, D., 123, 126, *131*, 153, *165*
Hall, G., 24, *54*, 133, *165*, 170, 171, 191, *194*, 387, 396, 399, *403*
Hall, H., 370, *384*
Hallman, H., 260, *267*
Hammond, G. R., *403*
Hanford, P. V., 399, *403*
Hankins, W. G., 227, 233, 253, 254, *266, 267, 270*
Hansen, G., 304, *321*
Hargrave, G. E., 227, 233, *267*
Harris, R. T., 361, 363, *381*
Hart, M. M., 196, *223*
Hartl, P., 139, 157, *163*, 173, 189, *192*, 299, *319*, 387, 399, *402*
Hayden, M., 61, *71*
Hazell, P., 367, *379*
Hearst, E., 75, *102*, 187, *193*, 196, 198, 209, 210, 218, 220, 222, *223, 224*, 298, *320*, 389, *404*
Hebb, D. O., 246, *267*, 395, *403*
Heistad, G. T., 373, *379, 380*
Hendersen, R. W., 123, *131*
Hendry, J., 134, 135, 142, *164*
Henne, D. R., 276, *292*
Henriksson, B. G., 363, *380*
Henton, W. W., 13, *20*
Hernandez, L. L., 365, *380*
Heth, C. D., 134, 135, 142, 143, *165*, 221, *224*
Hinderliter, C. F., 363, *380*
Hinson, R. E., 31, *55*, 59, *71*, 109, 128, *131*
Hirschhorn, I. D., 365, *380*

Hirsh, R., 401, *403*
Ho, B. T., 360, 365, 376, *378, 380, 383*
Hobson, G. N., 109, *131*
Hoffman, H. S., 142, *164*
Holland, P. C., 2, 5, *20*, 25, 26, 27, *55, 56,* 159, *165,* 178, *193,* 253, *267*
Hollinger, M., 247, *267*
Holloway, F. A., 363, 370, *380,* 400, *403*
Holmgren, B., 363, 364, *380*
Holmstrom, L. S., 227, *266*
Holohean, A. M., 365, *380*
Honig, W. K., 225, *267,* 307, *320,* 353, *354*
Hopkins, B. L., 326, *354*
Huang, J. T., 368, *380*
Hull, C. L., 1, *20,* 23, 49, *55,* 74, *102,* 115, *131,* 274, *292,* 326, *354,* 386, *403*
Hulse, S. H., 275, 276, 277, 279, 280, 284, 289, 290, *292*
Humpal, J., 279, 280, 284, 289, 290, *292*
Hunt, E. L., 227, 234, *266*
Hutton, R. A., 227, *271*
Hyde, T. S., 227, *267*

I

Idrobo, F., 180, *193*
Imada, I., 171, 173, *193*
Infurna, R. N., 401, *403*
Irwin, J., 253, *265*
Isaacson, R. L., 389, *405*
Isen, A. M., 369, *380*
Israel, M., 337, *354*
Iversen, S. D., 260, *268*
Iwahara, S., 361, *380*
Iwens, J., 234, *270*
Izquierdo, I., 400, *403*

J

Jackson, F. D., 370, *380*
Jackson, R. L., 58, *71*
Jacobs, W. J., 115, 129, *131, 132,* 399, *403*
Järbe, T. U. C., 260, 261, *264,* 363, 365, *380*
Jarrard, L. E., 391, *403*
Jarvik, M. E., 371, *379*
Jenkins, H. M., 12, 13, *21,* 39, 43, 49, *54, 55,* 188, 190, 191, *193,* 196, 213, 216, 217, 220, *223,* 307, 308, *321,* 400, *404*
Jenkins, J. J., 162, *164*
Jennings, W. A., 246, *267*
Jerison, H., 401, *404*

Jewell, N. P., 365, *382*
Jones, C. N., 376, *380*
Jones, D. R., 247, *268*
Jones, L. E., 370, *381*
Jones, M. R., 274, 279, *292*
Jonsson, G., 260, *267*
Joy, R. M., 368, *380*

K

Kaczender, E., 370, *383*
Kalat, J. W., 243, 247, *267*
Kamin, L. J., 24, *55,* 73, 76, 77, 78, *101, 102,* 108, 127, 129, *130, 101,* 137, 144, *163, 165,* 180, *193,* 234, 252, *267,* 307, 320
Kaplan, P., 187, *193,* 198, 210, 218, 222, 223
Karp, L., 369, *380*
Karpicke, J., 389, *404*
Kasprow, W. J., 139, 146, 157, 160, *163, 165,* 175, 182, *192, 193,* 387, 400, *402*
Katz, J. J., 344, *354*
Keele, S. W., 344, *355*
Kehoe, E. J., 225, *267*
Keightley, S., 394, *405*
Kelfer, D. A., 399, *403*
Keller, R. J., 60, 69, *71*
Kenfield, M., 233, *267*
Kilbey, M. M., 361, 363, *381*
Kill, D., 394, *405*
Killeen, P., 14, *21*
Kimble, G. A., 109, 127, *131*
Kimeldorf, D. J., 227, 234, *266*
Kimmel, H. D., 24, 45, *55*
King, D. A., 137, 138, 139, 140, 141, 142, 144, 145, 146, 151, 154, 157, 158, 159, *164*
King, R. A., 299, *321*
Kinsbourne, M., 359, *383*
Kirk, R. E., 240, *267*
Kirschbaum, E. H., 234, 247, *268*
Klein, N. W., Jr., 360, 365, *382*
Klein, S. B., 371, *381, 383*
Koelling, R. A., 226, 227, 233, 234, 252, *266*
Kohler, W., 3, *21*
Komisaruk, B. R., 393, *403*
Konorski, J., 4, 13, *21,* 24, 32, 49, 52, *55,* 105, *131,* 134, 135, *165,* 172, *193,* 195, 198, 212, *223,* 386, 398, *404*
Kotovsky, K., 274, *293*

Kovacevic, N. S., 370, *383*
Kovner, R., 227, *266*
Kral, P. A., 227, *271*
Krebs, W. H., 370, *383*
Kremer, E. F., 69, *71, 75, 102*
Kubie, J. L., 391, 392, *404*
Kupalov, P. S., 13, *21*
Kurz, E. M., 394, *404*

L

Lal, H., 360, 365, 367, *381, 383*
Lambos, W. A., 12, *21*
Langford, A., 371, *381*
Larsen, J. D., 227, *267*
Larson, R. C., 371, *378*
Larue, C., 233, *267*
Lashley, K. S., 274, *292*
Laverty, R., 367, *379*
Lazar, R., 316, *321*
Leclerc, R., 220, *223*
Lehr, P. P., 371, *381*
Leibmann, S., 371, *378*
Leight, K. A., 369, *381*
Leiman, A., 360, 362, *378*
Leith, N. J., 370, *377*
Lett, B. T., 253, *267*
Levine, S., 370, *381*
Levis, D. J., 369, *381*
Levitsky, D. A., 394, *404*
Levy, C. J., 247, *265*
Leyland, C. M., 24, *55*
Lindblom, L. L., 12, 13, *21,* 39, *55,* 196, 213, 216, 217, *223*
Little, L., 337, *355*
Liu, S. W., 335, *355*
Locurto, C., 13, *21,* 81, 91, 94, *102*
Loftus, E. F., 178, *192*
Logan, F. A., 73, 74, *103,* 387, *404*
Logie, L. C., 234, *269*
Logue, A. W., 262, *267*
LoLordo, V. M., 11, *21,* 26, 31, *55,* 59, *71,* 80, 81, *102,* 106, 108, 109, 110, 111, 115, 129, *131, 132,* 154, *165,* 168, *194,* 295, 314, *320*
Lomo, T., 391, *402*
Lopez, L. J., 298, 309, *321*
Lorden, J. F., 233, 261, *267*
Lovett, D., 233, *267*
Lubow, R. E., 24, *55,* 247, *267,* 387, 394, 396, 399, *404*

Lynch, G., 391, *404*
Lyons, J., 304, 313, *321*
Lysle, D. T., 187, *193*

M

MacDonald, L., 394, *404*
Macht, M. L., 369, *381*
Mackay, B., 247, *267*
Mackintosh, N. J., 3, 9, 10, *21,* 24, 26, *54, 55,* 68, *71,* 80, 82, 85, 91, 101, *102,* 110, 127, 129, *130,* 133, 144, *165,* 170, *193,* 225, 226, 238, 252, 255, 262, *265, 268, 270,* 298, 301, 304, 307, 318, *320,* 329, 337, *355, 356,* 398, *404*
Macnish, R., 372, *381*
Macrides, F., 233, *270*
Mah, W., 313, 314, 319, *321*
Mahoney, W. J., 60, 69, *71*
Maier, S. F., 88, 89, *102*
Makous, W., 227, *271*
Marlin, D. W., 247, *265*
Marlin, N. A., 171, 190, *193, 400, 404*
Martin, J. C., 234, *268*
Mason, S. T., 260, *268*
Mayes, A. R., 371, *381*
Mayse, J. F., 361, 371, *378, 381*
McAllister, D. E., 2, 11, 16, *21,* 180, *193,* 241, *268*
McAllister, W. R., 2, 11, 16, *21,* 180, *193,* 241, *268*
McAuley, K., 136, *166*
McCutcheon, L. E., 246, *267*
McEwen, B. S., 399, *404*
McGowan, B. K., 227, 252, *266*
McGrath, M., 335, *354*
McIntyre, D. C., 368, 371, *381*
McKelvie, A. R., 309, 310, 311, 312, 313, 314, 315, 316, 318, 319, *321*
McKim, W. A., 363, *381*
McNaughton, B. L., 391, 395, *404*
McNaughton, N., 260, *268*
Medin, D. L., 49, *55,* 160, *165,* 172, 178, *193,* 329, 331, 332, 335, 337, 338, 339, 341, 342, 345, 346, 348, 353, *355*
Mercier, P., 7, *20,* 80, 81, 84, 85, 88, 89, 90, *102,* 115, 116, 118, 129, *130,* 143, 159, *163,* 171, *192*
Merrill, H. K., 24, *54,* 141, *164*
Mervis, C. B., 344, 348, *355*
Micco, D. J., 399, *404*

Mickley, G. A., 227, *265*
Miksic, S., 367, *381*
Mikulka, P. J., 253, *268*
Miles, C. G., 307, *320*
Mill, J., 324, 325, *355*
Miller, H., 369, *384*
Miller, J. T., 303, 304, *321*
Miller, N. E., 247, *268, 373, 377, 381*
Miller, R. R., 139, 146, 157, 160, *163, 165,*
    171, 173, 174, 175, 182, 189, *192, 193,*
    299, *319,* 387, 399, 400, *402*
Mis, R. W., 109, 111, 129, *131*
Mitchell, D., 234, 246, 247, 259, *268*
Mitchell, L. K., 259, *268*
Mod, L., 389, *403*
Modrow, H. E., 361, 363, *381*
Monk, T. H., 370, *379*
Monteiro, K. P., 369, *378*
Moore, A. V., 247, *267*
Moore, J. W., 109, 111, 129, *131,* 376, *378,*
    396, *405*
Morishita, M., 171, 173, *193*
Morris, L. W., 371, *378*
Morris, R. G. M., 390, 396, *404*
Morrison, G. R., 234, *268*
Moschovakis, A., 400, *403*
Moye, T. B., 310, 311, 312, 315, 318, 319,
    321
Mulvaney, D. E., 399, *403*
Mumma, R., 337, *355*
Murphy, A. L., 58, *71*
Murphy, D. L., 369, *384*

N

Nachman, M., 233, 234, 247, *268, 269,* 371,
    381
Nadel, L., 106, *131,* 141, *165,* 172, *193,* 371,
    381, 385, 386, 387, 390, 391, 393, 394,
    395, 398, 399, 400, 401, *403, 404, 405*
Nakajima, S., 370, *381*
Navarick, D. J., 247, *269*
Nawrocki, T. M., 276, *292*
Neely, J. H., 39, *55,* 371, *383*
Nevitt, J. R., 362, *378*
Newlin, R. J., 298, 304, 305, 318, *320*
Newman, F. L., 300, *320*
Nilsson, L.-G., 135, *163,* 230, 231, 232, 233,
    234, 236, 237, 238, 239, 242, 243, 244,
    245, 246, 247, 250, 260, *264*

Noel, R. C., 303, *320*
Noguchi, S., 361, *380*

O

Oberdieck, F., 396, *404*
O'Connell, D. N., 369, *379*
Odling-Smee, F. J., 7, 11, *21,* 26, *55,* 69, *71,*
    79, 80, *102,* 139, 143, 159, *165,* 171, 173,
    194, 400, *405*
O'Farrell, T., 141, *163*
Ohlin, G. Ch., 365, *380*
O'Keefe, J., 385, 386, 387, 390, 391, 394,
    396, 398, 400, *404, 405*
O'Leary, D, K., 276, 279, *292*
O'Leary, K. D., 123, *132*
Olson, R. K., 291, *292*
Olton, D. S., 391, *405*
Orne, M. T., 369, *379*
Osborne, B., 253, *266*
Osborne, G. L., 370, *378*
Osgood, C. E., 338, *355*
Otis, L. S., 370, *381*
Overall, J. E., 234, *269*
Overmier, J. B., 7, *21, 56*
Overton, D. A., 359, 360, 361, 362, 363,
    364, 365, 366, 367, 368, 369, 370, 371,
    373, *381, 382*
Owren, M. J., 218, *223*

P

Pain, J. F., 233, *269*
Pan, S., 167, *194*
Parker, L. A., 234, 247, *266, 269*
Parkinson, J. K., 338, 339, *355*
Patterson, J., 7, *21*
Pavlov, I. P., 1, *21,* 77, *102,* 105, 113, 123,
    127, 129, *131,* 167, 169, *194,* 225, 246,
    269
Pearce, J. M., 133, *165,* 170, 171, 191, *194,*
    396, *403*
Peck, J. H., 368, 370, *382*
Pelleymounter, M. A., 261, *267*
Pepperberg, I., 279, *292*
Perkins, C. C., Jr., 180, *194,* 296, *320*
Perry, R. L., 234, 247, *268*
Petersen, R. C., 362, *382*
Peterson, D. W., 367, *379*
Peterson, G. B., 332, *355,* 389, *404*
Phifer, R., 362, *378*

Philput, C., 253, *268*
Pitts, E., 253, *268*
Ponzio, F., 260, *267*
Posner, M. I., 344, *355*
Postal, P. M., 344, *354*
Pote, R., 371, *379*
Prakash, I., 233, *265*
Premack, D., 291, *292*
Price, T., 73, 74, *103*
Prinz, P. N., 368, *380*
Prokasy, W. F., 106, *131*

Q

Quinsey, V. L., 75, *102*, 142, *165*

R

Rabinowitch, V., 247, *269*
Rabinowitz, F. M., 335, *354*
Ranck, J. B., Jr., 391, 392, *404, 405*
Randford, G. G., 233, *265*
Randich, A., 11, *21*, 26, 31, *55*, 59, *71*, 80,
    81, 87, *102*, 106, 108, 109, 110, 111, 112,
    114, 115, 118, 123, 126, 128, 129, *131,
    132*, 153, 154, 158, *165*, 168, *194*
Ranney, M., 310, 311, 312, 315, 318, 319,
    321
Rauschenberger, J., 233, 234, *268, 269*
Rauzin, R., 316, *321*
Rawlins, J. N. P., 396, *404*
Ray, O. S., 370, *377*
Ray, R. L., 24, 45, *55*
Razran, G., 225, *269*
Reberg, D., 134, 135, 142, *165*, 217, 220,
    223, 224
Reed, S. K., 345, *355*
Reed, V. G., 371, *382*
Reichart, H., 368, 371, *381*
Reid, L. S., 370, *384*
Rescorla, R. A., 2, 3, 6, 9, 12, 18, *21*, 23,
    24, 25, 26, 31, 35, 40, 41, 42, 52, 53, *54,
    55, 56*, 57, 69, *71*, 73, 74, 75, 76, 79, 100,
    103, 106, 107, 108, 110, 113, 114, 118,
    119, 121, 122, 123, 127, 128, 129, 130,
    132, 133, 134, 135, 137, 141, 142, 143,
    146, 148, 150, 151, 156, 158, 159, *165,
    166*, 167, 169, 170, 171, 180, 181, 182,
    183, 188, 189, 190, 191, *194*, 195, 196,
    197, 198, 200, 203, 209, 213, 217, 218,
    220, 221, 222, *224*, 226, 230, 252, 253,

    254, 255, 256, 257, 262, 263, *266, 269,
    271*, 298, 299, 307, 308, 318, *320*, 352,
    354, 386, 398, 400, *405*
Restle, F., 274, 276, *293*
Revusky, S. H., 227, 233, 234, 247, 252,
    259, 262, *269, 270*
Reynolds, T. J., 338, 339, 341, 342, 353, *355*
Rhor-Stafford, I., 61, *71*
Ribot, T., 372, *382*
Riccio, D. C., 167, *194*, 296, *321*
Richards, D. W., III, 360, *380*
Richards, R. W., 146, 160, *166*, 311, *321*
Rickert, E. J., 261, *267*
Rifkin, B. 24, *55*, 387, 394, 396, 399, *404*
Riley, A. L., 129, *132*, 259, *269*
Riley, E. P., 371, *383*
Rizley, R. C., 255, 256, 257, *269*
Roberts, L. J., 247, *267*
Roberts, W. A., 338, *355*
Robinson, T. E., 390, 392, *405*
Rohles, F. H., 234, *269*
Roitblat, H. L., 401, *405*
Roll, S. K., 359, *378*
Rolls, B. J., 246, *269*
Rolls, E. T., 246, *269*
Romano, C., 365, *382*
Rosch, E., 344, 348, *355*
Rosecrans, J. A., 360, 365, *378, 380, 382*
Rosenberg, L., 234, *270*
Rosenthal, J., 370, *379*
Ross, R. T., 118, *132*
Ross, S. B., 260, *267, 269*
Rozin, P., 234, 243, *267, 270*
Rudy, J. W., 233, 234, *270*
Rusiniak, K. W., 227, 233, 253, 254, *266,
    267, 270*
Rzóska, J., 247, *270*

S

Sachs, E., 360, 365, *382*
Salm, A., 361, 363, *381*
Sandell, J. H., 234, *270*
Santrock, J. W., 369, *377*
Sargent, D. M., 146, 160, *166*
Schachtman, T., 146, 160, *165*
Schaffer, M. M., 345, 346, *355*
Schechter, M. D., 376, *383*
Schmaltz, L. W., 389, *405*
Schneider, A. M., 371, *383*
Schnur, P., 396, *404*

Schubert, P., 391, *404*
Schwam, K. I., 61, *71*
Schwanenflugel, P. J., 348, *354*
Schwartz, A. L., 6, 11, 12, 13, *20*, 26, 43, *54*, 58, 70, *71*, 245, 246, *264*, 312, *320*, 394, *402*
Schwartz, B., 79, *103*
Scott, D. W., 259, *268*
Sears, R. J., 133, *164*
Sebestyen, G. S., 348, *355*
Seligman, M. E. P., 88, 89, *102*, 143, 159, *166*, 227, *270*
Semon, R., 373, *383*
Seybert, J. A., 370, *379*
Shalker, T. D., 369, *380*
Sheafor, P. J., 143, *166*, 241, *270*
Shearman, G., 365, 367, *381*, *383*
Sheffield, F. D., 26, *56*
Shein, W., 399, *404*
Shepard, R., 277, *293*
Shepp, B. E., 332, 354, *355*
Sherman, J. E., 150, 153, *166*
Shillito, E. E., 386, *405*
Shmavonian, B. H., 373, *383*
Shor, R. E., 369, *379*
Sidman, M., 316, *321*
Siegel, A., 393, *403*
Siegel, S., 59, *71*, 109, *132*, 158, *166*, 247, *266*, *270*, 372, *383*
Silverman, P. B., 365, *383*
Simmelhag, V. L., 30, *56*, 60, *71*
Simon, H. A., 274, *293*
Simson, P. C., 233, *265*, *270*
Singer, J. J., 371, *379*
Sjödén, P.-O., 135, 157, *163*, 230, 231, 232, 233, 234, 236, 237, 238, 239, 240, 242, 243, 244, 245, 246, 247, 248, 249, 250, 251, 253, 254, 255, 257, 258, 259, 260, *264*, *270*
Skinner, B. F., 1, *21*, 30, *56*, 274, *293*, 295, *321*
Slangen, J. L., 360, 364, 365, *378*
Sledjeski, M., 360, 362, *378*
Slotnick, B. M., 227, 230, *270*
Smith, E. E., 346, *355*
Smith, G. J., 4, *21*, 170, *194*, 361, *383*
Smith, J. C., 243, 247, 259, *264*, *265*, *270*
Smith, N. F., 125, *131*
Smith, S., 167, *194*
Smith, S. M., 159, 161, *166*, 222, *224*
Solomon, P. R., 396, *405*

Solomon, R. L., 107, 110, 129, *132*
Somjen, G., 233, *270*
Spear, N. E., 4, *21*, 159, 161, *166*, 170, 172, 178, 180, 182, *194*, 309, *321*, 361, 369, 371, *381*, *383*
Spence, K. W., 49, *56*, 134, 146, *166*, 325, 332, 345, *356*
Spencer, W. A., 107, 110, *132*
Spiker, C. C., 332, 335, *356*
Springer, A. D., 182, *193*
Squire, L. R., 391, 395, 398, *405*
Staddon, J. E. R., 30, *56*, 60, *71*, 225, *267*
Stein, L., 363, *377*
Steinman, F., 180, *194*
Stephan, F. K., 370, *383*
Stewart, J., 370, *383*
Stillman, R. C., 363, 369, *379*, *384*
Stroebel, C. F., 370, *383*
Strouthes, A., 247, *269*, *270*
Sturgis, R. D., 370, *380*
Suboski, M. D., 371, *379*
Sullivan, P., 141, *163*
Supak, T. D., 233, *270*
Sutherland, N. S., 252, *270*, 329, *356*
Sutter, J., 246, *268*
Sutterer, J. R., 115, *131*
Svinicki, J. G., 300, 302, 303, *321*
Svinicki, M. D., 300, 302, *321*
Swanson, J. M., 359, *383*
Switalski, R. W., 304, 313, *321*
Szwejkowska, G., 134, 135, *165*

T

Tailby, W., 316, *321*
Tarte, R. D., 396, *404*
Taukulis, H. K., 233, *270*
Taylor, J. A., 59, *71*, 109, 111, 127, 129, *132*
Taylor, R., 369, *383*
Teasdale, J. D., 369, *383*
Terrace, H. S., 9, 13, *21*, 81, 91, 94, *102*, *103*
Thomas, D. R., 24, 45, *56*, 167, *194*, 296, 298, 299, 300, 301, 302, 303, 304, 305, 306, 307, 308, 309, 310, 311, 312, 313, 314, 315, 316, 318, 319, *320*, *321*
Thomas, E., 196, *224*
Thompson, C. I., 371, *383*
Thompson, R. F., 107, 110, *132*
Thorndike, E. L., 1, *21*

Thune, G. E., 370, *378*
Tidd, G. E., 373, *377*
Timmons, J. K., 180, *192*
Timmons, R., 4, *21*, 170, *194*, 361, *383*
Todd, R. C., 274, *293*
Tolman, E. C., 24, *56*, 89, *103*, 385, 400, *405*
Tomie, A., 6, 12, *21*, 26, 31, *56*, 58, 59, 61, 70, *71*, 80, 88, *103*, 107, *132*, 143, *166*, 245, *270*, 296, 299, 304, 306, 307, 308, 312, 318, *321*
Torres, A. A., 373, *380*
Trainer, J. E., 289, 290, *293*
Trapold, M., *56*, 332, *355*
Travers, T., 13, *21*
Trowill, J. A., 371, *382*

U

Uhl, C. N., 148, *166*
Underwood, B. J., 181, *194*
Urda, M., 167, *194*, 293, *321*

V

Van Houten, R., 123, *132*
Verry, D. R., 276, *292*
Vitz, P. C., 274, *293*
Vogel, J. R., 247, *265*
Vom Saal, W., 307, 308, *321*
Vospalek, D. M., 376, *380*

W

Wagner, A. R., 3, 6, 12, 18, *21*, 24, 25, 31, 35, 39, 40, 41, *54*, *55*, *56*, 57, 69, *71*, *72*, 73, 74, 76, 79, 100, *103*, 106, 107, 108, 110, 113, 114, 118, 119, 121, 122, 123, 127, 128, 129, 130, *132*, 133, 134, 141, 143, 146, 148, 156, 158, *164*, *166*, 167, 169, 170, 171, 188, *194*, 196, 197, 200, 209, 217, 222, *224*, 226, 230, 252, 255, *269*, *270*, *271*, 298, 299, 307, 308, 318, *320*, 373, *377*, 386, 396, 398, *405*, *406*
Walker, E., 196, 218, *223*
Wann, P. D., 371, *383*
Wansley, R. A., 370, *380*
Warren, J. M., 337, *355*
Wasserman, E. A., 196, 198, *224*

Watson, J. B., 167, *194*
Webb, W. B., 370, *383*
Weiner, I., 396, *404*
Weingarten, M., 360, 365, *382*
Weingartner, H., 363, 369, *379*, *384*
Weisman, R. G., 213, *224*
Weiss, S. J., 123, *132*
Weissman, A., 365, 366, *378*
Welker, R. L., 136, *166*, 296, 306, 307, 308, 318, *321*
Werner, T. J., 177, *192*
Westbrook, R. F., 253, *265*
Weyant, R. G., 180, *194*, 296, *320*
Wheatley, K. L., 303, *321*
Wheeler, R. L., 332, *355*
White, B. N., 335, *356*
Whitman, D., 371, *381*
Wickens, D. D., 323, *356*, 370, *384*
Wilcoxon, H. C., 227, *271*
Williams, B. A., 60, 61, *72*
Williams, D. R., 31, *54*
Williams, K, D., 246, *268*
Willner, J., 106, *131*, 141, *165*, 172, *193*, 234, *271*, 385, 386, 387, 393, 396, 398, 399, 400, *404*, *405*, *406*
Wilson, N. E., 227, 252, *266*
Winiczai, Z., 389, *403*
Winslow, F., 372, *384*
Winzenz, D., 274, *292*
Witcher, E. S., 60, 69, *70*, *72*
Wittlin, W. A., 247, *271*
Wolf, D., 141, *163*
Wolfe, H. L., 49, *55*
Wollman, M. A., 227, *266*
Woods, S. C., 227, *271*
Wyers, E. J., 401, *406*
Wyrwicka, W., 326, *356*

Y,Z

Yadin, E., 196, *224*
Yamazaki, A., 171, 173, *193*
Zeaman, D., 335, *354*
Zeiler, M. D., 335, *355*
Zenick, H., 361, *384*
Zentall, T. R., 387, *406*
Zimmer-Hart, C. L., 53, *56*, 197, 217, 218, *224*
Zola-Morgan, S., 398, 401, *404*

Subject Index

A

Acquisition
  of context-US association, 11, 177, 249
  of inhibition, 195–196
Activity
  as CR, 8, 14, 26, 27, 41, 43, 65, 70, 205, 214
  relationship to CR, 16–18, 60, 65, 200, 204
Adaptation. *See* Habituation
Additivity of cues. *See* Summation
Approach–withdrawal
  from CS, 198
Association
  context-CS, 2, 24–25, 40, 171, 255, 262
  context-US, 2, 10, 11, 16, 24, 25, 115, 169, 177, 249, 256, 262
  CS–US, 2
  direct associations to elements, 326
  hierarchical, 2, 4, 5, 18, 24, 45, 53, 160, 178, 327, 399
Attention, 204
  competition for, 3, 24
  selective, 260
  See also Latent inhibition; Learned irrelevance
Autoshaping, 11, 70, 190

B

Backward conditioning, 128

B (right column)

Blocking, 26, 73
  by context, 3, 13, 23, 31, 45, 59, 87, 99, 109, 118, 143–144, 171
  of context, 82
  of instrumental stimulus control, 303

C

Choice
  between contexts, 7, 26, 115, 139, 145, 151
Classification learning, 344
  context model, 345
  prototype theory, 345
Comparator function of context, 4, 15, 24, 123, 181, 197
  and summation, 188
Competition
  between CRs, 15, 70
  between stimuli, 68, 170, 196, 400
  for association, 3, 24, 74, 393
  for attention, 3, 24
Conditional discrimination, 10, 24, 45, 177, 297, 326
  transverse pattern, 336
Conditioned emotional response, 70, 81, 115, 190
Conditioned response
  topography of, 5, 13, 15, 30, 60, 65, 69
Conditioned suppression. *See* Conditioned emotional response
Configuring, 136, 168, 179, 325, 327, 333

417

Context
  bodily states, 366–372, 401
  as conditional cue, 10, 45
  context-CS association. *See* Association
  context preference test, 7, 26, 80, 139, 145,
    151
  context-shift test, 6, 33–34, 38, 58, 84,
    118, 139, 172
  context-US association. *See* Association
  differential reinforcement of, 10, 28, 32,
    41, 137, 151, 172, 184
  drugs, 357
  elements of, 229, 233–242, 324
  extinction of, 8, 68, 83, 112, 152, 198,
    201, 204, 210
  extra-experimental, 10, 75, 296
  hierarchical, 2, 91, 275, 327, 386
  and inhibition, 75, 195
  learning rate, 10, 108–109, 177, 249, 394
  reinforcement, 275, 400
  temporal relationship to CS and US, 242,
    316, 353
  tone height, 284–288
Contingencies, 90, 181
  and hippocampus, 400
  negative CS–US, 76, 195
  noncontingent procedures, 12, 35, 58, 74,
    113
  positive CS–US, 113
Counterconditioning, 90, 213, 216
CS–US correlations. *See* Contingencies

D

Discrimination learning
  instrumental, 273, 295, 314–320
    between contexts, 273, 306
    between CSs, 273, 295
    information theory of, 329
    shifts, 337
  Pavlovian
    between contexts, 28, 32, 41, 118, 137,
      151, 172, 184
    between CSs, 32, 177, 208
Discriminative stimuli, 295
  threshold, 361
Disinhibition, 220
Drug discrimination, 359

E,F,G

Escape
  from context, 115

Extinction
  of context, 8, 68, 83, 112, 152, 198, 201,
    204, 210
  of CS, 61–63, 66, 138, 142, 146
    context-specificity of, 135, 207, 230, 250
  of inhibition, 217
Facilitator, 46
Generalization, 2, 5, 23, 179, 281, 289, 295,
    298, 325, 364, 398
Gibbon–Balsam model. *See* Scalar Expectancy
    Theory

H,I

Habituation
  sensory, 168, 389
  US, 107, 110, 129
Higher order conditioning, 26, 42, 171, 255
Hippocampus, 385
  and contingencies, 400
  and Theta activity, 391
  place cells, 387
Incidental stimuli, 296–297, 335
Information
  serial acoustic, 277
Inhibition
  conditioned, 40, 52, 75, 128, 137, 186, 196
  external, 130
Interstimulus interval, 259
Intertrial interval, 169, 204

L

Latent inhibition
  of context, 141
  of CS, 24, 41, 65, 140, 387, 396
Learned helplessness, 88
Learned irrelevance, 58, 60, 68, 88
Learning theory, 1
Learning vs. performance, 115, 121–123, 182,
    191, 221, 400
  inhibitory control, 196, 212

M,N,O

Masking, 299
Medial-entorhinal cortex, 261
Memory, 18, 159
  and emotion, 369
  CS representation, 49
  US representation, 50, 110, 134, 142, 159–
    160

Neophobia, 246
Noradrenalin, 260
Occasion setting, 2, 5, 24, 45, 295
Overshadowing, 114, 171, 226, 252. *See also*
    Blocking
in conditional discrimination, 313

P

Partial reinforcement, 36
Perceptual organization, 3, 277, 394
Pitch perception, 281–284
Place learning, 385
Potentiation, 252
Preference. *See* Choice
Proactive interference, 88, 213, 340

R

Random control. *See* Contingencies
Reacquisition, 61, 148
Reinforcement
    patterning, 275
Reinstatement, 142, 154, 202–203, 207
    context-specificity, 143
Renewal effect, 135
Rescorla–Wagner model, 3, 24, 35, 69, 74,
    100, 107, 113, 121, 127, 133, 148–
    149, 156, 158, 307, 386
Resistance to reinforcement, 6, 7, 58, 63, 67,
    78, 108
Retardation test. *See* Resistance to
    reinforcement
Retrieval, 2, 4, 124, 160, 167, 170, 172, 178,
    213, 230, 309, 327, 360, 373
    and drug states, 357
Retroactive interference and facilitation, 338
Rule learning, 276, 313

S

Scalar Expectancy Theory, 4, 24, 31, 35, 69,
    107, 113, 122, 204
Sensitization, 107, 246
Sensory preconditioning, 255
Serial pattern learning, 273
Simultaneous discrimination, 332
Spatial memory, 385
Spontaneous recovery
    of context CR, 8
State-dependent learning, 357
    learning set, 363
    overtraining, 361
    threshold, 361
Stimulus control (dimensional), 2, 6, 295
    masking by context, 299–303, 365
Successive discrimination, 332
Summation, 40
    of CS and context, 4, 7, 16, 75, 78, 126,
    134, 142, 146, 150, 167, 168, 325

T,U,V,W

Taste-aversion learning, 225
Time
    and contingency, 191
    and predictability, 91
    as a stimulus, 289, 353
    See also Scalar Expectancy Theory
Unconditioned stimulus (US)
    inflation, 150, 154
    intensity, 110–111, 126, 150
US-only procedure
    postexposure, 123, 147, 150, 154, 204
    preexposure, 12, 58, 80, 84, 106–108
Verbal behavior, 274
Wagner–Rescorla theory. *See* Rescorla–
    Wagner model